Salvage Excavations at Tel Qashish (Tell Qasis)
and Tell el-Wa'er (2010–2013)

Jezreel Valley Regional Project Studies

Series Editors
Matthew J. Adams
Margaret E. Cohen

NUMBER ONE

Salvage Excavations at Tel Qashish (Tell Qasis)
and Tell el-Wa'er (2010–2013)

Salvage Excavations at Tel Qashish (Tell Qasis) and Tell el-Wa'er (2010–2013)

Edited by

Edwin C. M. van den Brink and Matthew J. Adams

LOCKWOOD PRESS

Columbus, Georgia

2023

Salvage Excavations at Tel Qashish (Tell Qasis) and Tell el-Waʻer (2010–2013)

Copyright © 2023 by Lockwood Press

All rights reserved. No part of this work may be reproduced or transmitted in any form or by any means, electronic or mechanical, including photocopying and recording, or by means of any information storage or retrieval system, except as may be expressly permitted by the 1976 Copyright Act or in writing from the publisher. Requests for permission should be addressed in writing to Lockwood Press, PO Box 1080, Columbus, GA 31901, USA.

ISBN: 978-1-948488-65-5

Cover design by Susanne Wilhelm. Cover image: Aerial view of Tel Qashish and Tell el-Waʻer from the south. Photograph by Matthew J. Adams.

Library of Congress Cataloging-in-Publication Data

> Names: Brink, Edwin C. M. van den, editor. | Adams, Matthew J. (Matthew Joel), editor.
> Title: Salvage excavations at Tel Qashish (Tell Qasis) and Tell el-Waʻer (2010-2013) / edited by Edwin C. M. van den Brink and Matthew J. Adams.
> Description: Columbus, Georgia : Lockwood Press, 2023. | Series: Jezreel Valley regional project studies ; number 1 | Includes bibliographical references and index.
> Identifiers: LCCN 2022052512 (print) | LCCN 2022052513 (ebook) | ISBN 9781948488655 (hardcover) | ISBN 9781948488662 (pdf)
> Subjects: LCSH: Qashish Site (Israel) | Waʻer Site (Israel) | Excavations (Archaeology)--Israel--Jezreel Valley. | Bronze age--Israel--Jezreel Valley. | Jezreel Valley (Israel)--Antiquities.
> Classification: LCC DS110.Q317 S25 2023 (print) | LCC DS110.Q317 (ebook) | DDC 956.94--dc23/eng/20221114
> LC record available at https://lccn.loc.gov/2022052512
> LC ebook record available at https://lccn.loc.gov/2022052513

This paper meets the requirements of ANSI/NISO Z39.48-1992 (Permanence of Paper).

In Memoriam

Sharon Zuckerman
(1965–2014)

Photograph courtesy of Amnon Ben-Tor

Contents

List of Figures   IX
List of Tables   XV
Preface   XVII
Acknowledgments   XIX
Abbreviations   XXI

Part I: Introduction

Chapter 1   Introduction: The History of the Project and Overview of the Sites   3
(*Matthew J. Adams and Edwin C. M. van den Brink*)

Chapter 2   The Environs of Tel Qashish: Physiography and Geomorphology   13
(*Oren Ackermann and Noam Greenbaum*)

Part II: Tel Qashish West (Middle Paleolithic and Epipaleolithic)

Chapter 3   Middle Paleolithic and Epipaleolithic Flint Procurement and Associated Workshops West and South of Tel Qashish (*Alla Yaroshevich, Dan Kirzner, Hamudi Khalaily, Oren Ackermann, and Noam Greenbaum*)   25

Part III: Tell el-Waʻer (Early Bronze Age)

Chapter 4   Early Bronze Age I Settlement Remains at Tell el-Waʻer   55
(*Orit Segal, Dan Kirzner and Uzi ʻAd*)

Chapter 5   The Early Bronze Age Pottery Assemblage from Tell el-Waʻer   69
(*Edwin C. M. van den Brink*)

Chapter 6   Groundstone and Metal Tools from Tell el-Waʻer (*Edwin C. M van den Brink*)   79

Chapter 7   Lithic Artifacts from Tell el-Waʻer (*Polina Spivak*)   85

Chapter 8   Faunal Remains from Tell el-Waʻer (*Ronit Zuckerman-Cooper*)   89

Chapter 9   Salvage Excavations at Tell el-Waʻer: Discussion and Conclusions   91
(*Orit Segal and Edwin C. M. van den Brink*)

Part IV: Tel Qashish (Early Bronze Age)

Chapter 10   The Tel Qashish Late Early Bronze Age I Salvage Excavations: Introductory Notes   95
(*Edwin C. M. van den Brink*)

Chapter 11   Tel Qashish Areas A–D: Stratigraphy and Structural Features (2010 Excavations)   99
(*Edwin C. M. van den Brink, Uzi ʻAd, Dan Kirzner, Eli Yannai, Mohammed Hater, and Orit Segal*)

Chapter 12   Tel Qashish Areas F and E South: Stratigraphy and Structural Features South   115
(2010 Excavations) (*Eli Yannai*)

Chapter 13	Tel Qashish Area E North: Stratigraphy and Structural Features (2011 Excavations) (*Edwin C. M. van den Brink, Uzi ʻAd, Dan Kirzner, Eli Yannai, Mohammed Hater, and Orit Sega*l)	121
Chapter 14	Pottery from Tel Qashish Areas A, B, C and D (*Edwin C. M. van den Brink*)	133
Chapter 15	Pottery from Tel Qashish Areas E South and F (*Netanel Paz*)	161
Chapter 16	Pottery from Tel Qashish Area E North (*Edwin C. M. van den Brink*)	177
Chapter 17	Petrographic Analysis of the Early Bronze Age Pottery from Tel Qashish (*Anat Cohen-Weinberger*)	217
Chapter 18	A Cylinder Seal Impression from Tel Qashish Area E North (*Edwin C. M. van den Brink*)	223
Chapter 19	The Groundstone Assemblage from Tel Qashish (*Ianir Milevski*)	227
Chapter 20	The Late Early Bronze Age I Flint Assemblages from Tel Qashish Areas A–F (*Alla Yaroschevich*)	239
Chapter 21	Faunal Remains from the Margins of Tel Qashish, Area E (*Nuha Agha*)	269
Chapter 22	Microvertebrate Remains from the Margins of Tel Qashish, Area E South (*Lior Weisbrod*)	281
Chapter 23	Plant Remains from Late Early Bronze Age I Deposits from Tel Qashish Area E South (*Ehud Weiss and Yael Mahler-Slasky*)	285
Chapter 24	Salvage Excavations at Tel Qashish: Discussion and Conclusions (*Edwin C. M. van den Brink*)	297

Part V: A Late Bronze Age II Cultic Repository at Tel Qashish

Chapter 25	A Late Bronze Age II Cultic Repository near Tel Qashish in the Jezreel Valley, Israel (*Orit Segal, Uzi ʻAd, and Edwin C. M. van den Brink*)	307
Chapter 26	Petrographic Study of Late Bronze Age II Vessels from the Cultic Repository near Tel Qashish (*Anat Cohen-Weinberger*)	395
Chapter 27	The Cypriot Pottery from the Late Bronze Age II Cultic Repository near Tel Qashish (*Celia J. Bergoffen*)	403
Chapter 28	Provenience of Late Bronze Age II Pottery from the Cultic Repository near Tel Qashish (*Joseph Yellin, Matthew T. Boulanger, and Michael D. Glascock*)	407
Chapter 29	Residue Analysis of Chalices from the LBA IIA Cultic Cache from Tel Qashish (*Dvory Namdar*)	417

Index   423

List of Figures

Fig. 1.1.	General map of the southern Levant.	4
Fig. 1.2.	Map of the Jezreel Valley.	4
Fig. 1.3.	Map of Tel Qashish region with the locations of the salvage excavations by permit number.	5
Fig. 1.4.	Map of Tel Qashish and adjacent sites.	5
Fig. 1.5.	Aerial view of Qashish region after the completion of infrastructure works, looking north-northwest through the Kishon water gap.	6
Fig. 1.6.	Aerial view of Qashish region after the completion of infrastructure works, looking south toward Yoqne'am.	7
Fig. 1.7.	Aerial View of the hillock of Tell el-Wa'er.	8
Fig. 1.8.	Map of Tel Qashish showing excavation Areas A–F over 2020 orthophoto.	10
Fig. 2.1.	Location of the site and main geographical features.	14
Fig. 2.2.	Air photograph of the area and location of the studied sections.	14
Fig. 2.3.	Square ZY29, looking east.	15
Fig. 2.4.	Square L29: Trench probe.	15
Fig. 2.5.	Square L29.	16
Fig. 2.6.	Square D16, looking at azimuth 210°.	16
Fig. 2.7.	Trench probe section TQ1.	16
Fig. 2.8.	Trench probe section TQ2.	17
Fig. 2.9.	Trench probe section TQ3.	17
Fig. 3.1.	Location map of the sites mentioned in the text.	26
Fig. 3.2.	Aerial view of the region with indications of the sites mentioned in the text.	27
Fig. 3.3.	TQW during the excavations, looking southeast.	28
Fig. 3.4.	TQW, stratigraphic sequence in Square C6 during excavation.	28
Fig. 3.5.	TQW Levallois core made on homogeneous brown flint.	29
Fig. 3.6.	TQW, Levallois core, on nonhomogeneous flint.	29
Fig. 3.7.	TQW, Levallois point, made on homogeneous brown flint.	29
Fig. 3.8.	TQW, retouched Levallois flake on nonhomogeneous flint.	29
Fig. 3.9.	TQW, Levallois flake on homogeneous flint with concentric bands, seen on dorsal surface.	29
Fig. 3.10.	TQW, retouched Levallois flake made on homogeneous flint with concentric bands.	30
Fig. 3.11.	TQW, Levallois flake made on homogeneous coarse-grained flint.	30
Fig. 3.12.	TQW, Levallois core, hinged at the beginning of the reduction.	30
Fig. 3.13.	TQW, hinged Levallois core on balk.	30
Fig. 3.14.	TQW, cortical tools and debitage.	30
Fig. 3.15.	TQW, tested flint nodule.	31
Fig. 3.16.	TQW, Levallois cores.	31
Fig. 3.17.	TQW, Levallois cores.	31
Fig. 3.18.	TQW, Levallois cores.	32
Fig. 3.19.	TQW, Levallois points.	32
Fig. 3.20.	TQW, Levallois products.	32
Fig. 3.21.	TQW, naturally backed knives; some exhibit signs of modification or use.	32
Fig. 3.22.	TQW, blade core and bladelet core.	33
Fig. 3.23.	TQW, tools on PE and cortical items.	33

Fig. 3.24.	TQW, the hand axe.	33
Fig. 3.25.	TQW, distribution of Levallois cores, products, and NBK according to length.	34
Fig. 3.26.	TQS during the second excavation season, looking south.	35
Fig. 3.27.	TQS, stratigraphic sequence.	35
Fig. 4.1.	Location map of Tell el-Waʻer.	56
Fig. 4.2.	Aerial photograph showing the location of Tell el-Waʻer.	56
Fig. 4.3.	Tel Qashish and Road 70 to the southeast of the excavation site. Looking southeast.	56
Fig. 4.4.	Plan and sections of the exposed Early EB I village.	57
Fig. 4.5.	Aerial view of squares A/B 13–16, building units 10–11.	58
Fig. 4.6.	Aerial view of squares A/B 18–25, building units 3–9, 13–15.	58
Fig. 4.7.	Square A10, unit 1.	59
Fig. 4.8.	Square A11, unit 2.	59
Fig. 4.9.	Squares B18/19, unit 3.	59
Fig. 4.10.	Square A19, unit 4.	59
Fig. 4.11.	Square B/C24, unit 5.	60
Fig. 4.12.	Square B/C24, B25, units 5 and 6.	60
Fig. 4.13.	Square B24/25, units 5 and 6.	60
Fig. 4.14.	Squares A24/25, unit 7.	61
Fig. 4.15.	Squares A15, A/B16, unit 10.	61
Fig. 4.16.	Squares A20–A21, unit 13.	62
Fig. 4.17.	Squares B20–B22, unit 14.	62
Fig. 4.18.	Square B20, unit 14.	62
Fig. 5.1.	Bowls.	71
Fig. 5.2.	Holemouth jars and kraters.	72
Fig. 5.3.	Necked jars and pithoi.	74
Fig. 5.4.	Handles.	76
Fig. 6.1.	Selection of groundstone vessels from Tell el-Waʻer.	80
Fig. 6.2.	The two axe heads before cleaning (L214, B2033.1–2).	80
Fig. 6.3.	The two axe heads after cleaning (L214, B2033.1–2).	81
Fig. 6.4.	Locus 214, Basket 2033.1–2.	81
Fig. 7.1.	Chalcolithic–Early Bronze Age sickle blades from Tell el-Waʻer.	86
Fig. 7.2	A Chalcolithic tabular fan scraper, PPNB sickle blade, and Late Chalcolithic sickle blade from Tell el-Waʻer.	86
Fig. 10.1.	Map showing the location of Tel Qashish in northern Israel.	96
Fig. 10.2.	Plan of excavation Areas A–F around Tel Qashish.	96
Fig. 10.3.	Aerial view of Areas E South and North in the southeast margin of Tel Qashish.	97
Fig. 11.1.	Plan of excavation Areas A–F around Tel Qashish.	100
Fig. 11.2.	Area A1. Aerial view.	101
Fig. 11.3.	Area A1. Plan, trenches and sections.	101
Fig. 11.4.	Area A2. Plan and sections.	102
Fig. 11.5.	Area B. Plan and sections.	103
Fig. 11.6.	Area B. Aerial photograph.	104
Fig. 11.7.	Area D. LB II repository during excavation.	104
Fig. 11.8.	Area C. Squares G29–H29.	104
Fig. 11.9.	Area C. Squares L28/29–P28/29.	105
Fig. 11.10.	Area C. Plan of Squares R28/29/30–V28/29/30.	106
Fig. 11.11.	Area C. Plan and sections of Squares W28/29–ZD28/29.	108
Fig. 11.12.	Area C. Plan of Squares ZI29–ZJ29.	109
Fig. 11.13.	Aerial view of Area C and the tell of Qashish.	109

Fig. 11.14.	Aerial view of Areas C and D.	109
Fig. 11.15.	Area C. Square L29, small-limestones surface (Locus 311).	109
Fig. 11.16.	Area C. Square L28. Installation L348 during excavation.	109
Fig. 11.17.	Area C. Square L28. Installation L348 after excavation.	110
Fig. 11.18.	Area C. Small-limestones surface and W30 and W31.	110
Fig. 11.19.	Area C. Small-limestones surface and W30 and W31.	110
Fig. 11.20.	Area C. Aerial view of Squares R28/29/30–V28/29/30.	110
Fig. 11.21.	Area C. General view of Squares U28/29–V28/29.	111
Fig. 11.22.	Area C. Square U28. Stone-paved installation/W35 and W33.	111
Fig. 11.23.	Area C. Squares U28/29–V28/29.	111
Fig. 11.24.	Area C. Square X29. Remains of a partially preserved installation.	111
Fig. 11.25.	Area C. Square Y29, Locus 347.	111
Fig. 11.26.	Area D. Square ZM29, plan and section.	111
Fig. 11.27.	Area D. Squares ZP29–ZS29, plan and sections.	112
Fig. 11.28.	Area D. Square ZY29. Plan.	113
Fig. 11.29.	Area D. Squares ZP29–ZS29.	113
Fig. 12.1.	Area F. Plan and sections.	116
Fig. 12.2.	Area F, Square J24, L6059.	116
Fig. 12.3.	Area F, Square J24, L6049.	116
Fig. 12.4.	Area F, Square H26, L6013.	117
Fig. 12.5.	Area F, Square H29, Locus 6048.	117
Fig. 12.6.	Plan of Area E South.	118
Fig. 12.7.	Area E, Squares I64–J64, Loci 5023 and 5047.	119
Fig. 12.8.	Area E, Square J64, L5047, W506.	119
Fig. 12.9.	Area E, Square I64, Locus 5023, W501.	119
Fig. 12.10.	Area E, Square I62, L5003.	119
Fig. 12.11.	Area E, Square M57, L5050.	119
Fig. 12.12.	Area E, Square K54, L5017.	119
Fig. 12.13.	Area E, Square K54, L5017.	120
Fig. 12.14.	Area E, Square K54, L5045.	120
Fig. 13.1a	(spread). Plan of Area E South.	122
Fig. 13.1.b.	E–W cross-sections 1-1 and N–S cross-sections 2-2 of Area E South.	124
Fig. 13.2.	Tel Qashish. Bird eye's view of Area E.	125
Fig. 13.3.	Tel Qashish. Aerial view of Area E at the end of the excavation.	125
Fig. 13.4.	Area E, Square L55, Locus 5138, W518.	126
Fig. 13.5.	Area E, Square L56, Locus 5102.	126
Fig. 13.6	Area E, Square M56, Locus 5050.	126
Fig. 13.7.	Area E, Square K58, W516, W521, and W522, and Locus 5131.	127
Fig. 13.8.	Area E, Squares K/L59–60.	128
Fig. 13.9.	Area E, Square K58.	128
Fig. 13.10.	Area E, Square L60, W517.	128
Fig. 13.11.	Area E, Squares K–L59–L60–61, M59–60, N59–62, O60–63.	128
Fig. 13.12.	Area E, Squares M–O/59–63.	129
Fig. 13.13.	Area E, Squares M–O/59–60.	129
Fig. 13.14	Area E, Square O62, W500.	130
Fig. 14.1.	Areas A1–2. Selection of Late EB I pottery. Bowls and Jars.	137
Fig. 14.2.	Area B. Selection of Late EB I pottery. Bowls and Holemouth jars.	138
Fig. 14.3.	Area B. Selection of Late EB I pottery. Jars.	140
Fig. 14.4.	Area C. Chart showing numeric breakdown of Late EB I vessel types.	141

Fig. 14.5.	Area C. Selection of Late EB I pottery. Bowls and kraters.	142
Fig. 14.6.	Area C. Selection of Late EB I pottery. Other bowls.	144
Fig. 14.7.	Area C. Selection of Late EB I pottery. Holemouth jars.	146
Fig. 14.8.	Area C. Selection of Late EB I pottery. Holemouth jars (cont.).	148
Fig. 14.9.	Area C. Selection of Late EB I pottery. Bow-rim jars.	150
Fig. 14.10.	Area C. Selection of Late EB I pottery. Bow-rim jars (cont.).	152
Fig. 14.11.	Area C. Selection of Late EB I pottery. Other necked jars, handles.	154
Fig. 14.12.	Area C. Selection of Late EB I pottery. Other necked jars, handles.	156
Fig. 14.13.	Area D. Selection of Late EB I pottery.	158
Fig. 15.1.	Areas E (South) and F. Bowls and kraters.	167
Fig. 15.2.	Areas E (South) and F. Small closed vessels: gourd jars and teapots.	168
Fig. 15.3.	Areas E (South) and F. Holemouth jars with simple rim.	168
Fig. 15.4.	Areas E (South) and F. Holemouth jars with thickened rim.	170
Fig. 15.5.	Areas E (South) and F. Holemouth jars with ridged and squared-off rims.	171
Fig. 15.6.	Areas E (South) and F. Storage jars with short straight necks and short everted necks.	172
Fig. 15.7.	Areas E (South) and F. Bow-rim storage jars.	173
Fig. 15.8.	Areas E (South) and F. Storage Jars with simple rounded and cut rims; pithoi.	174
Fig. 15.9.	Areas E (South) and F. Handles.	175
Fig. 15.10.	Main vessel-type frequency in Area E (South).	176
Fig. 15.11.	Main vessel-type frequency in Area F.	176
Fig. 15.12.	Main vessel-type frequency for Areas E (South) and F.	176
Fig. 16.1.	Total number of body sherds vs. diagnostic sherds.	178
Fig. 16.2.	Frequency of diagnostic potsherds.	179
Fig. 16.3.	Area E North. Bowls and kraters.	180
Fig. 16.4.	Area E North. Red-slipped bowls or kraters with profiled rim, and small knobbed bowls.	182
Fig. 16.5.	Area E North. Gray burnished ware bowls.	184
Fig. 16.6.	Area E North. Small bowls.	186
Fig. 16.7.	Area E North. Holemouth jars and cooking jars with potmarks and slashes.	188
Fig. 16.8.	Area E North. Holemouth jars with applied rope decoration below rim's exterior.	190
Fig. 16.9.	Area E North. Holemouth jars with applied rope decoration below rim's exterior (cont.)	192
Fig. 16.10.	Area E North. Holemouth jars with continuous ridge below rim's exterior.	194
Fig. 16.11.	Area E North. Plain holemouth jars.	196
Fig. 16.12.	Area E North. Plain holemouth jars, flattened rim.	198
Fig. 16.13.	Area E North. Plain holemouth jars.	200
Fig. 16.14.	Area E North. Bow-rim jars.	202
Fig. 16.15.	Area E North. Bow-rim jars (cont.).	204
Fig. 16.16.	Area E North. Bow-rim jars (cont.).	206
Fig. 16.17.	Area E North. Bow-rim jars. Bases.	208
Fig. 16.18.	Area E North. Amphoriskoi, jugs, tall-necked jars.	210
Fig. 16.19.	Area E North. Jug/small jar bases, short-necked jars, pithoi.	212
Fig. 16.20.	Area E North. Indented ledge handles and loop handles.	214
Fig. 18.1.	Tel Qashish, Area E North. Neck-shoulder fragment of medium-sized jar bearing a cylinder seal impression.	225
Fig. 18.2.	1. Full picture of the jar fragment from Tel Qashish, Area E North. 2. Vessel fragment of indeterminate type from Megiddo bearing a cylinder seal impression.	225
Fig. 19.1.	Lower and upper grinding stones.	234
Fig. 19.2.	Mortars.	235
Fig. 19.3.	Hammerstones, pounders, and perforated stones.	236
Fig. 19.4.	Tournettes and Chalcolithic-period bowls.	237

Fig. 19.5.	Early Bronze Age I bowls.	238
Fig. 19.6.	Varia: A bell-shaped object.	238
Fig. 20.1.	Location map of the areas excavated on the margins of Tel Qashish.	240
Fig. 20.2	a–d. A variety of tools exemplifying the flint varieties used at the site.	240
Fig. 20.3	a–j. Representative Canaanean blades and sickle blades (fragments).	242
Fig. 20.4.	Knife on Canaanean blade.	243
Fig. 20.5.	Large cortical blade with gentle retouch and faceted platform and two knives.	243
Fig. 20.6.	End scraper with cortex remains.	244
Fig. 20.7.	The Canaanean blade core from Har Ḥaruvim.	244
Fig. 20.8.	Canaanean sickle blade made on coarse-grained flint with tiny black spots.	244
Fig. 20.9.	A core at the beginning of the reduction sequence.	244
Fig. 20.10.	Sickle blades and blade cores from Areas E South and F.	253
Fig. 20.11.	Cores from Areas C and D.	254
Fig. 20.12.	Bladelet cores and burin from Areas C, D, and E North.	255
Fig. 20.13.	Levallois point and retouched flakes from Area D. Middle Paleolithic intrusion.	256
Fig. 20.14.	Middle Paleolithic and Epipaleolithic/Upper Paleolithic intrusions.	257
Fig. 20.15.	Canaanean blades and tools: Characteristics of edge damage.	258
Fig. 20.16.	Canaanean blades and sickle blades: Distribution according to width.	259
Fig. 20.17.	Canaanean blades and sickle blades: Distribution according to thickness.	259
Fig. 20.18.	Canaanean blades and tools: Thickness according to fragment type.	260
Fig. 20.19.	Canaanean blades and tools: Width according to fragment type.	260
Fig. 20.20.	Canaanean blades and sickle blades: Width and thickness distribution according to fragment.	261
Fig. 20.21.	ʽEn Esur knife, sickle blades and truncated blade from Areas C and D.	262
Fig. 20.22.	Tools from Area C.	263
Fig. 20.23.	A knife and Canaanean sickle blades from Area E North.	264
Fig. 20.24.	Tools from Areas E South and F.	265
Fig. 20.25.	Bifacial tools from Areas E North and C.	266
Fig. 20.26.	Tools on PE from Areas C and E North.	266
Fig. 20.27.	End scrapers from Area E North.	267
Fig. 20.28.	Side scrapers and end scraper from Area C.	268
Fig. 21.1.	Survival profile of cattle (excluding cattle burial).	272
Fig. 21.2.	Area E, Locus 5105. Cattle remains in original anatomic articulation.	274
Fig. 22.1.	*Microtus* molar.	282
Fig. 23.1.	Location plan of Tel Qashish.	286
Fig. 23.2.	Plan of Area E South.	286
Fig. 23.3.	Locus 5043 in Area E South.	287
Fig. 23.4.	Emmer wheat (*Triticum dicoccum*) grains.	287
Fig. 23.5.	Emmer wheat (*T. dicoccum*), spikelet fork.	287
Fig. 23.6.	Bristle-spiked canary grass (*Phalaris paradoxa*) grains.	288
Fig. 23.7.	*cf. Lolium persicum* grain.	288
Fig. 23.8.	Compositae achene.	289
Fig. 23.9.	Grapevine (*Vitis vinifera*) pip.	289
Fig. 23.10.	Lentil (*Lens culinaris*) seeds.	289
Fig. 23.11.	*Galium* sect. *Kolgyda* (probably *G. tricornutum*) mericarp.	289
Fig. 25.1.	Location map.	308
Fig. 25.2.	Area B, plan and sections.	309
Fig. 25.3.	Aerial view of Area B after completion of the excavation with repository cave.	310
Fig. 25.4.	Cross-section through the cave.	310

Fig. 25.5.	The repository cave toward the end of excavation.	311
Fig. 25.6.	The shallow bedrock pocket with additional pottery vessels.	311
Fig. 25.7.	Area B, Locus 226. Shallow bedrock pocket with additional ceramic vessels.	312
Fig. 25.8.	Area B, the repository cave during excavation.	312
Fig. 25.9.	The cave during excavation.	313
Fig. 25.10.	Bowls types BL Ia–c, IIa–b.	336
Fig. 25.11.	Bowls types BL IIIa–b from Locus 225.	338
Fig. 25.12.	Bowls types BL IIIb (cont.), IIIc.	340
Fig. 25.13.	Bowls type BL IV.	342
Fig. 25.14.	Bowls types BL V, VIa–b, VII.	344
Fig. 25.15.	Bowls type BL VIII (Locus 225).	346
Fig. 25.16.	Chalices types CH Ia–b.	348
Fig. 25.17.	Chalices types CH IIa–c, III.	350
Fig. 25.18.	Goblets types GO I–IV.	352
Fig. 25.19.	Goblets types GO V–VI.	354
Fig. 25.20.	Goblets type GO VI (cont.).	356
Fig. 25.21.	Goblets types GO VI (cont.), VII.	358
Fig. 25.22.	Human-head goblet, restored.	360
Fig. 25.23.	Human-head goblet fragment prior to restoration.	361
Fig. 25.24.	Drawing of the vessels at the bottom of the repository cave.	361
Fig. 25.25.	Kraters type K Ia (Locus 225).	362
Fig. 25.26.	Kraters types K Ib, II.	364
Fig. 25.27.	Cooking pots.	366
Fig. 25.28.	Storage jar type SJ I (Locus 225).	368
Fig. 25.29.	Jugs type J Ia (Locus 225).	369
Fig. 25.30.	Jugs types J Ib, II–III (Locus 225).	370
Fig. 25.31.	Juglets.	372
Fig. 25.32.	Flasks.	374
Fig. 25.33.	Cup and saucer (Locus 219).	374
Fig. 25.34.	Lamps type LP Ia (Locus 225).	375
Fig. 25.35.	Lamps type LP Ia (cont.), Ib (Locus 225).	376
Fig. 25.36.	Stand type ST I (Locus 225).	377
Fig. 25.37.	Stands type ST II (Locus 225).	378
Fig. 25.38.	Stand type St II (cont.) (Locus 225).	379
Fig. 25.39	Stands type ST III (Locus 225).	380
Fig. 25.40	Stand type ST IV and incense burner (Locus 225).	382
Fig. 25.41.	Mycenaean pottery: Piriform jar and flasks (Locus 225).	383
Fig. 25.42.	Mycenaean pottery: Stirrup jars (Locus 225).	384
Fig. 25.43.	Cypriot pottery.	386
Fig. 25.44.	Small faience bowl (Locus 225).	388
Fig. 25.45.	Section of the repository cave showing the height range of the types found in the cache.	389
Fig. 25.46.	Pie chart showing the numerical distribution of pottery types in the cave's repository.	389
Fig. 26.1.	Stand. Petrographic Group A.	398
Fig. 26.2.	Bowl. Petrographic Group A.	398
Fig. 26.3.	Goblet. Petrographic Group B.	398
Fig. 26.4.	Goblet. Petrographic Group C.	398
Fig. 26.5.	Goblet. Petrographic Group C.	399
Fig. 26.6.	Cooking pot. Petrographic Group D.	399
Fig. 26.7.	Cooking pot. Petrographic Group D.	399

Fig. 26.8.	Bowl. Petrographic Group E.	399
Fig. 28.1.	Diamond drills used to sample pottery.	408
Fig. 28.2.	Vessel B.2156 after sampling.	408
Fig. 28.3.	Vessel B.2156 before sampling.	408
Fig. 28.4.	REE pattern for three Tel Qashish pottery vessels classified on stylistic grounds as Mycenaean.	410
Fig. 28.5.	REE pattern for three local and imported pots from Area B.	410
Fig. 29.1.	Schematic map of northern Israel on which the location of the site is marked.	418
Fig. 29.2.	The items found in the cave.	418
Fig. 29.3.	Sampling during excavation.	418
Fig. 29.4	A–E. Chromatograms of the analyzed samples.	419

List of Tables

Table 2.1.	Square ZY29, general description.	18
Table 2.2.	Probe trench section, Square L29, general description.	19
Table 2.3.	Square L29, luminescence OSL dating results.	20
Table 2.4.	Square D16, general description.	21
Table 2.5.	Probe trench section, TQ1, general description.	21
Table 2.6.	Probe trench section, TQ2, general description.	22
Table 2.7.	Probe trench section, TQ3, general description.	22
Table 3.1.	TQW: General Composition of the Flint Assemblage.	43
Table 3.2.	TQW: Composition of the Tools Assemblage.	43
Table 3.3.	TQW: Levallois Cores and Products according to Blank and Mode of Preparation.	44
Table 3.4.	TQW: Metric Characteristic of Levallois Cores according to Blank Removed.	44
Table 3.5.	TQW: Metric Characteristics of Levallois Products according to Blank kind.	45
Table 3.6.	TQW: Striking Platform of Levallois Products.	45
Table 3.7.	TQW: Metric Characteristics of Levallois Cores according to Mode of Preparation.	46
Table 3.8.	TQW: Metric Characteristics of Levallois Products according to Mode of Preparation.	47
Table 3.9.	TQS: General Composition of the Flint Assemblage.	48
Table 3.10.	TQS: Typological Composition of the Tools Assemblage.	48
Table 3.11.	TQS: Levallois Cores and Products according to Blank and Mode of Preparation.	49
Table 3.12.	TQS: Striking Platform of Levallois Products.	49
Table 3.13.	TQS: Metric Characteristics of Levallois Cores according to Mode of Preparation.	50
Table 3.14.	TQS: Metric Characteristics of Levallois Products according to mode of Preparation.	51
Table 5.1.	Tell el-Waʻer: Pottery diagnostics account per type.	77
Table 6.1.	Tell el-Waʻer. Groundstone objects, by locus (bowls excluded).	82
Table 6.2.	Tell el-Waʻer. Basalt bowl fragments.	83
Table 15.1.	Area E South. Secure loci list.	162
Table 15.2.	Area F. Secure loci list.	162
Table 17.1.	Inventory of analyzed vessels and results of the petrographic analysis.	218
Table 19.1.	Distribution of raw materials by area.	231
Table 19.2.	Areas A and B: Distribution of stone objects by type.	231
Table 19.3.	Areas C, D, and F: Distribution of stone objects by type.	232
Table 19.4.	Area E (North and South): Distribution of stone objects by type and stratum.	232
Table 19.5.	General distribution of types by area.	233

Table 20.1.	General composition of the assemblage.	249
Table 20.2.	Distribution of core types.	250
Table 20.3.	Typological composition of the assemblage.	251
Table 20.4.	Metric characteristics of Canaanean blades and tools.	252
Table 21.1.	Faunal remains per locus.	270
Table 21.2.	Faunal remains by taxa and stratigraphic context.	271
Table 21.3.	Ageing of cattle based on bone fusion, excluding the cattle burial.	272
Table 21.4.	Distribution of skeletal remains.	273
Table 21.5.	Measurements of faunal remains. Following von den Driesch 1976.	278
Table 22.1.	List of samples of microvertebrate remains from Tel Qashish, Area E South, including description of the skeletal remains.	284
Table 23.1.	Plant species in EB IB Tel Qashish, Area E South.	296
Table 24.1.	Presence (+)/absence (-) dichotomy of bow-rim and neckless rail/roll rim jars/pithoi from selected late EB I sites in western Galilee, the northern Jordan Valley, and the north Coastal Plain, listed from north to south.	299
Table 24.2.	Radiocarbon dates of Tel Qashish seeds from Area E (South).	301
Table 25.1.	List of restored pottery vessels.	390
Table 26.1.	Inventory of analyzed vessels.	397
Table 28.1.	Pottery from Area B analyzed by INAA.	414
Table 28.2.	Rare earth composition of pottery from Area B and references.	415
Table 28.3.	Concentration of barium and calcium in percent.	416
Table 29.1.	List of on-site samples, during the excavation.	421
Table 29.2.	List of the compounds identified in the lipid extracts of five chalices from Qashish.	422

Supplementary Table 19.6 available online at https://doi.org/10.5913/2022655.t19.

Preface

This volume is the first to appear in the *Jezreel Valley Regional Project Studies* series, which was conceived to be a venue for the publication of the extensive new primary and synthetic data generated by teams under the collaborative framework of the Jezreel Valley Regional Project (JVRP), including archaeological reports, environmental studies, and historical analyses. The (JVRP) is a long-term, multi-disciplinary survey and excavation project investigating the history of human activity in the Jezreel Valley from the Paleolithic through the Ottoman period. The project strives for a total history of the region using the tools and theoretical approaches of such disciplines as archaeology, anthropology, geography, history, ethnography, and the natural sciences, within an organizational framework provided by landscape archaeology. The project is also a framework for collaboration, facilitating interaction, collegiality, publication, and resources-sharing among its independent member projects, which currently include the *Castra Legionis VI Ferrata* Excavations, The Tel Aviv University Megiddo Expedition, The Tel Shimron Excavations, and The Tell Abu Shusha Excavations, as well as other initiatives currently in development.

The current volume brings to publication together several final reports of salvage excavations carried out by the Israel Antiquities Authority (IAA) in the vicinity of Tel Qashish between the years 2010 and 2013. These excavations, carried out in advance of major national development projects, provide a rare window into the archaeological remains within the landscape between tells which usually receive such little attention from research excavations. These remains between tells have much to contribute to the overall story of the region, contributing data either non-existent or inaccessible on multi-period settlement sites. They are also the remains that are at the most risk of destruction by modern development. As the national body responsible for the antiquities of Israel, the IAA carries out hundreds of excavations across the country every year, a majority of them in the landscape between tells and is therefore the most important producer of knowledge concerning these understudied components of the archaeological landscape. The salvage excavations presented herein reveal new data on the Paleolithic period, Early Bronze Age, and Late Bronze Ages in the Jezreel Valley and contribute greatly to our knowledge thereof.

Additional volumes in the JVRP Studies series currently in preparation include *Tel Megiddo East 1: The 2010-2013 Seasons*; *Castra Legionis VI Ferrata 1: The Principia and Related Studies*; *Stability and Change in the Jezreel Valley from 1200 to 900 BCE*; and *Current work in the Jezreel Valley 2022*.

Matthew J. Adams
Margaret E. Cohen

Series Editors,
Jezreel Valley Regional Project Studies

Acknowledgments

We wish to thank collectively the various members of the excavation teams for their hard work during the years of excavation and the preparation of this publication. We recognize that salvage excavations can be both rewarding and thankless, and we wish to extend our warm gratitude to all of those who participated in the projects presented herein. Each are thanked individually in the chapters relevant to their work.

Special thanks are also due to Dr. Viviana Moscovich who worked tirelessly over many months to bring order and harmony to the varied reports assembled here. Her invaluable assistance is greatly appreciated.

Finally, this publication would not have been possible without the support of the Israel Antiquities Authority's technical staffers and without the courteous consent of its Publication Committee, the latter presently headed by Dr. Zvi Greenhut.

The Editors

Abbreviations

ÄAT	Ägypten und Altes Testament
ABS	Archaeology and Biblical Studies
ADPV	Abhandlungen des Deutschen Palästinavereins
AnSt	*Anatolian Studies*
ASL	above sea level
BARIS	British Archaeological Reports International Series
BASOR	*Bulletin of the American Schools of Oriental Research*
BASORSup	Bulletin of the American Schools of Oriental Research Supplement Series
BBSAJ	*Bulletin of the British School of Archaeology in Jerusalem*
BSA	*Bulletin on Sumerian Agriculture*
CHANE	Culture and History of the Ancient Near East
CTE	core trimming elements
ErIsr	*Eretz Israel*
GBW	gray burnished ware
HA-ESI	*Hadashot Arkheologiyot-Excavations and Surveys in Israel*
HUJ	Hebrew University of Jerusalem
IAA	Israel Antiquities Authority
IEJ	*Israel Exploration Journal*
ill(s).	illustration(s)
INAA	instrumental neutron activation analysis
JArS	*Journal of Archaeological Science*
JPOS	*Journal of the Palestine Oriental Society*
JVRP	Jezreel Valley Regional Project
LBNL	Laurence Berkeley National Laboratory
MNI	minimum number of individuals
MP	Middle Paleolithic
MURR	University of Missouri Research Reactor
NEA	*Near Eastern Archaeology*
NBK	naturally backed knives
NISP	number of identified specimens
OBO	Orbis Biblicus et Orientalis
OIP	Oriental Institute Publications
OJA	*Oxford Journal of Archaeology*
OSL	optically stimulated luminescence
PE	primary elements
PEQ	*Palestine Exploration Quarterly*
pers. comm.	personal communication
PPN	Pre-Pottery Neolithic
REE	rare earth elements
SAOC	Studies in Ancient Oriental Civilization

SMNIA	Sonia and Marco Nadler Institute of Archaeology Monograph Series
TA	*Tel Aviv*
TDA	total diagnostic assemblage
TQS	Tel Qashish South
TQW	Tel Qashish West
UP	Upper Paleolithic
ZDPV	*Zeitschrift des Deutschen Palästina-Vereins*

Part I

Introduction

Chapter 1

Introduction: The History of the Project and Overview of the Sites

Edwin C. M. van den Brink (*Israel Antiquities Authority*)
Matthew J. Adams (*The W.F. Albright Institute of Archaeological Research*)

This volume is the first volume of the Jezreel Valley Regional Project Studies series, bringing together several final reports relating to salvage excavations carried out by the Israel Antiquities Authority (IAA) between the years 2010 and 2013. These followed in the wake of a number of intensive infrastructure development plans that were envisioned in the immediate environs of Tel Qashish in the northern Jezreel Valley, and that have since come to fruition (figs. 1.1–4). These plans included construction of a transnational natural gas pipeline, a new major highway intersection, and the new *Rakevet HaEmek*, "Valley Railway," linking Haifa–'Afula–Bet She'an, the latter being a reinvention of one of the most important segments of the Ottoman Hejaz railway. The gas line and the railway were planned to pass within 150 m of the northern and western flanks of Tel Qashish before crossing the Kishon River to the south. The new intersection expanding the cross-Israel Highway 6 and the widening of Highway 70 was located immediately to the west of Tel Qashish. Considering the known remains at Tel Qashish and the considerable density of archaeological remains in the Jezreel Valley generally, trial excavations were conducted by the IAA at key locations in the landscape to be impacted by the infrastructure plans, and salvage excavations carried out as needed.

Setting of the Sites

Given the present excavations' close proximity to Tel Qashish (NIG 210349-732351/210675-732569), the latter will serve as a natural point of departure and reference in the landscape (figs. 2.2–4). The environs of this tell and the landscape history are described by Oren Ackermann and Noam Greenbaum (ch. 2, this volume, with additional discussion in ch. 3). Tel Qashish (Hebrew, תל קשיש, from Arabic, تل القشيش, "Mound of the Husk") is a relatively small, elongated tell about 270 × 160 m at its base (ca. 28 m ASL) and rising to about 28 m (56 m ASL) above the surrounding plain. It is located in the northwestern part of the Jezreel Valley, on the northern bank of the perennial Kishon River that circumscribes its west and south flanks (figs. 1.3–5). The Kishon, the second largest river in Israel reaching the Mediterranean, is the primary drainage vehicle for the Jezreel Valley and the surrounding mountains of Manasseh on the west and south and the Gilboa and Nazareth ranges on the east and north. After passing Tel Qashish, the river enters the narrow Kishon water gap between Mount Carmel and the Tiv'on hills before entering the Akko plain and debouching into the Mediterranean next to Haifa, in the Kishon estuary north of the Carmel Ridge (fig. 1.5; Artzy 2006). The site's strategic location at the mouth of this pass between the Jezreel Valley and the Akko plain was probably key to its long history.

A natural spring, 'En Qashish, is located about 100 m south of the mound that invited habitation in this area already during the Levantine Middle Paleolithic where two sites have been discovered, 'En Qashish and 'En Qashish South (fig. 1.3; part 2, this volume). About 500m northwest of Tel Qashish, on the opposite side of the Kishon, is the small mound of Tell el-Waʻer (Hebrew: תל אל-וער, Arabic: تل الوعر; part 3, this volume). Two kilometers to the south of Tel Qashish is the prominent mound of Tel Yoqneʻam (Hebrew: תֵּל יָקְנְעָם) or Tell Qamun (Arabic: تل قامون), the largest and longest lived site (Early Bronze Age through Ottoman) close to the salvage projects reported on here (fig. 1.6; Ben-Tor, Avissar, and Portugali 1996; Ben-Tor, Zarzecki-Peleg, and Cohen-Anidjar 2005; Ben-Tor, Ben-Ami, and Livneh 2005).

Previous Archaeological Research at and around Tel Qashish

Tel Qashish

Trial excavations (two trenches) were conducted in Tel Qashish as early as in the 1920s (Garstang 1922) yielding solely Early Bronze Age pottery. The site was surveyed in the early 1950s by Raphael Giveon (1954) who found pottery ranging from the Middle Bronze Age to the Hellenistic period. Another survey of the site was conducted in the 1970s (Raban 1982; site 11) identifying architectural remains from the Middle Bronze, Iron Age, and Persian periods, as well as material culture from all periods from the Chalcolithic through "Arabic periods" (Raban 1982, xi). As part of the Yoqneʻam Regional Project Amnon Ben-Tor and Yuval Portugali (1987) surveyed

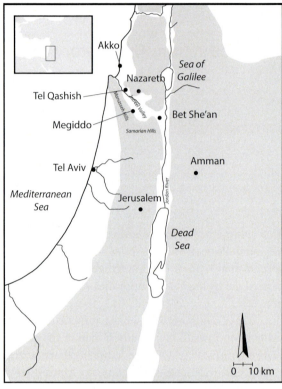

Fig. 1.1. General map of the southern Levant.

Fig. 1.2. Map of the Jezreel Valley. Courtesy of Google Earth.

1. Introduction: The History of the Project and Overview of the Sites

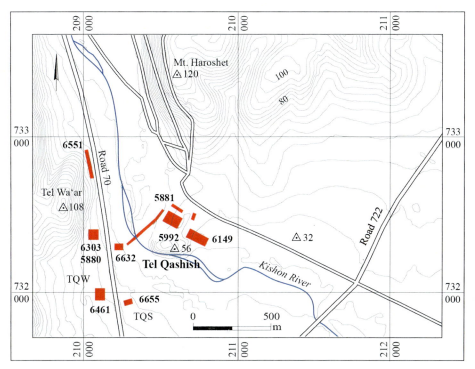

Fig. 1.3. Map of Tel Qashish region with the locations of the salvage excavations by permit number.

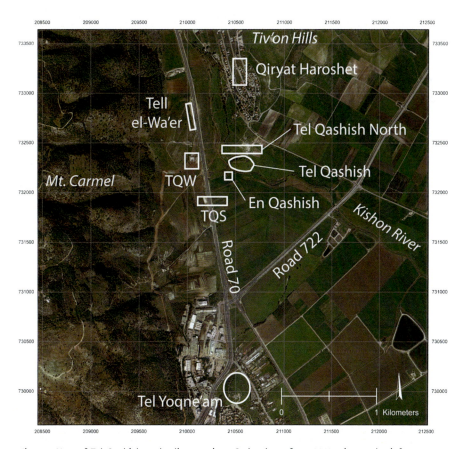

Fig. 1.4. Map of Tel Qashish and adjacent sites. Orthophoto from 2011 prior to the infrastructure construction works, courtesy of the JVRP.

Fig. 1.5. Aerial view of Qashish region after the completion of infrastructure works, looking north-northwest through the Kishon water gap, with the plain of Akko and the coast in the distance. Courtesy of the JVRP.

the site and between 1978 and 1987 carried out eight seasons of excavation. The project identified fifteen distinctive archaeological strata with remains dating to the late Early Bronze Age I (EB IB) through the Ottoman period (Ben-Tor, Bonfil, and Zuckerman 2003).

Two specific periods of occupation at Tel Qashish should be mentioned at the outset in the context of the presentation of the salvage excavations to be submitted, the Early Bronze Age I and the Late Bronze Age IIB. The earliest in situ remains excavated at Tel Qashish are from the late Early Bronze Age I (EB IB; Strata XIII–XV). While only narrowly exposed, late EB I Qashish consisted of large well-built houses, and the surveys found EB IB pottery extensively beyond the topographical boundaries of the mound, suggesting the site during that period was larger than the tell itself (Ben-Tor and Bonfil 2003). During the succeeding EB II–III period, the site contracted to the boundaries of the tell and was fortified. In the Late Bronze Age (Strata VII–V), the site has the typical material cultural assemblages of nearby sites such as Megiddo and Yoqne'am, and suffered the similar fate of being destroyed in the LB IIB (Stratum V; Ben-Tor, Bonfil, and Zuckerman 2003).

While the site was tentatively identified with "Helkath" mentioned in the list of 119 cities conquered by Pharaoh Thutmose III (Aharoni 1959), Amnon Ben-Tor, Ruhama Bonfil, and Sharon Zuckerman (2003,1) propose the site to be "Dabbesheth" from the Book of Joshua (Josh 19:11). However, no conclusive identification of the site with an ancient toponym has been made and these equations remain speculative.

Qiryat Haroshet

While not the subject of the reports in this volume, it is worth mentioning the salvage excavation at Qiryat Haroshet, 1.5 km northwest of Tel Qashish (figs. 1.4–5). Prior to a development project initiated by the municipality of Qiryat Haroshet on the western slopes of the ridge of the Tiv'on Hills, two seasons of excavation during 1998–1999 were carried out by the Recanati Institute for Maritime Studies of the

Fig. 1.6. Aerial view of Qashish region after the completion of infrastructure works, looking south toward Yoqne'am. Courtesy of the JVRP.

University of Haifa (Salmon 2008). These revealed four burial caves that appear to be part of a larger burial ground that was started during the EB IA and remained in use until at least the EB IB (Salmon 2008). The excavator suggested that the cemetery was part of the funerary landscape of EB Qashish. One may assume that the mortuary population derived from the nearby EB IA site at Tell el-Wa'er (see below) and from late EB I Tel Qashish itself.

Tell el-Wa'er and Tel Qashish West

Tell el-Wa'er, situated on a hillock 500 m northwest of Tel Qashish on the opposite side of the Kishon (figs. 1.3–4, 7; 3.1–2), was identified more than a century ago (Conder and Kitchener 1881–1883, maps; von Mülinen 1908, 211). Pottery sampled from its surface during an archaeological survey for the map of Yagur included sherds from the Iron, Persian, Hellenistic, Roman, Byzantine, and Early Islamic periods (Olami, Sender, and Oren 2004, 61*, site 189). In addition, two caves were identified on this hillock (site 188). Excavations at the foot of Tell el-Wa'er were conducted in 2010 by the IAA, and uncovered EB IA settlement remains (part 3, this volume). Another locality nearby, also excavated in 2010, was labeled Tel Qashish West (TQW) by its excavators, and revealed Mousterian finds (ch. 3, this volume; Yaroshevich, Khalaily, and Kirzner 2011).

'En Qashish

The site of 'En Qashish, some 100 meters south of the mound and the Kishon River (figs. 1.3–5; 3.1–2) was identified during a survey conducted in 2004 by the IAA around the junction of Yoqne'am. It was subsequently probed in a series of excavations conducted by a team from the Hebrew University, Jerusalem in 2005, 2009–2011, yielding the remains of an open-air Mousterian campsite from the Middle Paleolithic (70,000–60,000 YBP; Hovers et al. 2008; ch. 3, this volume). The site was further extensively probed in 2013 by the IAA (permit A6866/2013; Barzilai et al. 2015; Ekshtain et al. 2019), revealing a sequence of seasonal, short-lived Middle and Upper Paleolithic camp site occupations (ch. 3, this volume).

Fig. 1.7. Aerial View of the hillock of Tell el-Wa'er. The Tell el-Wa'er excavations were conducted near the northern base of the hill near the highway (right) and the TQW excavations were conducted near the southern base of the hill near the infrastructure installation (left).

'En Qashish South

Archaeological test trenching performed prior to the construction of a highway segment at 300 m south of the eponymous spring of 'En Qashish were followed in 2012–2013 by trial and salvage excavations conducted by the IAA (figs. 1.3–4; permit A6655/2013), initially in five distinct subareas marked A–E. Epipaleolithic *in situ* deposits were found in Areas D and E. These two subareas were subsequently extended into Areas E/F (southern area) and D/G (northern area), each covering *about* 120m², exposing further open-air in situ Epipaleolithic occupation remains (Yaroshevich et al. 2014, 2016).

The 2010–2013 Excavations

Between the years 2010–2013 five salvage excavations were conducted in the vicinity of Tel Qashish by the IAA, revealing Middle and Epipaleolithic at Tel Qashish West and Tel Qashish South (part 2, this volume), early Early Bronze Age I at Tell el-Wa'er (EB IA; part 3, this volume), late Early Bronze Age I at Tell Qashish (EB IB; part 4, this volume), Late Bronze Age II at Tel Qashish (part 5, this volume), and some early Roman remains (ch. 11, this volume). The final reports of these excavations form the core of the present volume.

Tel Qashish West: The Middle Paleolithic Excavations

The salvage excavations conducted by the IAA (permit A5880/2010) at Tel Qasish West (figs. 1.3–4, 7; 3.1–2), located at the foot of Tell el-Wa'er and distanced just a few hundred meters from a natural flint source, were carried out prior to the construction of a natural gas terminal. Three excavation areas were opened in the area and sixteen squares were excavated (part 2, this volume), revealing three layers; Only the middle one (Layer 2) contained in situ remains, yielding rich flint assemblages characterized by an abundance of Levallois items diagnostic of the Middle Paleolithic. The site is roughly contemporary with the nearby occupation of 'En Qashish referred to above. Both indicate the in-situ occupation of Neandertals who used these two sites alternately according to the seasonal flooding of the Kishon.

Tel Qashish South: The Middle Paleolithic/ Epipaleolithic Excavations

The site labeled Tel Qashish South (figs. 1.3–4; 3.1–2) was probed in 2012 by the IAA (permits A6461/2012, A6506/2012, and A6632/2012) in three separated localities about 300–400 m south from Tel Qashish, yielding mixed flint assemblages, with Levallois items appearing side by side with bladelet-oriented debitage characteristic of the Epipaleolithic (Yaroshevich 2012, 2013, 2014, 2015; part 2, this volume).

Tell el-Wa'er: The Early Bronze Age IA Excavations

Salvage excavations on behalf of the IAA were conducted by the IAA (permit A6551/2012), in a 10 m × 80 m strip of cultivated land at the northeastern edge of Tell el-Wa'er (figs. 1.3–4, 7; 3.1–2; 4.1; part 3, this volume), along a segment of the planned route of the Haifa–'Afula railway line and Highway 6, and parallel and west of Road 70, revealing segments of fifteen oval buildings of a hitherto unknown Early Bronze Age IA settlement almost immediately beneath the present-day surface, founded on the sloping bedrock (fig. 4.4). The site should be viewed alongside Yiftah'el Stratum II as representative of the early phase of the Early Bronze Age I (chs. 5–6, this volume), and suggestive of the changes in settlement patterns following this early phase into the later phase, where extensive areas in and around Tell Qashish were preferred. Chapters 4–9 present the final publication of these excavations.

Tel Qashish North, Areas A–F: The Early Bronze Age IB Excavations

Excavations were conducted by the IAA over six distinct areas north of Tel Qashish (Areas A–F; figs. 1.3–6, 8; 10.1–4) over the course of three subsequent trial and salvage excavations (permits A5881/2010, A5992/2010, and A6149/2011; part 4, this volume; van den Brink and 'Ad 2011). Seventy squares distributed over four adjoining areas (A–D) within the cultivated fields north and west of Tel Qashish were probed initially (fig. 1.8). Subsequently additional eighty squares were excavated in Areas F and E.

A dense spread of late EB I dwelling remains and several storage facilities, clearly part of a settlement, less than 100 m north of the actual Tel of Qashish, that is, in Areas E South/North and F, seem to have constituted the core of the site. In order to distinguish the former from the contemporary settlement remains at Tel Qashish, Strata XV–XIV, Areas E and F were designated as "the lower village," and the Tel Qashish, Strata XV–XIV remains as "the upper village." The remaining four areas probed slightly further to the west (Areas C and D) and north (Areas A and B), seem to be peripheral to it. Areas C and D, characterized by an almost continuous spread of small limestone surfaces and a single, rectangular structure can best be typified as a late EB I agricultural activity area. Outlying Areas A and B yielded only sporadic late EB I potsherds near or close to the natural limestone bedrock. The only structural remains here are a segment of an early Roman stone-paved road in Area A1, and a bedrock cavity containing a Late Bronze Age II ritual pottery cache in Area B (see below).

Overall, these excavations outside the boundaries of Tel Qashish are complementary to the finds from the tell, Strata XV–XIV. In the Early Bronze Age IB, the settlement consisted of a core of well-built houses on the tell, which sprawled into the lower village of the salvage excavations, which included additional domestic units and grain storage facilities (Areas E North and South–F) as well as agricultural installations and industrial areas (Areas C–D).

In the transition to the EB II/III, the core of the tell proper was fortified and its margins abandoned. This is a phenomenon that can be seen at EB I–II transitional sites around the region (e.g. Yoqne'am and Megiddo, Level J-4 to Level J-5; Adams 2013).

Tel Qashish North, Area B: The Late Bronze Age II Excavation

Nine squares were excavated down to natural bedrock in Area B, revealing mainly spreads of EB IB pottery without any structural remains (figs. 1.3–6, 8). In one of the squares a narrow bedrock cavity (depth ca. 3 m) was excavated, containing a cache of locally produced and imported ritual ceramic ves-

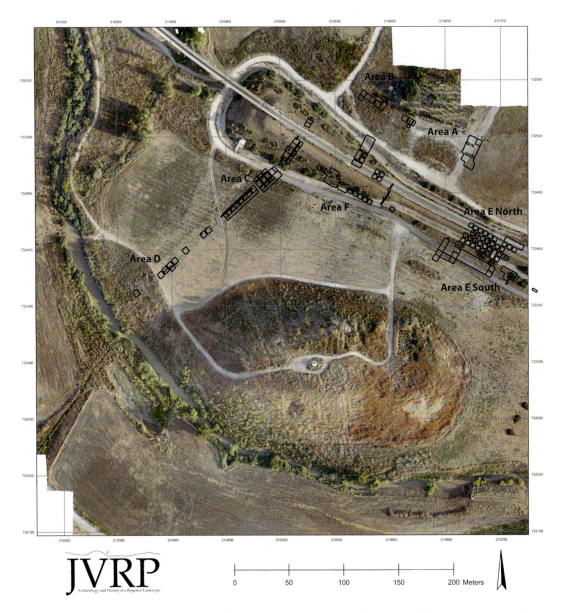

Fig. 1.8. Map of Tel Qashish showing excavation Areas A–F over 2020 orthophoto, post infrastructure construction. Courtesy of the JVRP.

sels, dating to the Late Bronze Age II (part 5, this volume; van den Brink, Segal, and Ad 2012; Ziffer et al. 2018)). The study of the ceramic assemblage indicates that the cache resulted from the disposal of temple objects in a one-time event. The deposit was done carefully and in an organized fashion not typical of more haphazard cultic favissae know from other sites, and the excavators suggest that the cache indeed is not a typical cultic favissa. They conclude that this was a deliberate concealment of the cultic vessels, probably in the face of a specific threatening event in the region. It is tempting to interpret this alongside the destruction of Tel Qashish Stratum V, and the collapse of LBA society across the region.

After this brief introductory overview, in the following chapters we will delve deeper, in chronological order, into the various find categories and findings deriving from the five above-mentioned relevant sites, starting with the Middle Paleolithic and ending with the Late Bronze Age II.

References

Adams, Matthew J.
2013 "Area J, Part III: The Main Sector of Area J." In *Megiddo V: The 2004–2008 Seasons*, edited by Israel Finkelstein, David Ussishkin, and Eric Cline, 47–118. 3 vols. SMNIA 31. Tel Aviv: Institute of Archaeology.

Aharoni, Yohanan
1959 "Zephath of Thutmose." *IEJ* 9: 110–22.

Artzy, Michal
2006 "The Carmel Coast during the Second Part of the Late Bronze Age: A Center for Eastern Mediterranean Transshipping." *BASOR* 343: 45–63.

Barzilai, Omry, Ariel Malinski-Buller, Ravid Ekshtain, and Erella Hovers
2015 "'En Qashish ('Ein Qashish)." *HA-ESI* 127. http://www.hadashot-esi.org.il/report_detail_eng.aspx?id=24852&mag_id=122.

Ben-Tor, Amnon, and Ruhama Bonfil
2003 "The Stratigraphy of the Early Bronze Age." In *Tel Qashish: A Village in the Jezreel Valley; Final Report of the Archaeological Excavations (1978–1987)*, edited by Amnon Ben-Tor, Ruhama Bonfil, and Sharon Zuckerman, 10–30. Qedem Reports 5. Jerusalem: Hebrew University of Jerusalem.

Ben-Tor, Amnon, and Yuval Portugali
1987 *Tell Qiri: A Village in the Jezreel Valley; Report of the Archaeological Excavations 1975–1977*. Qedem 24. Jerusalem: Hebrew University of Jerusalem.

Ben-Tor, Amnon, Miriam Avissar, and Yuval Portugali
1996 *Yoqneʿam I: The Late Periods*. Qedem Reports 3. Jerusalem: Hebrew University of Jerusalem.

Ben-Tor, Amnon, Doron Ben-Ami, and Ariella Livneh
2005 *Yoqneʿam III: The Middle and Late Bronze Ages; Final Report*. Qedem Reports 7. Jerusalem: Hebrew University of Jerusalem.

Ben-Tor, Amnon, Ruhama Bonfil, and Sharon Zuckerman
2003 *Tel Qashish: A Village in the Jezreel Valley; Final Report of the Archaeological Excavations (1978–1987)*. Qedem Reports 5. Jerusalem: Hebrew University of Jerusalem.

Ben-Tor, Amnon, Anabel Zarzecki-Peleg, and Shlomit Cohen-Anidjar
2005 *oqneʿam II: The Iron Age and Persian Period; Final Report of the Archaeological Excavations (1977–1988)*. Qedem Reports 6. Jerusalem: Hebrew University of Jerusalem.

Brink, Edwin C. M. van den, and Uzi ʿAd
2011 "Tel Qashish," *HA-ESI* 123. http://hadashot-esi.org.il/report_detail_eng.aspx?id=1894&mag_id=118.

Brink, Edwin C. M. van den, Orit Segal, and Uzi ʿAd
2012 "A Late Bronze Age II Repository of Cultic Paraphernalia from the Environs of Tel Qashish in the Jezreel Valley, Israel." In *Temple Building and Temple Cult in the Levant (2.–1. Millennium BC)*, edited by Jens Kamlah, 421–34, pls. 55–62. ADPV 41. Weisbaden: Harrassowitz.

Conder, C. R., and H. H. Kitchener
1881–1883 *The Survey of Western Palestine: Maps*. 3 vols. London: Committee of the Palestine Exploration Fund.

Ekshtain, Ravid, Ariel Malinsky-Buller, Noam Greenbaum, Netta Mitki, Mareike C. Stahlschmidt, Ruth Shahack-Gross, Nadav Nir, Naomi Porat, Daniella E. Bar-Yosef Mayer, Reuven Yeshurun, Ella Been, Yoel Rak, Nuha Agha, Lena Brailovsky, Masha Krakovsky, Polina Spivak, Micka Ullman, Ariel Vered, Omry Barzilai and Erella Hovers
2019 "Persistent Neanderthal Occupation of the Open-Air Site of 'Ein Qashish, Israel." *PLoS ONE* 14(6): e0215668. DOI: 10.1371/journal.pone.0215668.

Garstang, John
1922 "Report: Tell el Kussis." *BBSAJ* 2: 16–17.

Giveon, Raphael
1954 "'Emeq Yizrael." *Teva Va-Aretz* 10: 515–18. [Hebrew]

Hovers, Erella, Ariel Malinsky-Buller, Ravid Ekshtain, Maya Oron, and Reuven Yeshurun
2008 "Ein Qashish—A New Middle Paleolithic Open-Air Site in Northern Israel." *Journal of the Israel Prehistoric Society* 38: 7–40.

Mülinen, Eberhard Graf von
1908 "Beiträge zur Kenntnis des Karmels." *ZDPV* 31: 1–258.

Olami, Yaʿaqov, Shlomo Sender, and Eldad Oren
2004 *Map of Yagur (27): Archaeological Survey of Israel*. Jerusalem: Israel Antiquities Authority. http://www.antiquities.org.il/survey/newmap_en.asp#zoom=8.0000;xy:34.80852508545,31.298049926757;mapname=27.

Raban, Avner
1982 *Archaeological Survey of Israel: Nahalal Map (28) 16–23*. Jerusalem: Archaeological Survey of Israel.

Salmon, Yossi
2008 "Qiryat Harosheth—An Early Bronze Age Cemetery in the Vicinity of Tel Qashish." *Contract Archaeology Reports* 3: 5*–31*. http://excavations.haifa.ac.il/html/html_eng/Qiryat_Harosheth_1998.pdf.

Yaroshevich, Alla
2012 "Tel Qashish (South)." *HA-ESI* 124. http://www.hadashot-esi.org.il/Report_Detail_Eng.aspx?id=2168.
2013 "Tel Qashish (South)." *HA-ESI* 125. http://www.hadashot-esi.org.il/Report_Detail_Eng.aspx?id=2240.
2014 "Tel Qashish (South)." *HA-ESI* 126. http://www.hadashot-esi.org.il/Report_Detail_Eng.aspx?id=9568.
2015 "Tel Qashish (South) (B)." *HA-ESI* 127. http://www.hadashot-esi.org.il/report_detail_eng.aspx?id=23822&mag_id=122.

Yaroshevich, Alla, Hamudi Khalaily, and Dan Kirzner
2011 "Tel Qashish (West) Preliminary Report." *HA-ESI* 123. http://www.hadashot-esi.org.il/report_detail.asp?id=1842&mag_id=118. [Hebrew]

Yaroshevich, Alla, Nuha Agha, Elisabetta Boaretto, Lena Brailovsky, Valentina Caracuta, Noam Greenbaum, Dan Kirzner, Aviram Oshri, Naomi Porat, Yoel Roskin, Ariadna Shukrun, Polina Spivak, Katia Zutovsky, and Omry Barzilai
2014 "Investigating Pre-Agricultural Dynamics in the Levant: A New Stratified Epipaleolithic Site at 'En Qashish South, Jezreel Valley, Israel." *Antiquity Project Gallery* 88(342). https://www.antiquity.ac.uk/projgall/yaroshevich342.

Yaroshevich, Alla, Ofer Bar-Yosef, Elisabetta Boaretto, Valentina Caracuta, Noam Greenbaum, Naomi Porat, and Joel Roskin
2016 "A Unique Assemblage of Engraved Plaquettes from Ein Qashish South, Jezreel Valley, Israel: Figurative and Non-Figurative Symbols of Late Pleistocene Hunters-Gatherers in the Levant." *PLoS ONE* 11(8): e0160687. DOI: 10.1371/journal.pone.0160687.

Ziffer, Irit, Edwin C. M. van den Brink, Orit Segal, and Uzi Ad
2018 "A Unique Human Head-Cup from the Environs of Tel Qashish in the Jezreel Valley, Israel." In *The Adventures of the Illustrious Scholar: Papers Presented to Oscar White Muscarella*, edited by Elizabeth Simpson, 406–20. CHANE 94. Leiden: Brill.

Chapter 2

The Environs of Tel Qashish: Physiography and Geomorphology

Oren Ackermann (*Ariel University*)
Noam Greenbaum (*University of Haifa*)

General Environmental Background

The site of Tel Qashish is located on a chalky hill (ca. 35m ASL) east of Road 70 and north of the modern city of Yoqne'am (figs. 2.1 and 2.2). The site is located at the juncture of four main geographical structures: (1) the Mount Carmel ridge to the west, (2) the Tiv'on hills (part of the lower Galilee) to the northeast, (3) the Jezreel Valley to the southeast, and (4) the adjacent meander of the Kishon River.

The Kishon River, the second largest river crossing the Coastal Plain in Israel, with a channel length of 70 km, and drainage area of 1100 km^2 (Kishon Authority 2012), drains the Jezreel Valley to the Mediterranean Sea. Near the site of Tel Qashish, the channel and the valley change dramatically, with the channel direction shifting from northwest to north, and the valley narrowing from about 13 km to less than 700 m, as the channel enters the Kishon Water Gap between Mount Carmel and the Tiv'on hills.

Geologically, the site is located next to and parallel to the Carmel fault, which stretches along the eastern side of Mount Carmel. Various rock-formation exposures occur in the site's environs: the Carmel slope, composed mainly of limestone of the Turonian Age Binna Formation, a few small exposures of chalk of the of the Senonian Age Paleocene Epoch Mount-Scopus group, and chalk of the Adulam and Maresha Formations of the Eocene Epoch (Segev and Sass 2009).

The Kishon floodplain is composed of thick Quaternary alluvium covered by thick vertisols. The Tiv'on hills are composed mainly of Adulam and Maresha formations chalk of the Eocene Epoch. A few Miocene basalt exposures occur within the Jezreel Valley and on the contact line between the southeast part of the Tiv'on hills and the Jezreel Valley (Sneh, Bartov, and Rosensaft 1998).

The slopes of Mount Carmel and the Tiv'on hills are covered by rendzina soils with abundant patches of terra rossa soil covering limestone and dolomite. The Jezreel Valley is composed of grumusol (vertisols) and hydromorphic and gley soils (Dan et al.1975; Dan, Fine, and Lavee 2007; Singer 2007).

The climate is Mediterranean, characterized by hot, dry summers and cold, rainy winters. The annual mean temperature is 17°C, with mean temperatures of 13°C in January and 25°C in August (Shahar 2007). The rainy season generally lasts from October to May, with a mean annual rainfall of 600 mm (Israel Meteorological Service 1990). On the eastern slopes of Mount Carmel, the vegetation is composed of Mediterranean maqui as well as dwarf and dense shrubs. The most abundant species are pine (*Pinus halepensis*), kermes oak (*Quercus calliprinos*), terebinth (*Pistacia terebinthus*), bay laurel (*Laurus nobilis* L.), Judas tree (*Cercis siliquastrum* L.), Syrian maple (*Acer obtusifolium* Sm.), and strawberry tree (*Arbutus andrachne* L.). On the Tiv'on hills, the primary tree species is Tabor oak (*Quercus ithaburensis*), with the occurrence of a variety of annuals and geophytes (Ministry of Environmental Protection 2011). The Jezreel Valley is dominated by agricultural cultivation.

Research Aims

In this study, we conducted a geomorphological field study in order to describe the geomorphological and paleo-landscape of the environs of Tel Qashish, and to study the connection between the physical structure of the site's environs and its location. A separate study was conducted in the area of Tel Qashish West with relevance for the Middle Paleolithic site west of the Kishon (see ch. 3, this volume). The present study was conducted in collaboration with the salvage excavations of the Early Bronze Age settlement at Tell Qashish (Areas A–F; see Part IV, this volume).

Methodology

The geomorphological and landscape history of the site was reconstructed through a geomorphological field survey. The following representative sections were tested from west to east within the areas of the Tel Qashish excavations (fig. 2.2):

Area D, Square ZY29
The lowest point of the excavation area, near the Kishon River channel, which encountered the Kishon floodplain.

Area C, Square L29
The central part of the excavation area, in the west part of the site.

Area B, Square D16
Near the top of the excavation area, in the west part of the site.

Fig. 2.1. Location of the site and main geographical features.

Fig. 2.2. Air photograph of the area and location of the studied sections.

2. The Environs of Tel Qashish: Physiography and Geomorphology

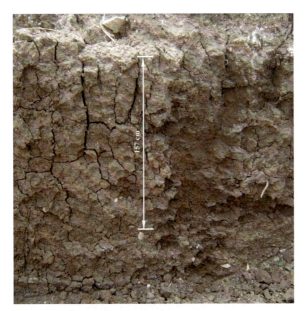

Fig. 2.3. Square ZY29, looking east.

Fig. 2.4. Square L29: Trench probe.

Area A
The highest point of the excavation area.

Area E, Sections TQ1-3E
The slopes on the east part of the site.

In the field, sediments were described according to their structure, texture, gravel content and type, sediment compaction, pedological characterizations, unit boundaries, and color. In the laboratory, the distribution of fine material (grains <2 mm) was measured by sedimentation using the hydrometer method (Klute 1986). Dating of the sedimentary units was based on flint artifacts and ceramic finds in the relevant strata. The optically stimulated luminescence (OSL) dating method was applied to one section in Square L29 to date the grumusol (which was void of ceramic finds) below the archaeological level.[1] The study of the effect and benefits of the physical structure of the site's environs on its location was conducted through field survey and analysis of the shaded relief image (fig. 2.1).

Results

The results are summarized and presented in tables 2.1–7 at the end of the chapter. In general, it seems that the Early Bronze Age remains at Tel Qashish were located on the ancient floodplain of the Kishon River and the western and eastern slopes of the tell (fig. 2.2).

Geomorphology and Sedimentology

The Kishon Floodplain: Area D, Square ZY29

This section was cut in the lowest area of the excavation adjacent to the Kishon River channel (figs. 2.2, 2.3; table 2.1). The exposure, which includes gray mottling and alluvial sediments with laminae of granular grains (fig. 2.4), suggests low-energy flows and flooding events of the Kishon River.

The Main Site Slopes

Square L29
A section in a mechanically dug trench close to Square L29, on the western slope of the tell (figs. 2.2, 2.4, 2.5; tables 2.2–3), revealed chalky bedrock at a depth of 220 cm. The bedrock is overlain by a 120 cm layer of clayey grumusol (the lower grumusol)

---

1 The analysis was conducted at the OSL dating laboratory of the Geological Survey of Israel, Jerusalem.

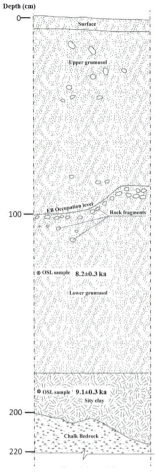

Fig. 2.5. Square L29.

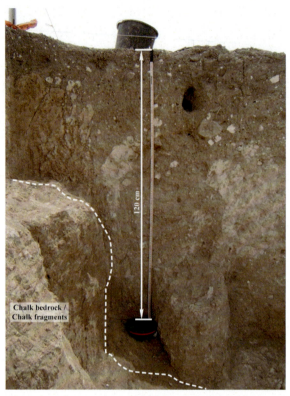

Fig. 2.6. Square D16, looking at azimuth 210°. The dashed line marks the contact between the chalky bedrock and the chalky fill sediment.

Fig. 2.7. Trench probe section TQ1.

dated by OSL (table 2.3) to about 8–9 ka BP. The Early Bronze Age occupation level was found on top of this layer. After the late EB I occupation was abandoned, a 70-cm layer of grumusol (the upper grumusol) covered this part of the site.

Square D16
This section, cut into the higher part of the western slope (figs. 2.2, 2.6; table 2.4), revealed that the chalky bedrock is situated about 60 cm below the present surface. The bedrock is overlain by chalky colluvial pale rendzina.

Area A
This area, the highest excavation point at 37.29 m ASL, is located on the topographic saddle north of the tell (fig. 2.2). Rounded pebbles and cobble-sized gravels were found deposited over the chalky bedrock, probably representing a former level and location (on a geological time scale) of the Kishon River,

Fig. 2.8. Trench probe section TQ2.

Fig. 2.9. Trench probe section TQ3.

about 17 m above the current channel and northeast of the main EB I site.

Area E, Sections TQ1–3

Testing the soil and the sediments in the eastern part of the main site through three mechanically dug trenches (figs. 2.2, 2.7–9; tables 2.5–7) revealed that the surface was composed of colluvial/alluvial soil. This soil deepens to the east, toward a small buried tributary (fig. 2.2), from about 25 cm to about 115 cm. Archaeological deposits diminish toward the east, while the soil depth increased. The colluvial/alluvial soil overlies Eocene chalk and Miocene lower basalt. During the Early Bronze Age, the surface in this part of the site was apparently about 50 cm lower than today, with an active small tributary to the east of the site (fig. 2.9).

Advantages of the Site's Location

The tell is located at the strategic Kishon Water Gap, an ancient pass leading from the coastal bay of Haifa inland to the Jezreel Valley, which further connected to other inland valleys, such as the Jordan River Valley (figs. 2.1–2). The value of the site's location in the EB I (and perhaps later) can be determined by a combination of the following physiographic characteristics: (1) the relatively high location in the landscape, about 17 m above the surrounding area, and overlooking the Kishon Water Gap pass; (2) the site was protected by the Kishon River on the western and southern sides and by a small (now buried) tributary channel on the east. These channels may have had perennial flows in the past, thus, serving as a natural defensive feature; (3) the Kishon River served as a permanent water source for the inhabitants of Tel Qashish and its immediate environs. It is important to note, however, that flow energy of the river at this point was relatively low due to a low channel gradient of less than 0.5 percent (Vachtman 2005). The narrow Kishon Water Gap contributed to the water low-energy flows in the past due to coastal sand intrusion and blockage or slowing down of the streamflow (Greenbaum et al. 2014), and, as observed over the last few decades, due to the large sediment yields sourcing from the cultivated areas upstream (Vachtman 2005).

References

Dan, Joel, Zvi Raz, Dan H. Yaalon, and Hanna Koyumdjisky
1975 *The Soil Association Map of Israel, 1:500,000.* Bet Dagan: Volcani Institute.

Dan, Joel, Pinchas Fine, and Hanoch Lavee
2007 *The Soils of the Land of Israel.* Tel Aviv: Tel Aviv University; Eretz. [Hebrew, English abstract]

Greenbaum, Noam, Ravid Ekshtain, Ariel Malinsky-Buller, Naomi Porat, and Erella Hovers
2014 "The Stratigraphy and Paleogeography of the Middle Paleolithic Open-Air Site of 'Ein Qashish, Northern Israel." *Quaternary International* 331: 203–15.

Israel Meteorological Service
2000 *Precipitation (mm): Average Annual Amount, Map 11. Period 1961-1990.* Jerusalem: State of Israel, Ministry of Transport.

Kishon Authority. http://www.kishon.org.il/.

Klute, Arnold, ed.
1986 *Methods of Soil Analysis: Part I—Physical and Mineralogical Methods*, 2nd ed. Agronomy Monographs 9.1. Madison, WI: American Society of Agronomy.

Ministry of Environmental Protection
30.11.2011 *Interactive Map: State of Israel.* http://gis.sviva.gov.il/website/moe/html/gis/interactiveMap1.htm#4$0&40 (accessed November 30, 2011). [Hebrew]

Segev, Amit, and Eytan, Sass
2009 *Geological Map of Israel 1:50,000. Sheet 3-III, Atlit.* Jerusalem: Geological Survey of Israel.

Shahar, Arieh
2007 *Universal Carta Atlas.* Jerusalem: Carta. [Hebrew]

Singer, Arieh
2007 *The Soils of Israel.* Berlin: Springer.

Sneh, Amihai, Yosef Bartov, and Marcelo Rosensaft
1998 *Geological Map of Israel 1:200,000, Sheet 1.* Jerusalem: Geological Survey of Israel.

Vachtman, Dina
2005 "Transport of Suspended Sediments in Nahal Kishon and Nahal Alexander to the Continental Shelf of Israel." MA thesis, University of Haifa. [Hebrew]

Table 2.1. Square ZY29, general description.

Unit	Depth from the surface (cm)[a]	Color[b]	Texture	Structure	Note
Grumusol	0–30				
	0–10	10YR 5/1 gray (dry)	Clay loam	Granular and massive, subangular blocky	Surface layer; soft lower transition to the layer below is gradual to clear.
	10–30	10YR 4/2 dark grayish brown	Silty clay loam	Subangular blocky	Anthropogenic chalk fragments (their utility is not understood); transition to the layer below according to the lower line of the rock fragments.
Hydromorphic grumusol	30–175	10YR 3/1 very dark gray	Clay (depth 30–150 cm), Sandy clay loam (depth 150–175 cm)	Subangular blocky to prismatic	Glay stains in the following colors: 7.5YR 4/1 dark gray, 7.5YR 3/3 dark brown, 7.5YR 3/1 very dark brown; at depths of 130–135 cm and 150–157 cm, grit to granular lamina.

a Absolute height of top of section is 23.80 m ASL. Absolute height of bottom of section is 21.78 m ASL.
b Based on the Munsell Soil Color Chart. Sample color was checked in dry conditions unless stated otherwise.

Table 2.2. Probe trench section, Square L29, general description.

Unit	Depth from the surface (cm)[a]	Color[b]	Texture	Structure	Note
Upper grumusol	0–10		Clay	Granular and massive to subangular blocky	Surface layer.
	10–70		Clay		Soil peds slightly hard to hard, with clay skin and diagonal cracks.
Early Bronze Age occupation level	70–100		Clay	Subangular blocky to prismatic	Occupation level with archaeological finds, subrounded rock fragments up to 15% of the layer; calcium carbonate sediments coat the rock fragments; signs of secondary calcium carbonated.
Lower grumusol	100–220		Clay changes to silty clay at 180 cm		Similar to the description of 10–70 and 70–100 cm; rock fragments are present at a depth of 130–220 cm; land snails are found in clumps at depth 130–220 cm; abrupt and wavy boundary to bedrock. OSL dating: 130–140 cm: 8.2±0.3 ka 185–190 cm: 9.1±0.3 ka
Chalk					Bedrock.

a Absolute height of top of section is 27.07 m ASL.
b Based on the Munsell Soil Color Chart. Sample color was checked in dry conditions unless stated otherwise.

Table 2.3. Square L29, luminescence OSL dating results.

GSI lab no.	Description	Depth (cm)	Moisture (%)	K (%)	U (ppm)	Th (ppm)	Ext. α (µGy/a)	Ext. β (µGy/a)	Ext. γ (µGy/a)	Cosmic (µGy/a)	Total dose (µGy/a)	No. of aliquots	O-D (%)	De (Gy)	Age (ka)
ACK-21	Grumusol	130–140	10	0.91	1.4	7.4	8	710	591	177	1486±40	17/18	14	12.3±0.4*	8.2±0.3*
ACK-22	Grumusol	185–190	10	0.69	1.5	8.7	10	800	674	166	1950±43	18/18	8	15.1±0.4*	9.1±0.3*

- Quartz samples (88–125 mm). De was obtained using the single aliquot regeneration (SAR) dose protocol on 2 mm aliquots, using preheats of 10 s @ 180–280°C. γ, β and α dose rates were calculated from the concentration of U, Th and K, and the cosmic dose estimated from sample burial depth.
- No. of aliquots: The number of measured aliquots used for De calculations.
- O-D: Overdispersion, the degree of scatter.
* For samples with OD <20 percent De (and ages) were calculated using the central age model.

Table 2.4. Square D16, general description.

Unit	Depth from the surface (cm)[a]	Color[b]	Texture	Structure	Note
Chalky soil	0–10	10YR 6/1 gray	Clay loam	Granular and massive	Surface layer, soft; low boundary is gradual to clear.
	10–40	10YR 7/1 light gray	Silty clay	Granular and massive to subangular blocky	Angular to subangular chalk fragments; the transition to the layer below according to the appearance of ceramic sherds at a depth of 40 cm.
Chalky fill sediments	40–120	10YR 7/1 light gray	Clay	Granular and massive to subangular blocky	Fill in a depression/trench, slightly hard, with chalky fragments; the layer contains ceramic sherds from the Early Bronze Age; sharp and wavy low boundary.
Chalk	From ~60 cm to 120cn			Bedrock fragments	Part of the unit composed of chalky fragments; a massive chalk bedrock at the side and the bottom a massive chalk bedrock.

a Absolute height of top of section is 34.98 m ASL.
b Based on the Munsell Soil Color Chart. Sample color was checked in dry conditions unless stated otherwise.

Table 2.5. Probe trench section, TQ1, general description.

Unit	Depth from the surface (cm)	Color (wet)[a]	Texture	Structure	Note
Basalt brown soil	0–15	10YR 4/2 dark grayish brown	Clay loam	Granular and massive	Eroded basalt gravel, gradual low boundary.
	15–75	10YR 4/2 dark grayish brown	Clay loam	Granular and massive	Sharp low boundary.
Chalky/Marl	75–160	10YR 7/3 Very pale brown		Bedrock	Eocene? Chalky marl; "aked" upper level characterized by reddish color (hue?) and baked rounded pebbles, up to 20 cm long; the pebbles are natural, evidence of unconformity line.

a Based on the Munsell Soil Color Chart. Sample color was checked in dry conditions unless stated otherwise.

Table 2.6. Probe trench section, TQ2, general description.

Unit	Depth from the surface (cm)	Color (wet)[a]	Texture	Structure	Note
Brown dark soil	0–25	10YR 3/2 Very dark grayish brown	Clay	Granular to subangular blocky and massive	Colluvial soil covering the Early Bonze Age site, with fragments of carbonates and eroded basalt; the number of basalt fragments increases relatively with depth; the low boundary is clear and wavy.
Very eroded basalt	20–50	7.5YR 4/2 brown	Sandy loam		The layer contains eroded basalt fragments up to 3–4 cm long; sign of carbonate sediment; gradual low boundary.
Basalt bedrock	50–160	clay 7.5YR 5/4 brown basalt 2.5YR 5/1 gray brown		Bedrock	Basalt fragments coated in between by carbonate clay veins.

a Based on the Munsell Soil Color Chart. Sample color was checked in dry conditions unless stated otherwise.

Table 2.7. Probe trench section, TQ3, general description.

Unit	Depth from the surface (cm)	Color (wet)[a]	Texture	Structure	Note
Dark brown soil	0–70	10YR 3/2 very dark grayish brown	Clay	Granular to subangular blocky and massive	Alluvial soil with limestone fragments; gradual low boundary; slightly hard.
B–horizon	70–115	7.5YR 4/2 brown	Clay	Columnar to prismatic	The layer contains a few rock fragments; slight hard; sharp and straight low boundary, unconformity or truncated line.
Weathered basalt	115–215			Eroded bedrock	Weathered basalt fragments.
Vesicular basalt	215–230			Bedrock	Hard bedrock; slightly eroded vesicular basalt.

a Based on the Munsell Soil Color Chart. Sample color was checked in dry conditions unless stated otherwise.

Part II

Tel Qashish West
(Middle Paleolithic and Epipaleolithic)

Chapter 3

Middle Paleolithic and Epipaleolithic Flint Procurement and Associated Workshops West and South of Tel Qashish

Alla Yaroshevich (*Israel Antiquities Authority*), Dan Kirzner (*Israel Antiquities Authority*),
Hamudi Khalaily (*Israel Antiquities Authority*), Oren Ackermann (*Ariel University*),
and Noam Greenbaum (*University of Haifa*)

Tel Qashish, surrounded by the perennial Kishon River, is located in a constriction of the Jezreel Valley, between Mount Carmel and Tiv'on Hills (figs. 3.1–2).[1] This setting constitutes a classical ecotone attractive for prehistoric hunter-gatherers. El-Khiam and Jericho arrowheads recovered during the excavations conducted on the tell (Rosen 2003) indicate that the site was used during the Pre-Pottery Neolithic period (11.5–8.5 ka BP) when the subsistence of incipient agriculturalists still depended on hunting. Recent extensive infrastructure-development projects conducted to the east and the west of the Road 70 separating the foothills of Mount Carmel and the Jezreel Valley led to important discoveries showing that the area adjacent to the tell was intensively used during the Paleolithic.

The discoveries east of Road 70 concern two sites with in situ remains, labeled 'Ein Qashish and 'Ein Qashish South. The first, adjacent to the Kishon River where it meanders around the tell, was occupied by Neandertals during the late Middle Paleolithic (MP) between 70 and 60 ka BP (Hovers et al. 2008; Malinski-Buller, Ekshstain, and Hovers 2014; Been et al. 2017; Ekshtain et al. 2019). The proximity to the river, in combination with the sedimentological composition of the site suggest occupation during the dry season, between early summer and early autumn (Hovers et al. 2014; Ekshtain et al. 2019). The second site, 'Ein Qashish South, located a few hundred meters south of the tell and the Kishon River, revealed an entire Epipaleolithic sequence—a period encompassing the transformation from mobile hunter-gatherers to sedentary foragers and first agriculturalists (c.25–11.5 ka BP; Yaroshevich et al. 2014, 2016). Also, a singular radiocarbon date obtained so far from a deep trench (unpublished) indicates that the site was initiated during the Upper Paleolithic (UP). All these data together indicate a virtually continuous use of the area throughout the prehistoric sequence, encompassing the late MP, UP, Epipaleolithic, and Early Neolithic periods.

The present contribution focuses on two sites discovered west of Road 70, on the foothills of Mount Carmel. The first, Tel Qashish West, is located on the lower slope of Tell el-Wa'er, a hillock adjacent to the mountain. This site yielded dense deposits rich in diagnostic MP (Levallois) artifacts, natural flint nodules, and cortical elements (Yaroshevich, Khalaily, and Kirzner, 2011) indicating on-site knapping from the beginning of the reduction sequence. Situated on top of the old alluvial fan of

---

1 The excavations at Tel Qashish West (TQW) were underwritten by the Netivey Gaz Company; the Derekh Eretz Company Ltd. financed the excavations at Tel Qashish South. We would like to thank K. Said, L. Talmi, and the late D. Ya'aqov-Jam for their administrative and logistical support during the excavations; L. Zieger and M. Smilanski for the flint drawings; P. Partouche for the aerial photographs; and E. C.M. van den Brink for editing the English of the manuscript. We are especially obliged to Giora Gal for his kind invitation to visit Bustan Gal and permission to conduct the survey focusing on the flint sources.

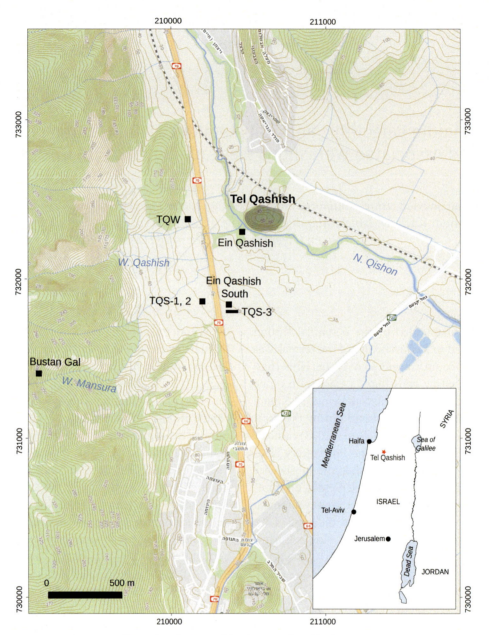

Fig. 3.1. Location map of the sites mentioned in the text.

Wadi Qashish previously dated to 74+/−10 ka BP (Zilberman et al. 2008; Greenbaum et al. 2014), this site is roughly contemporaneous with 'Ein Qashish, the Neandertal occupation on the bank of the Kishon River. The second site, Tel Qashish South (TQS), located on the alluvial fan of Wadi Mansura, yielded mixed flint assemblages, with Levallois items appearing side by side with bladelet-oriented debitage characteristic of the Epipaleolithic or Upper Paleolithic (Yaroshevich 2012, 2013, 2014). Similarly to TQW, the assemblages are characterized by numerous natural nodules and cortical flakes.

This study incorporates the results of the survey conducted on the slope of the mountain in the area of a private farm—Bustan Gal—and along the tributaries draining the slope, including Wadi Qashish and Wadi Mansura and their associated alluvial fans (figs. 3.1–2). Combined with techno-typological analyses of the Levallois component, the survey's results are employed to identify the function of the sites and their formation processes. In particular, the pos-

3. Middle Paleolithic and Epipaleolithic Flint Procurement and Associated Workshops

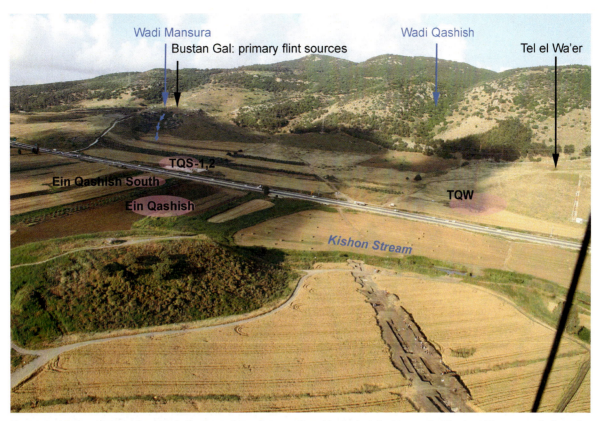

Fig. 3.2. Aerial view of the region with indications of the sites mentioned in the text, looking south. The short blue arrows indicate the track of the flint nodules detached from their primary source (Bustan Gal farm) down the slope to the locality of their accumulation (TQS).

sibility that both sites could be associated with the secondary source of flint raw material accumulating in the area due to the detachment of the flint fragments from the bedrock upslope, and their transport by gravity and by tributary flows to the valley (e.g., Ekshtain et al. 2014) is evaluated. Comparison with the published assemblages of the Neandertal occupation at ʿEin Qashish, in terms of the main techno-typological characteristics, was performed to assess the possibility that these neighboring sites, located in different topographic settings, were inhabited on a complementary, probably seasonal basis. The results of this study shed new light on the land-use strategies applied during the late Middle Paleolithic and later prehistoric periods in the area.

Geological Background

Tel Qashish West and Tel Qashish South are located on the southeastern edge of a semioval valley along the north–south Yoqneʿam–Jalame segment of the Carmel fault, close to the city of Yoqneʿam. The valley is surrounded by hard Turonian carbonate rocks, mainly limestone and dolomite of the Bina Formation along its northern and western border, and by relatively soft chalk with some flint concentrations and nuclei of the Senonian ʿEn-Zetim Formation along its southern border. Four steep first to second order tributaries drain into the valley from the Mount Carmel slope. In the northern part of the valley, the northwestern tributaries drain mainly hard limestone and dolomite exposures, thus containing mostly angular carbonate gravel. Together, these tributaries formed the old alluvial fan of Wadi Qashish, which was OSL-dated to between 123+/−13 ka (bottom) and 74+/−10 ka (top; Zilberman et al. 2008; Greenbaum et al. 2014). TQW, characterized by dense Middle Paleolithic deposits, is located on top of this old alluvial fan.

The southernmost tributary draining into the valley (figs. 3.1–2), called Wadi Mansura, separates between the eponymous tell and Bustan Gal, a private farm located on its northern bank. The alluvial fan associated with the southern tributaries and

Fig. 3.3. TQW during the excavations, looking southeast.

containing the mixed MP-Epipaleolithic/UP deposits excavated at TQS has not been dated.

Tel Qashish West

Excavation and Stratigraphy

The salvage excavations conducted at TQW were carried out prior to the construction of a natural gas terminal (fig. 3.3). Fifteen 4 × 4 m squares were opened, subdivided into 2 × 2 m units excavated in 5 cm splits. All sediments were dry-sieved through a 5 mm mesh. A 40-L sediment sample (volume equal to a split of 1 × 1 m, 1 cm deep), taken from the main archaeological layer (layer 2, see below), was wet-sieved through a 2 mm mesh. The debris, that is, chips (flakes smaller than 2.5 cm) and chunks, as well as nodules of flint raw material, were counted for each excavation unit and eventually left behind at the site.

The stratigraphic sequence of TQW is composed of three main layers (fig. 3.4):

Layer 1

Dark brown massive silty clay grumusol (vertisol), 30–70 cm thick, containing a few small- to medium-sized limestone clasts, and flint artifacts in a low density. This layer was removed using mechanical equipment.

Fig. 3.4. TQW, stratigraphic sequence in Square C6 during excavation.

Layer 2

Light-gray clay, increasing in thickness from a few centimeters to 25–30 cm toward the northeast and consisting of many small- to medium-size limestones, flint, and a few basalt clasts. The layer, very rich in knapped flint artifacts, also contained several poorly preserved (animal?) bone fragments. The matrix contains large amounts of carbonates.

Layer 3

Yellowish gray clay, rich in basalt and limestone clasts of various sizes up to boulder size. Flint artifacts are present, but in a considerably lower frequency than in Layer 2, and their number decreases with depth. A deep sounding performed at the easternmost edge of the excavated area showed this layer to be over three meters thick.

Fig. 3.5. TQW Levallois core made on homogeneous brown flint.

Fig. 3.6. TQW, Levallois core, on nonhomogeneous flint.

Fig. 3.7. TQW, Levallois point, made on homogeneous brown flint.

Fig. 3.8. TQW, retouched Levallois flake on nonhomogeneous flint.

Fig. 3.9. TQW, Levallois flake on homogeneous flint with concentric bands, seen on dorsal surface.

About seventy thousand artifacts, including debris, natural nodules, and numerous debitage and tools, were retrieved during the excavations (figs. 3.5–23). Levallois cores and products are virtually the only diagnostic artifacts present in the assemblage. A singular handaxe, the fossil type of the Lower Paleolithic Acheulian culture, was collected from the topsoil (fig. 3.24). For the present study, the assemblage culled from square C1 was analyzed, located in the northeastern part of the site where the prominent, 25–30 cm thick light-gray layer 2, rich in flint artifacts, was uncovered. In this square, layer 3 is 32 cm thick.

Flint Assemblage: General Composition and Physical Traits

The majority of the flint artifacts are patinated and abraded to various degrees. A calcite crust and a kind of luster were often observed. A few burnt artifacts were also recorded. Fresh or almost fresh items are not numerous (figs. 3.5–15), impeding detailed description of flint-type variability: Nonhomogeneous kinds with chalky inclusions appear to be common (figs. 3.6, 8), while homogeneous brown fine-grained flint is also frequently encountered (figs. 3.5, 7), and brown flint with wide stripes close to the cortex probably belongs to the latter variant (fig. 3.14). The homogeneous beige-brown, coarse-grained flint (fig. 3.11) occurs only sporadically. The same applies to the flint with concentric reddish stripes (figs. 3.9–10) which most probably originates in the nearby Menashe Hills, Adulam Formation (Ekshtain et al. 2014, fig. 6), or near the Nazareth Mountains, Timrat Formation (Ekshtain et al. 2014, fig. 5). The flint type with characteristic concentric reddish stripes can also be observed on the less weathered side of the singular handaxe found within the topsoil (fig. 3.24).

The majority of the assemblage is composed of debris, this group incorporating knapped artifacts that could not be affiliated with any technological group (table 3.1; all tables can be found at the end of the chapter) and natural flint nodules. Some of these appear to have been tested (fig. 3.15). Flakes dominate (56.6 percent) within the debitage group, followed by primary elements (PE, cortex covering more than 50 percent of the surface), which make up 17.7 percent. The frequency of naturally backed knives (NBK, 3.7 percent) is also relatively high.

Fig. 3.10. TQW, retouched Levallois flake made on homogeneous flint with concentric bands.

Fig. 3.11. TQW, Levallois flake made on homogeneous coarse-grained flint.

Fig. 3.12. TQW, Levallois core, hinged at the beginning of the reduction.

Fig. 3.13. TQW, hinged Levallois core on balk.

Fig. 3.14. TQW, cortical tools and debitage.

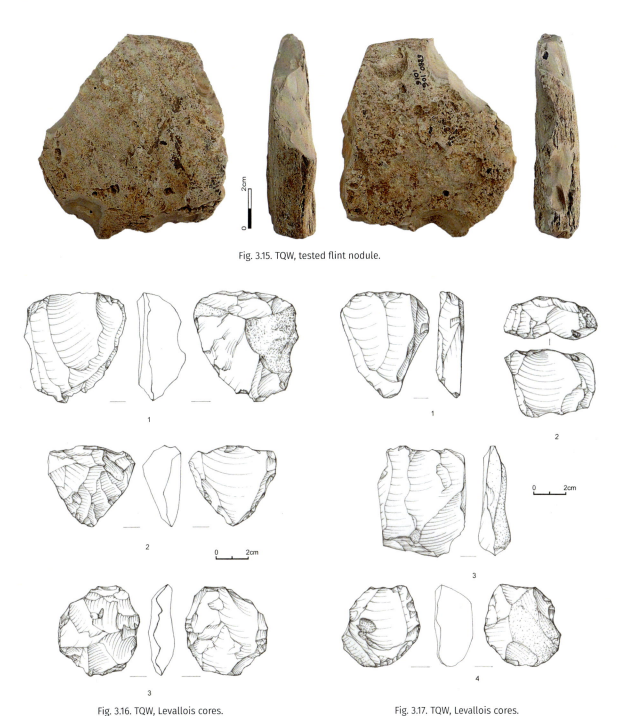

Fig. 3.15. TQW, tested flint nodule.

Fig. 3.16. TQW, Levallois cores.

Fig. 3.17. TQW, Levallois cores.

Blades and bladelets are not numerous, making up 2.5 percent and 0.2 percent, respectively. Levallois cores (figs. 3.16–18) make up more than half of the total cores present in the sample (see below for a detailed description). Amorphous cores, followed by cores on flakes, dominate the remainder of the group. Blade and bladelet cores are few. One blade/bladelet core found in the analyzed sample was made on a primary flake (fig. 3.22.1). In another case, blades and bladelets were removed from a thick tabular piece (fig. 3.22.2). The number of CTE (core trimming elements) is twice as high compared to the number of cores. The typological composition (table 3.2) shows a predominance of retouched flakes, followed by notches-denticulates. Formal tools modified by a substantial amount of retouch

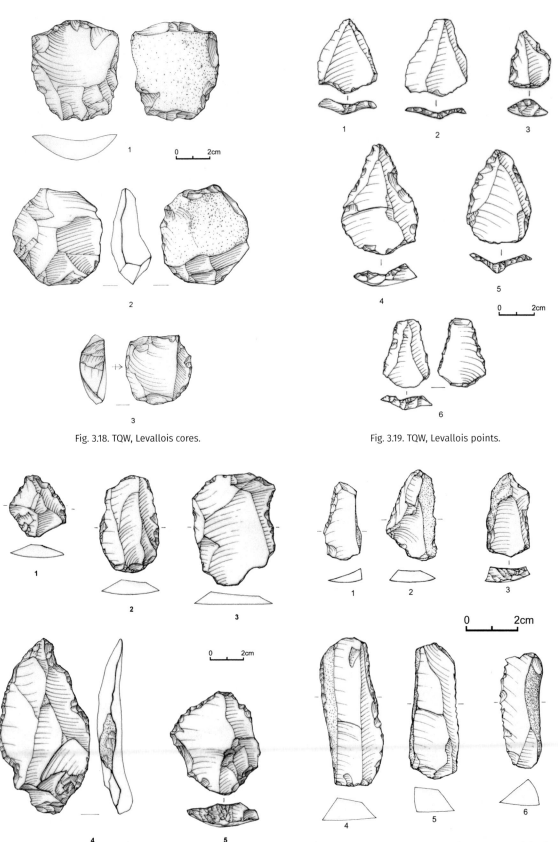

Fig. 3.18. TQW, Levallois cores.

Fig. 3.19. TQW, Levallois points.

Fig. 3.20. TQW, Levallois products.

Fig. 3.21. TQW, naturally backed knives; some exhibit signs of modification or use.

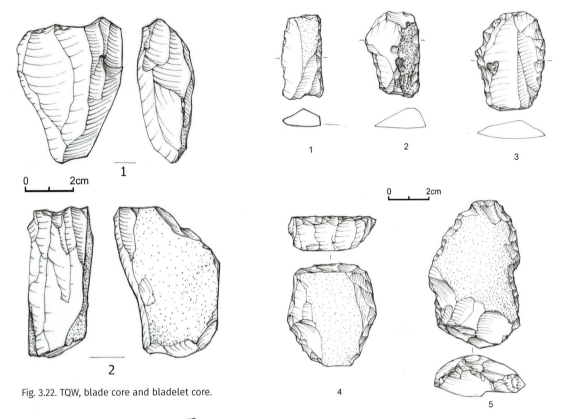

Fig. 3.22. TQW, blade core and bladelet core.

Fig. 3.23. TQW, tools on PE and cortical items.

Fig. 3.24. TQW, the hand axe.

are very rare. Of notice is the frequent use of PE as blanks for tool production (fig. 3.23).

Levallois Technology

The assemblage of Levallois artifacts obtained from square C1 includes thirty-four cores and seventy-eight products, that is, blanks and tools (table 3.3; figs. 3.16–20). Among the artifacts retaining their "Chapeau de gendarme," platform and faceting occur most frequently (table 3.4). Cores for flakes are almost five times more numerous than cores for points. Blade cores are absent in the assemblage. Flakes also predominate among the products, whereas blades and points appear in relatively low frequencies (table 3.3). Cores for flakes show lower values virtually in all metric characteristics compared to cores for points (table 3.5); among the products, however, flakes are larger than points, both on average and maximal values (table 3.6).

Bidirectional and centripetal methods of preparation are equally present (N=13 each) in the analyzed assemblage, while the unidirectional method (N=8) is the least numerous (table 3.3). Cores with a unidirectional scar pattern have the highest values in all the metric characteristics, including the size of the dominant scar alongside the lowest number of scars on their flaking surface (table 3.7). Some of these were apparently discarded at the beginning of the reduction sequence due to the hinge removal (figs. 3.12–13). Cores with a centripetal pattern are the smallest bearing the smallest dominant scar alongside the highest number of scars (table 3.7). Bidirectional and unidirectional patterns dominate among products, while centripetal is the least

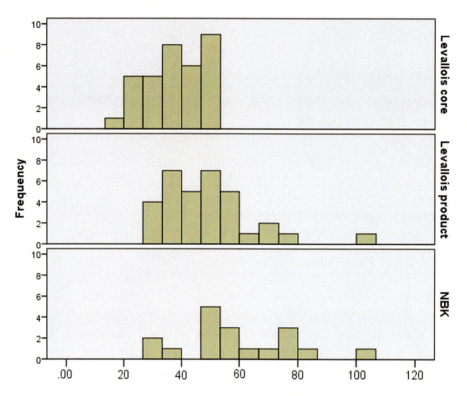

Fig. 3.25. TQW, distribution of Levallois cores, products, and NBK according to length.

common. As with cores, products with a centripetal scar pattern are the smallest and show the highest number of scars, whereas unidirectional and bidirectional ones show considerably higher values for all metric characteristics, alongside a lower number of scars on their surface (table 3.8). These observations indicate that the unidirectional mode was applied at the beginning of the core reduction sequence, whereas the centripetal one was applied at the final stage. Notably, cortex was observed on eight flakes (ca 10 percent of the Levallois products in the sample), six of these bearing a unidirectional scar pattern. Among cores, cortex was observed only on the maintenance surface. While products are consistently larger compared to the dominant scar on the corresponding cores, NBK are considerably larger, on average, compared to both cores and products (fig. 3.25).

Tel Qashish South

Excavation and Stratigraphy

The first and the second excavation seasons at Tel Qashish South were conducted in proximity to the olive groves west of Road 70 (figs. 3.1–2; Yaroshevich 2012, 2013). The third season was conducted east of this road, that is, within the valley (Yaroshevich 2014). The densest and largest accumulation of flint artifacts was obtained during the second season (Yaroshevich 2013). Seven 2 × 2m squares were excavated in 5 mm splits (fig. 3.26). The material was dry-sieved through a 5 mm mesh. A sample of a single excavation unit was wet-sieved through a 2 mm mesh.

Four main layers were documented (fig. 3.27):

Layer 1
A 1.6-m thick, dark brown-gray clay-silt layer (grumusol), removed using mechanical equipment.

Layer 2
A discontinuous, up to 40 cm thick layer/lens of matrix-supported brown clay layer, comprising up to 20 percent limestone clasts of various sizes, removed using mechanical equipment (track excavator).

Layer 3
A 50–60 cm thick layer of limestone clasts of various sizes mixed with knapped flint items.

3. Middle Paleolithic and Epipaleolithic Flint Procurement and Associated Workshops

Fig. 3.26. TQS during the second excavation season, looking south, on Wadi Mansura draining the slope of Mount Carmel.

Fig. 3.27. TQS, stratigraphic sequence.

Layer 4
Pale yellow clay with scant amounts of small limestone clasts, archaeologically sterile. A deep trench dug by mechanical equipment on the eastern margin of the area indicates that this layer thickens to more than 3 m.

The excavation yielded some fifteen thousand flint items, including debris and natural nodules. Levallois artifacts appear side by side with a bladelet-oriented industry characteristic of the Epipaleolithic/Upper Paleolithic (figs. 3.28–34), a feature observed in each square and excavation unit. A techno-typological analysis for this report was conducted on the assemblage culled from square C5.

Flint Assemblage: General Composition and Physical Traits

Virtually all items are covered with patina and bear signs of abrasion (figs. 3.28–32); some are heavily worn. This situation impedes reliable estimations concerning raw-material variability. Notably, bladelet cores appear to be less abraded compared to Levallois items.

The assemblage from square C5 comprises 4,574 items, the absolute majority being debris (table 3.9). Flakes make up more than a third of the debitage group (36.5 percent), followed by cores and PE (16.9 percent and 16.1 percent, respectively). While NBK are relatively numerous (3.5 percent), the frequencies of blades (1.2 percent) and bladelets (1.0 percent) are low. The majority of cores are amorphous; only 13 Levallois cores were found, alongside 20 bladelet cores (figs. 3.28–34). Retouched flakes, mostly non-Levallois, followed by notches/denticulates, dominate the tool assemblage (table 3.10). While retouched blades are relatively common, endscrapers (fig. 3.32), scrapers, and burins are present in very low numbers. Two fragmented backed bladelets and a single truncation complete the assemblage.

Levallois Technology

The assemblage of Levallois items includes thirteen cores and forty-eight products (figs. 3.28–34). Most cores show flake removal; only two cores for points and one for blades were recorded (table 3.11. Flakes are also the most frequent among products, while blades and points are present in considerably lower numbers. Almost a third of the products lack their proximal part. Preparation of the platform by faceting (25 percent) is the most frequent (table 3.12); 22.9 percent of the products have a plain platform; "Chapeau de gendarme" platform occurs only in 6.3 percent of the products.

Most cores exhibit bidirectional preparation, while the products are dominated by a unidirectional scar pattern (table 3.11). The centripetal method is represented by a single core and a single flake. Items with bidirectional and unidirectional scars exhibit similar values in their metric characteristics—a pattern characterizing both cores and products (tables 3.13–14). The size of the products is consistently larger compared to the dominant scar on corresponding cores. Blades and points show higher metric values compared to flakes, which dominate the products assemblage. Finally, NBK are considerably longer, on average, compared to both cores and products (fig. 3.35). Cortex was observed only on the maintenance surface of six out of thirteen Levallois cores. Cortex was recorded on three items within the products category.

Fig. 3.28. TQS, patinated Levallois core.

Fig. 3.29. TQS, abraded Levallois core.

Fig. 3.30. TQS bladelet core, slightly patinated.

Fig. 3.31. TQS, abraded bladelet core.

Fig. 3.32. TQS, end scraper on primary flake.

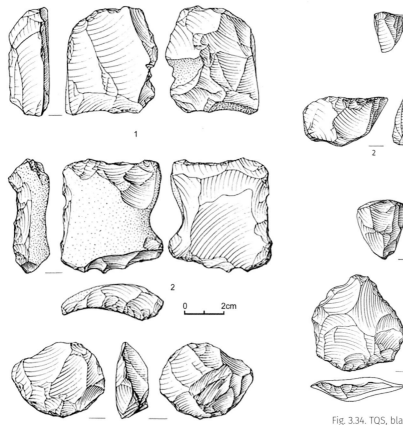

Fig. 3.33. TQS, Levallois cores.

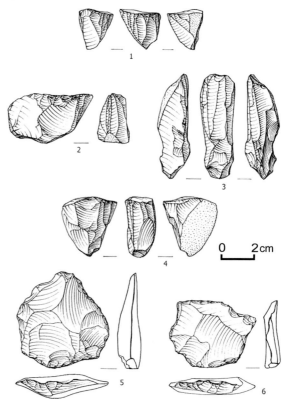

Fig. 3.34. TQS, bladelet cores and Levallois products.

Field Survey

A first survey, restricted to the area of Bustan Gal farm, was conducted during the second season of excavations at TQS (IAA permit A-6461; Yaroshevich 2013). The survey revealed primary flint sources containing small- to medium-sized nodules (up to cobble size), some fragmented but still embedded within the natural bedrock (fig. 3.36a–d). In particular, homogeneous brown and nonhomogeneous beige flint with chalky inclusions were observed. Furthermore, veins and nodules of a homogeneous brown high-quality flint were observed within an artificial, historic-era cave located on the farm (fig. 3.37). The visual similarity between certain flint types in TQW and TQS on the one hand and the sources detected in the farm area on the other suggests that these outcrops could have been a source for the raw material exploited by Paleolithic groups.

These nodules could be quarried directly from the outcrops, an option requiring climbing up the mountain slope. Another possibility is that the nodules, naturally, selectively weathered out from the rock, eroded and transported downslope by gravitational forces as well as by water flows along the tributaries, accumulated in the alluvial fan and composed a secondary source of raw material more readily available for the inhabitants of the valley. To evaluate these two scenarios, a second survey was conducted by two of the authors (Alla Yaroshevich and Noam Greenbaum) starting from the farm area and continuing along the tributaries draining the slope of Mount Carmel and the associated alluvial fans.

The results showed that Wadi Mansura—the southernmost tributary draining chalky areas and adjacent to Bustan Gal farm—indeed transports chalk and flint gravel into the southern part of the small, oval valley adjacent to the eastern mountain slope. In that area, about 5 percent of the gravel is composed of yellowish angular flint pebbles and cobbles (up to about 15 cm in size). Flint nodules were specifically found in the olive grove adjacent to TQS excavated during the second season, as well

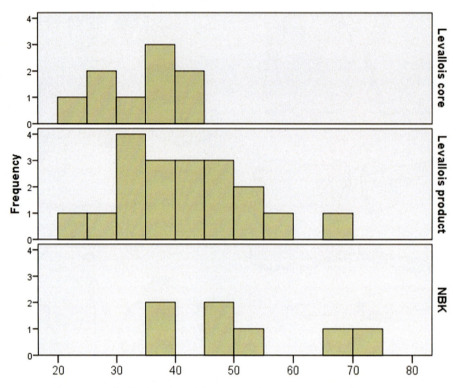

Fig. 3.35. TQS, distribution of Levallois cores, products, and NBK according to length.

as in the heaps of stones removed from the groves (figs. 3.38–40). Importantly, the flint types observed in the grove and the heaps are similar to those recorded in the area of the Bustan Gal farm.

The abundance of flint artifacts observed in the alluvial fan of Wadi Mansura, in the southern part of the valley, is in striking contrast to their virtual absence in the tributaries and the associated fan surveyed to the north, including that of Wadi Qashish. These observations provide valuable insights into the formation of TQW and TQS and the strategies of raw material procurement selected by the Paleolithic inhabitants of the valley (see discussion).

Comparison with ʻEin Qashish

Techno-typological comparison between TQW and ʻEin Qashish—the Neandertal occupation on the bank of the Kishon River (e.g., Malinski-Buler, Ekshtain, and Hovers 2014)—can help to evaluate the possibility that these roughly contemporary sites were complementary. A prominent difference appears in the frequency of PE, which is considerably higher in TQW (ca. 17.7 percent) versus around 7 percent in ʻEin Qashish (Malinski-Buler, Ekshtain, and Hovers 2014, table 1). At the same time, in terms of Levallois technology the sites exhibit several points of similarity. First, in both TQW and ʻEin Qashish, the absolute majority of Levallois cores show flake reduction. Second, in both sites bidirectional and centripetal modes of core preparation are the most common. Third, Levallois products mostly exhibit a unidirectional scar pattern. Furthermore, the shift from unipolar to centripetal flaking during the core reduction sequence was identified in both sites (e.g., Hovers et al. 2008; see also Yaroshevich et al. 2018 where this pattern is described in association with a workshop). Another point of similarity between TQW and ʻEin Qashish West can be followed in the tool assemblages predominated by minimally retouched blanks, with only low numbers of formal types.

The differences in the degree of raw material exploitation between the sites are not prominent. Thus, Levallois cores from TQW (48.4 mm long and 47.9 mm wide) are virtually identical to ʻEin Qashish (48.7 mm long and 46.1 mm wide; Malinski-Buler, Ekshtain, and Hovers 2014, table 5) even though the size of the dominant scar in TQW is larger: 37 mm long and 31 mm wide versus 29.7 mm long and

3. Middle Paleolithic and Epipaleolithic Flint Procurement and Associated Workshops

Fig. 3.36 a–d. Flint outcrops at Bustan Gal.

Fig. 3.37. Flint nodules inside artificial cave, Bustan Gal.

27.2 mm wide in ʿEin Qashish (2014, table 5) and the number of scars is lower: 6.1 on cores for flakes and 5.5 on cores for points versus 7.7 on average in ʿEin Qashish (2014, 237). While Levallois flakes from TQW (49.8 mm long and 35.6 mm wide) are slightly larger compared to ʿEin Qashish (39.8 mm long and 28.5 mm wide; 2014, table 6)—Levallois blades from TQW are shorter: 48.4 mm long and 27.4 mm wide versus 61.1 mm and 28.2 mm in ʿEin Qashish (2014, table 6).

Discussion and Conclusions

The data presented in this study provide insight into the function of the TQS and TQW sites, the process-

Fig. 3.38. Stone heap containing flint nodules on the alluvial fan of Wadi Mansura.

Fig. 3.39. Tested flint nodule from the stone heap on the alluvial fan of Wadi Mansura.

Fig. 3.40. Flint nodule from the stone heap on the alluvial fan of Wadi Mansura.

es that lead to their formation, and their possible association with the in situ occupations of nearby 'Ein Qashish and 'Ein Qashish South.

Our survey indicated that TQS was associated with the secondary source of flint accumulated on the alluvial fan of Wadi Mansura. The nodules could originate in the area of Bustan Gal farm, where a variety of raw flint were observed embedded within the chalky bedrock. The mixed nature of TQS can be attributed to the continuous activity of Wadi Mansura, which obviously disturbed and mixed the MP and Epipaleolithic/UP localities presumably spatially separated and/or stratified at first. It is quite possible that the secondary nodule accumulation available during the late MP was much more abundant, intense, and spatially extended than the one exposed during the TQS excavation which took place in proximity to Road 70.

The tributaries associated with TQW—Wadi Qashish and the next tributary to its north—are virtually devoid of flint nodules, suggesting that the formation process of that virtually clean MP site was different. A possible scenario would be the deliberate/purposeful collecting of flint nodules accumulated on the fan of Wadi Mansura (i.e., at TQS), and carrying them a few hundred meters away to the piedmont of Tell el-Wa'er for further reduction. The fact that the Levallois cores, products, and NBK exposed in TQW are larger in size compared to those of the TQS sample indicates that the largest flint nodules were selected for transportation to TQW. Nevertheless, the use of primary sources located up the slope of the mountain (e.g., Bustan Gal farm) cannot be excluded. In any case, the variability of flint types observed in TQW indicates that these local sources were not the only ones accessed by the inhabitants of TQW.

The TQW flint assemblage shows numerous points of similarity with 'Ein Qashish—the in situ occupation of Neandertals located a few hundred meters to the east on the bank of the Kishon River. The similarity is expressed in a variety of technological traits and in the composition of the tools assemblage. Furthermore, the differences in the intensity of the raw material exploitation are not prominent, suggesting that the same source/sources of flint raw material could have been used in both sites. The most profound difference—in the frequencies of PE—indicates intensive decortication in TQW as opposed to Ein Qashish where this activity is underrepresented (Malinski-Buler, Ekshtain, and Hovers 2014). These observations suggest the possibility/scenario of a complementary use of the two sites, apparently connected to environmental season-related variability, in particular the annual flooding of the Kishon River. While occupation at 'Ein Qashish is located in the proximity of the river and therefore was restricted to the summer and early autumn (Hovers et al. 2014; Ekshtain et al. 2019), TQW—located on a higher elevation up the slope of Tel el-Wa'er—could have been used during all seasons, winter included. Moreover, this particular location does not seem to be accidental since it provides the inhabitants, on the one hand, with a good view over the entire area, while offering shelter from the wind on the other.

The study of TQW and TQS presented here was conducted based on selected samples of flint artifacts. Abundant material for a more detailed, in-depth investigation of both sites is available. The connection between TQS and the Epipaleolithic/UP site of 'Ein Qashish South is still unclear at present, mostly because of the absence of microlithic tools at the former site. Future studies of flint assemblages deriving from different cultural contexts at 'Ein Qashish South will hopefully shed more light on land use by the last mobile hunter-gatherers roaming the area and also add to our understanding of the processes that eventually resulted in the abandonment of a mobile way of life based on hunting and gathering in favor of sedentary settlements and food production.

References

Been, Ella, Erella Hovers, Ravid Ekshtain, Ariel Malinsky-Buller, Nuha Agha, Alon Barash, Daniella E. Bar-Yosef Mayer, Stefano Benazzi, Jean-Jacques Hublin, Lihi Levin, Noam Greenbaum, Netta Mitki, Gregorio Oxilia, Naomi Porat, Joel Roskin, Michalle Soudack, Reuven Yeshurun, Ruth Shahack-Gross, Nadav Nir, Mareike C. Stahlschmidt, Yoel Rak, and Omry Barzilai
2017 "The First Neanderthal Remains from an Open-Air Middle Palaeolithic Site in the Levant." *Scientific Reports* 7.1: article 2958. DOI: 10.1038/s41598-017-03025-z.

Ekshtain, Ravid, Ariel Malinsky-Buller, Shimon Ilani, Irina Segal, and Erella Hovers
2014 "Raw Material Exploitation around the Middle Paleolithic Site of 'Ein Qashish." *Quaternary International* 331: 248–66. DOI: 10.1016/j.quaint.2013.07.025.

Ekshtain, Ravid, Ariel Malinsky-Buller, Noam Greenbaum, Netta Mitki, Mareike C. Stahlschmidt, Ruth Shahack-Gross, Nadav Nir, Naomi Porat, Daniella E. Bar-Yosef Mayer, Reuven Yeshurun, Ella Been, Yoel Rak, Nuha Agha, Lena Brailovsky, Masha Krakovsky, Polina Spivak, Micka Ullman, Ariel Vered, Omry Barzilai, and Erella Hovers
2019 "Persistent Neanderthal Occupation of the Open-Air Site of 'Ein Qashish, Israel." *PLoS ONE* 14(6): e0215668. DOI: 10.1371/journal.pone.0215668.

Greenbaum, Noam, Ravid Ekshtain, Ariel Malinsky-Buller, Naomi Porat, and Erella Hovers
2014 "The Stratigraphy and Paleogeography of the Middle Paleolithic Open-Air Site of 'Ein Qashish, Northern Israel." *Quaternary International* 331: 203–15. DOI: 10.1016/j.quaint.2013.10.037.

Hovers, Erella, Ariel Malinsky-Buller, Ravid Ekshtain, Maya Oron, and Reuven Yeshurun
2008 "Ein Qashish—A New Middle Paleolithic Open-Air Site in Northern Israel." *Journal of the Israel Prehistoric Society* 38: 7–40.

Hovers, Erella, Ravid Ekshtain, Noam Greenbaum, Ariel Malinsky-Buller, Nadav Nir, and Reuven Yeshurun
2014 "Islands in a Stream? Reconstructing Site Formation Processes in the late Middle Paleolithic Site of 'Ein Qashish, Northern Israel." *Quaternary International* 331: 216–33. DOI: 10.1016/j.quaint.2014.01.028.

Malinsky-Buller, Ariel, Ravid Ekshtain, and Erella Hovers
2014 "Organization of Lithic Technology at 'Ein Qashish: A Late Middle Paleolithic Open Air Site in Israel." *Quaternary International* 331: 234–47. DOI: 10.1016/j.quaint.2013.05.004.

Rosen, Steven A
2003 "The Chipped Stone Artifacts from Tel Qashish." In *Tel Qashish, A Village in the Jezreel Valley*, edited by Amnon Ben-Tor, Ruhama Bonfilj, and Sharon Zuckerman, 395–412. Qedem Reports 5. Jerusalem: Institute of Archaeology, Hebrew University.

Yaroshevich, Alla
2012 "Tel Qashish (South)." *HA-ESI* 124. http://www.hadashot-esi.org.il/report_detail_eng.aspx?id=2168&mag_id=119.
2013 "Tel Qashish (South)." *HA-ESI* 125. http://www.hadashot-esi.org.il/report_detail_eng.aspx?id=2240&mag_id=120.
2014 "Tel Qashish (South)." *HA-ESI* 126 http://www.hadashot-esi.org.il/report_detail_eng.aspx?id=9568&mag_id=121.

Yaroshevich, Alla, Hamudi Khalaily, and Dan Kirzner
2011 "Tel Qashish (West)." *HA-ESI* 123. http://www.hadashot-esi.org.il/report_detail_eng.aspx?id=1842&mag_id=118.

Yaroshevich, Alla, Nuha Agha, Elisabetta Boaretto, Lena Brailovsky, Valentina Caracuta, Noam Greenbaum, Dan Kirzner, Aviram Oshri, Naomi Porat, Yoel Roskin, Ariadna Shukrun, Polina Spivak, Katia Zutovsky, and Omry Barzilai
2014 "Investigating Pre-Agricultural Dynamics in the Levant: A New Stratified Epipaleolithic Site at 'En Qashish South, Jezreel Valley, Israel." *Antiquity Project Gallery* 88.342. https://www.antiquity.ac.uk/projgall/yaroshevich342.

Yaroshevich, Alla, Ofer Bar-Yosef, Elisabetta Boaretto, Valentina Caracuta, Noam Greenbaum, Naomi Porat, and Joel Roskin
2016 "A Unique Assemblage of Engraved Plaquettes from Ein Qashish South, Jezreel Valley, Israel: Figurative and Non-Figurative Symbols of Late Pleistocene Hunters-Gatherers in the Levant." *PLoS ONE* 11.8: e0160687. DOI: 10.1371/journal.pone.0160687.

Yaroshevich, Alla, Maayan Shemer, Naomi Porat, and Joel Roskin
2018 "Flint Workshop Affiliation: Chronology, Technology and Site-Formation Processes at Giv'at Rabbi East, Lower Galilee, Israel." *Quaternary International* 464: 58–80. DOI: 10.1016/j.quaint.2017.03.001.

Zilberman, Ezra, Noam Greenbaum, Yoav Nahmias, Naomi Porat, and Lana Ashqar
2008 "Late Pleistocene to Holocene Tectonic Activity along the Nesher Fault, Mount Carmel, Israel." *Israel Journal of Earth Sciences* 57: 87–100.

Table 3.1. TQW: General Composition of the Flint Assemblage.

	N	%
PE	221	17.7
NBK	46	3.7
Flake	705	56.6
Blade	31	2.5
Bladelet	2	0.2
Core	29	2.3
CTE	146	11.7
Levallois core	34	2.7
Levallois blank	32	2.6
Total debitage	**1246**	**100 (20.9% of total assemblage)**
Tools on Levallois blank	46	23.1
Tools, other	153	76.9
Total tools	**199**	**100 (3.3% of total assemblage)**
Chips	1439	31.8
Chunks	3085	68.2
Total debris	**4524**	**100 (75.9% of total assemblage)**
Total assemblage	**5969**	**100**

Table 3.2. TQW: Composition of the Tools Assemblage.

	Levallois blank	Non-Levallois blank	Total N	%
Retouched blank	28	86	114	57.3
Notch-denticulate	14	54	68	34.2
Scraper	4	7	11	5.5
Truncation	0	3	3	1.5
Awl	0	1	1	0.5
Backed item	0	1	1	0.5
Burin	0	1	1	0.5
Total	**46**	**153**	**199**	**100**

Table 3.3. TQW: Levallois Cores and Products according to Blank and Mode of Preparation.

	Mode of preparation	Blade	Flake	Point	Total N	%
Levallois core	Bidirectional		10	3	13	38.2
	Centripetal		13	0	13	38.2
	Unidirectional		5	3	8	23.6
	Total		**28**	**6**	**34**	**100**
Levallois product	Bidirectional	3	29	3	35	44.9
	Centripetal	0	5	0	5	6.4
	Unidentifiable	0	7	2	9	11.5
	Unidirectional	4	21	4	29	37.2
	Total	**7**	**62**	**9**	**78**	**100**

Table 3.4. TQW: Metric Characteristic of Levallois Cores according to Blank Removed.

		Length	Maximal width	Maximal thickness	Length of dominant scar	Width of dominant scar	N of scars
Flake	Mean	47.52	47.87	19.01	35.98	30.86	6.14
	N	28	28	28	28	28	28
	Std. Dev.	8.36	5.99	5.93	8.96	7.35	1.53
	Minimum	32.30	37.80	10.20	17.30	19.00	4
	Maximum	63.90	57.90	33.50	49.00	51.00	10
Point	Mean	52.62	48.05	21.53	47.12	33.17	5.50
	N	6	6	T6	6	6	6
	Std. Dev.	5.16	6.46	5.47	5.07	3.85	1.05
	Minimum	48.20	37.90	13.30	37.10	29.80	4
	Maximum	62.30	53.80	27.80	50.70	40.20	7
Total	Mean	48.42	47.90	19.45	37.95	31.26	6.03
	N	34	34	34	34	34	34
	Std. Dev.	8.07	5.98	5.85	9.39	6.87	1.47
	Minimum	32.30	37.80	10.20	17.30	19.00	4
	Maximum	63.90	57.90	33.50	50.70	51.00	10

Table 3.5. TQW: Metric Characteristics of Levallois Products according to Blank kind.

		Length	Maximal width	Maximal thickness	N of scars
Flake	Mean	49.86	35.68	8.71	5.04
	N	26	57	62	56
	Std. Dev.	16.50	8.98	2.36	1.19
	Minimum	27.30	19.90	4.80	3
	Maximum	104.20	57.60	14.60	10
Blade	Mean	48.45	27.40	7.56	4.57
	N	2	7	7	7
	Std. Dev.	4.74	4.96	1.39	1.13
	Minimum	45.10	22.40	5.80	3
	Maximum	51.80	37.40	9.80	6
Point	Mean	44.08	31.75	7.90	3.56
	N	5	8	9	9
	Std. Dev.	10.33	5.68	2.16	.74
	Minimum	32.00	22.80	5.10	3
	Maximum	60.00	41.60	11.20	5
Total	Mean	48.90	34.43	8.51	4.81
	N	33	72	78	72
	Std. Dev.	15.21	8.71	2.28	1.23
	Minimum	27.30	19.90	4.80	3
	Maximum	104.20	57.60	14.60	10

Table 3.6. TQW: Striking Platform of Levallois Products.

		Broken	Chapeau de gendarme	Cortical	Dihedral	Facetted	Plain	Total
Blade		3	1	0	1	1	1	7
Flake		12	15	3	6	15	11	62
Point		3	2	0	2	2	0	9
Total	N	18	18	3	9	18	12	78
	%	23.1	23.1	3.8	11.5	23.1	15.4	100

Table 3.7. TQW: Metric Characteristics of Levallois Cores according to Mode of Preparation.

		Length	Maximal width	Maximal thickness	Length of dominant scar	Width of dominant scar	N of scars
Unidirectional	Mean	55.62	50.40	22.32	45.19	31.05	5.00
	N	8	8	8	8	8	8
	Std. Dev.	7.40	5.84	4.81	4.47	6.69	.93
	Minimum	45.00	41.00	15.20	37.10	22.00	4
	Maximum	63.90	54.80	27.80	49.50	40.20	7
Bidirectional	Mean	48.18	46.57	19.24	39.25	33.35	5.54
	N	13	13	13	13	13	13
	Std. Dev.	7.60	5.87	7.48	10.59	7.08	.88
	Minimum	32.30	37.80	10.20	17.30	24.50	4
	Maximum	59.30	53.90	33.50	50.70	51.00	7
Centripetal	Mean	44.22	47.70	17.91	32.20	29.31	7.15
	N	13	13	13	13	13	13
	Std. ev.	5.96	6.15	4.06	6.78	6.69	1.519
	Minimum	33.00	39.30	10.60	23.20	19.00	5
	Maximum	55.20	57.90	24.00	43.00	39.90	10
Total	Mean	48.42	47.90	19.45	37.95	31.26	6.03
	N	34	34	34	34	34	34
	Std. Dev.	8.07	5.98	5.85	9.39	6.87	1.47
	Minimum	32.30	37.80	10.20	17.30	19.00	4
	Maximum	63.90	57.90	33.50	50.70	51.00	10

Table 3.8. TQW: Metric Characteristics of Levallois Products according to Mode of Preparation.

		Length	Maximal width	Maximal thickness	N of scars
Unidirectional	Mean	51.08	37.29	9.13	4.43
	N	9	27	29	28
	Std. Dev.	16.43	8.78	2.33	.92
	Minimum	27.30	21.50	5.10	3
	Maximum	74.00	57.60	14.50	6
Bidirectional	Mean	50.25	32.17	8.20	4.88
	N	19	32	35	34
	Std. Dev.	15.67	8.45	2.45	.81
	Minimum	32.40	19.90	4.80	4
	Maximum	104.20	54.80	14.60	7
Centripetal	Mean	42.83	36.15	8.48	7.75
	N	3	4	5	4
	Std. Dev.	10.99	5.91	1.32	2.06
	Minimum	35.70	29.80	6.90	6
	Maximum	55.50	43.50	9.70	10
Unidentifiable	Mean	35.35	33.15	7.70	4.17
	N	2	9	9	6
	Std. Dev.	4.74	9.00	1.47	1.32
	Minimum	32.00	22.80	6.10	3
	Maximum	38.70	47.10	10.10	6
Total	Mean	48.90	34.43	8.51	4.81
	N	33	72	78	72
	Std. Dev.	15.21	8.71	2.28	1.23
	Minimum	27.30	19.90	4.80	3
	Maximum	104.20	57.60	14.60	10

Table 3.9. TQS: General Composition of the Flint Assemblage.

	N	%
PE	137	16.1
NBK	30	3.5
Flakes	310	36.5
Blade	10	1.2
Bladelet	9	1.0
Levallois blank	48	5.6
Cores	144	16.9
Levallois core	13	1.5
CTE	149	17.5
Total debitage	850	100 (18.6% of total assemblage)
Tools	159	100 (3.5% of total assemblage)
Chips	160	4.5
Chunks	3405	95.5
Total debris	3565	100 (77.9% of total assemblage)
Total assemblage	4574	100

Table 3.10. TQS: Typological Composition of the Tools Assemblage.

	Levallois blank	Non-Levallois blank	Total N	%
Retouched flake	17	88	105	67.3
Retouched blade		11	11	7.1
Retouched blank, other		12	12	7.7
Notch-denticulate		13	13	8.3
Scraper		5	5	3.2
Endscraper		4	4	2.6
Truncation		1	1	0.6
Burin		3	3	1.9
Microliths		2	2	1.3
Total	17	139	156	100

Table 3.11. TQS: Levallois Cores and Products according to Blank and Mode of Preparation.

		Blade	Flake	Point	Total N	Total %
Levallois core	Bidirectional	1	6	2	9	69.2
	Centripetal	0	1	0	1	7.7
	Unidentifiable	0	1	0	1	7.7
	Unidirectional	0	2	0	2	15.4
	Total	1	10	2	13	100
Levallois product	Bidirectional	3	10	1	14	29.2
	Centripetal	0	1	0	1	2.0
	Unidentifiable	0	7	1	8	16.7
	Unidirectional	2	21	2	25	52.1
	Total	5	39	4	48	100

Table 3.12. TQS: Striking Platform of Levallois Products.

		Broken	Chapeau de gendarme	Cortical	Dihedral	Facetted	Plain	Total
Blade		2	0	0	1	1	1	5
Flake		11	3	1	5	11	8	39
Point		2	0	0	0	0	2	4
Total	N	15	3	1	6	12	11	48
	%	31.3	6.3	2.1	12.5	25.0	22.9	100.0

Table 3.13. TQS: Metric Characteristics of Levallois Cores according to Mode of Preparation.

		Length	Maximal width	Maximal thickness	Length of dominant scar	Width of dominant scar	N of scars
Unidirectional	Mean	43.55	31.00	14.20	37.85	26.10	5.00
	N	2	1	2	2	1	2
	Std. Dev.	7.14	.	4.10	2.76	.	1.41
	Minimum	38.50	31.00	11.30	35.90	26.10	4.00
	Maximum	48.60	31.00	17.10	39.80	26.10	6.00
Bidirectional	Mean	42.73	39.02	24.52	35.36	29.74	6.57
	N	6	5	6	5	5	7
	Std. Dev.	6.96	4.52	5.44	8.06	8.20	2.82
	Minimum	33.50	33.50	16.40	24.70	20.40	4.00
	Maximum	51.60	44.60	31.20	43.30	39.70	11.00
Centripetal	Mean	32.30	28.90	9.30	29.80	28.40	8.00
	N	1	1	1	1	1	1
Unidentifiable	Mean	35.50	45.00	12.20	32.20	43.20	8.00
	N	1	1	1	1	1	1
Total	Mean	41.13	37.50	19.70	34.94	30.80	6.54
	N	10	8	10	9	8	11
	Std. Dev.	6.91	6.16	7.67	6.32	8.07	2.42
	Minimum	32.30	28.90	9.30	24.70	20.40	4.00
	Maximum	51.60	45.00	31.20	43.30	43.20	11.00

Table 3.14. TQS: Metric Characteristics of Levallois Products according to mode of Preparation.

		Length	Maximal width	Maximal thickness	N of scars
Unidirectional	Mean	42.07	31.30	8.82	5.27
	N	12	25	25	22
	Std. Dev.	10.50	6.15	2.20	1.67
	Minimum	23.60	20.70	4.20	3
	Maximum	58.00	48.60	14.50	8
Bidirectional	Mean	43.30	28.9923	8.4786	5.69
	N	4	13	14	13
	Std. Dev.	18.01	7.98	2.12	1.49
	Minimum	30.00	17.50	4.70	3
	Maximum	68.70	48.40	11.90	8
Centripetal	Mean	40.00	30.00	7.00	11.00
	N	1	1	1	1
Unidentifiable	Mean	33.75	30.77	8.31	5.33
	N	2	8	8	3
	Std. Dev.	3.75	7.40	3.14	2.52
	Minimum	31.10	24.70	4.20	3
	Maximum	36.40	47.10	13.90	8
Total	Mean	41.34	30.54	8.59	5.56
	N	19	47	48	39
	Std. Dev.	11.40	6.76	2.30	1.85
	Minimum	23.60	17.50	4.20	3
	Maximum	68.70	48.60	14.50	11

Part III

Tell el-Waʻer
(Early Bronze Age)

Chapter 4

Early Bronze Age I Settlement Remains at Tell El-Waʻer

Orit Segal, Dan Kirzner and Uzi ʻAd (*Israel Antiquities Authority*)

Introduction

Salvage excavations were conducted in 2012, in a 10 × 80 m strip of cultivated land at the northeastern edge of Tell el-Waʻer (Segal 2019), alongside and parallel to Road 70, on behalf of the Israel Antiquities Authority.[1] The excavations revealed structural remains of a hitherto unknown Early Bronze Age IA settlement almost immediately beneath the present-day surface, founded on the sloping bedrock and covered with a thin layer of occupational debris. The tell, rising on a natural limestone hillock on the eastern slope of Mount Carmel (map ref. 210056–62/732715–74), is about 3 km north of Yoqneʻam and 500 m northwest of and opposite Tel Qashish, on the west bank of the Kishon River separating the two (figs. 4.1–2).

The central part of Tell el-Waʻer, identified well over a century ago (Conder and Kitchener 1881–1883; von Mülinen 1908, 211), is occupied by some building remains surrounded by many Ottoman burials. Pottery sampled from its surface during an archaeological survey for the map of Yagur includes sherds from the Iron Age and the Persian, Hellenistic, Roman, Byzantine, and Early Islamic periods (Olami, Sender, and Oren 2004: 61*, site 189). At least two caves have been identified on this hillock (Olami, Sender and Oren 2004: 61*, site 188). Excavations in this area, west of the Kishon River, were conducted in 2010 by Hamudi Khalaily and Alla Yaroshevich, revealing Mousterian finds (Yaroshevich, Khalaily, and Kirzner, 2011). For an overview of excavations carried out in the past on the opposite, east side of the Kishon River, that is, on and in the margins of Tel Qashish, see, for example, Ben-Tor, Bonfil and Zuckerman 2003, 1–2; van den Brink, Segal, and ʻAd 2012; Segal, ʻAd, and van den Brink, ch. 25, this volume; van den Brink and ʻAd 2011; and van den Brink 2014.

The Excavation

Along the lower slope of Tell el-Waʻer, within an excavation grid of two fourteen-squared adjoining rows (Squares A and B/10–11, 13–16, 18–22) covering an 80 × 10 m area (figs. 4.2–3), the stone foundations segments of fifteen structures (some oriented north–south, others east–west) were exposed (Units 1–15, figs. 4.3-6). Fifty-six loci (L100–132, 200–222) and 194 baskets (B1000–1142, 2000–2050), the smallest 3-D excavation units (cf. Braun and Goph-

---

[1] The excavations were conducted from 15.7.12 through 30.07.12 and resumed from 09.12.12 through 24.12.12, undertaken on behalf of the Israel Antiquities Authority and financed by the Israel Railways and Cross-Israel Highway companies under the direction of Orit Segal (permit A-6551/2013) and with the participation of Dan Kirzner and Uzi ʻAd (area supervisors), E. Bachar and Y. Amrani (administration), R. Mishayev and M. Kahan (surveying), A. Peretz (photography), M. Shuiskaya (pottery and ground stones drawings), M. Smilansky (flint tools drawings), C. Amit (studio photography), and E. Belashov (plans).

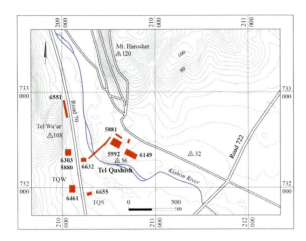

Fig. 4.1. Location map of Tell el-Wa'er.

Fig. 4.2. Aerial photograph showing the location of Tell el-Wa'er on the west side of the Kishon River and opposite Tel Qashish. Looking north. Source: Google Earth.

Fig. 4.3. Tel Qashish and Road 70 to the southeast of the excavation site. Looking southeast.

na 2004, 189), were allotted (see appendix: List of Loci and Baskets).

Stratigraphy and Description of the Structural Remains

The accumulation of anthropogenic deposits immediately on or very close to the natural, sloping bedrock, associated with the sparsely preserved and deflated EB IA settlement remains, is rather shallow. Although significant vertical stratigraphic built-up of the site is lacking, the horizontal distribution of the settlement remains (fig. 4.4) evidence at least two or possibly three building subphases, indicated by some wall segments apparently cutting into others. However, in Unit 14 (floor L214, see below), the original floor levels of the various structures were missing. Most of the site's wall remains were found deflated down to the foundation's last one to three stone courses.

4. Early Bronze Age I Settlement Remains at Tell El-Wa'er

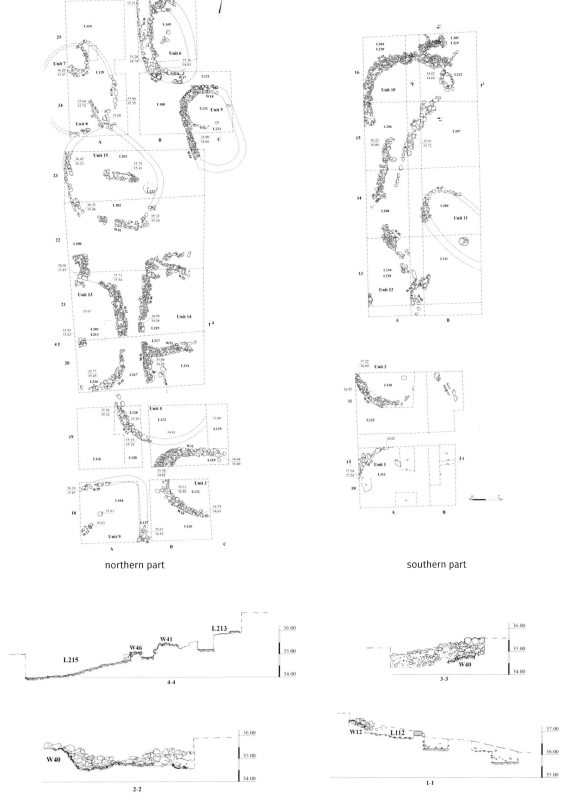

Fig. 4.4. Plan and sections of the exposed Early EB I village.

Fig. 4.5. Aerial view of squares A/B 13–16, building units 10–11.

Fig. 4.6. Aerial view of squares A/B 18–25, building units 3–9, 13–15.

Units 1 and 2 (Squares 10, 11)

These not fully excavated structures, oriented northeast–southwest and separated by an almost 2-m empty space, are represented by two counteropposed, curvilinear wall segments protruding from the north and west balks of Square A10 (Unit 1, W12) and the northwest corner of Square A11 (Unit 2, W10; fig. 4.4, Sec. 1-1).

Wall 12, 0.65 m wide and preserved to a height of one course (height 0.1–0.3m), has two clear but only partially extant faces. It was built of a double row of fieldstones measuring 0.35 × 0.25 × 0.15 m on average (fig. 4.7) on the natural limestone bedrock. The fill associated with this wall (L112) is composed of small limestone chunks, originally possibly serving as foundation for a missing floor. A large, flat, natural limestone in the northeast part of Square A10 perhaps originally served as a base for a roof-supporting post, or else may be an isolated remnant of a stone pavement. Based on the surviving north part of this structure, its original diameter is estimated at about 10 m.

Wall 10, 0.55 m wide, preserved to a height of one course (0.2 m high), is built of a double row of small- and medium-sized fieldstones and has two clear, but only partly extant, faces (fig. 4.8). It rests on a thin layer of small limestones (L118), perhaps serving for leveling the surface, directly overlaying the natural limestone bedrock. There is no indication of a conceivable floor.

Fig. 4.7. Square A10, unit 1. Curvilinear wall segment W12 protruding from the north and west balks of the square, looking north.

Fig. 4.9. Squares B18/19, unit 3. Curvilinear wall segments W11 and W19 forming the western apse of this unit, looking west.

Fig. 4.8. Square A11, unit 2. Curvilinear wall segment W10 in the northwest corner of the square, looking south.

Fig. 4.10. Square A19, unit 4. Curvilinear wall segment W13 in the northeast corner of the square, looking southeast.

Unit 3 (Squares B18/19)

Only the western part of this rather large, east–west oriented oval building could be excavated, its east part/end being located beyond the present excavation area's east border and still awaiting excavation (figs. 4.4, 6). The curvilinear wall, composed of W11 and W19 (width 0.6–0.9 m) and built from small, natural limestones, forms the western apse of the building. It is exposed over a length of 11 m and an internal maximum width of 4 m (fig. 4.9). The wall was not built on natural bedrock but on a layer of small limestones (L132), possibly used for leveling the surface. Depending on its position on the slope, one to four courses of the wall were preserved, up to a maximum height of 0.7 m. Based on the excavated wall remains, an original length of 15 m was estimated for this particular building.

Unit 4 (Square A19)

A curvilinear wall segment (W13), in the northeast corner of Square A19, is all that is left to indicate the presence of yet another structure (fig. 4.4). The two-faced wall is built of two parallel rows of slightly hewn fieldstones (0.15 × 0.3 × 0.3 m; total width 0.6 m). Only the first course, resting on a layer of small-sized limestones directly overlaying the natural bedrock (L123), was preserved (fig. 4.10). Although a few additional stones belonging to W13 were exposed in the area occupied by the north and east balks of the square, its expected extension was absent in the surrounding squares excavated in tandem.

Unit 5 (Squares B/C24)

The curvilinear, two-faced W18 (Square B24), together with W44, its western, linear extension to the

Fig. 4.11. Square B/C24, unit 5. Curvilinear wall segment W18 and its western, linear extension to the south (W44) forming the western apse. Looking west.

Fig. 4.12. Square B/C24, B25, units 5 (foreground) and 6 (background), looking northwest.

Fig. 4.13. Square B24/25, units 5 (background) and 6 (foreground), looking southeast.

south (Squares B/C24 and C24), form the western apse (estimated cross diameter 5 m) of this not fully excavated oval building (fig. 4.4). The walls are preserved to a height of three to four courses and consist of two parallel rows of natural, medium-sized limestones with some open spaces in between filled up with smaller limestones (figs. 4.11–13). The walls are built upon a layer of small-sized limestones immediately overlaying natural bedrock. The curvilinear alignment of limestones abutting the east face of W18 might be all that is left of an internal partition wall separating the west apse from the other part or parts of the building. Wall 44, the southern extension of W18, could be traced in the balk area between Squares B24 and B23 and in the northeast corner of B23, dissolving after this. The fill inside the building (L131 and L221) consists of a featureless, brown-grayish soil layer, clearly indicating that the floor was not preserved here.

Unit 6 (Squares B24/25)

The two-faced wall segments W16, W17, and W45 seem to form part of the southwest end of a rather large building (fig. 4.4), an impression based on the substantial width of the walls, varying locally between 0.8–1.1 m. The fill inside this building (L109) consists of many small-sized fieldstones embedded in an otherwise featureless brown soil layer, perhaps the foundation of a floor pavement (fig. 4.12). The surviving wall segments are built of two parallel rows of small-sized, slightly dressed limestones (0.2 × 0.2 × 0.3 m), preserved to a maximum height of three courses, with intermediate empty spaces filled up with smaller limestones (fig. 4.13).

A large limestone slab, about midway between the curvilinear parts of W16 and W17 (fig. 4.4) might originally have served as a column base for roof support. The northern extension of this building lay beyond the present excavation's northern border and remains unexcavated.

Fig. 4.14. Squares A24/25, unit 7. Curvilinear wall segment W15, looking southeast.

Fig. 4.15. Squares A15, A/B16, unit 10. Curvilinear wall segment W43 and slightly curvilinear wall segment W40, looking south.

Another interpretation of the existing plan of this unit is that of a rather small, curvilinear structure (ca. 5 meter in diameter), its north and south extremes being defined by the curved parts of W16 and W17. These walls abut or are partly founded on the more rectilinear W45 segment, which may have formed part of a larger structure/building awaiting future excavation in the adjoining areas beyond the excavation's present north and east borders.

Unit 7 (Square A24/25)

This apparently small, curvilinear structure (ca. 1.1 m in diameter; fig. 4.4) is evidenced by the two-faced curvilinear W15 segment (width 0.7 m), built of small, natural limestones (0.3 × 0.3 × 0.2 m), and preserved to a height of one course resting on a sterile soil fill directly overlaying natural bedrock (fig. 4.14). Whether it represents an isolated feature, for example, a small storage facility, or perhaps part of Unit 8 (see below), remains unclear.

Unit 8 (Square A24)

This unit is represented by a curvilinear wall segment, W14 (fig. 4.4), preserved to a height of one course and set on the natural bedrock, most likely originally built of two rows of natural large-sized limestones (0.15 × 0.2 × 0.5 m), of which only the easternmost row survived, with the interspaces filled with smaller limestones. Wall 21, exposed to a length of almost 2 m (fig. 4.4) and originally composed of two rows of natural small-sized limestones (0.2 × 0.1 × 0.1 m), is preserved to a height of one course (max. height 0.1 m) and could have served as an internal partition wall. Several limestone slabs (0.5 × 0.7 m), close to the north face of W21, might represent remnants of the original floor (stone pavement).

Unit 9 (Square A18)

Two wall segments (W20 and W22) might be part of the north apse of a northeast–southwest oriented building extending beyond the present excavation's west and south borders, and thus remaining unexcavated. This is supported by the position of the short W22 segment uncovered in the balk area between Squares A18 and B18, and the fact that both segments are founded on a sterile soil layer overlaying natural bedrock. Wall 20 (length 2.5 m, width 0.3 m), protruding from the north and west balks of the square (fig. 4.4), was preserved to a height of one to two courses (0.1–0.3 m high). The short, northeast–southwest oriented wall segment W23, protruding into the square from its west balk, might have served as an internal partition wall. A single, isolated limestone slab (0.35 × 0.35 × 0.15 m) near the center of the square might originally have served as a base for a post supporting a roof.

Unit 10 (Squares A15, A/B16)

The two-faced curvilinear W43 (figs. 4.4, 15, Sec. 2-2, 3-3), built of small- and medium-sized natural

Fig. 4.16. Squares A20–A21, unit 13. Curvilinear wall segment W41, looking northeast.

Fig. 4.17. Squares B20–B22, unit 14. Segments of a western perimeter wall (W46), including a possible entrance way, looking west.

Fig. 4.18. Square B20, unit 14. East–west oriented partition wall (W51), looking north.

limestones resting on a sterile soil layer overlaying the natural bedrock, seems to form the northwest apse of a rather large, oval building with a small, semicircular stone-built silo (diam. 1 m) preserved to a height of two courses, adjacent to the internal face of the wall. It is unclear whether and how the north–south oriented wall segment W40, to the south of W43 and built of a double row of natural limestones, relates to this building. Wall 40 is built on a brown soil layer extending on both sides of the wall (L206 and L207), clearly indicating that no conceivable floor survived.

Unit 11 (Squares B13 and B14)

The badly preserved remains of a curvilinear wall segment (W47; fig. 4.4), built of two parallel rows of natural, small- and medium-sized limestones (width 0.3–0.6 m) on brown sterile soil overlaying the bedrock, and preserved to a height of only one course, possibly represent the northwest apse of an oval building. A large limestone slab, perhaps a post base for supporting a roof, was found nearby, in L211 (Square B13, fig. 4.4), although it is impossible to know whether it was associated with this incompletely preserved structure or not.

Unit 12 (Squares A13/14)

Several wall segments (W48–W50) were exposed, difficult to interpret (fig. 4.4). A column base for a post supporting a roof protrudes from the west balk of Square A13.

Unit 13 (Squares A20–A21)

The two wall segments W41 (with a possible entranceway), built on a sterile, brown layer of soil (similar to that exposed in the adjoining Loci 203 and 213), and preserved to a height of one course, protrude into Square A20 from its south balk (fig. 4.4, Sec. 4-4) and continue in Square A21 to their north. Together, they constitute the eastern and nearly continuous perimeter wall of an oval, north-south oriented building (fig. 4.16). The surviving segments (length 8 m, width 0.7 m) enclose a 3.5-m wide area. Inside this building, slightly off-center, a circular stone arrangement (0.5 m in diameter) possibly served as a post base for supporting the roof. The west part of this building is located beyond the excavation's western limit and therefore remains unexcavated.

Unit 14 (Squares B20–B22)

Two segments of a western perimeter wall (W46, length ca. 8.9 m, width 0.6 m), preserved to a height of only one course and with a possible entranceway opposite the probable entranceway in Unit 13, rest on a layer of brown soil mixed with small-sized limestones (fig. 4.17). The southern wall segment (Square 20), together with the northern segment extending from Square 21 into Square 22 and uncovered 1.5–3 m east of Unit 13, may form part of an oval building with two internal partition walls (fig. 4.4, W51 and W52). The east–west oriented partition W51 (fig. 4.18) is 4 m long and 0.6 m wide. The southern end of W46 is missing but probably would have stopped short before W11 of Unit 3. Two well-preserved copper axes (B2033; fig. 6.2–4; van den Brink, ch. 6, this volume) were found together on Floor L214, close to the east face of W46, south of partition W52.

Unit 15 (Squares A22–23 and B22)

The segments of a two-faced, curvilinear perimeter wall (W42) were uncovered, oriented northwest–southeast, preserved to a height of only one course, to a length of 6.7 m, and a width of 2.8 m. The wall, resting on brown, sterile soil, like the one exposed in the adjoining Loci 201 and 202, protrudes into Square 23 from its west balk and forms a unicellular structure (fig. 4.4). L222 is a small probe excavated below the foundation level of W42 down to bedrock.

References

Ben-Tor, Amnon, Ruhama Bonfil, and Sharon Zuckerman
2003 *Tel Qashish: A Village in the Jezreel Valley; Final Report of the Archaeological Excavations (1978–1987)*. Qedem Reports 5. Jerusalem: Hebrew University of Jerusalem.

Braun, Eliot, and Ram Gophna
2004 "Excavations at Ashqelon, Afridar—Area G." *'Atiqot* 45: 185–241.

Brink, Edwin C. M. van den
2014 "Tel Qashish (Rakevet ha-Emeq): Preliminary Report." *HA-ESI* 126. http://www.hadashot-esi.org.il/Report_Detail_Eng.aspx?id=14714&mag_id=121.

Brink, Edwin C. M. van den, and Uzi 'Ad
2011 "Tel Qashish: Preliminary Report." *HA-ESI* 123. http://www.hadashot-esi.org.il/report_detail_eng.aspx?id=1894&mag_id=118.

Brink, Edwin C. M. van den, Orit Segal, and Uzi 'Ad
2012 "A Late Bronze Age II Repository of Cultic Paraphernalia from the Environs of Tel Qashish in the Jezreel Valley, Israel." In *Temple Building and Temple Cult in the Levant (2.–1. Millennium BC)*, edited by Jens Kamlah, 421–34, pls. 55–62. ADPV 41. Wiesbaden: Harrassowitz.

Conder, C. R., and H. H. Kitchener
1881–1883 *The Survey of Western Palestine: Maps*. 3 vols. London: Committee of the Palestine Exploration Fund.

Mülinen, Eberhard, Graf von
1908 "Beiträge zur Kenntnis des Karmels." *ZDPV* 31: 1–258.

Olami, Ya'aqov, Shlomo Sender, and Eldad Oren
2004 *Map of Yagur (27): Archaeological Survey of Israel*. Jerusalem: Israel Antiquities Authority. http://www.antiquities.org.il/survey/newmap_en.asp#zoom=8.0000;xy:34.80852508545,31.298049926757;mapname=27.

Segal, Orit
2019 "Tel el-Wa'ar, Preliminary Report". *HA-ESI* 131. http://www.hadashot-esi.org.il/report_detail_eng.aspx?id=25666&mag_id=127.

Yaroshevich, Alla, Hamudi Khalaily, and Dan Kirzner
2011 "Tel Qashish (West)." *HA-ESI* 123. http://www.hadashot-esi.org.il/report_detail.aspx?id=1842&mag_id=118. [Hebrew]

Appendix: List of Loci and Baskets

Square	Locus	Elevations	Description	Baskets
A10	100	37.53 36.29	Exposure of small- and medium-sized stones after mechanical removal of the sterile topsoil.	1000, 1011, 1021, 1044, 1089
B10	101	36.43 35.64	Exposure of stones in the west half of the square after mechanical removal of the sterile topsoil.	1001, 1012, 1023
A11	102	37.26 36.09	Exposure of a stony surface after mechanical removal of the sterile topsoil.	1002, 1014, 1013, 1022, 1033
B11	103	36.37 35.71	Exposure of stones in the western half of the square after mechanical removal of the sterile topsoil.	1003, 1024, 1034, 1045, 1050
A18	104	36.61 35.40	Exposure of a stony surface after mechanical removal of the sterile topsoil.	1025, 1035, 1063, 1077, 1108
B18	105	35.72 34.60	Exposure of W19 after mechanical removal of the sterile topsoil in the north part of Square B18.	1016, 1026, 1064, 1066, 1078, 1088, 1094, 1109
B19	106	35.39 34.70	Exposure of a stony surface and W11 in the southern part of Sqare B19.	1006, 1017, 1027, 1066, 1086, 1097
A24	107	35.91 35.70	Exposure of stony surface after mechanical removal of the sterile topsoil.	
B/C24	108	35.76 34.20	Exposure of stones and wall (W44) after mechanical removal of the sterile topsoil.	1019, 1029, 1039, 1068, 1085, 1142
B25	109	35.45 34.40	Exposure of W16 after mechanical removal of the sterile topsoil.	1009, 1030, 1103, 1104, 1116, 1117, 1118, 1130
A25	110	36.40 35.60	Exposure of washed-down stone debris from the slope after mechanical removal of the sterile topsoil.	1031, 1084, 1099, 1100, 1115, 1120
A24	111	35.76 35.63	Removal of stony surface L107.	1082, 1091, 1114
A10	112	36.94 36.65	Removal of a stone collapse and exposure of W12.	1032, 1046. 1071, 1073, 1074, 1075, 1089, 1090, 1092
A24	113	35.90 35.72	Removal of a stone collapse and exposure of W21.	1038, 1042, 1043, 1098

4. Early Bronze Age I Settlement Remains at Tell El-Wa'er

Square	Locus	Elevations	Description	Baskets
A11	114	36.80 36.70	South of W10.	1049, 1121
A11	115	36.66 36.09	Limited test probe northeast of W10.	1057, 1062
A19	116	35.58 35.23	Exposure of stones in the eastern part of the square.	1095
A10	117	36.29 36.19	Small probe down to bedrock in the southern part of the square.	1061
A11	118	36.64 36.44	North of W10.	1076, 1107
B19	119	35.00 34.50	South of W11.	1096, 1133
A19	120	35.30 35.20	Removal of stones in the northeastern part of the square and exposure of W13.	1080
B/C24	121	35.11 34.00	Exposure of W17 in the northern part of the square.	1081, 1102, 1112, 1128
A18	122	35.94 35.59	Removal of a stone collapse and excavation underneath.	1105
B19	123	35.72 34.80	Stony surface north of W11.	1106, 1111
A24/25	124	36.20 35.97	Removal of balk between squares A24–25 and exposure of W15	1119, 1131
A11	125	36.75 36.70	South of W10	1122
B18	126	34.79 34.60	Removal of a stone collapse and exposure of W19.	1123
A/B18	127	35.65 35.45	Balk between squares A18 and B18.	
A19	128	35.23 35.30	East of W13.	
B19	129	34.40 33.60	Probe northeast of W11, from its foundation level downward.	

Square	Locus	Elevations	Description	Baskets
B/C24	130	34.40 34.30	Removal of stones and exposure of W18.	1129
B/C24	131	34.30 34.22	Excavation inside unit 5 (W18).	1132
B18	132	35.11 34.80	North of W19.	
A22	200	36.06 35.85	Excavation between two "stone platforms" after mechanical removal of the sterile topsoil.	2000
A/B23	201	35.79 35.43	Exposure of stones after mechanical removal of the sterile topsoil.	2001
A/B22-23 B23	202	36.35 35.98 36.22 36.01	Cleaning of the surface and exposure of W42.	2002, 2020
A21	203	35.77 35.71	Cleaning of the surface and exposure of fieldstones.	2003
A16	204	36.32 36.11	Cleaning of the surface and exposure of W43.	2004, 2013, 2021, 2038
B16	205	35.36 35.11	Exposure of stones and W43.	2005
A15	206	36.26 36.05	Exposure of a stony surface after mechanical removal of the sterile topsoil.	2006, 2014, 2043, 2047
B15	207	35.93 35.72	Exposure of W40 in the northwestern part of the square after mechanical removal of the sterile topsoil.	2007, 2015
A14	208	36.13 35.81	Exposure of a stony surface after mechanical removal of the sterile topsoil.	2008, 2016, 2040
B14	209	35.59 34.75	Cleaning of the surface and exposure of W47.	2009, 2017, 2027
A13	210	36.35 35.86	Exposure of stone tops.	2010, 2018, 2023, 2039, 2044
B13	211	35.02 34.82	Cleaning after the mechanical removal of the sterile topsoil.	2011, 2019, 2026

Square	Locus	Elevations	Description	Baskets
B16	212	35.11 34.42	Excavation beneath stones L205.	2012, 2022, 2025, 2031
A20	213	36.07 35.95	West of W41, inside Unit XIII.	2024
B20	214	34.84 34.31	Beaten earth floor, south of W51.	2028, 2032, 2033 (2 metal axes), 2036, 2041
B20	215	34.99 34.00	Excavation east and beneath the base level of W46.	2029, 2030, 2035, 2042
A20	216	35.83 35.67	Limited probe north of W41.	2034
B20	217	35.13 34.79	Cleaning of W41 and W46.	2037
A13	218	35.86 35.76	South of W49.	2048
B16	219	34.68 34.60	Exposure of a surface with potsherds, perhaps a floor.	2045
A16	220	35.83 35.69	North of W43.	2046
C24	221	34.80 34.66	East of W44.	2049
B23	222	35.32 3510	Removal of a stone collapse in unit 15.	2050

Chapter 5

The Early Bronze Age Pottery Assemblage from Tell El-Wa'er

Edwin C. M. van den Brink (*Israel Antiquities Authority*)

A small collection of ninety-four chrono-typologically diagnostic potsherds—rims, handles, and bases of various ceramic vessel types—were collected during excavations at Tell el-Wa'er (table 5.1), all dating from an early phase of the Early Bronze Age I (EB IA). A selection of these (n= 42) is presented and illustrated below (figs. 5.1–4).

Typology

Bowls

Only one of the six preserved bowl rim fragments (6.38 percent of the total diagnostic assemblage—henceforth TDA) was sufficiently preserved to reliably estimate its diameter (fig. 5.1.2). The rims are tapered (fig. 5.1.1), round (fig. 5.1.2, 4), or flat (fig. 5.1.3).

One rim had been finger-indented (fig. 5.1.3), a decoration method common in early EB I assemblages and applied to both open and closed vessel forms (e.g., Golani and van den Brink 1999, 5; figs. 5.2.6–13; 5.3.12–15; 5.4.1–3). In another case (fig. 5.1.1), the interior surface of a bowl had been red slipped. Figure 5.1.4 represents part of a gray burnished ware bowl, one of the main and foremost hallmarks of the early EB I (Braun 2012, 6–12).

Holemouth Jars

The holemouth jars (n=16 or 17.01 percent of TDA) in this assemblage include thin-walled vessels with plain and often tapered rims (fig. 5.2.1–5), jars with indented-decorated rims (fig. 5.2.6–10, 12) or with a continuous indented band(s) of clay immediately below the rim's exterior (fig. 5.2.11, 13), characteristic of early EB I assemblages (e.g., Yiftah'el, Braun 1997, fig. 9.8–11). While these jars are often red slipped on their exterior surfaces (e.g., Braun 1997), all relevant sherds in the Tell el-Wa'er collection were not slipped. The flattened, red-painted rim/wall fragment illustrated in figure 5.2.15 may represent a fragment of a holemouth krater.

Necked Jars and Pithoi

Necked jars with plain, tapered, or rounded, outfolded rims (n=23 or 24.48 percent of TDA; fig. 5.3.1–11), and pithoi with plain or indented rims, or with an applied indented band of clay ("rope decoration") around their neck (n=13 or 13.83 percent of TDA; fig. 5.3.12–15) predominate this small assemblage. Notable once again is that, but for one rim fragment (fig. 5.3.4), the exterior surfaces of all other relevant samples were left plain, that is, unslipped, contrasting with the many similar but slipped vessels found both in the north and center regions of the country (cf. Braun 1997, figs. 9.15–20; Golani and van den Brink 1999, figs. 5.9, 12, 17). A broad, flattened rim fragment (fig. 5.3.16), with a possibly indented outer edge, belongs to a thin-walled jar that does not fit any of the jar types presented above.

Handles

Most handles (ten out of eighteen or 19.15 percent of TDA) are finger-indented ledge handles (fig. 5.4.1–3). Diminutive knobs, either single or in a pair (fig. 5.4.4–5), found on several body sherds, are probably decorative rather than functional. Loop handles are rare in this small assemblage.

Noteworthy are two small loop-handle fragments with prefiring incisions (fig 5.4.6–7), understood as belonging to the Tel Erani C cultural horizon associated with a postearly EB I phase, namely the onset of the late EB I (EB IB1). These two fragments should be either considered intrusive, indicating a post-EB IA activity in this area for which, to date, no other evidence was found at the site, or else as an integral part of the present EB IA assemblage. The latter case would imply such-like diagnostic Erani C-contemporary vessels were produced already in the early EB I, perhaps toward its very end (EB IA2), at the interface with EB IB1 (for the nomenclature used, see Yekutieli 2000, 129–30).[1]

Discussion

Morphologically, this small assemblage comfortably fits the early EB I ceramic repertoire in the region, best illustrated by the shape and style similarities of pottery vessels retrieved from Yiftah'el, Stratum II, the contemporary key reference (Braun 1997, 60–89). Both assemblages include, inter alia, gray burnished ware bowls, finger-indented holemouth jars—sometimes with an occasional, finger-indented band of clay ("rope-decoration") added to the upper part of jars' exterior—and pithoi with a finger-indented, outfolded, tapered rim and a rope-decorated, tall neck/shoulder.

Looking at table 5.1, and excluding the handles (n=18) and base fragments (n=18), each making up 19.15 percent of all diagnostics, respectively, the closed vessels (n=52) clearly predominate over open ones (n=6), a pattern that repeats itself in various other early EB I ceramic assemblages, not only in the country's northern region, as illustrated by Yiftah'el, Stratum II (Louhivouri 1997, 44, table 7.1), but also the central coastal plain, for example, at Azor (Golani and van den Brink 1999, table 1).

The legitimate question raised by the two Tel Erani C-horizon decorated handle fragments found within the early EB I Tell el-Wa'er pottery assemblage of whether these are to be considered intrusive or indicate a stage at the interface of the EB IA1 with the EB IB1 remains open due to the lack of absolute dates from this site.

---

[1] A similar situation occurred at Ḥorbat Ḥammim near Modi'in in the Foothills/Shephala, where two Erani C handles were collected from a small cave yielding predominantly early EB I (EB IA) pottery remains (van den Brink et al., in press; see also van den Brink 2007).

References

Braun, Eliot
1997 *Yiftah'el: Salvage and Rescue Excavations at a Prehistoric Village in Lower Galilee, Israel.* IAA Reports 2. Jerusalem: Israel Antiquities Authority.
2012 "On Some South Levantine Early Bronze Age Ceramic Wares and Styles." *PEQ* 144: 5–32.

Brink, Edwin C. M. van den
2007 "Ḥorbat Ḥammim (South)." *HA-ESI* 119 (December 2007). http://www.hadashot-esi.org.il/report_detail_eng.aspx?id=676&mag_id=112.

Brink, Edwin C. M. van den, Liora Kolska Horwitz, Ofer Marder, and Henk K. Mienis
In press "Early Bronze Age IA Settlement Remains at Ḥorbat Ḥammim (South), Modi'in." *'Atiqot*.

Golani, Amir, and Edwin C. M. van den Brink
1999 "Salvage Excavations at the Early Bronze Age IA Settlement of Azor." *'Atiqot* 38: 1–49.

Louhivuori, Mikko
1997 "The EB I Pottery Sample from Yiftah'el II." In *Yiftah'el. Salvage and Rescue Excavations at a Prehistoric Village in Lower Galilee, Israel*, edited by Eliot Braun, 43–50. IAA Reports 2. Jerusalem: Israel Antiquities Authority.

Yekutieli, Yuval
2000 "Early Bronze Age I Pottery in Southwestern Canaan." In *Ceramics and Change in the Early Bronze Age of the Southern Levant*, edited by Graham Philip and Douglas Baird, 129–52. Levantine Archaeology 2. Sheffield: Sheffield Academic.

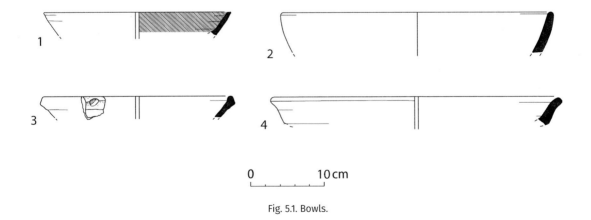

Fig. 5.1. Bowls.

No.	Locus	Basket	Description	Remarks
1	218	2018.2	Obliquely scraped rim/wall fragment of bowl	Traces of red slip inside; many coarse white grits.
2	125	1122.2	Tapered rim/wall fragment of bowl	Plain, light orange surface; many coarse white (calcrete) grits.
3	118	1072.1	Slightly flattened, indented rim/wall fragment of bowl	Plain, light orange surface; small calcrete grits.
4	125	1122.4	Everted rim/carinated wall fragment of gray burnished ware bowl	Plain, gray surface; small and coarse white grits; some glimmers.

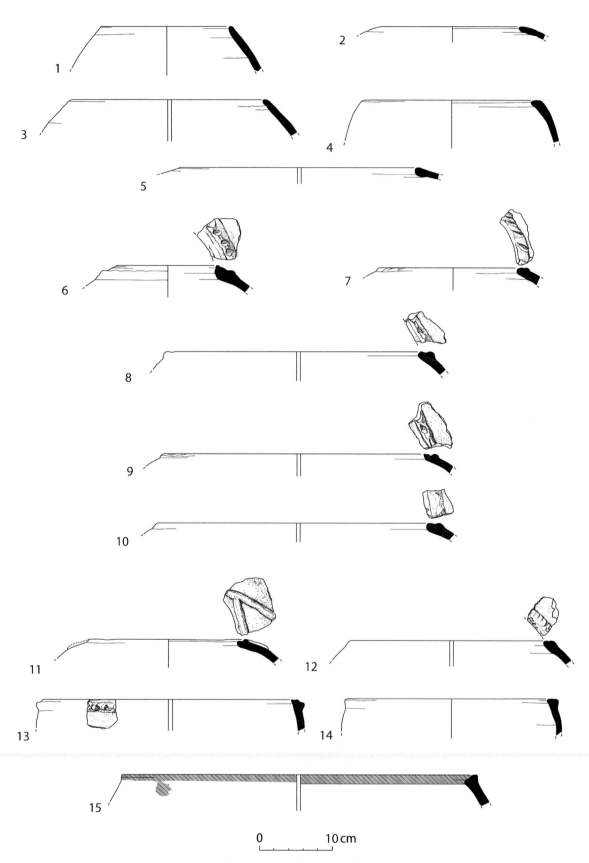

Fig. 5.2. Holemouth jars and kraters.

No.	Locus	Basket	Description	Remarks
1	125	1122.1	Tapered rim/wall fragment of a thin-walled holemouth jar	Plain, light orange surface; thick, gray core, thin light orange oxidation zones; small white (calcrete) grits and few glimmers.
2	118	1107.2	Tapered rim/wall fragment of a smallish holemouth jar	Plain, light orange surface; many small dark (chert?) grits and some glimmers (quartzite?).
3	101	1012.1	Tapered rim/wall fragment of a thin-walled holemouth jar	Plain, light orange surface; small and coarse white grits; many small, empty pores.
4	102	1033.1	Slightly infolded rim/wall fragment of a holemouth jar	Plain, light orange surface and core; many small calcrete inclusions and some glimmers.
5	112	1048.3	Rounded, slightly thickened rim/wall fragment of a holemouth jar	Plain, light orange surface; many small dark (chert) grits; few coarse white grits; some glimmers.
6	210	2044.1 2044.2	Two conjoining rim/wall fragments of a rope-decorated holemouth jar (cooking pot)	Indented band of clay ca. 1 cm below rim's exterior; plain, grayish surface; many small white and gray grits and glimmers.
7	215	2055	Rounded, indented rim/wall fragment of a holemouth jar	Well-fired; plain, light orange surface; few coarse white and even fewer gray grits.
8	214	2038.10	Slightly flattened rim with applied rope decoration below it/wall fragment of a holemouth jar	Plain, light orange surface; thick, gray core; light orange oxidation zones; small and few coarse, white grits.
9	220	2046.2	Tapered rim/wall fragment of a holemouth jar with an indented band of clay applied directly below rim's exterior	Plain, orange surface; small white grits; some glimmers.
10	220	2018.2	Tapered rim/wall fragment of a holemouth jar with an indented band of clay applied just below rim's exterior	Plain, orange surface.
11	214	2036.7	Rim/wall fragment of a holemouth vessel with applied bands of clay parallel and oblique to rim's exterior	Plain, orange surface; many and coarse small white grits.
12	230	2046.1	Indented rim/wall fragment of a medium-sized holemouth jar	Plain, orange surface; some white and gray grits.
13	214	2036.3	Flattened, slightly guttered rim and wall fragment of a restricted holemouth krater with rope decoration	Plain, light orange surface.
14	217	2037.3	Flattened, plain rim/wall fragment of a holemouth vessel	Plain, orange surface; many coarse white grits.
15	204	2013	Flattened rim/wall fragment of a holemouth krater	Red-painted rim; light orange surface; many small calcrete inclusions.

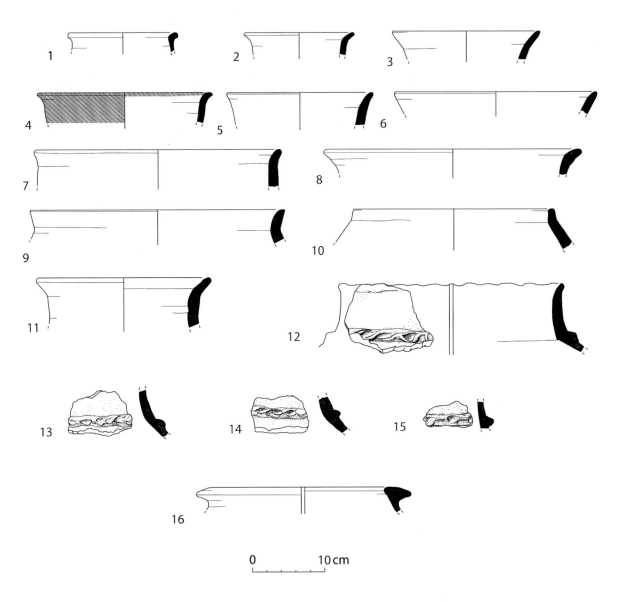

Fig. 5.3. Necked jars and pithoi.

No.	Locus	Basket	Description	Remarks
1	112	1032.1	Rim/short neck/shoulder fragment of a small closed vessel	Orange, coarse throughout; very few, minute, white grits.
2	101	1032.3	Everted rim/short neck/shoulder fragment of a small jar/jug	Plain, light orange surface.
3	112	1075.2	Tapered, everted rim/neck/wall fragment of a smallish jar	Plain, light orange surface; small and coarse white grits and small glimmers.
4	217	2037.1	Tapered, everted rim, short neck/shoulder fragment of a medium-sized jar	Red-painted exterior; small white grits.
5	114	1121	Tapered and everted rim/neck fragment of a medium-sized jar	Plain, light orange surface; orange core throughout; small calcrete grits.
6	101	1032.1	Rounded rim/neck fragment of a medium-sized jar	Plain, light orange surface; many coarse white grits.
7	214	2028.3	Rounded, everted rim/neck fragment of a largish jar	Plain, light orange surface; many small calcrete inclusions.
8	112	1075.1	Everted, tapered rim/neck fragment of a largish jar	Plain, light orange surface; small and coarse gray grits; some glimmers.
9	112	1092.1	Everted rim/neck/shoulder fragment of a largish jar	Plain, light orange surface; many small white (calcrete) and fewer gray inclusions; some glimmers.
10	214	2236.6	Rounded, everted rim/short neck/shoulder fragment of a jar	Plain, orange surface; many white, small grits.
11	114	1049.3	Everted tapered rim/short neck/shoulder fragment of large jar	Plain, light orange surface; gray core, light orange oxidation zones; many small and few coarse calcrete inclusions.
12	112	1092.2	Finger-indented, everted tapered rim/rope-decorated, tall neck/shoulder fragment of a pithos	Plain, grayish surface; many small dark (chert?) grits; few white grits and glimmers (quartzite?).
13	112	1075.4	Rope-decorated neck/wall fragment of a storage jar/pithos	Plain light orange surface; thick, orange core; many small calcrete grits; very few dark grits.
14	112	1075.3	Rope-decorated neck/wall fragment of a storage jar/pithos	Plain, light orange surface; many small dark (chert?) grits; few glimmers (quartzite?).
15	125	1122.3	Neck/shoulder fragment of a jar with rope application	Plain, light orange surface; many small gray and fewer white grits; some glimmers.
16	118	1107.1	Broad, flattened rim/ thin wall fragment of a jar; outer edge of rim possibly indented	Plain light orange surface; thick, gray core; many small and coarse calcrete grits; very few dark specks.

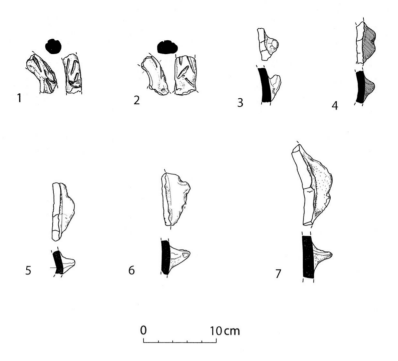

Fig. 5.4. Handles.

No.	Locus	Basket	Description	Remarks
1	104	1077.1	Incised, near-cylindrical loop handle fragment	Plain, orange surface; many small calcrete grits and some glimmers.
2	104	1077.2	Incised, oval loop handle fragment	Plain, orange surface; many small calcrete grits and some glimmers.
3	110	1084	Knobbed body sherd of closed vessel	Plain, light orange surface; orange core throughout; small calcrete grits.
4	214	2041.3	Red-painted body sherd with two small knobs	Traces of red paint on exterior; small white grits; N.B. Late Chalcolithic.
5	214	2036.5	Fragment of an indented ledge handle	Plain, light orange surface; small white grits.
6	208	2040.1	Fragment of a small, indented ledge handle	Plain, light orange surface; coarse white and fewer gray grits; few glimmers.
7	115	1057.3	Wall fragment of a jar with indented ledge handle	Plain, light orange surface; small and few coarse white and gray grits; some glimmers.

5. The Early Bronze Age Pottery Assemblage from Tell El-Wa'er

Table 5.1. Tell el-Wa'er: Pottery diagnostics account per type.

Locus	Bowl rims	Holemouth jars with plain rims	Holemouth jars with indented/rope-decorated rims	Large-necked jars with indented rims	Small-necked jars: rims	Small-necked jars: neck/shoulder fragments	Pithoi/rope-decorated: rims	Pithoi: rope-decorated: neck/shoulder fragments	Handles	Flat bases	Total
101		1			1	1				1	4
102		1			1	1 rope-decorated fragment			2 indented ledge handles; 1 loop handle	1 (jar); 4	11
104									2 loop handles		2
106	1										1
108					1			1			2
110						3 rope-decorated fragments			1 indented ledge handle; 1 knob		5
112		1		1	2		3		1 loop-handle fragment	5	13
113									1 incised loop handle		1
114					2	1				1	4
115	1				1	1 rope-decorated fragment			1 indented ledge handle	2 (jars)	5
118	1	1						1			4
123										1	1
125	2	1						1	1 large red-painted loop handle		5
204			1								1

77

Locus	Bowl rims	Holemouth jars with plain rims	Holemouth jars with indented/ rope-decorated rims	Large-necked jars with indented rims	Small-necked jars: rims	Small-necked jars: neck/ shoulder fragments	Pithoi/rope-decorated: rims	Pithoi: rope-decorated: neck/shoulder fragments	Handles	Flat bases	Total
208									1 indented ledge handle		1
210			1					2	2 indented ledge handles		5
212						1 rope-decorated fragment			1 indented ledge handle		2
214			4		2	1		4	2 indented ledge handles; 1 (body sherd with 2 small knobs)	2	16
215			1			1 rope-decorated fragment				1	3
217		1			1	1 rope-decorated fragment		1			4
218	1										1
220			2								2
230			1								1
Total (n=; %)	6 6.38%	6 6.38%	10 10.63%	1 1.06%	11 11.71%	11 11.71%	3 3.19%	10 10.64%	18 19.15%	18 19.15%	94 100%

Chapter 6

Groundstone and Metal Tools from Tell El-Wa'er

Edwin C. M. van den Brink (*Israel Antiquities Authority*)

The Groundstone Assemblage

Thirty groundstone items were recovered at Tell el-Wa'er, most of them made of basalt (tables 6.1–2). In addition to fourteen basalt bowl fragments (table 6.2; fig. 6.1.1–2), the assemblage includes six dense basalt fragments of upper grinding stones (manos), four dense and vesicular basalt fragments of basalt grinding slabs (metates), two pounder/abrader stones (one made of basalt and the other of flint; figs. 6.1.3 and 6.1.4, respectively), one basalt nodule and one bipolar drilled dense basalt item, both of unknown function, one nondistinct red stone fragment and two nondistinct limestone items.

Insofar as the basalt bowl fragments are diagnostic, they belong to flat-based bowls with slightly splayed walls and flattened rims (Braun 1990; type IA), considered a hallmark of the EB I. As seemingly corroborated by the other finds from Tell el-Wa'er, they appear early in the EB I sequence, also exemplified, for instance, at Yiftah'el Stratum II (Braun 1997, 97–100). A single, small ring-stand fragment of a fenestrated pedestal basalt bowl (L108/B1039; cf. table 6.2) belongs to the Late Chalcolithic horizon and should be considered intrusive.

Two Metal Axe Heads

Two metal axe heads (L214/B2033.1–2; figs. 6.2–4) were found together on a beaten-earth floor (L214), close to the east face of W46 in unit 14 (ch. 4, this volume). Metallurgical analyses of the two axes, conducted by D. Abu-Salah (IAA), are still in progress, and the results thereof will be published elsewhere. Notably, two near-identical metal axes were found at contemporary Yiftah'el, Stratum II, and analyzed for their metallurgical and metallographic data (Shalev and Braun 1997, 93–96, fig. 11.3).

References

Braun, Eliot
1990 "Basalt Bowls of the EB I Horizon in the Southern Levant." *Paléorient* 16: 87–96.
1997 *Yiftah'el. Salvage and Rescue Excavations at a Prehistoric Village in Lower Galilee, Israel*. IAA Reports 2. Jerusalem: Israel Antiquities Authority.

Shalev, Sariel, and Eliot Braun
1997 "The Metal Objects from Yiftah'el II." In *Yiftah'el: Salvage and Rescue Excavations at a Prehistoric Village in Lower Galilee, Israel*, by Eliot Braun, 92–96. IAA Reports 2. Jerusalem: Israel Antiquities Authority.

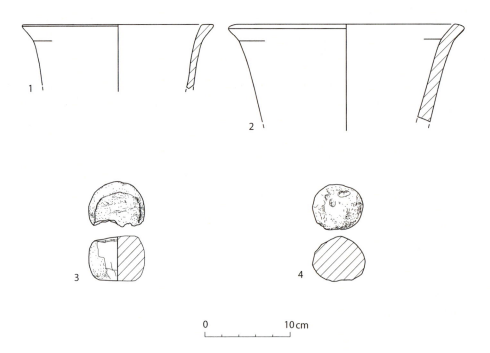

Fig. 6.1. Selection of groundstone vessels from Tell el-Wa'er: Basalt bowl rims (1–2); basalt abrader (3); flint pounder (4).

Fig. 6.2. The two axe heads before cleaning (L214, B2033.1–2).

6. Groundstone and Metal Tools from Tell El-Waʻer 81

Fig. 6.3. The two axe heads after cleaning (L214, B2033.1–2).

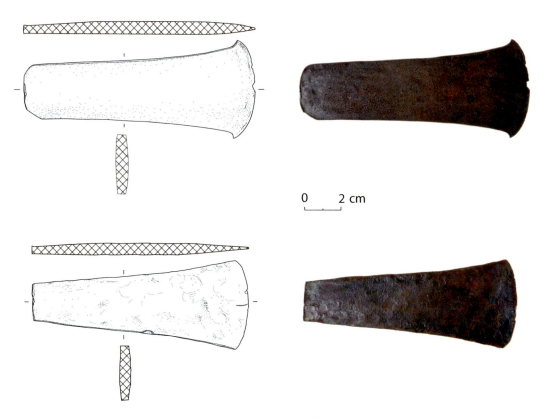

Fig. 6.4. Locus 214, Basket 2033.1–2.

Table 6.1. Tell el-Waʻer. Groundstone objects, by locus (bowls excluded).

Locus	Basket	Square	Description	Remarks
100	1089	A10	Fragment of a plano-convex (?), dense-basalt upper grinding stone (mano); 8 × 13 × 8 cm	Small fragment; only the flat bottom face is preserved; the upper face and all edges are broken.
103	1045	B11	Fragment of a plano-convex, dense-basalt upper grinding stone (mano); 14 × 13 × 6 cm	Partly preserved (half).
105	1016	B18	Fragment of a slightly convex dense-basalt grinding slab (metate); 14 × 12 × 55.5 cm	Only one slightly convex surface and a small part of one rounded edge are preserved.
105	1134	B18	Fragment of a flat vesicular-basalt grinding slab (metate); 11 × 9.5 × 3.6 cm	One rounded edge is preserved.
111	1091	A24	A rounded, small basalt "nodule," ca. 2.5 cm in diameter	Function unknown.
112	1073	A10	Fragment of a slightly convex vesicular-basalt grinding slab (metate); 17 × 8 × 3.6 cm	One rounded edge is preserved.
112	1074	A10	Fragment of a slightly convex basalt grinding slab (metate); 8 × 5 × 4 cm	Possibly belonging to fragment B1073 (same vesicular basalt).
113	1042	A24	Bipolar drilled dense-basalt item; 6 × 5 cm; both holes are slightly off-center (each ca. 2.5 cm wide at the top, and ca. 2 cm deep)	
124	1131	A24	Rectangular fragment of a red stone object; 9 × 7 × 4.5 cm	
206	2006	A15	Five fragments of a dense-basalt grinding stones	Two fragments of manos, showing the plano-convex shape in section.
208	2080/10	A14	Round flint pounder; ca. 5 × 5 cm	See fig. 6.1.4; slightly abraded.
208	2040	A14	Rectangular, soap-bar-like/sized limestone object	Abraded on one side (lime cortex missing).
210	2044	A13	Fragment of a dense-basalt upper grinding stone (mano); 10 × 8.5 × 7 cm; and an additional fragment probably belonging to the same mano	Plano-convex; parts of both the convex/top and the flat bottom faces are preserved.
212	2031	B16	Fragment of plano-convex, slightly vesicular-basalt upper grinding stone (mano); 11.5 × 15 × 6 cm	Partly preserved (half).
214	2036	B20	Round basalt abrader; 6 × 4.5 × 5 cm	See fig. 6.1.3; two flat surfaces.
218	2048.1	B20	Limestone fragment of a cylindrical item, ca. 9.5 cm in diameter, preserved height 2.6 cm	The item has a flat, polished (?) base and inclined "wall"; perhaps a pedestal segment?

Table 6.2. Tell el-Wa'er. Basalt bowl fragments.

Locus	Basket	Square	Description	Remarks
105	1088	B18	Nondistinct base fragment of a bowl	
108	1039	B24/C24	Ring stand fragment of a small basalt bowl on a fenestrated pedestal 1.6 × 2.1 cm in section	Late Chalcolithic.
109	1104	B25	Wall fragment of a basalt bowl; 6 × 4 × 1.2 cm	
110	1084	A25	Six conjoining but nondistinct base fragments of a bowl	
110	1120	A25	Flat base/wall fragment (ca. half preserved) of a flat-based dense-basalt bowl; 17.5 cm in diameter outside and 15 cm inside; 5-cm-thick base; partly preserved wall (1.5 cm thick; preserved height ca. 6 cm)	
112	1089	A10	Flaring, flat rim/wall fragment of a basalt bowl; wall ca.1.3 cm thick; preserved height ca. 6 cm	Braun 1990, type Ia.
112	1090	A10	Wall fragment of basalt bowl; 5.5 × 3.5 × 1.4 cm	
113	1043	A24	Complete base of a flat-based dense-basalt bowl; 13 cm in diameter outside and 10.5 cm inside; ca. 4-cm thick base; the walls are broken	
204	2013	A16	Flaring, flat rim/wall fragment of a basalt bowl; wall ca.1 cm thick; preserved ca. 6 cm high and 4 cm wide	Braun 1990, type Ia.
206	2006.1	A15	Flaring flat rim/wall fragment of a basalt bowl; wall ca.0.7 cm thick; preserved ca. 8 cm high	See fig. 6.1.1; Braun 1990, type Ia.
206	2006.2	A15	Flaring flat rim/wall fragment of a basalt bowl; wall ca.1.5 cm thick; preserved ca. 11.5 cm high	Fig. 6.1.2; Braun 1990, type Ia.
206	2006.4–.7	A15	Four bowl wall fragments belonging to at least two distinct bowls	Braun 1990, type Ia.
206	2043.1	A15	Flat base/wall fragment of a flat-based dense-basalt bowl; 14 cm in diameter outside and 10 cm inside; 3.5-cm thick base; partly preserved wall (2 cm thick; preserved height ca. 2.5 cm)	
206	2043.2	A15	Flat base/wall fragment of a flat-based dense-basalt bowl; 15 cm in diameter outside and 13 cm inside; 3.5-cm thick base; partly preserved wall (1.5 cm thick; preserved height ca. 4 cm)	Ca. a third is preserved.

Chapter 7

Lithic Artifacts from Tell El-Wa'er

Polina Spivak (*Israel Antiquities Authority*)

During the excavations at Tell el-Wa'er, a small assemblage of fifty-three flint items was retrieved from a single stratum dated to the Early EB I. All the deposits were dry-sieved through a 5 mm mesh.

Raw Material

The major part of the flint assemblage, primarily composed of sickle blades, is made from a fine-grained, brown-colored, high-quality homogeneous flint. Among the sickle blades, a lighter, smoother flint variety is most frequent, while a low-quality coarse flint variety is most recurrent among chunks. The vast majority of implements are sharp and fresh. Only a few objects showed fire damage.

Only a few rolled flint pieces were recorded, most of them with a heavy typical yellowish patina and probably originating in nearby Middle Paleolithic sites (Hovers et al. 2008, 2014; Yaroshevich, Khalaily, and Kirzner 2011). Some rolled pieces were seemingly reused in later periods, either at the site, at an issue location (see below), or at nearby Epipalaeolithic localities (Yaroshevich 2012).

The Assemblage

The assemblage is predominated by tools (33.9 percent), namely sickle blades. Only a relatively small number of debris and debitage elements were documented. Flakes outnumber blades in a 3:1 ratio. Primary elements are common (13.2 percent), indicating in situ, ad hoc knapping. Two recovered cores were made on rolled flint pieces covered by yellow patina, most likely representing reused chunks. One small, pyramidal core was used for bladelet production. The other, larger core presents only flake scars.

Tools

Sickle blades, making up 70 percent of the tools, were mostly fashioned on relatively short and thin blades. Most blades were backed by abrupt and semiabrupt retouch. The working edges were finely denticulated and gloss is limited to the denticulation (fig.7.1). Nibbling is common. Truncations were found on all unbroken ends. Such sickles have been assigned to the Wadi Raba type C by Ran Barkai and Avi Gopher (2012, 800; Barkai 1996, 20), dated to the Early Chalcolithic period. Steven Rosen (1997, 138–40) refers to these blades as proto-Canaanean, most common during the Chalcolithic period and the Chalcolithic–Early Bronze transition. The proto-Canaanean sickles are not as standardized and uniform as the Canaanean products. Most do not have the typical trapezoidal cross-section, and, even when two scar ridges are present along the back, they can hardly be considered parallel. The Canaanean industry took over completely during the Early Bronze period (Rosen 1997, 141–42).

Two isolated sickle blades, of other types, were also collected at the site: a small fragment of a thick, bipolar blade (fig. 7.2.1) prepared on a different flint

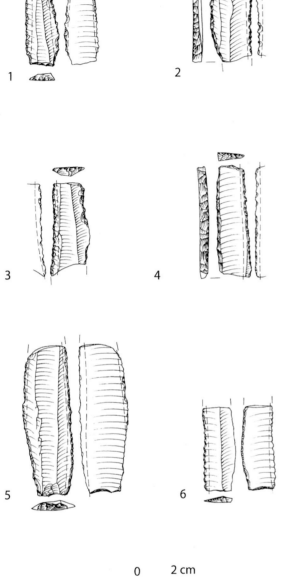

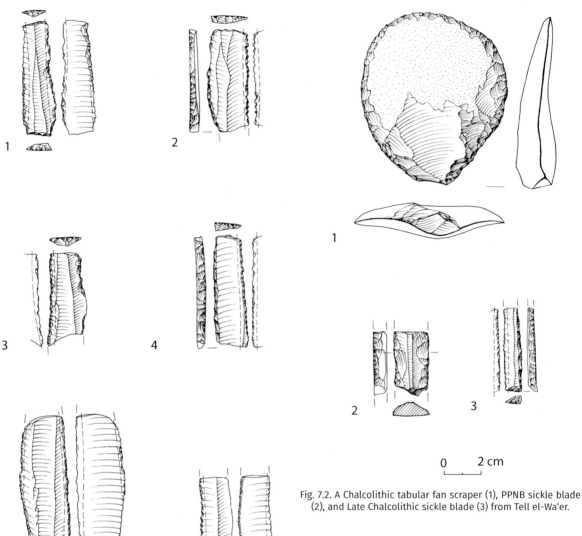

Fig. 7.2. A Chalcolithic tabular fan scraper (1), PPNB sickle blade (2), and Late Chalcolithic sickle blade (3) from Tell el-Wa'er.

Fig. 7.1. Chalcolithic–Early Bronze Age sickle blades from Tell el-Wa'er.

type and typologically diagnostic of the PPNB period, and an extremely narrow backed sickle blade, typical of the (Ghassulian) Late Chalcolithic period (fig. 7.2.2).

Among the remaining tools, scrapers are the most frequent. One tabular flint scraper—often referred to in the literature as a fan-scraper—was manufactured on a flat cortical flake (fig. 7.2.1). This fan-shaped type is typically associated with the Chalcolithic period (Rosen 1983) but can also be characteristic of Early Bronze Age flint assemblages.

Discussion

The relatively high blade-to-flake ratio (3:1), associated with the blade intended industry, and the total lack of debitage (related cores and CTE) in the assemblage indicate that the blades used as sickles were made elsewhere and imported to the site. This assumption is reinforced by the superior light and smooth flint used for the sickle blades, and the presence of the beautifully executed fan-scraper, also imported (Rosen 1983). Material-goods trade and dispersion is a well-known scenario, usually applied to Canaanean blades (Rosen 1983; 1997, 107–8; 2003; Milevski 2013). Although, as mentioned, most blades and sickles from Tell el-Wa'er do not exhibit true Canaanean technological characteristics, finding them without the presiding chaîne-opératoire elements is typical of a vast majority of sites with Canaanean finds (Bankirer 2003,180; Rosen and Vardi 2014, 330–32; Eisenberg 2012, 59; Milevski et al. 2012, 107–17). The same is true for the tabular scrapers (Rosen 1983).

The phenomenon of lack of production waste and use of nonlocal raw material has generated regular debates and proposals of distribution-system models of specialized and semispecialized productive goods in the Early Bronze Age (Rosen 1983; 1997, 107–8; 2003; Yellin, Levy, and Rowan 1996; Milevski 2013; Shimelmitz 2009 and references therein).

Tell el-Waʻer is a single-stratum site dated to the beginning of the Early Bronze Age (EB I). However, the diagnostic flint tools seem to point to an earlier phase, possibly the Chalcolithic–Early Bronze transition, although it should be noted that Canaanean and proto-Canaanean industries recorded in clear Chalcolithic contexts (Barkai 2004; Rowan and Levy 1994; Vardi and Gilead 2013) have often been considered intrusive (Milevski et al. 2011). Still, the origins of proto-Canaanean technology being as uncertain (Shimelmitz and Mendel 2008; Shimelmitz 2009) as the sources and distribution curves of the Early Bronze Age trading routes (Rosen 1983; Rosen, Tykot, and Gottesman 2005, 2011; Yellin, Levy, and Rowan 1996), it is evident that unique, imported flint tools had an exceptionally long life. Clearly, the centralized manufactured products may have changed hands several times before finally reaching their final destination.

It is safe to argue that the Tell el-Waʻer's flint assemblage comprises the most typical toolkit components of both the Chalcolithic period and the Early Bronze Age: Imported, highly standardized objects on the one hand and local ad hoc tools on the other. Both represent the cause and effect of the extensive trade system that flourishing into the following Middle Bronze Age.

References

Bankirer, Rina Y.
2003 "The Flint Assemblage." In *Salvage Excavations at the Early Bronze Age Site of Qiryat Ata*, edited by Amir Golani, 171–82. IAA Reports 18. Jerusalem: Israel Antiquities Authority.

Barkai, Ran
1996 "The Flint Assemblage from Nahal Zehora I, A Wadi Raba Site in the Menashe Hills: The Implications of a Technological and Typological Analysis." MA thesis, Tel Aviv University.
2004 "The Chalcolithic Lithic Assemblage." In *Givʻat Ha-Oranim: A Late Chalcolithic Site*, edited by Naʻama Scheftelowitz and Ronit Oren, 87–109., Salvage Excavation Reports 1. Tel Aviv: Tel Aviv University.

Barkai, Ran, and Avi Gopher
2012 "Flint Assemblages from Naḥal Zehora II: Techno-Typological Changes during the PN." In *Village Communities of the Pottery Neolithic Period in the Menashe Hills, Israel. Archaeological Investigations at the Sites of Naḥal Zehora*, edited by Avi Gopher, 2 vols., 757–869. SMNIA 29. Tel Aviv: Tel Aviv University.

Eisenberg, Emanuel
2012 "The Early Bronze Age IV Site at Shaʻar Ha-Golan." *Atiqot* 69:1–73.

Hovers, Erella, Ravid Ekshtain, Noam Greenbaum, Ariel Malinsky-Buller, Nadav Nir, and Reuven Yeshurun
2014 "Islands in a Stream? Reconstructing Site Formation Processes in the Late Middle Paleolithic Site of ʻEin Qashish, Northern Israel." *Quaternary International* 331: 216–33. DOI: 10.1016/j.quaint.2014.01.028.

Hovers, Erella, Ariel Malinsky-Buller, Ravid Ekshtain, Maya Oron, and Reuven Yeshurun
2008 "Ein Qashish—A New Middle Paleolithic Open-Air Site in Northern Israel." *Journal of the Israel Prehistoric Society* 38: 7–40.

Milevski, Ianir
2013 "The Exchange of Flint Tools in the Southern Levant during the Early Bronze Age." *Lithic Technology* 38.3: 202–19.

Milevski, Ianir, Elisabetta Boaretto, Anat Cohen-Weinberger, Elisheva Kamaisky, Hamoudi Khalaily, Nili Liphschitz, Moshe Sade, and Sariel Shalev
2012 "Er-Rujum (Shaʼalabim East): An Intermediate Bronze Age (EB IV) Site in the Ayyalon Valley." *Atiqot* 69: 75–140.

Milevski, Ianir, Peter Fabian, and Ofer Marder
2011 "Canaanean Blades in Chalcolithic Contexts of the Southern Levant?" In *Culture, Chronology and the Chalcolithic: Theory and Transition*, edited by

Jaimie Lea Lovell, and Yorke M. Rowan, 149–59. Levant Supplementary Series 9. Oxford: Oxbow.

Rosen, Steven A.
1983 "A Model of Material Cultural Dispersion." *BASOR* 249: 79–86.
1997 *Lithics after the Stone Age: A Handbook of Stone Tools from the Levant*. Walnut Creek, CA: Alta Mira.
2003 "Early Multi-resource Nomadism: Excavations at the Camel Site in the Central Negev." *Antiquity* 77: 749–60. DOI: 10.1017/S0003598X0006169X.

Rosen, Steven A., Robert H. Tykot, and Michael J. Gottesman
2005 "Long-Distance Trinket Trade: Early Bronze Age Obsidian from the Negev." *Journal of Archaeological Science* 32: 775–84. DOI: 10.1016/j.jas.2005.01.001.
2011 "The Camel Site Obsidian: Analyses, Synthesis and Implications." In *An Investigation into Early Desert Pastoralism: Excavations at the Camel Site, Negev*, edited by Steven A. Rosen, 133–46. Los Angeles: Cotsen Institute of Archaeology.

Rosen, Steven A., and Jacob Vardi
2014 "The Chipped Stone Assemblage from Be'er Resisim–A Final Report." In *Excavation at the Early Bronze IV Sites of Jebel Qa'aqir and Be'er Resisim*, edited by William G. Dever, 327–39. Winona Lake, IN: Eisenbrauns.

Rowan, Yorke M., and Thomas E. Levy
1994 "Proto-Canaanean Blades from the Chalcolithic Site of Gilat." *Levant* 26: 167–74.

Shimelmitz Ron
2009 "Variability in Specialized Canaanean Blade Production of the Early Bronze Age Levant." In *Techniques and People. Anthropological Perspectives on Technology in the Archaeology of the Proto-Historic and Early Historic Periods in the Southern Levant*, edited by Steven A. Rosen and Valentine Roux, 133–54. Paris: de Boccard.

Shimelmitz, Ron, and Shlomo Mendel
2008 "A Chalcolithic Workshop for the Production of Blades and Bi-facial Tools at Khirbet Yoah, the Manasseh Hills." *Journal of the Israel Prehistoric Society* 38: 229–56.

Vardi, Jacob, and Isaac Gilead
2013 "Chalcolithic-Early Bronze Age Transition in the Southern Levant: The Lithic Perspective." *Paléorient* 39: 111–23.

Yaroshevich, Alla
2012 "Tel Qashish (South)." *HA-ESI* 124. http://www.hadashot-esi.org.il/report_detail_eng.aspx?id=2168&mag_id=119.

Yaroshevich, Alla, Hamudi Khalaily, and Dan Kirzner
2011 "Tel Qashish (West), Preliminary Report." *HA-ESI* 123. http://www.hadashot-esi.org.il/report_detail_eng.aspx?id=1842&mag_id=118.

Yellin, Joseph, Thomas E. Levy, and Yorke M. Rowan
1996 "New Evidence on Prehistoric Trade Routes: The Obsidian Evidence from Gilat, Israel." *Journal of Field Archaeology* 23: 68–361. DOI: 10.1179/009346996791973873.

Chapter 8

Faunal Remains from Tell El-Wa'er

Ronit Zuckerman-Cooper (*Israel Antiquities Authority*)

This report describes the forty-two animal bone fragments and teeth remains recovered in the excavations undertaken at the Early Bronze Age I site of Tell el-Wa'er.

Method

All the bones were identified in the Laboratory of Archaeozoology at the University of Haifa. Identification was attempted for most bone fragments, except for shaft fragments smaller than 4 cm. Standard measurements were possible only for one bone and were taken following Angela von den Driesch's (1976) guidelines. Bone specimens were identified to the highest possible resolution in terms of taxonomic or body-size categories, with small-sized representing animals such as rabbits, medium-sized representing animals such as goats, sheep, pig, or gazelle, and large-sized representing animals such as cattle, or horses/donkeys.

Age-at-death estimation was possible only for caprine and relies on Annie Grant's (1982) dental-wear stages.

All the bones were examined for surface modifications resulting from human activities (e.g., cutting, burning, and breaking), animal activities (e.g., gnawing, predation, and digestion), and other factors (such as weather, vegetation, and pathologies).

Results

The medium-sized specimens (n=21; 50 percent) represent the largest group of faunal remains, followed by large-sized specimens (n=12; 28.6 percent) comprising mostly long-bone shaft fragments. Taxonomic identification was available for caprine (sheep or goat) (n=5; 11.9 percent) and cattle remains (n=2; 4.8 percent). Taxonomic frequencies point to the vast majority of the large-sized specimens probably being cattle, with medium-sized specimens being caprine. Small quantities of other taxa were also found, such as a horse or a donkey (n=1; 2.4 percent) and a small-sized specimen (n=1; 2.4 percent).

Due to the small sample sizes of the teeth available for aging assessment (three caprine teeth from the right mandible, M1–M3), these data should be treated with some caution. Based on dental eruption and wear data, the caprine population seems to have consisted of juvenile and subadult animals (aged 13–24 months).

In terms of skeletal elements, the assemblage was predominated by long-bone shaft fragments (81 percent) of small, medium, and large-sized specimens. The identified species—caprine, cattle, and equid—are represented mainly by teeth, though some long bones, such as caprine humerus and tibia, were also present (measurement for the tibia: Bd=42.1). Toes are poorly represented, and only a single second phalange (cattle) was documented.

All bones were examined for surface modifications resulting from human activities (e.g., butchery and burning), animal activities (e.g., gnawing), and other factors (e.g., weather and pathologies). Two burnt fragments belonging to medium-sized specimens make up only 4.8 percent of the total number of bone fragments in the assemblage. These fragments were found in L214, a beaten-earth floor south of W51. The bones show nonuniform burning and variations in their color and the extent of the burnt surfaces. Furthermore, all the long-bone fragments present surface modifications caused by exposure, on the land surface, to weather conditions. No butchery marks, carnivore gnawing, or pathology deformations were observed in the assemblage.

Conclusions

The bone assemblage retrieved from Tell el-Waʻer is composed primarily of caprine, cattle, and other similarly sized animals. The limited data available on the mortality profile of caprine suggest a preference for the slaughter of immature animals, a pattern usually associated with herd-management aimed at meat production. The taphonomic analysis revealed that a relatively long exposure on the land surface had damaged the bones before being finely covered by sediment. Due to the small size of the current assemblage, no further analysis could be conducted, nor additional conclusions drawn.

References

Driesch, Angela, von den
1976 *A Guide to Measurement of Animal Bones from Archaeological Sites: As Developed by the Institut für Palaeoanatomie, Domestikationsforschung und Geschichte der Tiermedizin of the University of Munich.* Peabody Museum Bulletin 1. Cambridge: Peabody Museum of Archaeology and Ethnology.

Grant, Annie
1982 "The Use of Tooth Wear as a Guide to the Age of Domestic Ungulates." In *Ageing and Sexing Animal Bones from Archaeological Sites*, edited by Bob Wilson, Caroline Grigson, and Sebastian Payne, 91–108. BARIS 109. Oxford: British Archaeological Reports.

Chapter 9

Salvage Excavations at Tell El-Wa'er: Discussion and Conclusions

Orit Segal and Edwin C. M. van den Brink (*Israel Antiquities Authority*)

The very distinct, curvilinear architecture that characterizes the structural remains uncovered at Tell el-Wa'er, and the associated pottery, ground stone assemblages, and copper axe heads, strongly resemble those discovered in Yiftah'el Stratum II (Braun 1997), an example par excellence and a key site for the early northern EB I in this region. Based on the Tell el-Wa'er findings, the two settlements may be considered contemporary.

Lacking absolute dates for both sites, we have to content ourselves with the notion that, in the (near) absence of rectilinear architecture, the deposits at Tell el-Wa'er postdate the latest phase of the Late Chalcolithic (i.e., LC 2) and predate the later phases of the EB I when the curvilinear building tradition was abandoned and rectilinear architecture reintroduced.

Given the shallow depths of the early EB I deposit at Tell el-Wa'er, and notwithstanding some architectural subphasing evident at the site, we may surmise that this settlement was short-lived, abandoned, and never resettled. The earliest vestiges of human habitation in subsequent, later phases of the EB I are to be found in and around Tel Qashish, just opposite Tell el-Wa'er, on the other (east) side of the Kishon River (chs. 11–24, this volume; Ben-Tor, Bonfil, and Zuckerman 2003, 10–57).

References

Ben-Tor, Amnon., Ruhama Bonfil, and Sharon Zuckerman
2003 *Tel Qashish: A Village in the Jezreel Valley; Final report of the Archaeological Excavations (1978–1987)*. Qedem Reports 5. Jerusalem: Hebrew University of Jerusalem.

Braun, Eliot
1997 *Yiftah'el: Salvage and Rescue Excavations at a Prehistoric Village in Lower Galilee, Israel*. IAA Reports 2. Jerusalem: Israel Antiquities Authority.

Part IV

Tel Qashish
(Early Bronze Age)

Chapter 10

The Tel Qashish Late Early Bronze Age I Salvage Excavations: Introductory Notes

Edwin C. M. van den Brink (*Israel Antiquities Authority*)

Tel Qashish is located in the northwestern portion of the Jezreel Valley, Israel, approximately 15 km southeast of Haifa, 2.5 km north of Yoqneʿam, and 18 km west of Nazareth (fig. 10.1; ch. 1, this volume). Excavations on the tell from 1978 to 1987 revealed a stratigraphic sequence from the Early Bronze Age I through the Persian period (Ben-Tor, Bonfil, and Zuckerman 2003). While reached in only a limited area, the late EB I remains at the site and the analyses of the finds suggest that the site was a significant village of the period in the Jezreel Valley (Ben-Tor and Bonfil 2003; Zuckerman 2003).

Parts of a projected trajectory of a transnational, natural gas pipeline, passing within a range of less than 150 m of Tel Qashish's north and west flanks before crossing the Kishon River, were subjected in the late spring of 2010 to initial archaeological inspection by means of mechanical trenching (IAA permit A-5881/2010). Seventy 5 × 5 m squares, distributed over four adjoining areas (A–D) within the cultivated fields north and west of Tel Qashish were subsequently probed (figs. 10.2–3). These revealed a foundation segment of either a Roman road or platform (Area A; ch. 11, this volume), a Late Bronze Age II cultic pottery cache with over four hundred intact vessels (Area B; Part V, this volume), and structural remains of late Early Bronze Age I agricultural installations (Areas C–D).

Later in that same year, additional salvage excavations were conducted less than 30 m east of Area C, in anticipation of the construction of a 10-m-wide segment of a railroad track (Rakevet HaʿEmeq), in two further areas (IAA permit A-5992/2010; fig. 10.2): Area F, along an approximately 70-m-long, northeast–southwest 5-m-wide transect, locally extended 5 m north and south; and Area E South, some 65 m further to the east, within the same grid lines but separated from the Area F by a dirt path leading up to the tell of Qashish. After revealing a spread of agricultural storage structures in Area E South, the area was further extended and probed (Area E North) within a grid of thirty 5 × 5 m squares in 2011 in a third, and thus far final, salvage excavation (IAA permit A-6149). A single stratum of dense structural remains of an extensive, late EB I settlement was revealed, founded on sterile, weathered basalt soil (fig. 10.3).

This part (IV) of the book focuses exclusively on the late EB I remains (with a brief note on the Roman road in ch. 11). Due to the progression of the salvage excavations and the various IAA archaeologists tasked with the projects, the stratigraphy and pottery chapters are divided up according to the individuals responsible for the areas. Consequently, there are also differing approaches to the material in each of these chapters. The stratigraphy and structural features of Areas A–F are presented in chapters 11–13. The pottery assemblages deriving from these areas and the petrographic analysis of selected items are presented in chapters 14–18; the groundstone and chipped stone tools and the faunal and floral remains (the latter including over 7600 seeds) are presented in chapters 19–23 respectively, followed by a final, brief discussion and conclusions in chapter 24.

Fig. 10.1. Map showing the location of Tel Qashish in northern Israel.

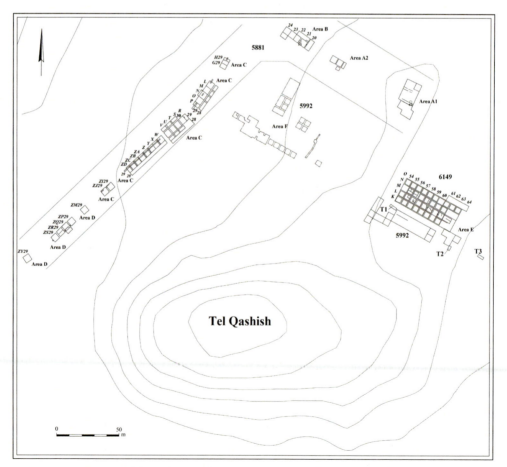

Fig. 10.2. Plan of excavation Areas A–F around Tel Qashish.

10. The Tel Qashish Late Early Bronze Age I Salvage Excavations: Introductory Notes

Fig. 10.3. Aerial view of Areas E South and North in the southeast margin of Tel Qashish. Looking south.

The combined picture emerging from these salvage excavations in the margins of Tel Qashish, along with those on the tell, exposes a thriving rural village and its immediate hinterland, eventually abandoned and never resettled again. It significantly supplements the findings deriving from other contemporary late EB I settlement sites in the region, which include the Tel Qashish Strata XV–XIV "upper village," Megiddo Levels J-2–4; Qiryat Ata Strata III–II, 'En Shadud Strata II–I, 'En Esur Stratum II, and Tel Beth Shean Strata M3–M2.

References

Ben-Tor, Amnon, Ruhama Bonfil, and Sharon Zuckerman
2003 *Tel Qashish: A Village in the Jezreel Valley; Final Report of the Archaeological Excavations (1978–1987)*. Qedem Reports 5. Jerusalem: Hebrew University of Jerusalem.

Ben-Tor, Amnon, and Ruhama Bonfil
2003 "The Stratigraphy of the Early Bronze Age." In *Tel Qashish: A Village in the Jezreel Valley; Final Report of the Archaeological Excavations (1978–1987)*, edited by Amnon Ben-Tor, Ruhama Bonfil, and Sharon Zuckerman, 10–30. Qedem Reports 5. Jerusalem: Hebrew University of Jerusalem.

Zuckerman, Sharon
2003 "Tel Qashish in the Early Bronze Age I." In *Tel Qashish: A Village in the Jezreel Valley; Final Report of the Archaeological Excavations (1978–1987)*, edited by Amnon Ben-Tor, Ruhama Bonfil, and Sharon Zuckerman, 57–60. Qedem Reports 5. Jerusalem: Hebrew University of Jerusalem.

Chapter 11

Tel Qashish Areas A–D: Stratigraphy and Structural Features (2010 Excavations)

Edwin C. M. van den Brink, Uzi ʻAd, Dan Kirzner, Eli Yannai, Mohammed Hater, Orit Segal
(*Israel Antiquities Authority*)

Tel Qashish is situated east of Road 70 and about 2 km northeast of Tel Yoqneʻam (fig. 10.1) and known to contain habitation levels dating at least from the Early Bronze through the Iron Ages (Ben-Tor, Bonfil, and Zuckerman 2003). Sections of a planned transnational natural gas pipeline passing within 150 m of Tel Qashish's north and west flanks were subjected to initial archaeological inspection by means of mechanical trenching in the late spring of 2010 (ch. 10, this volume; IAA permit A-5881/2010). The presence of archaeological remains off of the tell was borne out by the initial survey and subsequent salvage excavations. Seventy 5 × 5 m squares distributed over the four adjoining Areas A–D were probed within the cultivated fields north and west of Tel Qashish (fig. 11.1). Excavation Areas E and F concern subsequent salvage excavations presented in chapters 12 and 13.

Area A

Area A1 (Figures 11.2–3)

At about 0.2–0.3 m below the present surface level, an extensive, flat, and carefully paved surface built of one course of densely packed, natural and semihewn limestones (Loci 120, 122, and 125) was exposed in all nine probed squares (Squares B5–6, C5–6, D4–6, E6, and F5; figs. 11.2–3). Two distinct stone sizes were roughly used: 0.42 × 0.40 × 0.30 m, and 0.12 × 0.10 × 0.08 m. This 23 m long and 7.5–8 m wide surface is locally delineated on its eastern side by a 13.5-m-long single row of medium-sized fieldstones, oriented northeast–southwest (W10). The function of this built surface, almost leveled with the surrounding natural bedrock, is unclear; it may have been part of an ancient road or platform.

Only a few potsherds were found deposited on and in-between the stones of this feature. Two east-west cross sections (Locus 128 in Squares D4–D6, and Loci 133 and 136 in Squares C5–C6), were cut through it (fig. 11.3, sections 1-1 and 2-2) to examine its internal structure hoping to extract sealed pottery from below the stone surface.

Underneath the stone surface, a thin soil fill layer directly rested on the natural bedrock. None of the potsherds retrieved from this fill (ch. 14, this volume) postdate the second century CE, providing a *terminus post quem* date for the stone surface. Also, outside the confines of this surface, late Early Bronze Age I sherds (ch. 14, this volume; fig. 14.1) were found wherever deeper-lying bedrock pockets were exposed, with no structural remains and probably residual to attested late EB I activities elsewhere at the site (in particular Area E, see chs. 12–13, this volume).

Area A2 (Figures 11.2, 4)

Area A2 was opened less than 50 m northwest of Area A1 (fig. 11.2). In four probes (squares D15, D16, D17, and E16), soft chalky bedrock was ex-

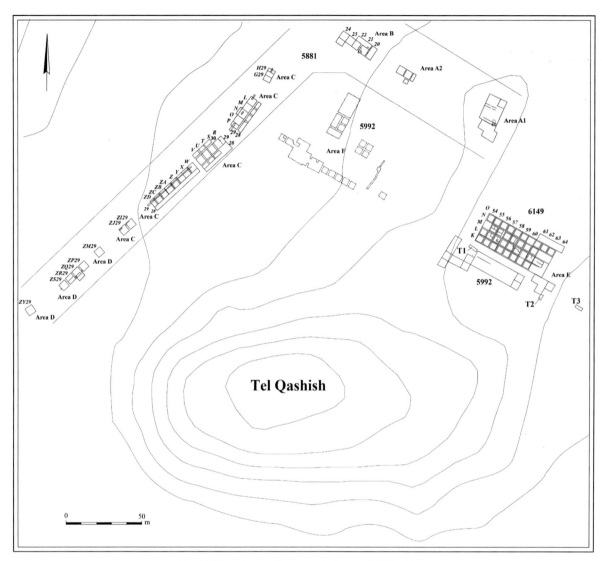

Fig. 11.1. Plan of excavation Areas A–F around Tel Qashish.

posed only a few centimeters below the present surface. No features were revealed, except for a 5.5 m long, 1.5 m wide, and about 1 m deep straight segment of a north–south-oriented ancient cut in the soft bedrock (Squares D16 and E16; Loci 123 and 132). This apparently manmade trench yielded, besides some possibly intrusive potsherds dating from the late EB I, three large, almost perfectly round (ballista-like) very heavy stones, not dissimilar in shape from the scores of much smaller round (sling?) stones exposed in the nearby Area B (see below). A causal relationship between these stones and the nearby platform in Area A1 could be suggested, but given the absence of more conclusive, datable finds, the date and function of this partially excavated feature remains obscure.

Area B (Figures 11.2, 5–7)

About 135 m north of the northern edge of Tel Qashish, nine squares (figs. 11.2, 5: C20–22; D20–24; E24) were excavated down to the natural white chalky bedrock. The bedrock gently slopes in a northwest–southeast direction from 29.8 m ASL to 28.7 m ASL (a 1.1 m difference in absolute height over a 20 m distance; fig. 11.5, section 1-1), and is covered by a 0.25–0.5-m-thick layer of alluvial sediments. Three features of archaeological interest,

Fig. 11.2. Area A1. Aerial view.

Fig. 11.3. Area A1. Plan, trenches and sections.

dating from two distinct periods, were noticed and excavated in this area:

1. A local spread of small, fist-sized limestones was found just below the present plow zone, with numerous potsherds on and in between the stones dating exclusively from the late Early Bronze Age I (ca. 3000 BCE) (fig. 11.5: Squares C20, D20–21; Loci 200, 222, 224, 227, 228).

Below this approximately 0.25-m-thick stony layer, further late EB I ceramics were found on the bedrock. Structural remains were absent. In Areas C and D, similar and often discontinuous spreads of small stones have been exposed over larger areas, sometimes associated with structural remains (see below). The presence and nature of scores of mostly small (diameter ca. 5 cm), heavy, round (quartz?) stones found in the fill above the stony layer and on natural bedrock remains unclear. Although apparently natural, their clustering in this excavation area clearly indicates that they were deliberately selected and collected, perhaps due to their rather uniform size and weight, and possibly modified (pecked) in ancient times. They are too small to have functioned as pounding stones but might have been used, for example, as sling stones during hunting or warfare.

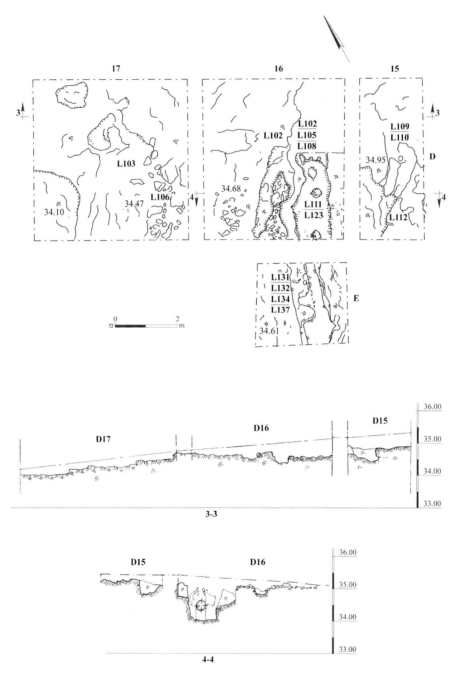

Fig. 11.4. Area A2. Plan and sections.

2. A narrow, approximately 3-m-deep bedrock cavity (figs. 11.5–6: Square D21, Loci 212, 218, 219, and 225) with a stepped entrance on the southwest, which accommodated a LB II repository of ritual ceramic vessels (fig. 11.7). Its ceiling, with evidence of a late EB I occupation on top, had collapsed in antiquity, creating a depression that, over time, filled up and was sealed by fine, alluvial sediments concealing the cave. Based on the chrono-typological range of both the locally produced and imported ceramic vessels in the assemblage, the repository can be dated to a noninitial phase within the LB II. These findings have already been selectively discussed in the past (van den Brink, Segal, and 'Ad 2012; Ziffer et al. 2018), and a separate, final report concerning this repository is published in this volume (Part V).

11. Tel Qashish Areas A–D: Stratigraphy and Structural Features (2010 Excavations)

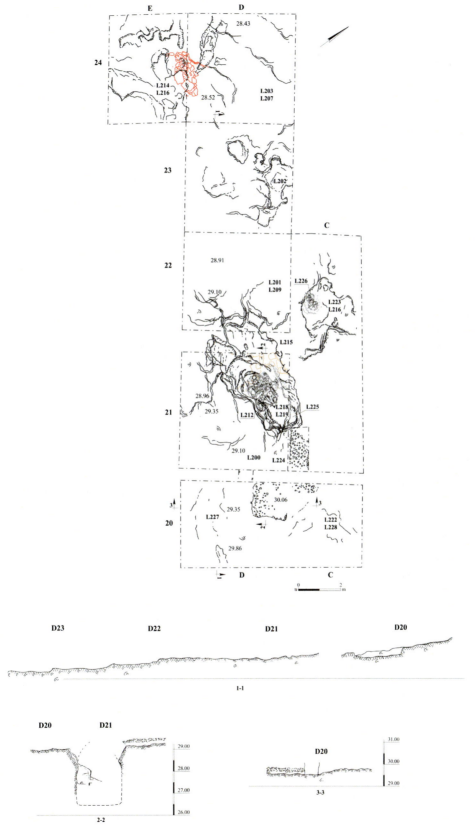

Fig. 11.5. Area B. Plan and sections.

Fig. 11.6. Area B. Aerial photograph, looking southwest.

Fig. 11.7. Area B. LB II repository during excavation.

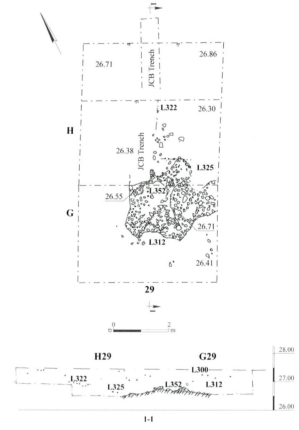

Fig. 11.8. Area C. Squares G29–H29.

3. A natural bedrock depression (fig. 11.5: Square C22, Loci 223 and 226) just 4 m north of the repository cave, containing additional LB II ceramic vessels, including numerous disk-based bowls, a pilgrim's flask, and a dipper juglet, possibly associated with the repository cave and reflecting the leftovers of a ritual or ceremony performed each time cultic paraphernalia was brought to the cave (cf. Segal, 'Ad, and van den Brink, ch. 25, this volume).

11. Tel Qashish Areas A–D: Stratigraphy and Structural Features (2010 Excavations)

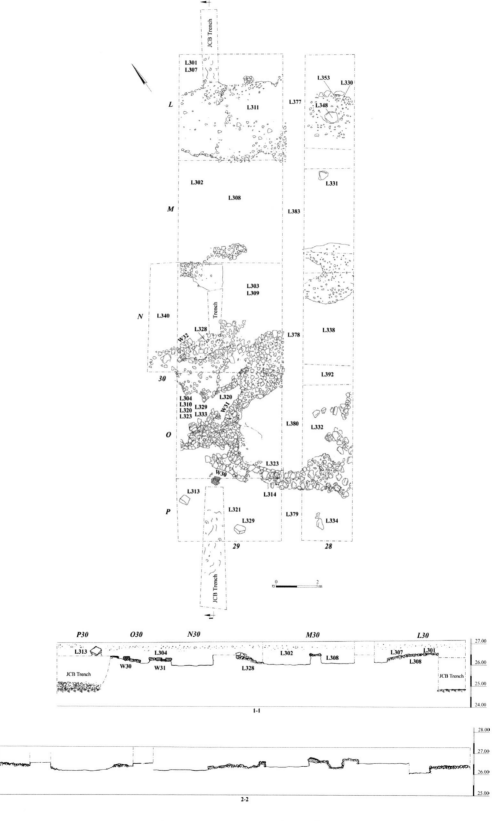

Fig. 11.9. Area C. Squares L28/29–P28/29.

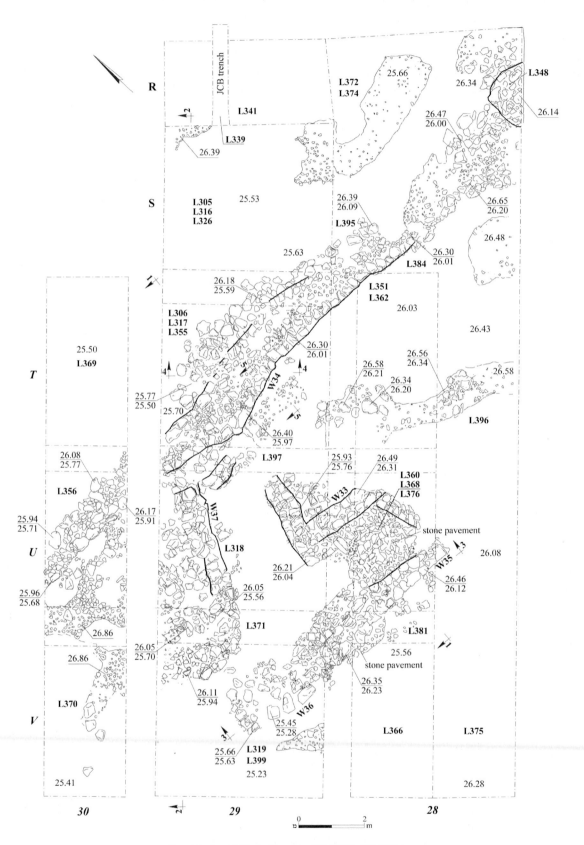

Fig. 11.10. Area C. Plan of Squares R28/29/30–V28/29/30.

Area C (Figures 11.2, 8–25)

Forty-two squares (fig. 11.8: G29–H29; fig. 11.9: L28–29, M28–29, N28–30, O28–29, P28–29; fig. 11.10: R28–29, S28–29, T28–30, U28–30, V28–30; fig. 11.11: W28/29–ZD28/29; fig. 11.12: ZI29/ZJ29) were opened in the excavation's core area, 100 m east of the present streambed of the Kishon River and less than 80 m west of the contact zone between the northern edge of Tel Qashish and the surrounding alluvium soil area (figs. 11.13–14).

In this area, the natural limestone bedrock lies about 1.5–2 m below the present plow-zone levels and is covered by thick deposits of dark brown, grumusol alluvial soils. A single and continuous anthropogenic level/horizon stretching over an area at least 130-m long was identified embedded in these deposits, about 0.5–0.7 below the present surface (i.e., covered by and resting on similar sterile sediments overlaying the natural bedrock). The main archaeological feature consists of spreads of small fieldstones locally associated with stone-built walls, installations, or structures interspersed with high densities of almost exclusive late EB I potsherds (see below). Ground stone tools are also common (see Milevski, ch. 19, this volume), but flints (see Yaroshevich, ch. 20, this volume) and animal bones (see Agha, ch. 21, this volume) are scarce.

In the northernmost two squares (G29–H29, fig. 11.8), a rather amorphous 3.0 × 3.5 m single layer of small, natural limestones (L352) was exposed between a top layer of sterile, grumic soils (max. 1 m thick; Loci 312, 322, and 325) and similar sterile sediments below (fig. 11.8, section 1–1). This layer locally protruded from the east balks of both squares and was slightly damaged on the northeast by a test trench mechanically dug prior to excavation.

The next, double row of five excavation squares (L28/L29–P28/P29, fig. 11.9), 12 m southwest of Square G29, shows a similar and slightly clearer picture (because of the larger exposure) of what appears to be two separate units of stone spreads, each with additional features.

Over the full length of Squares L28/L29, an 8.5 × 3.5 m continuous spread of small field limestones (figs. 11.9, 11.15: L311; figs. 11.9, 11.16: L353) was exposed below a thick layer of sterile grumic soil sediments (Loci 301, 307, 330, and 377). This single continuous unit with more or less well-defined parallel north and south margins could represent the foundation of a floor. The northwest and southeast ends of this stony surface protrude from the west balk of Square L29 and the east balk of Square L28, beyond the excavated area confined to the borders of the projected gas pipeline.

Embedded in this stony surface is an installation (figs. 11.16–17: L348, Square L28) of unclear function consisting of a single, obliquely set round stone slab (diameter 0.6 m) facing and distanced about 0.7 m from four medium-sized field limestones set in a curvilinear row on the surface's north margin. Two interpretations would normally be applied to such an installation. The slab may have been used as a semistationary grinding surface, though striations resulting from grinding were not observed on its surface. Alternatively, the stone could have served as a base to support a wooden column. However, the absence of structural (wall) remains nearby, would seem to mitigate against such an interpretation—though such remains may simply not be preserved.[1]

An approximately 7 m empty space (coinciding mainly with Squares M28/M29) separates between Surface L311/L353 and the remains of a second stony surface, 8.5 × 7.5 m, exposed below the same thick layer of grumic topsoil sediments in Square N29 (Loci 303 and 309) and Squares O28–O29 (Loci 304, 310, and 320 in Square O29; Locus 332 in Square O28) and showing roughly the same orientation as the one described above (L311, L353). Its west end protrudes from the west balk of Square O29 and could thus not be exposed to its full extent.

The surface's south end covers a poorly preserved, rectilinear wall segment (W30) built of a double row of medium-sized field limestones with smaller limestones in between, preserved to a height of two courses and a width of 0.65 m, and exposed for a length of 4.6 m (figs. 11.9, 18–19). Another surviving wall segment (W31) abuts but does not bond with the north face of W30. Since both wall segments were found topped with the same limestone spread (L328) making up the stony surface exposed in Squares N29 and O28/O29, these two walls (W30 and W31) seemingly belong to an earlier occupational phase. This is one of the only few

---

1. Stone column bases have been uncovered in Area F (see ch. 12, this volume).

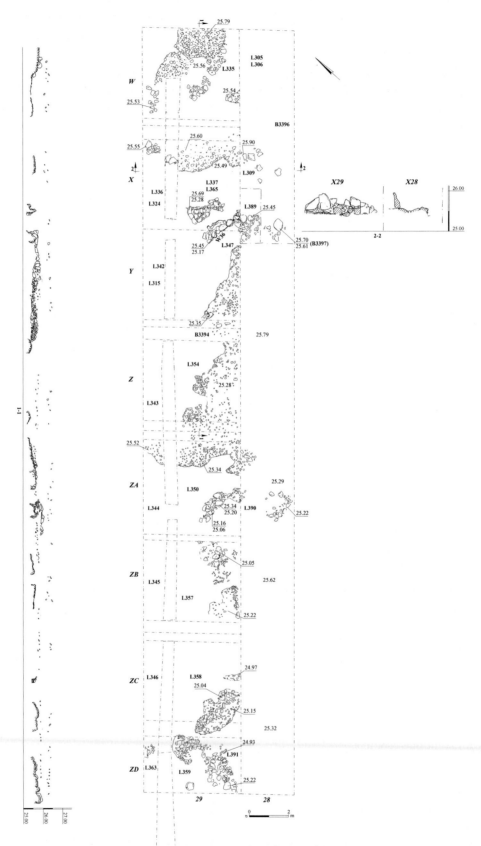

Fig. 11.11. Area C. Plan and sections of Squares W28/29–ZD28/29.

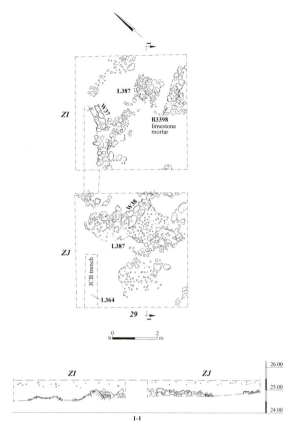

Fig. 11.12. Area C. Plan of Squares ZI29–ZJ29.

Fig. 11.13. Aerial view of Area C and the tell of Qashish, looking south.

Fig. 11.14. Aerial view of Areas C and D, looking southwest.

Fig. 11.15. Area C. Square L29, small-limestones surface (Locus 311), looking southwest.

Fig. 11.16. Area C. Square L28. Installation L348 during excavation, looking southwest.

instances (see below) where two separate, superimposed phases of occupation at the site could be distinguished. Based on the pottery finds (see ch. 14, this volume), both phases are to be dated to the late EB I. A third wall segment (W32 in Squares N29/N30), covered by a thick layer of grumic, sterile topsoil (L340), was exposed underneath the stony surface's northwestern end. Wall 32 may have belonged to the same structure as wall segments W30 and W31.

Excavation of a third, triple row of squares (fig. 11.10, R28–29, V28–30), 12 m south of Squares P28–P29, revealed additional remains of small limestone surfaces below the same thick top layer of sterile, grumic soil (Loci 305, 306, 318, 356, 360, 372) found in the previously described areas. The central surface, L355 (Sq T29), is delineated on the southwest by a 15-m long east–west-oriented stone fence (W34) built of a single row of stones. This fence, preserved to a height of only two courses and running the full length of three adjoining squares, protrudes from their outer opposite balks. The wall's south face is fairly clear and pronounced, while its north face is not. Against and alongside the latter were seemingly haphazardly piled up, instead, numerous smaller and larger fieldstones. A cross-section through this stone pile shows that the wall/fence rests directly on sterile, grumusols (fig. 11.10, section 4–4), while the stone debris piled up against it locally overlays an apparent depression (a pit or channel?) filled with small fieldstones (fig. 11.10, section 5–5), perhaps for leveling off the area.

The various stone surfaces exposed on both sides of this fence are slightly undulating because of post-dispositional twisting, possibly due to subsoil warping—as also observed at other nearby archaeological sites such as 'En Shadud (Braun 1985, 19, pls. II, IV.B)—resulting in severe distortion of these rather poorly preserved structural remains and hindering correct interpretation.

Adjacent to the northeastern end of W34, in Square S28, part of a circular, carefully stone-paved installation (L348; estimated diameter 2.5 m) was exposed, its west part protruding from the east balk of the square.

Less than 4 m south of the stone fence W34 (Squares U28–U29), structural remains include segments of two parallel stone walls (W33 and W35), each built of a double row of fieldstones and preserved to a maximum height of two courses. These possibly represent the remains of an earlier partly preserved structure later integrated into a rectangular stone-built structure or installation of unknown function with a carefully laid, stone-paved floor (Loci 368/376; figs. 11.10, 20–23). The unnamed wall with which W33 seems to make a straight corner (fig. 11.10) is more apparent than factual; W33 being earlier than the unnamed wall, W33 abutting the latter one.[2] A paved floor segment (L319) of yet

Fig. 11.17. Area C. Square L28. Installation L348 after excavation, looking east.

Fig. 11.18. Area C. Small-limestones surface and W30 and W31, looking southeast.

Fig. 11.19. Area C. Small-limestones surface and W30 and W31, looking northwest.

Fig. 11.20. Area C. Aerial view of Squares R28/29/30–V28/29/30, looking east.

---

2. The divergence seen between fig. 11.10 (plan of Squares U/V 28–29) and fig. 11.20 (photograph of the same squares), concerning this additional stone pavement segment, is due to the fact that the photograph shows a later stage during excavation that is not reflected in fig. 11.10.

Fig. 11.21. Area C. General view of Squares U28/29–V28/29, looking west.

Fig. 11.24. Area C. Square X29. Remains of a partially preserved installation, looking east.

Fig. 11.22. Area C. Square U28. Stone-paved installation/W35 and W33, looking west.

Fig. 11.25. Area C. Square Y29, Locus 347. Portable limestone mortar (B3395).

Fig. 11.23. Area C. Squares U28/29–V28/29. Segment of a stone pavement possibly related to a second installation, looking north.

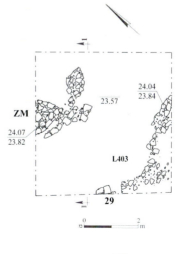

Fig. 11.26. Area D. Square ZM29, plan and section.

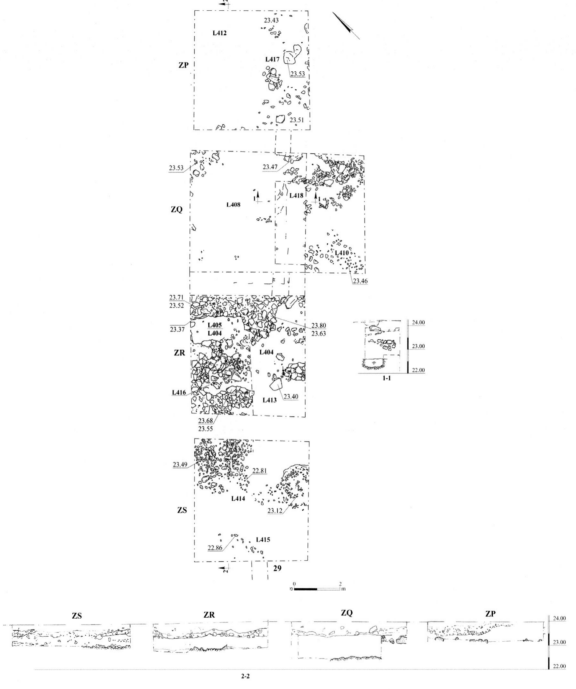

Fig. 11.27. Area D. Squares ZP29–ZS29, plan and sections.

another possible installation bordered the western end of the first structure (fig. 11.18). A notable find, the upper part of a basalt tournette, or slow potter's wheel (Milevski, this volume, ch. 19, fig. 19.4.1), was uncovered in secondary use in Square V29 (L319, B3041).[3]

---

3. A similar item was uncovered at the tell, in an EB III context (Ben-Tor, Bonfil, and Zuckerman 2003, 80–82, fig. 41; with thanks to Ianir Milevski for this reference).

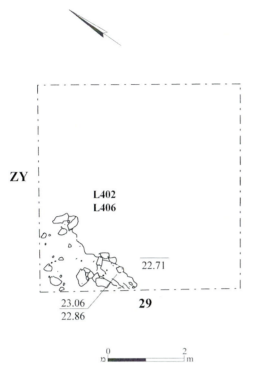

Fig. 11.28. Area D. Square ZY29. Plan.

Fig. 11.29. Area D. Squares ZP29–ZS29, looking northeast.

Three additional discontinuous small stone surfaces, all with a similar northwest–southeast orientation, were exposed over eight (4.5 × 5 m) squares (W28/29–ZD28/29; fig. 11.11), 3 m south of Squares V28–30. The largest, continuous (though far from complete) exposure of such a surface spreads over three adjoining squares (Squares Y29–Z29–ZA29). The remains of a wall (W36, Squares X29–Y29) and a possible stone pavement (fig. 11.11, section 2–2; Square X29; fig. 11.24), representing the scant remains of yet another possible installation, were found between this large stone surface and the next one exposed in Squares W29–X29. Basalt grinding slabs/stones (L389, B3396, and B3397; L347, B3395) and a portable limestone mortar (L347, B3394; fig. 11.25) were found in situ on two stony surfaces (cf. Milevski, ch. 19, this volume).

Remains of yet another stone surface and three small wall segments (W37, W38, and unnumbered wall), one apparently slightly curvilinear (W37), were exposed in two adjoining squares (ZI29–ZJ 29; fig. 11.9), 16 m southwest of Square ZD29. A portable limestone mortar (Milevski, ch. 19, this volume; fig. 19.2.2) was found embedded in a slightly oblique position on top of this stone surface in Square ZI29 (fig. 11.12, L387/B3398), a situation reminiscent of that noted in Square Y29 (fig. 11.25). The presence of these ground stone tools clearly shows that food processing activities took place in this area.

Area D (Figures 11.26–29)

Six squares (ZM29, ZP29–ZS29, ZY29) were opened just north of and very close to the Kishon River, less than 50 m west of the western edge of Tel Qashish. Below an approximately 0.4 m top layer of sterile grumusol was exposed a horizontal spread of recent, chalky stone debris with some modern iron rods and broken glass embedded in it, and, notably, inter alia, Middle-Paleolithic flints (Levallois technique).[4] Underneath, a single layer of surfaces built of small

---

4. We would like to thank Dr. Alla Yaroshevich (IAA) for her kind assistance in identifying the relevant flint materials. A Middle Paleolithic site was excavated by her in 2010 on the opposite side of Road 70 and north of the Kishon River (permit A-5880), as well as two additional prehistoric sites in the close vicinity of Tell Qashish and north of the Kishon River, i.e., an Epipaleolithic site (permits A-6303, A-6461), and an Early–Middle Paleolithic site (permit A-6655) coexcavated with Omry Barzilai (IAA).

stones and some wall remains was uncovered, remains similar to ones recorded throughout Area C. This layer overlaid the sterile, grumusol accumulated on the natural bedrock (fig. 11.29). As with Area C, the pottery associated with this layer dates almost exclusively from the late EB I (van den Brink, ch. 14, this volume, fig. 14.13). It seems clear, therefore, that the EB I remains exposed in Area D represent but the southernmost extension of the late EB I layer exposed in Area C.

References

Ben-Tor, Amnon, Ruhama Bonfil, and Sharon Zuckerman
2003   *Tel Qashish: A Village in the Jezreel Valley; Final Report of the Archaeological Excavations (1978–1987)*. Qedem Reports 5. Jerusalem: Hebrew University of Jerusalem.

Braun, Eliot
1985   *'En Shadud: Salvage Excavations at a Farming Community in the Jezreel Valley, Israel*. BARIS 249. Oxford: British Archaeological Reports.

Brink, Edwin C. M. van den, Orit Segal, and Uzi 'Ad
2012   "A Late Bronze Age II Repository of Cultic Paraphernalia from the Environs of Tel Qashish in the Jezreel Valley." In *Temple Building and Temple Cult: Architecture and Cultic Paraphernalia of Temples in the Levant (2–1. Mill B.C.E.)*, edited by Jens Kamlah, 421–34. ADPV 41. Wiesbaden: Harrassowitz.

Ziffer, Irit, Edwin C. M. van den Brink, Orit Segal, and Uzi 'Ad
2018   "A Unique Human-Head Cup from the Environs of Tel Qashish in the Jezreel Valley, Israel." In *The Adventure of the Illustrious Scholar: Papers Presented to Oscar White Muscarella,* edited by Elizabeth Simpson, 406–20. CHANE 94. Leiden: Brill. DOI: 10.1163/9789004361713_023.

Chapter 12

Tel Qashish Areas F and E South: Stratigraphy and Structural Features (2010 Excavations)

Eli Yannai (*Israel Antiquities Authority*)

In 2010, test and salvage excavations were conducted north of Tel Qashish as part of preparatory works for the construction of the Haifa–'Afula Railway line. The excavation (IAA permit A-5992/2010) aimed at discovering the extent of the archaeological remains at the site and defining their nature. Two excavation areas were defined: Area F, on the western flank of the slope, which consists of limestone rock of the Eocene formation, and Area E South on the eastern flank of the slope, which consists of a young basalt layer of rock of the Miocene period. The upper part of the western flank is not settled, although several natural caves—likely formed through karstic activities—were discovered. No evidence of human exploitation of these caves was found.

Area F

The excavation in Area F was conducted in a 60-m-long, northwest–southeast 5-m-wide transect (Squares I26–I35), locally extended in a 5 m grid to the north (Squares J24–J30, J39, K26–K28, N–S 29/30, and N–O 33/34) and south (Squares H26–H30; figs. 10.3, 12.1). The architectural remains exposed in this area are consequently very fragmentary, and the results limited.

Square J24

Three walls (W603/W608, W611, and W612) of a single building were found in this square, located in the westernmost, highest part of the excavation area (fig. 12.1). A north–south oriented wall segment (W603/W608; 0.9m wide), built of a double row of large-sized (0.4–0.5 m) fieldstones was exposed. Its western face (W603) was slightly eroded and locally detached from its eastern face (W608). On the south, protruding from the south balk of the square, a similarly built wall segment (W611) abuts W603 at a straight angle. Another straight alignment, of a single row of smaller-sized (0.35–0.4 m) fieldstones (W612), abuts the west face of W603 in its middle point.

Further wall segments of the same building were noticed on the surface outside the actual excavation area. A beaten-earth floor (L6059), with a small number of finds on it (fig. 12.2), was exposed in the western part of this building. This floor is delineated by walls W603, W612, and W611 on the east, north, and south, respectively. The area immediately to the east of it (L6049; fig. 12.3) was found deflated.

Squares H26–I26

Protruding from both the north and west balks of Square H26 and continuing into Square I26, west of Locus 6013 (figs. 12.1, 4), a northwest–southeast-oriented single straight wall segment (W610; ca. 3 m long and 1 m wide) was uncovered, built of two parallel rows of varying-sized fieldstones with a core of smaller limestones in between, clearly part of a structure.

Squares J27–K27

In this part of the excavation area, two linear and parallel, stone-built wall segments were uncovered (fig. 12.1). The west wall (W600), partially preserved, was built of a single row of large fieldstones (0.35–0.5 m) oriented southwest. Its west face was missing and could not be reconstructed. This wall extends to the south into a virtually unexcavated area, and only a single row of large-sized fieldstones had survived. The total width of the south part of this wall segment, as was the case with that of its north extreme, cannot be reconstructed. East of W600, and almost parallel to it, wall segment W601 was uncovered, consisting of a double row of smaller-sized fieldstones (0.35–0.4 m). These two walls delineated a beaten-earth floor (L6043) with potsherds, stone chips, and a small number of other finds.

The area west of W600 was defined as floor L6026 and east of W601 as L6044. North of both walls, a straight alignment of a single row of fieldstones (W605) was found, and 0.5 m further south a second alignment of a single row of fieldstones were exposed. W605 was found seriously damaged and weathered, and it is difficult to know whether this wall was part of an enclosure wall or the eroded north extreme of the structure.

Squares H–I29–30

Two perpendicular wall segments (W603, W604) were uncovered in Squares I–H29 (fig. 12.1). Protruding from both the north and south balks of Square I29, the 6-m-long and 1-m-wide segment of W604, oriented northeast–southwest, is built of a double row of large-sized (0.4–0.5 m) fieldstones with a core of small- and medium-sized limestones. The 4-m-long linear east–west oriented wall segment W603, which abuts the east face of W604, consists of a double row of large-sized (0.3–0.5 m) fieldstones with a core of small limestones. A northeast–southwest alignment of a single row of fieldstones (W606) abuts the middle of W603 from the north. This wall, together with W604 and W606, form a single room (L6046).

Between L6050 and L6054, both located east of W606, a single row of fieldstones was found, but it is uncertain whether this was part of a wall. L6053 is located northeast of where wall W604 intersects

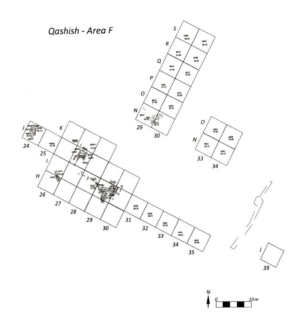

Fig. 12.1. Area F. Plan and sections.

Fig. 12.2. Area F, Square J24, L6059. Small room formed by W603, W611, and W612. Looking west.

Fig. 12.3. Area F, Square J24, L6049. Looking west.

Fig. 12.4. Area F, Square H26, L6013. Area east of W610. Looking southwest.

Fig. 12.5. Area F, Square H29, Locus 6048. Floor segment southwest of W603 and W604. Note the stone slab (column base) in the center. Looking west.

with W603. L6047 is located southwest of where wall W604 intersects with W603. On the floor segment L6048, located southwest of the juncture of W604 and W603, a large stone column-base was found (fig. 12.5). L6037 is located east of this column-base. Another straight wall segment (W607), oriented northwest–southeast, was uncovered protruding from the west balk of Square I29. Several nondistinct, large- and small-sized fieldstone concentrations were found north of Square I29.

Summary of Area F

The structural remains found in Area F are very fragmentary and severely eroded. It was not possible to make any meaningful connections between them. The built-up area was limited to the lower two-thirds of the hill's west slope.

The three, possibly four partially preserved structures consisted of straight, wide, and narrow wall segments. In contrast to Area E South (see below), no curvilinear architecture was found in this area. It seems reasonable to assume that the wider walls were the external walls of the structures while the narrow walls served, perhaps, as internal division walls. Only in one of the structures (floor L6048), was a pillar base (for roof support) found.

The poor preservation conditions of the structural remains are most likely due to the steepness of the eroding western slope on which they were located, just slightly north of Tel Qashish proper.

Area E South

Area E is located southeast of Area F, on a mildly eastward descending slope. Structural remains in this area were uncovered at three separate locations, each one of a completely different architectural nature.

Squares I–J63/64

In the southeasternmost, lowest part of the excavation area, the stone foundations and floors of two circular stone structures (Loci 5023 and 5047) were exposed (figs. 12.6–7). The walls of these structures (W501 and W506) were originally built of two rows with a core of small-sized fieldstones in between. The preserved external faces of these walls were built of large-sized fieldstones (up to 0.3 m in diameter), while the internal rows consisted of smaller fieldstones (up to 0.2 m).

The northern structure (L5047) (figs. 12.6–8) is defined by its external circular W506 (0.40–0.50 m wide), of which only short segments survived (fig. 12.8). The southwestern part of the structure was found intact, while its northeast part had eroded away. Many potsherds (nonrestorable) were found lying on this structure's floor.

A second circular structure (L5023), defined by the circular W501 (figs. 12.6–7, 9), was found 2 m south of the first one. The structure was well preserved on its west side, but its down-sloping eastern side had completely eroded away (fig. 12.9). Large fragments of late EB I storage jars (rims and bases; see Paz, ch. 15, this volume) containing a large number of seeds, mainly hulled emmer wheat (*Triticum*

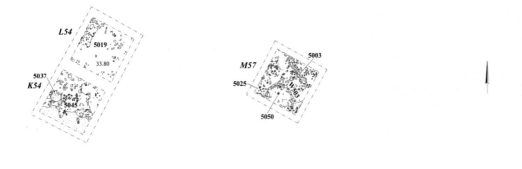

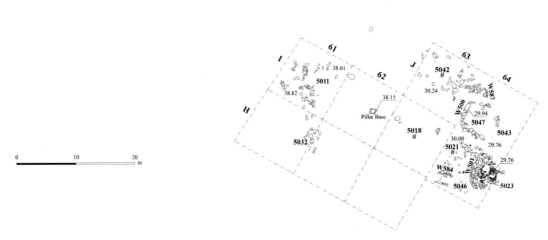

Fig. 12.6. Plan of Area E South.

dicoccum; see Weiss and Mahler-Slasky, ch. 23, this volume), were found in situ inside this structure (for radiocarbon dating of samples from this deposit, see van den Brink, ch. 24, this volume). A significant amount of plant remains, similar in composition to that found within the installation (L5023), was found on a floor (L5021) immediately west of it. Both structures appear to have been used as silos for storing jars containing agricultural produce.

Squares H–I61/63

Packed-earth floor segments (Loci 5018 and 5042) were exposed northwest of the two circular silos. Six column bases were found sunk into those floors. These were of two distinct types: Four were made of stone slabs and the other two consisted of circles of small stones (L5023; figs. 12.6, 10).

On the western side of the area (Squares H61–I61), some concentrations of small fieldstones were found (Loci 5011 and 5032), oriented southeast–northwest. These concentrations seem to mark the western border of the open area that extended west to the two circular silos. This border is aligned with the two silos, and the area between them was seemingly occupied by sheds or tent-like structures made of organic materials and supported by columns.

12. Tel Qashish Areas F and E South: Stratigraphy and Structural Features (2010 Excavations)   119

Fig. 12.7. Area E, Squares I64–J64, Loci 5023 (W501) and 5047 (W506). The two circular structures (silos). Looking southwest.

Fig. 12.10. Area E, Square I62, L5003. The floor with column bases. Looking west.

Fig. 12.8. Area E, Square J64, L5047, W506. The northern circular structure with jars. Looking west.

Fig. 12.11. Area E, Square M57, L5050. The semicircular row of fieldstones (W503) and the floor level to its north. Looking south.

Fig. 12.9. Area E, Square I64, Locus 5023, W501. The southern circular structure. Looking southeast.

Fig. 12.12. Area E, Square K54, L5017. Pit. Looking west.

Fig. 12.13. Area E, Square K54, L5017. Pit. Looking east.

Fig. 12.14. Area E, Square K54, L5045. Earthen floor segment in open space with in situ potsherds and other finds around pit L5017. Looking west.

Squares M57 and K–L54

Six squares were probed in the higher part of the excavation area (fig. 12.6), where large zones of weathered, grooved bedrock, full of natural depressions, were uncovered.

A floor (L5025) containing large fragments of several storage jars and very few carbonized grains and a semicircular alignment (W503; 2 m in diameter) of medium-sized fieldstones (0.2 × 0.2 m) were exposed in Square M57. The semicircular row of stones was open to the south and did not extend to the southern square (L57). This stone alignment, consisting of a single row of fieldstones, was not a wall nor a circular wall segment. The inner part of the circle consisted of a floor with a plastered pit (L5050; (figs. 12.6, 11). On this floor two in situ storage jars were uncovered. together yielding large amounts of lentil seeds (*L. culinaris*; see Weiss and Mahler-Slasky, ch. 23, this volume; for radiocarbon dating of samples from this deposit, see van den Brink, ch. 24, this volume). However, those segments and the stones that surrounded them were not part of structures but mere rubble (including L5003) and rock surfaces.

A partially pebble-paved, rock-hewn pit was found in Square K54 (L5037, figs. 12.12–14) yielding few carbonized seeds. Around this pit were found segments of an earthen floor with in situ potsherds (L5045; fig. 12.14) and some additional grains (see ch. 23, this volume). The area around the pit was very similar in nature to the one around the semicircular row of fieldstones (W503) in Square M57.

These two squares and surroundings areas seem to form part of a large open space used for activities associated with yet unidentified buildings.

An irregular spread of small and medium-sized stone (L5019) was uncovered in Square L54 immediately below present topsoil level.

Summary of Area E South (A-5992)

Area E South can be divided into two very distinct parts. In the lower, southeastern part of the excavation area, there is a dense spread of agricultural storage structures comprising several storage jars filled with various kinds of grains (Weiss and Mahler-Slasky, ch. 23, this volume) and forming part of a dwelling complex more fully uncovered in the third excavation season, in Area E North (IAA permit A-6149; see van den Brink et al., ch. 13, this volume). Structures similar to the two circular silos uncovered in Squares I–J63/64 have been found in many other late EB I sites, such as Giv'at Rabbi, Qiryat Ata, and 'Ein Asawir (Golani and Yannai 2016). In the upper, northwestern part of the excavation area, evidence was found for intensive activities in an open space.

References

Golani, Amir, and Eli Yannai
2016 "Storage Structures of the Late Early Bronze I in the Southern Levant and the Urbanisation Process." *PEQ* 148: 8–41.

Chapter 13

Tel Qashish Area E North: Stratigraphy and Structural Features (2011 Excavations)

Edwin C.M. van den Brink, Uzi 'Ad, Dan Kirzner, Eli Yannai, Mohammed Hater, Orit Segal
(*Israel Antiquities Authority*)

A grid of thirty-nine 4 × 4 m squares (figs. 13.1–2; Squares K53–60, L53–61, M53–60, N53–62, O59–60, 62–63), situated immediately north of two rows of squares probed before in 2010 by Yannai (Area E South, ch. 12, this volume; and fig. 15.2), was, for the most part, manually excavated within seventeen days by sixty workers (permit A-6149/2011). A total of 106 loci (Loci 5051–5156) were opened and 356 baskets (B50395–B50720) allotted.[1] Nineteen walls or segments thereof were identified (W508–W526).

Generally speaking, a single layer of structural remains was uncovered 0.20–0.85 m below the present plow zone, with a moderate sloping of 33.36–29.97 m ASL (fig. 13.1b: cross-sections 1-1, 2-2).

The topsoil consisted of thick deposits of dark brown, grumusol sediments (Ackermann and Greenbaum, ch. 2 this volume) mixed with large amounts of late Early Bronze Age I potsherds. Underneath, the main features in this area consisted of spreads of medium and large limestone fieldstones, locally associated with segments of rectilinear and semicurvilinear stone-wall foundations (fig. 13.3) resting on virgin, weathered basalt bedrock. A west-east description of the main structural features follows.

The Structural Remains

In the northwestern end of the excavation area, 0.2 m below a thick layer of grumic dark brown topsoil sediments, a north–south oriented spread of small and medium-sized limestone pebbles (Loci 5098, 5107, and 5108) was uncovered in Square N53. Protruding from both the north and south balks of the square and located 6 m northeast of the main structural remains in this area (see below), this stony 0.2 m high surface covers an area about 4 m long and 2 m wide.

After removal of a 0.45–0.75 m thick top layer of grumusol, no special features were noticed in Squares K54 and L54 (Loci 5064 and 5096) except for a small number of potsherds dating from the late EB I and resting on the sterile weathered basalt soil probed in Square L54 (L5103). In Squares M54, N54, K55, L55, M55, and N55 (Loci 5114, 5078, 5138, 5132, 5086, 5097, and 5099), a local, nondistinct spread of small and medium-sized limestones was uncovered 0.45–0.65 m below the present surface, resting on sterile, weathered basalt soil. This stony layer possibly represents the collapse/stone debris of wall foundations.

In the northeast corner of Square L55, a single straight row of medium-sized fieldstones protruding from the east balk of the square and oriented northwest–southeast was uncovered (fig. 13.4), representing a 2 m long, 0.2 m wide, and 0.1 m high wall segment (W518) preserved to a height of only

---

1. Loci 5000–5050 were allotted to Area E South by Yannai in his 2010 excavation at the site (A-5992; see ch. 12, this volume).

Fig. 13.1a (spread). Plan of Area E South.

13. Tel Qashish Area E North: Stratigraphy and Structural Features (2011 Excavations) 123

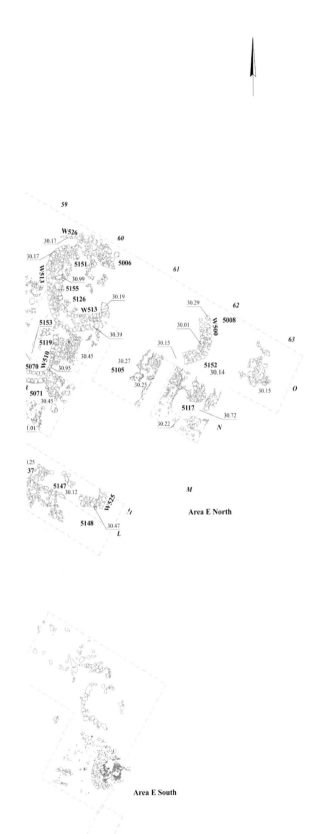

one course.[2] Underneath the same thick top layer of grumic soils already mentioned above (Loci 5052, 5062, 5068, 5072, 5077, 5089), the excavation in Squares K56, L56, N56, K57, M56, M57, N57, M58, and N58 revealed additional, nondescript, high concentrations of small and medium-sized limestones (Loci 5066, 5094, 5102 [fig. 13.5], 5115, 5080, 5135, 5133, 5106, 5109, 5101, 5124, 5125), some associated with segments of stone wall foundations (W514 and W524).[3] The stone spreads are apparently of the same nature as those revealed in the northeastern squares, mixed with small amounts of late EB I potsherds and one basalt grinding stone (L5066, B50431).

In Square M56, structural remains of an agriculture installation had already been exposed (W503, Loci 5003, 5025, and 5050) during the previous salvage excavation season (see Yannai, ch. 12, this volume). In this square, a rounded wall segment W503 (Locus 5050; fig. 13.6), built of fieldstones of varying sizes, was found embedded in thick dark brown soil deposits containing some late EB I potsherds (Locus 5140). Immediately northwest of W503, the typical grumic soil was mixed with burnt soil (Loci 5050 and 5154) comprising high concentrations of broken pieces of restorable EB I storage jars (some burnt) that contained charred lentils (cf. Weiss and Mahler-Slasky, ch. 23, this volume), and further associated with a complete basalt bowl (B50697; Milevski, ch. 19: fig. 19.5.1, this volume).

In Squares K58, L57–58 (Loci 5053, 5084, 5090, and 5145), better-preserved architectural remains were uncovered. In Squares L57–L58 (Loci 5134, 5113, 5112, and 5136), three semirounded wall segments (W512, W515, and W520) were exposed:

1. W515, in Square L57. A 2 m long and 0.65 m wide double row of medium-sized fieldstones with a core of smaller limestones, preserved to a height of one course (0.1 m). Its northern end protrudes from the balk of Squares L57/M57, and its southeastern end is cut by the western face of W512.

---

2. Note that on the photograph fig. 13.4 is erroneously written (Square) L56; it should correctly read (Square) L55.
3. Note that on the photograph fig. 13.5 is erroneously written (Square) L57; it should correctly read (Square) L56.

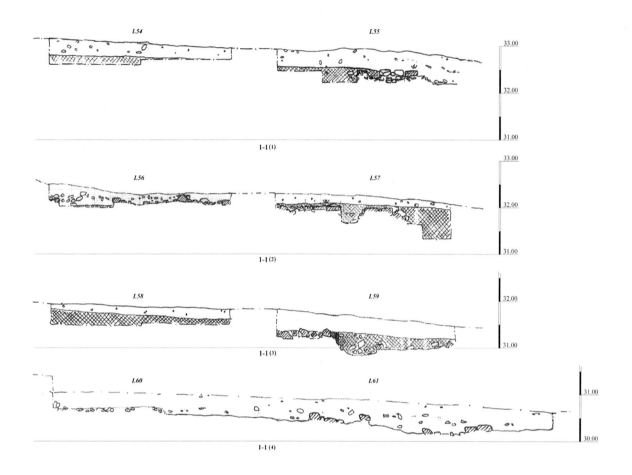
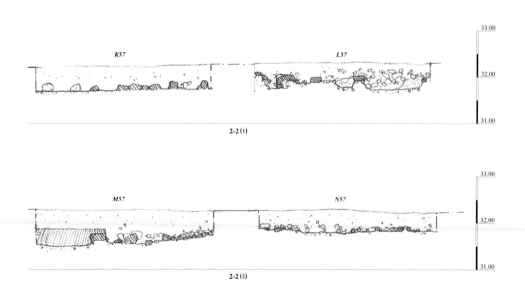

Fig. 13.1.b. E–W cross-sections 1-1 and N–S cross-sections 2-2 of Area E South.

13. Tel Qashish Area E North: Stratigraphy and Structural Features (2011 Excavations)

Fig. 13.2. Tel Qashish. Bird eye's view of Area E, looking southeast.

Fig. 13.3. Tel Qashish. Aerial view of Area E at the end of the excavation, looking southwest.

Fig. 13.4. Area E, Square L55, Locus 5138, W518, looking east.

Fig. 13.6 Area E, Square M56, Locus 5050, rounded wall segment W503, looking south; note basalt bowl B50697 in the right, lower corner of the photo.

Fig. 13.5. Area E, Square L56, Locus 5102. Looking east.

2. The semirounded, 3.6 m long and 0.70 m wide segment of W512, in Square L57, oriented northwest–southeast, built of a double row of medium-sized fieldstones with a core of smaller limestones, preserved one course high (0.1 m). Its southeastern edge abuts W520.

3. A poorly preserved segment of W520, measuring 2.7 m long, 0.65 m wide, and 0.20 m high. This northeast–southwest oriented wall, similar to W512 and making a corner with it, runs under the balks of Squares L57–L58 (Locus 5145). Only a single course was preserved, resting on sterile weathered basalt soil.

These three walls may represent the foundation level of two distinct constructions with rounded corners: W515 was apparently earlier than W512, which, along with W520, created a structure that included at least two rooms or inner spaces (L5112 and L5145).

East of W520, in Square L58 (L5136), the main feature consists of nondistinct spreads of limestone fieldstones of varying sizes, containing small amounts of potsherds dating from the Late EB I and some animal bones. These stone spreads, resting on sterile weathered basalt soil, possibly represent the collapse/stone debris of wall W520.

In Square K58, southeast of W520, the topsoil contained some Late EB I potsherds, animal bones, and flint (Loci 5054 and 5123). Underneath, at depths varying between 0.45 m and 0.65 m, three small wall segments (W516, W521, and W522; fig. 13.7) of unclear plan and resting on sterile, weathered basalt soil were uncovered beneath a thick concentration of fieldstones of varying sizes (Loci 5130, 5131 and 5156):[4]

1. W522, in the northwest corner of Square K58, consists of a semirounded double row of medium-sized fieldstones with a core of smaller limestones. This 1.7 m long, 0.75 m wide and 0.1 m high, east–west/southwest–northeast-oriented wall protrudes from the west side of the balk between Squares K58 and K57 and is preserved to a height of one course.

2. W521, 2.3 m long, 0.2 m wide, and 0.05–0.1 m high and preserved only one course high, is built of a single row of medium-sized fieldstones. This

---

4. Note that on the photograph fig. 13.7 is erroneously written (Square) K59; it should correctly read (Square) K58.

wall, oriented southeast–northwest, abuts, on its northern end, the south face of W522.

3. W516, in the northeast corner of Square K58, is also built of a semirounded double row of medium-sized fieldstones filled with a core of smaller limestones. It protrudes from the south side of the balk between Squares K58 and L58, and it is oriented north–south/northeast–southwest. This 2.1 m long, 0.5–0.2 m wide, and 0.15 m high wall segment is preserved only one course high and abuts, on the southwest, the eastern face of W521. Only the northern row of fieldstones was preserved in the wall's final 0.6 m on the west.

These three poorly preserved wall foundation segments may represent the remains of contemporary small rounded dwellings with inner partitions, or else a larger structure with several small rooms.

Just two meters south and southeast of W516, better preserved architectural remains, including a large segment of a massive wall and associated stone pavement, were uncovered in Squares K58/59, K59, K59/L59, L59, K59/60, K60, L59/60, L60, L60/61, L61, L61/62, and L62, 0.20–0.85 m below present topsoil that contained some Late EB I potsherds, animal bones and flint (Loci 5156, 5061, 5137, 5139, 5149, 5144, 5147, 5148, 5056, 5057, 5091).

In the southwest corner of Square K59 and the balk area between Squares K58 and K59 (Loci 5156 and 5061), a poorly preserved, 3.9 m long, 0.35 m wide, and 0.2 m high north–south wall foundation segment (W523) was uncovered, built of a single row of medium-sized fieldstones and preserved one course high. A large stone pavement (F5122; figs. 13.8–9) measuring 5.2 m long from east to west and 2.5 m wide from north to south, built of large-sized, natural, nonmodified stone slabs, abuts the eastern face of W523 on its northern end.[5] On the north, the pavement abuts the southern face of W517 (fig. 13.10), while on the east it abuts the western face of W519.

North of the stone pavement F5122, in Squares L59 and K59/L59 (Loci 5137 and 5139), the western

---

5. Note that on the photograph fig. 13.9 is erroneously written (Square) K60; it should correctly read (Square) K59.

Fig. 13.7. Area E, Square K58, W516, W521, and W522, and Locus 5131 (east of W516). Looking east.

part of a massive stone alignment representing the east–west oriented foundations of W517 was uncovered. It was built of a double row of large- and medium-sized fieldstones, filled with a core of smaller limestones. Preserved one-course high (0.1–0.2 m) and measuring 11.6 m long and 0.9–1.3 m wide, it continues to the east crossing Squares L59–61 (Loci 5137, 5139, 5141, 5142, 5144, and 5147). In the central-west part of Square L59 (L5120), close to the northern face of W517, a concentration of limestones of varying size, resting on sterile weathered basalt soil, was uncovered, possibly representing the collapsed stone debris of W517.

In the northwest corner of Square K60 and the north part of Squares K59/60 (Loci 5149 and 5121 respectively), east of the stone pavement F5122, a stone alignment, a segment of the foundation of W519, was revealed. Only the western face of this wall was preserved, built of a row of large- and medium-sized natural fieldstones. This wall segment, preserved to a height of one course and oriented north–south, measures 4.3 m long, 0.45 m wide, and 0.1–0.15 m high. W519 was seemingly a semirounded or curved wall creating the northeast rounded corner of a larger structure with a stone-paved floor (F5122). The northern end of W519 bonded with W517.

South and east of Square L60 and 1 m below present topsoil containing a small amount of late EB I potsherds and flint (Loci 5057 and 5121), a nondistinct concentration of variably sized limestones was uncovered, resting on sterile, weathered basalt soil. This stony layer could represent the stone collapse/debris of a wall foundation situated outside the southmost boundary of the excavated area.

Fig. 13.8. Area E, Squares K/L59–60. Segment of a stone-slab-paved (F 5122) structure cutting into a straight wall segment (W517) of another building to its north. Looking northwest.

Fig. 13.9. Area E, Square K58. Detail of the stone-slab pavement F5122. Looking northeast.

Fig. 13.10. Area E, Square L60, W517. Looking east.

Fig. 13.11. Area E, Squares K–L59–L60–61, M59–60, N59–62, O60–63. Aerial view of east part of excavation area with W517 and stone pavement F5122. Looking east.

Excavation in Squares L59/60, and L60 (Loci 5141, 5142, 5144), revealed the eastern extension of wall W517 (figs. 13.10–11) while reaching sterile weathered basalt soil at both its south (L5141) and north faces (L5142). North of W517, a nondistinct concentration of variably sized limestones were unearthed (L5142), possibly representing the wall's collapsed stone debris of W517's foundations and its small-sized limestones core, or else a living surface/floor, containing a small number of potsherds dating from the late EB I period and some animals bones, flint, and shells.

Below a 0.3-m-thick top layer of grumic dark-brown sediments mechanically removed in Squares L60/61, L61, and L62 (Loci 5147 and 5148), the eastern extreme of W517's foundations was uncovered, together with nondistinct concentrations of variably sized limestones. This stony layer possibly delineates the continuation of W517 to the east, and perhaps stone debris of nonpreserved collapsed walls, but this is hard to assert since, due to lack of time, these squares were not properly excavated.

In the north part of Square L62 (L5148), an angular stone alignment (W525) was uncovered, consisting of a double row of large- and medium-sized fieldstones with a core of smaller limestones, oriented north–south/east–west. This wall segment, preserved to a height of only one course, is 3.2 m long, 0.6 m wide, and 0.1 m high, representing the remains of an additional structure.

In Squares M59, M60, N60–N63, and O59–O63, 0.35–0.75 m below the topsoil containing some late EB I potsherds, animal bones, and flint (Loci 5057–5060, 5069, 5073, 5076, 5077, 5088, 5092, 5093, 5110, 5111, 5128, 5146, 5150, and 5152), segments

Fig. 13.12. Area E, Squares M–O/59–63. Stone wall foundations (W500, W508–W511, W513, and W526) of three separate structures with rounded corners, one cutting into the other. Looking southeast.

Fig. 13.13. Area E, Squares M–O/59–60. Stone wall foundations W508, W509, and W513 of two rectangular buildings with rounded corners. Looking east.

of seven distinct stone wall foundations (W508–W511, W513, W500, and W526), resting on sterile, weathered basalt soil, were uncovered. These are the remains of three or four partly uncovered Late EB I architectural units, probably dwellings (fig. 13.12).

In Squares M59 and M60 (Loci 5127–5129, 5092, 5093, and 5146), a meter from the northeast corner of Square M59, a 5.9 m long, 0.3–0.71 m wide, and 0.1 m high semirounded wall (W509) built of a double row of medium-sized fieldstones with a core of smaller limestones was uncovered, preserved to a height of only one course. It was oriented northwest–southeast, crossing the balk area between Squares M59 and M60, and extending to the northern part of Square M60 (W508), and extending into Square N60 (W510; fig. 13.13).

Another, smaller semirounded wall built of a double row of small and medium-sized fieldstones (W511) abuts the western face of W509, thus creating a small 1×1 m inner space (L5127), which yielded a large amount of Late EB I potsherds and a complete basalt grinding stone (B50610; see Milevski, ch. 19, table 19.6, this volume, accessible online at https://doi.org/10.5913/2022655.t19.6). W511, 2.1 m long, 0.3–0.45 m wide, and oriented southwest–northeast, is preserved only one course high (0.1 m).

W509 bonds with the southern end of W508 (Squares M59–M60 and N60), forming the southwestern corner of a structure. Both walls are of identical construction.

W508 is 6.3 m long, 0.85 m wide, and 0.1 m high. Its northern extremity abuts the south face of W513 at its semicircular corner. This large 11.4 m long and 1.15 m wide curvilinear wall segment, with two rounded corners, preserved to a height of 0.35 m, is built of a double row of large- and medium-sized fieldstones, with a core of limestones of various sizes. Preserved to a maximum height of two courses and roughly oriented east–west (Squares N60, N60/O60), south–north (Squares N60, N59/60, and O59/60), and west–east (O60), it creates a large dwelling structure with rounded corners. The inner space of the structure (5 × 7 m) was partly excavated as L5151, yielding a large amount of Late EB I potsherds (Loci 5126 and 5155, including large fragments of a jar [B50700]).

In the structure located southwest of W513 and created by W509 on the west, W508 on the south, and W513 to the east, Loci 5070, 5092, 5119, 5129, 5150, 5151, and 5153 were excavated. The sizeable inner space (8 × 5 m) of this structure yielded a large amount of Late EB I potsherds, as well as a large concentration of reddish-brown mud-brick fragments (L5092) at the northern end of W509, the latter possibly representing the remains of a mud-brick wall originally resting on the stone foundation W509, or perhaps the collapsed ceiling debris.

Slightly north of the northeastern extremity of W513, the foundation course of W526 was partly uncovered (Squares O59–60; figs. 13.1, 12), consisting of a single row of large- and medium-sized fieldstones oriented east–west, measuring 3.4 m long, 1.15 m wide and preserved to a maximum height of two courses (0.5 m). W526 was apparently built of two parallel rows of fieldstones, but only the southern row was uncovered, its north part located beyond the excavated area. The connection between W513 and W526 remains unclear.

Fig. 13.14 Area E, Square O62, W500. Looking southeast.

Northeast of these walls, the main feature in this area (Square O60) consists of nondistinct spreads of limestone fieldstones of varying sizes.

Southeast of W513, in Squares N61 and N62 (Loci 5105 and 5117), another indistinct spread of limestone fieldstones of various sizes was uncovered, resting on sterile weathered basalt soil.

In Squares N62/O62, O62, and O62/63 (L5152), excavation of the southeastern semirounded corner of W500 (Loci 5008 and 5152), only partly exposed during the previous salvage excavation season (see Yannai, ch. 12, this volume), was completed. W500, 4.1 m long, 0.85 m wide and oriented north–south/east–west, is built of a double row of medium-sized fieldstones, with a core of smaller limestones (fig. 13.14).[6] The wall was preserved to a height of only one course (0.1 m). The soil around it contained only a small amount of late EB I potsherds and a complete basalt grinding stone (B50720). These indistinct stone spreads southeast of W500 resting on sterile, weathered basalt soil (L5152), possibly represent the debris of the collapsed W500 foundations and the remains of a floor, or, alternatively, other walls situated outside the excavated area.

Summary

The continued excavations in Area E North revealed a single stratum of structural remains pertaining to a large, late EB I settlement set on the sterile, weathered basalt soil. Based on the data collected during the short excavation, it is hard or often even impossible to determine with certainty the number of building phases exposed, although we are confident that at least two phases can be distinguished, both dating from the late EB I. The north and northwest parts of the excavated area are characterized by stone debris of collapsed buildings, with high concentrations of limestone fieldstones that are difficult to interpret. However, these can certainly be considered as the remains of structures, including collapsed walls, floors, and installations.

The main features in the southern part of the excavation include particularly dense remains of large structures built on massive stone wall foundations, characterized by rounded corners and situated adjacent to one another. These remains were only partially exposed due to the limited time available for excavation.

The various wall remains revealed the well-preserved foundations of at least two, and possibly three large domestic structures, as well as a courtyard (Square N61) where a nearly complete skeleton of a cow was unearthed (see Agha, ch. 21, this volume). In the southwest part of one of the exposed structures, a well-built floor, paved by large stone slabs, is notable. Other structural features such as the presence of a few mud-bricks in the center of the excavated area, of charred lentils associated with several storage jars in proximity to a rounded installation (silo), and of basalt ground stone tools and Canaanean flint knives point to a well-organized and specialized agricultural community with extensive on-site human activities.

It should be stressed that only a small part of the site was revealed during excavations. Based on the exposed structural remains, this habitation area spread in all directions beyond the present excavation's borders.

---

6. Note that on the photograph fig. 13.14 is erroneously written (Square) O63; it should correctly read (Square) O62.

The large-scale salvage excavations conducted at 'En Esur ('Ein Asawir) between 2018 and 2020, nine years after the Tel Qashish salvage excavations, revealed remains of an extensive late EB I settlement (Elad and Paz 2018; Elad, Paz, and Shalem 2018, 2019) not unlike the one presented in this chapter.

References

Elad, Itai, and Paz Yitzhak
2018 "'En Esur (Asawir)." *HA-ESI* 130 (July 2018). http://www.hadashot-esi.org.il/report_detail_eng.aspx?id=25453&mag_id=126.

Elad, Itai, Yitzhak Paz, and Dina Shalem
2018 "'En Esur (Asawir), Area M." *HA-ESI* 133 (December 2018). http://www.hadashot-esi.org.il/report_detail_eng.aspx?id=25495&mag_id=126.
2019 "'En Esur (Asawir), Area O." *HA-ESI* 131 (July 2019). http://www.hadashot-esi.org.il/report_detail_eng.aspx?id=25576&mag_id=127.

Chapter 14

Pottery from Tel Qashish Areas A, B, C, and D

Edwin C. M. van den Brink (*Israel Antiquities Authority*)

The pottery described below was culled during the excavations carried out at Tel Qashish in 2010 (IAA permit A-5881) from four separate excavation areas, namely Area A (with 40 loci and 130 baskets, the smallest 3D excavation unit), Area B (with 29 loci and 177 baskets), Area C (with 101 loci and 394 baskets), and Area D (with 22 loci and 87 baskets). The pottery from Area A mainly concerns Early Roman pottery found in association with a stone platform (see ch. 11, this volume) that is beyond the scope of the present chapter. The pottery deriving from Area B includes over four hundred ceramic Late Bronze Age II vessels found in two caches to be presented in Part V, chapter 25. The pottery from Areas C and D, almost exclusively dated to the late EB I, was found in association with structural agricultural remains (see ch. 11, this volume), and forms the main thrust of the present chapter.

The Pottery

Area A (Figure 14.1)

The finds from this area are marginal to this report's main concern, that is, the late EB I ceramic remains. The major part of the pottery uncovered in this area dates to the Early Roman period, with a total number of 1081 body sherds and 96 type-diagnostic sherds. The relatively few EB I potsherds (635 body sherds and 47 diagnostics) from this period, retrieved from a bedrock layer found below the Early Roman stone platform (see ch. 11, this volume), include bowls with incurved rims (fig. 14.1.1), plain holemouth jars (fig. 14.1.2), bow-rim jars (fig. 14.1.3), and a few other types of necked jars (fig. 14.1.4–5). All the bases are flat (fig. 14.1.6).

Area B (Figures 14.2–3)

This area is the farthest from the actual tell of Qashish, and no structural late EB I remains were found in it. The relatively limited late EB I assemblage from Area B (2,495 body sherds, 330 vessel-diagnostic sherds) is comparable, in composition, to those of Areas C (below) and E (see ch. 15, this volume). It includes, among others, fragments of a bowl with conoid projection (fig. 14.2.1), a gray burnished ware bowl (fig. 14.2.2), and several holemouth jars with and without rope decoration (fig. 14.2.3–10). One rim/wall fragment of a holemouth jar (fig. 14.2.11) shows two prefiring, incised, nearly vertical slashes below the rim's exterior.

Several bow-rim jar fragments (fig. 14.3.1–3) and rims and bases of other types of necked jars (fig. 14.3.4–8) conclude the assemblage. One indented ledge handle shows prefiring-applied circular punctures (fig. 14.3.9), in the same vein as the handles found in Areas C (fig. 14.12.7) and E (fig. 16.20.11).

Area C (Figures 14.4–12)

Area C yielded 22,584 potsherds, 3,163 of these (making up 14 percent of all sherds retrieved in this area) being so-called diagnostics (rim, handle, and base fragments, as well as decorated—mainly with finger-indented bands of clay—body sherds). The frequently applied red slip to the vessels' exterior and/or interior surfaces are considered by the author as a functional rather than a decorative feature. For the break-up of the diagnostic potsherds into distinct vessel types, see figure 14.4.

No attempts were made to further subdivide flat-bases fragments (n=1292 or 40.8 percent of all diagnostics) according to vessel types, and, therefore, these have—together with the handle fragments (n=188 or 5.9 percent of all diagnostics) and decorated body sherds (n=255 or 8.1 percent of all diagnostics)—been excluded from the differential count of diagnostic rim/vessel types (n=1428 or 45.2 percent of all diagnostics).

The most common vessel in the assemblage retrieved from Area C is the holemouth jar (n=910 or 63.7 percent) followed, far behind, by the bow-rim jars (n=354 or 24.8 percent). The remainder rim diagnostics (n=164 or 11.5 percent) consist of various types of bowls, jugs, and necked jars other than bow-rim jars. Following is a presentation and discussion of the Area C pottery assemblage, invariably dating from the late EB I. The typological division follows Sharon Zuckerman's (2003, 35–48) typology for the late EB I Strata XV–XIV at Tel Qashish (upper village).[1]

Open Vessels

Bowls and Kraters (Figs. 14.5–6)
Compared to holemouth and bow-rim jars, the number of rim fragments of shallow and deep bowls and kraters (n=42 or 3 percent) is few and far between in Area C. These fragments consist of both shallow and deep bowls and kraters (Zuckerman's types B I, B IIa, and K II respectively, 2003, 35, 37) with rounded/tapering, slightly incurved (n=26; fig. 14.5.1–13), and sometimes sharply incurved rims (n=3; fig. 14.5.14–16). Bowls with sharply incurved rims can perhaps be considered the predecessors of the somewhat later (EB II) platters. One bowl with slightly incurved rim has a small knob applied just below the rim's exterior (fig. 14.5.7).

Other bowl types include profiled, gutter-rim bowls (n=5, fig. 14.5.17–20; Zuckerman type IIb), all red-slipped and burnished outside and on the inside of the rim; bowls with conoid projections (n=3; fig. 14.6.1–2; Zuckerman type B IIc), and gray burnished ware bowls (n= 5; fig. 14.6.3–5; Zuckerman 2003, 36, type B III). Only one small bowl was found in Area C (fig. 14.6.6) (Zuckerman type B IV), a type slightly more common in Area E (see ch. 16, this volume).

Restricted Vessels

Neckless Jars: Holemouth Jars (Figs. 14.7–8)
With 910 rim fragments of distinct holemouth jars (64 percent), these vessels—used for both cooking and storage—represent the most common vessel type in the Area C assemblage. The same applies to the late EB I ceramic assemblage from Tel Qashish Strata XV–XIV (the upper village; Zuckermann 2003, 37). As with the latter (37), rounded bases are absent in Area C, and, in fact, in all the excavated areas north and west of the tell. Therefore, all holemouth jars can be considered having been flat-based.

Based on Zuckerman's holemouths classification (2003, 27, fig. 19), the rims are either simple (e.g., figs. 14.7.4, 7; 14.8.8–10) or thickened (e.g., figs. 14.7.3, 5–6; 14.8.2–3, 7) (Zuckerman types H I and H II respectively), both either rounded/tapering (types H Ia and H IIa) or sharpened (H Ib and H IIb). Upturned rims and squared-off rims (Zuckerman types H III and H V respectively) are notably absent, while only very few examples of plain, ridged rims (fig. 14.7.11–12; Zuckerman's type H IV) were found, a feature relevant also for the assemblage of Area E (see ch. 16, this volume). Only three examples of spouted holemouth jars (fig. 14.8:14–16; Zuckerman type H VI) were identified. Not a single complete holemouth jar was found.

Although the crusted surface of many sherds makes it difficult to assess their final surface treatment, several jars clearly had red-slipped exterior surfaces, in ratios lower than contemporary examples from the nearby Area E (see ch. 16, this volume). Soot stains preserved on the outside of some rim fragments plainly indicate their function as cooking pots.

---

1. For the distinction made in her report between the upper and lower villages at Tel Qashish, see p. 50.

A plastic decoration consisting of a horizontal (continuous?) strip or band of finger-indented clay applied to the exterior surface of the jars around the shoulder is not uncommon (fig. 14.7.2–5). A few jars show prefiring incised simple marks just below the rim's exterior, possibly potters' marks (fig. 14.7.6–7). Only two rim fragments with a small knob applied below the rim's exterior were found in Area C (fig. 14.7.8–9). Another rare decoration mode is the application of small, finger-impressed round patches of clay, again below the rim's exterior (fig. 14.7.10).

Necked Jars: Bow-rim Jars (Figs. 14.9–10)
With 94 rims and 260 diagnostic neck/shoulder fragments (25 percent), storage jars with restricted rim/curved neck (so-called bow-rim jars; Zuckerman's type SJ II, 2003, 38, fig. 21.2–3) constitute the second most frequent vessel type found in Area C (and in Area E, see ch. 15, this volume). Rims are either rounded/tapering (figs. 14.9.1; 14.10.1–2; Zuckerman type SJ IIa) or cut/trimmed (figs. 14.9.2–10; 14.10.3; Zuckerman type SJ IIb). In principle, it would have been possible to further subdivide the rim/neck/shoulder fragments based on the varying degree of the necks' curvatures. Although the often-crusted surface of the sherds obfuscates the observation of final surface treatment, many jar fragments are red-slipped on the outside and, less frequently, on the inside of the neck. In a single case, a small knob was applied to the shoulder's exterior (fig. 14.10.3). All bow-rim jars have wide, flat bases.

Other Necked Jars (Figs. 14.11–12)
Other necked jars are represented by 108 sherds (8 percent). Apart from a very few rim, base, and indented ledge-handle fragments of small jugs or juglets and perhaps a single "teapot" (fig. 14.12.1–7; Zuckerman types NJ and T), relevant rim fragments include both medium- and large-sized vessels, either short-necked (fig. 14.11.1–5, 13–15 or tall-necked (fig. 14.11.6–12), coinciding with Zuckerman's (2003, 38) types NJ, SJ I, and SJ III. All the vessels are frequently red-slipped on the outside, and, sometimes, also on the inside of the neck.

Handles (Figs. 14.11.16; 14.12.2,7)
Among the handles and handle fragments (n=188), indented ledge handles are most frequent (n=135) while loop handles (n=48), lug handles (n=3), and knob handles (n=2) are much less so. One loop handle shows two horizontal parallel rows, with seven prefiring incised, vertical slashes in each (fig. 14.11.16). For a similar but not identically slashed loop handle from Area E, see figure 15.20.13. An indented ledge handle shows prefiring impressed circular punctures on its top side (fig. 14.12.7), similarly to handles found in Area B (fig. 14.3.6, 9).

Area D (Figure 14.13)

The late EB I pottery assemblage from Area D (including 1,632 body sherds and 130 vessel-shape diagnostic sherds), the area closest to the tell, differs somewhat from that of Areas C and E for it notably seems to lack bow-rim jars yet comprises a type of large, necked storage jars with applied decoration around their neck (fig. 14.13.11–13), absent in Areas A–C and E South (see ch. 15, this volume).

Among the several bowl fragments is a single gray burnished ware bowl (fig. 14.13.1). Jars include generic examples of holemouth jars (fig. 14.13.2–6) and necked jars (fig. 14.13.7–13). Also of interest are some fragments of small jars with rolled rims (fig. 14.13.9–10), which were not found in any other excavation area at the site. Bases are typically flat (fig. 14.13.14–15). A single flat base fragment of a small vessel with applied, continuous finger-impressed (rope) decoration (fig. 14.13.16) is seemingly the sole fragment of this vessel-type found at the site.

Summary

Although Areas A and B yielded small pottery assemblages of late EB I pottery retrieved mainly from bedrock levels without any structural contexts, the bulk of the late EB I pottery derives from Areas C and D, where they were found in association with various structural remains (see ch. 11, this volume). Closed vessels predominate over open shapes. Comparison with the published pottery record, foremost of Tel Qashish itself (Ben-Tor, Bonfil, and Zuckerman, 2003), clearly shows that the Areas C–D assemblages can be considered contemporary with the Strata XV–XIV remains on the tell of Qashish and that these areas can be considered part of the tell's agricultural hinterland.

References

Ben-Tor, Amnon, Ruhama Bonfil, and Sharon Zuckerman
2003 *Tel Qashish: A Village in the Jezreel Valley; Final Report of the Archaeological Excavations (1978–1987)*. Qedem Reports 5. Jerusalem: Hebrew University of Jerusalem.

Zuckerman, Sharon
2003 "The Early Bronze Age Pottery." In *Tel Qashish: A Village in the Jezreel Valley; Final Report of the Archaeological Excavations (1978–1987)*, edited by Amnon Ben-Tor, Ruhama Bonfil, and Sharon Zuckerman, 35–56. Qedem Reports 5. Jerusalem: Hebrew University of Jerusalem.

14. Pottery from Tel Qashish Areas A, B, C, and D

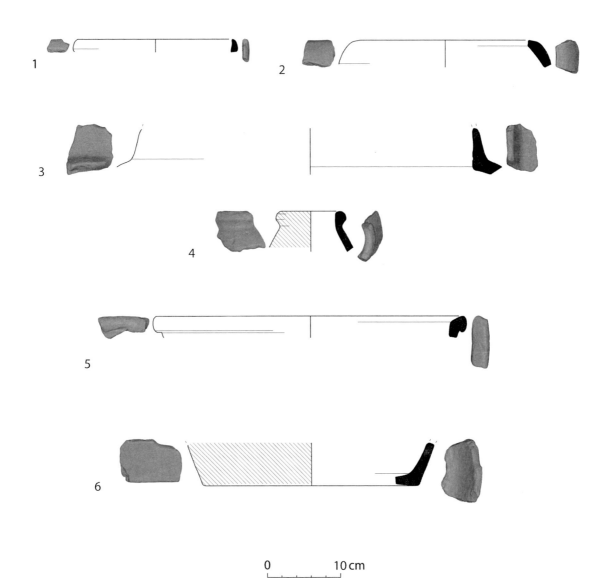

Fig. 14.1. Areas A1–2. Selection of Late EB I pottery. Bowls and Jars.

No.	Vessel	Locus	Basket	Description
1	Bowl	104	1020	Incurved rim fragment. Plain, buff-orange surface; many small and fewer coarse white grits.
2	Holemouth Jar	126	1083	Guttered rim/wall fragment. Plain, buff-orange surface; light brown core, buff-orange oxidation zones; white grits.
3	Bow-rim jar	104	1053	Neck/shoulder fragment. Possible traces of slip outside; eroded surface; gray core, buff-orange oxidation zones; many white grits.
4	Small (globular?) jar	133	1111	Rim/neck/wall fragment. Traces of red slip outside; buff-orange surface; coarse white and small gray grits.
5	Jar	127	1093	Everted rim/neck fragment. Traces of red slip outside and on rim inside; light brown core throughout; small, dark inclusions.
6	Jar	102	1006	Flat base/wall fragment. Red-slipped outside; plain buff-orange surface; gray core throughout; small and coarse white grits.

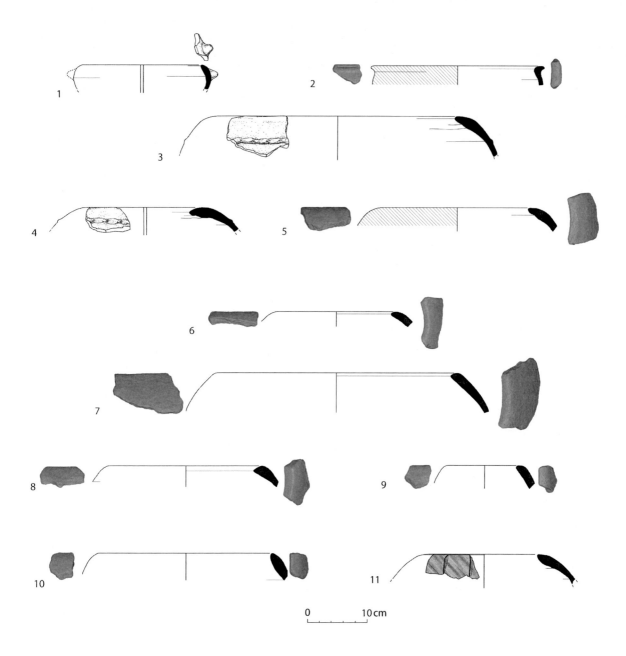

Fig. 14.2. Area B. Selection of Late EB I pottery. Bowls and Holemouth jars.

No.	Vessel	Locus	Basket	Description
1	Knobbed bowl	223	2069	Tapering rim/wall fragment. Eroded, buff-orange surface; many gray grits; fired at low temperature.
2	GBW bowl	217	2058	Rim/wall fragment. Traces of slip outside; gray surface; gray core; few grits.
3	Holemouth jar	212	2024	Tapering rim/rope-decorated wall fragment. Eroded, buff-orange surface; thick, light brown core, thin, buff-orange oxidation zones; many white, coarse grits.
4	Holemouth jar	200	2000	Tapering rim/rope-decorated wall fragment. Possible traces of red slip outside; eroded, buff-orange surface; many small and coarse white grits; tool or finger marks visible on inside (photo detail).
5	Holemouth jar	200	2000	Tapering rim/wall fragment. Red-slipped outside; plain, buff-orange surface; many small and coarse white grits.
6	Holemouth jar	208	2010	Tapering rim/wall fragment. Plain, buff-orange surface; many white grits.
7	Holemouth jar	222	2080	Tapering rim/wall fragment. Crusted, buff-orange surface; orange core, buff-orange oxidation zones; many small and coarse, angular grits; some glimmer (quartz?).
8	Holemouth jar	217	2052	Rim/wall fragment. Plain, buff-orange surface; gray core, light brown and then buff-orange oxidation zones; small and coarse, white and gray grits; some glimmers.
9	Holemouth jar	207	2017	Rim/wall fragment. Eroded, orange surface; many small and coarse white grits.
10	Holemouth jar	210	2020	Rim/wall fragment. Eroded, buff-orange surface; gray core, buff-orange oxidation zones; small and few coarse, white grits.
11	Holemouth jar	222	2080	Tapering rim/incised wall fragment. Outside; two slightly oblique-vertical prefiring incised slashes; orange core throughout; small and coarse white grits.

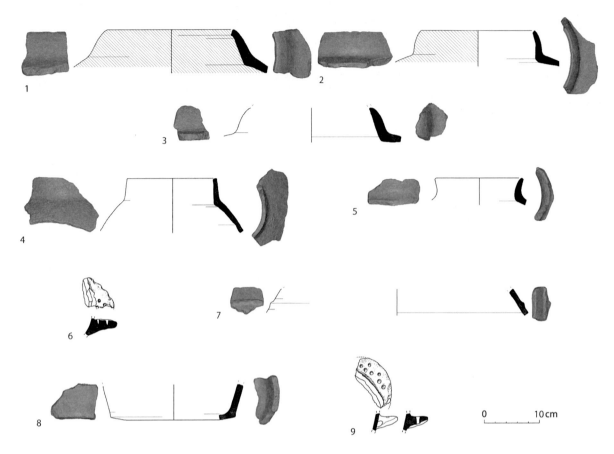

Fig. 14.3. Area B. Selection of Late EB I pottery. Jars.

No.	Vessel	Locus	Basket	Description
1	Bow-rim jar	217	2054	Guttered rim/neck/shoulder fragment; traces of red slip outside and on inside of the neck; buff-orange surface; thick, light brown core, thin, buff-orange oxidation zones; many white, coarse grits.
2	Bow-rim jar	218	2053	Slightly guttered rim/neck/shoulder fragment; traces of red slip outside; buff-orange surface; thick, light brown core, thin, buff-orange oxidation zones; many white and gray grits.
3	Bow-rim jar	210	2014	Neck/shoulder fragment; eroded, buff-orange surface; light brown core throughout; many small and coarse white grits.
4	Jar	222	2083	Flattened rim/neck/shoulder fragment; crusted surface; gray, inner core with one buff-orange oxidation zone on the outside; many gray grits, glimmers.
5	Jar	213	2035	Tapering rim/neck/shoulder fragment; eroded, buff-orange surface; white and gray grits; some glimmers.
6	Jar	213	2035	Indented ledge handle fragment with circular impressions on one side; plain, buff-orange surface; traces of soot on upper surface of handle; many white grits.
7	Jar	200	2000	Body sherd with applied rope decoration; eroded, orange surface; many small and coarse white grits.
8	Jar	213	2035	Flat base/wall fragment of jar; plain, orange surface; orange core throughout; white grits.
9	Jar	221	2061	Indented ledge handle fragment with prefiring applied perforations on the topside; Eroded, buff-orange surface.

14. Pottery from Tel Qashish Areas A, B, C, and D

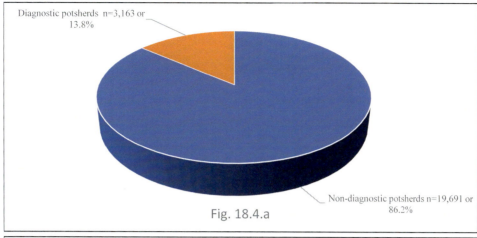

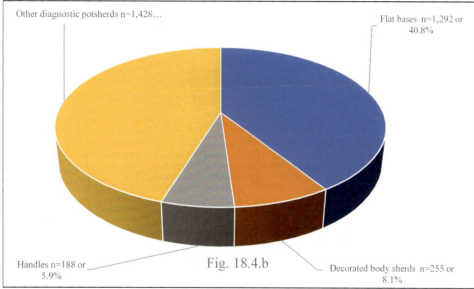

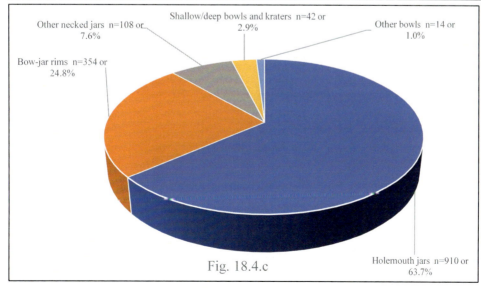

Fig. 14.4. Area C. Chart showing numeric breakdown of Late EB I vessel types.

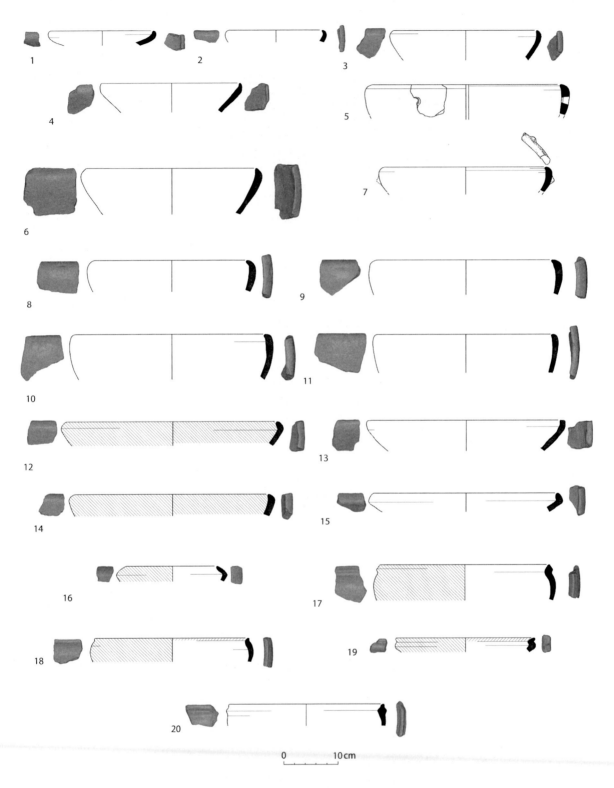

Fig. 14.5. Area C. Selection of Late EB I pottery. Bowls and kraters.

No.	Vessel	Locus	Basket	Description
1	Bowl	397	3369	Tapering, incurved rim; plain, light brown surface; thin, light brown core with alternating orange and light brown oxidation zones.
2	Bowl	316	3038	Incurved rim/wall fragment; plain, orange surface; thin, gray core, buff-orange oxidation zones; small white and gray grits; few coarse white and gray grits.
3	Bowl	323	3060	Tapering, incurved rim/wall fragment; possible traces of red slip in and outside; eroded, buff-orange surface; light brown core throughout; white grits.
4	Bowl	338	3119	Tapering, incurved rim/wall fragment; eroded, plain surface; interior surface and exterior surface until just below rim curvature orange; below external rim curvature light-brown, possibly indicating that this bowl was stacked inside another vessel/bowl in the kiln; thick, gray core, thin, buff-orange oxidation zones; many coarse, white grits.
5	Thick-walled bowl	311	3017	Tapering, incurved rim/wall fragment; postfiring, drilled hole just below rim; many coarse, and fewer small white grits, few gray grits; thick, orange core with thin, buff-orange, exterior oxidation zones.
6	Large bowl/krater	392	3350	Tapering, incurved, thickened rim/wall fragment; eroded, plain buff-orange surface; orange core; small white grits.
7	Large bowl	337	3188	Incurved rim/wall fragment with external, small knob; plain, buff-orange surface; strong, light-brown core with buff-orange oxidation zones; small and coarse white grits.
8	Large bowl/krater	388	3355	Tapering, incurved rim and wall fragment; plain, light brown surface; grayish-light brown core throughout; small gray grits; some glimmers; inside of incurved rim irregular, i.e., not fully smoothed.
9	Large thick-walled bowl/krater	388	3371	Tapering, incurved rim; possible traces of red slip outside; gray core throughout (secondary?); white grits.
10	Large bowl	324	3067	Rim/wall fragment; possible traces of red slip/paint outside and inside; surface buff-orange; gray core, light brown oxidation zones; white grits.
11	Deep bowl/krater	324	3067	Slightly incurved rim/wall fragment; plain, buff-orange surface; thick, gray core; thin, buff-orange oxidation zones; small and fewer coarse white grits.
12	Thick-walled bowl	317	3128	Tapering, incurved rim/wall fragment; red slipped inside and outside; buff-orange surface; light-brown-orange core, with thin, orange oxidation zones and buff-orange surface; many small, few coarse white grits.
13	Bowl	338	3119	Flattened, incurved rim/wall fragment; buff-orange core; orange oxidation zones and buff-orange, plain surface; small and coarse white grits.
14	Bowl	397	3369	Tapering, incurved rim; red-slipped inside and outside; surface buff-orange; thick gray core, thin, buff-orange oxidation zones; white grits.
15	Flat bowl	350	3240	Carinated rim/wall fragment; eroded, plain, buff-orange surface; thick light brown core, thin buff-orange oxidation zones; white grits.
16	Platter (EB II?)	362	3321	Tapering, carinated rim/wall fragment; red-slipped exterior; thick gray core, thin buff-orange oxidation zones; gray and very few white grits.
17	Large bowl (Qashish Type B IIb)/krater	395	3368	Flattened, outward folded rim/shoulder fragment; red-slipped outside; buff-orange surface; light brown core throughout; many small gray grits.
18	Large bowl/krater	388	3380	Rim/wall fragment; red slipped and burnished outside and on inside of rim; buff-orange core throughout; small gray grits.
19	Large bowl	386	3324	Rim/wall fragment; traces of slip inside and outside; light brown-buff-orange core throughout; small, gray grits.
20	Krater	336	3094	Guttered ledge rim/wall fragment; eroded, buff-orange surface; light brown–buff-orange core throughout; very fine dark inclusions.

144 Salvage Excavations at Tel Qashish (Tell Qasis) and Tell el-Wa'er (2010–2013)

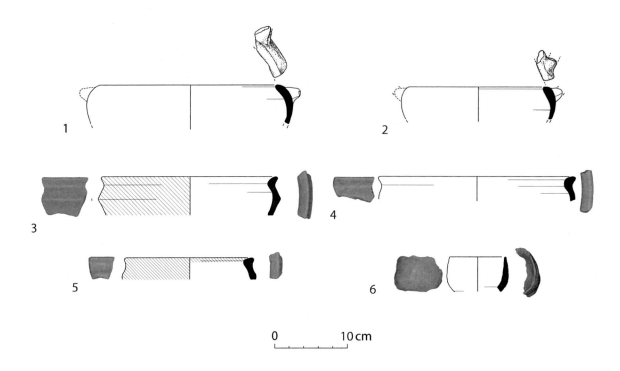

Fig. 14.6. Area C. Selection of Late EB I pottery. Other bowls.

No.	Vessel	Locus	Basket	Description
1	Knobbed bowl	367	3278	Eroded, grayish surface; light brown–grayish core throughout; small gray grits gray core throughout; many small gray grits.
2	Knobbed bowl	377	3291	Eroded, grayish surface; gray core throughout; many small gray grits.
3	GBW bowl	367	3279	Traces of slip outside; grayish core throughout, small gray grits.
4	GBW bowl	355	3200	Plain surface; inside soot stains, outside brownish; white and gray grits.
5	GBW bowl	366	3207	Traces of slip preserved on rim; ware is not typical GBW, but rather buff-orange; thin, gray core; buff-orange thick oxidation zones; small gray grits.
6	Small bowl	359	3226	Very asymmetrical, preserved half; gray core with many white, fewer gray grits and some glimmer; external oxidation zones (plain surface) buff-orange.

146 Salvage Excavations at Tel Qashish (Tell Qasis) and Tell el-Wa'er (2010–2013)

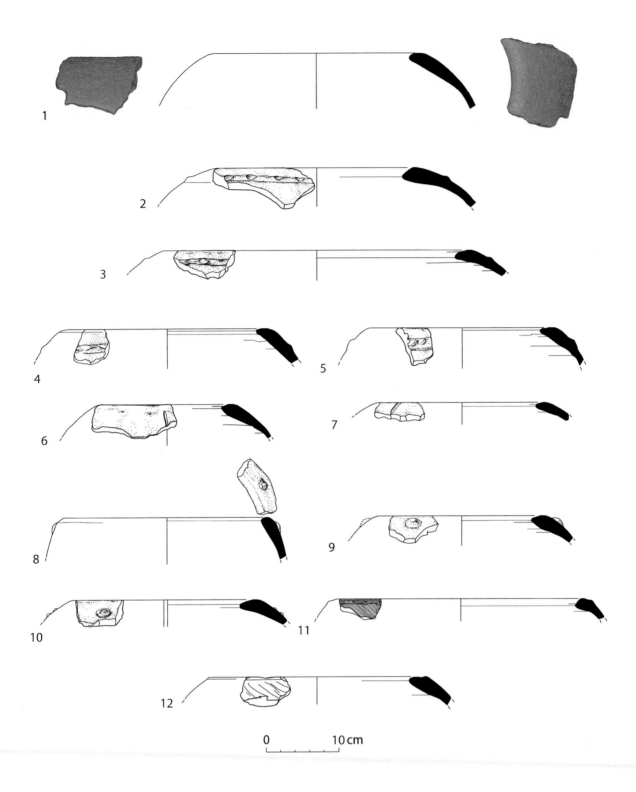

Fig. 14.7. Area C. Selection of Late EB I pottery. Holemouth jars.

No.	Vessel	Locus	Basket	Description
1	Holemouth jar	320	3048	Thick-walled rim/wall fragment; possible traces of red slip outside; buff-range surface; brownish core throughout; many small, fewer coarse white and gray grits, and few glimmers.
2	Holemouth jar	335	3160	Tapering rim/wall fragment with applied indented rope decoration; plain, orange surface; orange core, with single, buff-orange exterior oxidation zone; white angular grits.
3	Holemouth jar	395	3360	Thickened rim/wall fragment with applied rope decoration; traces of red slip outside; eroded, buff-orange surface; buff-orange core throughout; fired at high temperature.
4	Holemouth jar	388	3358	Rim/rope-decorated wall fragment; plain, buff-orange surface; thick, light brown core; orange oxidation zones; coarse white, angular grits.
5	Holemouth jar	353	3179	Thickened rim/wall with applied rope decoration fragment; plain buff-orange surface; thick, light brown core, thin, orange oxidation zones; white, and few dark inclusions.
6	Holemouth jar	365	3188	Large, thin-walled; prefiring applied potmark; well fired; possible traces of red slip outside; buff-orange surface; thick, light brown core, buff-orange oxidation zones; white grits.
7	Holemouth jar	376	3335	Tapering rim fragment; potmark; prefiring, obliquely incised slash/mark; plain, buff-orange surface; gray core, buff-orange oxidation zones; white inclusions.
8	Holemouth jar	327	3079	Rounded rim/wall fragment; small knob just below the rim; plain, buff-orange surface; light brown core throughout; many white grits.
9	Holemouth jar	329	3082	Tapering rim/wall fragment; small knob below rim; eroded, plain, buff-orange surface; thick, light-brown core, orange oxidation zones; small and coarse white grits.
10	Holemouth jar	395	3360	Tapering rim/wall fragment; circular decoration; possible traces of red slip outside; buff-orange surface; buff-orange core; orange surface/oxidation zones; few white grits.
11	Holemouth jar	376	3322	Rim/wall fragment with incisions; traces of red slip outside; small, prefiring-impressed indentations along ridge below rim; buff-orange surface; light brown core throughout; small, gray grits.
12	Holemouth jar	375	3262	Tapering rim/ridged wall fragment (EB II?); Plain, orange surface; gray core, orange oxidation zones; small and few coarse white grits; fired at high temperature.

148 Salvage Excavations at Tel Qashish (Tell Qasis) and Tell el-Wa'er (2010–2013)

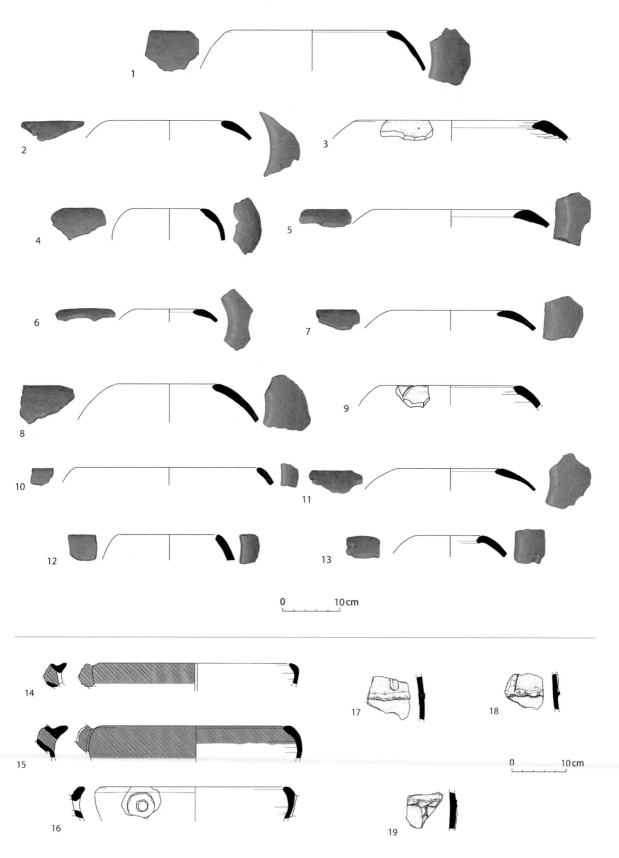

Fig. 14.8. Area C. Selection of Late EB I pottery. Holemouth jars (cont.).

No.	Vessel	Locus	Basket	Description
1	Holemouth jar	335	3182	Thin-walled; tapering rim/wall fragment; crusted, buff-orange surface; orange core; white grits.
2	Holemouth jar	323	3060	Thin-walled; thickened rim/wall fragment; plain, orange surface; light brown core; buff-orange oxidation zones; many white grits, small and coarse.
3	Holemouth jar	367	3255	Thickened rim/wall fragment; plain cream-yellow surface; gray core throughout (secondary?); white grits.
4	Holemouth jar	357	3241	Tapering rim/wall fragment; eroded, plain buff-orange surface; light brown-buff-orange core throughout; white coarse grits, some glimmers.
5	Holemouth jar	388	3323	Rim/wall fragment; plain, buff-orange surface; horizontal tool marks visible on inside; light brown core, buff-orange oxidation zones; white grits; fired at high temperature.
6	Holemouth jar	319	3041	Thin-walled; tapering rim/wall fragment; possible traces of red slip outside; buff-orange surface; light brown core throughout; small and fewer coarse, white grits; fired at high temperature.
7	Holemouth jar	386	3302	Thin-walled; thickened rim/wall fragment; plain, buff-orange surface; gray core, orange oxidation zones; small and coarse white grits.
8	Holemouth jar	389	3365	Tapering rim/wall fragment; plain, buff-orange surface; buff-orange core throughout; many white grits; some glimmers.
9	Holemouth jar	308	3018	Tapering rim fragment with incision; plain, orange-buff surface; small white and gray grits; prefiring incised, diagonal slash outside near the rim (potmark?).
10	Holemouth jar	387	3328	Rim/wall fragment; plain, buff-orange surface; gray core, buff-orange oxidation zones; white grits.
11	Holemouth jar	367	3279	Thin-walled; thickened rim/wall fragment; plain, buff-orange surface; orange core throughout; many coarse white grits; fired at high temperature.
12	Holemouth jar	308	3046	Flattened rim fragment of holemouth jar or rim/neck fragment of bow-rim jar; plain, buff-orange surface; gray core, with a single, buff-orange interior oxidation zone; small and medium-sized white grits.
13	Holemouth jar	377	3315	Bowl? Incurved rim/wall fragment with postfiring drilled hole; plain, buff-orange surface; light brown core, with single, interior orange oxidation zone; white grits and some glimmers.
14	Holemouth jar	350	3191 drawn	Tapering rim/spout fragment; traces of red slip outside; eroded, buff-orange surface; gray core, buff-orange oxidation zones; small, gray grits.
15	Holemouth jar	350	3240 drawn	Tapering rim/spout/wall fragment; red-slipped and burnished outside, and on the inside of the rim, upper part of wall; many small gray and few white grits.
16	Holemouth jar	308	3071 drawn	Tapering rim/spout attachment/wall fragment; eroded, buff-orange surface; spout is broken off at the very place of its attachment to the jar's wall; many small gray grits.
17	Holemouth Jar	335	3171 drawn	Body sherd with two perpendicularly applied bands of finger-impressed rope decoration; eroded, buff-orange surface; gray core, with only one, exterior, buff-orange oxidation zone; small white grits; some large (organic?) inclusions.
18	Holemouth jar	332	3101 drawn	Body sherd with two perpendicularly applied bands of finger-impressed rope decoration; eroded, buff-orange surface; buff-orange core throughout; small white grits.
19	Holemouth jar	357	3241 drawn	Body sherd with two perpendicularly applied bands of finger-impressed rope decoration; eroded, buff-orange surface; gray core, buff-orange oxidation zones; small white grits.

150 Salvage Excavations at Tel Qashish (Tell Qasis) and Tell el-Wa'er (2010–2013)

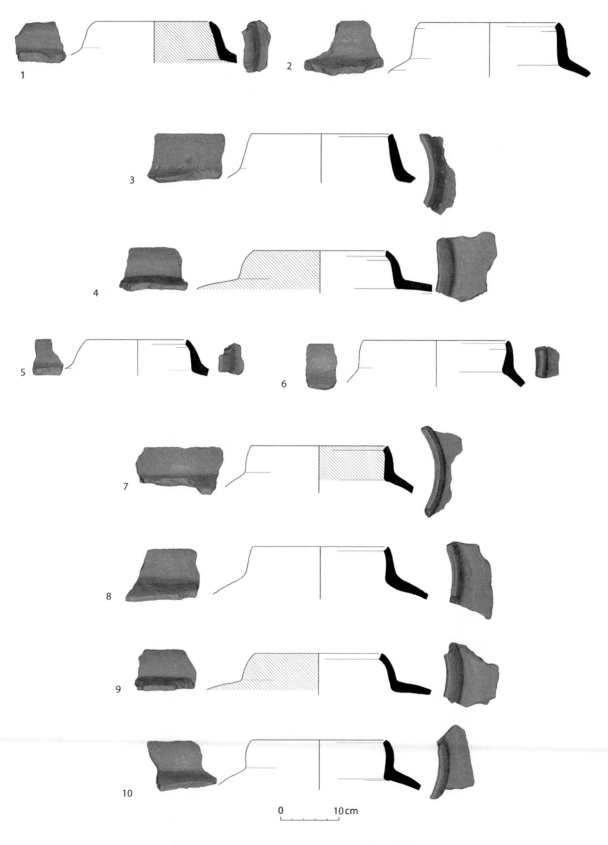

Fig. 14.9. Area C. Selection of Late EB I pottery. Bow-rim jars.

No.	Vessel	Locus	Basket	Description
1	Bow-rim jar	388	3364	Tapering rim/neck/shoulder fragment; red-slipped on inside of the neck; no traces of red slip (preserved) on the outside; strong, gray core, with single, interior, buff-orange oxidation zone; white, angular grits; few glimmers.
2	Bow-rim jar	367	3278	Slightly guttered rim/neck/shoulder fragment; possible traces of red slip outside; buff-orange interior; light brown exterior surface; white grits.
3	Bow-rim jar	379	3314	Flattened rim/tall neck/shoulder fragment; plain, buff-orange surface; strong, gray core, with buff-orange oxidation zones; white grits.
4	Bow-rim jar	380	3283	Slightly guttered rim/neck/shoulder fragment; red-slipped outside; soot stains outside; light brown core throughout; light brown core, with only one, interior, buff-orange oxidation zone; many small and coarse white grits; tool/scraping marks visible on inside of the wall.
5	Bow-rim jar	331	3084	Medium-sized; obliquely flattened slightly guttered rim neck/shoulder plain, buff-orange surface; grayish core, buff-orange oxidation zones; white grits.
6	Bow-rim jar	308	3018	Flattened rim/neck/shoulder fragment; plain, buff-orange surface; gray external, buff-orange internal oxidation zone; small and fewer medium-sized white grits; neck/shoulder joint on inside not smoothed.
7	Bow-rim jar	394	3340	Flattened rim/neck/shoulder fragment; traces of red slip on inside of the neck; interior joint between neck and shoulder not smoothed that is clearly visible; plain, buff-orange surface; dark brown core, buff-orange oxidation zones; possible traces of red slip/paint on inside of the neck.
8	Bow-rim jar	392	3384	Guttered rim/neck/shoulder fragment; plain, buff-orange surface; orange core; few white grits; fired at high temperature.
9	Bow-rim jar	392	3384	Guttered rim/neck/shoulder fragment; traces of red slip outside; plain, buff-orange surface; orange core; small and coarse white grits; fired at high temperature.
10	Bow-rim jar	310	3011	Flattened rim/neck/shoulder fragment; eroded, plain, buff-orange surface; neck-shoulder joint inside not smoothed; gray core, alternating light brown and buff-orange oxidation zones; many small to medium-sized white, and fewer gray grits.

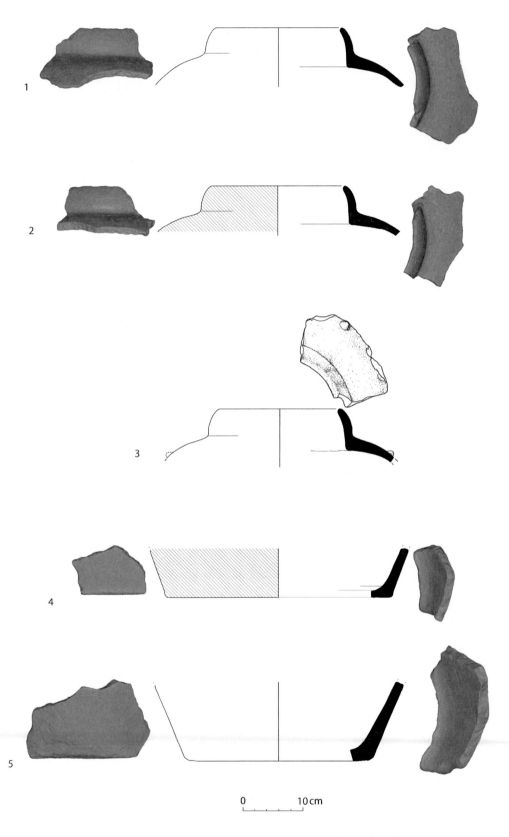

Fig. 14.10. Area C. Selection of Late EB I pottery. Bow-rim jars (cont.).

No.	Vessel	Locus	Basket	Description
1	Bow-rim jar	320	3066	Tapering rim/neck/shoulder/wall fragment; light-brown core; buff-orange, exterior oxidation zones; many coarse, fewer small white grits; interior joint between neck and shoulder only roughly smoothed; scraping tool marks visible on inside.
2	Bow-rim jar	310	3034	Rim/neck/shoulder fragment; traces of red slip outside; eroded, buff-orange surface; light-brown core; many small and coarse white and dark grits; fired at high temperature.
3	Bow-rim jar	320	3066	Obliquely flattened rim/neck/shoulder fragment with small knob(s?) in shoulder; eroded, plain, buff-orange surface; thin gray core, buff-orange oxidation zones; many white grits; interior neck/shoulder joint not smoothed.
4	Bow-rim jar	320	3048	Base/wall fragment of large jar; traces of red-slip outside; many small and few coarse dark grits, few small white grits and some glimmers; light brown core with thick exterior buff-orange oxidation zones.
5	Bow-rim jar	328	3096	Flat base/wall fragment of large jar; crusted buff-orange surface; thick gray core, alternating light brown and buff-orange exterior oxidation zone, thin, interior light brown oxidation zone; small to coarse white inclusions.

154 Salvage Excavations at Tel Qashish (Tell Qasis) and Tell el-Wa'er (2010–2013)

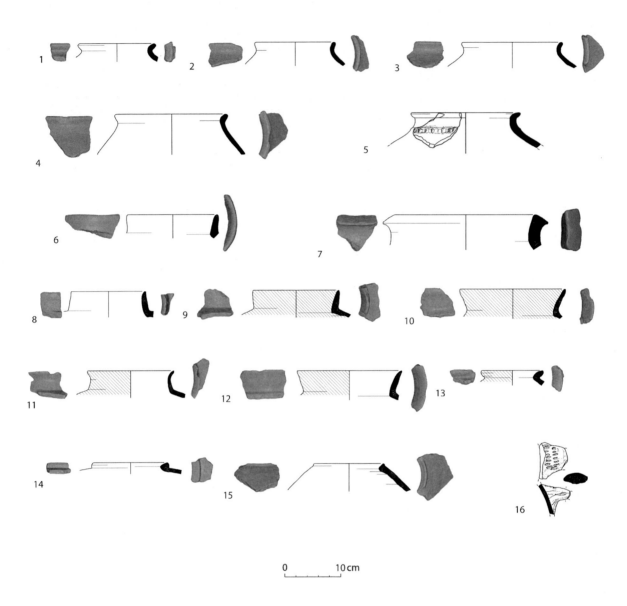

Fig. 14.11. Area C. Selection of Late EB I pottery. Other necked jars, handles.

No.	Vessel	Locus	Basket	Description
1	Medium-sized jar	367	3279	Rounded, everted rim/shoulder fragment; plain, buff-orange surface; thick gray core, thin, buff-orange oxidation zones; few white grits.
2	Thin-walled jar	362	3204	Rounded, everted rim/neck/shoulder fragment; eroded, brown surface; grayish core throughout; small white and gray grits; some glimmers.
3	Thin-walled jar	357	3265	Thin-walled; rounded, everted rim/neck/shoulder fragment; plain, buff-orange surface; soot stains on neck outside; gray core, with single, interior, buff-orange oxidation zone; small and fewer coarse white and gray grits.
4	Medium-sized jar (cooking pot? perhaps EB II?)	362	3344	Everted rim/neck/shoulder/wall fragment; plain buff-orange surface; soot stains outside; gray core, with single, interior, buff-orange oxidation zone; many white grits.
5	Medium-to-large-sized jar (EB II?)	367	3209	Rim/short neck/decorated shoulder fragment; horizontal row of finger-impressed indentations; brown exterior surface; buff-orange interior surface; thick gray core, thin buff-orange oxidation zones; small white and very few coarse white grits; fired a high temperature.
6	Jar	389	3391	Rim/neck/shoulder fragment; strong, light brown core, buff-orange oxidation zones; white grits; horizontal tool marks visible on inside.
7	Thick-walled pithos	396	3367	Flat, curving rim/neck/shoulder; plain, light brown surface; thick gray core, buff-orange oxidation zones; small, gray grits and glimmers.
8	Medium-sized jar	399	3383	Tapering and slightly everted rim/neck/shoulder fragment; eroded, plain surface; thick light brown core, buff-orange oxidation zones; fired at high temperature.
9	Medium-sized jar	353	3167	Tapering rim/flaring neck/shoulder fragment; the neck/shoulder joint is well visible on the inside with an apparently additional strip of clay for support (photo detail); traces of red slip outside, and on the neck inside; buff-orange surface; buff-orange core throughout; many white angular grits.
10	Jar	335	3171	Tapering rim/flaring neck/shoulder fragment; traces of red slip outside and inside the neck; interior joint neck/shoulder clearly visible, not smoothed; orange core; white grits.
11	Thin-walled, small jar	392	3349	Rim/neck/shoulder fragment; traces of red slip outside; buff-orange surface; light brown core many small-coarse white grits; fired at high temperature.
12	Teapot (?)	332	3085	Tapering rim/flaring neck/shoulder fragment; red-slipped outside; orange-buff surface; buff-orange core throughout; many gray grits.
13	Small, short-necked jar	317	3039	Tapering, everted rim/neck/shoulder fragment; buff-orange surface; traces of red slip outside; orange core throughout; many small gray and few white grits.
14	Small jar/jug	384	3306	Everted, flattened rim/shoulder fragment; possible traces of red slip outside; buff-orange surface; buff-orange core throughout; small gray, and very few white grits.
15	Medium-sized jar	388	3390	Rim/shoulder/wall fragment; plain, buff-orange surface; buff-orange core throughout; white grits; fired at high temperature; horizontal tool marks visible on inside.
16	Handle	367	3279	Fragmented loop handle with two parallel, horizontal rows of seven vertical slashes, incised prefiring; plain orange surface.

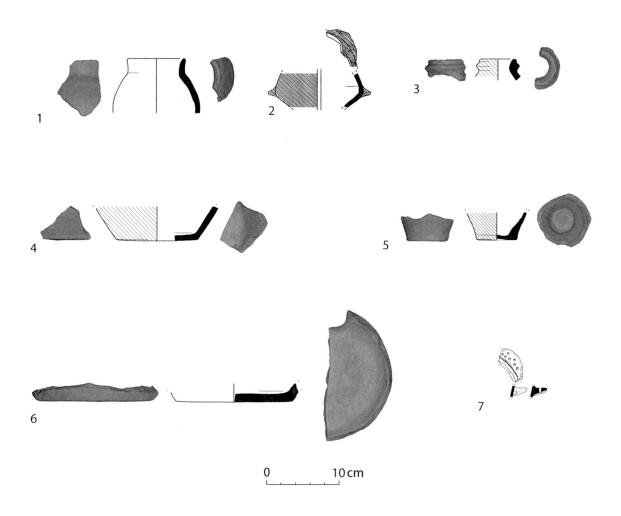

Fig. 14.12. Area C. Selection of Late EB I pottery. Other necked jars, handles.

14. Pottery from Tel Qashish Areas A, B, C, and D

No.	Vessel	Locus	Basket	Description
1	Small jar/juglet	331	3099	Rim/neck shoulder/wall fragment; plain, buff-orange surface; light brown core, buff-orange oxidation zones; small, white grits.
2	Handle/wall fragment of small vessel	347	3143	Red-slipped outside.
3	Teapot (?)	340	3149	Rim [sic]/neck fragment; red slipped and burnished outside; light brown core with buff-orange oxidation zones; small white grits.
4	Jug (EB II?)	367	3209	Slightly amphaloid base/wall fragment; red-slipped and burnished; gray core with buff-orange oxidation zones; small white and gray grits; thrown omphalos in center of base.
5	Small, thin-walled jar	319	3107	Flat base/wall fragment; red slipped and burnished outside; interior surface buff-orange; exterior surface light-brown; buff-orange core throughout; many coarse gray and few small white grits; fired at high temperature.
6	Jar	362	3373	Flat base; plain, buff-orange-light brown surface; strong, gray core; thin buff-orange oxidation zones.
7	Indented ledge handle	317	3128	Fragment; punctured design; eroded, buff-orange surface.

158 Salvage Excavations at Tel Qashish (Tell Qasis) and Tell el-Wa'er (2010–2013)

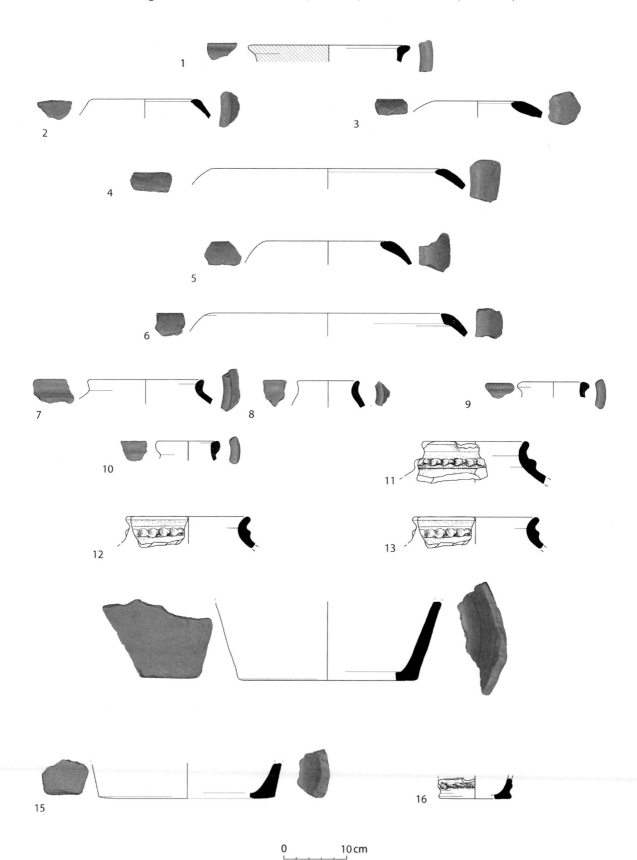

Fig. 14.13. Area D. Selection of Late EB I pottery.

No.	Vessel	Locus	Basket	Description
1	GBW bowl	403	4021	Traces of slip outside; gray surface; gray core; white grits.
2	Holemouth jar	403	4011	Tapering rim/wall fragment; eroded, buff-orange surface; thin, light brown core, buff-orange oxidation zones; many small (and one very large) white grits.
3	Holemouth jar	406	4035	Tapering rim; eroded, buff-orange surface; light brown core throughout; gray core, buff-orange oxidation zones; small and coarse white grits.
4	Holemouth har	403	4011	Tapering rim/wall fragment; plain, buff-orange surface; white grits and glimmers.
5	Holemouth har	401	4006	Tapering rim/wall fragment; plain, orange surface; small white grits.
6	Holemouth har	419	4082	Tapering internal ledge rim/wall fragment; plain, orange surface; core orange throughout; coarse white grits.
7	Jar (EB II?)	403	4014	Tapering, everted rim/neck/shoulder fragment; soot (?) stained, gray surface out and on rim inside; gray core throughout (secondary?); white grits; few glimmers; fired at high temperature.
8	Small jar	403	4021	Rim/neck/shoulder fragment; eroded, buff-orange surface; thin orange core; thick, buff-orange oxidation zones.
9	Small jar	405	4028	Rim/neck fragment; plain, buff-orange surface; thin, light brown core with strong, buff-orange oxidation zones; white grits.
10	Small jar	418	4075	Flattened rim/neck/shoulder fragment; plain, buff-orange surface; white grits.
11	Jar	410	4042	Everted rim/neck/rope-decorated shoulder fragment; plain, buff-orange surface; gray grits.
12	Jar	418	4077	Everted rim/neck/rope-decorated shoulder fragment; possible traces of slip outside; buff-orange surface; light brown core; single, gray, exterior oxidation zone; white grits; few glimmers.
13	Jar	418	4069	Everted rim/neck/rope-decorated shoulder fragment; plain, brownish surface; strong, gray core, thin oxidation zones; white grits.
14	Large jar	400	4005	Flat base/wall fragment; possible traces of red slip outside; buff-orange surface; strong, light brown core, with buff-orange oxidation zones; small and coarse white grits.
15	Thick-walled jar	414	4071	Thin, flat base/wall fragment; eroded, orange surface; thick, gray core, thin buff-orange oxidation zones; many small and coarse white grits.
16	Small, unusual vessel	400	4005	Disk-shaped base/decorated wall fragment; indented rope decoration around the base; core and surface orange; white grits and glimmers.

Chapter 15

Pottery from Tel Qashish Areas E South and F

Netanel Paz
(*Computational Archaeology Laboratory, Institute of Archaeology, The Hebrew University of Jerusalem*)

Introduction

Presented below is a typological study of the ceramic assemblage from Areas E and F in Tel Qashish, recovered during the excavations led at the site by Eli Yannai (IAA permit A-5992; see above, ch. 12). Figures 15.1–9 depict only sherds from secure loci (see tables 15.1–2); no complete vessels were found or restored.

The typological analysis is based on morphology and surface treatment. Due to the archaeological remains being close to the surface, the pottery is rather badly preserved; most sherds are worn-out, making it difficult to trace, when visible, any surface decoration (e.g., slip and burnish).

All the potsherds were scanned and drawn at the Computerized Archeology Lab of the Institute of Archaeology, the Hebrew University of Jerusalem, using 3D high-end cameras and dedicated software developed at the lab (Karasik and Smilansky 2011; Grosman et al. 2014). Out of 6134 potsherds recovered from both Area E and Area F, 369 (6 percent) are diagnostics (not including bases and handles), and 383 were scanned. The assemblage included 130 bases, which make up 2.1 percent of the overall assemblage, and 60 handle fragments, which make up 0.9 percent of the assemblage, both not typologically defined.

The typological classification is mostly based on the ceramic report of Tel Qashish Strata XV–XIV (Zuckerman 2003). For further comparative purposes, the assemblages of Beth Shean Strata M3–M2 (Rotem 2012), Qiryat Ata Strata III–II (Golani 2003), 'En Shadud (Braun 1985), and 'En Esur ('Ein Asawir; Yannai, Lazar-Shorer, and Grosinger 2006) were used.

Typology

Bowls
(n=23, making up 6.2 percent of the total; fig. 15.1)

Type B I: Shallow Bowls with a Simple Rim
(n=11, making up 3 percent of the total; fig. 15.1.1–3). This type has curved sides and a simple straight rim. Most examples are not decorated; one specimen is red-slipped inside and out. These bowls comprise a very small percentage of the assemblage, both in area E (2 percent) and area F (3 percent).

Parallels: Qashish Strata XV–XIV (Zuckerman 2003, fig. 17.1); Beth Shean Strata M3–M2 (Rotem 2012, pls. 2.9; 18.14); Qiryat Ata Strata III–II (Golani 2003, fig. 4.1.4–5).

Type B II: Deep Bowls
This type comprises the two following subtypes:

Type B IIa: Deep bowls with a simple rim
(n=10, making up 2.7 percent of the total; fig. 15.1.4–6). Not a common type. Red slip is visible on the inside and the outside.

Parallels: Qashish Strata XV–XIV (Zuckerman 2003, fig. 17.4); Beth Shean Strata M3–M2 (Rotem 2012, pls. 18.18, 21, 28); 'En Shadud Strata II–I (Braun 1985, fig. 15.15–17).

Type B IIb: Deep bowls with conical projections
(n=2, 0.5 percent of the total; fig. 15.1.7).
Bowls with a rounded body, an inverted rim, and a conical projection below the rim. Some examples, such as the one in figure 15.1.7, are red slipped on the outside. This bowl type is very common in the northern valleys during the EB I. Previously considered an imitation of the gray burnished ware (GBW) bowls (Wright's type 4), this is no longer so since both types appear together in some sites and the same contexts and made of the same material, as in Tel Qashish Strata XV–XIV (Zuckerman 2003).

Douglas Esse (1989) claimed that these bowls should be dated to a post-GBW phase, based on their later date at Tel Beth-Yeraḥ. Eliot Braun (1996) suggested attributing the type to an earlier phase within the EB IB, namely the 'En Shadud Horizon. Sharon Zuckerman ruled out these two options based on the presence of both Wright's type 4 GBW bowls and bowls with a conical-projection in the same EB IB strata at Tel Qashish, a phase that, according to Zuckerman, includes the 'En Shadud Horizon and the later phases of the EB I.

The presence of the bowls with a conical projection in Beth Shean Strata M3 and M2 further strengthens the claim that this type continued to be in use up to the very end of the EB IB (Rotem 2012, 131).

Parallels: Qashish Strata XV–XIV (Zuckerman 2003, fig. 17.7); Beth Shean Strata M3–M2 (Rotem 2012, pls. 2.10; 18.16); 'En Shadud Strata II–I (Braun 1985, fig. 18.8–10).

Kraters
(Fig. 15.1)

K I: Krater with an inverted rim
(n=14, making up 3.8 percent of the total; fig. 15.1.8–10).
Very scarce in the assemblage, these vessels are similar to the type B II deep bowls but are larger in diameter.

Parallels: Qashish Strata XV–XIV (Zuckerman 2003, fig. 18.2–3); Beth Shean strata M3–M2 (Rotem 2012, pls. 3.6–9); 'En Shadud Strata II–I (Braun 1985, fig. 14.2).

Table 15.1. Area E South. Secure loci list.

Locus No.	Context
5003	Rock surface on topsoil
5004	Rock surface on topsoil
5015	Dismantling of rock surface
5026	West of circular rock surface
5028	Floor
5029	Floor
5030	Floor
5037	Hewn pit
5045	Floor
5047	Silo
5048	Area around Silo 5047
5049	Floor

Table 15.2. Area F. Secure loci list.

Locus No.	Context
6011	Floor
6012	Floor
6013	Floor
6025	Floor
6026	Floor
6027	Floor
6029	Pit
6032	Floor
6033	Floor
6044	Area near W601
6045	Floor
6046	Area near W603
6048	Room
6049	Floor
6051	Floor
6056	Floor
6059	Room
6060	Area between W608 and W609

Small Closed Vessels
(Fig. 15.2)

Type GJ: Gourd jars
(n=2, making up 0.5 percent of the total; fig. 15.2.1). Also referred to as amphoriskoi (Golani 2003, 97; Yannai, Lazar-Shorer, and Grosinger 2006, 89), this type has a rounded and squat body, horizontal shoulders, and a sharply everted neck. The straight handles extend from the top of the neck to the shoulder. The vessels are usually red slipped on the outside. In this assemblage, gourd jars are represented only by body sherds showing the distinctive horizontal shoulder.

Parallels: Qashish Strata XV–XIV (Zuckerman 2003, fig. 20.6–7); Qiryat Ata Strata III–II (Golani 2003, fig. 4.8.5–6); 'En Esur I Stratum II (Yannai, Lazar-Shorer, and Grosinger 2006, fig. 4.60.1–2); 'En Shadud Strata II–I (Braun 1985, fig. 20.2–4).

Type T: Teapots
(n=4, making up 1.1 percent of the total; fig. 15.2.2–3) Rare in the assemblage, these vessels show a ridged neck and, usually, a bent spout, although straight ones have also been found. Most vessels are red slipped. In this assemblage, these vessels are represented mostly by bent spouts.

Parallels: Qashish Strata XV–XIV (Zuckerman 2003, fig. 20.5); Beth Shean Strata M3 (Rotem 2012, pls. 14.5; 17.9); Qiryat Ata Strata III–II (Golani 2003, fig. 4.8.9–14); 'En Esur I Stratum II (Yannai, Lazar-Shorer, and Grosinger 2006, fig. 4.60.18, 21–24).

Holemouth Jars
(n=267, making up 72.4 percent of the total; fig. 15.3–5)

Holemouth jars are the most common vessel type in the assemblage. These have a round or elliptical body, a flat or round base, and a small variety of rim shapes. Contrary to most other vessel types, holemouth rims do not provide clear chronological anchors (Zuckerman 2003). Four subtypes were found, defined by their rim shapes:

Type H I: Holemouths with a Simple Rim (fig. 15.3)
The rim is a direct continuation of the body. Two subtypes are present:

Type H Ia: Holemouths with a simple, rounded rim
(n=86, making up 23.3 percent of the total; fig. 15.3.1–4).

Parallels: Qashish Strata XV–XIV (Zuckerman 2003, fig. 19.1); Beth Shean Strata M3–M2 (Rotem 2012, pls. 21.7; 28.3); Qiryat Ata Strata III–II (Golani 2003, fig. 4.5.1–6); 'En Esur I Stratum II (Yannai, Lazar-Shorer, and Grosinger 2006, fig. 4.56.9); 'En Shadud Strata II–I (Braun 1985, fig. 21.10–11).

Type H Ib: Holemouths with a rim sharpened at the edge
(n=93, making up 25.2 percent of the total; fig. 15.3.5–10).

Parallels: Qashish Strata XV–XIV (Zuckerman 2003, fig. 19.2); Beth Shean Strata M3–M (Rotem 2012, pls. 21.9; 26.13); Qiryat Ata Strata III–II (Golani 2003, fig. 4.5.7–9); 'En Esur I Stratum II (Yannai, Lazar-Shorer, and Grosinger 2006, fig. 4.56.14); 'En Shadud Strata II-I (Braun 1985, fig. 21.14).

Type H II: Holemouths with a Thickened Rim (fig. 15.4)
The rim is thicker than the body. There are two subtypes:

Type H IIa: Holemouth with a rounded rim
(n=26, making up 7 percent of the total).
The rim is thickened and rounded at the edge (fig. 15.4.1–4).

Parallels: Qashish Strata XV–XIV (Zuckerman 2003, fig.19.3); Beth Shean Strata M3–M2 (Rotem 2012, pls. 4.6–7; 5.3, 6); Qiryat Ata Strata III–II (Golani 2003, fig. 4.6.7, 9); 'En Esur I Stratum II (Yannai, Lazar-Shorer, and Grosinger 2006, fig. 4.56.1–6).

Type H IIb: Holemouth with a sharpened rim
(n=46, making up 12.5 percent of the total).
The rim is thickened and sharpened at the edge (fig. 15.4.5–7).

Parallels: Qashish Strata XV–XIV (Zuckerman 2003, fig. 19.4–5); Beth Shean Strata M3–M2 (Rotem 2012, pls. 7.5–7); Qiryat Ata Strata III–II (Golani 2003, fig. 4.7.1–5); 'En Esur I Stratum II (Yannai, Lazar-Shorer, and Grosinger 2006, fig. 4.56.10–13, 15–16).

Type H III: Holemouths with a Ridged Rim
(n=1, making up 0.3 percent of the total; fig. 15.5)
In this type, a ridge is seen below the rim (fig. 15.5.1).

Parallels: Qashish Strata XV–XIV (Zuckerman 2003, fig. 19.7); Beth Shean Strata M3–M2 (Rotem 2012, pls. 6.8; 17.7); Qiryat Ata Strata III–II (Golani 2003, fig. 4.7.8–10); 'En Esur I Stratum II (Yannai, Lazar-Shorer, and Grosinger 2006, fig. 4.56.19); 'En Shadud Strata II–I (Braun 1985, fig. 21.19–20).

Type H IV: Holemouths with a Squared-off Rim
(n=15, making up 4.1 percent of the total, fig. 15.5)
In these vessels, the rim was cut into a square shape (fig. 15.5.2–5).
Parallels: Qashish Strata XV–XIV (Zuckerman 2003, fig. 19.8); Beth Shean Strata M3–M2 (Rotem 2012, pls. 5.9; 8.1); Qiryat Ata Strata III–II (Golani 2003, fig. 4.7.11–14).

Storage Jars
(Figs. 15.6–8)

Storage jars (n=58, making up 16 percent of the total) are the second most common vessel type in the assemblage—although significantly less than holemouth jars—making up 23.8 percent of the total in Area E and 11.3 percent in Area F. Two types were found in these areas, types SJ I and SJ II:

Type SJ I: Storage Jars with a Short Neck (fig. 15.6)
This jar type, with a relatively short neck, usually has a rope/thumbed decoration around the shoulder, below the neck. There are two subtypes:

Type SJ Ia: Storage jars with a short straight neck
(n=11, making up 3 percent of the total; fig. 15.6.1–3).
Parallels: Beth Shean Strata M3–M2 (Rotem 2012, pls. 11.7, 9; 24.1); Qiryat Ata Strata III–II (Golani 2003, fig. 4.12.6); 'En Esur I Stratum II (Yannai, Lazar-Shorer, and Grosinger 2006, fig. 4.58.4, 6); En Shadud Strata II–I (Braun 1985, fig. 20.10, 13).

Type SJ Ib: Storage jars with a short everted neck
(3 percent, n=11; fig. 15.6.4–6).
Parallels: Beth Shean Strata M3–M2 (Rotem 2012, pls. 11.11; 12.2–6) Qiryat Ata Strata III–II (Golani 2003, fig. 4.12.11–12); 'En Esur I Stratum II (Yannai, Lazar-Shorer, and Grosinger 2006, fig. 4.58.1–3); 'En Shadud Strata II–I (Braun 1985, fig. 20.9).

Type SJ II: Bow-rim Jars (figs. 15.7–8)
This jar, with a short or high convex neck, drooping shoulder, and an oval body, are sometimes red slipped on the outside. Some examples are also red slipped on the interior, at the neck. This type has two subtypes determined by rim shape:

Type SJ IIa: Storage jars with a simple rounded rim
(n=11, making up 3 percent of the total; figs. 15.7.1; 15.8.1–2).
Parallels: Qashish Strata XV–XIV (Zuckerman 2003, fig. 21.2); Qiryat Ata Strata III–II (Golani 2003, fig. 4.10); 'En Esur I Stratum II (Yannai 2006, fig. 4.59.2, 4); 'En Shadud Strata II–I (Braun 1985, fig. 23.10–11).

Type SJ IIb: Storage jars with a cut rim
(n=25, making up 7 percent of the total).
In this subtype, the rim is cut into a square/gutter shape, and the neck is sometimes shorter than in subtype SJ IIa (fig. 15.8.3–5).
Parallels: Qashish Strata XV–XIV (Zuckerman 2003, fig. 21.3); Qiryat Ata Strata III–II (Golani 2003, fig. 4.11); 'En Esur I Stratum II (Yannai, Lazar-Shorer, and Grosinger 2006, fig. 4.59.14).

Pithoi
(Fig. 15.8)

Type PT I: Rail-rim Pithoi (n=1)
Only one example of this vessel type, with a straight neck and a thick ring-shaped rim, was found in the assemblage. An incised decoration is visible below the rim (fig. 15.8.5).
Parallels: Beth Shean Strata M3–M2 (Rotem 2012, pls. 9.1–2); 'En Shadud Strata II–I (Braun 1985, fig. 23.3).

Handles
(n=60, making up 0.9 percent of the total; fig. 15.9)

Type HD I: Ledge Handles
(n=42, making up 0.7 percent of the total)
The ledge handle makes its first appearance in the Neolithic Yarmukian and Jericho XIII cultures. This type, found throughout the country, has five main variants (Amiran 1963, 56–60). These handles were usually used for large vessels such as storage jars, holemouth jars, and kraters, and are a well-known

indicator of the EB I. Some are red slipped; one example has an incised decoration, and another one is thumb-indented (fig. 15.9.1–2). This type makes up 1.4 percent of the Area-E assemblage and 0.8 percent of the Area-F assemblage.

Parallels: Qashish Strata XV–XIV (Zuckerman 2003, fig. 22.1–2); Beth Shean Strata M3–M2 (Rotem 2012, pls. 12.17–23); 'En Esur I, Stratum II (Yannai, Lazar-Shorer, and Grosinger 2006, fig. 4.60.28–30); 'En Shadud Strata II–I (Braun 1985, fig. 25.1–6).

Type HD II: Pierced Lug Handles (n=3)
This type, very scarce in the assemblage, was used on small vessels, for example, teapots and bowls. These handles are small, sometimes red slipped, perforated from one side to the other using a round and elongated tool (fig 15.9.5).

Parallels: Qashish Strata XV–XIV (Zuckerman 2003, fig. 22.3–4); Beth Shean Strata M3–M2 (Rotem 2012, pl. 2.10).

Type HD III: Loop Handles
(n=15, making up 0.2 percent of the total)
These handles can be found on a large variety of vessels, both large and small. Many are decorated with red slip (fig. 15.9.3–4).

Parallels: Qashish Strata XV–XIV (Zuckerman 2003, fig. 22.5–8); Beth Shean Strata M3–M2 (Rotem 2012, pl. 14.3).

Discussion

Chronology

The pottery assemblage from Areas E and F (A-5992) can be associated, with a high degree of certainty, with a late phase in the EB I, sometimes termed EB IB. Although the assemblage originates from two separate excavation areas, the lack of typological qualitative or quantitative differences indicates that they belong to the same short time span within the EB I and may also allude to a similar function.

The EB IB dating of this assemblage is based on—and strengthened by—its high similarity to other assemblages from northern Early Bronze Age settlements dated to a late phase in the EB I, such as Tel Qashish Strata XV–XIV (Zuckerman 2003), Tel Beth Shean Strata M3–M2 (Rotem 2012), Qiryat Ata Strata III–II (Golani 2003), 'En Shadud Strata II–I (Braun 1985), and 'En Esur Stratum II (Yannai, Lazar-Shorer, and Grosinger 2006).

The assemblage comprises a rather small variety of types (figs. 15.10–12), yet some are clear indicators of the EB IB in the northern valleys, such as the bow-rim storage jars (type SJ II), and, in a lower frequency, the deep bowls with conical projections (type B IIb) and the teapots. The assemblage also lacks any indicators of the previous EB IA period seen, for example, in Yiftah'el Stratum II (Braun 1997).

Production Materials and Technological Characteristics

Most vessels were made of a light-buff material with white and gray grits, a light-brown ware also being sometimes used. Some holemouths were made of a dark-brown ware perhaps similar to that of the brown holemouth type originating in the Golan Heights and identified and characterized by Mark Iserlis and Yitzhak Paz (2011). If the sherds from Qashish are indeed of the same type (see petrography, ch. 17, this volume), provenance and chronology questions are raised since the brown holemouths have been dated to the EB II, whereas only an EB IB phase was recognized in Areas E and F.

Rope decoration appears on 1 percent (n=61) of the total number of sherds in the assemblage; red slip makes up 1.2 percent (n=73), and band slip appears on 0.1 percent of the sherds (n=5). The predominance of red-slip decoration is present in other northern sites of both the EB IB and the previous EB IA.

It should be stressed that the eroded condition of the pottery assemblage, caused by its proximity to the surface, makes it difficult to recognize signs of surface treatment and thus portrays a distorted picture of the frequency and the variety of decorations.

Function

Storage vessels make up 87 percent (holemouths 71 percent; storage jars 16 percent) of the ceramic assemblage of Areas E and F, testifying to the function of these areas mainly for the storage and distribution of foodstuffs. Although holemouth jars were also used as cooking pots, this is not the case here, since their ware does not include the usual white crystalline inclusions commonly found in cooking ware, nor were there any distinguishable soot marks on the vessels.

The architectural remains from these areas further strengthen this perception. The circular structures (ch. 12, this volume), containing large restorable fragments of storage jars full of burnt wheat (ch. 23, this volume), and the open earthen floors, with no traces of relating walls, topped by column bases and a large amount of pottery (mainly holemouth jars), are best suited for the storage and dissemination of produce. The minuscule percentage of open vessels in the assemblage negates the possibility of other domestic activities.

The ceramic and architectural finds from Areas E south and F point to a communal storage and distribution area. Since such an area was not exposed on top of the actual tell, it probably served the entire settlement.

References

Amiran, Ruth
1963 *Ancient Pottery of the Holy Land: From Its Beginnings in the Neolithic Period to the End of the Iron Age*. Jerusalem: Bialik Institute; Israel Exploration Society.

Braun, Eliot
1985 *En Shadud: Salvage Excavations at a Farming Community in the Jezreel Valley, Israel*. BARIS 249. Oxford: BAR.

Esse, Douglas
1989 "Village Potters in Early Bronze Palestine: A Case Study." In *Essays in Ancient Civilization Presented to Helene J. Kantor*, edited by Albert Leonard and Bruce Williams, 77–92. SAOC 47. Chicago: Oriental Institute of the University of Chicago.

Golani, Amir
2003 *Salvage Excavations at the Early Bronze Age Site of Qiryat Ata*. IAA Reports 18. Jerusalem: Israel Antiquities Authority.

Grosman, Leore., Avshalom Karasik, Ortal Harush, and Uzy Smilansky
2014 "Archaeology in Three Dimensions: Computer-Based Methods in Archaeological Research." *Journal of Eastern Mediterranean Archaeology and Heritage Studies* 2: 48–64.

Karasik, Avshalom, and Uzy Smilansky
2011 "Computerized Morphological Classification of Ceramics." *Journal of Archeological Science* 38: 2644–57.

Iserlis, Mark, and Yitzhak Paz
2011 "Urban Cooking Pot in the Early Bronze Age II-III: A Comparative Technological Perspective." In *Eretz-Israel. Amnon Ben-Tor Volume*, edited by Y. Aviram, S. Gitin, A. Mazar, N. Neeman, S. Zuckerman, and E. Stern. Jerusalem. (Hebrew).

Rotem, Yael
2012 "The Early Bronze Age Ib Pottery from Strata M-3 and M-2." In *Excavations at Tel Beth-Shean 1989–1996: Vol. IV, The 4th and 3rd Millennia BCE*, edited by Amihai Mazar, 123–235. Jerusalem: Israel Exploration Society; Hebrew University of Jerusalem.

Yannai, Elie, Dorit Lazar-Shorer, and Zohar Grosinger
2006 "The Pottery Assemblages." In *'En Esur ('Ein Asawir) I: Excavations at a Protohistoric Site in the Coastal Plain of Israel*, edited by Elie Yannai, 63–178. IAA Reports 31. Jerusalem: Israel Antiquities Authority.

Zuckerman, Sharon
2003 "The Early Bronze Age Pottery." In *Tel Qashish: A Village in the Jezreel Valley; Final Report of the Archaeological Excavations (1978–1987)*, edited by Amnon Ben-Tor, Ruhama Bonfil, and Sharon Zuckerman, 35–56. Qedem Reports 5. Jerusalem: Hebrew University of Jerusalem.

15. Pottery from Tel Qashish Areas E South and F

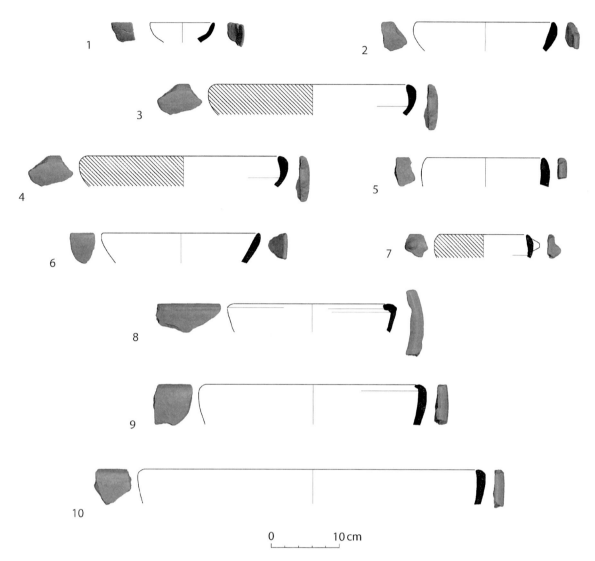

Fig. 15.1. Areas E (South) and F. Bowls and kraters.

No.	Type	Locus	Reg. No.	Description
1	B I	6013	60074-6	Light-orange material; gray grits; light-orange core. Red slip on the interior and exterior.
2	B I	6044	60309-3	Light-orange material; gray grits; light-orange core.
3	B I	6044	60333-9	Light-brown material; brown grits; light gray core. Red slip on the exterior.
4	B IIa	6011	60072-3	Orange material, orange core. Red slip on interior and exterior.
5	B IIa	5049	50385-3-10	Light-brown material; white grits; gray core.
6	B IIa	6012/14	6014-2	Brown material; white and gray grits; gray core.
7	B IIb	6013	60332-3	Light-buff material; gray grits; buff core. Protruding knob, red slip on the exterior.
8	K I	6013	60044-5	Brown material; brown core.
9	K I	5003	50121-1	Light-buff material; white grits; buff core.
10	K I	5045	50309	Light-orange material; white grits; gray core.

168 Salvage Excavations at Tel Qashish (Tell Qasis) and Tell el-Wa'er (2010–2013)

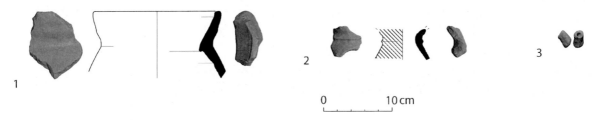

Fig. 15.2. Areas E (South) and F. Small closed vessels: gourd jars and teapots.

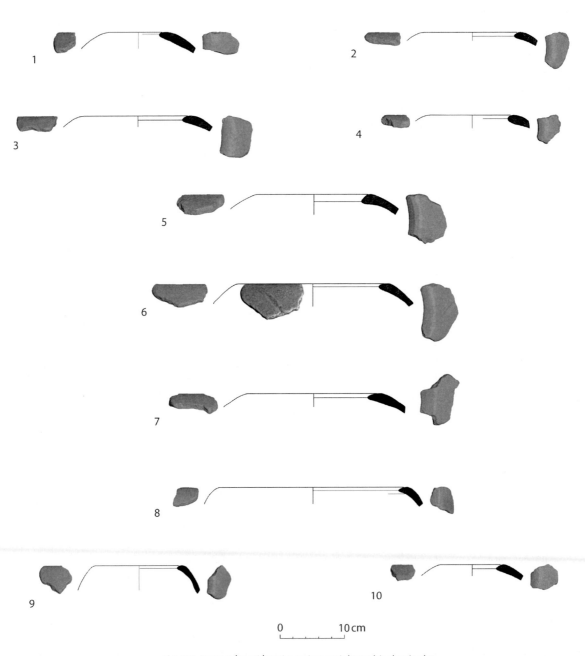

Fig. 15.3. Areas E (South) and F. Holemouth jars with simple rim.

No.	Type	Locus	Reg. No.	Description
1	GJ	6044	60333-1	Light-buff material; white grits; gray core.
2	T	6034	60260-1	Light-buff material; gray grits; buff core. Ridge on neck, red slip on the exterior.
3	T	6026	60135-5	Light-gray material; white grits; gray core. Red slipped.

No.	Type	Locus	Reg. No.	Description
1	H Ia	5003	50050-2	Light-brown-buff material; white grits; light-gray core.
2	H Ia	5048	50386-4-7b	Light-brown-buff material; white and gray grits; light-gray core
3	H Ia	6011	60062-2	Light-gray material; white grits; gray core.
4	H Ia	6013	60332-6	Light-orange material; white grits; buff core.
5	H Ib	6014	60119-1	Light-orange material; white and gray grits; gray core.
6	H Ib	6013	60332-4b	Light-buff material; white grits; buff core. Potters mark.
7	H Ib	6056	60312-11	Light-buff material; white grits; buff core.
8	H Ib	5045	50266	Orange-brown material; gray and grits; black-gray core.
9	H Ib	6044	60309-2	Light-brown material; white grits; light-gray core.
10	H Ib	5048	50386-1-4	Buff material; white and gray grits; light-gray core.

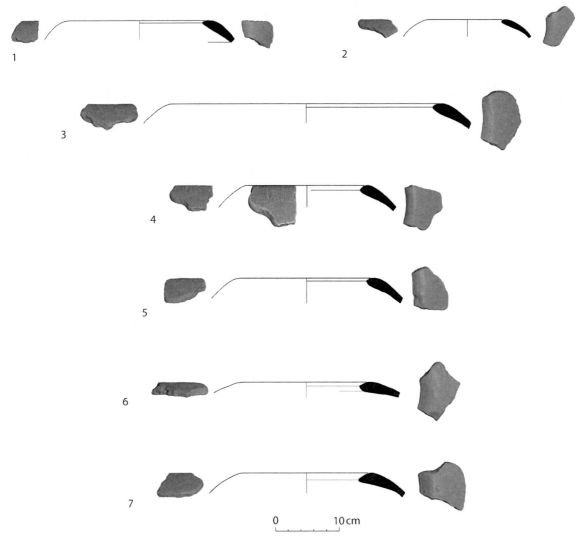

Fig. 15.4. Areas E (South) and F. Holemouth jars with thickened rim.

No.	Type	Locus	Reg. No.	Description
1	H IIa	5048	50392-8	Light-brown material; white and gray grits; gray core.
2	H IIa	5028	50188+50181-1	Gray material; white grits; light-gray core.
3	H IIa	5030	50185-1	Light-brown-buff material; white grits; buff core.
4	H IIa	5049	50385-3-5	Light-orange material; white grits; light-brown core. Potters mark.
5	H IIb	6013	60332-8	Light-buff material; white grits; buff core.
6	H IIb	6014	60251-4	Gray material; white grits; gray core.
7	H IIb	6043	60334-3	Light-buff material; white grits; light-gray core.

15. Pottery from Tel Qashish Areas E South and F

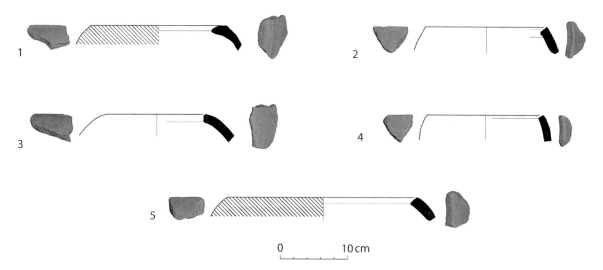

Fig. 15.5. Areas E (South) and F. Holemouth jars with ridged and squared-off rims.

No.	Type	Locus	Reg. No.	Description
1	H III	6014	60043-3	Light-buff material; gray grits; buff core. Red slip on the exterior.
2	H IV	6013	60030-1	Orange material; white and gray grits; orange core.
3	H IV	5047	50382-7	Orange material; white and gray grits; orange-brown core.
4	H IV	6033	60210-1	Light-buff material; gray grits; gray core.
5	H IV	6044	60333-8	Light-brown-buff material; brown and gray grits; light-brown core. Red slip on the exterior.

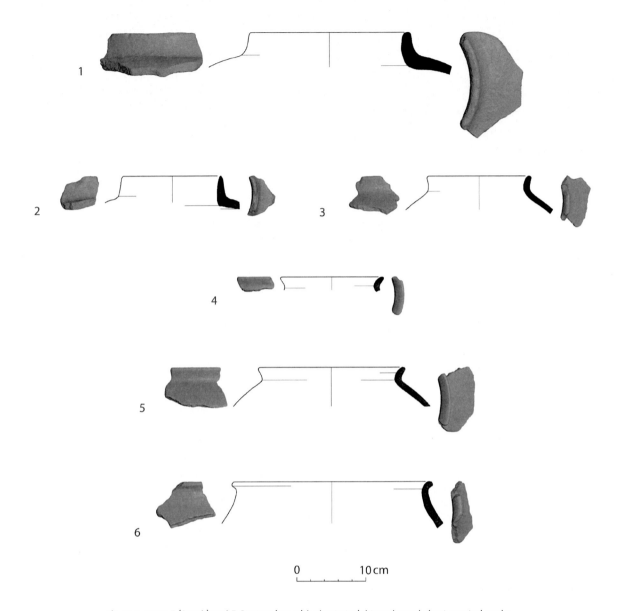

Fig. 15.6. Areas E (South) and F. Storage jars with short straight necks and short everted necks.

No.	Type	Locus	Reg. No.	Description
1	SJ Ia	5049	50385-4-1	Light-brown material; gray and white grits; gray core.
2	SJ Ia	5049	50385-3-12	Orange-brown material; white grits; orange core.
3	SJ Ia	6056	60312-13	Brown material; gray grits; light-gray core.
4	SJ Ib	6011	60062-1	Gray material; white grits; dark-gray core.
5	SJ Ib	6045	60388-1	Gray material; white grits; dark-gray core.
6	SJ Ib	6056	60312-1	Orange material; white grits; black-gray core.

15. Pottery from Tel Qashish Areas E South and F

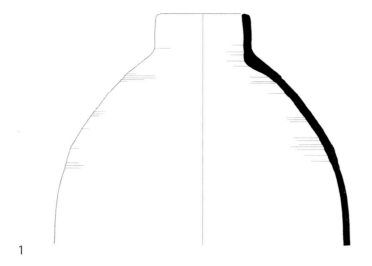

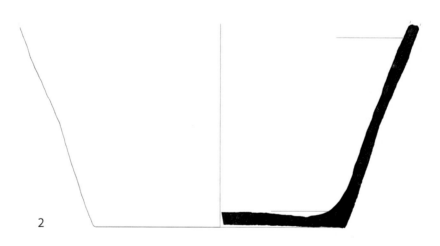

Fig. 15.7. Areas E (South) and F. Bow-rim storage jars.

No.	Type	Locus	Reg. No.	Description
1	SJ IIa	5023	50321	Light-buff material; white grits; buff core.
2	SJ Base	5050	50391-7	Light-buff material; white grits; buff core.

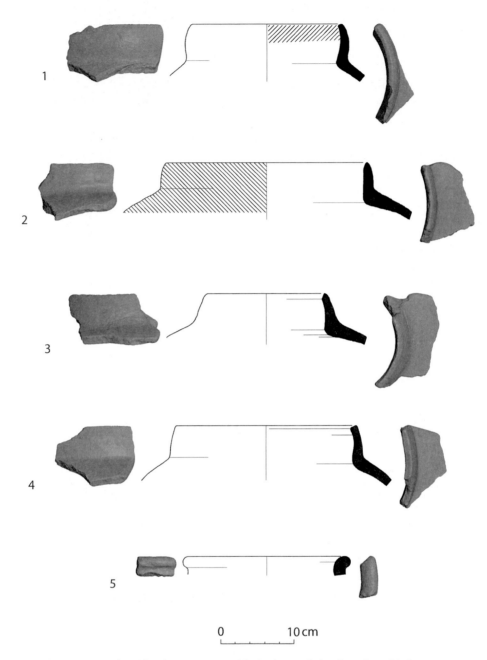

Fig. 15.8. Areas E (South) and F. Storage Jars with simple rounded and cut rims; pithoi.

No.	Type	Locus	Reg. No.	Description
1	SJ IIa	6014	60289-2	Light-buff material; white grits; buff core. Red slip on interior of rim.
2	SJ IIa	6014	60269-1	Light-buff material; white grits; buff core. Red slip on the exterior.
3	SJ IIb	6013	60074-1	Orange-buff material; white grits; light-gray core.
4	SJ IIb	6045	60311-2	Buff material; white grits; buff core.
5	PT I	6048	60283-2	Light-orange material; white and gray grits; light-gray core. Incised line below rim.

15. Pottery from Tel Qashish Areas E South and F

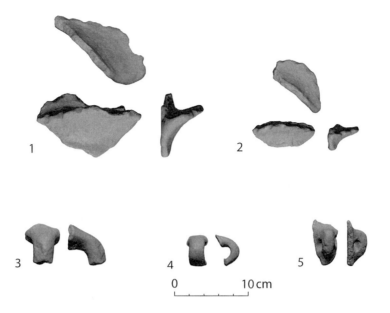

Fig. 15.9. Areas E (South) and F. Handles.

No.	Type	Locus	Reg. No.	Description
1	HD I	6013	60321-25	Orange-buff material; white grits; gray core.
2	HD I	6043	60334-2	Light-buff material; gray grits; light-gray core. Red slip on exterior.
3	HD III	6014	60073-9	Gray material; white grits; gray core.
4	HD III	6044	60333-12	Buff material; gray grits; buff core. Red slipped.
5	HD II	5047	50384-1c	Light-brown coarse material; gray grits; pink core.

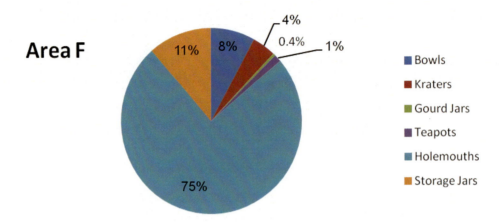

Fig. 15.10. Main vessel-type frequency in Area E (South).

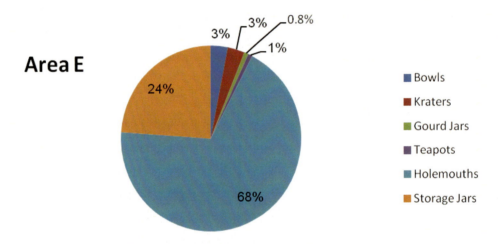

Fig. 15.11. Main vessel-type frequency in Area F.

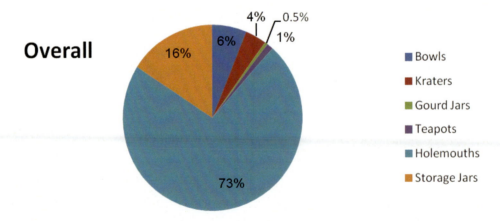

Fig. 15.12. Main vessel-type frequency for Areas E (South) and F.

Chapter 16

Pottery from Tel Qashish Area E North

Edwin C. M. van den Brink (*Israel Antiquities Authority*)

The excavations in the north part of Area E (permit A-6149)—just a few meters north of Eli Yannai's excavation (Area E South, ch. 12, this volume)—revealed substantive remains of domestic architecture (coined "the lower village," as opposed to the contemporary "upper village" remains on the tell proper, Strata XV–XIV). These yielded 30,401 potsherds, 5,580 of these diagnostics (rim, handle, base fragments, and decorated body sherds; fig. 16.1). As in Area C (ch. 14, this volume), the frequently noted application of red slip to the vessels' exterior and(or) interior surface is considered functional, not decorative. For a breakdown of the diagnostic sherds, see fig. 16.2. The flat base fragments (n=2205, making up 39.5 percent of the total diagnostics) have not been further subdivided to vessel types, and, together with the handle fragments (n=373, making up 6.7 percent of the total diagnostics) and the decorated body sherds (n=316, making up 5.7 percent of the total diagnostics) have, therefore, been excluded from the differential count of diagnostic types.

As with Area C, the most common vessel in Area E (North) is the holemouth jar (n=1742 rim fragments making up 64.8 percent of the total), distantly followed by bow-rim jars (n=816, making up 30.4 percent of the total). The remaining diagnostics (n=128, 4.8 percent) comprise various types of bowls, jugs, and necked jars other than bow-rim jars. Below follows a presentation and discussion of the pottery assemblage from this area, invariably dating from the late EB I. The typological division below follows that presented by Sharon Zuckerman (2003, 35–48) for the late EB I Tel Qashish (upper village) Strata XV–XIV.

Typology

Open Vessels

Bowls (figs. 16.3–5)
Compared to holemouths (n=1742) and bow-rim jars (n=816), rim fragments of bowls and kraters (n=75 or 2.8 percent) are few and far between in Area E (North), similarly to Area C (see ch. 14, this volume). These include both shallow and deep bowls and kraters (Zuckerman's [2003, 35, 37] types B I, B IIa, and K II, respectively) with rounded/tapering, slightly incurved rims (n=31; fig. 16.3.1–16). Bowls with sharply incurved rims, possibly heralding the platters common in the EB II, are absent in this area, in contrast to the few specimens found in Area C. Other bowl types include a few profiled, gutter-rim bowls (n=5; fig. 16.4.1–4; Zuckerman type IIb), all red-slipped and burnished outside and on the rim's interior; bowls with conoid projections (n=3; fig. 16.4.5–7; Zuckerman type B IIc), and a relatively large number of gray burnished ware bowls (n= 32; fig. 16.5.1–29; Zuckerman's type B III). Only four small bowl rim fragments were found (fig. 16.6.1–4; Zuckerman type B IV), one with soot stains (fig. 16.6.2) indicating a possible function as an oil container/lamp.

But for a single specimen of a deep GBW bowl with wide, flaring rim (fig. 16.5.1), all the sufficiently diagnostic GBW bowl fragments (that is, those fragments with at least partially preserved carinated walls) are less flaring and deep, with their sharp or sinuous carination close to the bowls' aperture (fig. 16.5.3–12). Only one GBW bowl base was found (fig. 16.5.2).

Restricted Vessels

Neckless Jars

Holemouth Jars (figs. 16.7–13)
With 1742 rim distinct fragments of holemouth jars (64.8 percent), these vessels, used both for cooking and storage, predominate the Area E (North) assemblage, as in Area C, with rounded jar bases being likewise absent. Thus, all holemouth jars can be considered flat based.

The recovered sherds are somewhat better preserved than those revealed in Area C, with less crusted surfaces, making it easier to observe whether or not a vessel was originally red slipped. Soot stains preserved on the outside of various rim fragments indicate they were part of cooking pots.

Following Zuckerman's (2003, 27, fig. 19) holemouth classification, the rims are either simple (figs. 16.7.1–4, 6–8, 12–19; 16.8.1–2, 4–12; 16.9.2, 4–9; 16.10.1–4, 6–8, 10, 12–15; 16.11.1, 4–6, 8–18, 13–14; 16.12.2, 5–7, 11, 13, 16–18; 16.13.1–3, 5–7, 9–13) or thickened (figs. 16.7.1, 9–11, 20; 16.8.3; 16.9.1, 3, 10–12; 16.10.5, 9, 11; 16.11.2–3, 7, 11–12, 15–16; 16.12.14–15; 16.13.4, 8; Zuckerman types H I and H II), each type either rounded/tapering (types H Ia and H IIa) or sharpened (types H Ib and H IIb). As with Area C, upturned rims and squared-off rims (Zuckerman types H III and H V, respectively) are notably absent, while only a few examples of plain, ridged rims (figs. 16.10.1–7; 16.12.10; Zuckerman's type H IV) have been noticed.

In addition to various rim fragments with prefiring simple incisions just below their exterior edges (fig. 16.7.5–20), several more show complex incised signs, all to be possibly understood as potters' marks (fig. 16.7.1–4). A plastic decoration, consisting of a horizontal (continuous?) strip or band of finger-indented clay applied to the exterior surface of the jars around the shoulder, is very common (n=316; fig.

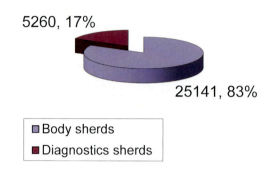

Fig. 16.1. Total number of body sherds vs. diagnostic sherds.

16.9.1–12). In one case, such decoration was applied obliquely (fig. 16.9.1) rather than horizontally, and, in another case, it was horseshoe-shaped (fig. 16.9.2).

An uncommon decoration, a ridge—rather than a horizontally applied indented strip of clay— was sometimes noted just below the rims' exterior (figs. 16.10.1–6; 16.12.10). In two cases, a prefiring continuous grove was applied (fig. 16.10.7–8). Another rare decoration method, already noted in Area C, is the application of small, finger-impressed round patches of clay, also below the rim's exterior (fig. 16.10.9, 11). Besides the two examples found in Area C (see ch. 14, this volume), three other rim fragments with a small knob applied below the rim's exterior were found (fig. 16.10.10, 12–13). In two cases, the attachment of a (now broken off) knob handle was noted (fig. 16.10.14–15). Plain holemouth rims are illustrated in figs. 16.11–13. In some cases, postfiring drilled perforations were discerned below the rim (fig. 16.12.8, 18).[1]

Only one spout fragment, notably with two opposite, postfiring drilled perforations and probably originally attached to a holemouth jar (Zuckerman type H VI), was found in Area E (North; fig. 16.13.13).

Necked Jars

Bow-rim Jars (figs. 16.14–17)
With 816 rims and diagnostic neck/shoulder fragments (30.4 percent), storage jars with a restricted

---

1. Twelve nondiagnostic body sherds show a single, postfiring drilled hole. Single or double postfiring drilled holes were further observed below the rims of two holemouth and two bow-rim jars (fig. 16.15.13).

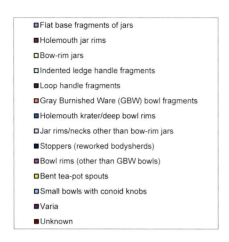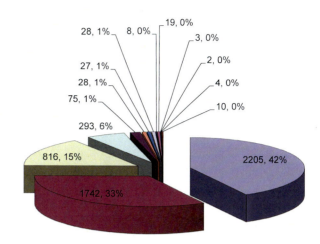

Fig. 16.2. Frequency of diagnostic potsherds.

rim/curved neck (so-called bow-rim jars; Zuckerman 2003, 38, fig. 21.2–3, type SJ II) represent, as in Area C, the second most frequent vessel type in Area E (North). Rims are rounded (figs. 16.15.11–12, 14–16; 16.16.1) or tapering (fig. 16.16.2, 4,10; Zuckerman type SJ IIa) or, more frequently, cut/trimmed (in the relevant antiplates indicated as flattened/ guttered: figs. 16.14.1–7; 16.15.1–10; 16.16.3, 5, 7–9, 11–12; Zuckerman type SJ IIb). Because of the significantly larger number of bow-rim jars found in this area, a greater variety is noticeable in jar size and neck curvature compared to Area C. Many jar fragments are red slipped on the outside, and, less frequently, on the inside of the curved neck. In rare instances, a postfiring drilled perforation was noted in the neck (fig. 16.15.13). The bases are characteristically wide and flat (fig. 16.17.1–8).

Necked Jars Other than Bow-Rim Jars (figs. 16.18–19) Only 44 (1.6 percent) rim fragments of jars other than holemouths and bow-rim jars were found in Area E (North). These include a few examples of relatively small vessels like amphoriskoi (fig. 16.18.1–5; Zuckerman 2003, 38, gourd jars, types GJ); a single high loop-handled vessel (fig. 16.18.6); three spouts of distinct teapots (fig. 16.18.7–9; Zuckerman type T); and a miniature juglet (fig. 16.18.10). The bases are flat (fig. 16.19.1–9). Rim fragments belonging to both medium-sized and large vessels, either short-necked or tall-necked (figs. 16.18: 11–27, 16.19: 10–18; Zuckerman's [2003, 38] types NJ, SJ I, and SJ III), are frequently red-slipped on the outside, and sometimes also on the neck's inside.

Handles (Figure 16.20)

The indented ledge handle (n=293; fig. 16.20.1–10) is the most frequent handle type in Area E (North), as in Area C, while loop handles (n=75; fig. 16.20.12–13) are much less frequent. Small strap handles were attached to amphoriskoi (fig. 16.19.1–5).

Almost all ledge handles, frequently red slipped, are rather large and undoubtedly belong to large holemouth cooking pots, and holemouth and necked storage jars.

One indented ledge handle shows prefiring circular impressions applied in a single row (fig. 16.20.11), similar to the examples found in Areas B (fig. 14.3.6, 9) and C (fig. 14.12.7). A small, singular indented ledge handle attached near the flat base of a small vessel (fig. 16.20.2) is unique to the site. A single, large loop handle shows prefiring incisions (fig. 16.20.13).

References

Zuckerman, Sharon
2003 "The Early Bronze Age Pottery." In *Tel Qashish: A Village in the Jezreel Valley; Final Report of the Archaeological Excavations (1978–1987)*, edited by Amnon Ben-Tor, Ruhama Bonfil, and Sharon Zuckerman, 35–56. Qedem Reports 5. Jerusalem: Hebrew University of Jerusalem.

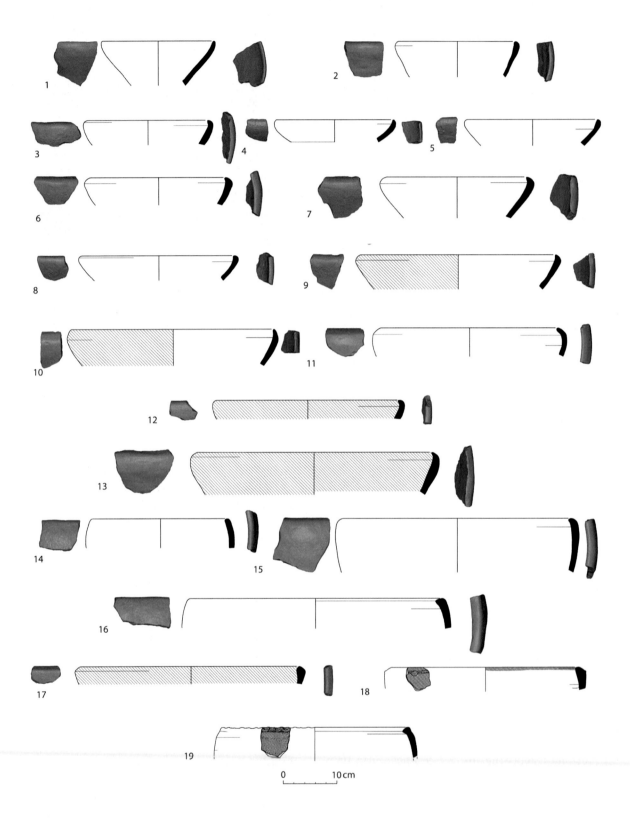

Fig. 16.3. Area E North. Bowls and kraters.

No.	Vessel	Locus	Basket	Description
1	Bowl	5113	50549	Slightly incurved, tapering rim/wall fragment. Plain, buff-orange surface; light gray core, buff-orange oxidation zones; many white angular grits.
2	Bowl	5078	50600	Thickened rim/wall fragment. Possible traces of red slip inside; thin gray core, thick buff-orange oxidation zones; white grits.
3	Bowl	5135	50652	Tapering, incurved rim/wall fragment. Plain, buff-orange surface; gray core, buff-orange oxidation zones; small and coarse white grits.
4	Bowl	5136	50638	Tapering, incurved rim/wall fragment. Plain, orange surface; thin, light brown core; orange oxidation zones; many white grits.
5	Bowl	5102	50650	Tapering, incurved rim/wall. Plain buff-orange surface; grayish-light brown core, buff-orange oxidation zones; many small white grits.
6	Bowl	5115	50598	Incurved rim/wall fragment. Plain, buff-orange surface; thin, gray core, buff-orange oxidation zones; white grits, some coarse; fired at high temperature.
7	Large bowl	5076	50520	Tapering, incurved rim/wall fragment. Plain, buff-orange surface; thick buff-orange core, orange oxidation zones; small white grits.
8	Bowl	5065	50505.2	Rounded rim/wall fragment. Plain, buff-orange surface; light brown core with only one, exterior, buff-orange oxidation zone; few white and dark grits; few glimmers.
9	Bowl	5064	50566	Tapering, incurved rim/wall fragment. Red-slipped outside; thick, light brown core; buff-orange oxidation zones; few small gray grits; few glimmers.
10	Bowl	5066	50499	Tapering, incurved rim/wall fragment. Traces of red slip outside; light-brown/buff orange core; orange oxidation zones.
11	Bowl	5066	50431	Rounded, incurved rim/wall fragment. Plain, buff-orange surface; gray core, buff-orange oxidation zones; small and few coarse white grits.
12	Bowl	5080	50569	Tapering, incurved rim/wall fragment. Red slipped inside and outside; buff-orange core throughout; gray and white grits; few glimmers.
13	Large bowl	5109	50623	Tapering, incurved rim/wall fragment. Red-slipped inside and outside; thick gray core; buff-orange oxidation zones; many small and few very coarse white grits.
14	Deep, restricted bowl/krater	5059	50483	Rounded rim/wall. Plain buff-orange surface; buff-orange core all through; small and coarse white grits.
15	Deep, large bowl	5138	50681	Rim/wall fragment. Possible traces of slip outside; thick gray core; brown oxidation zones.
16	Thick-walled, deep bowl/krater	5059	–	Rim/wall fragment. Buff-orange, plain surface; gray core; buff-orange oxidation zones; few white grits; fired at high temperature.
17	Deep bowl/krater	5099	50516	Obliquely flattened rim/wall fragment. Red-slipped outside and inside; grayish core, buff-orange oxidation zones; gray, and fewer white grits; few glimmers.
18	Thick-walled, deep bowl/krater	5065	50434.14	Indented rim/wall fragment. Traces of red slip/paint outside, and on inside of the rim; light brown surface and core; small and coarse dark grits.
19	Deep bowl/krater	5026	50680	Flattened, indented rim/wall fragment. Traces of red slip outside; orange core throughout; small and coarse white grits.

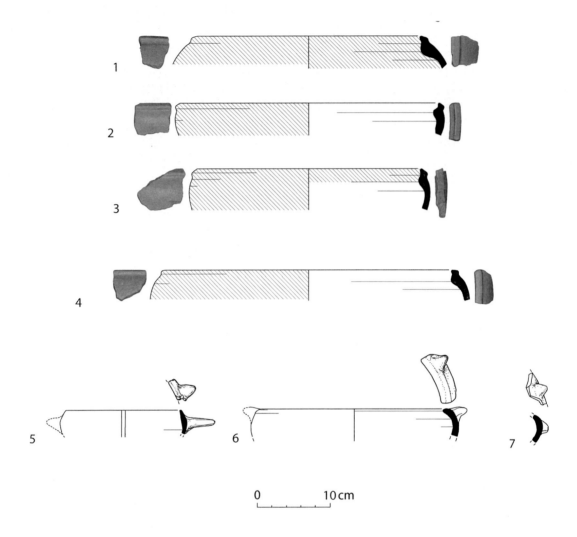

Fig. 16.4. Area E North. Red-slipped bowls or kraters with profiled rim, and small knobbed bowls.

No.	Vessel	Locus	Basket	Description
1	Deep bowl/krater	5126	50712	Profiled rim/wall fragment. Red-slipped outside, and on inside of the rim; buff-orange core (wall) throughout; gray core in rim area, with buff-orange oxidation zones.
2	Large bowl/krater	5065	50477	Profiled rim/wall, densely red-slipped fragment. Densely red-slipped exterior and inside of the rim; buff-orange surface; grayish core; buff-orange oxidation zones; many small gray grits.
3	Large bowl/krater	5026	50680	Profiled rim/wall fragment. Burnished red slip outside and on inside of the rim; thin gray core, thick buff-orange oxidation zones; small dark inclusions.
4	Large bowl/krater	5059	50413.11	Profiled rim/wall fragment. Red slip/paint on exterior rim and wall; buff-orange surface; thick gray core; thin, buff-orange oxidation zones; few white grits.
5	Smallish bowl	5084	50532	Tapering rim/conical knob/wall fragment. Gray core throughout; small gray grits (fabric similar to that of the GBW bowls).
6	Small-knobbed bowl	5097	50591	Tapering rim, conical knob, wall fragment. Traces of red slip [sic] outside; gray core; grayish oxidation zones; small gray grits.
7	Knobbed bowl	5146	50689	Wall fragment. Eroded body sherd; buff-orange core, with only one, exterior, light-brown oxidation zone.

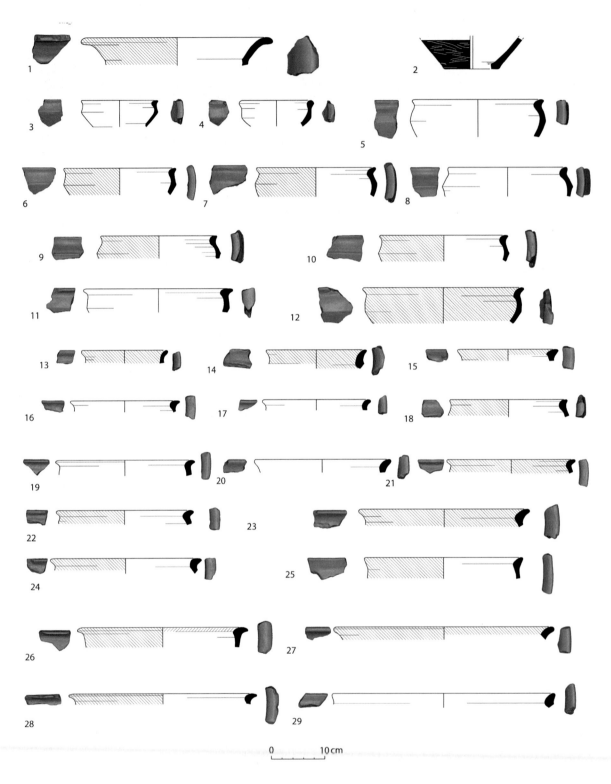

Fig. 16.5. Area E North. Gray burnished ware bowls.

No.	Vessel	Locus	Basket	Description
1	Bowl	5093	50576	Rounded, everted rim/flaring neck fragment of a large GBW bowl. Fragment is preserved until the very beginning of the carination; traces of slip outside; gray core throughout; some white grits, very few gray grits.
2	Bowl	5102	50622	Flat base/wall fragment of a deep GBW bowl. Gray-slipped and burnished exterior; interior left plain; thick, gray core with buff-orange oxidation zones; few white grits.
3	Bowl	5136	50638	Rim/wall fragment of GBW bowl. Traces of red [sic] slip outside and inside; gray core throughout; few white grits; pores of burnt-out (organic?) material; some glimmers.
4	Bowl	5109	50623	Rim/carinated wall fragment of small GBW bowl. Crusted surface; grayish-brown core throughout; few small white and gray grits.
5	Bowl	5059	50460	Everted rim/carinated wall fragment of GBW bowl. Traces of grayish slip outside; thick gray core; very thin, light brown oxidation zones; few white and still fewer gray inclusion.
6	Bowl	5066	50471	Rim/carinated wall fragment of GBW bowl. Traces of cream-white slip outside; buff-orange core, grayish oxidation zones; small gray grits.
7	Bowl	5135	50683	Rim/carinated wall fragment of GBW bowl. Traces of slip outside; gray core throughout; few white grits.
8	Bowl	5059	50483	Everted rim/carinated wall fragment of GBW bowl. No traces of slip remained; grayish-light brown surface; gray core all through; small gray grits.
9	Bowl	5059	50439	Everted rim/carinated wall fragment of GBW bowl. Traces of grayish slip outside and on inside of the rim; small gray grits.
10	Bowl	5059	50439	Everted rim/carinated wall fragment of GBW bowl. Slipped, and horizontally burnished exterior, and inside of rim; gray core; buff-orange oxidation zones; small, gray grits.
11	Bowl	5080	50514	Rim/carinated wall fragment of GBW bowl. Traces of slip preserved outside; gray core throughout; small gray grits.
12	Bowl	5109	50623	Rim/carinated wall fragment of GBW bowl. Traces of slip inside and outside; gray core throughout; small gray grits.
13	Bowl	5147	50692	Rim/wall fragment of GBW bowl. Traces of slip inside and outside; gray core throughout; very few white grits.
14	Bowl	5136	50638	Rim/wall fragment of GBW bowl. Traces of red [sic] slip outside and inside; gray core throughout; few white grits; pores of burnt-out organic material; some glimmers.
15	Bowl	5058	50447	Rim/wall fragment of GBW bowl. Joint rim/neck on inside of the bowl is irregular, that is, not smoothed; traces of slip outside and on the rim; gray core throughout; few small white and gray grits.
16	Bowl	5138	50681	Rim fragment of GBW bowl. Plain, gray surface; gray core throughout; white grits.
17	Bowl	5066	50666	Rim fragment of GBW bowl. Traces of grayish slip outside; light brown core throughout; small gray grits.
18	Bowl	5059	50439	Everted rim/wall fragment of GBW bowl. Traces of grayish slip; buff-orange surface; small, gray grits.
19	Bowl	5066	50527	Rim/wall fragment of GBW bowl. Grayish surface; gray core throughout; some white grits; some glimmers.
20	Bowl	5071	50620	Rim/wall fragment of GBW bowl. Grayish surface; gray core throughout; few small white grits; few small dark (organic?) inclusions.

continued on p. 187

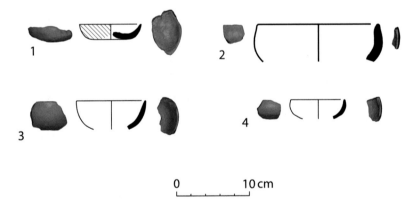

Fig. 16.6. Area E North. Small bowls.

No.	Vessel	Locus	Basket	Description
21	Bowl	5150	50688	Rim/wall fragment of GBW bowl. Traces of slip inside and outside; darkish gray core, lighter gray oxidation zones; small gray grits.
22	Bowl	5071	50521	Rim/wall fragment of GBW bowl. Traces of gray slip; gray core with few, small white grits and some dark (organic) inclusions.
23	Bowl	5137	50646	Rim/wall fragment of GBW bowl. Traces of slip inside and outside; gray core throughout; few white grits; few glimmers.
24	Bowl	5142	50691	Rim/wall fragment of GBW bowl. Traces of slip outside; thin gray core; brown oxidation zones; many small gray grits, very few white grits.
25	Bowl	5066	50450.5	Rim/wall fragment of GBW bowl. Traces of slip outside; gray surface; gray core throughout; small gray grits.
26	Bowl	5078	50523	Rim/wall fragment of GBW bowl. Traces of slip outside; thick gray core; very thin-buff-orange oxidation zones; small and coarse white grits.
27	Bowl	5074	50508.7	Rim fragment of GBW bowl. Traces of dark slip outside and inside; brown-grayish core; small white and coarse gray grits.
28	Bowl	5109	50642	Rim fragment of GBW bowl. Traces of slip outside; gray core throughout; few glimmers.
29	Bowl	5078	50548	Rim fragment of GBW bowl. Grayish core throughout; small gray grits.

No.	Vessel	Locus	Basket	Description
1	Very small bowl/cup	5107	–	Tapering rim/wall fragment. Plain, buff-orange surface; buff-orange core throughout; very few, small white grits.
2	Very small hemispheric bowl	5066	–	Tapering rim/wall fragment. Traces of red slip outside; soot traces outside on base; grayish core (secondary?) throughout; some glimmers.
3	Very small hemispheric bowl	5066	50450	Tapering rim/wall fragment. Light brown surface; traces of red slip inside; light brown core throughout; small gray grits.
4	Small hemispherical bowl/cup	5126	50712	Tapering rim/wall fragment. Possible traces of red-slip outside; orange core throughout; very few white grits.

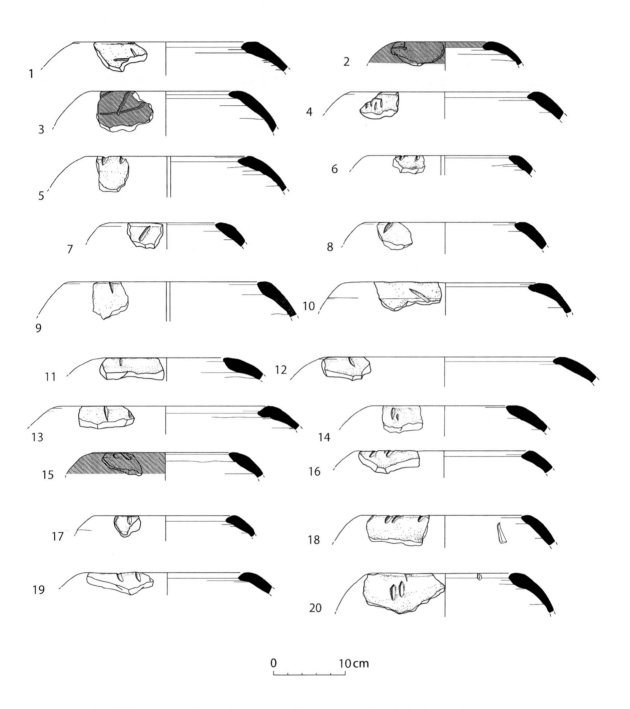

Fig. 16.7. Area E North. Holemouth jars and cooking jars with prefiring incised potmarks and slashes.

16. Pottery from Tel Qashish Area E North

No.	Vesssel	Locus	Basket	Description
1	Holemouth jar	5080	50488	Simple rim/potmark incised wall fragment. Prefiring incised incompletely preserved potmark below the rim's exterior; plain, buff-orange surface; thick gray core; thin buff-orange oxidation zones; many white coarse grits.
2	Holemouth jar	5059	50460	Tapering rim/incised mark on wall fragment. Traces of slip outside; buff-orange surface; light brown core; buff-orange oxidation zones; small and coarse white grits.
3	Holemouth jar	5136	50638	Tapering rim/prefiring incised wall fragment. Traces of red slip outside; thick, light brown core; thin buff-orange oxidation zones; small white grits, few coarse ones.
4	Thick-walled holemouth jar	5065	50442	Rim/wall fragment with prefiring incised potmark. Buff-orange surface; small and coarse white grits.
5	Holemouth cooking jar	5113	50601	Tapering, thickened rim/prefiring incised wall fragment. Soot stains outside; plain buff-orange surface; dark brown-reddish core, with (secondary) gray exterior oxidation zone; many small white grits.
6	Holemouth jar	5059	50460	Tapering rim/incised mark on wall fragment. Plain brown-orange surface; brown-orange core all through; very small white grits.
7	Holemouth jar	5107	50616	Tapering rim/prefiring incised wall fragment. Soot stains inside and outside; gray core throughout (secondary?); many white grits, some coarse.
8	Holemouth jar	5070	50550	Tapering rim/prefiring incised wall fragment. Obliquely incised slash below rim outside; Plain, buff-orange surface; thick gray core; buff-orange oxidation zones, white grits, some very coarse.
9	Holemouth jar	5114	50553	Thickened rim/prefiring incised wall fragment. Traces of slip outside; gray core; brownish oxidation zones; many small white grits.
10	Holemouth jar	5080	50587	Thickened rim/prefiring incised wall fragment. Traces of red slip outside; prefiring, incompletely preserved incision below the rim's exterior.
11	Holemouth jar	5088	50510	Tapering, thickened rim/prefiring incised wall fragment. Prefiring incised, vertical slash below rim's exterior; plain surface; orange core throughout; small and coarse white and gray grits; some glimmers.
12	Holemouth jar	5066	50471	Tapering rim/incised wall fragment. Plain, buff-orange surface; orange core throughout; small white grits.
13	Holemouth jar	5066	50499.4	Tapering, incurved rim/incised wall fragment. Plain, buff-orange surface; thin, light brown core, buff-orange oxidation zones.
14	Holemouth jar	5074	50459	Tapering rim/prefiring incised wall fragment. Prefiring incised vertical slash below rim's exterior.
15	Holemouth jar	5146	50689	Tapering rim/prefiring incised wall fragment. Traces of red slip outside; thick gray core, with very thin buff-orange oxidation zones; small and coarse white grits.
16	Holemouth jar	5066	50471.2	Rim/wall fragment with incisions near the rim. Plain, buff-orange surface; thick, gray core; buff-orange oxidation zones; coarse white grits; many glimmers; some pores of burnt-out organic inclusions.
17	Holemouth jar	5120	50602	Tapering rim/prefiring incised wall fragment. Plain, buff-orange exterior surface; gray core with only one, exterior, buff-orange oxidation zone; few white grits, some coarse.
18	Holemouth jar	5068	50430	Tapering rim/prefiring incised wall fragment. Plain, buff-orange surface; orange core throughout; small white and gray grits; some glimmers.
19	Holemouth jar	5107	50544	Tapering rim/prefiring incised wall fragment. Plain, buff-orange surface; thick, gray core, thin inner, and thicker exterior, buff-orange oxidation zones; many white grits; few glimmers.
20	Holemouth jar	5132	50625	Tapering, thickened rim/prefiring incised wall fragment. Plain, buff-orange surface; thick, light brown core, very thin, buff-orange oxidation zones; small and coarse white grits.

190 Salvage Excavations at Tel Qashish (Tell Qasis) and Tell el-Wa'er (2010–2013)

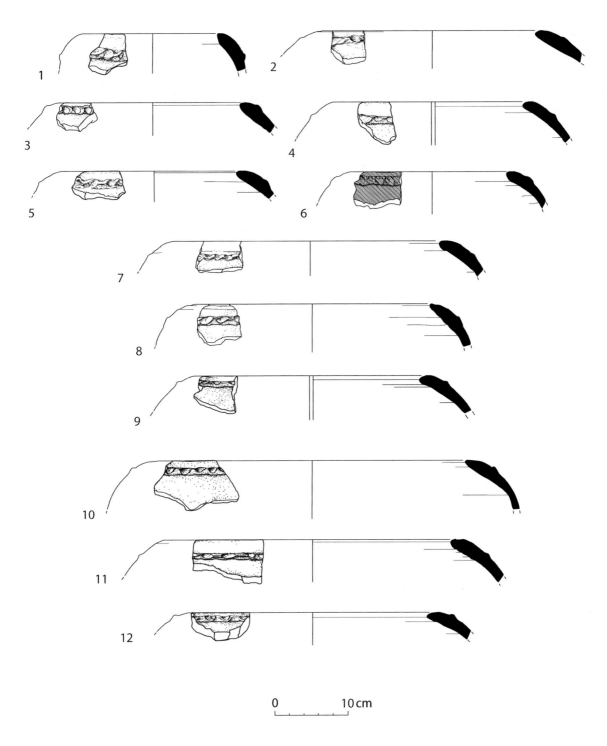

Fig. 16.8. Area E North. Holemouth jars with applied rope decoration below rim's exterior.

No.	Vessel	Locus	Basket	Description
1	Jar	5123	50605	Tapering rim/rope-decorated wall fragment. Traces of red slip outside; light gray core with only one, exterior light brown oxidation zone; many small and coarse white grits.
2	Jar	5051	50448	Tapering rim/rope-decorated wall fragment. Possible traces of red slip outside; thin, light brown core, buff-orange and light brown oxidation zones; small white grits.
3	Jar	5152	50717	Tapering, thickened rim/rope-decorated wall fragment. Plain surface; buff-orange core throughout; many white grits.
4	Jar	5056	50548	Tapering rim/rope-decorated wall fragment. Traces of red slip; thin, light brown core, buff-orange oxidation zones; small and few coarse white grits.
5	Jar	5136	50638	Tapering rim/rope-decorated wall fragment. Plain, buff-orange surface; thin gray core, with alternating light brown and buff-orange oxidation zones; many small white grits.
6	Jar	5078	50552	Tapering rim/rope-decorated wall fragment. Traces of red slip outside; gray core; buff-orange oxidation zones; many small, fewer coarse white grits.
7	Jar	5006	50678	Tapering rim/rope-decorated wall fragment. Plain, buff-orange surface; gray core; light brown and buff-orange oxidation zones; small and few coarse white grits; some glimmers.
8	Jar	5055	50443.6	Tapering rim/rope-decorated wall fragment. Plain, buff-orange surface; Light brown core; buff-orange oxidation zones; small and coarse white grits.
9	Jar	5126	50678	Tapering rim/rope-decorated wall fragment. Grayish core, buff-orange oxidation zones; few white grits; some glimmers.
10	Jar	5066	50499	Tapering rim/rope-decorated wall fragment. Plain, buff-orange surface; buff-orange core throughout; many small and coarse white grits.
11	Jar	5136	50648	Tapering rim/rope-decorated wall fragment. Plain, buff-orange surface; gray core, buff-orange oxidation zones; many small and coarse, angular white grits.
12	Jar	5126	50719	Tapering rim/rope-decorated wall fragment. Plain, light-brown surface; light-brown core throughout; some white grits.

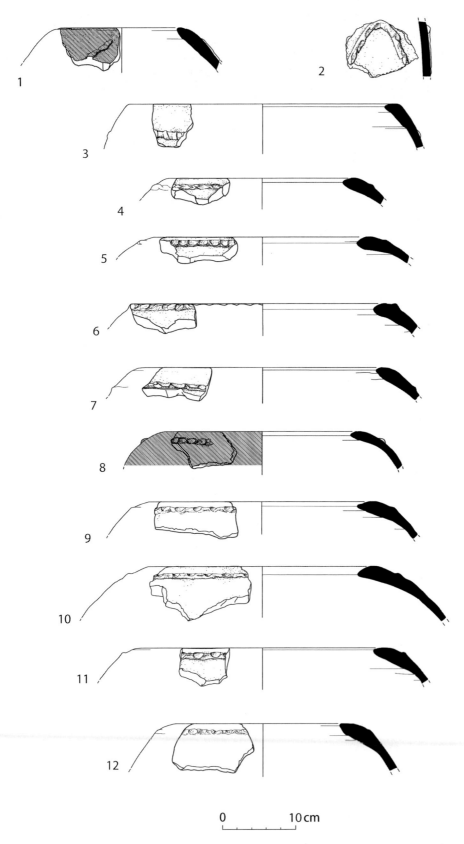

Fig. 16.9. Area E North. Holemouth jars with applied rope decoration below rim's exterior (cont.)

16. Pottery from Tel Qashish Area E North

No.	Vessel	Locus	Basket	Description
1	Jar	5066	50431	Thickened, tapering rim/rope-decorated wall. Traces of red slip outside; diagonal applied rope decoration on exterior; many white grits.
2	Jar	5126	50619	Wall fragment with applied horse-shoe shaped, indented rope decoration. Possible traces of red slip outside.
3	Jar	5080	50541	Thickened rim/rope-decorated wall fragment. Plain buff-orange surface; buff-orange core throughout; many small white grits.
4	Jar	5106	50540	Thickened rim/rope-decorated wall fragment. Plain, buff-orange surface; orange core throughout; many white angular grits; fired at high temperature.
5	Jar	5127	50610	Thickened rim/rope-decorated wall fragment. Possible traces of red slip outside; thick gray core, buff-orange oxidation zones; many small white grits, few are coarse.
6	Jar	5106	50540	Tapering rim/rope-decorated wall fragment. Plain, buff-orange surface; orange core throughout; many white angular grits.
7	Jar	5114	50553	Tapering rim/rope-decorated wall fragment. Plain, buff-orange surface; light brown core; buff-orange oxidation zones; many white grits, few are coarse.
8	Jar	5132	50615	Tapering rim/rope-decorated wall fragment. Red-slipped outside; orange core throughout; white grits, some coarse.
9	Jar	5088	50510	Tapering rim/rope-decorated wall fragment. Plain, light brown surface; (buff-)orange core throughout, white grits, mainly coarse.
10	Jar	5059	50460	Thickened, tapering rim/applied rope-decorated wall fragment. Plain buff-orange surface; buff-orange-light brown core; small and coarse white grits.
11	Jar	5075	50455.2	Tapering thickened rim/rope-decorated wall fragment. Plain, buff-orange surface; wall: buff-orange core throughout; light brown core, buff-orange oxidation zones.
12	Jar	5127	50610	Tapering thickened rim/rope-decorated wall fragment. Crusted surface; gray core, alternating light brown and buff-orange oxidation zones; small white grits, few are coarse.

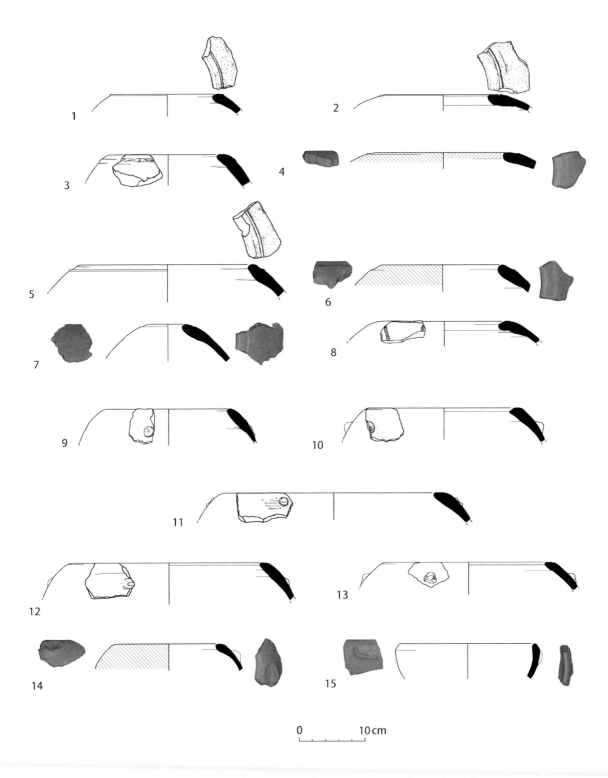

Fig. 16.10. Area E North. Holemouth jars with continuous ridge below rim's exterior.

No.	Vessel	Locus	Basket	Description
1	Jar	5149	50689	Rim/ridged wall fragment. Dark brown surface; dark gray core; reddish-brown oxidation zones; many small, fewer coarse white grits; rather gritty fabric.
2	Jar	5121	50653	Tapering rim/ridged wall. Dark brown surface; gray core, buff-orange oxidation zones; coarse white grits; some glimmers.
3	Jar	5088	50538	Tapering rim/ridged wall fragment. Possible traces of slip outside; light brown core; buff-orange oxidation zones; white and few gray grits; many glimmers.
4	Jar	5121	50670	Rim/ridged wall fragment. Red-slipped outside and on inside of the rim; thick, gray core, thin buff-orange oxidation zones; white grits and dark (organic?) inclusions.
5	Jar	5101	50659	Thickened rim/ridged wall fragment. Slipped outside; soot stains outside; gray core throughout (secondary?); few white, still fewer gray grits; some glimmers.
6	Jar	5135	50635	Rounded rim, slightly ridged wall fragment. Red-slipped outside; thick, light brown core; buff-orange oxidation zones; small and few coarse white grits.
7	Jar	5071	50595	Tapering rim/ridged wall fragment. The internal rim/wall interface has not been smoothed; plain buff-orange surface; buff-orange core throughout; small and very few coarse white grits.
8	Jar	5130	50634	Tapering rim/incised "negative ledge" wall fragment. Plain, buff-orange surface; thick gray core, thin, buff-orange oxidation zones; white grits.
9	Jar	5059	50439	Thin-walled. Thickened, tapering rim/wall fragment with applied round clay patch. Plain, buff-orange surface; orange core; buff-orange oxidation zones; coarse white grits.
10	Jar	5155	50667	Tapering rim/knobbed wall fragment. Plain, buff-orange surface; thick, light brown core, thin buff-orange oxidation zones; few white grits; few dark inclusions.
11	Jar	5093	50584	Tapering, thickened rim/decorated wall fragment. Applied, finger-impressed round patch of clay just below the rim's exterior; horizontal, parallel striations visible around the rim outside (wheel toolmarks); thick light brown core, thin buff-orange oxidation zones; small, angular white grits.
12	Jar	5136	50703	Tapering rim/knobbed wall fragment. Traces of red slip outside; small knob below rim; thick gray-light brown core, buff-orange oxidation zones; white grits.
13	Jar	5071	50595	Tapering rim/knobbed wall fragment. Traces of red slip outside.
14	Jar	5080	50514	Tapering rim, wall with loop handle attachment. Traces of red slip outside.
15	Jar	5026	50680	Rounded rim/loop-handled wall fragment. Traces of slip outside; attachment of large loop handle just below the rim outside; gray core throughout; small gray grits (fabric looks similar to that of the GBW bowls).

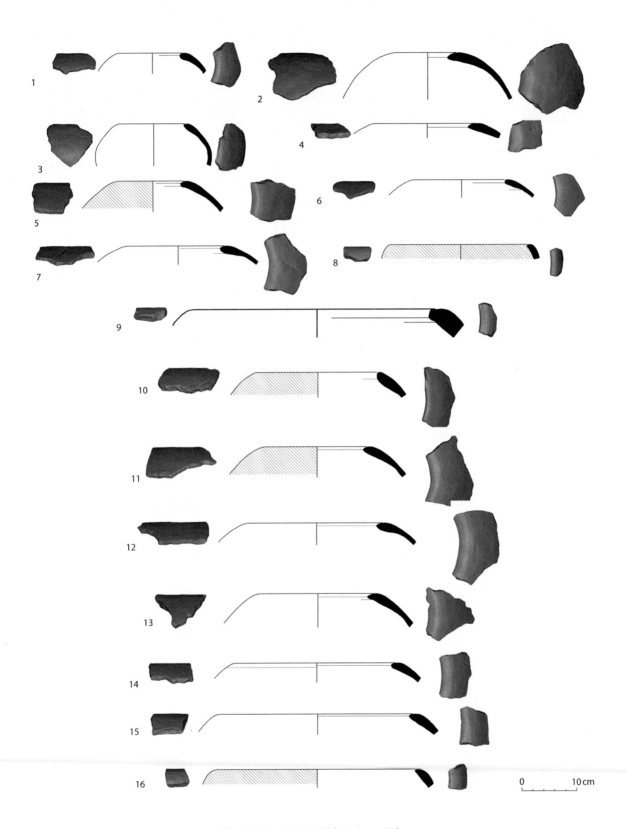

Fig. 16.11. Area E North. Plain holemouth jars.

No.	Vessel	Locus	Basket	Description
1	Jar	5051	50448	Rim/wall fragment. Possible traces of red slip outside; orange core throughout; small white grits.
2	Jar	5113	50549	Tapering, thickened rim/wall fragment. Plain, buff-orange surface; light brown-buff orange core throughout; many small, angular grits.
3	Jar	5066	50678	Tapering, slightly thickened rim/wall fragment. Plain, buff-orange surface thick gray core, thin, buff-orange oxidation zones; small white grits.
4	Jar	5059	50413.10	Thin-walled. Tapering rim/wall fragment. Plain, buff-orange surface; three finger(?) impressions visible on exterior thin, gray core; small white grits.
5	Jar	5135	50652	Slightly flattened rim/wall fragment. Traces of red slip outside; gray core, buff-orange oxidation zones; few white grits.
6	Jar	5114	50606	Thin-walled. Rounded rim/wall. Plain, buff-orange surface; gray core (rim), buff-orange oxidation zones.
7	Jar	5055	50493	Tapering, thickened rim/wall fragment. Plain buff-orange–light brown surface; light brown core throughout; small white grits.
8	Jar	5080	50514	Tapering rim/wall fragment. Traces of red slip outside and [sic] inside; buff-orange core throughout; gray grits; few glimmers.
9	Jar	5135	50652	Guttered rim/wall fragment. Plain, buff-orange surface; thin, gray core, thick orange oxidation zones; small gray, fewer white grits; some glimmers.
10	Jar	5121	50670	Thick-walled. Rim/wall fragment. Light brown-buff orange core; coarse white and gray grits; some glimmers.
11	Jar	5138	50681	Tapering, thickened rim/wall fragment. Traces of red slip outside; gray core in rim area with buff-orange oxidation zones; wall's core buff-orange throughout.
12	Jar	5138	50681	Tapering, thickened rim/wall fragment. Crusted surface; thick, grayish core, thin buff-orange oxidation zones; small and coarse white, angular grits.
13	Jar	5123	50605	Tapering rim/wall fragment. Plain, orange surface; light brown core, buff-orange oxidation zones; white grits, few are coarse.
14	Jar	5071	50595	Tapering rim/wall fragment. Plain, buff-orange surface; gray core, buff-orange oxidation zones; many small and coarse white grits.
15	Jar	5135	50683	Tapering, slightly thickened rim/wall fragment. Plain, buff-orange surface; gray-brownish core, buff-orange oxidation zones; many white, small and coarse, angular grits.
16	Jar	5138	50681	Tapering, thickened rim/wall fragment. Red slip outside; gray-brownish core, thick exterior, thin interior buff-orange oxidation zones; many small and coarse white grits.

198 Salvage Excavations at Tel Qashish (Tell Qasis) and Tell el-Wa'er (2010–2013)

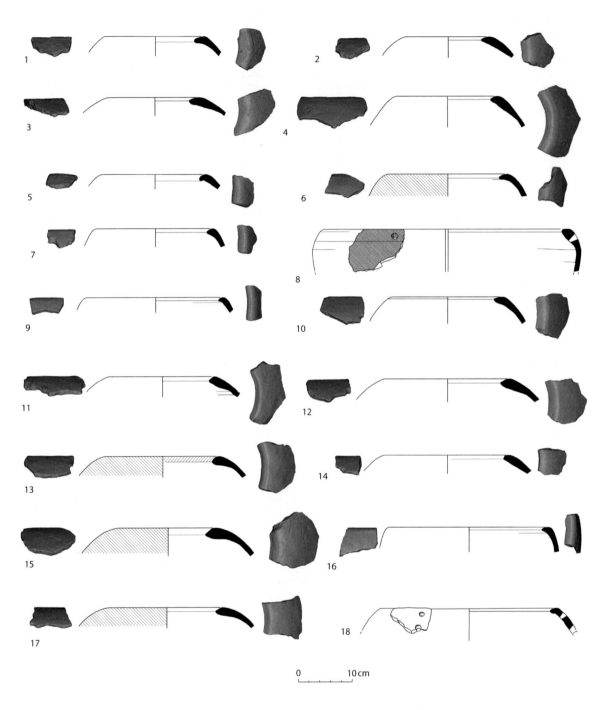

Fig. 16.12. Area E North. Plain holemouth jars, flattened rim.

16. Pottery from Tel Qashish Area E North

No.	Vessel	Locus	Basket	Description
1	Jar	5066	50450	Thickened, tapering rim/wall fragment. Plain buff-orange surface; buff-orange core throughout; small white grits; some glimmers; tool marks visible on the inside.
2	Jar	5136	50703	Rim/wall fragment. Crusted surface; thin gray core, thick buff-orange oxidation zones; small and coarse white grits.
3	Jar	5059	50439	Thin-walled. Thickened, tapering rim/wall fragment. Plain, buff-orange surface; gray core; buff-orange oxidation zones; coarse white grits.
4	Jar	5102	50533	Tapering, thickened rim/wall fragment. Plain, buff-orange surface; thin, grayish core, buff-orange oxidation zones; fired at high temperature.
5	Jar	5071	50521	Small jar. Folded rim/neck fragment. Buff-orange core throughout; very few, small white grits.
6	Jar	5132	50615	Tapering rim/wall fragment. Traces of red slip outside; light brown-buff orange core throughout; few white grits; fired at high temperature.
7	Jar	5142	50691	Tapering rim/wall fragment. Plain, buff-orange surface; thin, light brown core, orange oxidation zones; small and coarse white grits.
8	Jar	5074	50459	Thickened rim/wall fragment. Postfiring drilled hole (from outside inward); traces of red slip outside; buff-orange core throughout; few small, fewer coarse white grits.
9	Jar	5078	50600	Rim/wall fragment. Traces of soot outside; gray core (secondary?) throughout; small and few coarse white grits.
10	Jar	5071	50595	Tapering rim/ridged wall fragment. The internal rim/wall interface has not been smoothed; plain buff-orange surface; buff-orange core throughout; small and very few coarse white grits.
11	Jar	5097	50542	Slightly guttered rim/wall fragment. Soot stains outside; thick gray core, thin buff-orange oxidation zones; small and coarse white grits; few gray grits.
12	Jar	5074	50536	Thickened rim/wall fragment. Plain, buff-orange surface; light brown-buff-orange core throughout; small white grits.
13	Jar	5126	50712	Slightly guttered rim/wall fragment. Plain, buff-orange surface; orange core, buff-orange oxidation zones; white grits; many glimmers.
14	Jar	5130	50634	Thickened rim/wall fragment. Traces of red slip outside and on the inside of the rim; light brown core with only one, interior, buff-orange oxidation zone; few white grits.
15	Jar	5130	50686	Thickened, tapering rim/wall fragment. Traces of red slip outside; light brown core throughout; small and coarse white grits.
16	Jar	5074	50536	Sharply in-folded rim/wall fragment. Plain, buff-orange surface; light brown core; orange oxidation zones; small and coarse white grits.
17	Jar	5153	50718	Tapering, and externally slightly flattened rim/wall fragment. Traces of slip outside; buff-orange core throughout; white, angular grits.
18	Jar	5074	50459	Rim/drilled wall fragment. Two postfiring drilled holes (from the outside inward) below rim; soot stains inside and outside; brown-grayish core throughout (secondary?); small and coarse white grits.

200 Salvage Excavations at Tel Qashish (Tell Qasis) and Tell el-Wa'er (2010–2013)

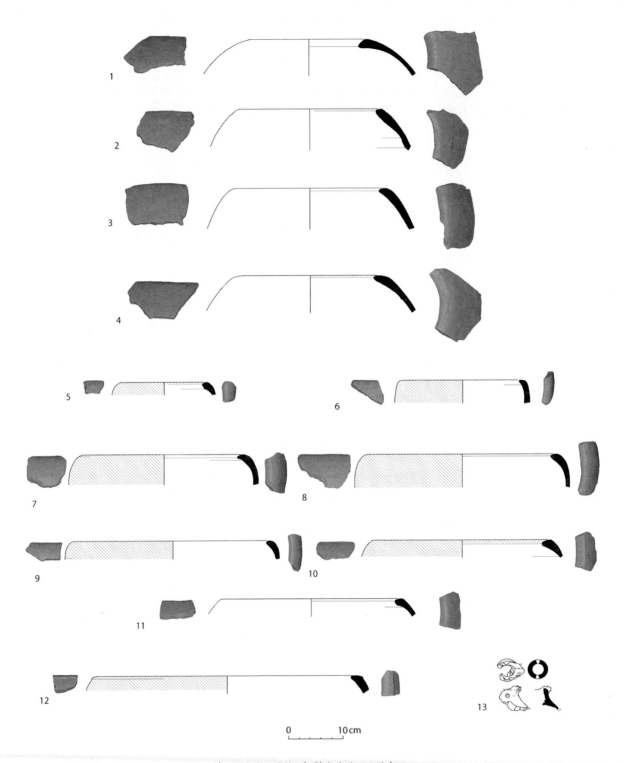

Fig. 16.13. Area E North. Plain holemouth jars.

No.	Vessel	Locus	Basket	Description
1	Jar	5135	50667	Thin-walled. Tapering, incurved rim/wall fragment. Plain, buff-orange surface; strong gray core in rim area, but light brown in wall area; buff-orange oxidation zones; many coarse and fewer small white grits.
2	Jar	5126	50719	Rounded rim/wall fragment. Plain, buff-orange surface; buff-orange core throughout; many small white grits.
3	Jar	5078	50470	Rim/wall fragment. Plain, buff-orange surface; gray core; buff-orange oxidation zones; small and coarse white grits.
4	Jar	5066	50639	Tapering, slightly thickened rim/wall fragment. Plain, light brown surface; orange core throughout; small white grits; few glimmers; fired at high temperature.
5	Jar	5146	50689	Rim/wall fragment. Red-slipped outside and on the inside of the rim; orange core throughout; no grits.
6	Jar	5080	50541	Tapering rim/wall fragment. Traces of red slip outside; buff-orange core throughout; white grits.
7	Bowl/krater	5106	50592	Tapering, incurved rim/wall fragment. Traces of red slip outside; buff-orange core throughout; small dark grits; some glimmers.
8	Jar	5076	50520	Tapering, thickened rim/wall fragment. Burnished red slip outside; buff-orange core throughout; small gray grits, and few coarse white grits.
9	Jar	5066	–	Rim/wall fragment. Densely red-slipped outside and on rim; light brown core throughout; small gray grits, few coarse white grits.
10	Jar	5142	50705	Sharply infolded rim/wall fragment. Red-slipped outside and on inside of the rim; light brown core throughout; small gray grits.
11	Jar	5138	–	Rim/wall fragment. Buff-orange core, with only one, exterior light brown oxidation zone; small, angular white grits.
12	Krater	5065	50469.10	Red slip outside, and on inside of the rim; gray core; buff-orange oxidation zones; small gray grits.
13	Jar	5149	50687	Large spout fragment. Traces of red slip outside; two opposite postfiring drilled holes; orange core throughout; very small white grits; few coarse dark inclusions.

202 Salvage Excavations at Tel Qashish (Tell Qasis) and Tell el-Wa'er (2010–2013)

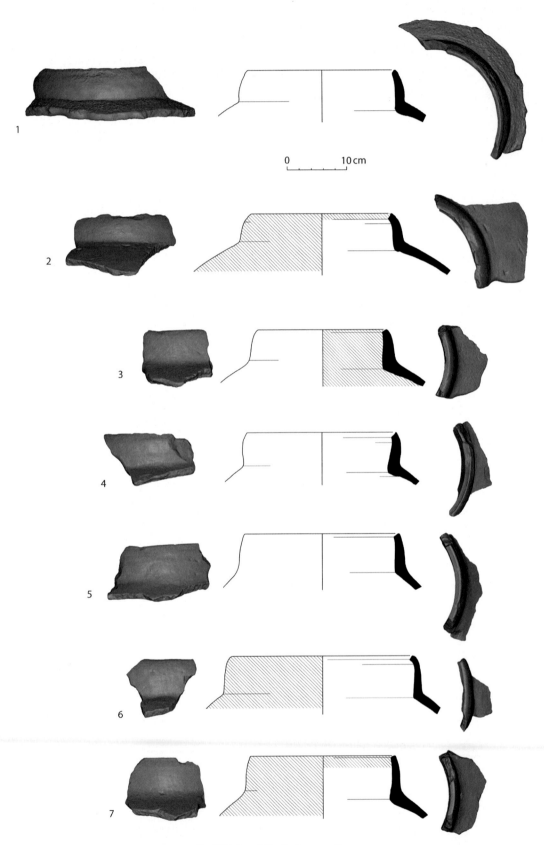

Fig. 16.14. Area E North. Bow-rim jars.

No.	Locus	Basket	Description
1	5130	50668	Large. Obliquely flattened rim/neck/shoulder fragment. Plain buff-orange surface; thick gray core, buff-orange oxidation zones; many small, and fewer white grits.
2	5074	50508.5	Guttered rim/neck/shoulder fragment. Neck/shoulder joint on the inside of the fragment clearly visible; red-slipped outside, and on rim; thick, light brown core; thin buff-orange oxidation zones.
3	5152	50709	Obliquely flattened rim/neck/shoulder fragment. Traces of red slip outside and on inside of the rim/neck; light brown-grayish core, buff-orange oxidation zones; many dark grits; some glimmers.
4	5078	50523	Guttered rim/neck/wall fragment. Red slip outside; light brown core; buff-orange oxidation zones; small and coarse white grits; fired at high temperature.
5	5066	50471	Slightly guttered rim/neck/shoulder fragment. Plain, buff-orange surface; thick, light brown core, buff-orange oxidation zones; many small and coarse white grits.
6	5092	50511.13	Obliquely flattened rim/neck/shoulder fragment. Traces of red slip outside; light brown core with only one, exterior, buff-orange oxidation zone; small gray, few white grits; some glimmers.
7	5074	50508.8	Obliquely flattened rim/neck/shoulder fragment. Traces of red slip on inside of neck; the obliquely flattened rim is irregular edged inside; striation marks (wheel-made) on inside of the neck.

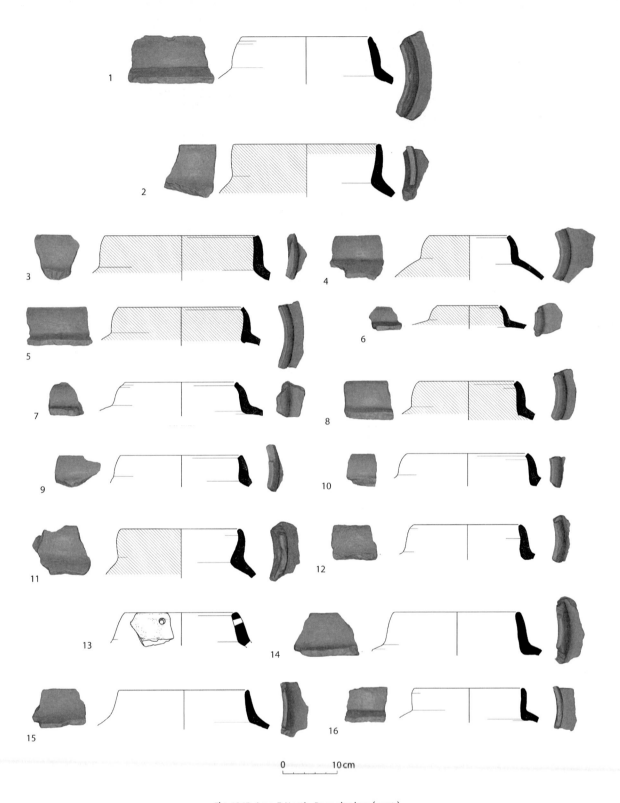

Fig. 16.15. Area E North. Bow-rim jars (cont.).

16. Pottery from Tel Qashish Area E North

No.	Vessel	Locus	Basket	Description
1	Jar	5050	50682	Slightly guttered rim/neck/shoulder fragment. Plain, buff-orange surface; thin gray core, thick exterior and thin interior buff-orange oxidation zones; small, white grits.
2	Jar	5152	50717	Obliquely flattened rim/neck/shoulder fragment. Traces of red slip outside and on inside of the rim/neck.
3	Jar	5132	50625	Thick-walled. Slightly guttered rim/neck/shoulder fragment. Red-slipped outside, and on the inside of the neck; thick gray core, buff-orange oxidation zones; many white grits.
4	Jar	5129	50643	Obliquely flattened rim/neck/shoulder fragment. Traces of red slip outside; buff-orange core throughout; white, angular grits.
5	Jar	5113	50549	Guttered rim/neck/shoulder fragment. Traces of red slip outside and on inside of neck; interior neck/shoulder joint visible.
6	Jar	5138	50681	Small. Flattened rim/neck/shoulder fragment. Red-slipped outside and inside of neck.
7	Jar	5135	50652	Obliquely flattened rim/neck/shoulder fragment. Plain, orange surface; thick gray core, thin orange oxidation zones; many white, angular grits.
8	Jar	5109	50546	Slightly guttered/neck/shoulder fragment. Traces of red slip outside and on the inside of the neck; thick, light grayish core (almost laminated-like), buff-orange oxidation zones; white angular grits.
9	Jar	5078	50523	Slightly guttered rim/neck/wall fragment. Plain, buff-orange surface; thick gray core, thin buff-orange oxidation zones; white grits; possible some grog inclusions.
10	Jar	5074	50482	Obliquely flattened rim/neck/shoulder fragment. Plain, buff-orange surface; light brown core, buff-orange oxidation zones; many small and coarse white grits.
11	Jar	5152	50695	Rounded rim/neck/shoulder fragment. Traces of red slip outside.
12	Jar	5091	50559	Rounded rim/neck/shoulder fragment. Possible traces of slip and/or soot stains; light brown core throughout; small and coarse white grits; very few gray grits; some glimmers.
13	Jar	5141	50672	Slightly flattened rim/postfiring drilled neck/wall fragment. Traces of slip outside; thick gray core, with alternating, exterior buff-orange and gray (secondary?) oxidation zones and buff-orange interior oxidation zone; many small white grits.
14	Jar	5138	–	Rounded rim/neck/wall fragment.
15	Jar	5109	50546	Rounded rim/neck/wall fragment. Plain, buff-orange surface; thick gray core, thin buff-orange oxidation zones; few white and gray grits; few glimmers.
16	Jar	5126	50678	Rounded rim/neck/shoulder fragment. Plain, yellowish-brown surface; very thin, gray core, thick buff-orange oxidation zones; many small and coarse white grits.

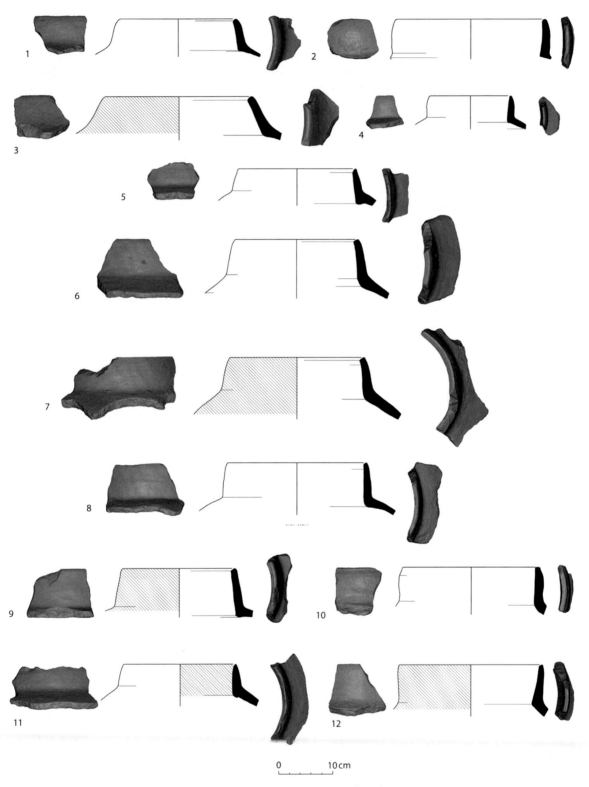

Fig. 16.16. Area E North. Bow-rim jars (cont.).

16. Pottery from Tel Qashish Area E North

No.	Vessel	Locus	Basket	Description
1	Jar	5147	50692	Rounded rim/neck/shoulder fragment. Interior joint neck/shoulder not smoothed; plain, yellowish-cream surface; light brown core throughout, few white grits.
2	Jar	5092	50507	Tapering rim/neck/shoulder fragment. Surface crusted; very thick, light brown core with thin buff-orange oxidation zones; small white and gray grits; some glimmers.
3	Jar	5105	50537	Flattened rim/neck/shoulder fragment. Traces of red slip outside; thin gray core, brown oxidation zones; small and coarse white grits; glimmers.
4	Jar	5074	–	Small. Tapering rim/neck/shoulder fragment. Plain, buff-orange surface.
5	Jar	5059	50413.4	Slightly guttered rim/neck/shoulder fragment. Plain surface; soot outside; light brown/grayish core and oxidation zones; the gray color maybe secondary, from heating on fireplace/hearth.
6	Jar	5146	50675	Large. Flattened rim/neck/shoulder fragment. Crusted surface; thick grayish core, buff-orange oxidation zones, the exterior one thicker than the interior one.
7	Jar	5080	50541.2	Obliquely flattened rim/neck/shoulder fragment. Traces of red slip outside; thick gray core; buff-orange oxidation zones; many coarse white grits.
8	Jar	5050	50714	Obliquely flattened rim/neck/shoulder fragment. Plain, orange surface; orange core throughout; small gray grits, very few white grits; few glimmers.
9	Jar	5109	50623	Slightly guttered rim/neck/shoulder fragment. Red-slipped outside; thick gray core, buff-orange oxidation zones; small dark grits, very few white grits.
10	Jar	5071	50620	Tapering rim/flaring neck/shoulder fragment. Possible traces of red slip outside; buff-orange core throughout; small gray, fewer white grits; some glimmers.
11	Jar	5138	50681	Slightly guttered rim/neck/shoulder fragment. Traces of red slip preserved on inside of the neck; neck/shoulder joint inside clearly visible; fired at high temperature.
12	Jar	5071	50557	Slightly guttered rim/neck/shoulder fragment. Traces of red slip outside; buff-orange surface; grayish core; buff-orange oxidation zones; small white grits; some glimmers.

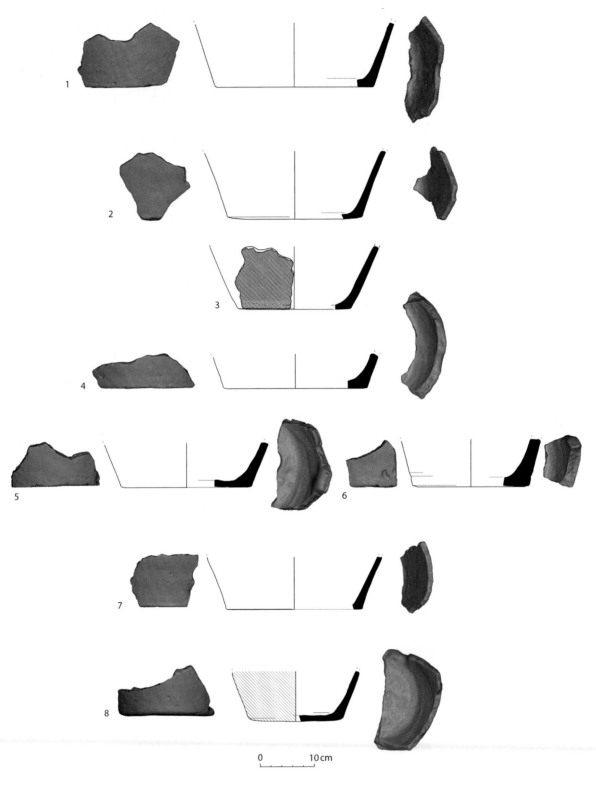

Fig. 16.17. Area E North. Bow-rim jars. Bases.

No.	Vessel	Locus	Basket	Description
1	Jar	5113	50549	Flat base/wall fragment of large jar. Light brown core, gray core with exterior buff-orange oxidation zone; many white grits.
2	Jar	5074	50459	Flat base/wall fragment. Plain, buff-orange surface.
3	Jar	5126	50619	Flat base/wall fragment. Red-slipped outside; grayish core, buff-orange oxidation zones; few small white grits; some glimmer.
4	Jar	5135	–	Flat base/wall fragment. Gray core with only one, exterior buff-orange oxidation zone; white and gray grits.
5	Jar	5130	–	Flat base/wall fragment. Crusted surface; light gray core, buff-orange oxidation zones; small white grits.
6	Jar	5059	50483	Flat base/wall fragment of large, thick-walled jar. Plain, buff-orange surface; orange core; white, coarse grits.
7	Jar	5102	50533	Flat base/wall fragment of large cooking pot/jar. Soot stains outside; plain, buff-orange surface; gray core (secondary?) with single, interior, buff-orange oxidation zone.
8	Jar	5050	50716	Flat base/wall fragment of large jar. Red slip on exterior surface; plain, buff-orange surface; break: inside gray, outside buff-orange; many small white grits; few glimmers.

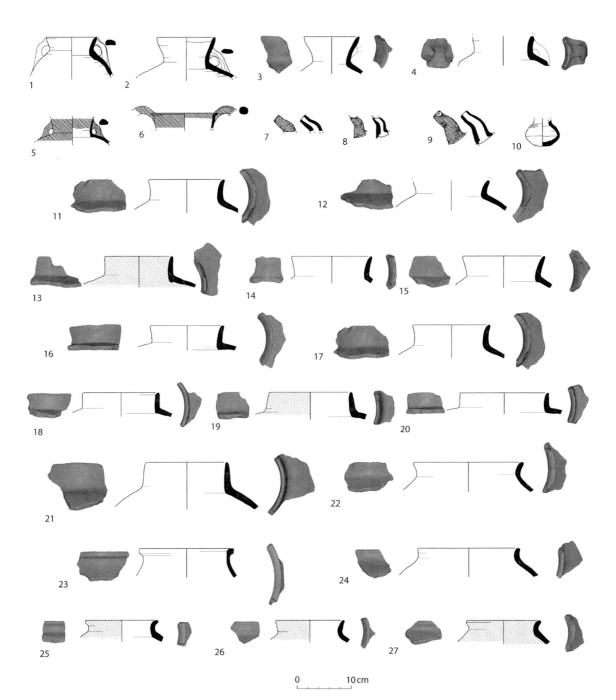

Fig. 16.18. Area E North. Amphoriskoi, jugs, tall-necked jars.

No.	Vessel	Locus	Basket	Description
1	Amphoriskos	5115	50598	Rim/handle/neck/shoulder fragment. Plain cream-light brown surface; buff orange core throughout; many small gray, fewer white grits; some glimmers.
2	Amphoriskos	5121	50670a	Rim/neck/shoulder/handle fragment. Possible traces of red-slip outside; external gray, internal buff-orange zone; with and gray grits; some glimmers; fired at high temperature.
3	Amphoriskos	5121	50670b	Rim/neck/shoulder/handle fragment; possibly part of 50670a. Possible traces of red-slip outside; external gray, internal buff-orange zone; with and gray grits; some glimmers; fired at high temperature.

No.	Vessel	Locus	Basket	Description
4	Amphoriskos	5105	50537	Neck/handle/shoulder fragment. Plain surface; buff-orange core, orange oxidation zones; many white, angular grits.
5	Amphoriskos	5074	50482	Neck/shoulder/handle fragment. Red-slipped and burnished outside.
6	Jug	5078	50523	Everted rim/neck/high loop handle fragment. Red-slipped (and burnished?) outside, and on inside of the rim.
7	Teapot	5107	50544	Small spout. Red-slipped outside.
8	Teapot	?	?	Small, bent spout. Red-slipped outside.
9	Teapot	5006	50678	Large bent spout. Red-slipped outside.
10	Miniature Juglet	5080	50587	Neck/wall/rounded base fragment. Plain, buff-orange surface.
11	Necked Jar	5130	50634	Tapering rim/flaring neck/shoulder fragment. Crusted surface; light brown core, buff-orange oxidation zones; white grits.
12	Tall Necked Jar	5135	50635	Flaring neck/shoulder fragment. Traces of red slip outside; orange core throughout; small gray, fewer white grits.
13	Necked Jar	5080	50514	Tapering rim/flaring neck/shoulder fragment. Neck/shoulder joint on the inside clearly noticeable; traces of red slip outside, and on inside of the rim; buff-orange core all through; white grits.
14	Necked Jar	5151	50694	Tapering rim/flaring neck/shoulder fragment. Neck/shoulder interior joint not smoothed; light brown surface; light brown core throughout; many small and few coarse white grits.
15	Necked Jar	5153	50708	Tapering rim/flaring neck/shoulder fragment. Crusted surface; buff-orange core throughout; white, coarse grits.
16	Thin-walled necked jar	5059	50460	Tapering rim/slightly flaring neck/shoulder fragment. Plain, buff-orange surface; orange core; buff-orange oxidation zones; small and coarse white grits.
17	Thin-walled necked jar	5059	50413.8	Tapering rim/flaring neck/shoulder fragment. Plain, buff-orange surface; traces of soot outside; orange core; white, coarse grits.
18	Necked jar	5059	50413.11b	Tapering rim/neck/wall fragment. Plain, buff-orange surface; thick, orange core; thin, buff-orange oxidation zones; fired at high temperature; interior neck/shoulder joint well visible, that is, not smoothed.
19	Necked jar	5066	50527	Tapering rim/neck/shoulder fragment. Traces of red slip outside; buff-orange core throughout; small and coarse white grits.
20	Necked jar	5126	50678	Rim/slightly flaring neck/shoulder fragment. Plain, buff-orange surface; thin, gray core, buff-orange oxidation zones; few, small gray grits; some glimmers.
21	Necked jar	5066	50499	Tapering rim/neck/wall fragment. Exterior surface buff-orange; interior surface gray (secondary; from cooking); gray core, buff-orange oxidation zones; small and coarse white grits fired at high temperature; few glimmers.
22	Necked jar	5074	50536	Tapering rim/flaring neck/shoulder fragment. Soot around rim's exterior as well on wall's exterior.
23	Thin-walled cooking pot/jar	5064	50566	Flattened rim/neck/shoulder fragment. Soot stains inside and outside; gray core throughout (secondary?); small, white grits; few glimmers.
24	Necked jar (cooking pot)	5122	50604	Rounded rim/neck/shoulder fragment. Gray core throughout (secondary?); few small white grits.
25	Necked jar	5080	50514	Everted, tapering rim. Traces of red slip outside; buff-orange core throughout; gray and fewer white small grits; few glimmers.
26	Medium-sized necked jar	5138	50681	Tapering rim/flaring neck/shoulder fragment. Red-slipped outside; very thin, light brown core; thick, orange oxidation zones.
27	Necked jar	5109	50623	Rounded rim/flaring neck/shoulder fragment. Traces of red slip outside, and on the inside of the rim; thick light brown core, thin buff-orange oxidation zones; very few white grits; some dark glimmers.

212 Salvage Excavations at Tel Qashish (Tell Qasis) and Tell el-Wa'er (2010–2013)

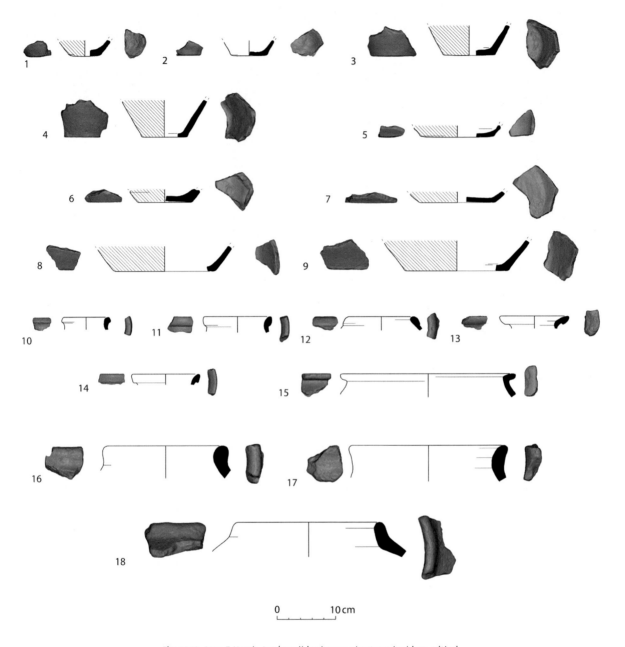

Fig. 16.19. Area E North. Jug/small jar bases, short-necked jars, pithoi.

16. Pottery from Tel Qashish Area E North

No.	Vessel	Locus	Basket	Description
1	Small jar/jug	5071	–	Flat base/wall. Red-slipped surface outside; light brown core throughout; small gray, fewer white grits.
2	–	5147	50692	Small. Flat base/wall fragment. Plain, buff-orange surface; orange core throughout, coarse, angular white grits.
3	Small jar/jug	5148	50693	Flat base/wall fragment. Red-slipped exterior; gray core; light brown oxidation zones; very few, small white grits.
4	Small jar/jug	5135	50635	Flat base/wall fragment. Red-slipped outside; thin gray core, buff-orange oxidation zones; white angular grits.
5	Small jar/jug	5080	50514	Flat base/wall fragment. Red slipped outside; thin gray core, buff-orange oxidation zones outside; small gray grits; one red grit.
6	Small jar	5065	–	Flat base/red-slipped wall fragment. Buff orange surface and core; small gray grits, and occasional coarse white grits; fired at high temperature.
7	Small jar/jug	5080	–	Flat base/wall fragment. Traces of slip outside and on the base's outside as well.
8	Small jar/jug	5099	50543	Flat base/wall fragment. Red-slipped outside; gray core; buff-orange oxidation zones; small gray grits.
9	Small jar/jug	5074	–	Flat base/wall fragment. Wall red-slipped outside until ca. 1 cm above the actual base; buff-orange core throughout; many pores (burnt-out organic inclusions?).
10	Small jar	5065	50419.7	Rim/neck fragment. Plain buff-orange surface; white grits.
11	Smallish jar	5135	50652	Rim/neck fragment. Plain, orange surface; light brown core, buff-orange oxidation zones; white grits.
12	Small jar	5071	50521	Folded rim/neck fragment. Buff-orange core throughout; very few, small white grits.
13	Medium-sized jar	5079	50463.5	Everted, tapering rim/neck. Plain, buff-orange surface; buff-orange core throughout; very few small white and gray grits.
14	Small (Egyptianized?) jar	5065	50477	Profiled rim/neck fragment. Plain, buff-orange surface; gray core; buff-orange oxidation zones; few white and dark grits/inclusions.
15	Jar	5062	50473	Flat, externally folded rim//neck/wall fragment. Dark, almost laminated-like core, buff-orange oxidation zones; small gray grits.
16	Pithos	5066	50471.17	Rim/neck fragment. Traces of red slip preserved on inside rim; buff-orange surface; strong grayish core, thin buff-orange oxidation zones; small gray and, fewer, coarse white grits; some glimmers.
17	Pithos	5066	50431.15	Rim/neck fragment. Plain, buff-orange surface; thick, gray core with thin, buff-orange oxidation zones; few coarse white grits; many small brown grits (grog?); some glimmers.
18	Pithos	5153	50708	Rim/flaring neck/shoulder fragment. Crusted surface; gray core throughout; very few white grits; pores of burnt-out organic inclusions; many small glimmers.

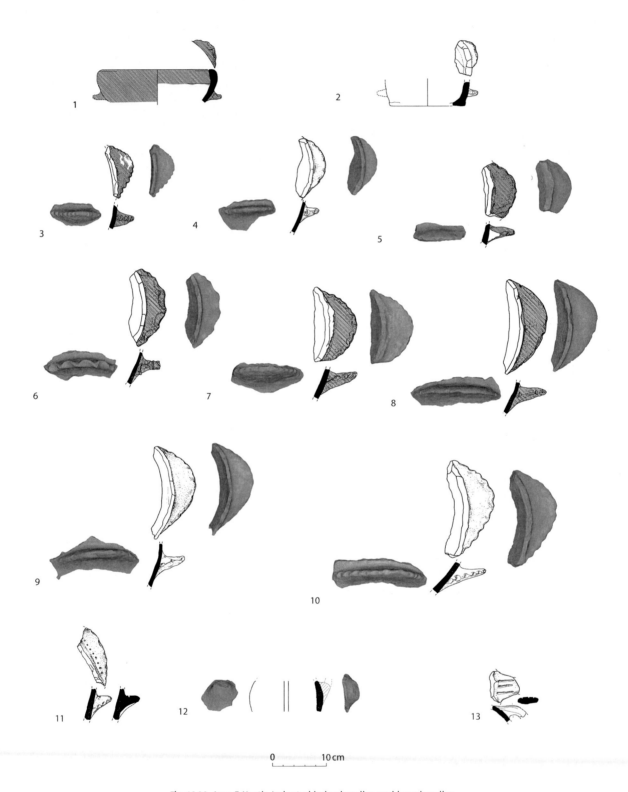

Fig. 16.20. Area E North. Indented ledge handles and loop handles.

No.	Handle	Locus	Basket	Description
1	Indented ledge handle of krater	5153	50718	Flattened rim; neck or wall fragment. Red-slipped outside and on the inside of the rim or neck; thick gray core; buff-orange oxidation zones; no visible inclusions.
2	Small indented ledge handle of small jar/jug	5121	50631	Flat base/wall. Plain, buff-orange surface; thick, gray core, thin buff-orange oxidation zones; small and coarse white grits.
3	Indented ledge handle	5121	50653	Traces of red slip on both surfaces; white grits.
4	Indented ledge handle/wall fragment of medium-sized jar	5059	–	Plain buff-orange surface; light brown core; buff-orange oxidation zones; small and few coarse white grits.
5	Indented ledge handle	5066	50666	Traces of red slip on both surfaces; thick orange core, thin buff-orange oxidation zones; many small, fewer coarse white grits.
6	Indented ledge handle of jar	5066	50685	Traces of red slip outside; orange core throughout; gray and fewer white grits.
7	Indented ledge handle/wall fragment of jar	5066	50527	Traces of red slip outside; buff-orange core throughout; white grits.
8	Large indented ledge handle of jar	5126	50678	Traces of red slip on both surfaces; buff-orange core throughout; many small and coarse white grits.
9	Large indented ledge handle	5059	50460	Plain, light brown surface; orange core with light brown oxidation zones; many small white grits; fired at high temperature.
10	Large indented ledge handle of jar	5050	50682	Plain, buff-orange surface; traces of soot on bottom side of handle; brownish core; buff-orange oxidation zones; many small gray grits; some glimmers.
11	Indented ledge handle	5150	50688	Red-slipped surface. A prefiring row of circular punctures on the top side of the handle.
12	Loop handle	5066	50685	Red slipped; buff-orange core throughout; small gray and fewer white grits.
13	Large loop handle	5121	50603	Three prefiring incised parallel, vertical slashes; gray-brownish core; plain buff-orange surface; buff-orange oxidation zones; small gray and white grits; some large glimmers.

Chapter 17

Petrographic Analysis of the Early Bronze Age Pottery from Tel Qashish

Anat Cohen-Weinberger (*Israel Antiquities Authority*)

The present study presents the results of the petrographic analysis of twenty Early Bronze Age I samples taken from pottery collected at Tel Qashish during the three excavation seasons carried out in 2010–2011. The samples were taken from gray burnished ware bowls, a single knobbed bowl, jars, holemouth jars, cooking pots, and one "teapot" (table 17.1).[1]

The cooking pots are reminiscent of the later (EB II) Golanite "brown cooking pots" (Paz and Iserlis 2009), and identifying their provenance is crucial for understanding Golan–Galilee interregional connections during the Early Bronze I (see pottery description of Areas E [South] and F, permit A-5992, ch. 15, this volume). Thus, the main goal of this study is to characterize the raw material of these cooking pots and identify their provenance. For the present analysis, it is important to compare the raw material of these cooking pots to other pottery found at the same site and to assess the geological setting of the excavated site (see below).

The petrographic method is based on the assumption that ancient potters used local clay units and tempers which must reflect the geology of the production site (e.g., Arnold 1985; Braekmans and Degryse 2017). Hence, the fabric of the vessels is compared to the site's geological characteristics.

Geological Setting

The site is covered with alluvial sediments derived from the surrounding sedimentary and volcanic rocks. North and northeast of the site, sedimentary rocks, mainly chalk and limestone of the lower Galilee Eocene Adulam, Timrat, and Maresha formations are exposed. These formations are also exposed in Tel Qashish (Sneh, Bartov and Rosensaft 1998; Amihai Sneh, pers. comm. 2012).

The Jezreel Valley, southeast of the site, is characterized by alluvium and a few Miocene basalt exposures. West of the site, the northeastern flank of Mount Carmel presents mainly chalk of the Cenomanian Isfye and Arqan formations, and dolomite and limestone of the Turonian Bina Formation (Sneh, Bartov and Rosensaft 1998; Segev and Sass 2009). On a hill sloping eastward from Mount Carmel and facing Tel Qashish, on the western side of Road 70, chalk of the Mount Scopus Group is exposed. The Mount Carmel sedimentary rocks are accompanied, in several localities, by volcanic intercalations of basalts and tuffs (Picard 1956; Sass 1968, 115–16; Bein and Sass 1980; Segev and Sass 2009). The dominant volcanic rocks are pyroclastics of basic composition, demonstrating undersea explosion (Sass 1980). Located about 2 km southwest of the site, and in Naḥal Raqefet, are Late Cretaceous basaltic flows, tuff, and a spilitic basalt outcrop (Segev and Sass 2009). Senonian to Paleocene chalk and marls of the Ghareb and Taqiye formations are ex-

---

1. This chapter was submitted in 2014, and only minor updates were made in 2020.

Table 17.1. Inventory of analyzed vessels and results of the petrographic analysis.

Number	Permit	Locus	Basket	Type	Figure	Petrographic Group
1	A-5881	320	3066	Rim/neck/shoulder fragment of bow-rim jar, with small external knob	14.10.3	C
2	A-5881	353	3179	Holemouth jar rim with applied rope decoration	14.7.5	C
3	A-5881	367	3209	Rim/short neck/decorated shoulder fragment of medium-to-large-sized jar (EB II?)	14.11.5	B (variant)
4	A-5881	367	3278	Incurved rim/wall fragment of knobbed bowl	14.6.1	B
5	A-5881	375	3262	Holemouth jar rim with exterior ridge	14.7.12	E (variant)
6	A-5881	376	3335	Holemouth jar rim with prefiring incised mark below the rim's exterior	14.7.7	C
7	A-5881	410	4042	Outfolded rim/neck/rope-decorated shoulder fragment of jar	14.13.11	D
8	A-5881	418	4077	Outfolded rim/neck/rope-decorated shoulder fragment of jar	14.13.12	D
9	A-5992	60	60244	Brown holemouth jar		E
10	A-5992	6014	60043	Brown holemouth jar		E
11	A-5992	6014	60275	Brown holemouth jar		E
12	A-5992	6027	60759	Brown holemouth jar		E
13	A-5992	6044	60333	Brown holemouth jar		E
14	A-6149	5006	50678	Large bent spout of teapot	16.18.9	B
15	A-6149	5075	50455.2	Holemouth jar rim with applied rope decoration	16.9.11	C
16	A-6149	5078	50523	Outfolded rim/neck/high loop handle fragment of jug	16.18.6	B
17	A-6149	5080	50541.2	Obliquely flattened rim/neck/shoulder fragment of bow-rim jar	16.16.7	C
18	A-6149	5093	50576	Rounded, outfolded rim/flaring neck fragment of large GBW bowl	16.5.1	A
19	A-6149	5109	50623	Rim/carinated wall fragment of GBW bowl	16.5.4	A
20	A-6149	5971	50557	Slightly guttered rim/neck/shoulder fragment of bow-rim jar	16.16.12	C

posed about 3 km south of the site on the southern slope of Naḥal Yoqneʻam.

The main soils in the vicinity of the studied site are composed of brown and light rendzina, which develops on the chalk units northeast and east of the site, of alluvial brown grumusols in the Kishon River and the Jezreel Valley, and of terra rossa and rendzina soils on Mount Carmel (Ravikovitch 1969; Dan and Raz 1970; Dan, Yaalon, and Koyumdjisky 1975).

Results

The analyzed vessels belong to five distinct petrographic groups (A–E), the samples in each group sharing similar petrographic properties of clay and tempers. The proposed origin of each group relies on the mineralogical and lithological properties of the clay and tempers and their suggested geological contexts.

Group A

This group is characterized by optically active calcareous clay extremely rich in foraminifers. Upper Cretaceous foraminifers such as the genus Hetrohelix were identified. The nonplastic components (f:c ratio {0.062 mm} ≈ 90:10) contain poorly sorted grog fragments and crushed calcite, as well as a few chalk and bone fragments. A single basalt fragment was found in one sample (table 17.1.18). The clay is identified as marl, and its exact source cannot be determined. There are limited Upper Cretaceous foraminiferous marl units. These include the exposures of the Senonian Kabri member in west Galilee, the Turonian Yirka Formation in the north and northwest Galilee, and the Cenomanian Deir Hanna Formation that includes marl units and crop out in the Galilee Mountains (Sneh, Bartov, and Rosensaft 1998). Notably, no petrographic data of these units are yet available. Two gray burnished ware bowls (table 17.1.18–19; fig. 16.5.1, 4) are related to this group.

Group B

This group is characterized by an optically active calcareous clay, extremely rich in foraminifers. The nonplastic components (f:c ratio {0.062 mm} ≈ 80:20) consist of mainly poorly sorted rounded to subangular basalt fragments and basalt derived minerals. Alterations to iddingsite and chlorite are common. A few calcareous rock fragments and crushed calcite are also present. Additionally, grog appeared in the paste of one jar (table 17.1.16). The matrix of this group is similar to that of group A and originates from an unidentified marl unit. The raw material of this group broadly fits the geology of the Jezreel Valley and lower Galilee. A knobbed bowl, a red-slipped jar, and a "teapot" are all related to this group (table 17.1.4, 14, 16; figs. 14.6.1, 16.18.9, 6). An additional single jar (table 17.1.3; fig. 14.11.5) represents a variant of this petrographic group, as crushed calcite fragments were deliberately added to the paste as nonplastic components.

Group C

This group is characterized by calcareous clay, rich in foraminifers. The nonplastic components (f:c ratio {0.062 mm} ≈ 80:20) consist of poorly sorted, crushed calcite fragments deliberately added to the paste. The clay is similar to that of groups A and B and was identified as marl. The nonplastic components are nonindicative for provenance determination. Three holemouth jars and three bow-rim jars are related to this group (table 17.1.1–2, 6, 15, 17, 20; figs. 14.10.3; 14.7.5; 14.7.7; 16.9.11; 16.16.7, 12).

Group D

This group is characterized by calcareous clay with about 5 percent silt-sized quartz grains and a few silt- to fine-sand-sized basalt derived minerals. The nonplastic components (f:c ratio {0.062 mm} ≈ 80:20) consist of poorly sorted, crushed calcite fragments, as well as mollusk shells and a few limestone fragments and, rarely, silicified foraminifers. This raw material represents an unidentified soil with deliberately added calcite fragments that fit some areas in northern Israel interfacing volcanic rocks exposures. Two jars are related to this group (table 17.1.7–8; fig. 14.13.11–12).

Group E

This group is characterized by ferruginous optically active clay with silt-sized quartz grains and basaltic derived minerals. The nonplastic components are poorly sorted holocrystalline, medium-grained basalt fragments showing intergranular texture, and sand-sized basalt derived minerals. Alterations to iddingsite are common. One sample (table 17.1.5) contains a few calcareous rock fragments and some sand-sized discrete foraminifera. The raw material of this group was identified as a soil derived from the weathering of the primary basalt minerals. The silt-sized quartz grains derived from aeolian dust (Adan-Bayewitz and Wieder 1992; Wieder and Adan-Bayewitz 2002; Singer 2007). Basaltic brown Mediterranean soils, basaltic vertisols, and regosols appear in the eastern part of the lower Galilee, along the Jordan River in upper Galilee, on the Golan Heights and, to a limited extent, in the Jezreel and Ḥarod Valleys (Dan and Raz 1970; Dan et al. 1975; Singer 2007, 153). Five cooking pots are related to this group (table 17.1.5, 9–13; fig. 14.7.12).

Summary and Discussion

The raw materials of groups A–D are typical to pottery from sites in the Jezreel Valley and the Galilee, as shown in many previous petrographic studies (e.g., Zuckerman, Ziv-Esudri, and Cohen-Weinberger 2009, 148–50), as well as in the petrography of EB II and EB III pottery from Tel Qashish (Porat 2003).

The results of previous petrographic studies of GBW, from many sites, pointed to different manufacture places and traditions in the Jezreel Valley, the Galilee, and the eastern Samaria regions (e.g., Goren 1991; Fischer 2000, 204–6; Goren and Zuckermann 2000, 174–75; Getzov, Nagar, and Cohen-Weinberger 2015). The results of the current study concur with the previous results of the petrographic analysis of GBW bowls from Tel Qashish (Goren and Zuckermann 2000, 180–81). Although the exact source cannot be determined, the characteristic raw material repeatedly appears in samples from multiple sites, suggesting a single tradition and, most likely, a restricted number of manufacturing places.

The cooking pots related to the petrographic group E are reminiscent of the Golanite brown cooking pots defined by Yitzhak Paz and Mark Iserlis (2009) and known from EB II contexts. Previous studies—which tried to establish a pottery manufacturing place in the Golan Heights rather than in the Galilee—claimed that calcareous components are usually present in the basalt-bearing pottery made in Galilee but are absent from vessels made in the Golan (Cohen-Weinberger 2013, 389; Paz and Iserlis 2009, 106). Moshe Wieder and David Adan-Bayewitz (2002, 407, 409) explained the absence of carbonate in pottery produced from basaltic-derived soil in the Galilee as a material leached of carbonates. Basalt rock fragments usually appear as nonplastic components in the pottery made in Galilee or the Jezreel Valley together with sedimentary rock fragments and usually embedded in calcareous clay.

Petrographic analysis of pottery from various periods from sites located in the Golan Heights did not report any calcareous components in the paste (e.g., Adan-Bayewitz 1993, 196–97; Porat 1998; Porat and Killebrew 1999; Osband 2014, 128; Shalem et al. 2019, 344).[2] Pottery made of noncalcareous basaltic soils is unusual in sites of the Jezreel Valley and Galilee, and the provenance of the current brown cooking pots in the Golan Heights is thus more likely. However, some exceptional examples are known, such as the Early Bronze Age III Khirbet Kerak ware vessels found in the Jezreel Valley, which were produced from the local basalt-derived soils but with no calcareous components in their raw material (Zuckerman, Ziv-Esudri and Cohen-Weinberger 2009, 146–51). Similar basaltic soil was used for making a Late Bronze Age II cooking pot found at Tel Qashish (Cohen-Weinberger, ch. 26, this volume).

Confirming or refuting a plausible provenance from the Golan Heights, the Jezreel Valley, or eastern Galilee should be done with caution. Placing the origin of the cooking pots in the Golan Heights should be carefully further tested for it poses new significant chronological implications for the interregional relations between the Golan and the Jezreel Valley (see also pottery description of Areas F [South] and F, permit A-5992, ch. 15, this volume).

---

2. Limestone inclusions were identified in a petrographic study of the Early Bronze Age pottery from Leviah in the southern Golan (Paz and Shoval 2012).

References

Adan-Bayewitz, David
1993 *Common Pottery in Roman Galilee: A Study of Local Trade*. Bar-Ilan Studies in Near Eastern Languages and Culture. Ramat Gan: Bar-Ilan University Press.

Adan-Bayewitz, David, and Moshe Wieder
1992 "Ceramics from Roman Galilee: A Comparison of Several Techniques for Fabric Characterization." *Journal of Field Archaeology* 19: 189–205.

Arnold, Dean E
1985 *Ceramic Theory and Cultural Process*. New Studies in Archaeology. Cambridge: Cambridge University Press.

Bein, Amos, and Eytan Sass
1980 "Geology." In *Atlas of Haifa and Mount Carmel*, edited by Arnon Sofer and Barukh Kipnis, 14–17. Haifa: Applied Scientific Research Co., University of Haifa.

Braekmans, Dennis, and Patrick, Degryse
2017 "Petrography: Optical Microscopy." In *The Oxford Handbook of Archaeological Ceramic Analysis*, edited by Alice Hunt, 233–65. Oxford: Oxford University Press.

Cohen-Weinberger, Anat
2013 "Provenance of Clay Ossuaries and Other Vessels." In *Peqi'in: A Late Chalcolithic Burial Site, Upper Galilee, Israel*, by Zvi Gal, Dina Shalem, and Howard Smithline, 387–90. Land of Galilee 2. Jerusalem: Ostracon.

Dan, Joel, and Zvi Raz
1970 *Soil Association Map of Israel. 1:250,000*. Beit Dagan: Volcani Institute.

Dan, Joel, Zvi Raz, Dan H. Yaalon, and Hanna Koyumdjisky
1975 *The Soil Association Map of Israel, 1:500,000*. Beit Dagan: Volcani Institute.

Fischer, Peter. M
2000 "The Early Bronze Age at Tell Abu al-Kharaz, Jordan Valley: A Study of Pottery Typology and Provenance, Radiocarbon Dates, and Synchronism." In *Breaking with the Past: Ceramics and Change in the Early Bronze Age of the Southern Levant*, edited by Graham Philip, and Douglas Baird, 201–32. Levantine Archaeology 2. Sheffield: Sheffield Academic.

Getzov, Nimrod, Yossi Nagar, and Anat Cohen-Weinberger
2015 "A Burial Cave of the Late Chalcolithic and Early Bronze Age I at Midrakh 'Oz, Western Jezreel Valley." *'Atiqot* 82:21*–46*. [Hebrew]

Goren, Yuval
1991 "The Beginnings of Pottery Production in Israel: Technology and Typology of Proto-Historic Ceramic Assemblages in Eretz-Israel (6th–4th Millenia BCE)." PhD diss., Hebrew University of Jerusalem.

Goren, Yuval, and Sharon Zuckerman
2000 "An Overview of the Typology, Provenance and Technology of the Early Bronze Age I 'Grey Burnished Ware.'" In *Breaking with the Past: Ceramics and Change in the Early Bronze Age of the Southern Levant*, edited by Graham Philip, and Douglas Baird, 165–82. Levantine Archaeology 2. Sheffield: Sheffield Academic.

Osband, Mechael
2014 "Ceramic Ecology of the Golan in the Roman and Early Byzantine Periods." PhD diss., Bar-Ilan University.

Paz, Yitzhak, and Mark Iserlis
2009 "Golanite Production and Distribution Center of Cooking Pots during the Early Bronze Age II." In *Techniques and People: Anthropological Perspectives on Technology in the Archeology of the Proto-historic and Early Historic Periods in the Southern Levant,* edited by Steven A. Rosen and Valentine Roux, 99–110. Paris: de Boccard.

Paz, Yitzhak, and Shlomo Shoval
2012 "Miniature Votive Bowls as the Symbolic Defense of Leviah: An Early Bronze Age Fortified Town in the Southern Levant." In *Time and Mind: The Journal of Archaeology, Consciousness and Culture* 5: 7–18.

Picard, Leo
1956 *Geological Map of Israel, Series C, Zikhron Ya'akov, 1:100,000*. Jerusalem: Ministry of Development, Geological Survey of Israel.

Porat, Naomi
1998 "Pottery Analyses from Site 12." Pp. 344–46. In *The Chalcolithic Culture of The Golan*, edited by Claire Epstein. IAA Reports 4. Jerusalem: Israel Antiquities Authority.
2003 "Petrography of the Early Bronze Age II–III Pottery." In *Tel Qashish: A Village in the Jezreel Valley; Final Report of the Archaeological Excavations (1978–1987)*, edited by Amnon Ben-Tor, Ruhama Bonfil, and Sharon Zuckerman, 161–64. Qedem Report 5. Jerusalem: Institute of Archaeology, Hebrew University Jerusalem

Porat, Naomi, and Ann E. Killebrew
1999 "Petrographic Analyses of Late Antique and Islamic Fine and Coarse Wares from Qasrin." In *The*

Practical Impact of Science on Near Eastern and Aegean Archaeology, edited by Scott Pike and Seymour Gitin, 127–42. Wiener Laboratory Monograph 3. London: Archetype.

Ravikovitch, Shlomo
1969 *Israel: Soil Map, 1:250,000*. Reḥovot: Hebrew University of Jerusalem, Faculty of Agriculture.

Sass, Eytan
1968 "Geology of the Umm El Fahm Area, Northern Israel." *Israel Journal of Earth Sciences* 17: 115–30.
1980 "Late Cretaceous Volcanism in Mount Carmel, Israel." *Israel Journal of Earth-Sciences* 29: 8–24.

Segev, Amit, and Eytan Sass
2009 *Geological Map of Israel 1:50,000. Sheet 3-III, Atlit*. Jerusalem: Geological Survey of Israel.

Shalem, Dina, Anat Cohen-Weinberger, Bernardo Gandulla, and Ianir Milevski
2019 "Ceramic Connections and Regional Entities: The Petrography of Late Chalcolithic Pottery from Sites in the Galilee (Israel)." In *"Isaac Went Out … to the Field" (Genesis 24:63): Studies in Archaeology and Ancient Cultures in Honor of Isaac Gilead*, edited by Haim Goldfus, Mayer I. Gruber, Shamir Yonah, and Peter Fabian, 262–77. Oxford: Archaeopress Archaeology.

Singer, Arieh
2007 *The Soils of Israel*. Berlin: Springer.

Sneh, Amihai, Yosef Bartov, and Marcelo Rosensaft
1998 *Geological Map of Israel 1:200,000, Sheet 1*. Jerusalem: Geological Survey of Israel.

Wieder, Moshe, and David Adan-Bayewitz
2002 "Soil Parent Materials and the Pottery of Roman Galilee: A Comparative Study." *Geoarchaeology* 17: 393–415.

Zuckerman, Sharon, Adi Ziv-Esudri, and Anat Cohen-Weinberger
2009 "Production Centers and Distribution Patterns of KKW in the Southern Levant: A Typological and Petrographic Perspective." *TA* 36: 135–80.

Chapter 18

A Cylinder Seal Impression from Tel Qashish Area E North

Edwin C. M. van den Brink (*Israel Antiquities Authority*)

Among the many pottery body sherds retrieved from Area E (North; IAA permit A-6149), a single, in situ red-polished neck/shoulder fragment of a medium-sized jar (L5071, B50645) bore a cylinder seal impression with a naturalistic animal file (Ben-Tor 1978, class IIA) depicting two four-legged animals striding and facing left (figs. 18.1, 18.2.1), one with two long horns. A segment of a matching cylinder seal impression was found ex-situ, at Megiddo (reg.no. 34.2754), more than eighty years ago (fig. 18.2.2; Engberg and Shipton 1934, 36, figs. 10 C; 11 C; Ben-Tor 1978, no. IIA-4; Braun 2004, 2013, 106, pl. 78.a).[1] As first noticed by Eliot Braun (pers. comm. 2013), both examples were rolled from the same cylinder seal. Alexander Joffe (2001, 355–56, fig. 19.1) tentatively identified the two wild animals on the Megiddo fragment as a lion or leopard pursuing an ibex. For an interpretation of the symbolic and ideological intent of the iconography displayed, see Joffe 2001, 360–61.

Another late EB I cylinder seal impression showing an animal file was recovered ex-situ in the upper village of Tel Qashish, Stratum IX (Ben-Tor 2003, fig. 73.5), displaying, unlike the one at issue here, a tête-bêche arrangement and regarded as the product of a distinctive Jezreel Valley workshop.

---

1. This fragment is presently kept at the Rockefeller Museum, Jerusalem. I would like to thank Eliot Braun for drawing my attention to this sherd, and Alegre Savariego for facilitating its photography side by side with the Qashish fragment. The photos (figs. 18.1 and 18.2.2) were taken by Clara 'Amit. The Qashish fragment (fig. 18.1) was drawn by Irina Lidsky-Reznikov.

References

Ben-Tor, Amnon
1978 *Cylinder Seals of Third-Millennium Palestine.* BASORSup 22. Cambridge: American Schools of Oriental Research.
2003 "The Early Bronze Age Cylinder-Seal Impressions and a Stamp Seal." In *Tel Qashish: A Village in the Jezreel Valley; Final Report of the Archaeological Excavations (1978–1987)*, edited by Amnon Ben-Tor, Ruhama Bonfil, and Sharon Zuckerman, 165–73. Qedem Reports 5. Jerusalem: Hebrew University of Jerusalem.

Braun Eliot
2004 "More Evidence for Early Bronze Age Glyptics from the Southern Levant." *Levant* 36: 13–30.
2013 *Early Megiddo on the East Slope (the "Megiddo Stages"): A Report on the Early Occupation of the East Slope of Megiddo; Results of the Oriental Institute's Excavations, 1925–1933.* OIP 139. Chicago: Oriental Institute of the University of Chicago.

Engberg, Robert M., and Geoffrey M. Shipton
1934 *Notes on the Chalcolithic and Early Bronze Age Pottery of Megiddo.* SAOC 10. Chicago: University of Chicago Press.

Joffe, Alexander
2001 "Early Bronze Age Seal Impressions from the Jezreel Valley and the Problem of Sealing in the Southern Levant." In *Studies in the Archaeology of Israel and Neighboring Lands, in Memory of Douglas L. Esse*, edited by Samuel R. Wolff, 355–75. SAOC 59. ASOR Books 5. Chicago: Oriental Institute of the University of Chicago.

18. A Cylinder Seal Impression from Tel Qashish Area E North

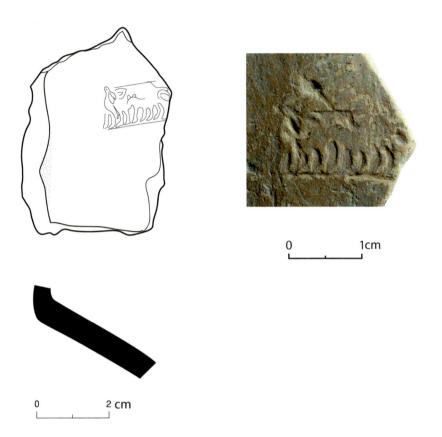

Fig. 18.1. Tel Qashish, Area E North. Neck-shoulder fragment of medium-sized jar bearing a cylinder seal impression (Square M61, Locus 5071, Basket 50645).

Fig. 18.2. 1. Full picture of the jar fragment from Tel Qashish, Area E North. 2. Vessel fragment of indeterminate type from Megiddo bearing a cylinder seal impression (Square U17, below Locus 1371, reg.no. 34.2754/P5554).

Chapter 19

The Groundstone Assemblage from Tel Qashish

Ianir Milevski (*Israel Antiquities Authority*)

The excavations carried out at the margins of Tel Qashish yielded a total of ninety-seven groundstone objects. The assemblage described in this chapter, retrieved from all excavated areas, includes tools, vessels, and tournettes used for the fabrication of pottery. Architectural stone objects, such as door sockets, are not included in this report.

Most loci are either topsoil or belong to EB I contexts. Vessel fragments from the Chalcolithic period were mostly found in topsoil contexts. One of these vessels, from Area B, is to be dated to the Late Bronze Age based on the pottery assemblage found there and dated to this period.

The illustrations of the objects (figs. 19.1–6) were arranged not only typologically but also contextually, giving primacy to items originating in the EB I occupation levels. Parallels of the objects in other sites in the country are brought mainly for vessels and specific artifacts. Tools are not covered in extenso, and parallels for them from other sites will be presented only in particular cases.

Defining the raw materials from which the artifacts were produced and their provenience will help understand not only the overall groundstone system, but also, and mainly, the exchange relations of the site and other regions of the country. The typological definitions largely follow the technological and typological considerations put forward by Katherine Wright (1992a, b), Erella Hovers (1996), Yorke Rowan (1998), and a previous study carried out by the author (Milevski 1998).

Tables 19.1–5 (at the end of the chapter) present the distribution of stone objects and raw materials according to areas and types. The complete list of stone objects appears in table 19.6 (accessible at https://doi.org/10.5913/2022655.t19.6), ordered by object number, and includes all the relevant data for each object.

Statistical data of the objects—according to type, contexts, and areas—will sometimes be brought to reveal general tendencies in the assemblages and probable functional divisions at the site. The minimum number of individuals (MNI) applied to stone objects is determined according to typological differences and the condition of the items. In most cases, a minimalist approach will be used, taking into account only complete and broken objects.

Raw Materials

Basalt and vesicular basalt (table 19.1) were the main raw materials (ca. 61 percent) used for making groundstones. Although no figures are given, it would seem that this was also the case at Qiryat Ata, where most of the illustrated Early Bronze stone objects were made of basalt (Rowan 2003). Since basalt sources are not local, these groundstones probably originated in areas located to the east of Qashish in the basalt outcrops of the Yarmuk River, near the Kinneret, or in the Golan Heights (Rowan 1998, Phillip and Williams-Thorpe 2001). Limestone, chalk, and flint (sometimes pebbles and cobbles from the water streams near the site) make up the remainder of the groundstones' raw materials. Pebbles, cobbles, and nodules, as blanks, are a large component of the assemblage, making up about 28 percent of the total items. Limestone and flint probably originated in the Cenomanian or Eocene geological layers close to the site (Picard and Golani 1992).

Technology

Technological aspects of the groundstone industries from the southern Levant have rarely been discussed in research. In his article on groundstones from Mexico, John Clark (1988, 83, quoted by Hovers 1996, 172) defined groundstones as artifacts produced by pecking, grinding, abrading, and polishing. Wright (1992a, 53) added to this list also flaking (a common characteristic of chipped flints), drilling, and incising. In defining grinding technology, Jennie Adams (1998) outlined three different categories for objects involved in it: artifacts used to reduce substances, artifacts used to shape other artifacts, and artifacts shaped with groundstones.

The different aspects of stone-tool and vessel fabrication are not addressed in this chapter, but the "Manufacture" column in table 19.6 (https://doi.org/10.5913/2022655.t19.6) is dedicated to technique observations relating to the final form of the object. Blanks for tool preparation are indicated in the column describing the condition of the object.

Typology

Lower and Upper Grinding Stones

Lower and upper grinding stones, mostly made of vesicular basalt, are a significant component of the groundstones assemblage. The number of lower grinding stones (n=17) is almost three times higher than that of the upper grinding stones (n=6). In general, the working surface of the lower grinding stones is flat (fig. 19.1.1), slightly convex (fig. 19.1.2), or concave shallow (fig. 19.1.3).

Upper grinding stones are usually loaf-shaped (fig. 19.1.4), dome-shaped (fig. 19.1.5), or elongated (fig. 19.1.6).

Mortars

Two mortars, clearly stationary, were found in Area C, made of massive blocks of limestone with round and shallow working surfaces (fig. 19.2.1–2).

Hammerstones

Six hammerstones were found in Areas E (North and South) and F, either spherical-like (fig. 19.3.1) or cubical (fig. 19.3.2). These tools, made of flint nodules, limestone, or basalt, were intended for battering. Some show scars or grooves on their working surfaces.

Pounders

Twelve pounders—a different type of battering tool— were uncovered in Areas B, C, E North, and F, most of them ovoid or elongated. They are divided into three subtypes according to size: heavy (n=1), medium (n=7), and small (n=4).

The heavy pounder (134 × 130 × 78+ mm), found in Area A and made of chalk and with an ovoid body (fig. 19.3.3), was probably intended for heavy-duty tasks. The small pounders are generally oval and measure less than 30 mm long (fig. 19.3.4). A concentration of pounders (n=7), most of them medium-sized, was found in Area E North, hinting perhaps to a specific activity in that area.

Worked Pebbles, Cobbles

The assemblage comprises four worked pebbles and cobbles of unclear function (two may be considered rubbing stones), made of limestone or quartzolite, some of them exhibiting polishing marks. The cobbles are over 50 mm long.

Perforated Stones

Nine perforated stones were found in Areas E (North and South; n=5) and F (n=4). Five are spindle whorls (fig. 19.3.5–7). One of these (Fig. 19.3.7), a whorl probably utilized for spinning, has a molded rim around the perforation. Some perforated stones (e.g., Fig. 19.3.8–9) may have been used as weights, but some of them are small mace-head-shaped stones of unclear function.

Tournettes

Two basalt tournettes (potter's wheel) were found, one in Area C and the second in Area E (South). The tournette from Area C (Fig. 19.4.1), representing an upper wheel, bears a groove in the center. It was unfortunately found broken, but its diameter could be reconstructed to about 28 cm. Similar objects were found in EB III contexts at Khirbet el-Batrawy (Fiaccavento 2013).

The second tournette, from Area E (South), the base of a basalt bowl, was converted into a lower potter's wheel (not illustrated). This phenomenon, that is, taking a (broken?) bowl and recycling its base into a potter's wheel, is very well known in the southern Levant, seen in sites such as Qiryat Ata (Rowan 2003) and Ashkelon Barnea (Rosenberg and Golani 2014, fig. 6.2). It is also present in other assemblages, such as those of Tel Miqne (Milevski forthcoming), Ḥorbat Petura (Milevski and Baumgarten 2008, fig. 8.3), and ʿEn Zippori (Milevski and Getzov 2014). During the excavations of the Hebrew University in the upper part of Tel Qashish (Ben-Tor, Bonfil, and Zuckerman 2003, 80–82, fig. 41, pl. 9.20), a lower potter's wheel was found in an EB III context.

While large numbers of lower parts of potter's wheels have been found in the southern Levant, the upper parts are less common. An almost complete list of upper and lower potter's wheels has been published by Chiara Fiaccavento (2013, table 1). The potter's wheels from the present Qashish excavations show that the pottery was produced at the site, at the foot of the tell. This situation probably changed during the EB III when workshops were present in the upper part of the city.

Bowls

Bowls have a high representation rate in the Qashish assemblage (n=25). Five fragments date from the Ghassulian Chalcolithic, while the remainder (n=18) are dated to the Early Bronze. All were made of nonvesicular basalt.

Some Chalcolithic bowls are hemispherical (fig. 19.4.2–3), and others (fig. 19.4.6) have fenestrated bases. Two items (fig. 19.4.4–5) could be earlier, probably from what some colleagues call the Late Pottery Neolithic or Early Chalcolithic (Rowan 1998). Most of these early items were found in topsoil contexts.

The Early Bronze bowls have everted rims (fig. 19.5.1–3) and thick bases (Fig. 19.5.4–5). A complete, finely made, and relatively low bowl is worth noting (Braun 1990; Rowan 1998).

Varia

The function of the twelve items included in this category, found in all areas, was difficult to establish. However, based on the worked surfaces they exhibit, they were clearly part of the stone tools.

One item worth noting, bell-shaped and made of chalk (fig. 19.6.1; repeat link), has a groove dividing it into two parts. This groove, probably intended for tying a string, indicates that the item could have been a pendant. Its hollow body shows two perforations on one side and one on the opposite side, giving the object the semblance of a nozzle. No coeval parallel for this item was found, but two stone pendants, one bell-shaped (Matskevich and Milevski 2003, fig. 8.2) and one globular (Lechevallier 1978, fig. 35.7) were found in the Neolithic site of Abu Ghosh.

Summary

The groundstone assemblage retrieved from the settled area near Tel Qashish is relatively small. Most items seem to belong to the EB I occupation, although a few earlier ones clearly date from the Chalcolithic period. Two industry types were discerned at the site: one based on imports, with objects made of basalt (vesicular or nonvesicular), represented mainly by grinding stones and bowls; and a local one, based on the exploitation of limestone and flint nodules, pebbles, and cobbles.

Areas E (North and South) and F seem to have been the most active in grinding and utilizing stone vessels. However, this could be the result of the more extensive excavations carried out in these two specific areas compared to the rest of the site.

The tool types present at the site show a relative balance between grinding activities, evidenced by the presence of lower and upper grinding stones, and pounding/hammering, represented by hammers, pounders, and other tools. The low number of mortars present at the site can be either due to these activities not being carried out on-site or that they were conducted in yet unexcavated parts of the site.

Acknowledgments

I am indebted to Viviana Moscovich and Matthew J. Adams for editing this text.

References

Adams, Jennie L.
1998 "Ground Stone Artifacts." In *Archaeological Investigations of Early Village Sites in the Middle Santa Cruz Valley: Analyses and Synthesis Part I*, edited by Jonathan B. Mabry, 357–422. Anthropological Papers 19. Tucson: Center for Desert Archaeology.

Ben-Tor, Amnon, Ruhama Bonfil, and Sharon Zuckerman
2003 *Tel Qashish: A Village in the Jezreel Valley; Final Report of the Archaeological Excavations (1978–1987)*. Qedem Reports 5. Jerusalem: Hebrew University of Jerusalem.

Braun, Eliot
1990 "Basalt Bowls of the EB I Horizon in the Southern Levant." *Paléorient* 16: 87–96.

Clark, John E.
1988 *The Lithic Artifacts of La Libertad, Chiapas, Mexico: An Economic Perspective*. Papers of the New World Archaeological Foundation 52. Provo: New World Archaeological Foundation.

Fiaccavento, Chiara
2013 "Potters' Wheels from Khirbet Al-Batrawy: A Reconsideration of Social Contexts." *Vicino Oriente* 17: 75–103.

Hovers, Erella
1996 "The Groundstone Industry." In *Excavations at the City of David 1978–1985 Directed by Yigal Shiloh, Vol. IV: Various Reports*, edited by Donald T. Ariel and Alon de Groot, 171–203. Qedem 35. Jerusalem: Hebrew University of Jerusalem.

Lechevallier, Monique
1978 *Abou Gosh et Beisamoun: Deux gisements du VIIe millénaire avant l'ère chrétienne en Israël*. Paris: Association Paléorient.

Matskevich, Zinovi, and Ianir Milevski
2003 "Stone Imagery Items." In *The Neolithic Site of Abu Ghosh: The 1995 Excavations*, edited by Hamoudi Khalaily and Ofer Marder, 74–76. IAA Reports 19. Jerusalem: Israel Antiquities Authority.

Milevski, Ianir
1998 "The Groundstone Tools." In *Villages, Terraces, and Stone Mounds: Excavations at Manahat, Jerusalem, 1987–1989*, by Gershon Edelstein, Ianir Milevski, and Sara Aurant, 61–77. IAA Reports 3. Jerusalem: Israel Antiquities Authority.

Forthcoming "The Stone Tools and Vessels from Tel Miqne-Ekron—Final Report." In *Tel Miqne-Ekron Object and Material Culture Monograph: MB II–Iron Age II*, edited by Trude Dothan and Seymour Gitin. Ekron Limited Edition Series 14. Jerusalem: W.F. Albright Institute of Archaeological Research; Hebrew University of Jerusalem.

Milevski, Ianir, and Yaakov Baumgarten
2008 "Between Lachish and Tel Erani: Horvat Ptora, a New Late Prehistoric Site in the Southern Levant." In *Proceedings of the 5th International Congress on the Archaeology of the Ancient Near East, Vol. 2*, edited by Joaquín Córdoba Zoilo, Miquel Molist, Carmen Pérez Aparicio, Isabel Rubio de Miguel, and Sergio Martínez Lillo, 609–26. 3 vols. Madrid: Universidad Autónoma de Madrid.

Milevski, Ianir, and Nimrod Getzov
2014 "'En Zippori: Preliminary Report." *HA-ESI* 126. http://www.hadashot-esi.org.il/Report_Detail_Eng.aspx?id=13675.

Picard, Leo Y., and U. Golani
1992 *Geological Map, Northern Sheet*. Jerusalem: Geological Survey of Israel.

Philip, Graham, and Olwen Williams-Thorpe
2001 "The Production and Consumption of Basalt Artefacts in the Southern Levant during the 5th–4th Millennia BC: A Geochemical and Petrographic Investigation." In *Archaeological Sciences 97; Proceedings of the Conference Held at the University of Durham, 2–4 September 1997*, edited by Andrew Millard, 11–30. BARIS 939. Oxford: Archaeopress.

Rosenberg, Danny, and Amir Golani
2014 "Groundstone Tools of a Copper-Smiths' Community: Understanding Stone-Related Aspects of the Early Bronze Age Site of Ashqelon Barnea." *Journal of Mediterranean Archaeology* 25: 27–51.

Rowan, Yorke M.
1998 "Ancient Distribution and Deposition of Prestige Objects: Basalt Vessels during Late Prehistory in the Southern Levant." PhD diss., University of Texas, Austin.

2003 "The Groundstone Assemblage." In *Salvage Excavations at the Early Bronze Age Sites of Qiryat Ata*, edited by Amir Golani, 183–202. IAA Reports 18. Jerusalem: Israel Antiquities Authority.

Wright, Katherine
1992a "A Classification System for Ground Stone Tools from the Prehistoric Levant." *Paléorient* 18: 53–81.
1992b "Ground Stone Assemblage Variation and Subsistence Strategies in the Levant 22,000–5,000 B.P." PhD diss., Yale University.

Table 19.1. Distribution of raw materials by area.

Type	Area A	Area B	Area C	Area D	Area E (North and South)	Area F	Total	Percent
Limestone	1	1	3		3	2	10	10.3
Chalk	1				3	1	5	5.1
Pebbles and cobbles			2	1	7	3	13	13.4
Flint					5	3	8	8.3
Basalt	1		6	3	24	5	39	40.2
Vesicular basalt			6		12	2	20	20.6
Varia					2		2	2.1
Subtotal	3	1	17	4	56	16	97	100

Table 19.2. Areas A and B: Distribution of stone objects by type.

Type	Area A	Area B	Total
Grinding stones	1		1
Pounders	1	1	2
Bowl	1		1
Subtotal	3	1	4

Table 19.3. Areas C, D, and F: Distribution of stone objects by type.

Type	Area C	Area D	Area F	Total
Lower grinding stones	3	1	2	6
Upper grinding stones		1	1	2
Mortars	2			2
Pounders	2		1	3
Hammerstones			3	3
Worked pebbles/cobbles	1	1		2
Spindle whorls/perforated items			4	4
Tournette	1			1
Varia	3	1	2	6
Bowls	3		3	6
Chalcolithic bowls	2			2
Subtotal	17	4	16	37

Table 19.4. Area E (North and South): Distribution of stone objects by type and stratum.

Type	Stratum 1	Stratum 2	Total
Lower grinding stones	3	8	11
Upper grinding stones	1	3	4
Hammerstones		2	2
Pounders	4	4	8
Rubbing stones	1	1	2
Worked pebbles/cobbles	2		2
Spindle whorls/perforated items	2	3	5
Tournettes		1	1
Varia	3	3	6
Bowls	5	7	12
Chalcolithic bowls	3		3
Subtotal	24	32	56

Table 19.5. General distribution of types by area.

Type	Area A	Area B	Area C	Area D	Area E (North and South)	Area F	Total	Percent
Lower grinding stones			3	1	11	2	17	17.5
Upper grinding stones				1	4	1	6	6.2
Mortars			2				2	2.1
Hammerstones					2	3	5	5.1
Pounders	1	1	2		8	1	13	13.4
Rubbing stones					2		2	2.1
Worked pebbles/cobbles			1	1	2		4	4.1
Spindle whorls/perforated items					5	4	9	9.3
Tournettes			1		1		2	2.1
Varia	1		3	1	6	2	13	13.4
Chalcolithic bowls			2		3		5	5.1
Bowls	1		3		12	3	19	19.6
Subtotals	**3**	**1**	**17**	**4**	**56**	**16**	**97**	**100.0**

Supplementary Table 19.6 available online at https://doi.org/10.5913/2022655.t19.6.

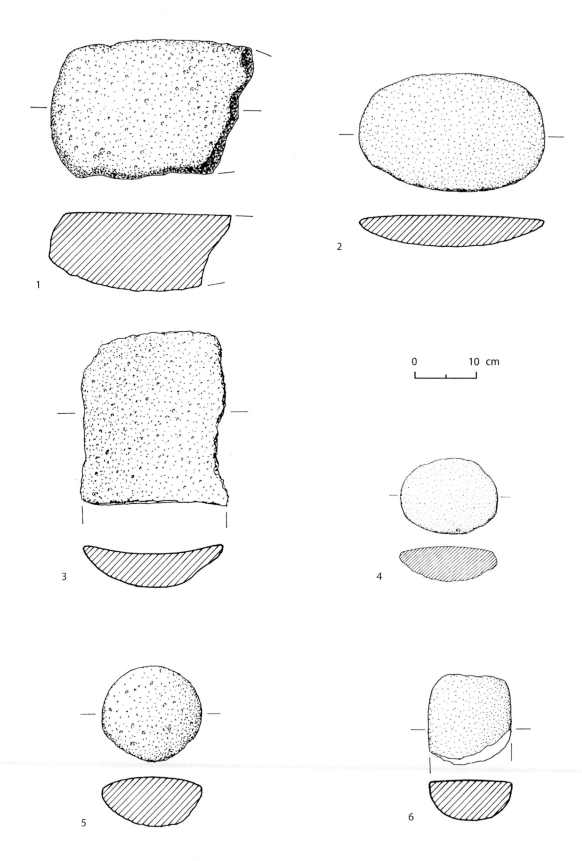

Fig. 19.1. Lower and upper grinding stones.

19. The Groundstone Assemblage from Tel Qashish 235

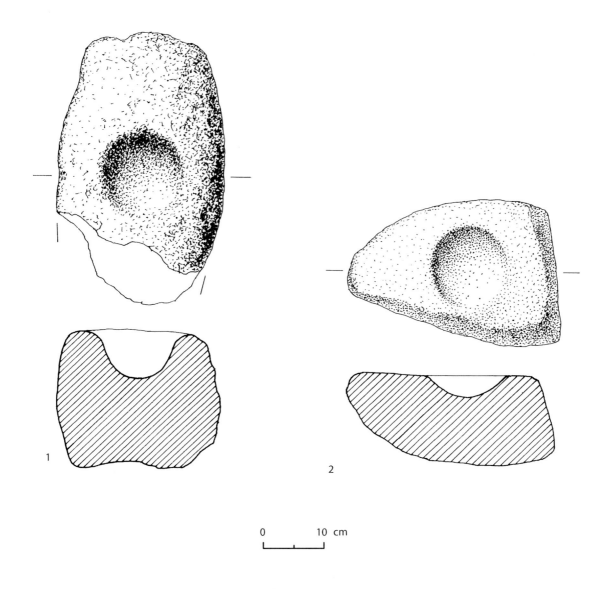

Fig. 19.2. Mortars.

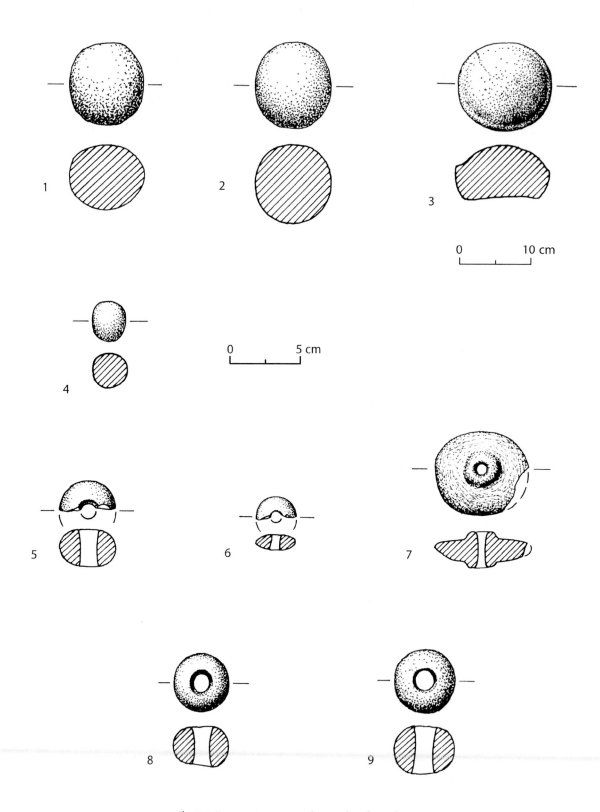

Fig. 19.3. Hammerstones, pounders, and perforated stones.

19. The Groundstone Assemblage from Tel Qashish

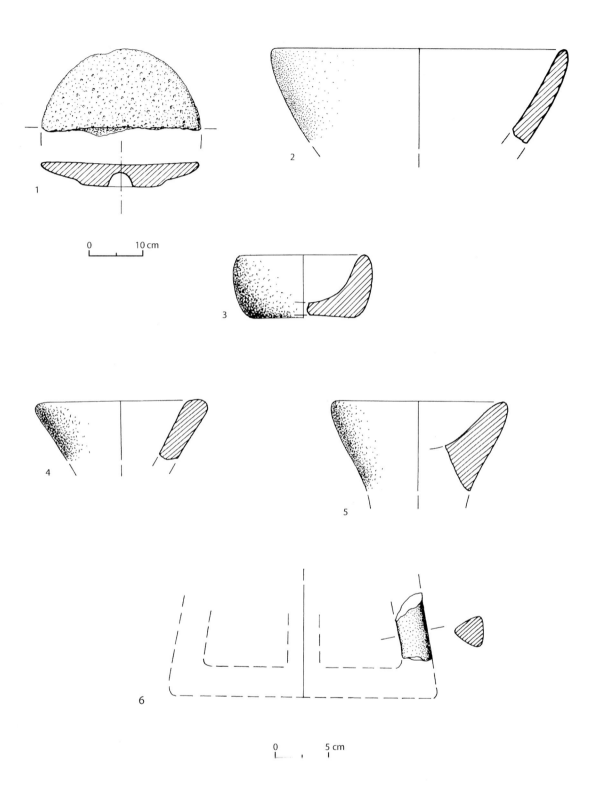

Fig. 19.4. Tournettes and Chalcolithic-period bowls.

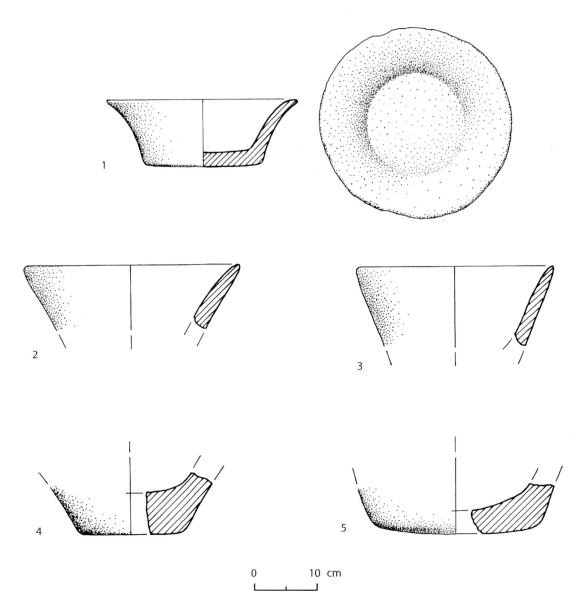

Fig. 19.5. Early Bronze Age I bowls; complete (1), rims (2–3), and bases (4–5).

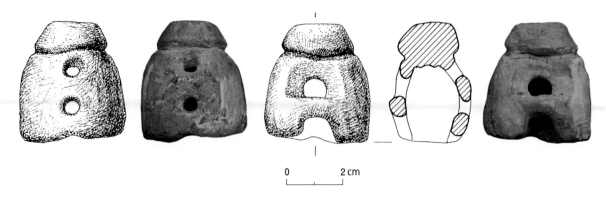

Fig. 19.6. Varia: A bell-shaped object.

Chapter 20

The Late Early Bronze Age I Flint Assemblages
from Tel Qashish Areas A–F

Alla Yaroshevich (*Israel Antiquities Authority*)

This report describes the flint assemblages recovered during three seasons of salvage excavations conducted in 2010–2011 in the margins of Tel Qashish, in Areas A–D (IAA permit A-5881), Areas E South and F (IAA permit A-5992), and Area E North (IAA permit A-6149; cf. chs. 15–17, this volume).

Excluding the remarkable Late Bronze Age II repository of cultic pottery objects excavated in Area B (Part V, this volume), and the Early Roman stone pavement in Area A1 (ch. 11, this volume), all the in situ remains exposed during these seasons date to the late Early Bronze Age I (EB IB).

A variety of flint sources can be found around Tel Qashish, on Mount Carmel, the Menashe Hills, and the Nazareth Mountains (Ekshtain et al. 2013; and ch. 3, this volume). Of particular importance is the proximity of the site to Har Ḥaruvim, a center of Canaanean-blades production located in Menashe Hills (Meyerhof 1960; Shimelmitz, Barkai, and Gofer 2000; Shimelmitz 2009; Milevski 2013), only a few km south of Tel Qashish and initially associated with the EB II horizon (Meyerhof 1960). However, recent surveys conducted at the site yielded a sufficient number of pottery sherds diagnostic of the EB I (Milevski, pers. comm.) to suggest that this workshop could have indeed supplied Tel Qashish during that period. This possibility is supported by the visual similarity of some Canaanean blades derived from Tel Qashish with blade cores from Har Ḥaruvim in terms of the raw material. Considering the proximity of the Har Ḥaruvim workshop, the parameters indicating the value of the Canaanean blades in the eyes of the Tel Qashish inhabitants are of especial interest. In particular, metric characteristics, edge damage, and evidence of recycling shed light on the degree of exploitation of these artifacts, highlighting certain aspects related to their production system and their use-related variability.

The relatively large areas exposed during the excavations allow analyzing the spatial distribution of the various flint categories. Their subsequent comparison with the assemblage revealed at the tell (Rosen 2003) sheds light on the use of the entire site during the EB IB.

The flint assemblage recovered in Areas A–F has a considerable intrusive component, predominantly of Middle Paleolithic (MP) and Epipaleolithic/Upper Paleolithic (UP) origins. While in situ MP and Epipaleolithic/UP sites are present in the vicinity of the tell (see ch. 3, this volume), the physical characteristics of the intrusive artifacts recorded in the assemblage (patination and varying degrees of abrasion) point to their affiliation with two redeposited sites excavated on the foothills of Mount Carmel, a few hundred meters to the west and south of Tel Qashish (see ch. 3, this volume). One of them, Tel Qashish West (TQW), is characterized by abundant MP deposits (fig. 20.1). The other, Tel Qashish South (TQS), yielded a secondary source of flint raw material apparently exploited during the MP and

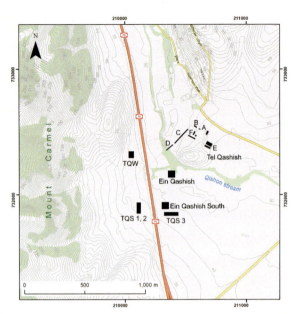

Fig. 20.1. Location map of the areas excavated on the margins of Tel Qashish and the prehistoric sites excavated in its vicinity.

Epipaleolithic/UP periods (fig. 20.1). Several diagnostic Chalcolithic and PPN artifacts (see below) complement the intrusive component.

Methodology

Most sediments were not sieved, but selected loci, in particular those related to grain storage facilities (silos) in Area E South (ch. 12, this volume), were sieved through a 2 mm mesh to recover microfaunal remains (ch. 22, this volume). This sieving also yielded a considerable amount of flint chips, that is, small flakes with a maximal length of 1.5 cm. These were not counted, but their presence certainly indicates on-site knapping.

The assemblage (N=1544) is presented per the main techno-typological categories and accompanied by data on their distribution in each excavated area. Following Steven Rosen (2003), Canaanean blades were affiliated with the debitage group.

Results

Raw Material

About a third of the artifacts exhibit various degrees of patination. There is a clear correlation between the frequency of patinated items and the topography of the site. In Areas C and D, the lowest topo-

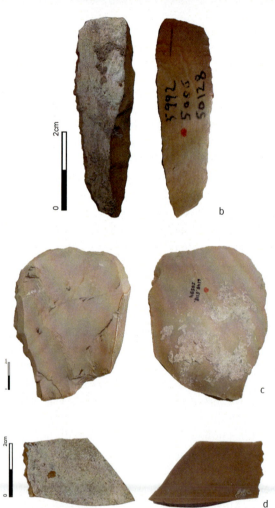

Fig. 20.2a–d. A variety of tools exemplifying the flint varieties used at the site: a. Scraper (Area C, L394, B3340); b. Backed and truncated sickle blade on PE (Area E South, L5006, B50128); c. End scraper (Area E North, L6149, B5118); d. A fragment of a tabular scraper (Area E South, L5025, B50222)

graphical area, half of the debitage and a third of the ad hoc tools are patinated. The majority of the diagnostic MP and Epipaleolithic/UP artifacts were exposed in these areas. In Areas E and F, the highest topographical areas, a third of the debitage and a fifth of the ad hoc tools exhibit patina.

Fresh artifacts exhibit several flint categories. The first refers to a nonhomogeneous gray–beige flint, often with chalky inclusions. Several flint varieties within this category were observed in primary and secondary sources on Mount Carmel, in particular at Bustan Gal, the private farm located on the slope of the mount and facing the valley (ch. 3, this volume). These nonhomogeneous varieties are present almost exclusively among the ad hoc tools and the debitage. A high-quality beige flint, often with distinctive orange to brown narrow concentric bands, is common as well (fig. 20.2a–d). This flint probably originates in the Menashe Hills (Adulam Formation), a few kilometers south of the site (Ekshtain et al. 2013, fig. 6), though similar-looking material, known as "Solelim flint" (or Timrat Formation; Ekshtain et al. 2013, fig. 5), is abundantly present near Nazareth as well.

Canaanean blades and sickle blades are made on high-quality, very bright beige to gray and brown flint, homogeneous or with bands (figs. 20.3a–j; 20.4–5). Certain types look similar to the Canaanean blade cores from the Har Ḥaruvim workshop presently on exhibit in the archaeological museum of Kibbutz Ramat HaShofet (figs. 20.6–7). Two distinctively large cortical tools, namely an end scraper and a wide retouched blade with a faceted platform (figs. 20.5–6), are of especial interest. The similarity in raw material of these large artifacts and some of the Canaanean blade cores from Har Ḥaruvim is apparent not just in color, texture, and the striped pattern, but also in the cortex, which is thin and smooth, orange-brown or whitish on the surface and brown in its interior. A few Canaanean blades are made on a coarse-grained, bright-beige material with tiny black points (fig. 20.8).

Fine-grained gray, pinkish, and purple flint fragments apparently represent a PPN intrusion. This period was revealed in a particular context on the tell (Rosen 2003, 396). Limestone, weathered flint, and burnt items are present in low numbers. A few pieces of quartz and transparent flint complement the variability of the raw material categories.

Technology

Flint artifacts are not numerous in Areas A (N=46) and B (N=29), both heavily disturbed or destroyed in the post-EB period (table 20.1; all tables can be found at the end of the chapter). The most abundant assemblages were exposed in Areas C and D (N=754 and N=277, respectively). Area E (South and North, combined) yielded 312 flint artifacts, and another 128 items were found in Area F.

In all areas, debitage is dominated by flakes, which make up about a third of the assemblage. The frequency of Canaanean blades in Areas C–D (1.8 percent) is very low compared to Areas E and F, where these artifacts make up 22.3 percent and 29.17 percent of debitage, respectively. Plain blades appear in low numbers varying from 2.1 percent to 7.0 percent. Bladelets are very rare: their frequencies vary from 0.6 percent to 2.3 percent in different areas.

Cores constitute 14.4 percent, 10.6 percent, and 10.5 percent of debitage in Areas C–D, E, and F, respectively. Amorphous cores predominate the assemblage (table 20.2), and their majority shows small or very small flake removal; a few exhibit flake and blade removals. Flake cores with a single striking platform represent the second, most common group. One of the flake cores, abandoned at the beginning of the reduction sequence (fig. 20.9), allows estimating the original size of the nodules. The frequencies of CTE are remarkably high in all areas, indicating intensive core use. The relatively high frequencies of PE show on-site knapping from the beginning of the reduction sequence.

Blade cores are rare. One of these, made of high quality, homogeneous beige flint, is quite exhausted but has a somewhat regular pyramidal shape and a modified striking platform (fig. 20.10.5). A similar find from 'En Esur Stratum II was interpreted as an on-site attempt to remove prismatic Canaanean-like blades (Milevski et al. 2006, 197). The only fresh core indicating bladelet removals (together with those of small flakes) was found in topsoil in Area D (fig. 20.11.1).

Patinated bladelet cores with one or two platforms and a few patinated bladelets represent Epipaleolithic intrusions (fig. 20.12). The intrusive bladelet-oriented industry, together with Levallois flakes, tools, and cores (figs. 20.13; 20.14.1–2), were

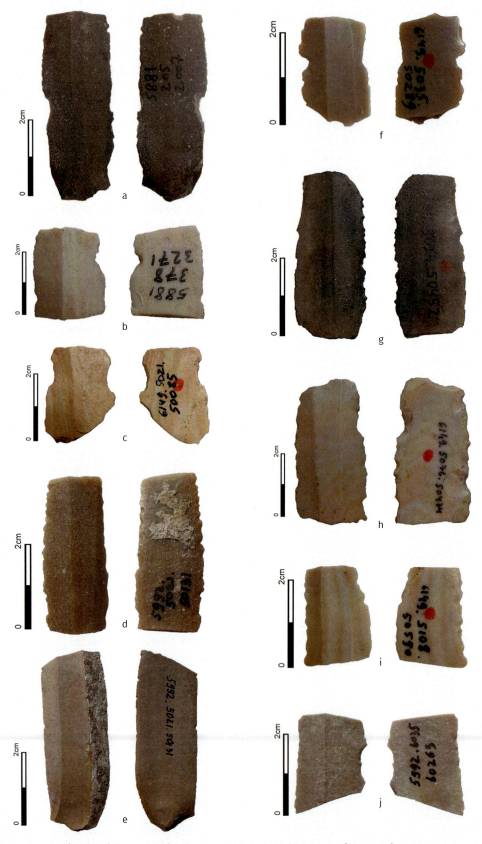

Fig. 20.3a–j. Representative Canaanean blades and sickle blades (fragments).

20. The Late Early Bronze Age I Flint Assemblages from Tel Qashish Areas A–F

Fig. 20.4. Knife on Canaanean blade (Area E North, L6149, Basket 50601).

Fig. 20.5. Large cortical blade with gentle retouch and faceted platform (Area C, L379, B3319) and two knives (Area E North, L5113, B50601; and Area C, L347, B3181).

found mostly in Areas C and D. This pattern is not coincidental since these areas, topographically the lowest, are the closest to the alluvial fan containing the redeposited MP and Epipaleolithic artifacts uncovered at TQS and TQW (ch. 3, this volume). A blade core with bidirectional removals characteristic of the PPNB, made on high-quality beige flint (fig. 20.11.2), was also found in Area C.

Canaanean blades (N=81) are represented mostly by medial fragments (N=59); another twenty items constitute proximal parts. Only six Canaanean blades show no edge damage. The majority (ca. 80 percent) exhibits signs of use (nibbling) and about 60 percent of the Canaanean blades exhibit nibbling on both cutting edges (fig. 20.15).

Canaanean blades are 35.1 mm long, 19.5 mm wide, and 4.9 mm thick on average (table 20.4). The width and thickness distribution indicate two distinctive groups (figs. 20.16–17). The majority varies from 15 mm to 20 mm in width and 3.5 mm to 6.0 mm in thickness. The less-numerous group includes items 20 to 30 mm in width and 6.0 mm to 8.5 mm in thickness. Figures 20.18–20 show the metric characteristics of the fragment categories (proximal, medial, distal). While proximal fragments are wider and thicker than medial ones on average (figs. 20.18–19), the widest and the thickest fragments occur mostly among medial fragments (fig. 20.20). These observations show that the bimodal pattern does not correlate with fragmentation (i.e., medial vs. proximal) but characterizes the assemblage in general.

Typology

The typological composition of the assemblage is presented in table 20.3. There is a sharp contrast between Areas C–D, where the ad hoc assemblage constitutes close to 95 percent, and Areas E–F where formal types, particularly Canaanean sickle blades (19.2 percent and 33.3 percent of the tools, respectively), are prominent. The description below starts with the formal tool types (figs. 20.3a–j; 20.4; 20.10; 20.21–25), followed by the ad hoc group (figs. 20.26–28).

Canaanean sickle blades

(N=28, figs. 20.10; 20.21–24)—twenty-five Canaanean sickle blades consist of medial fragments; the

Fig. 20.6. End scraper with cortex remains (right; Area E North, L5118, B 50594) next to the Canaanean blade core from Har Ḥaruvim (left). The core is exhibited at the archaeological museum of Kibbutz Ramat HaShofet.

Fig. 20.7. The Canaanean blade core from Har Ḥaruvim, exhibited at the archaeological museum of Kibbutz Ramat HaShofet.

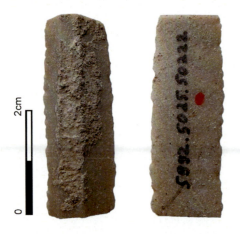

Fig. 20.8. Canaanean sickle blade made on coarse-grained flint with tiny black spots.

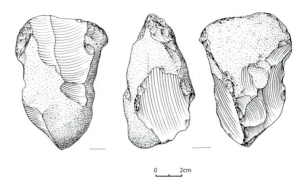

Fig. 20.9. A core at the beginning of the reduction sequence (Area C, L310, B3011).

remaining three have one truncated extremity. No proximal (bulbar) fragments with gloss were observed. Notches are often present on one or both edges (figs. 20.3b–c, f, h, j; 20.23.4). The artifacts with two opposed notches may represent a fragmented 'En Esur knife—a type recently delineated during the large-scale excavations of the eponymous site (Brailovsky, Elad, and Paz 2020).

Five sickle blades show gloss on both edges; resharpening in the form of serration or retouch is often present (fig. 20.15). In most cases, the non-glossed edge exhibits nibbling, retouch, or both.

Canaanean sickle blades are 27.4 mm long, 16.5 mm wide, and 3.9 mm thick on average (table 20.4). These values are lower in comparison to Canaanean blades; moreover, the comparison between medial segments also indicates that the Canaanean sickle blades are narrower and thinner than thee Canaanean blades (figs 20.18–19). Furthermore, sickle blades exhibit lower values of standard deviation (SD) in all metric characteristics (length, width, and thickness), indicating that these tools are more standardized as a group (table 20.4). The relatively high standardization of Canaanean sickle blades compared to Canaanean blades is evident in width and thickness distribution (figs. 20.16–17). Thus, most sickle blades fall between 15 mm and 20 mm in width and 3.0 mm and 5.0 mm in thickness. No sickle blades corresponding to the group of the large (i.e., wide and thick) Canaanean blades were recorded (fig. 20.20).

Knives
(N=2)—two complete blades with gentle retouch and nibbling on both edges were present in the assemblage. One of them has a triangular cross-sec-

tion and a slightly curved lateral profile. This item, 152 mm long, 20.5 mm wide, and 7.5 mm thick, is made on high quality, homogeneous beige-brown flint with curved bands (figs. 20.23.1; 20.4k). The other knife, produced on a secondary ridge blade with a faceted platform, has two notches on its distal proximity (fig. 20.21.1). This distinctive tool, 113 mm long, 19.2 mm wide, and 6.3 mm thick, represents a complete example of an 'En Esur knife (Brailovsky, Elad, and Paz 2020) made on a raw material characterized by a regular pattern of straight parallel bands.

Retouched Canaanean blades

(N=7)—this group encompasses retouched and truncated items, two of them complete (figs. 20.21.4; 20.22.2; 20.24.1). In one case, the truncation appears on the proximal (bulbar) fragment. These tools are diverse in terms of their metric characteristics, in particular in width and thickness. All exhibit signs of use or modification on their edges.

Backed and truncated sickle blades

(N=5, figs. 20.10.2; 20.21.2–3; 20.22.2, 20.24.2)—these narrow and elongated tools were found either on the bedrock exposed beneath the topsoil or at the top level of the layer bearing archaeological artifacts uncovered after most of the topsoil layer had been mechanically removed. Of interest is a sickle blade on PE with the cutting edge modified by a serration that removed only a very narrow part of the cortex, (fig. 20.24.2). A parallel was found in 'En Esur, Stratum IV, associated with the Late Chalcolithic (Milevski et al. 2006, 197).

A geometric sickle blade

(fig. 20.10.1)—this is a singular item, wide and short, modified by truncation and invasive ventral retouch along the edge, apparently indicating a hafting-related thinning. Though found in a sealed EBI context, it may represent a Middle Bronze intrusion.

Tabular scrapers

(N=4)—this group is represented by cortical fragments produced on high-quality flint, either beige or beige with a banded pattern, commonly used for the production of Canaanean blades (fig. 20.2d). In one case, there is indication of cortex grinding. No incisions were observed. Some of the tools affiliated with the ad hoc group (see below) may represent recycled tabular scrapers.

Microliths

(N=6)—besides three patinated retouched bladelets, apparently Epipaleolithic in origin, two micro end scrapers were found, both made on fine-grained homogeneous gray flint. One of the latter was exposed on a floor together with a fragment of a backed bladelet (fig. 20.24.7–8).

Bifacial tools

(N=3)—one of the tools is an adze made on a piece of tabular flint (fig. 20.25.1). The second is the burnt fragment of a bifacial tool with signs of polishing (fig. 20.25.2). These two artifacts are abraded and patinated. The third item is the preform of a bifacial tool on a massive flake, fresh in appearance.

Ad hoc tools

Retouched flakes

(n=111)—this is the most prominent group in the assemblage, encompassing a variety of blanks with numerous PE and CTE. More than half are made on homogeneous beige or beige with a banded pattern flint. While the majority are small, fully in accordance with the dominant core types, medium- to large-sized items are also present, mostly among the PE and cortical flakes (fig. 20.26.1). As mentioned above, some of these tools may represent recycled tabular scrapers.

Retouched blades

(n=14)—the low numbers of retouched blades in the assemblage is in accordance with the frequency of blade cores. Outstanding is the distinctively large, wide cortical blade with a faceted platform (figs. 20.5; 20.27.1). Its raw material closely resembles the one used for the Canaanean blade cores from Har Ḥaruvim. The similarity appears in the banded pattern, color, texture, and the cortex, which is thin, whitish on the surface and brown in its inner part. The retouch is partial, probably due to wear rather than intentional modification.

Notch–denticulates

(n=65)—these form the second largest group of tools. The majority are made on flakes, some rather massive and thick. Primary flakes, as well as blades and CTE, were also often used.

End scrapers
(n=16)—a couple of patinated items may represent Epipaleolithic/UP intrusions (fig. 20.14.2–3). Among fresh artifacts, steep tools on thick blanks are prominent (fig. 20.26). Some of them, modified by removal of elongated flakes, can be defined as core scrapers. The exceptionally large end scraper retaining part of the thin orange-brown cortex (figs. 20.6; 20.27.3) closely resembles Canaanean blade cores from Har Ḥaruvim in terms of raw material.

Multiple tools
(n=12)—this group shows a variety of combinations: awls with scrapers, with denticulates, or with truncation; denticulates with scrapers, or with truncation. A variety of blanks were applied, including PE, blades, and CTE.

Burins
(N=11)—these are diverse, both typologically and in blank selection, which includes CTE. Three burins are patinated, including one intrusive Epipaleolithic tool (fig. 20.12.4).

Awls
(n=7)—three of these tools are made on flakes, two on CTE, and two on primary flakes. One of these probably represents a recycled tabular scraper (fig. 20.27.2), made on a beige flint with a banded pattern commonly used at the site.

Side scrapers
(n=5)—three patinated tools may represent a Paleolithic intrusion. The remaining two were modified by steep retouch (fig. 20.28.1–2).

Discussion and Conclusions

The assemblages recovered in the margins of Tel Qashish (Areas A–F) contain abundant ad hoc and Canaanean blade industries alongside a much less prominent tabular scrapers and bladelet-oriented production. The most common raw material found at the site visually correlates with the sources located in the Menashe Hills referred to as the 'Adulam Formation (Ekshtain et al. 2013). The mostly flake-oriented ad hoc industry exhibits diverse raw materials, including nonhomogeneous kinds originating in Mount Carmel. The techno-typological composition, together with the raw material variability, clearly indicates that ad hoc tools were produced on-site. The Canaanean blades picture is more complicated. On the one hand, the absence of Canaanean cores suggests that the blades were imported. On the other hand, the presence of exceptionally large cortical tools (the wide blade and the end scraper), which resemble the Canaanean blade cores from Har Ḥaruvim in terms of the flint characteristics, indicates the possibility of on-site event/events of blade production.

The analysis of the metric characteristics, the edge damage, and the fragmentation of the Canaanean blade products revealed certain patterns of interest. Compared to Canaanean blades, Canaanean sickle blades have lower length, width, and thickness values, as well as lower standard deviation values indicating that sickle blades are more standardized as a group. The absence of proximal fragments among Canaanean sickle blades provides another strong indication for a deliberate choice of blanks for sickle-blade production, in contrast to Canaanean blanks where proximal fragments constitute as much as a quarter of the artifacts. Furthermore, the comparison between the medial fragments indicates a preference for narrow and thin artifacts for the production of sickle blades. All these patterns apparently reflect hafting-related constraints. Canaanean blades without gloss often exhibit nibbling, suggesting they were actually used and do not represent blanks to be transformed into sickle blades at a later point in time, or leftovers of sickle-blade production.

The frequent use of both cutting edges, edge resharpening, the virtual absence of complete blanks, the high degree of segmentation (at least 1:5 based on the ratio between proximal and medial fragments), and instances of recycling, such as notches produced on glossed edges, indicate an economic or cost-efficient approach toward Canaanean blade products.

Similar technological and use-related traits can be seen in the EB flint assemblage retrieved from Tel Qashish itself (Rosen 2003), where proximal fragments are extremely rare among sickle blades (three out of the sixty-two measurable items, Rosen 2003,

404) while abundant among Canaanean blades (30 percent, Rosen 2003, 404 and table 28). Canaanean blades (42.3 mm long, 19.9 mm wide, and 4.8 mm thick on average) and Canaanean sickle blades (39 mm long, 17.4 mm wide, and 4.7 mm thick on average; Rosen 2003) from the tell of Qashish are similar in their metrics to the corresponding groups retrieved in the tell's margins, Areas A–F (table 20.4). Another point of similarity refers to the metrics of the complete artifacts Canaanean blades (12.9 cm, 8.2 cm, and 11.9 cm; Rosen 2003, 397), which are comparable to the knives exposed in Areas C and E.

Finally, the Early Bronze assemblage from the tell is characterized by the frequent use of both cutting edges (almost half of the items show double gloss; Rosen 2003), edge resharpening, and a high degree of segmentation, indicating a cost-effective approach to Canaanean blades.

Indeed, the cost-effective approach to Canaanean blade products, in particular, the frequent appearance of double gloss and evidence of edge resharpening, characterize assemblages from other contemporary sites in the area (e.g., Shimelmitz, and Rosen 2014; Bankirer, 2003). At Tel Qashish and its margins this phenomenon is especially prominent due to the proximity of the site to high-quality natural flint sources and the Har Ḥaruvim workshop in particular. Such an economic approach indicates that the blades were not readily available to the farmers and emphasizes the highly specialized nature of Canaanean blades production and their high value in the eyes of the site's inhabitants. There are not enough data to reconstruct how the system of Canaanean blade production and distribution exactly operated. If the large cortical tools (the wide blade and the endscraper) represent the on-site reduction of Canaanean blade cores, then the scenario of itinerant knappers would be one of several possibilities, as suggested in the literature (Manclossi, Rosen, and de Miroschedji 2016; Manclossi, Rosen, and Milevski 2019).

The varying frequencies of the main artifact groups per excavation area, together with the data deriving from the tell itself (Rosen 2003), shed light on the spatial organization of the site. In Area D, topographically the nethermost area, only a few Canaanean blades and sickle blades were found, whereas the absolute majority of the assemblage is composed of ad hoc tools and debitage. In Area C, the presence of Canaanean blades and sickle blades is more prominent, even though these artifacts still constitute a very small portion of the retrieved debitage and tools, respectively. In contrast, in Areas E and F—topographically the highest—Canaanean blade products, blades, and sickle blades combined are much more numerous compared to the ad hoc groups. This pattern suggests that most of the activities related to the valued Canaanean blade products—hafting, retooling, resharpening—took place in the topographically higher-lying Areas E and F, in association with storage and dwelling structures. Interestingly, in the assemblage from the tell itself, the gap between the Canaanean blade products and the ad hoc group is even more prominent: 110 blades and 68 sickle blades against 46 ad hoc tools (after Rosen 2003).

The frequencies of tabular scrapers emphasize this topography-based hierarchy: Only four fragments were found in the tell's margins (1.3 percent of tools, excluding a few probably recycled artifacts), against eleven on the tell (excluding two intrusive Middle Bronze Age artifacts, ca. 5 percent of the tools, Rosen 2003, 404). Moreover, complete items and items with incisions were found only on the tell. This pattern is of especial interest considering the suggestion that tabular scrapers could have had a ritual function (McConaughy 1979, 1980; see also Elliott 1977 as summarized in Rosen 1997, in Shimelmitz and Adams 2014, in Yerkes et al. 2016), a hypothesis based on tabular scrapers and their spalls being found within or close to sacral areas, for example, the court of the EB IB temple at Tell Megiddo, which yielded numerous spalls indicating frequent resharpening of these tools (Shimelmitz and Adams 2014). More research is required to confirm the topography-related variability of the activities carried out at the margins of Tel Qashish. The study of tabular scrapers from 'Ein Zippori, indicating that these tools were most often used to butcher and skin animals (Yerkes et al. 2016), provides an interesting perspective in this regard.

Use-wear analysis can also shed light on the possibility that at least some Canaanean blades from the present site represent actual tools and not merely blanks for sickle blades or leftovers of sickle-blade production. The variety of functions of Canaanean blades identified in previous studies (e.g., Gurova 2013; Groman-Yaroslavski, Iserlis, and Eisenberg 2013) suggest that this possibility is viable.

Insights into the technological variability of Canaanean-blade production provided by recent studies (Manclossi, Rosen, and Milevski 2019; Manclossi, Rosen, and de Miroschedji 2016, Shimelmitz 2009; Shimelmitz and Rosen 2014) in combination with the possibility to differentiate between flint sources (e.g., Ekshtain et al. 2013) can be particularly helpful in reconstructing the manufacture and distribution systems of these artifacts. Such studies applied to Tel Qashish assemblage may confirm on-site Canaanean-blade reduction; alternatively, they could identify technological variations within the same workshop that supplied the site or the import of artifacts from different workshops. The latter, that is, importing from a variety of sources, is further suggested by the flint variability exhibited by the Canaanean blade products in Tel Qashish's margins.

The high value of the Canaanean blades at the site identified in the present study close to the workshop highlights the importance of these issues for reconstructing the EB IB economic and social aspects of lifestyle in the Jezreel Valley and beyond.

References

Bankirer, Rina Y.
2003 "The Flint Assemblage." In *Salvage Excavations at the Early Bronze Age Sites of Qiryat Ata*, edited by Amir Golani, 171–82. IAA Reports 18. Jerusalem: Israel Antiquities Authority.

Brailovsky, Lena, Itai Elad, and Yitzhak Paz
2020 "The "En Esur Knives': A New Tool Type from the Early Bronze Age Ib Period Site of 'En Esur ('Ein Asawir)." *Mitekufat Haeven* 50: 209–22.

Ekshtain, Ravid, Ariel Malinsky-Buller, Shimon Ilani, Irina Segal, and Erella Hovers
2013 "Raw Material Exploitation around the Middle Paleolithic site of 'Ein Qashish." *Quaternary International* 331: 248–66.

Elliott, Carolyn
1977 "The Religious Beliefs of the Ghassulians c. 4000–3100 B.C." *PEQ* 109: 3–25.

Gurova, Maria
2013 "Tribulum Inserts in Ethnographic and Archaeological Perspective: Case Studies from Bulgaria and Israel." *Lithic Technology* 38: 179–201.

Groman-Yaroslavski Iris, Mark Iserlis, and Michael Eisenberg
2013 "Potters' Canaanean Flint Blades during the Early Bronze Age." *Mediterranean Archaeology and Archaeometry* 13: 171–84.

Manclossi, Francesca, Steven A. Rosen, and Ianir Milevski
2019 "Canaanean Blade Technology: New Insights from Horvat Ptora (North), an Early Bronze Age I Site in Israel." *Mitekufat Haeven* 49: 284–315.

Manclossi, Francesca, Steven A. Rosen, and Pierre de Miroschedji
2016 "The Canaanean Blades from Tel Yarmuth, Israel: A Technological Analysis." *Paléorient* 42: 49–74.

McConaughy, Mark A.
1979 "Formal and Functional Analysis of Chipped Stone Tools from Bab edh-Dhra', Jordan." PhD diss., University of Pittsburgh.
1980 "Chipped Stone Tools." In "Preliminary Report of the 1979 Expedition to the Dead Sea Plain, Jordan," edited by Walter E. Rast and R. Thomas Schaub. *BASOR* 240: 57–58.

Meyerhof, Ezra L.
1960 "Flint Cores from Har HaHaruvim." *Mitekufat Haeven* 1: 23–26. [Hebrew]

Milevski, Ianir
2013 "The Exchange of Flint Tools in the Southern Levant during the Early Bronze Age." *Lithic Technology* 38: 202–19.

Milevski, Ianir, Ofer Marder, Hamoudi Khalaily, and Flavia Sonntag
2006 "The Flint Assemblages." In *'En Esur ('Ein Asawir) I: Excavations at a Protohistoric Site in the Coastal Plain of Israel*, edited by Eli Yannai, 179–210. IAA Reports 31. Jerusalem: Israel Antiquities Authority.

Rosen, Steven A.
1997 *Lithics after the Stone Age: A Handbook of Stone Tools from the Levant*. Walnut Creek, CA: AltaMira.
2003 "The Chipped Stone Artifacts from Tel Qashish." In *Tel Qashish: A Village in the Jezreel Valley; Final Report of the Archaeological Excavations (1978–1987)*, edited by Amnon Ben-Tor, Ruhama Bonfil, and Sharon Zuckerman, 395–412. Qedem Reports 5. Jerusalem: Hebrew University of Jerusalem.

Shimelmitz, Ron
2009 "Variability in Specialized Canaanean Blade Production of the Early Bronze Age Levant." In *Techniques and People: Anthropological Perspectives on*

Technology in the Archaeology of the Proto-Historic and Early Historic Periods in the Southern Levant, edited by Steven A. Rosen and Valentine Roux, 135–56. Mémoires et Travaux du Centre de Recherche Français à Jerusalem 9. Paris: de Boccard.

Shimelmitz, Ron, Ran Barkai, and Avi Gopher
2000 "A Canaanean Blade Workshop at Har Haruvim, Israel." *TA* 27: 3–22.

Shimelmitz, Ron, and Matthew J. Adams
2014 "Flint Knapping and the Early Bronze Age I Temple of Megiddo, Israel: Some Aspects of the Organization of Late Prehistoric Cult." *Journal of Mediterranean Archaeology* 27: 51–78.

Shimelmitz, Ron, and Steven A. Rosen
2014 "The Flint Assemblage." In *Bet Yerah: The Early Bronze Age Mound, Volume II: Urban Structure and Material Culture 1933–1986 Excavations*, edited by Raphael Greenberg, 151–88. IAA Reports 54. Jerusalem: Israel Antiquities Authority.

Yerkes, Richard W., Ran Barkai, Avi Gopher, and Katia Zutovski
2016 "The Use of Fan Scrapers: Microwear Evidence from Late Pottery Neolithic and Early Bronze Age Ein Zippori, Israel." *Journal of Lithic Studies*, 3: 185–205. DOI: 10.2218/jls.v3i1.1447.

Table 20.1. General composition of the assemblage.

	Area A, disturbed	Area B, disturbed	Area C	Area D	Total C-D A-5881		Area E South A-5992	Area E North A-6149	Total Area E		Area F A-5992		Total	
	N	N	N	N	*N*	%	N	N	*N*	%	*N*	%	*N*	%
PE	5	0	57	21	*78*	12.5	8	15	*23*	12.2	*6*	7.0	*112*	*11.9*
Flakes	9	13	171	65	*236*	37.9	30	34	*64*	34.0	*23*	26.7	*345*	*36.5*
Blades	1	0	9	4	*13*	2.1	5	4	*9*	4.8	*6*	7.0	*29*	*3.1*
Canaanean blades	0	3	11	0	*11*	1.8	32	10	*42*	22.3	*25*	29.1	*81*	*8.6*
NBK	1	0	1	2	*3*	0.5	2	0	*2*	1.1	*0*	0	*6*	*0.6*
Bladelets	0	0	4	0	*4*	0.6	2	0	*2*	1.1	*2*	2.3	*8*	*0.8*
CTE	7	6	132	54	*186*	29.9	9	17	*26*	13.8	*15*	17.4	*240*	*25.4*
Burin spall	0	0	2	0	*2*	0.3	0	0	*0*	*0*	*0*	*0*	*2*	*0.2*
Cores	3	0	67	23	*90*	14.4	7	13	*20*	10.6	*9*	10.5	*122*	*12.9*
Total Debitage (% of Total)	26	22	454	169	*623*	100 (60.4)	95	93	*188*	100 (60.2)	*86*	100 (68.7)	*945*	*100 (61.3)*
Chunks	7	5	148	55	*203*	19.4	29	43	*72*	23.1	*10*	7.8	*297*	*19.2*
Tools	13	2	152	53	*205*	24.3	27	25	*52*	16.7	*30*	23.4	*302*	*19.5*
Total	46	29	754	277	*1031*	100	151	161	*312*	100	*126*	100	*1544*	*100*

Table 20.2. Distribution of core types.

	Area A, disturbed	Area B, disturbed	Area C	Area D	Total C-D A-5881		Area E South A-5992	Area E North A-6149	Total Area E		Area F A-6149		Total	
	N	N	N	N	*N*	%	N	N	*N*	%	N	%	*N*	%
Levallois	0	0	5	2	*7*	*7.8*	0	0	*0*	*0*	0	0	7	5.7
One platform, flakes	0	0	7	1	*8*	*8.9*	0	4	*4*	*20*	0	0	12	9.8
One platform, blades	0	0	3	0	*3*	*3.3*	0	1	*1*	*5*	1	11.1	5	4.1
One platform, bladelets	0	0	0	0	*0*	*0*	0	1	*1*	*5*	1	11.1	2	1.6
One platform, mixed	0	0	1	1	*2*	*2.2*	0	0	*0*	*0*	0	0	2	1.6
Two platforms and more	0	0	3	4	*7*	*7.8*	0	0	*0*	*0*	1	11.1	8	6.6
Amorphous	2	0	38	13	*51*	*56.7*	7	7	*14*	*70*	3	33.3	70	57.4
Discoidal	1	0	2	0	*2*	*2.2*	0	0	*0*	*0*	0	0	3	2.5
On flake	0	0	8	2	*11.1*	*10.8*	0	0	*0*	*0*	3	33.3	13	10.7
Total	3	0	67	23	*90*	*100*	7	13	*20*	*100*	9	100	*122*	100

Table 20.3. Typological composition of the assemblage.

	Area A, disturbed	Area B, disturbed	Area C	Area D	Total C, D A-5881		Area E South A-5992	Area E North A-6149	Total Area E		Area F A-5992		Total	
	N	N	N	N	N	%	N	N	N	%	N	%	N	%
Canaanean sickle blades	0	1	6	1	7	3.4	5	5	10	19.2	11	33.3	28	9.3
Canaanean blades, retouched	0	0	0	0	0	0	3	1	4		1	3.3	7	2.3
Knives	0	0	1	0	1	0.5	0	1	1	1.9	0	0	2	0.7
Backed and truncated sickle blades	0	0	2	0	2	1.0	2	0	3	5.8	1	3.3	5	1.7
Geometric sickle blade	0	0	0	0	0	0	0	0	0	0	1	3.3	1	0.3
Tabular scrapers	1	0	1	0	1	0.5	1	1	2	3.8	0	3.3	4	1.32
Microliths	0	0	4	0	4	1.9	0	0	0	0	2	6.7	6	2.0
Bifacial	0	0	2	0	2	0.5	0	1	1	1.9	0	0	3	1.0
Retouched flakes	4	1	63	28	93	45.3	4	7	11	23.1	5	16.7	112	36.4
Retouched blades	1	0	6	2	8	3.9	2	0	2	3.8	3	10	14	4.6
Notch/denticulates	4	0	35	14	49	23.9	6	2	8	15.4	4	13.3	65	21.5
End scrapers	0	0	7	1	8	3.9	2	6	8	15.4	0	0	16	5.3
Multiple tools	0	0	8	2	10	4.9	1	0	1	1.9	1	3.3	12	4.0
Awls	1	0	5	1	6	2.9	0	0	0	0	0	0	7	2.3
Burins	0	0	8	3	11	5.4	0	0	0	0	0	0	11	3.6
Truncations	1	0	2	1	3	1.5	0	0	0	0	0	0	6	2.0
Side scrapers	1	0	0	0	0	0	2	1	3	5.8	1	3.3	5	1.7
Total	13	2	152	53	205	100	27	25	52	100	30	100	302	100

Table 20.4. Metric characteristics of Canaanean blades and tools.

Type		Length (mm)	Width (mm)	Thickness (mm)
Canaanean blades	Mean	35.1	19.531	4.9
	N	81	81	81
	Std. Deviation	13.4	3.7	1.1
Retouched Canaanean blades	Mean	35.0	21.3	6.1
	N	7	7	7
	Std. Deviation	11.8	4.2	0.9
Canaanean sickle blades	Mean	27.4	16.5	3.9
	N	28	28	28
	Std. Deviation	8.8	2.8	1.0
Knives	Mean	132.6	19.8	6.9
	N	2	2	2
	Std. Deviation	27.4	0.9	0.8

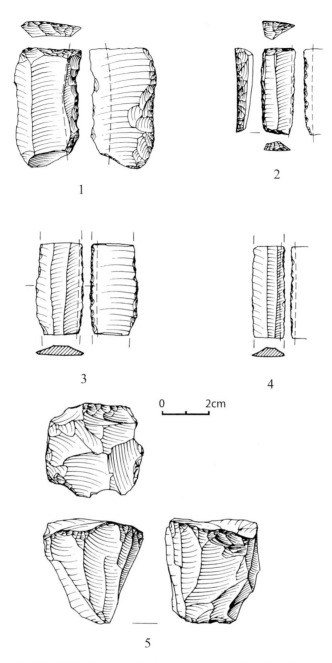

Fig. 20.10. Sickle blades and blade cores from Areas E South and F.

No.	Area	Locus	Basket	Description
1	F	6033	60220	Truncated sickle blade
2	E South	5012	50115	Backed and truncated sickle blade
3	E South	5025	50222	Canaanean sickle blade
4	E South	5025	50222	Canaanean sickle blade
5	F	6038	60205	Blade core

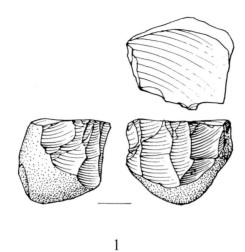

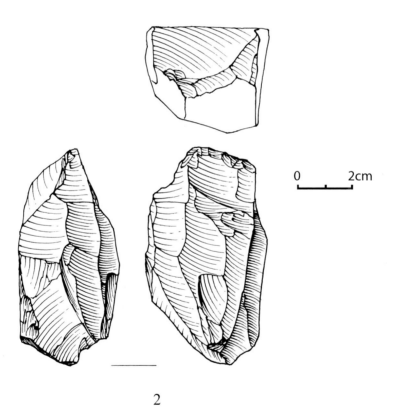

Fig. 20.11. Cores from Areas C and D.

No.	Area	Locus	Basket	Description
1	D	400	3385	Mixed bladelet-flakes core
2	C	397	3369	Blade core, PPNB

20. The Late Early Bronze Age I Flint Assemblages from Tel Qashish Areas A–F

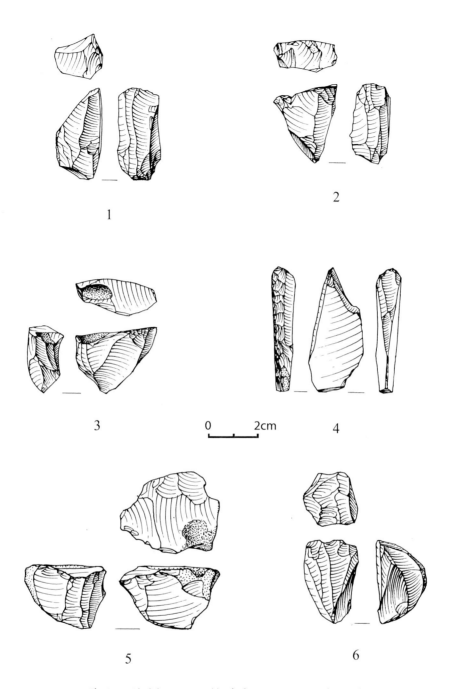

Fig. 20.12. Bladelet cores and burin from Areas C, D, and E North.

No.	Area	Locus	Basket	Description
1	D	403	4014	Bladelet core
2	D	411	4055	Bladelet core
3	D	414	4072	Bladelet core
4	D	414	4072	Burin
5	C	396	3367	Bladelet core
6	E North	5054	50452	Bladelet core

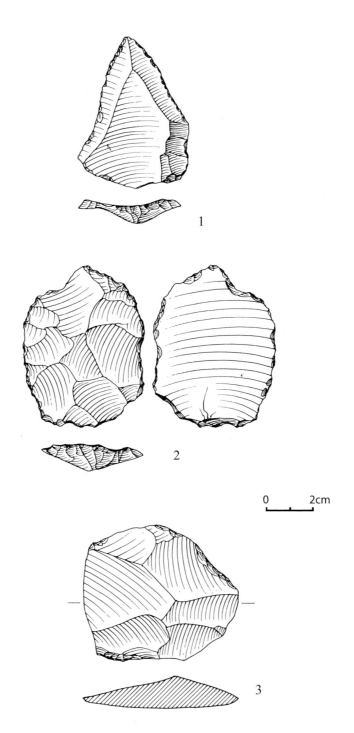

Fig. 20.13. Levallois point and retouched flakes from Area D. Middle Paleolithic intrusion.

No.	Area	Locus	Basket	Description
1	D	401	4001	Levallois point
2	D	401	4001	Levallois flake, retouched
3	D	401	4001	Levallois flake, retouched

20. The Late Early Bronze Age I Flint Assemblages from Tel Qashish Areas A–F

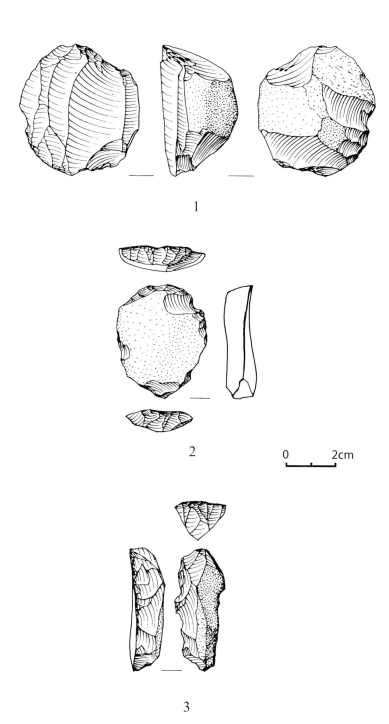

Fig. 20.14. Middle Paleolithic and Fpipaleolithic/Upper Paleolithic intrusions.

No.	Area	Locus	Basket	Description
1	D	409	4047	Levallois core
2	C	350	3240	End scraper
3	C	350	3175	End scraper

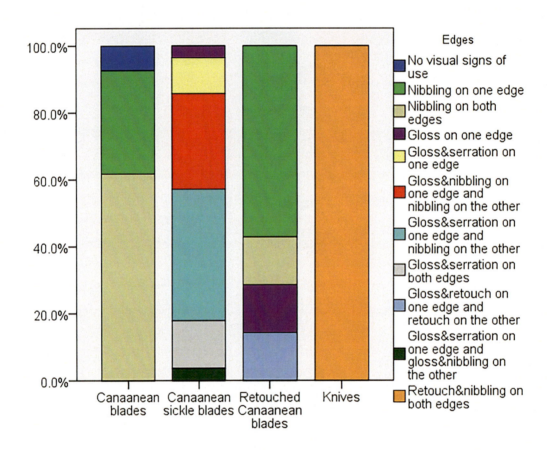

Fig. 20.15. Canaanean blades and tools: Characteristics of edge damage.

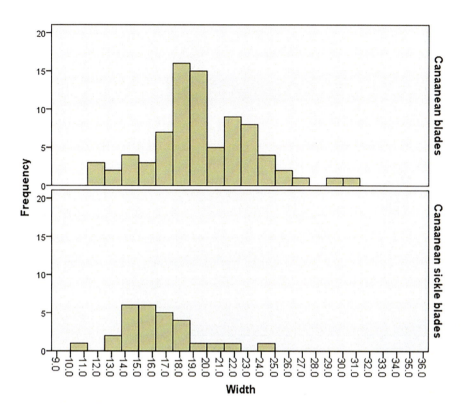

Fig. 20.16. Canaanean blades and sickle blades: Distribution according to width.

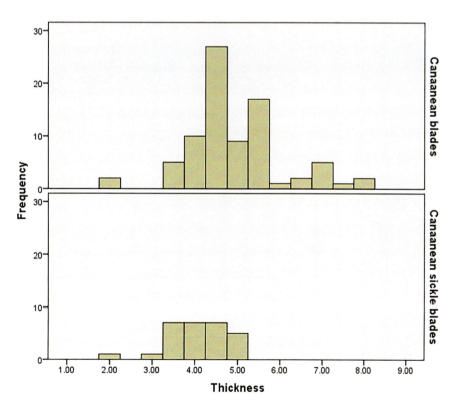

Fig. 20.17. Canaanean blades and sickle blades: Distribution according to thickness.

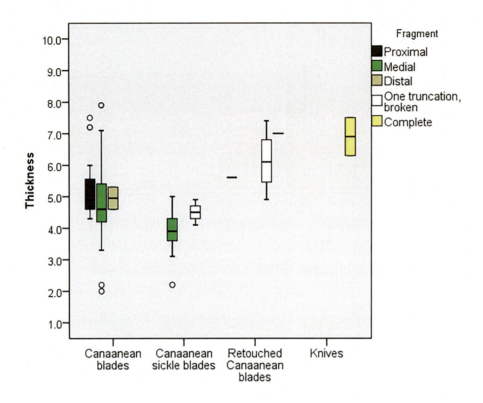

Fig. 20.18. Canaanean blades and tools: Thickness according to fragment type.

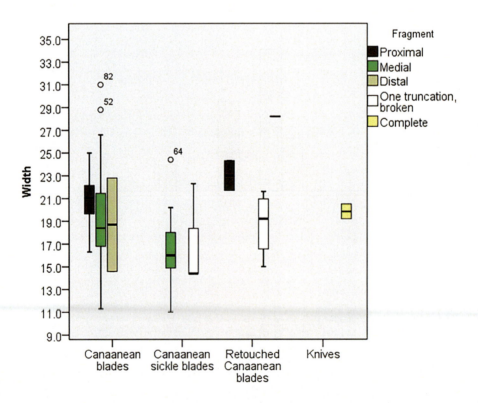

Fig. 20.19. Canaanean blades and tools: Width according to fragment type.

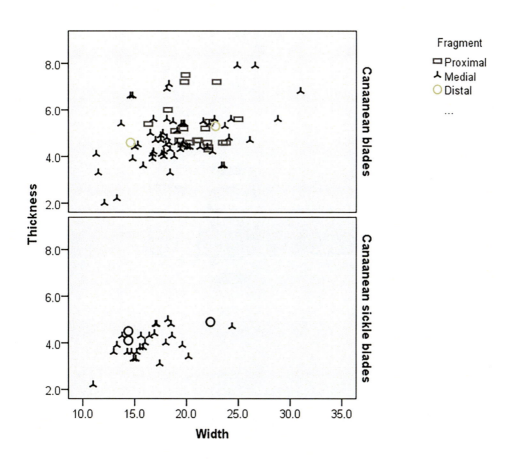

Fig. 20.20. Canaanean blades and sickle blades: Width and thickness distribution according to fragment.

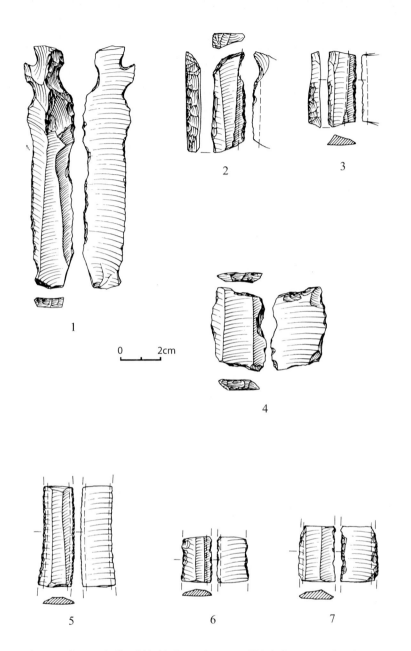

Fig. 20.21. 'En Esur knife, sickle blades and truncated blade from Areas C and D.

No.	Area	Locus	Basket	Description
1	C	347	3181	'En Esur knife
2	C	302	3348	Backed and truncated sickle blade
3	C	309	3055	Backed sickle blade
4	C	384	3343	Truncated Canaanean blade
5	C	383	3292	Canaanean sickle blade
6	C	383	3292	Canaanean sickle blade
7	D	403	4021	Canaanean sickle blade

20. The Late Early Bronze Age I Flint Assemblages from Tel Qashish Areas A–F

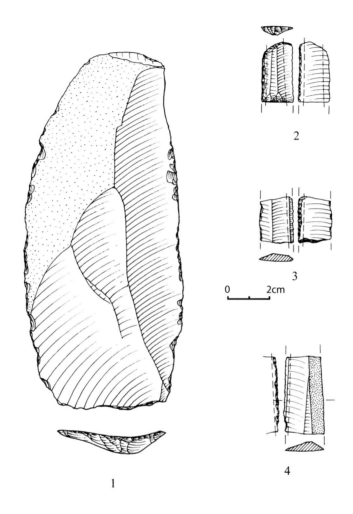

Fig. 20.22. Tools from Area C.

No.	Area	Locus	Basket	Description
1	C	379	3319	Retouched cortical blade
2	B	204	2006	Truncated sickle blade, double gloss
3	C	384	3342	Canaanean sickle blade
4	C	302	3003	Canaanean sickle blade

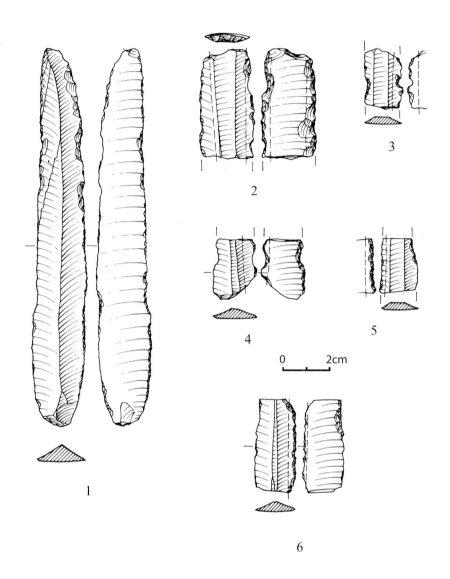

Fig. 20.23. A knife and Canaanean sickle blades from Area E North.

No.	Area	Locus	Basket	Description
1	E North	5113	50601	Retouched Canaanean blade
2	E North	5076	50474	Canaanean sickle blade, truncated
3	E North	5035	50289	Canaanean sickle blade, notched
4	E North	5021	50085	Canaanean sickle blade, notched
5	E North	5108	50590	Canaanean sickle blade
6	E North	5054	50452	Canaanean sickle blade

20. The Late Early Bronze Age I Flint Assemblages from Tel Qashish Areas A–F

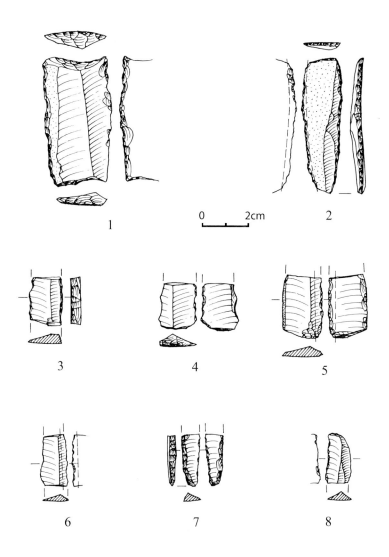

Fig. 20.24. Tools from Areas E South and F.

No.	Area	Locus	Basket	Description
1	E South	5038	50338	Canaanean blade, truncated
2	E South	5006	50128	Backed and truncated sickle blade, on PE
3	F	6031	60154	Backed blade fragment
4	F	6031	60154	Truncated blade fragment
5	F	6012	60089	Canaanean sickle blade
6	F	6017	60048	Canaanean sickle blade
7	F	6011	60118	Backed bladelet
8	F	6011	60118	Micro end scraper

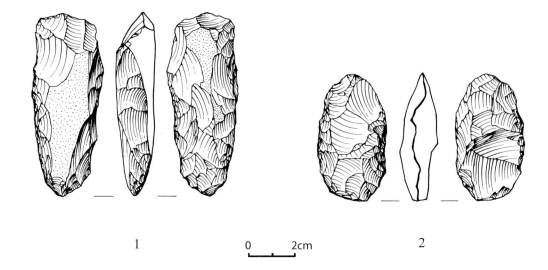

Fig. 20.25. Bifacial tools from Areas E North and C.

No.	Area	Locus	Basket	Description
1	E North	5138	50681	Adze
2	C	374	3294	Axe, partially polished

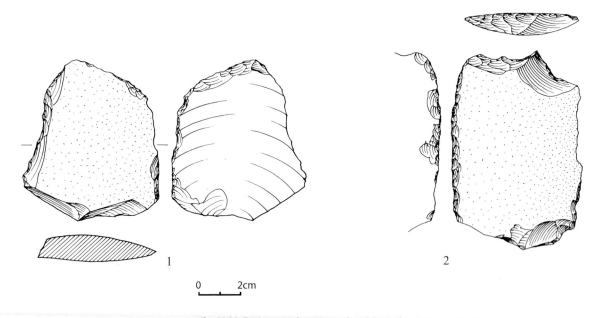

Fig. 20.26. Tools on PE from Areas C and E North.

No.	Area	Locus	Basket	Description
1	C	311	3017	Retouched primary flake
2	E North	5138	50681	Awl on retouched primary flake

20. The Late Early Bronze Age I Flint Assemblages from Tel Qashish Areas A–F

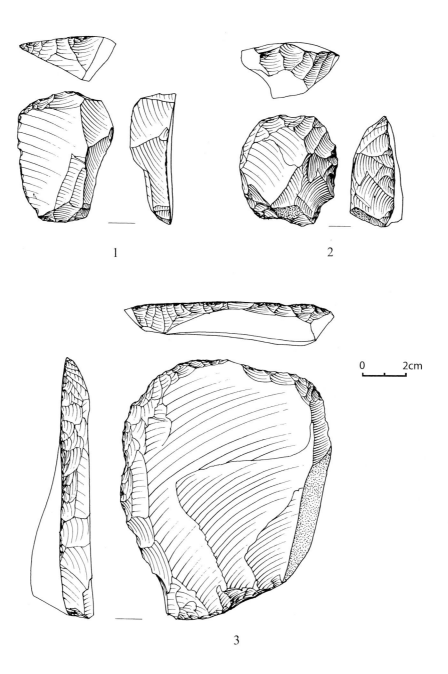

Fig. 20.27. End scrapers from Area E North.

No.	Area	Locus	Basket	Description
1	E North	5051	50405	End scraper
2	E North	5105	50574	End scraper
3	E North	5118	50594	End scraper

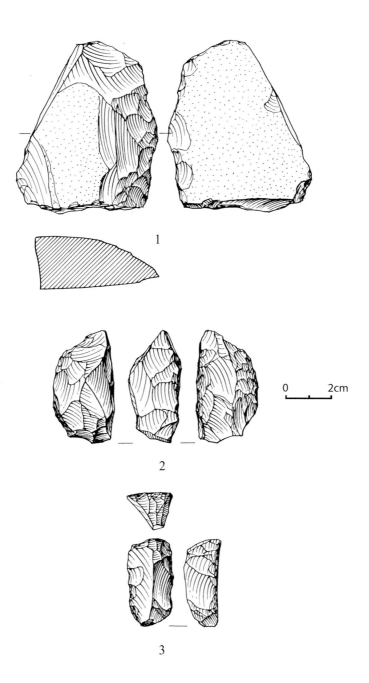

Fig. 20.28. Side scrapers and end scraper from Area C.

No.	Area	Locus	Basket	Description
1	C	374	3274	Side scraper
2	C	394	3340	Side scraper
3	C	375	3262	End scraper

Chapter 21

Faunal Remains from the Margins of Tel Qashish, Area E

Nuha Agha (*Israel Antiquities Authority*)

The faunal remains included in this report derive from the second and third seasons of the salvage excavations undertaken in the margins of Tel Qashish (permits A-5992 and A-6149; Yannai, ch. 12; and van den Brink et al., ch. 13, this volume). The site is located in the Mediterranean phytogeographic region, on the north bank of the Kishon River, and receives about 600–700 mm of rain per annum (Orni and Efrat 1980). Previous excavations at the site yielded rich faunal assemblages from a variety of periods (Horwitz 2003a). The present assemblage is rather small and is associated mainly with a late stage of the Early Bronze Age I (van den Brink et al., ch. 13, this volume).

No faunal remains were collected whatsoever during the first season of excavation (A-5881; Areas A–D). In Area F, only three bones were found, a number that did not allow for any meaningful analysis.[1] The lack of any faunal remains from over half of the total excavated area is thus striking. While deposition conditions along the Kishon River banks are not uniform (e.g., among the Middle Palaeolithic and Epipalaeolithic sites of 'Ein Qashish; Stahlschmidt et al. 2018 and personal observation),

it is hard to ascribe the lack of animal bones from Areas A–D to these conditions alone, since it is hard to expect the preservation condition within these areas to be heterogenic.

Given the above, this report focuses on the remains deriving from Area E (A-5992 and A-6149). These remains were collected from loci attributed to late EB I (NISP=153), topsoil (NISP=12), and insecure contexts (NISP=4); only late EB I material is analyzed here. Unfortunately, the small size of the late EB I assemblage and the fragmentary character of the excavated remains did not allow for an examination of distinct subunits such as separate strata or spatially different contexts. Furthermore, most loci (except L5105; see below) yielded only a few bones each—very often just one or two bones (table 21.1). Therefore, all the remains coming from loci that yielded late EB I finds are analyzed here as a single unit dated to this period, unless otherwise specified.

Methods

No calcite matrix covered the bones, so the cleaning procedure was limited to washing the bones in clean water, removing the remaining earth, and then letting them dry in a shaded area. Bones that had been broken, either in antiquity or during excavation, and whose parts remained close to each other, were refitted. This was made to minimize possible distortion of the results by counting the same element twice, and sometimes also helped to identify the bone.

---

[1]. The bones from Area F included a calcaneus of a large-sized animal (Locus 6014), a distal tibia fragment of a sheep/goat (Locus 6012), and a broken mandible of a goat (Locus 6009). The mandible had a sequence of teeth (dp4–M2). The level of abrasion on the dp4 tooth indicates an age ranging between one to two years.

The bones were identified to anatomical elements and attributed to taxons, as close as possible to the species level. When possible, identification was made by comparison of the archaeological specimen to the bones of modern animals stored at the comparative collection of the National Natural History Collections of the Hebrew University of Jerusalem. Remains that are not indicative of any particular species (diaphysis, vertebrae, ribs, cranial fragments, etc.) were attributed to size classes (Brain 1981). Severely damaged bone fragments, especially of joints, which could not be identified to taxon level, were also attributed to size classes. Three size classes were defined: large-sized mammals (such as cattle), dama-sized mammals (most probably of *Dama mesopotamica*), and medium-sized mammals (such as sheep/goat, gazelle, and pig).

Determination of anatomic position of long bone fragments was based on the division of these bones into five sections: the proximal epiphysis, the proximal shaft, the medial shaft, the distal shaft, and the distal epiphysis. Determination of anatomical position for the other bones was based on Keith Dobney and Kevin Rielly 1988, with an even more accurate anatomical position being recorded for some fragments. Whenever possible, the body side—left or right—was recorded as well. Completeness of the bone was calculated based on the surviving parts of the bone, and not as a percentage of the whole bone, to avoid a quantitative skew of the assemblage (Klein and Cruz-Uribe 1984).

All bones that survived to a satisfying degree were measured following Angela von den Driesch 1976, using a manual caliper with an accuracy of 0.1 mm. Several morphological and metrical methods were employed to distinguish between the bones of goats and sheep (Zeder and Lapham 2010 for references; Zeder and Pilaar 2010).

The two most common methods of ageing bones from archaeological excavations are based on the fusion of the bones (Silver 1969) and on patterns of eruption and abrasion of teeth. For the latter, age is determined according to three mandibular teeth that make a single sequence: Milk tooth dp4, which is the last one to fall; pre-molar P4 that replaces dp4; and the third molar, that erupts when dp4 falls, or slightly later (Reitz and Wing 1999). When dp4 is found, the specimen is defined as "young," while when P4 or M3 are found, the specimen is defined as "mature" or "old," depending on the height of the crown and its shape (Klein and Cruz-Uribe 1984). The patterns of teeth eruption and abrasion used here follow those published by Annie Grant (1982) for various domestic animals, and those published by Sebastian Payne (1973) for sheep/goat. Assignment of absolute age to the eruption and abrasion patterns was based on Anna Haber (Haber and Dayan 2004, tables 2–5).

Frequency of different body parts at the site, as expressed in the distribution of skeletal elements, may hint at the function of a site, its internal organization, and cultural preferences of its inhabitants (Speth 1983; Stiner 1991). Here, skeletal elements were divided into seven groups, following Mary Stiner (1991, 2002): cranial (antler/horn, skull, maxilla, mandible, and loose teeth), axis (pelvis, vertebrae, and rib), upper forelimb (scapula and humerus), lower forelimb (radius, ulna, carpals, metacarpal), upper hind limb (femur), lower hind limb (tibia, patella, calcaneum, astragalus, tarsal, metatarsal), and feet (phalanges).

The bone's surface bears traces of natural and cultural processes that affected its survival. Therefore, each identified bone was examined from all sides with a magnifying glass, under light (see Blumenchine, Marean, and Capaldo 1996), in the search for signs that may hint at cultural processes and postdepositional agents: human activity that left cutmarks and burning (Binford 1981), or agents such

Table 21.1. Faunal remains per locus.

Locus	NISP	Locus	NISP	Locus	NISP
5006	1	5080	15	5122	3
5023	3	5084	1	5123	3
5025	1	5088	1	5130	4
5050	1	5101	1	5135	1
5056	1	5102	2	5136	4
5066	5	5105	63	5137	2
5068	1	5106	1	5138	3
5071	5	5107	3	5141	1
5074	4	5108	2	5142	8
5076	5	5109	4	5148	1
5078	1	5114	1	5151	1

Table 21.2. Faunal remains by taxa and stratigraphic context.

Taxon/size class	?	Topsoil	Late EB I	Total
Bos sp.	1	6	66	73
Large-sized mammal	1	3	45	49
Dama mesopotamica			6	6
Dama size		1	4	5
Sus sp.			15	15
Capra/ovis sp.			5	5
Capra hircus		1		1
Medium-sized mammal	2	1	11	14
Gazella gazella			1	1
Total	4	12	153	169

as roots and natural elements (Behrensmeyer 1978), and gnawing by predators and rodents (Binford 1981; Blumenschine, Marean, and Capaldo 1996).

Results

The preservation level of the remains was not homogeneous. Following Anna Behrensmeyer's (1978) definitions, it may be stated that the preservation ranged from level 2 to level 4, with 87 percent of the bones fitting levels 2 and 3 in nearly equal numbers. Marks left by plant roots were visible on all bones. This biogenic process and the clay matrix in which the remains were deposited led to a generally poor bone-surface preservation.

Cutting marks were found on only five bones, revealing a low frequency (i.e., ca. 3.5 percent of the 142 relevant remains): three of cattle, one of a pig, and one of a dama-sized animal, all associated with the dismembering of the animal's carcass. Gnawing marks were also identified on five bones: four bones showed marks characteristic of rodents, possibly porcupines, and one showed the gnawing marks of carnivore teeth. Burning marks were identified only on two bones, but these were black, thus not necessarily indicating intentional burning (Shahack-Gross, Bar-Yosef, and Weiner 1997).

The identified remains were all of mammals, all of them ungulates (table 21.2). The vast majority belonged to livestock animals, represented by cattle (*Bos* sp.), pigs (*Sus* sp.), and ovi-caprines (*Ovis aries/ Capra aegagrus*). Wild animals were represented to a more limited extent and included Persian fallow deer (*Dama mesopotamica*), gazelle (*Gazella gazella*), and perhaps also wild boar (*Sus scrofa*; see below).

The analysis of the remains was limited by the small size of the samples, resulting from hand collection in the field. This is also evident in the taxonomic breakdown of the assemblages, where cattle, making up to more than half of the assemblage, are by far more frequent than pigs and ovi-caprines. These results (table 21.2) contrast with those of Liora Kolska Horwitz's (2003a, 433, table 39) analysis of the assemblages collected during the Hebrew University excavations at the site, on the high mound area, where cattle account for only 16 percent of the EB I remains. In addition, as the collection by hand—not supported by systematic sieving—is biased to larger, complete elements and taxa, small remains like those of small mammals, birds, fish, and reptiles were virtually absent from our sample, although they were present in the Hebrew University assemblage. Therefore, no attempt was made to reconstruct the natural environment of the site based on our results, but its proximity to the Kishon River must be noted.

Table 21.3. Ageing of cattle based on bone fusion, excluding the cattle burial.

Age group	Bone	Part	Fusion age	Fused	Unfused
7–18m	Scapula	Glenoid fossa	7–10m	2	0
	Humerus	Distal	12–18m	0	1
	Phalanx 1	Proximal	18m	1	0
	Phalanx 2	Proximal	18m	1	0
24–30m	Tibia	Distal	24–30m	0	1
	Metacarpus	Distal	24–30m	1	0
30–42m	Tibia	Proximal	30–48m	0	1
	Calcaneus		36–42m	1	2
42–48m	Femur	Distal	42–48m	0	1

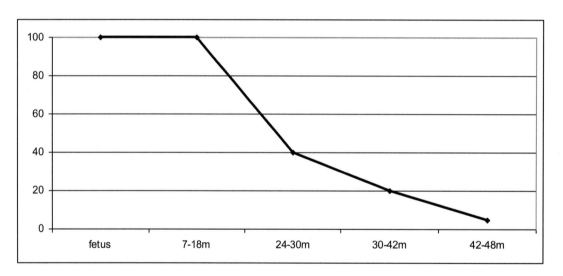

Fig. 21.1. Survival profile of cattle (excluding cattle burial).

Cattle

Within the cattle remains (NISP=111; including forty-five fragments of large-sized mammals), two separate groups are distinguished. In Locus 5105, two baskets (50574 and 50608) were identified by the excavators as representing a single deposition event and account for nearly half of all cattle remains (NISP=54). Analysis of these remains indicated that they represent one animal, supporting the excavators' conclusion. The remainder of the remains (NISP=57) represent a minimal number of individuals (MNI) of three animals, based on the identification of three right tibia bones. The remains deriving from the deposition in Locus 5105 were excluded from the analysis of skeletal part distribution and herd demography, as they represent a single animal and may thus skew the results.

The age profile for the cattle, based on bone fusion (table 21.3; fig. 21.1), points to the presence of both young and mature animals. It seems that most animals were culled upon reaching adult age, at about two to two-and-a-half years, but some were kept alive until much later. This may indicate that

Table 21.4. Distribution of skeletal remains.

	Capra/Ovis (+medium-sized mammal)		Bos sp. (+large-sized mammal)[a]		Sus sp.	
Skeletal Element	NISP	Percent	NISP	Percent	NISP	Percent
Cranial	1	6.3	3	5.8	6	40.0
Axis	5	31.3	6	11.5	3	20.0
Upper forelimb	2	12.5	12	23.1	2	13.3
Lower forelimb	2	12.5	9	17.3	1	6.7
Upper hind limb	1	6.3	1	1.9		0.0
Lower hind limb	3	18.8	17	32.7	3	20.0
Feet	2	12.5	4	7.7		0.0
Total	*16*	*100.0*	*52*	*100.0*	*15*	*100.0*

[a] Excluding the cattle burial (L5105, B50574, B50608) and five additional bones: four metapodial, and one bone of a large-sized animal the anatomical position of which could not be securely identified.

the herd was not limited to the production of meat, but that secondary products such as milk, and perhaps the use of the animals as traction animals, were also sought.

All skeletal parts were represented (table 21.4), but their relative proportions suggest the predominance of butchery refuse over food refuse. For example, lower hind limbs, poor in meat, account for nearly a third of all cattle remains, while upper hind limbs, considered meat-rich cuts, are seventeen times less frequent. The rarity of cut marks does not necessarily contradict this conclusion, as a carcass could be processed without leaving even a single cut mark (Shipman and Rose 1983). It is interesting to note that cut marks were also rare in the assemblage retrieved during the Hebrew University excavations at the site (Horwitz 2003a).

The complete remains of cattle (table 21.5a at the end of the chapter) were found to be in the range of domestic cattle (*Bos taurus*). Previous works dealing with faunal remains from other late EB I sites revealed a similar picture (Horwitz 2003b, 2013; Agha 2014; Maher 2014). However, it should be noted that the aurochs (*Bos primigenius*, wild cattle) are known in Israel until the Iron Age (Tsahar et al. 2009). In fact, several extremely large cattle bones from EB II–MB II contexts at the Tel of Qashish have been identified in the past as belonging to this wild beast (Horwitz 2003a, 434)

The most notable concentration of animal bones was uncovered in Locus 5105, where a large part of a single animal was found in original anatomic articulation (fig. 21.2). Unfortunately, there is little in the field documentation to shed light on the circumstances of deposition. In particular, it is regretful that the relation of the cattle remains to the stone layer stretching beneath the topsoil was not clarified, thus casting a shadow over the attribution of these bone remains to the EB I. However, the remains from Locus 5105 did not differ in their preservation and appearance from the rest of the faunal assemblage. A closer look at the content of Locus 5105 reveals that not all the cattle remains here belonged to the same animal. For example, the presence of two right proximal metacarpals points to the remains of at least two animals. The remains that can securely be attributed to a single deposition event (MNI=1) include only those excavated under Baskets 50574 and 50608. The material from these two baskets (NISP=55) was separated by the excavators from the rest and stored in a single box.

Except for a single fragment (a femur of a medium-sized animal), all identified skeletal remains from Baskets 50574 and 50608 belonged to *Bos* sp.

Fig. 21.2. Area E, Locus 5105. Cattle remains in original anatomic articulation.

or an animal of similar size. The remains represented all body parts: cranium, axis, upper and lower forelimb, upper and lower hind limb, and feet. Three bones were found to still be anatomically articulated during the analysis of the material: a right astragal and a distal fibula, a right unciform and cuneiform and one distal left radius and cuneiform. Not all skeletal parts were uncovered, though. Notably missing were the cranium (except for some mandibular fragments), some vertebrae, including the atlas and the axis, the sternum, the pelvis, and the phalanx bones (except for one). None of these bones were found in other baskets from Locus 5051.

All bones were found fused, indicating an animal that was older than three years at death. This is in accordance with the dental data, as both third lower molars (M3) had a similar abrasion level (L; following Grant 1982), indicating a senile age. Interestingly, none of the bones showed cutting marks, which may hint at a natural death of the specimen, possibly of old age.

Pigs

The pig remains (NISP=15) were all identified as belonging to the domestic pig (*Sus scrofa domestica*).

Nevertheless, there are strong reasons to believe that wild boars were also present in the faunal assemblage, as these animals are still found in the lower Galilee (Mendelson and Yom-Tov 1999) and were probably abundant in the past in the water-rich habitat along the Kishon riverbanks. As noted by Horwitz (2003a, 434), it may be hard to discriminate the boar remains from those of the domesticated species, especially when dealing with the remains of younger animals. As boar piglets are less aggressive and tend to stay with adult females until they are around twenty months old, several such animals can be easily trapped at the same time (Milevski et al. 2015, 118). It should also be noted that three bones from the previous excavations at the Tel of Qashish were thought to belong to boars (Horwitz 2003a, 434), and that a few bones and teeth suspected to belong to boars were documented at Qiryat Ata (Horwitz 2003b, 2013; Maher 2014).

Most of the pig remains may be classified as butchery waste, but the small sample size must be kept in mind (table 21.4). The only remains from which age data could be extracted were a dp4 tooth (abrasion level D; Grant 1982), an unfused distal humerus, and an unfused calcaneus. The age-at-death indicated by these remains are less than six months, less than one year and less than thirty months, respectively. Based on these limited data, it may be concluded that pigs were culled mainly while still young, less than one year in age, as also found in other contemporary sites (see Agha 2014).

Ovi-Caprines

The low number of ovi-caprine remains (NISP=6, MNI=1) offers little for reconstructing herd-growing strategies. For example, age-at-death could be deduced only from one unfused proximal tibia, indicating an age younger than forty-two months. None of the remains could be identified to the exact taxon level.[2] The distribution of skeletal parts (table 21.4) is indeed based on a small sample, but the high proportion of axis, feet, and lower limb bones is noteworthy; it may reflect the predominance of butchery refuse over food discard.

Wild animals

The central role played by domesticated species did not preclude hunting wild animals, as documented in the tell of Qashish (Horwitz 2003a) and in other EB I sites in the region such as Yiftah'el (Horwitz 1997). In the absence of sieving, the data from the present excavation are limited to the Persian fallow deer and mountain gazelle. The predominance of the first (NISP=6) over the second (NISP=1) is even more striking when taking into consideration the bones of *Dama*-sized animals (NISP=4). This, however, should not be taken for granted, as it may result from a bias toward larger bones (and thus larger animals) while hand-picking the bones.

Discussion

The analysis of the faunal remains from the margins of Tel Qashish contributes to our knowledge of this late EB I site in several aspects. The lack of sieving and the absence of any faunal remains from more than half of the excavated areas are unfortunate, but the Area E assemblage, while biased toward the representation of large bones and large species, still offers some important insights.

Overall, the assemblage fits well with the present knowledge of EB I economy, as reflected in other faunal assemblages from neighboring sites in the Jezreel Valley and adjacent areas in northern Israel, such as Yiftah'el (Horwitz 1997), 'En Shadud (Horwitz 1985), 'En Zippori (personal observation), and Qiryat Ata (Horwitz 2003b, 2013; Agha 2014; Maher 2014). In all these sites, ovi-caprines seem to have been the main livestock animal, providing meat and secondary products such as milk and wool. Pigs served as a convenient source of meat for sedentary communities. Hunting local wild species, such as the Persian fallow deer and the mountain gazelle, served both practical and perhaps cultural needs. The importance of cattle is not always reflected proportionally in faunal assemblages, as its meat contribution in weight surely surpassed that of ovi-caprines. The crucial role of cattle as a traction animal is also reflected in EB iconography (e.g., Eisenberg 1992; Sussman 1980).

The representation of cattle skeletal elements is of special interest. While all body parts are present, it would seem that several body parts rich in meat, particularly the upper hind limbs, are underrepresented, while parts poor in meat, such as feet and the lower hind limb, are overrepresented. A similar picture may be suggested for the ovi-caprine remains. This is in sharp contrast to the pattern observed in the assemblages from the Hebrew University excavations at the tell proper, where body parts rich in meat were frequent both in the EB II, EB III and MBIIA–B, suggestive of consumption discard (Horwitz 2003a, 432–34). When considering the location of the present excavation areas, one may suggest that slaughtering took place at the margins of the tell, while the consumption of the meat took place mainly at the tell itself.[3] Thus, the marginality of Area E, as reflected in the cattle remains, may have been not only geographical but also reflect a social hierarchy, that is, a lower availability of meat-rich cattle parts for the inhabitants of this downhill area. Unfortunately, this far-reaching hypothesis

---

2. A fragment of a lower jaw of a domesticated goat (*Capra hircus*) was found in an unstratified context.

3. Interestingly, this pattern is opposite to that identified in Egyptian sites, where cattle forelimbs were considered appropriate for the consumption of the elites (Allentuck 2015).

cannot be tested against data from the tell itself, as the small EB I sample of cattle from the Hebrew University excavations did not allow for any conclusions regarding body part representations.

The cattle remains from Locus 5105, representing the deposition of an old animal, cannot be fully understood at the moment. The proximity of the remains to the EB I dwellings, the large portion of the skeleton that survived in its original anatomic articulation, and the absence of any evidence for gnawing of predators, do not support the possibility that the animal died naturally off-site. Earlier burials of cattle in neighboring sites, such as in PPNB Kefar Ha-Ḥoresh (Horwitz and Goring-Morris 2004) and Late Neolithic ʻEn Ẓippori (personal observation; excavated by Milevski and Getzov) were clearly symbolic. In the EB, burial of donkeys appears (e.g., Greenfield, Shai, and Maeir 2012; Sapir-Hen, Gadot, and Lipschits 2017), but no burial of cattle was reported to date. If the cattle burial from the margins of Tel Qashish indeed dates to the EB I, it may be part of a wider regional phenomenon, as another burial was recently identified in the early EB I site of ʻAfula (Dalali-Amos and Getzov 2014). A complete bos primigenius was found buried in the cultic area of the Megiddo temples of Level J-3 or J-4 (late EB I; Adams 2013). The character of these burials and that of the remains from our Locus 5105, as well as the relation of the cattle burial to that of donkeys, are still to be clarified.

References

Adams, Matthew J.
2013 "Area J, Part III: The Main Sector of Area J [The Early Bronze Age, Stratigraphy and Architecture]." In *Megiddo V: The 2004-2008 Seasons*, edited by Israel Finkelstein, David Ussishkin, Eric Cline, M. Adams, E. Arie, N. Franklin, and M. Martin, 47–118. 3 vols. SMNIA 31. Tel Aviv: Institute of Archaeology.

Agha, Nuha
2014 "The Faunal Remains from the Early Bronze Age Site of Qiryat Ata—Area N." *ʻAtiqot* 79: 45–57.

Allentuck, Adam
2015 "An Acquired Taste: Emulation and Indigenization of Cattle Forelimbs in the Southern Levant." *Cambridge Archaeological Journal* 25: 45–62.

Binford, Lewis R.
1981 *Bones: Ancient Men and Modern Myths*. New York: Academic Press.

Behrensmeyer, Anna K.
1978 "Taphonomic and Ecologic Information from Bone Weathering." *Paleobiology* 4: 150–62.

Blumenschine, Robert J., Curtis Marean, and Salvatore D. Capaldo
1996 "Blind Tests of Inter-Analyst Correspondence and Accuracy in the Identification of Cut-Marks, Percussion-Marks and Carnivore Tooth Marks on Bone Surfaces." *JArS* 23: 495–507.

Brain, Charles K.
1981 *The Hunters or the Hunted? An Introduction to African Cave Taphonomy*. Chicago: University of Chicago Press.

Dalali-Amos, Edna, and Nimrod Getzov
2014 "ʻAfula." *HA-ESI* 126. http://www.hadashot-esi.org.il/report_detail_eng.aspx?id=9569&mag_id=121.

Dobney, Keith, and Kevin Rielly
1988 "A Method for Recording Archaeological Animal Bones: The Use of Diagnostic Zones." *Circaea* 5: 79–96.

Driesch, Angela von den
1976 *A Guide to Measurement of Animal Bones from Archaeological Sites: As Developed by the Institut für Palaeoanatomie, Domestikationsforschung und Geschichte der Tiermedizin of the University of Munich*. Peabody Museum Bulletin 1. Cambridge: Peabody Museum of Archaeology and Ethnology.

Eisenberg, Emanuel
1992 "An EB I Stamp Seal from Tel Kitan." *ErIsr* 23: 5–8. [Hebrew]

Grant, Annie
1982 "The Use of Tooth Wear as a Guide to the Age of Domestic Ungulates." In *Ageing and Sexing Animal Bones from Archaeological Sites*, edited by Bob Wilson, Caroline Grigson, and Sebastian Payne, 91–108. BAR British Series 109. Oxford: BAR.

Greenfield, Haskel J., Itzhaq Shai, and Aren Maeir
2012 "Being an 'Ass': An Early Bronze Age Burial of a Donkey from Tell es-Safi/Gath, Israel." *Bioarchaeology of the Near East* 6: 21–52.

Haber, Anna, and Tamar Dayan
2004 "Analyzing the Process of Domestication: Hagoshrim as a Case Study." *JArS* 31: 1587–601.

Horwitz, Liora Kolska
1985 "The En Shadud Faunal Remains." In *En Shadud: Salvage Excavations at a Farming Community in the Jezreel Valley, Israel*, edited by Eliot Braun, 168–77. BARIS 249. Oxford: BAR.
1997 "Faunal Remains." In *Yiftah'el: Salvage and Rescue Excavations at a Prehistoric Village in Lower Galilee, Israel*, edited by Eliot Braun, 155–71. IAA Reports 2. Jerusalem: Israel Antiquities Authority.
2003a "Fauna from Tel Qashish." In *Tel Qashish: A Village in the Jezreel Valley; Final Report of the Archaeological Excavations (1978–1987)*, edited by Amnon Ben-Tor, Ruhama Bonfil, and Sharon Zuckerman, Horwitz, 427–43. Qedem Reports 5. Jerusalem: Israel Antiquities Authority.
2003b "Early Bronze Age Animal Exploitation at Qiryat-Ata." In *Salvage Excavations at the Early Bronze Age Site of Qiryat*, edited by Amir Golani. 225–41. IAA Reports 18. Jerusalem: Israel Antiquities Authority.
2013 "Early Bronze Age Fauna from Qiryat Ata—Area O." *'Atiqot* 75: 61–70.

Horwitz, Liora Kolska, and Adrian Nigel Goring-Morris
2004 "Animals and Ritual during the Levantine PPNB: A Case Study from the Site of Kfar Hahoresh, Israel." *Anthropozoologica* 39: 165–78.

Klein, Richard G., and Kathryn Cruz-Uribe
1984 *The Analysis of Animal Bones from Archaeological Sites*. Chicago: University of Chicago Press.

Maher, Edward D.
2014 "Animal-Based Economy and Local Ecology: The Early Bronze Age II Fauna from Qiryat Ata––Area S." *'Atiqot* 79: 99–109.

Mendelssohn, Heinrich, and Yoram Yom-Tov
1999 *Fauna Palaestina: Mammalia of Israel*. Jerusalem: Publications of the Israel Academy of Sciences and Humanities.

Milevski, Ianir, Ofer Marder, Henk K. Mienis, and Liora Kolska Horwitz
2015 "Abu Ghosh, Jasmine Street: A Pre-Ghassulian Site in the Judean Hills." *'Atiqot* 82: 85–130.

Orni, Efraim, and Elisha Efrat
1980 *Geography of Israel*, 4th ed. Jerusalem: Israel Universities Press.

Payne, Sebastian
1973 "Kill-off Patterns in Sheep and Goats: The Mandibles from Aşvan Kale." *AnSt* 23: 281–303.

Reitz, Elizabeth J., and Elizabeth S. Wing
1999 *Zooarchaeology*. Cambridge Manuals in Archaeology. Cambridge: Cambridge University Press.

Sapir-Hen, Lidar, Yuval Gadot, and Oded Lipschits
2017 "Ceremonial Donkey Burial, Social Status, and Settlement Hierarchy in the Early Bronze Age III: The Case of Tel Azekah." In *The Wide Lens in Archaeology: Honoring Brian Hesse's Contributions to Anthropological Archaeology*, edited by Justin Lev-Tov, Paula Hesse, and Allan Gilbert, 259–70. Archaeobiology 2. Atlanta: Lockwood Press.

Shahack-Gross, Ruth, Ofer Bar-Yosef, and Steve Weiner
1997 "Black-Coloured Bones in Hayonim Cave, Israel: Differentiating between Burning and Oxide Staining." *JArS* 24: 439–46.

Shipman, Pat, and Jennie Rose
1983 "Early Hominid Hunting, Butchering, and Carcass-Processing Behaviors: Approaches to the Fossil Record." *Journal of Anthropological Archaeology* 2: 57–98.

Silver, Ian A.
1969 "The Aging of Domesticated Animals." In *Science in Archaeology*, edited by Don Brothwell and Eric Higgs, 283–302. London: Thames & Hudson.

Speth, John D
1983 *Bison Kills and Bone Counts: Decision Making by Ancient Hunters*. Chicago: University of Chicago Press.

Stahlschmidt, Mareike C., Nadav Nir, Noam Greenbaum, Tami Zilberman, Omry Barzilai, Ravid Ekshtain, Ariel Malinsky-Buller, Erella Hovers, and Ruth Schahack-Gross
2018 "Geoarchaeological Investigation of Site Formation and Depositional Environments at the Middle Palaeolithic Open-Air Site of 'Ein Qashish, Israel." *Journal of Palaeolithic Archaeology* 1: 32–53.

Stiner, Mary C.
1991 "Food Procurement and Transport by Human and Non-Human Predators." *JArS* 18: 455–82.
2002 "On in situ Attrition and Vertebrate Body Part Profiles." *JArS* 29: 979–91.

Sussman, Varda
1980 "A Relief of a Bull from the Early Bronze Age." *BASOR* 238: 75–77.

Tsahar, Ella, Ido Izhaki, Simcha Lev-Yadun, and Guy Bar-Oz
2009 "Distribution and Extinction of Ungulates during the Holocene of the Southern Levant." *PLOS ONE* 4(4): e5316. DOI: 10.1371/journal.pone.0005316.

Zeder, Melinda A., and Heather A. Lapham
2010 "Assessing the Reliability of Criteria Used to Identify Postcranial Bones in Sheep, Ovis, and Goats, Capra." *JArS* 37: 2887–905.

Zeder, Melinda A., and Suzanne E. Pilaar
2010 "Assessing the Reliability of Criteria Used to Identify Mandibles and Mandibular Teeth in Sheep, Ovis, and Goats, Capra." *JArS* 37: 225–42.

Table 21.5. Measurements of faunal remains. Following von den Driesch 1976.

a. Cattle.

	#	Locus	Notes	Measurements			
Scapula				*SLC*	*GLP*	*LG*	*BG*
	92	5059	F	53.2	68.1	58.3	46.6
	125	5066	F		67.1	56.5	44.3
Humerus				*Bd*	*BT*	*HDH*	
	4	5105	F	94.7	79.1	33.0	
Radius				*BP*	*BFp*		
	1	5105	F	86.4	76.3		
Ulna				*BPC*			
	30	5105		41.3			
Calcaneus				*GB*			
	82	5105	U	33.1			
	113	5105	F	43.9			
Metacarpal				*Bp*	*Dp*	*CW*	*TW*
	5	5105	F	63.1	34.9		
	9	5105	F	62.2	37.1	30.8	24.0
	71	5073	F	59.1	34.3		
	73	5107	F	52.4	30.6		
	80	5105	F	52.5			
	84	5090	F	62.3	35.0		
	117	5105	F			30.6	24.5
Metatarsal				*Bp*	*Dp*		
	49	5080	F	51.6	47.6		
	53	5137	F	46.6	43.6		
	81	5105	F	47.7	44.9		
First phalanx				*GLPe*	*Bp*	*SD*	*Bd*
	6	5105	F		32.5	27.9	27.6
	74	5107	F	62.1	29.6	25.2	
Second phalanx				*GL*	*Bp*	*SD*	
	55	5066	F	26.3	26.6	33.6	
Third phalanx				*MBS*			
	46	5142	F	12.5			

b. Persian fallow deer

	#	Locus	Notes	Measurements			
Metatarsal				*Bp*	*Dp*	*SD*	
	48	5080	F	27.5	30.5	18.8	
First phalanx				*GLpe*	*Bp*	*SD*	*Bd*
	112	5151	F	50.8	18.4	13.8	16.7
	120	5088		51.5	17.7	13.9	16.8

c. Gazelle.

	#	Locus	Notes	Measurements		
Astragalus				*GLl*	*Dl*	*Bd*
	133	5141	*Gazella*	29.8	15.5	17.9

d. Sheep/goat.

	#	Locus	Notes	Measurements	
First phalanx				*SD*	*Bd*
	62	5136	F	9.2	10.0

Chapter 22

Microvertebrate Remains from the Margins of Tel Qashish, Area E South

Lior Weissbrod

(*Laboratory of Archaeozoology, Zinman Institute of Archaeology, University of Haifa*)

A program for the systematic sampling of microvertebrate remains was conducted during salvage excavations at the margins of Tel Qashish. The program was initiated by Dr. Eli Yanai and Dr. Lior Weissbrod and focused on Area E (South, permit A-5992). A fairly large sample of sixty-one buckets, ten liters each, was collected from six different loci and subjected to fine (1 mm mesh) wet-sieving. Sorting of the resulting residue was undertaken at the Laboratory of Archaeozoology of the University of Haifa at the initiative of Dr. Edwin van den Brink and Dr. Weissbrod. The material was analyzed at the lab by Dr. Weissbrod.

Results

The sample produced a meager number of cranial and post-cranial identified specimens (NISP), seventeen in total, and a low taxonomic richness, including, in order of abundance, three species of rodents: *Microtus guentheri* (field vole), *Meriones tristrami* (jird), and *Spalax ehrenbergi* (mole rat), as well as squamata (snakes and lizards; table 22.1). The distribution of the remains showed a clear sample-size effect, that is, loci with larger numbers of buckets also generally produced more significant numbers of microvertebrate specimens. One exception is Locus 5045, in excavation Square K45, which had the highest number of buckets (n=15) but yielded an unexpectedly low number of specimens (n=1).

The skeletal material includes only isolated and ex-situ teeth, with no complete jaws. Long bones are also represented by fairly small fragments, indicating a high degree of fragmentation. Microscopic inspection of microtus molar teeth revealed some erosion of the enamel and exposure of underlying dentine along the salient angles, always on one side of the tooth (Fig. 22.1). Such erosion is reminiscent of the effect of gastric acid on the skeletal remains of small prey items in the digestive system of predators, as recorded by Peter Andrews (1990). Nonetheless, the consistent presence of this erosion on a single side of the teeth suggests that exposure occurred after they became isolated from the jaws and were deposited. A potential source for this phenomenon may be postdepositional chemical corrosion, which would have affected the exposed side of teeth lying on the surface of the site. Furthermore, the contribution of predators, which is typically manifested by high concentrations of microvertebrate remains and high taxonomic diversity (e.g., Weissbrod, 2013), is not likely in this case.

Discussion and Conclusions

The material described here represents the only systematically collected and published assemblage of microvertebrate remains from the Early Bronze Age I in Israel. The results of the excavation at the margins of Tel Qashish can be compared to a recently collected sample of microvertebrate remains from

Iron Age deposits at Tel Megiddo in the Jezreel Valley. This sample, retrieved from an equal sediment volume (610 liters), produced a considerably larger number of identified specimens, exceeding a NISP of one thousand (Weissbrod et al., 2013), and was further characterized by a somewhat broader representation of taxa. In addition to the taxa recorded at Qashish, the Megiddo sample included high numbers of house-mouse specimens (*Mus musculus domesticus*) and shrews of the Soricidae family. This assemblage was also characterized by better preservation conditions, including some intact or nearly intact long bones and jaws.

The exceedingly low numbers of specimens and taxa, together with the high fragmentation characterizing the Qashish assemblage, may reflect the remains' accumulation mode or the influence of the depositional environment at the site. The Qashish assemblage was collected from an off-tell context on the outskirts of the late Early Bronze Age I settlement, in an open area with evidence of outdoor activities (see van den Brink et al., ch.13, this volume). In contrast, the depositional environment of the Tel Megiddo assemblage reflected a dense Iron Age settlement residential area on the tell.

Two accumulation modes of the remains can be considered in the Qashish off-tell context:

1. The accumulation of remains of small animals that lived inside the settlement as human commensals and died there.
2. An accumulation resulting from later intrusions by burrowing species.

It is difficult to determine which of these two scenarios apply in this case, given the Qashish small sample size. Nevertheless, the presence of taxa such as vole, jird, and mole rat, all specialized burrowers, and the absence of commensal taxa such as the house mouse and shrews points to later intrusion as the likely mode of accumulation.

The meagerness of the Tel Qashish assemblage can be likely explained by:

1. A low rate of accumulation of microvertebrate remains, which could have resulted, for example, from rare occasions of animals dying inside their burrows;
2. Bad preservation conditions; or

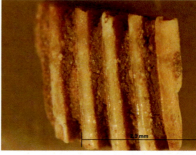

Fig. 22.1. *Microtus* molar showing fairly intact condition on lingual side (top) and some erosion on labial side (bottom).

3. A combination of these two factors.

The accumulation and preservation of microvertebrate remains were likely influenced by the characteristics of the depositional environment and by the fact that this part of the settlement was never again inhabited after the EB I. Since the deposits were not covered by layers of later occupations, this part of the site could have been subject to considerable erosion/deflation.

Given the nearby presence of the Kishon River, the absence of fish remains in Qashish is striking, as the Megiddo assemblage included hundreds of these. Several reasons can be suggested for this absence:

1. A lack of preservation of the delicate, fish remains
2. Fish-processing activities were conducted in other parts of the settlement, such as within residential quarters and not as part of outdoor activities
3. Fish was not consumed at Qashish during the Early Bronze Age.

Previous excavations at the tell of Qashish yielded very few fish remains (n=8), despite systematic sieving (Horwitz 2003). Only few other data sources on fish remains are available for Early Bronze Age I sites in Israel. At Tel Megiddo, only fifty-five remains from the whole Early Bronze Age sequence were found, while their number substantially increased in the Iron Age IB period, in the late second Millennium BCE (Lernau 2000, 2006).

At the same time, fairly large samples of fish remains were retrieved from Early Bronze Age I contexts at the coastal site of Ashkelon (Lernau 2004). Thus, the data point to the substantial use of marine fish resources on the coast, while at inland sites such as Tel Qashish, with access to small inland rivers, the level of fish exploitation may have remained quite low during the Bronze Age. Larger samples of fine-sieved material from both tell and off-tell contexts at Qashish are needed to address, in greater detail, important questions on economic strategies, settlement ecology, and the preservation bias of the various types of faunal finds.

References

Andrews, Peter
1990 *Owls, Caves, and Fossils: Predation, Preservation and Accumulation of Small Mammal Bones in Caves, with an Analysis of the Pleistocene Cave Faunas from Westbury-Sub-Mendip, Somerset, U.K.* Chicago: University of Chicago Press.

Horwitz, Liora Kolska
2003 "Fauna from Tel Qashish." In *Tel Qashish: A Village in the Jezreel Valley; Final Report of the Archaeological Excavations (1978–1987)*, edited by Amnon Ben-Tor, Ruhama Bonfil, and Sharon Zuckerman, 427–43. Qedem Reports 5. Jerusalem: Israel Antiquities Authority.

Lernau, Omri
2000 "Fish Bones." In *Megiddo III: The 1992–1996 Seasons*, edited by Israel Finkelstein, David Ussishkin, and Baruch Halpern, 463–77. 2 vols. SMNIA 18. Tel Aviv: Tel Aviv University.

2004 "Fish Remains from Early Bronze Age Ashqelon, Afridar." *'Atiqot* 45: 299–305.

2006 "Fish Remains." In *Megiddo IV: The 1998–2002 Season*, edited by Israel Finkelstein, David Ussishkin, and Baruch Halpern, 474–96. 2 vols. SMNIA 24. Tel Aviv: Tel Aviv University.

Weissbrod, Lior
2013 "The Micromammalian Remains." In *Megiddo V: The 2004–2008 Seasons*, edited by Israel Finkelstein, David Ussishkin, and Eric. H. Cline, 1210–14. 3 vols. SMNIA 31. Tel Aviv: Tel Aviv University.

Weissbrod, Lior, Guy Bar-Oz, Thomas Cucchi, and Israel Finkelstein
2013 "The Urban Ecology of Iron Age Tel Megiddo: Using Microvertebrate Remains as Ancient Bio-indicators." *JArS* 40: 257–67.

Table 22.1. List of samples of microvertebrate remains from Tel Qashish, Area E South, including description of the skeletal remains.

Square	Locus	Buckets with microfauna	Buckets without microfauna	Context	Specimens	Taxa	NISP
K54	5017	1	4	Bedrock lined pit in open area with evidence of outdoor activities.	*Microtus* left M_1 [erosion of enamel along salient angles on a single side].	*Microtus*	1
I64	5021	2	5	Round structure, partly preserved, containing lower parts of storage jars with burnt grains. Situated at the border, between the densely built residential area and open space, with evidence of various outdoors activities.	*Meriones* right talus; *Microtus* right M_1 & left M_1 [erosion of enamel along salient angles on the messial side only].	*Meriones*, *Microtus*	3
I64/65	5021	0	4	Round structure, partly preserved, containing lower parts of storage jars with burnt grains. Situated at the border, between the densely built residential area and open space, with evidence of various outdoors activities.			0
I64	5023	6	12	Round structure, partly preserved containing lower parts of storage jars with burnt grains. Situated at the border between densely built residential area and open space with evidence of various outdoors activities.	Left incisor 30%; 2 unidentified vertebrate remains; Squamata angular; 1 burnt unidentified vertebrate specimen; *Microtus* maxilla alveolar fragment.	*Micotus*, squamata	6
I64/65	5023	0	1	Round structure, partly preserved, containing lower parts of storage jars with burnt grains. Situated at the border, between the densely built residential area and open space, with evidence of various outdoors activities.			0
M57	5025	1	1	Stone circle in open area with evidence of outdoor activities.	*Microtus* left M^2 [erosion of enamel along salient angles on a single side].	*Microtus*	1
T54	5037	3	5	?	Squamata vert; *Spalax* Left humerus distal 1/4; Left incisor 30%; *Meriones* Left calcaneus; *Spalax* Left incisor 80%.	*Meriones*, *Spalax*, *Squamata*	5
K54	5045	1	14	Bedrock lined pit in open area with evidence of outdoor activities.	1 unidentifiable vertebrate specimen.		1
K57	5045	0	1	Part of the open area.			0
Total		14	47				17

Chapter 23

Plant Remains from Late Early Bronze Age I Deposits from Tel Qashish Area E South*

Ehud Weiss (*Archaeobotanical Laboratory, Institute of Archaeology, Bar-Ilan University*)
Yael Mahler-Slasky (*The Martin [Szusz] Department of Land of Israel Studies and Archaeology, Bar-Ilan University*)

During the salvage excavations carried out by the Israel Antiquities Authority northeast of Tel Qashish (fig. 23.1), in anticipation of the construction of a 10-m-wide segment of a railroad track (Rakevet ha-'Emeq), archaeobotanical remains were extracted from deposits in Area E South (permit A-5992, see Yannai, ch. 12, this volume; figs. 23.2–3). This area comprised the remains of a rural village dated to the late Early Bronze Age I (EB IB, ca. 3300 BCE) that was abandoned and never again resettled (see van den Brink chs. 10, 11, and 24, this volume).

Tel Qashish, located on the Kishon floodplain in the western part of the Jezreel Valley (fig. 23.1), at the juncture of three main landscape units (see Ackermann, ch. 2, this volume), is surrounded by fertile lands that allow the cultivation of a variety of crops.

Materials and Methods

A total of 114 samples were analyzed at the archaeobotanical laboratory of the Institute of Archaeology, Department of Land of Israel Studies and Archaeology, Bar-Ilan University, including 15 sediment samples sieved during the excavation and 99 samples floated by the excavators. Subsequently, light fraction samples were brought to the laboratory for processing.

All the samples were examined under an Olympus SZX9 stereo-microscope using magnifications up to x63.

Only forty-nine samples yielded charred plant remains, identified mainly by their external morphology, sorting them into types, sizes, shapes, and surface textures, and comparing these with plant organs in our reference collection. In addition, manuals and seed atlases were used for comparative purposes, sometimes also serving as preliminary guides (Bertsch 1941, 182; Beijerinck 1947), as well as the computerized key for grass grains of Israel and its adjacent regions (Kislev et al. 1995, 1997, 1999). Latin plant names appearing in the present report follow Avinoam Danin (2004), while common names follow Ori Fragman-Sapir, David Heller, and Avi Shmida (1999).

Results

Table 23.1 (at the end of the chapter) summarizes the plant remains found in Area E South. A total of around 7600 seeds were identified. The quantity of plant remains among the different samples was not homogeneous, some samples being rich in plant remains and others poor. Fifty samples contained no plant remains.

---

* We would like to thank Dr. Yoel Melamed for his help with the identification of the plant remains.

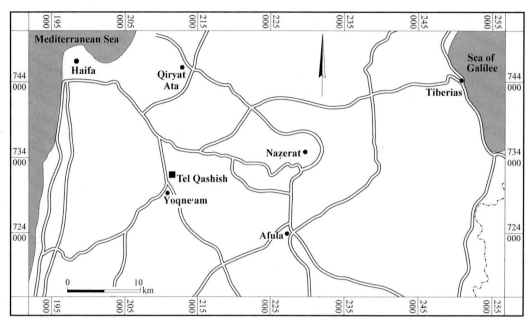

Fig. 23.1. Location plan of Tel Qashish.

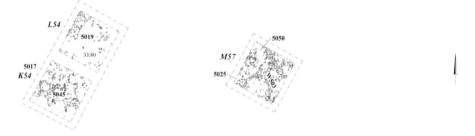

Fig. 23.2. Plan of Area E South.

23. Plant Remains from Late Early Bronze Age I Deposits from Tel Qashish Area E South

Fig. 23.3. Locus 5043 in Area E South.

Fig. 23.4. Emmer wheat (*Triticum dicoccum*) grains, dorsal view. The embryo (on the bottom) is missing in the right grain and its dent can be seen. The right grain shows the typical long and narrow shape of *T. dicoccum* grains, while the other two are wider, still in the general range of this species (Locus 5023).

Fig. 23.5. Emmer wheat (*T. dicoccum*), spikelet fork (Locus 5023).

Plant Remains by Locus

Locus 5023

Locus 5023 is the southernmost of two circular storage facilities exposed in Area E South (figs. 23.2–3; Yannai, ch. 12, this volume, figs. 12.9, 6). This structure was found well preserved on its west side but had completely eroded on the down-sloping east side of the site. In this structure, large fragments of rims and bases of restorable late EB I storage jars were found (see Paz, ch. 15, this volume). The plant remains were uncovered in situ above the jars' bases, indicating that the grains originated in these storage jars (for radiocarbon dating of samples from this deposit, see van den Brink, ch. 24, this volume).

The plant assemblage retrieved from this locus contains 3433 grains. Of these, about 2990 grains and 12 spikelet forks of hulled emmer wheat (*Triticum dicoccum*) were identified (figs. 23.4–5), as well as 8 grains of barley (*Hordeum vulgare*).

Many weeds, commonly found in cereal fields, were identified in this assemblage: 354 grains of bearded ryegrass (*Lolium* cf. *temulentum*), 60 grains of bristle-spiked canary grass (*Phalaris paradoxa*) (fig. 23.6), and 2 grains of wall barley (cf. *Hordeum glaucum*). One grain of *Lolium subulatum/rigidum* and 1 grain of *Lolium cf. persicum* (fig. 23.7) were also identified.

Only two seeds of legumes were found in this locus: one of lentil (*Lens culinaris*), and one of faba bean (*Vicia faba*).

The significant amount of wheat grains found in L5023 indicates that the rounded structure may have functioned as a silo, where jars for grain storage were kept.

This cache of wheat was not fully sorted and included mainly prime grains (i.e., wheat grains) and small seeds of various weed species. Cleaning was not performed at a high level, with 13 percent of the grains in Locus 5023 representing grains of weeds and other species accompanying wheat in a cereal field.

Apparently, the grains were stored after threshing and initial sieving meant to separate the grains from their spikelets. Only twelve spikelet forks of emmer wheat were found among the wheat grains, indicating that the separation of the grains from its spikelets was performed elsewhere before storing them. Since the pales and glumes that form the hulls of emmer wheat do not easily separate from the grains during threshing (Hillman 1981, 1984a, 1984b), the emmer spike breaks into individual spikelets that need to be subsequently broken by using a pestle and mortar to release the grains. The small number of spikelets in this assemblage may indicate that only a few grains had not been released from the spikelets before storing, and that the fire that apparently burned the silo caused the chaff to break and release their grains.

The eight barley grains found in the locus might represent residues of barley grains stored there beforehand. Alternatively, these may indicate admixture in the field.

A small assemblage of seventy-two seeds came from a single jar (Jar No. 8; B50261). These seeds were similar to those of the rest of the locus but comprised a higher percentage of weeds (36 percent). Including the general "leftovers" in the jar, that is, the small barley grains and wheat spikelet forks, their percentage reaches 40 percent.

Locus 5021

Locus 5021 is a floor located west of silo L5023 (see Yannai, ch. 12, this volume: figs. 12.6–7). The plant remains from L5021, very similar to those of L5023, contain 24 percent weeds from cereal fields. A nut-

Fig. 23.6. Bristle-spiked canary grass (*Phalaris paradoxa*) grains, lateral view. The grains are laterally compressed, and the embryo's dent (on the left) is rather long. The grains are irregular in shape (Locus 5023).

Fig. 23.7. *cf. Lolium persicum* grain, dorsal view (on the left) and ventral view (on the right) (Locus 5023).

let of *Adonis* sp. was also found. The plant remains found on this floor most likely represent the remainder of the grains left in the silo after some were taken for food preparation.

Locus 5025

Locus 5025 comprises the structural remains of an agricultural installation exposed in Square M57 (see van den Brink and 'Ad, 2011; Yannai, ch. 12, this volume, fig. 12.11). This locus is a floor covered with storage jars. Only two grains of a cereal weed species, *L.* cf. *temulentum*, were found in this locus, most probably representing leftovers from a cereal crop that had been stored in the jars.

Locus 5037

Locus 5037 is a pit with pottery (see Yannai, ch. 12, this volume, figs. 12.12–14). Only a small amount of seeds was found in this locus, also representing remains of sorted wheat grains. One *Compositae achene* seed was found, but it was not possible to identify it to species level (fig. 23.8).

Fig. 23.8. Compositae achene (Locus 5037).

Fig. 23.9. Grapevine (*Vitis vinifera*) pip, dorsal view (Locus 5045).

Fig. 23.10. Lentil (*Lens culinaris*) seeds. The charred seeds are round and rather compressed (Locus 5050).

Fig. 23.11. *Galium* sect. *Kolgyda* (probably *G. tricornutum*) mericarp (Locus 5050).

Locus 5045

Locus 5045 is a floor and a pit covered with pottery (see Yannai, ch. 12, this volume: figs. 12.6, 14). One grape (*Vitis vinifera*) pip was found (fig. 23.9), the only fruit found at the site, indicating that its inhabitants consumed grapes as part of their diet. At present, their exact form of consumption (fresh, raisins, or wine) cannot be deduced.

Locus 5050

Locus 5050 is a floor with two jars found in situ (see Yannai, ch. 12, this volume, figs. 12.6, 11; for radiocarbon dating of samples from this deposit, see van den Brink, ch. 24, this volume). In the north part of this floor were found a mud-plastered pit and plant remains.

The plant assemblage from this pit consists mainly of lentils (*L. culinaris*, 4085 seeds; fig. 23.10). Fourteen mericarps of *Galium* section Kolgyda—probably rough-fruited bedstraw (*Galium tricornutum*)—were found among these seeds (fig. 23.11). *G. tricornutum* is known as a weed present in legume fields (Garfinkel et al., 1988).

The lentil collection was clean and included only 0.3 percent of legume weeds, indicating that the collection had been strictly cleaned before storage. Thirty-eight barley grains and three emmer wheat grains were also identified in this locus. These cereal grains, together with the weed *L. cf. temulentum* often found in association with cereals in the field, might be residues of cereal crops grown in rotation with the lentils, in the same fields, in previous seasons.

The Diet of Tel Qashish

The assemblage of Tel Qashish contains five important crop species:

1. Emmer Wheat: Triticum dicoccum (Poaceae)

Wheats are the universal cereals of Old-World Mediterranean agriculture. They are superior to most other cereals for their high nutritional value. Their grains contain starch (60–80 percent carbohydrate) and a significant amount of protein (8–14 percent). The gluten proteins in cereal grains give wheat dough its stickiness and its ability to rise when leavened (Zohary, Hopf, and Weiss 2012, 23).

The individual spikelets are the product of threshing hulled, nonshattering emmer wheat (*T. dicoccum*). In domestic emmer, the grains remain invested by the pales and glumes. Threshing results in the breaking of the rachis of the ear at its weakest points below each spikelet. The emmer found at Tel Qashish represents a primitive stage in the group of domesticated *T. turgidum* wheats.

Hulled emmer was the principal wheat during the Neolithic and the Early Bronze Age in the Mediterranean basin, southwest Asia, and temperate Europe. Later, more advanced, naked free-threshing domestic types gradually replaced it (Zohary, Hopf, and Weiss 2012, 39–40). Emmer wheat grains are usually longer, narrower, and thinner than those of the naked wheat (*T. parvicoccum*).

Examples of ancient *T. dicoccum* were found, for example, in the Chalcolithic Cave of the Treasure (Zaitschek 1961), and the Pre-Pottery Neolithic C 'Atlit-Yam (Kislev, Hartmann, and Galili 2004).

2. Barley: Hordeum vulgare (Poaceae)

Domesticated barley, *H. vulgare* subsp. *vulgare*, is one of the main cereals in Mediterranean agriculture. Throughout its vast area of distribution, barley is a universal companion to wheat. However, compared to the latter, it is regarded as an inferior staple and poor person's bread. Barley is also the main cereal used for beer fermentation, and preparation of this beverage seems to be an ancient tradition (Hopf 1976; von Bothmer et al. 1991; Darby, Ghalioungui, and Grivetti 1977; Samuel 1996a, 1996b). This crop was and still is an important feeding supplement for domestic animals (Zohary, Hopf, and Weiss 2012, 51–52).

Ancient *H. vulgare* has been found, for example, in Iron Age Tel Aphek (Kislev and Mahler-Slasky 2009) and Iron Age II (604 BCE) Ashkelon (Weiss, Kislev, and Mahler-Slasky 2011).

3. Lentil: Lens culinaris (Fabaceae)

Lentils, like other legume species, are annual crops cultivated for their seeds and accompany the cereals in most regions of grain agriculture. They are an attractive cultivating option since, contrary to most other flowering plants, legumes can fix atmospheric nitrogen through symbiosis with the root bacterium rhizobium. Rather than reducing the amount of nitrogen, the pulses add it to the soil. Thus, by practicing rotation or mixing of legume crops and cereals, the cultivator can maintain higher levels of soil fertility. Another virtue is that the seeds of pulses are exceptionally rich in storage proteins, whereas grass grains are rich in starch, thus complementing each other as food elements and contributing, together, to a balanced human diet. In traditional agricultural communities, pulses served and continue to serve as the main substitute for meat, with a protein content of 25 percent (Zohary, Hopf, and Weiss 2012, 75, 77).

Lentils rank among the oldest and most appreciated grain legumes of the Old World. Compared to cereals, yields are relatively low, but lentil stands out as one of the most nutritious and tasty pulses.

Ancient *L. culinaris* is one of the common legumes found in archaeological sites, such as in Pre-Pottery Neolithic B Yiftah'el (Garfinkel, Kislev, and Zohary 1988), and Early Bronze Age Jericho (Hopf 1983).

4. Faba bean: Vicia faba (Fabaceae)

Faba beans, like lentils and other legume crops, constitute part of the main pulses of Old World agriculture. The erect, robust plant readily bears threshable pods and relatively large seeds, with a high protein content (about 20–25 percent). In some Asian and Mediterranean countries, the dry seeds of the faba bean provide a staple protein source for the poor. These seeds are also regarded as valuable animal food. *V. faba* is an annual crop. Faba bean taxonomists recognize three or four intergrading and interfertile main types of cultivar forms (Muratova 1931; Hanelt 1972). Forms with relatively small, rounded seeds measuring 6–13 mm are placed in *V. faba* var *minor*, while forms with medium-sized seeds, 2–15 mm long, 12–15 mm wide, and 5–8 mm thick, are placed in var. *major*. Almost all the seed remains from archaeological sites dating from the Neolithic through the Roman periods fall within the range of var. *minor* (Zohary, Hopf, and Weiss 2012, 89–90). Ancient *V. faba* seeds have been found in sites such as Pre-Pottery Neolithic B Yiftah'el (Garfinkel, Kislev, and Zohary 1988) and Middle Bronze Age IIA Tel Nami (Kislev, Artzy, and Marcus 1993). The larger faba seeds, var. *major*, which are prevalent these days, seem to have been cultivated at a relatively late date.

5. Grapevine: Vitis vinifara (Vitaceae)

Grapevine is one of the classic fruits of the Old World. Since the Early Bronze Age, grapes have contributed significantly to food production in this area, providing fresh fruits rich in sugar (the berries contain 15–25 percent sugar), easily stored dried raisins, and juice for fermenting wine. The latter became an important trade element in countries around the Mediterranean Sea (Zohary, Hopf, and Weiss 2012, 121). Examples of ancient *V. vinifara* have been found, for example, in Late Bronze IIB Tel Batash (Kislev, Melamed, and Langsam 2006) and Iron Age II Ashkelon (Weiss, Kislev, and Mahler-Slasky 2011).

Wild Plants and Weed Species

Adonis sp. (Ranunculaceae)

Adonis sp. are annual, perennial herbs. The fruits are elongated heads of wrinkled, short-beaked achenes. Five species of *Adonis* grow in Israel (Zohary 1966, 211). The achene found in Tel Qashish was broken, and its typical wrinkles were well-distinguished, though it was impossible to define its species because only this fragment was found.

Ancient remains of *Adonis* sp. are reported in Israel from as early as the 790,000 BP Acheulian site Gesher Benot Yaaqov (Alperson-Afil et al. 2009) and in other sites such as the Upper Paleolithic Ohalo II (Weiss et al. 2008) and Iron Age I Tel Aphek (Kislev and Mahler-Slasky 2009).

Galium sect. Kolgyda (Rubiaceae)

The genus *Galium* comprises annual and perennial herbs or small shrubs. The fruits of the *Galium* species have two mericarps. Fresh mericarps measure 2.5–6 mm in diameter (Feinbrun-Dothan 1978, 240–46), while the mericarps found in Tel Qashish are only about 1.5–2 mm in diameter (fig. 23.11). The latter, globose or hemispherical with ± elliptical hole on the flat side, are typical of section *Kolgyda*, which includes five *Galium* species growing in Israel, namely *G. aparine*, *G. pisiferum*, *G. samuelssonii*, *G. tricornutum*, and *G. verrucosum*, and also of the related genus *Asperula*. The hairs and tubercules surrounding the mericarp had been completely removed, possibly due to threshing or fire, preventing the exact identification of the *Galium* mericarps found in the Tel Qashish to the species level.

We assume that the *Galium* species found among the lentils in Tel Qashish belongs to *G. tricornutum*, as this species is a known weed in legume fields (Garfinkel, Kislev, and Zohary 1988). Ancient *G. tricornutum* was reported in several sites, such as Upper Paleolithic (23,000 BP) Ohalo II (Weiss et al. 2008), MB II–III Shiloh (Kislev 1993), and Iron Age II (604 BCE) Ashkelon (Weiss, Kislev, and Mahler-Slasky 2011).

Poaceae

Weeds and wild grasses species were defined using the reference collection at Bar-Ilan University and the computerized key for grass grains of Israel and its adjacent regions (Kislev et al. 1995, 1997, 1999). The dimensions of the grains to be defined were measured and processed by the computerized key, following the use of the reference collection for final identification.

cf. Hordeum glaucum (=H. murinum ssp. glaucum).

Hordeum glaucum is an annual grass growing in ruderal areas, roadsides, and near human habitations (Feinbrun-Dothan 1986, 182). The archaeological grains measure 4.2–4.28 mm long, 1.52–1.64 mm wide, and 1.08 mm thick. The grain is thin and wedge-shaped. Ancient *H. glaucum* was found in Israel at several sites, such as the Upper Paleolithic (23,000 BP) Ohalo II (Weiss et al. 2008) and LB IIB Tel Aphek (Kislev and Mahler-Slasky 2009).

cf. Lolium persicum

Lolium persicum is an annual grass. It is very rare in Israel, growing in the fields on basalt rocks and soil (Feinbrun-Dothan 1986, 233–34). Its grain is about three-and-a-half to five times longer than wide, and its ventral side is concave. The archaeological grain measures 4.08 mm long, 1.6 mm wide, and 1.16 mm thick (fig. 23.7). The only reported archaeological find of this species is from the Hellenistic/Parthian site Larsa, in Iraq (Neef 1989).

Lolium subulatum/rigidum

Lolium subulatum and *L. rigidum* are annual grasses growing in fields (Feinbrun-Dothan 1986, 231–32). The archaeological grain measures 4.6 mm long, 1.72 mm wide, and 0.92 mm thick. Ancient *L. rigidum* grains were found in Israel in sites such as Iron Age II Ashkelon (Weiss, Kislev, and Mahler-Slasky 2011) and Bronze Age Tel Beth Shean (Simchoni, Kislev, and Melamed 2007). No finds of *L. subulatum* in Israel have come to the authors' knowledge.

Lolium cf. temulentum

Lolium temulentum is an annual species. Its mature grains are oblong, often partly exposed, 4–7 mm, and about two to three times longer than wide (Feinbrun-Dothan 1986, 234). This species is reputed to be a noxious weed since ancient times (Kroll, 1983, 82–86; Kislev 1980). It exhibits many of the features of weeds, such as its annual growth pattern, loss of its ability to disperse, enlargement of grains, and loss of its primary habitat (Zohary 1962, 219).

The grains from Tel Qashish were not well preserved, and some deformation might have occurred from fire. The grains were generally similar in shape to recent *L. temulenum* grains but smaller. The dimensions of the wheat grains were also relatively smaller than in later periods. The direct relationship between the weeds' grain size and that of the wheat it accompanies has already been mentioned by Nikolai Vavilov (1926, 207). Ancient *L. temulentum* grains are very commonly found in association with cereals. In Israel, it was found almost in every site where cereal crops were present, the earliest site being the Upper Paleolithic Ohalo II (23,000 BP; Snir et al. 2015).

Phalaris paradoxa

P. paradoxa is an annual species. Its mature grains are laterally compressed and bear a narrow ventral groove. Its hilum is oblong, and its embryo is rather long and typically situated on the narrow side of its grain. In southwest Asia, *P. paradoxa* is a noxious weed in traditional agriculture since it is difficult for the farmer to separate its dispersal units from cereal grains (Bor, Guest, and Al-Rawi 1968, 368; Zohary 1941, 46–47).

The grains found in Tel Qashish are rather small compared to most *P. paradoxa* grains but are still within the species grain size-range (fig. 23.6). Ancient *P. paradoxa* grains were found at many sites in Israel in association with cereals, for example, MB IIB Tel Beth Shean (Simchoni, Kislev, and Melamed 2007) and Iron Age II (604 BC) Ashkelon (Weiss, Kislev, and Mahler-Slasky 2011).

Malva sp.

Malva spp. are annual and perennial herbs. Six *Malva* species grow in Israel. The fruit is a schizocarp with many indehiscent mericarps. The mericarps of the different species differ in size, shape, and texture, but the seeds of all the species are rather similar (Zohary 1972, 315).

In Tel Qashish, only one seed was found, with no mericarp, hence the identification to the genus level. Ancient mericarps and seeds of *Malva spp.* have been found in several sites in Israel, such as Upper Paleolithic Ohalo II (23,000 BP; Weiss et al., 2008) and Chalcolithic Tel Shiqmim (Kislev 1987).

Discussion and Summary

Two main collections of charred plant remains were found in the late Early Bronze Age I rural lower village of Tel Qashish, Area E South.

The first—a hulled wheat collection—was found in the southern circular structure L5023. Broken storage jars were found in the same context, indicating that this structure was a silo where cereal grains were stored in jars. The grains were stored after being separated from their spikelets and after manual sorting. However, the wheat pile was not completely clean and contained about 13 percent of weeds and other species. A similar plant assemblage was also found at the bottom of jar no. 8, uncovered in this locus. The higher percentage of weeds (36 percent) in the assemblage from this jar suggests it might be leftovers after taking out wheat grains for consumption.

The second collection was discovered in a mud-plastered pit (L5050) containing mainly lentils. This pile was rather clean, and included less than 1 percent of weeds, indicating a strict manual cleaning before storage. Lentil seeds, like other legume species, are exceptionally rich in proteins, and thus have been an important component of the human diet since ancient times.

The two collections are also distinct in their weed-crop assemblages. Cereal weeds, *L. temulenum* and *P. paradoxa*, were found mainly together with wheat grains, while the only legume weed at the site, *Galium* sect. *Kolgyda* (most probably *G. tricornutum*), was found with the lentil seeds.

The weed *L. temulenum* has poisonous properties known since antiquity, on account of its grains containing the alkaloid temulin. The flour made of cereals not properly cleaned and containing grains of *L. temulenum* sometimes caused fatal cases of food poisoning, especially in wet years. The poisonous properties of the *L. temulenum* grain are also known to be connected with the presence of a fungal mycelium between the seed coat and the aleurone layer (Feinbrun-Dothan 1986, 234–35). Besides the fact that this is a common weed in agricultural fields and archaeobotanical assemblages, it is an intriguing find considering that these grains could have been the cause of some disturbance among the Tel Qashish inhabitants.

Weeds such as *L. temulentum* and *P. paradoxa* are obligatory weeds, today growing only in cereal fields (Zohary 1950). These species are widely distributed throughout Israel and thus cannot serve to identify the location of the wheat fields. The only information they provide concerns the cereal's cleaning degree. *L. persicum* is a species growing in fields, but its distribution in Israel is restricted to Samaria, upper Galilee, and the Golan. Unfortunately, its preservation state did not enable certain identification. However, if this is indeed *L. persicum*, it can point to the presence of wheat originating in fields in those regions, far away from the site. This is an interesting find, considering that the valley fields are well known for their fertility throughout history, and a special reason was needed for such an import.

The cereals, legumes, and fruits from Tel Qashish indicate that the late EB I inhabitants of the site had a balanced vegetal diet that contained carbohydrates from cereals, proteins from pulses, vitamins A, B, and C, and the various minerals. No doubt, grapevine added energy, sugars, and vitamins to their diet, as well as wine for sacramental and joyous daily uses.

References

Alperson-Afil Nira, Gonen Sharon, Mordechai Kislev, Yoel Melamed, Irit Zohar, Shosh Ashkenazi, Rivka Rabinovich, Rebecca Biton, Ella Werker, Gideon Hartman, Craig Feibel, and Naama Goren-Inbar
2009 "Spatial Organization of Hominin Activities at Gesher Benot Ya'aqov, Israel." *Science* 326: 1677–80. DOI: 10.1126/science.1180695.

Beijerinck, Willem
1947 *Zadenatlas der Nederlandsche flora, ten behoeve van de botanie, palaeontologie, bodemcultuur en warenkennis: Omvattende, naast de inheemsche Flora, onze belangrijkate cultuurgewassen en verschillende adventiescorten*. Wageningen: Veenman.

Bertsch, Karl
1941 *Früchte und Samen: Ein Bestimmungsbuch zur Pflanzenkunde der vorgeschichtlichen Zeit*. Handbücher der praktischen Vorgeschichtsforschung 1. Stuttgart: Enke.

Bor, Norman L., Evan Guest, Ali al-Rawi
1968 *Flora of Iraq, Vol. 9, Gramineae*. Baghdad: Ministry of Agriculture of the Republic of Iraq.

Bothmer, Roland von, Niels Jacobsen, Rikke B. Jørgensen, Ib Linde-Laursen, and Claus Baden
1991 *An Ecogeographical Study of the Genus Hordeum*. Rome: International Board for Plant Genetic Resources.

Brink, Edwin C. M. van den, and Uzi 'Ad
2011 "Tel Qashish," *HA-ESI* 123. http://hadashot-esi.org.il/report_detail_eng.aspx?id=1894&mag_id=118.

Danin, Avinoam
2004 *Distribution Atlas of Plants in the Flora Palaestina Area*. Jerusalem: Israel Academy of Sciences and Humanities.

Darby, William J., Paul Ghalioungui, and Louis Grivetti
1977 *Food: The Gift of Osiris*. London: Academic Press.

Feinbrun-Dothan, Naomi
1978 *Flora Palaestina, Part 3: Ericaceae to Compositae*. Jerusalem: Israel Academy of Sciences and Humanities.

1986 *Flora Palaestina, Part 4: Alismataceae to Orchidaceae.* Jerusalem: Israel Academy of Sciences and Humanities.

Fragman-Sapir Ori, David Heller, and Avi Shmida
1999 *Checklist and Ecological Data-Base of the Flora of Israel and Its Surroundings: Including Israel, Jordan, the Palestinian Autonomy, Golan Heights, Mt. Hermon and Sinai.* Jerusalem: Society for the Protection of Nature.

Garfinkel, Yosef, Mordechai E. Kislev, and Daniel Zohary
1988 "Lentil in the Pre-Pottery Neolithic B Yiftah'el: Additional Evidence of Its Early Domestication." *Israel Journal of Botany* 37: 49–51.

Hanelt, Peter
1972 "Die intraspezifische Variabilität von Vicia faba L. und ihre Gliederung." *Kulturpflanze* 20: 75–128.

Hillman, Gordon C.
1981 "Reconstructing Crop Husbandry Practices from the Charred Remains of Crops." In *Farming Practice in British Prehistory*, edited by Roger J. Mercer, 123–62. Edinburgh: Edinburgh University Press.
1984a "Interpretation of Archaeological Plant Remains: The Application of Ethnographic Models from Turkey." In *Plants and Ancient Man: Studies in Palaeoethnobotany; Proceedings of the Sixth Symposium of the International Work Group for Palaeoethnobotany, Groningen, 30 May–3 June 1983*, edited by Willem van Zeist and Willem A. Casparie, 1–41. Rotterdam: Balkema.
1984b "Traditional Husbandry and Processing of Archaic Cereals in Recent Times: The Operations, Products and Equipment Which Might Feature in Sumerian Texts, Part 1; The Glume Wheats." *BSA* 1: 1–32.

Hopf, Maria
1976 "Bier." In *Reallexikon der Germanischen Altertumskunde*, edited by Heinrich Beck, Herbert Jahnkuhn, Kurt Ranke, and Reinhard Wenskus, 2:530–33. Berlin: de Gruyter.
1983 "Jericho Plant Remains." In *Excavations at Jericho*, edited by Kathleeen M. Kenyon and Thomas A. Holland, 576–621. London: British School of Archaeology in Jerusalem.

Kislev, Mordechai E.
1980 "*Triticum parvicoccum* sp. nov., the Oldest Naked Wheat." *Israel Journal of Botany* 28: 95–107.
1987 "Chalcolithic Plant Husbandry and Ancient Vegetation at Shiqmim." In *Shiqmim I: Studies Concerning Chalcolithic Societies in the Northern Negev Desert, Israel (1982–1984)*, edited by Thomas E. Levy, 251–79, 549–63. 2 vols. BARIS 356. Oxford: BAR.
1993 "Food Remains." In *Shiloh: The Archaeology of a Biblical Site*, edited by Israel Finkelstein, Shlomo Bunimovich, and Zvi Lederman, 354–61. SMNIA 10 Tel Aviv University: Institute of Archaeology.

Kislev, Mordechai E., Michal Artzy, and Ezra Marcus
1993 "Import of an Aegean Food Plant to a Middle Bronze IIA Coastal Site in Israel." *Levant* 25: 145–54.

Kislev, Mordechai E., Anat Hartmann, and Ehud Galili
2004 "Archaeobotanical and Archaeoentomological Evidence from a Well at Atlit-Yam Indicates Colder, More Humid Climate on the Israeli Coast during the PPNC Period." *JArS* 31: 1301–10.

Kislev, Mordechai E., and Yael Mahler-Slasky
2009 "Food Remains." In *Aphek-Antipatris II: The Remains on the Acropolis; The Moshe Kochavi and Pirhiya Beck Excavations*, edited by Yuval Gadot and Esther Yadin, 499–525. SMNIA 27. Tel Aviv University: Institute of Archaeology.

Kislev, Mordechai E., Yoel Melamed, and Yakov Langsam
2006 "Plant Remains from Tel Batash." In *Timnah (Tel Batash) III: The Finds from the Second Millennium BCE*, edited by Nava Panitz-Cohen and Amihai Mazar, 295–310. Qedem 45. Jerusalem: Hebrew University, Jerusalem.

Kislev, Mordechai E., Yoel Melamed, Orit Simchoni, and Mina Marmorstein
1997 "Computerized Key of Grass Grains of the Mediterranean Basin." *Lagascalia* 19: 289–94.
1999 "Computerized Keys for Archaeological Grains: First Steps." In *The Practical Impact of Science on Near Eastern and Aegean Archaeology*, edited by Scott Pike and Seymour Gitin, 29–31. London: Archetype.

Kislev, Mordechai E., Orit Simchoni, Yoel Melamed, and Mina Marmorstein
1995 "Computerized Key for Grass Grains of Israel and Its Adjacent Regions." In *Res Archaeobotanicae: International Workgroup for Palaeoethnobotany; Proceedings of the 9th Symposium Kiel 1992*, edited by Helmut Kroll and Rainer Pasternak, 69–79. Kiel: Oetker-Voges.

Kroll, Helmut
1983 *Kastanas: Die Pflanzenfunde Ausgrabungen in einem Siedlungshügel der Bronze- und Eisenzeit Makedoniens 1975–1979.* Prähistorische Archäologie in Südosteuropa 2. Berlin: Spiess.

Muratova, V. S.
1931 "Common Beans, Vicia faba L. A Botanical–Agronomical Monograph." *Bulletin of Applied Botany of Genetics and Plant-Breeding* 50 (Supplement): 1–295.

Neef, Reinder
1989 "Plant Remains from Archaeological Sites in Lowland Iraq: Hellenistic and Neobabylonian Larsa." In *Larsa, travaux de 1985*, edited by Jena-Louis Huot, 151–61. Paris: Editions Recherche sur les Civilisations.

Samuel, Delwen
1996a "Investigation of Ancient Egyptian Baking and Brewing Methods by Correlative Microscopy." *Science* 273: 488–90.
1996b "Archaeology of Ancient Egyptian Beer." *Journal of the American Society of Brewing Chemists* 54: 3–12.

Simchoni, Orit, Mordechai E. Kislev, and Yoel Melamed
2007 "Bet-Shean as a Trade Center of Crops in the Bronze Age: Botanical and Entomological Evidence." In *Excavations at Tel Bet-Shean 1989–1996, Vol. II: The Middle and Late Bronze Age Strata in Area R*, edited by Amihai Mazar and Robert Mullins, 702–15. Jerusalem: Israel Exploration Society; Hebrew University, Jerusalem.

Snir, Ainit, Dani Nadel, Iris Groman-Yaroslavski, Yoel Melamed, Marcelo Sternberg, Ofer Bar-Yosef, and Ehud Weiss
2015 "The Origin of Cultivation and Proto-Weeds, Long Before Neolithic Farming." *PLOS ONE* 10(7): e0131422. DOI: 10.1371/journal.pone.0131422.

Vavilov, Nikolai I.
1926 *Studies on the Origin of Cultivated Plants*. Leningrad: Institut de Botanique Appliquée et d'Amelioration des Plantes.

Weiss, Ehud, Mordechai E. Kislev, and Yael Mahler-Slasky
2011 "Plant Remains." In *Ashkelon 3: The Seventh Century B.C.*, edited by Lawrence E. Stager, J. David Schloen, and Daniel M. Master, 591–613. Winona Lake, IN: Eisenbrauns.

Weiss, Ehud, Mordechai E. Kislev, Orit Simchoni, Dani Nadel, and Hartmut Tschauner
2008 "Plant-Food Preparation Area on an Upper Paleolithic Brush Hut Floor at Ohalo II, Israel." *JArS* 35: 2400–2414.

Zaitschek, David V.
1961 "Remains of Cultivated Plants from the Cave of Nahal Mishmar: Preliminary Note." *IEJ* 11: 70–72.

Zohary, Daniel, Maria Hopf, and Ehud Weiss
2012 *Domestication of Plants in the Old World: The Origin and Spread of Domesticated Plants in Southwest Asia, Europe, and the Mediterranean Basin*, 4th ed. Oxford: Oxford University Press.

Zohary, Michael
1941 *The Weeds of Palestine and Their Control*. Tel Aviv: Hassadeh. [Hebrew]
1950 "The Segetal Plant Communities of Palestine." *Vegetatio* 2: 387–411.
1962 *Plant Life of Palestine*. New York: Ronald.
1966 *Flora Palaestina*. Jerusalem: Israel Academy of Sciences and Humanities.
1972 *Flora Palaestina*. Jerusalem: Israel Academy of Sciences and Humanities.

Table 23.1. Plant species in EB IB Tel Qashish, Area E South.

	Plant name	Organ	Locus 5021	Locus 5023	Locus 5023 jar no. 8	Locus 5023 total	Locus 5025	Locus 5037	Locus 5045	Locus 5050	Total
Cereals	*Hordeum vulgare*	grain		7	1	8				38	46
	Triticum dicoccum	grain	31	2950	43	2993		6		3	3033
	Triticum dicoccum	spikelet fork		10	2	12		3			15
Cereals total			31	2967	46	3013		9		41	3094
Pulses	*Lens culinaris*	seed		1		1		1		4085	4087
	Vicia faba	seed		1		1					1
Pulses total				2		2		1		4085	4088
Fruits	*Vitis vinifera*	pip							1		1
Wild plants and weeds	*Adonis* sp.	achene	1								1
	cf. *Compositae*	achene						1			1
	Galium sect. *Kolgyda*	mericarp								14	14
	cf. *Hordeum glaucum*	grain		2		2					2
	cf. *Lolium persicum*	grain		1		1					1
	Lolium cf. *temulentum*	grain	8	334	20	354	2	1	1	1	367
	Lolium subulatum/rigidum	grain		1		1					1
	Malva sp.	seed						1	1		1
	Phalaris paradoxa	grain	1	54	6	60		2			64
Wild plants and Weeds total			10	392	26	418	2	5	2	15	452
Grand total			41	3361	72	3433	2	15	3	4141	7635

Chapter 24

Salvage Excavations at Tel Qashish: Discussion and Conclusions

Edwin C. M. van den Brink (*Israel Antiquities Authority*)

The late Early Bronze Age I rural village of Tel Qashish (Stratum XV) was surveyed (Portugali 1982) and probed in the 1980s by a team of archaeologists of the Hebrew University in Jerusalem (Ben-Tor, Bonfil, and Zuckerman 2003; Zuckerman 2003b, 57–60) on the mound of the tell of Qashish at elevations between around 46.50 and 43.30 m ASL. Four salvage excavations were carried out in the immediate margins of Tel Qashish in 2010–2011. Excluding the data collected in Areas A and B, which mainly concerned the Roman period (ch. 11, this volume) and the Late Bronze Age II (Part V, this volume), one of the main findings of the three subsequent excavations was that this village clearly extended beyond the natural boundaries of the tell occupying a chalky outcrop, the east slope of a similar outcrop northeast of the mound (Areas E–F, at elevations between ca. 33.4 and 29 m ASL) and down its west slope toward the Kishon River (Areas C–D, at elevations between 13 and 22 m ASL).

The late EB I structural remains exposed in Areas C–F seem to represent part of an inhabited area located slightly further down on the east slope of the hill (henceforth "lower village"), with the late EB I settlement probed by Amnon Ben-Tor and colleagues (Ben-Tor and Bonfil, 2003, 10–30; Zuckerman, 2003a, 2003b) situated on the hilltop (the tell proper, henceforth "the upper village"). Both parts of the village most probably existed in symbiosis.

The lower village is characterized by two distinct activity zones. One was devoted to both habitation and for storage of surplus agricultural produce (Areas E North and South–F). It was located closest to the late EB I occupation on the tell and comprised partial remains of several apparently one-room rectangular dwellings with rounded corners, additional rectilinear structures oriented similarly to those on the tell and two circular silos containing several storage jars filled with grain. Somewhat farther away, an industrial, agricultural zone (Areas C–D) comprised several installations and some disconnected surfaces of small-sized fieldstones interspersed with groundstone basalt, limestone mortars, and grinding stones.

No complete plans of structures were found on the east slope, Areas E North and South. All that remained were the first courses of their stone foundations. With the exception of a carefully placed flagstone pavement, no floors could be discerned in these buildings (figs. 13.8–9, ch. 13, this volume). Mud-brick debris found inside three of the better-preserved structures clearly indicates they derived from the wall's superstructures. Their remains represent a single stratum but represented in two or three building phases (figs. 13.11–13). Unfortunately, their sequence could not be clarified as work had to be halted for lack of additional time. The earliest building remains rested directly on the sloping, virgin soil (consisting there of weathered basalt), while later remains rested on a thin layer of dark colluvial soil mixed with pottery sherds above the weathered basalt bedrock.

While the architectural remains represented a single stratum, the inner stratigraphic sequence of Area E (North) could not be clarified in its entirety within a very severe, and inadequate seventeen-day time limit set for the excavation of this area (permit A6149/2011). A look at figures 13.11–13 clearly shows that there are at least two, possibly three distinct building phases, evidenced by a wall/walls of one structure cutting into those of another building.

Three mechanically dug trenches set along an approximately 65 m east–west axis in Area E South (TQ 1–3; fig. 2.2, ch. 2, this volume) revealed the underlying subsoil stratigraphy of the site more clearly. The westernmost trench (TQ 1), situated nearest the top of the hill, revealed a relatively thin layer of weathered basalt deposited on the east slope over the chalk hill, becoming increasingly thicker downslope toward the east (Ackermann, ch. 2, this volume). This stands in stark contrast to Areas C and D, on the west slope of the same hill probed in 2010, where the basalt sediments are absent and where Miocene chalk bedrock is covered by deposits of alluvial/colluvial soils. It is notable that whereas the contemporary settlement on the tell continued into the succeeding EB II–III periods, the late EB I settlement on the east slope and contemporary activity areas on the west slope were apparently abandoned, never to be resettled.

However, higher up the slope, in the western extreme of Area E, several narrow wall segments, perhaps belonging to a phase following most of the settlement's abandonment were found embedded in extensive spreads of unworked, chalk and *nari* (layer of harder chalk/limestone covering chalk deposits) stones mixed with large chunks of late EB I pottery clearly in situ. The nature of the pottery spreads uncovered in Areas E South and North—large pieces of layered, broken pottery, mainly of holemouth jars and bow-rim storage jars—distinctly indicates that the sherds concern primary deposits. Taken together with the interspersed stone debris, it might, perhaps, represent the settlement's collapse by an earthquake, possibly the same one that destroyed the not-so-distant contemporary settlement at Tel Megiddo.[1]

Among the portable finds, pottery is predominant. Areas C (IAA permit A-5881) and E North (IAA permit A-6149) yielded 45,831 plain body sherds and 8,154 diagnostic sherds (including 3,497 flat base fragments).[2] The largest group is represented by holemouth jars (n=2,652 or 57 percent of all diagnostics, bases excluded) followed by bow-rim storage jars (n=1,170 or 25 percent), while the remainder (n=835 or 18 percent) is made up of smaller ceramic vessels: various types of kraters and bowls, the latter comprising gray burnished ware bowls, knobbed and small and hemispheric bowls; bow-rim jars and various types of necked jars; and few amphoriskoi and red-polished "tea-pots" with a bent spout. With 82 percent of all diagnostics belonging to holemouth and bow-rim jars, the assemblage is clearly domestic, that is, nonfunerary.[3] The composition and numerical breakdown of the pottery assemblage are comparable to those from the upper village on the tell, where holemouth jars are also the predominant type (Zuckerman 2003a, 49).

Whereas at contemporary, neighboring sites such as Qiryat Ata, ʽEn Shadud, Megiddo, ʽEn Zippori, and Naḥal Zippori 3, varying quantities of large jars (pithoi) with bow-rims *and* indented rail/roll rims were found (table 24.1; see Braun 1996, tables 3.5–7), the complete absence of the latter type at Tel Qashish is particularly noteworthy. Could this indicate that one of the production centers of bow-rim jars was located at or near the site? Nimrod Getzov (2004, 44) suggested a manufacturing center for the other, rail-rim type in the eastern Jordan Valley.

The red-polished neck/shoulder fragment of a medium-sized jar bearing a cylinder seal impression showing two four-legged animals (fig. 18.1, ch. 18, this volume), one with two long horns, has an identical parallel in a cylinder seal impression found at

---

1. For a different view of the earthquake hypothesis see Adams 2013.

2. Areas A, B, and D yielded only limited amounts of late EB I pottery, not taken into account here. The pottery found in the second (2010) season in Areas E (South) and F (IAA permit A-5992), making a total of 6134 potsherds, including 369 diagnostics, 130 flat bases, and 60 handles, is detailed in ch. 15 by Netanel Paz, and have not been included in the present account. The potsherd count for Area E (North) includes sherds retrieved in the third (2011) season of salvage excavations (IAA permit A-6149).

3. In funerary pottery assemblages, the smaller ceramic vessels specified above outweigh by far the large storage and cooking jars.

Table 24.1. Presence (+)/absence (−) dichotomy of bow-rim and neckless rail/roll rim jars/pithoi from selected late EB I sites in western Galilee, the northern Jordan Valley, and the north Coastal Plain, listed from north to south.

Sites	Rosh ha-Niqra	Abu ed-Dnahab, Strata III–II	Qiryat Ata	Tel Megadim (Tel Sahar)	Tel Kitan, Strata VII	Bet Yerah, Period B	Tel Qashish	'En Shadud, Strata I–II	Beth Shean	'En Esur	'Afula	Megiddo Level J4; East Slope	Giv'at Rabi/'En Zippori	Naḥal Zippori 3
Bow-rim pithoi	−	−	+ (many)	+ (many)	−	−	+ (many)	+	−	+	+	+	+ (few)	+ (many)
			Golani 2003, 101, figs. 4.10–11 (type SJII).	Gophna 1974, figs. 1.5–6; S. Wolff, pers. comm. 2020.			Zuckerman 2003a, 56, figs. 3.11–12; 4.5–6; 6.13; 9.13–14;10.12–13; 12.12–14; 22.3 (type SJII); ch. 14, this volume: figs. 14.9–10.	Braun 1985, fig. 23.8–12 (type 26).		Yannai, Lazar-Shorer, and Grosinger 2006, 89, figs. 4.59; 4.62.8; 4.74.8.	Sukenik 1948, pl. IV.1–3, 5–7, 9–11.	East slope Braun 2013, 86–89, fig. 27, pls. 58–59.	Getzov, pers. comm. 2011.	van den Brink, pers. comm. 2013.
Rail-rim pithoi	+	+	+		+	+ (many)	−	+	+	+ (few)	−	+	+	+ (many)
	Tadmor and Prausnitz 1959, fig. 6.1–4.	Getzov 20(4, 44, fig. 18.15	Golani 2003, 108, fig. 4.13.16–18 (type SJ VIII).		Eisenberg and Rotem 2016, figs. 11, 12.1–3.	Paz 2006, 283, fig. 7.24.11; Greenberg and Eisenberg 2006, 123, fig. 5.77.4.		Braun 1985, 115, fig. 23.3–7 (type 25).	Braun 2004, 52, pl. IV.17.	Yannai, Lazar-Shorer and Grosinger 2006, 88, fig. 4.57.3–4.		Level J4-J5 Joffe 2000, fig. 8.4.21; east slope Braun 2013, 89–90.		van den Brink, pers. comm. 2013.

Megiddo more than eighty years ago (fig. 18.2; Engberg and Shipton 1934, 36, figs. 10C, 11C), pointing to both examples being rolled from the same cylinder seal. Though rare, cylinder seal impressions are known from other late EB I contexts in the area, for example, ʻEn Shadud, Tel Kitan, Bet Yeraḥ, Meʻona, and Qiryat Ata (for references, see Joffe 2001, 360–61; Braun 2004; 2013, ch. 4).

Analysis of the flints collected during the three excavation seasons on the margins of Tel Qashish revealed certain trends in the technological characteristics of the artifacts and their spatial distribution. All three industries characteristic of the Early Bronze Age are present in the assemblage, namely the on-site produced, so-called ad hoc tools; Canaanean blades possibly imported from nearby Har Ḥaruvim, based on the strong affinities noted in the raw material with cores from that site; and tabular scrapers that may have functioned in a cultic context.

The groundstone tools found in Areas C–E consist mainly of basalt grinding stones (manos and metates), portable stone mortars, a single complete basalt bowl, and a fragment of the upper part of a tournette. The conspicuous, almost total absence of groundstone tools in contemporary habitation levels at the nearby tell/mound (Strata XV–XIV), excavated in the past by Ben-Tor and colleagues, seems to speak volumes as only a single fragment of a basalt grinding stone was found in late EB I deposits there (Ben-Tor and Bonfil 2003, 29, fig. 14.17). This implies that certain household-based activities such as food-processing, for instance, grinding of grain to make flour, were carried out on the outskirts of the actual habitation zone.

Cereals, legumes, and fruits were identified in varying quantities among the archaeobotanical assemblage, indicating a balanced vegetal diet containing carbohydrates from cereals, proteins from pulses, vitamins A, B, and C, and various minerals. Two main collections of charred plant remains were found in the lower village, in Area E (South). A hulled wheat collection (3433 grains) was retrieved from a circular silo (Locus 5023). The grains were stored after having been separated from their spikelets and manually sorted, activities that might very well have been carried out in Area C. Another collection derives from a mud-plastered pit (Locus 5050) containing mainly lentils (4085 seeds), known to have been an important component of human diet since ancient times because of their rich protein content. See below for radiocarbon dates from these collections.

Other categories of sparser finds include both macro- and microfaunal remains. Numerically, ovi-caprines were the predominant domestic livestock, providing meat and secondary products such as milk and wool. The actual meat contribution of cattle in terms of weight undoubtedly surpassed that of ovi-caprines, while pigs served as a supplementary source of meat. A notable feature in Area E South is an apparent cattle burial, perhaps part of a wider regional phenomenon. Hunting of local wild species, such as the Persian fallow deer and the mountain gazelle, served both dietary and perhaps also symbolic needs. The macrofaunal assemblage, indicates a mixed subsistence based on farming and herding at the site, which fits well with the present knowledge of EB I economy as reflected in other faunal collections from neighboring sites in the Jezreel Valley and adjacent areas in northern Israel.

The highly fragmented microvertebrate assemblage recovered from the site is of great interest since it is the only Early Bronze Age I assemblage in Israel to have been systematically collected, analyzed, and published. The number of specimens (seventeen) and taxa is exceedingly low, possibly resulting from postdepositional, environmental processes at the site. They include, in order of abundance, three species of rodents, field vole, jird, and mole-rat, as well as snakes and lizards.

Radiocarbon Dating of Seeds from Area E (South)

(Elisabetta Boaretto, Kimmel Center for Archaeological Science, Weizmann Institute of Science)

Four seeds from the seed caches from Area E (South) were sent for radiocarbon analysis. The radiocarbon results are summarized in table 24.2. Calibrated ages are relative to ±1 standard deviation (±1σ; a 68.2 percent probability that the true age is included in those limits) and ±2 standard deviation (±2σ; a 95.4 percent probability that the true age is included in those limits). Samples were prepared following Meirav Yizhaq et al. 2005 and measured at the D-REAMS Accelerator Laboratory of the Weizmann Institute (Rehovot, Israel).

Table 24.2. Radiocarbon dates of Tel Qashish seeds from Area E (South). Dates are calibrated with OxCal 4.4.2 ©Bron Ramsey 2020 using the calibration table in Reimer et al 2020.

Lab #	Field ID	Locus	Type	%C	C-14 age ±1σ year BP	Calibrated range ±1σ	Calibrated range ±2σ
RTD-7539	Qashish 2	5050	Seed *L. Culinaris*	72.8	4454+/-40	3327 (34.3%) 3230BCE 3182 (7.9%) 3156BCE 3110 (11.9%) 3075BCE 3066 (14.2%) 3026BCE	3340 (91.8%) 3010BCE 2981 (2.0%) 2961BCE 2951 (1.6%) 2935BCE
RTD-7540	Qashish 6	5050	Seed *L. Culinaris*	75.6	4435+/-43	3321 (24.7%) 3237BCE 3176 (3.8%) 3161BCE 3106 (36.5%) 3011BCE 2977 (1.9%) 2968BCE 2945 (1.4%) 2939BCE	3334 (30.1%) 3214BCE 3190 (8.0%) 3148BCE 3138 (57.3%) 2923BCE
RTD-7541	Qashish 4	5023	Seed *Triticum dicoccum*	65.0	4503+/-34	3339 (10.3%) 3314BCE 3296 (3.8%) 3286BCE 3240 (14.6%) 3206BCE 3198 (39.5%) 3104BCE	3358 (95.4%) 3093BCE
RTD-7542	Qashish 10	5023	Seed *Triticum dicoccum*	65.4	4499+/-33	3337 (10.6%) 3311BCE 3298 (5.3%) 3285BCE 3273 (1.7%) 3269BCE 3241 (13.2%) 3210BCE 3194 (37.5%) 3104BCE	3356 (94.5%) 3092BCE 3050 (1.0%) 3041BCE

C-14 ages are reported in conventional radiocarbon years BP (before present = 1950) in accordance with international conventions (Stuiver and Polach 1977). Thus, all the calculated 14C dates have been corrected for fractionation so the results will be equivalent with the standard δ 13C value of -25‰ (wood). Calibrated ages in calendar years were obtained following calibration tables in Reimer et al. 2013 by means of the OxCal v. 4.2 Bronk Ramsey Program (2010 version; Bronk-Ramsey 1995, 2001, 2010).

Summary

In light of their shared material culture, the present excavations have shown that the late EB I Stratum XV settlement at the tell of Qashish extended well beyond the mound's immediate, natural confines, both to the north and to the Kishon River on the west. The terms "upper village" and "lower village" were introduced to avoid confusion between the actual tell occupation and the one beyond its limits, the former representing the settlement on the actual mound and the second at its foot and slightly beyond this chalky outcrop and its accumulation of occupational deposits.

The structural remains of the lower village exposed in the extension of Tel Qashish's eastern slope (Area E North and South) are characterized by dwellings with rounded corners with stone-built foundations and mud-brick walls. While the custom of building houses with rounded corners is considered as the last echo of a curvilinear building tradition introduced during the formative stages of the EB I (Braun 1989, 2020; Golani 1999), early EB I remains are notably absent in both the upper and lower villages of Tel Qashish. However, remains of an early EB I settlement have recently been identified in salvage excavations at Tell el-Wa'er (ch. 4, this volume), a few hundred meters northwest of the present site (figs. 4.1, 10.1) along the west side of Road 70 (fig. 10.2), while some early EB I artifacts have been found in a nearby burial cave just slightly north of and opposite Tel Qashish (Salmon 2008, 16*, fig. 11).

Another notable feature revealed during excavations is the contrast between the continued occupation of the upper village in the EB II–III (Stratum XII and later), and the abandonment of the lower village's settlement and agricultural activity on the east (Areas E–F) and west (Areas C–D) slopes, which were never resettled. Thus, the subsequent, EB II settlement diminished in size, compared to the previous late EB I occupation, and was confined to within the fortification wall. This late EB I–EB II transition settlement-shrinking process is also observed at several other contemporary sites in the area such as Yoqneʻam, while during the same time other sites like Bet Yeraḥ, Yaqush, and Tel Reḥov grew, and others appear to have been abandoned (e.g., Megiddo).

References

Adams, Matthew J.
2013 "Area J, Part III: The Main Sector of Area J." In *Megiddo V: The 2004–2008 Seasons*, edited by Israel Finkelstein, David Ussishkin, and Eric Cline, 47–118. 3 vols. SMNIA 31. Tel Aviv: Institute of Archaeology.

Ben-Tor, Amnon, and Ruhama Bonfil
2003 "The Stratigraphy of the Early Bronze Age." In *Tel Qashish: A Village in the Jezreel Valley; Final Report of the Archaeological Excavations (1978–1987)*, edited by Amnon Ben-Tor, Ruhama Bonfil, and Sharon Zuckerman, 10–30. Qedem Reports 5. Jerusalem: Hebrew University of Jerusalem.

Ben-Tor, Amnon, Ruhama Bonfil, and Sharon Zuckerman
2003 *Tel Qashish: A Village in the Jezreel Valley; Final Report of the Archaeological Excavations (1978–1987)*. Qedem Reports 5. Jerusalem: Hebrew University of Jerusalem.

Braun, Eliot
1985 *En Shadud: Salvage Excavations at a Farming Community in the Jezreel Valley, Israel*. BARIS 249. Oxford: BAR.
1989 "The Problem of the Apsidal House: New Aspects of Early Bronze I Domestic Architecture in Israel, Jordan, and Lebanon." PEQ 121: 1–43.
1996 "Cultural Diversity and Change in the Early Bronze I of Israel and Jordan: Towards the Understanding of the Chronological Progression and Patterns of Regionalism in Early Bronze I Society." PhD diss., Tel Aviv University.
2004 *Early Beth Shan (Strata XIX–XIII): G. M. Fitz-Gerald's Deep Cut on the Tell*. University Museum Monograph 121. Philadelphia: University of Pennsylvania Museum of Archaeology and Anthropology.
2013 *Early Megiddo on the East Slope (the "Megiddo Stages"): A Report on the Early Occupation of the East Slope of Megiddo; Results of the Oriental Institute's Excavations, 1925–1933*. OIP 139. Chicago: Oriental Institute of the University of Chicago.
2020 "Reflections on South Levantine Early Bronze 1 Vernacular Architecture." https://www.academia.edu/42805562/Braun_EB_1_Vernacular_Architecture.

Bronk-Ramsey, Christopher
1995 "Radiocarbon Calibration and Analysis of Stratigraphy: The OxCal Program." *Radiocarbon* 37: 425–30. DOI: 10.1017/S0033822200030903.
2001 "Development of the Radiocarbon Calibration Program." *Radiocarbon* 43.2A: 355–63. DOI: 10.1017/S0033822200038212.
2010 "OxCal." https://c14.arch.ox.ac.uk/oxcal.html.

Eisenberg, Emanuel, and Yael Rotem
2016 "The Early Bronze Age IB Pottery Assemblage from Tel Kitan, Central Jordan Valley." *IEJ* 66: 1–33.

Engberg, Robert M., and Geoffrey M. Shipton
1934 *Notes on the Chalcolithic and Early Bronze Age Pottery of Megiddo*. SAOC 10. Chicago: University of Chicago Press.

Getzov, Nimrod
2004 "Notes on the Material Culture of Western Galilee in the Early Bronze Age IB in Light of the Abu edh-Dhahab Excavations." *ʻAtiqot* 48: 35–50.

Golani, Amir
1999 "New Perspectives on Domestic Architecture and the Initial Stages of Urbanization in Canaan." *Levant* 31: 123–33.
2003 *Salvage Excavations at the Early Bronze Age Site of Qiryat Ata*. IAA Reports 18. Jerusalem: Israel Antiquities Authority.

Gophna, Ram
1974 "The Settlement of the Coastal Plain of Eretz-Israel during the Early Bronze Age." PhD diss., Tel Aviv University. [Hebrew]

Greenberg, Raphael, and Emanuel Eisenberg
2006 "Area BS: The Bar-Adon Excavations, Southeast, 1951–1953." In *Bet Yerah: The Early Bronze Age Mound I; Excavations Reports, 1933–1986*, edited by Raphael Greenberg, Emanuel Eisenberg, Sarit Paz, and Yitzhak Paz, 117–234. IAA Reports 30. Jerusalem: Israel Antiquities Authority.

Joffe, Alexander H.
2000 "The Early Bronze Age Pottery from Area J." In *Megiddo III: The 1992–1996 Seasons*, edited by Israel Finkelstein, David Ussishkin, and Baruch Halpern, 161–85. 2 vols. SMNIA 18. Tel Aviv: Tel Aviv University.
2001 "The Early Bronze Age Seal Impressions from the Jezreel Valley and the Problem of Sealing in the Southern Levant." In *Studies in the Archaeology of Israel and Neighboring Land in Memory of Douglas L. Esse*, edited by Samuel Wolff, 355–75. SAOC 59. ASOR Books 5. Chicago: Oriental Institute of the University of Chicago; Boston: American Schools of Oriental Research.

Paz, Yitzhak
2006 "Area UN: The Ussishkin-Netzer Excavations, 1967." In *Bet Yerah: The Early Bronze Age Mound I; Excavations Reports, 1933–1986*, edited by Raphael Greenberg, Emanuel Eisenberg, Sarit Paz, and Yitzhak Paz, 277–338. IAA Reports 30. Jerusalem: Israel Antiquities Authority.

Portugali, Yuval
1982 "A Field Methodology for Regional Archaeology (the Jezreel Valley Survey, 1981)." *TA* 9: 170–88.

Reimer, P., W. Austin, E. Bard, A. Bayliss, P. Blackwell, C. Bronk Ramsey, M. Butzin, H. Cheng, R. Edwards, M. Friedrich, P. Grootes, T. Guilderson, I. Hajdas, T. Heaton, A. Hogg, K. Hughen, B. Kromer, S. Manning, R. Muscheler, J. Palmer, C. Pearson, J. van der Plicht, R. Reimer, D. Richards, E. Scott, J. Southon, C. Turney, L. Wacker, F. Adolphi, U. Büntgen, M. Capano, S. Fahrni, A. Fogtmann-Schulz, R. Friedrich, P. Köhler, S. Kudsk, F. Miyake, J. Olsen, F. Reinig, M. Sakamoto, A. Sookdeo, and S. Talamo
2020 "The IntCal20 Northern Hemisphere radiocarbon age calibration curve (0–55 cal kBP)." *Radiocarbon*, 62.

Salmon, Yossi
2008 "Qiryat Ḥaroshet: An Early Bronze Age Cemetery in the Vicinity of Tel Qashish." *Contract Archaeology Reports* 3: 5*–31*.

Stuiver, Minze, and Henry A. Polach
1977 "Discussion Reporting of C-14 Data." *Radiocarbon* 19: 355–63. DOI: 10.1017/S0033822200003672.

Sukenik, Eleazar L.
1948 "Archaeological Investigations at 'Affūla." *JPOS* 21: 1–71.

Tadmor, Miriam, and Moshe Prausnitz
1959 "Excavations at Rosh Hanniqra." *'Atiqot* 2 (English Series): 72–88.

Yannai, Ei, Dorit Lazar-Shorer, and Zohar Grosinger
2006 "The Pottery Assemblages." In *'En Esur ('Ein Asawir) I: Excavations at a Protohistoric Site in the Coastal Plain of Israel*, edited by Eli Yannai, 63–178. IAA Reports 31. Jerusalem: Israel Antiquities Authority.

Yizhaq, Meirav, Genia Mintz, Illit Cohen, Hamudi Khalaily, Steve Weiner, and Elisabetta Boaretto
2005 "Quality Controlled Radiocarbon Dating of Bones and Charcoal from the Early Pre-Pottery Neolithic B (PPNB) of Motza (Israel)." *Radiocarbon* 47: 193–206. DOI: 10.1017/S003382220001969X.

Zuckerman, Sharon
2003a "The Early Bronze Age I Architecture." In *Tel Qashish: A Village in the Jezreel Valley; Final Report of the Archaeological Excavations (1978–1987)*, edited by Amnon Ben-Tor, Ruhama Bonfil, and Sharon Zuckerman, 31–56. Qedem Reports 5. Jerusalem: Hebrew University of Jerusalem.
2003b "Tel Qashish in the Early Bronze Age I." In *Tel Qashish: A Village in the Jezreel Valley; Final Report of the Archaeological Excavations (1978–1987)*, edited by Amnon Ben-Tor, Ruhama Bonfil, and Sharon Zuckerman, 57–60. Qedem Reports 5. Jerusalem: Hebrew University of Jerusalem.

Part V

A Late Bronze Age II Cultic Repository
at Tel Qashish

Chapter 25

A Late Bronze Age II Cultic Repository near Tel Qashish in the Jezreel Valley, Israel

Orit Segal, Uzi 'Ad, and Edwin C. M. van den Brink (*Israel Antiquities Authority*)

Tel Qashish is a relatively small artificial mound built atop a natural bedrock outcrop located at the western limit of the Jezreel Valley (fig. 25.1; map ref. New Israel Grid 210349–732351/210675–732569)—a narrow passage between Mount Carmel to the west and the Shefar'am Hills to the east. It was surveyed in the 1950s by Raphael Giveon and in the 1970s by Avner Raban (1982), being probed already in the 1920s by John B. E. Garstang (1922). Amnon Ben-Tor of The Hebrew University of Jerusalem carried out extensive excavations along the northern slopes of the tell in the 1970s and the 1980s, when a sequence of fifteen strata covering various phases of the late Early Bronze Age I through the Persian period was recognized, including occupational layers ascribed to the Late Bronze Age IIB (Stratum V; Ben-Tor, Bonfil, and Zuckerman 2003a).

Yohanan Aharoni (1987, 15) identified the mound with the settlement of Helkath, which appears in the list of cities conquered by Thutmose III (fifteenth century BCE). Ben-Tor proposed identifying it with the settlement of Dabbesheth, mentioned in the tribe of Zebulun's territorial-boundaries description (Josh 19:10–11; Ben-Tor, Bonfil, and Zuckerman 2003b, 1).

In late spring and early summer 2010, the Israel Antiquities Authority surveyed and sounded, by mechanical means, the trajectory of a new pipeline for natural gas that approached the northern and western flanks of the tell. Subsequent salvage excavations in a grid system of seventy 5 × 5 m squares yielded mostly evidence of late Early Bronze Age I deposits (Areas A–D, van den Brink et al., ch. 11, this volume; Areas F and E South, Yannai, ch. 12 this volume; Area E North, van de Brink et al., ch. 13, this volume and van den Brink 2014; permits A-5992 and A-6149).[1]

The present report focuses on the surprise find of two repositories of Late Bronze Age II cult vessels excavated in tandem about 135 m north of the tell.[2]

Excavation of the Late Bronze II Repository

Nine squares (C 20–22, D 20–24, E24), opened about 135 m north of the northern edge of Tel Qa-

---

1. Salvage excavations were carried out along the north and west margins of Tel Qashish (NIG 210349-732351/210675-732569) from March 21 to May 31, 2010. Work was conducted on behalf of the Antiquities Authority by Edwin C. M. van den Brink and Uzi 'Ad (permit A-5881/2010), with the assistance of Mohammed Hater and Orit Segal (area supervisors), Limor Talmi and Karem Sa'id, and the participation of Eli Bachar and late Shlomo Ya'aqov-Jam (administrators), Rebekka Mishayev, Y. Nemichnitzer and Yakov Smidov (surveyors), Anjela Dagut (GPS), Assaf Peretz (field photography) and Sky View Photography Ltd. (aerial photography), Benyamin Agami (safety), Oren Ackermann and Naom Grinbaum (geologists), Alla Sheftelowicz (flints), Elisheva Kamaisky (pottery restoration in the field), Joseph Buchengolz (pottery restoration in the lab), P. Gendelman (identification of Roman pottery) and Danny Sion (metal detector). The excavations were financed by the Israel Natural Gas Lines Ltd.
2. See also van den Brink et al. 2012.

Fig. 25.1. Location map.

shish, were manually excavated down to the natural bedrock (figs. 25.2–3) in what was labeled Area B.[3] The area gently slopes in a southeast–northwest direction, from elevation 29.8 m ASL in the northwest to 28.7 m ASL in the southeast (fig. 25.2, section 1-1), that is, a 1.1 m difference in absolute height measured over a 20-m distance. The chalky white bedrock is covered by a 0.25–0.5-m thick layer of colluvial sediments.

Three features of archaeological interest—dating from two distinct periods—were noticed and excavated in this area:

1. A local spread of small, fist-size limestones just below the present plow zone, with numerous potsherds on and in between them, dating exclusively from the late Early Bronze Age I, in Squares C20–D20 and D21(fig. 25.2: Loci 200, 222, 224, 227, and 228). Below this stony approximately 25-cm-thick layer, more late EB I ceramics, directly resting on bedrock, were found. Architectural remains were absent (van den Brink 2014).

2. A narrow, about 3-m-deep natural bedrock cavity exposed in the soft Eocene chalk bedrock (fig. 25.2: Square D21, Loci 212, 218, 219, and 225; fig. 25.5). Its roof, with evidence of late EB I occupation atop, had caved in during antiquity, creating a depression. This depression filled up over time and was sealed by fine, colluvial sediments, thus concealing the cave that accommodated the main LB IIB repository.

3. A natural bedrock depression located outside of and about 4 m to the north of the repository cave, containing an additional cache of about twenty LB IIB ceramic vessels (fig. 25.2: Square C22, Loci 223 and 226, figs. 25.6–7) and considered as an overflow of the larger cache.

Some 225 m² were excavated around the two caches down to bedrock (fig. 25.3), but no evidence was found of further hidden deposits that would allude to similar events.

The Repository Cave

This natural cavity, artificially enlarged laterally—as indicated by the numerous chisel marks visible on large segments of its interior walls and its further deepened floor—was of irregular plan, about 3 m

---

3. During the excavation, four separate areas (A–D) were probed manually (van den Brink and 'Ad 2011).

25. A Late Bronze Age II Cultic Repository near Tel Qashish in the Jezreel Valley, Israel

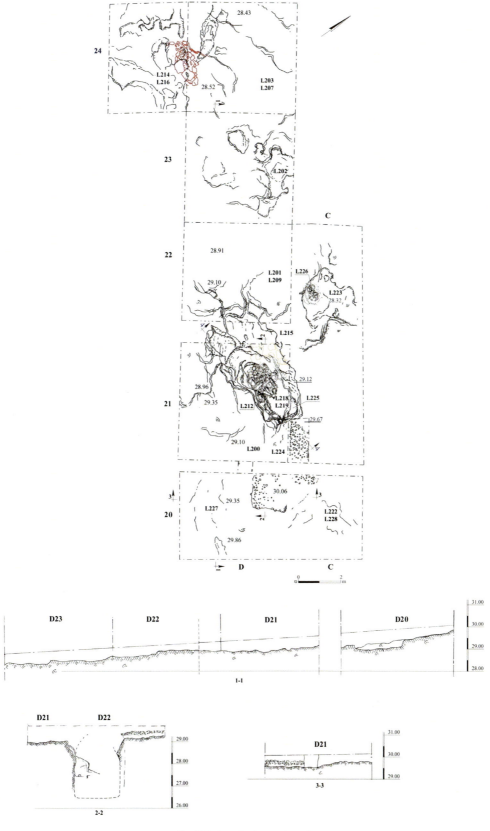

Fig. 25.2. Area B, plan and sections.

Fig. 25.3. Aerial view of Area B after completion of the excavation with repository cave visible at right-hand side of the photo.

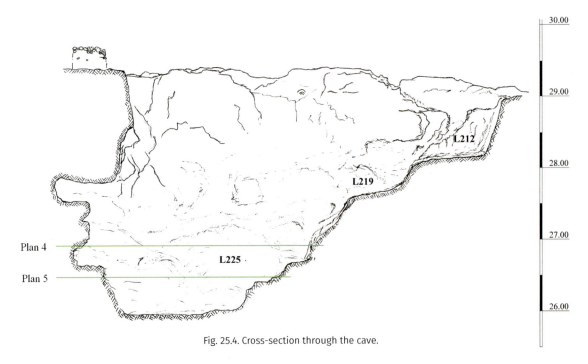

Fig. 25.4. Cross-section through the cave.

long and between 1.4–2.0 m wide, with a maximum height of 3 m (figs. 25.2–5). It was located about 0.5 m beneath the deeply plowed topsoil containing a random spread of small fieldstones mixed with pottery dating from the end of the EB I.

The excavation revealed three hewn steps (fig. 25.4, Loci 212 and 219; fig. 25.5) in the southwestern edge of the cave and leading into it. The cave accommodated a repository of approximately 236 complete ceramic vessels carefully deposited on its floor (fig. 25.2, L225), spilling over onto the hewn steps higher up in the cave (Loci 219 and 212; figs. 25.8–9), probably in an attempt to avoid stepping on and breaking the vessels that had already been deposited at the bottom of this small cave. The vessels were carefully set atop one another; bowls, for instance, were stacked inside each other up to half a meter in height.

The orderly placement of the vessels, some found still intact, and their internal arrangement into groups—for example, juglets of Cypriot provenance placed next to the southern edge of the cave, Myce-

Fig. 25.5. The repository cave toward the end of excavation, looking east.

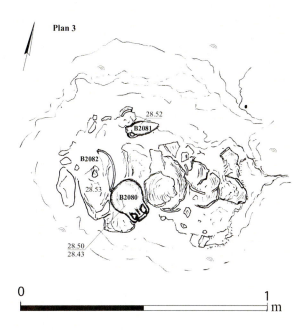

Fig. 25.6. The shallow bedrock pocket with additional pottery vessels (looking northwest).

naean vessels in its eastern corner, and a group of tall stands in the center of the cave near the second step—indicate they were deliberately deposited in a specific order. The absence of soil accumulations in between the packed clusters of vessels indicates this was done over a short period, perhaps even as a single event.

The Secondary Cache

Approximately 3.5 m northwest of this cave and its contents, a shallow, 0.9 × 0.5 m recess in the bedrock was exposed containing an additional, much smaller cache of about twenty similar pottery vessels (figs. 25.6–7, Square C23, L226), among them, bowls with a ring base, a flask, and dipper juglets. Based on several conjoining vessel fragments deriving from both localities, the smaller cache clearly relates to the larger one, having functioned perhaps as a repository for an overflow of vessels from the cave, or else, perhaps points to a ceremony that took place when the cave itself was being sealed.[4]

---

4. For signs of ceremonial activity during the sealing of the Yavneh *favissa* (Iron Age), see Panitz-Cohen 2010, 129.

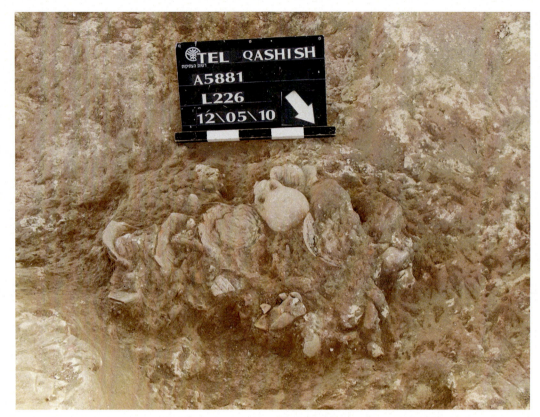

Fig. 25.7. Area B, Locus 226. Shallow bedrock pocket with additional ceramic vessels (looking northwest).

The Assemblage

Except for one small faience bowl, the assemblage contained only pottery vessels, more than 236 in total, some of these clearly cultic, while others, more quotidian, were used during worship and were therefore buried together with the cultic paraphernalia. Due to the collapse of the cave's roof, only a few vessels remained intact, while the majority was found complete but broken. The pottery was removed from its original find spot under the supervision of Elisheva Kamaiyski (IAA). Most of the vessels are from the southern Levant, while a few vessels are Mycenaean/Aegean and Cypriot imports. The absence of small finds such as metallic, stone, and bone items is conspicuous.

All the vessels were systematically recorded, mapped, and photographed in the field. Documentation also included recording the upper and lower elevations for each vessel (see antiplates to figs. 25.10–23, 25–44; figs. 25.10–47 can be found at the end of this chapter). Restoration of the pottery assemblage at the lab, skillfully handled by Joseph Buchengolz, was straightforward, and a large part

Fig. 25.8. Area B, the repository cave during excavation, looking southwest.

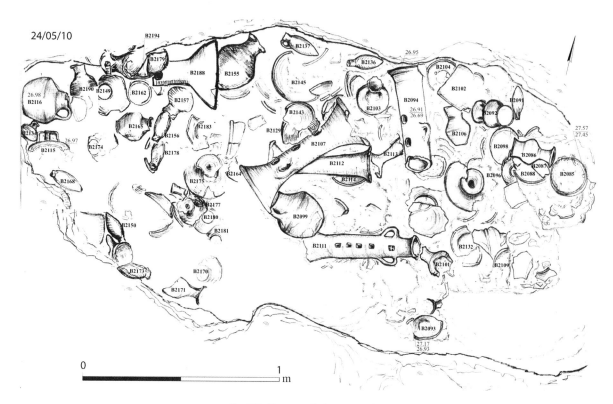

Fig. 25.9. The cave during excavation.

of the assemblage could be restored in a relatively short time. In the absence of sufficient funding, however, restoration of the whole assemblage was not feasible, and a selection had to be made. Broken vessels that belonged to repetitive types already present in the restored assemblage (e.g., lamps and bowls) were left, by necessity, unrestored.

All vessels, restored or otherwise, have been counted to establish the minimum number of items; the rims of nonrestored vessels were counted by calculating the relative size of the rim fragments in units of one-eighth of a full circumference.[5]

Finally, it was possible to compare the ceramic assemblage to nearby contemporary sites such as Tel Qashish Strata V and VI, Tel Yoqne'am Strata XIXa–b, and Tel Megiddo Strata VIIa–VIIb. Other nearby relevant sites included for such a comparison are Tel Abu Hawam Stratum V and Tel Mevorakh Stratum IX. Cultic assemblages of the period were similarly examined, such as the Stratum-Ib temple at Ḥaẓor the Fosse Temple at Lachish, and the Beth Shean temples in Israel, Transjordan (Deir 'Alla), and Syria (Tell Kazel).

The following presentation of the assemblages, deriving from both the repository cave and secondary cache, will be followed by a discussion and conclusions.

Typology

South Levantine Pottery

BOWLS (BL)

The assemblage comprises ninety-five bowls, making up 40 percent of all vessels recovered from the repository cave.[6] Most bowls (92.5 percent) are unrestricted, that is, open forms with either rounded or straight walls set on a disk base: sixty-eight out

---

5. Eight 1/8s representing an entire vessel, four 1/8s half a vessel, and so forth.

6. Of the ninety-five bowls, only thirty-seven were restored and drawn. Fifty-eight bowls remain unrestored and, therefore, have not been drawn.

of ninety bowls (75.50 percent) have disk bases and 17 percent have concave disk bases. Four percent of all bases are flat, two percent are shallow ring bases, and only one bowl has a molded ring base.

The bowls have been divided into eight main types according to their overall morphology, with further subdivisions based on differences in rim shape (e.g., simple, everted, internally thickened, tapered, and other):

1. Restricted hemispherical bowls (BL I; n=3).
2. Open straight-walled bowls (BL II; n=10).[7]
3. Open rounded bowls (BL III; n=26).
4. Large open bowls with oblique inward-folded rim (BL IV; n=8).
5. Closed carinated bowls (BL V; n=1)
6. Open carinated bowls (BL VI; n=10).
7. Shallow carinated bowls (BL VII; n=2).
8. Carinated bowls with a cyma–shaped profile (BL VIII; n=20).

Type BL I: Restricted, hemispherical bowls
Three subtypes, each represented by a single bowl, could be distinguished based on differences in rim shape:

1. BL Ia, with a simple rim (n=1).
2. BL Ib, with a tapered rim (n=1).
3. BL Ic, with a slightly internally thickened rim (n=1).

Type BL Ia. A rounded hemispherical bowl with simple rim (fig. 25.10.1)—the bowl's wall is rounded until the vessel's shape becomes hemispherical. The rim is simple and as thick as the vessel's wall. The bowl illustrated in figure 25.10.1, missing its base, is decorated with red short vertical lines around its orifice.

Hemispherical bowls are common in Beth Shean in all Area S strata (e.g., Stratum S-5), and make up as much as 24 percent of the bowls in Stratum N-3a (Panitz-Cohen 2009, 204–5, type 75). Parallels are also to be found in Megiddo Stratum VIIa (Loud 1948, pl. 65.9), while this bowl type becomes most common there in Strata VIb and VIa. They are known from LB II deposits in many other sites in the country, for example, in Lachish, Ashdod, Gezer, Bet El, Ḥaẓor (see Killebrew 1999a, 83, form CA 2). Bowls of this type continue into the twelfth to eleventh centuries BCE throughout the country (Panitz-Cohen 2009, 205).

Type BL Ib. A rounded bowl with a tapered rim (fig. 25.10.2)—this bowl, missing its base, has a thin wall and a tapered rim. No other rims of this type have been found. Bowls with tapered rims appear at Tel Qashish Strata VIII–VIIa (Bonfil 2003, 278, type B II) and in Tel Yin'am's Stratum-XIIA Building 2 from the mid-thirteenth century BCE (Liebowitz 2003, fig. 35.1).

Type BL Ic. A rounded bowl with a small inward-folded rim (fig. 25.10: 3)—only one bowl is attributed to this subtype. This small bowl (diam. 12 cm) has a tapered rim thickened on the inside. The bowl stands on a low ring base. Two similar bowls were found in Stratum VIIb of the tell in Qashish (Bonfil 2003, 279, type B VI c). Another example was found in Tel Miqne-Ekron (B5; Killebrew 1998, fig. III.III.2.9). Ann Killebrew ascribes a similar bowl to Form CA 8 (round hemispherical bowl), appearing at first at the end of the Late Bronze Age and continuing into the Iron Age I (Killebrew 1998, 89, Form CA 8).

Types BL II and BL III: Open Bowls

Open bowls are predominant in the assemblage, making up 39 percent of all open shapes (n=90). They are divided into two types, each with its own variants based on the various rim shapes:

1. Open straight-walled bowls (BL IIa–b, n=37)
2. Open rounded bowls (BL IIIa–c, n=53).

Type BL II: Open straight-walled bowls

Type BL IIa. Open straight-walled bowls with simple everted rims (fig. 25.10.4–12)—bowls with straight or slightly concave walls and simple rounded and usually everted rims. They stand either on a flat(?) or a concave disk base. In Tel Yoqne'am, similar vessels with a simple everted rim are the most common type among the straight-walled bowls appearing in ever-increasing numbers from Stratum XXI onward and becoming dominant toward the end of the LBA

---

[7]. Fifteen additional bowls can be defined as either type 2 or 3.

in Stratum XIXa (Ben-Ami and Livneh 2005, 253, type B CI a; Ben-Ami 2005, figs. III.8.8, III.18.24, III.24.7). Other parallels come from Tel Dan Strata VIIb and VIIa2 (Biran, Ben-Dov, and Arensburg 2002, fig. 2.29.16); Tel Qashish Stratum VIIa (LBI) and Stratum VI (LB IIA; Ben-Tor and Bonfil 2003, figs.107.10, 108.2); Aphek-Antipatris, Stratum X14, LBI/IIA (Gadot 2009, fig. 8.2.4); Hazor Area D, Stratum 2 (LB I) and LB II (Yadin et al. 1958, pls. XCV.12, CV.5–6, CXXXIII.5); Tell Abu Hawam Cemetery–LB II (Anati 1959, fig. 8.10).

Type BL IIb. An open straight-walled bowl with a folded rim (fig. 25.10.13)—the sole bowl representing this type has a straight wall thickening toward the disk base and a rim thickened on the inside. Bowls with folded rims are a common form in the terminal LB II strata at Tel Miqne-Ekron; however, they are absent in Iron Age I strata comprising Mycenaean IIIC:1b pottery (Killebrew 1999a, 82, form CA 1, figs. III.III.1.2, III.II.4.9). A parallel of this bowl was found in a Stratum-XIII open area west of Building 1 in Tel Yin'am (Liebowitz 2003, fig. 1.6).

Type BL III: Open rounded bowls

Type BL IIIa. Open rounded bowls with a simple rounded rim (fig. 25.11.1–2)—these bowls, measuring about 20 cm in diameter, have rounded walls and simple rims, both equally thick. Similar bowls appear on the mound of Tel Qashish in Strata VIII–V (Bonfil 2003, 277–78, type B Ia). Ruhama Bonfil (2003, 277–78) noted that the diameter of the bowls in these layers is 20 cm, whereas they measure 35 cm in diameter in Stratum VIII, beginning to shrink already in this stratum. This corroborates Olga Tufnell's conclusion that LBA bowls become smaller throughout the period. A similar conclusion was reached by Yuval Gadot (2009, 191, type BO1) for Tel Aphek.

Parallels: Tel Gezer (fourteenth to thirteenth centuries BCE, Panitz-Cohen and Maeir 2004, pl. 2.5); Tel Aphek Stratum X12 (LB IIb, Gadot 2009, figs. 8.2.1, 8.3.1) and fifty-three bowls of this type also found in the *favissa* ascribed to Stratum X14 (LB I/IIA, Gadot 2009, 190); Yoqne'am Stratum XXb (Ben-Ami 2005, fig. III.4.9); Tel Qashish Stratum VI (Ben-Tor and Bonfil 2003, fig. 112.2); Ḥazor Area C–Stratum 1b, Area D–Stratum 1 (Yadin et al. 1958, pl. LXXXV.6; 1960, pl. CXVII.7); Beth Shean, from the temple, level VII (Killebrew 1999a, figs. III. II.57.3, 61.7; III.III.1.6).

Type BL IIIb. Open rounded bowls with a simple everted rim (figs. 25.11.3–13, 25.12: 1–9)—most of these bowls stand on a flat disk base, but some have a concave disk base (figs. 25.11.5, 25.12.2) or a ring base (figs. 25.11.11, 25.12.7). This bowl type appears in Tel Qashish from Stratum IXa through Stratum VI (Bonfil 2003, 279, type B Va). At Tel Yoqne'am, most (over 95 percent) bowls of this type appear in the LBA strata, although they also occur already in MBA strata (Ben-Ami and Livneh 2005, 256, type B CIIm).

Parallels: Tel Qashish Strata VIIb, VIIa, IV/V (Ben-Tor and Bonfil 2003, figs. 100.5, 107.10, 108.5, 130.7); Tell Abu Hawam (Anati 1959, fig. 8:8; Balensi 1980, pl. 5.4, 6, 12); Tel Yoqne'am Strata XIXb, XIXa, XXa (Ben-Ami 2005, figs. III.8.8; III.14.14–16, 18; III.16.11–13; III.18.27); Ḥazorr Area C–Strata 1a, 1b; Area F–Stratum 1b (Yadin et al. 1958, pls. LXXXV.7; LXXXVII.2–3; LXXXIX.1; CV.24, 26; 1960, pls. CXVII.38; CXXVIII.16, 19); Tel Mevorakh Stratum X (Stern 1984, fig. 1.10); Megiddo Stratum F-7 (Ilan, Hallote, and Cline 2000, fig. 9.14.3); Tel Aphek Stratum X13–X12 (Gadot 2009, fig. 8.43.20); Tel Gezer LB IIA–B (Panitz-Cohen and Maeir 2004, pl. 2.11); Lachish (Tufnell, Inge, and Harding 1940, pl. XLIB.109).

Type BL IIIc. Open rounded bowls with an oblique rim (fig. 25.12.10–13)—bowls with tapered rims. The bowl illustrated in figure 25.12.13 has a disk base with a hole, made after the bowl ceased to function as such. In Yoqne'am, bowls of this type appear mainly in the MB IIC and toward the LB I (?), especially in Stratum XIX (Ben-Ami and Livneh 2005, 256).

Parallels: Yoqne'am Stratum XIXa (Ben-Ami 2005, fig. III.24.6); Ḥazor Area C–Stratum 1b (Yadin et al. 1958, pl. CV.29; 1960, pl. CXVII.28); Tell Abu Hawam, LB IIA–B (Anati 1959, fig. 8.5); Megiddo Stratum F-9 (Ilan, Hallote, and Cline 2000, fig. 9.10.18); Tel Yin'am–Building 1, Stratum XIIA, early to mid-thirteenth century BCE (Liebowitz 2003, fig. 30.1, 4).

Type BL IV: Large bowls with an oblique inward-folded rim

These bowls (n=8), with diagonal rims folded on the inside, curved walls, and either flat/concave disk bases or shallow ring bases, measure between 28 and 30 cm in diameter (fig. 25.13.1–6). The bowl illustrated in figure 25.13.5 is decorated on the inside with perpendicularly crossing red stripes and a red-painted rim. Red paint was also noted on the rim of bowls fig. 25.13.1, 6.

Similar large bowls appear in Tel Qashish in Strata VIIb, VIIa, and V (Bonfil 2003, 278, type IIIb1), and similar rims appear in Tel Yoqneʻam Stratum XIX on 71 percent of the bowls of this type, some being decorated (Ben-Ami and Livneh 2005, 256, type B CIIj). Killebrew (1998, 82) classifies bowls with inward-folded rims as form CA 1, most common in Tel Miqne at the end of the LB I, but absent in Iron Age I strata.

Parallels: Tel Miqne-Ekron: Stratum IX Phase 11D (Killebrew 1999a, fig. III.II.4.11, III.III.1.2); Tel Aphek Stratum X14 (LB I/IIA; Gadot 2009, fig. 8.2.8); Megiddo VIIb and Stratum F-9 (Ilan, Hallote, and Cline 2000, fig. 9.10.18); Yoqneʻam Strata XXb, XIXb, XIXa (Ben-Ami 2005, figs. III.4.16, III.16.7, III.18.15); Ḥaẓor Area C–Strata 2, 1b, Area F–Stratum 1b (Yadin et al. 1960, pls. CXVI.5, CXVII.37, CXXVIII.23–24); Gezer Tombs, dated to the LB IIb (Panitz-Cohen and Maeir 2004, 11–12, pl. 1.18, 20); Tel Qashish, from Stratum VIIb (LBI) to Stratum V/IV (LB IIB–Iron I; Ben-Tor and Bonfil 2003, figs. 100.7; 130.9), Giloh (Killebrew 1999a, fig. III.III.2.1); Dan, from Tomb 387, dated to the LB IIA (Biran, Ben-Dov, and Arensburg 2002, figs. 2.54.2, 11).

Types BL V–VIII: Carinated Bowls

Thirty-two carinated bowls (33 percent of the bowls assemblage) were found in the assemblage. These subdivide into twenty-five bowls with a cyma-shaped profile (26 percent of all bowls), and seven open or closed carinated bowls (7 percent of all the bowls). One of these seven bowls is a closed carinated vessel, while the other six are open carinated vessels with everted or vertical walls. Two bowls are carinated on the upper third of the wall.

Type BL V. A single closed carinated bowl

This single bowl (fig. 25.14.1), with a simple rounded rim and standing on a flat disk base, is carinated on the upper third of its wall, slanting inward above the carination. No slip or burnish signs are visible. Closed carinated bowls are unknown in the LBA; instead, they occur in earlier phases in a different form (e.g., Tel Qashish, types CB I–VI, Bonfil 2003, 280–81). Only very few parallels were found. The vessel is similar to the carinated bowls with a cyma-shaped profile, except for its noneverted rim and its profile rather resembling that of a goblet. One parallel was found in Megiddo Stratum F-9 (Ilan, Hallote, and Cline 2000, fig. 9.10.14). At Tel Dan, the upper part of a rim and shoulder of a similar vessel were ascribed to a goblet (Biran, Ben-Dov, and Arensburg 2002, fig. 2.30.7); however, since the aperture of the Tel Dan vessel is 23 cm, it should be classified as a bowl rather than a goblet.[8]

Type BL VI: Open carinated bowls

The open carinated bowls (n=10), with either a disk or a ring base, make up 9.5 percent of the bowls in the assemblage. The wall above the gentle carination is upright (and slightly flaring) or everted. They have no painted decoration and are not slipped or burnished. They are subdivided into two types, as follows:

Type BL VIa. Open, straight-wall carinated bowls (fig. 25.14.2–4)—these three bowls are gently carinated midway up their wall, which is upright above the carination. The bowl illustrated in fig. 25.14.3 has a wide disk base, while the bowl in fig. 25.14.2 has a ring base. In Yoqneʻam, these bowls occur mainly in Strata XXI–XIXa, becoming more prevalent in later strata (Ben-Ami and Livneh 2005, 252).

Parallels: Tel Aphek Stratum X14 (Gadot 2009, fig. 8.4.2); Ḥaẓor Area D–Stratum 1 (LB II), Area E–LB I, Area C–Stratum 1b (LB I–IIA), and Area A–Stratum 9a (LB I; Yadin et al. 1958, pls. XCVI.4–5, 7;

---

8. The upper opening of the Tel Qashish goblets ranges from 10 to 12 cm in diameter. The largest goblet (GO IV) has an opening measuring 18 cm in diameter.

CXXXVI.7; 1960, pl. CXVIII.8; Ben-Tor et al. 1997, fig. II.15.3).

Type BL VIb. Open, gently carinated bowls with flaring wall (fig. 25.14.5–11)—these bowls, with a simple rim, are mildly carinated midway up their wall or on the upper third of the vessel (fig. 25.14.10). The wall becomes everted above the carination. The rim and the wall are equally thick. These carinated bowls with a simple, everted rim are known throughout the country but are particularly common in the north (Killebrew 2005, 115 n. 24). They disappear at the end of the thirteenth century and are replaced by carinated bowls with a cyma-shaped profile (Killebrew 2005, 115, form CA 7). At Tel Qashish, bowls with a mild carination were found only in Strata VIIa–VI, and, based on the parallels, they can be dated to the LB I and early LB II (Bonfil 2003, 279, type OB IIb).

Parallels: In Yoqne'am, these bowls are common in all layers, from Stratum XXI (MB IIC) through Stratum XIXa (MB IIC–LB II; Ben-Ami and Livneh 2005, 252, type BII); Tel Miqne-Ekron Stratum IX (Phases 11B and 11C; Killebrew 1999a, fig. III.III.1.13). At Tel Yin'am, a parallel was found beneath the stone pavement of Stratum XIIB (late fourteenth century to early thirteenth century BCE) and in Stratum XIIA (mid-thirteenth century BCE; Liebowitz 2003, figs. 8.1, 20.1, 42.1); Tel Qashish (Ben-Tor and Bonfil 2003, figs. 104.5, 112.6; Bonfil 2003, fig. 130.1); Hazor Area C–Stratum 1b, Area D–LB II (Yadin et al. 1958, pls. XC.3, XCV.3, CV.9, CVI.6; 1960, pl. CXVIII.6, 11); Tel Dan from Tomb 387, dated to the LB IIA (Biran, Ben-Dov, and Arensburg 2002, figs. 2.19.17, 2.54.5); Tell Kazel, from the courtyard, level 6 (Badre and Gubel 1999–2000, fig. 22r); Megiddo Stratum VIIb (Loud 1948, pl. 65.15); Beth Shean Stratum VII and VI (Panitz-Cohen 2009, pl. 15.2, 23).

Type BL VII: Carinated, shallow bowls

These shallow bowls (n=2) are carinated right below the everted rim. They stand on a ring base (fig. 25.14.12) or a concave disk base (fig. 25.14.13). The bowl illustrated in figure 25.14.13 is decorated with red-painted strokes on top of the rim and a wavy line below it restricted to the upper third of the vessel. These bowls are known from the end of the Late Bronze Age II and especially from the Iron Age I (Killebrew 1998, 85, form CA 5). A parallel from Tel Yin'am comes from a post-Stratum XIIA deposit (end of the thirteenth century BCE; Liebowitz 2003, fig. 21.6).

Type BL VIII: Carinated bowls with a cyma-shaped profile

Approximately 26 percent of the bowls (n=20) in the assemblage belong to this type (fig. 25.15.1–13). They have a mild, S-shaped carination occurring immediately below the rim. A red and (or) black-painted decoration sometimes appears on the rim or below it. Bowls with a cyma-shaped profile developed from the vestigial carinated bowls of the Middle Bronze Age (Killebrew 1998, 87, form CA 7). They first appeared at the end of the thirteenth century and became common during the Iron Age I (Killebrew 1998, 87).

Parallels: Yoqne'am Strata XXa, XIXa (Ben-Ami 2005, figs. III.8.2; III.18.27, 34–35; III.24.10); Tel Qashish Stratum V/IV (Ben-Tor and Bonfil 2003, fig. 130.10); Ḥazor Area C–Stratum 1a, 1b, Area H–Stratum 1b (Yadin et al. 1958, pls. LXXXV.14, 16; LXXXVII.7; XC.2; 1961, pl. CCLXXII.27); Megiddo Stratum F-7 (Ilan, Hallote, and Cline 2000, fig. 9.14.4); Tel Yin'am Stratum XII (Liebowitz 2003, fig. 11.4).

CHALICES (CH)

The assemblage includes thirteen chalices, making up 6 percent of the total number of vessels. These are open bowls placed atop a high trumpet base. They are divided into three main types, CH I–III, further divided into five subtypes based on rim differences.

Type CH Ia–b

This type (n=6; fig. 25.16) consists of a wide, open bowl (diameter 20 cm) set on a high and smooth trumpet base. Both parts have either simple rounded or oblique carinated rims.

Type CH Ia. Chalices with a simple, rounded rim (fig. 25.16.1)—these undecorated chalices have a smooth trumpet base, on which an open bowl with a simple rounded rim was set.

Parallels: Ḥaẓor Area F–Tomb 8144-8145, dating from the LB II (Yadin et al. 1960, pl. CXXIX.19); Tell Deir ʿAlla, LB II Sanctuary (Franken 1992, fig. 5-3.10); Tell Abu-Hawam Phase Va (Balensi 1980, pl. 8.5).

Type CH Ib. Chalices with a flaring rim (fig. 25.16.2–4)—these chalices are similar to the previous type except for their everted rim, which is sometimes carinated along its lower edge. In Yoqneʿam, this type occurs in the late phase of the LBA (Strata XIXa–b; Ben-Ami and Livneh 2005, 264, type CH 1; Ben-Ami 2005, fig. III.18.39). Chalices with everted rims are known from Tell Abu Hawam Stratum V (with a ridge on the base of the bowl, Balensi 1980, pl. 8.7). A comparable chalice with a longer carinated rim was found in the temple assemblage of the LB IIB in Area G at Tel Nami (Yoselevich 2004, 33, type CH21, pl. 1.10); Megiddo Stratum VIb (Loud 1948, pl. 74.17).

Type CH IIa–c

Chalices belonging to this type (n=6; fig. 25.17.1–5) have a deeper bowl set on a tall trumpet pedestal. The bowls, ranging between 13 and 15 cm in diameter, are not as wide as those of type CH I. The rims are triangular, inverted, or hammer-shaped.

Type CH IIa. Chalices with a triangular rim (fig. 25.17.1)—these chalices have a round bowl with a thickened rim, triangular in cross-section and pointing outward. They have a red-painted wavy line along the edge of the rim and a trumpet base. The connection between bowl and base is thickened.

Parallels: Tel Mevorakh Stratum X (Stern 1984, fig. 1.23); Tell Abu Hawam Stratum V (Yoselevich 2004, pl. 2.4). This type is dated from the end of the LB II until the Iron Age I and onward (Yoselevich 2004, 42).

Type CH IIb. Chalices with a hammer-shaped rim (fig. 25.17.2–3)—two chalices belong to this type. They have hammer-shaped, everted rims, triangular in cross-section. The outer part of the chalice's rim in figure 25.17.2 is concave and decorated with a red-painted wavy line, while the chalice's rim in figure 25.17.3 is rounded on the outside, thicker, and undecorated. In Yoqneʿam, these chalices belong to the excavators' type II, and they constitute a chronological peg, since, except for one example from Stratum XIXb, all ascribe to Stratum XIXa which dates from the LB IIB (Ben-Ami and Livneh 2005, 264, type CH II).

Parallels: The LB II temple assemblage in Area G at Tel Nami (Yoselevich 2004, 33, type CH20c, pls. 1.6, 2.1); Megiddo Stratum VII and various LB II tombs (Loud 1948, pl. 72.12; Grutz 2007, fig. 7.3.1.2; Guy and Engberg 1938, pl. 60.30); Yoqneʿam (Ben-Ami 2005, fig. III.14.20); Tell Deir ʿAlla, the LB II sanctuary (Franken 1992, fig. 5.13.8).

Type CH IIc. Chalices with an incurved, plain rim (fig. 25.17.4–5)—two chalices belong to this type. The inclination left a ridge on the lower edge of the rim that protrudes from the side of the bowl.

Parallels: The LB II temple assemblage in Area G at Tel Nami (Yoselevich 2004, pl. 1.4); Tel Yinʿam, Building 1, Stratum XIIA (mid-thirteenth century BCE, Liebowitz 2003, fig. 27.3).

Depending on the type, connecting the bowls to the chalice's bases was done in various ways:

In type CH I, the chalice's pedestal was attached to the outside of the bowl while the clay was leather hard. In type CH II, characterized by a taller pedestal, the connection between the base and the bowl is thicker and more solid. Another technique can be seen in the chalice in figure 25.17.3, type CH IIb, where a protuberance, on the base of the bowl, was inserted into the pedestal.

Type CH III

Only one chalice belonging to this type (n=1; fig. 25.17.6), with an incurved, pinched rim, was found in the assemblage, representing a kind of hybrid between the tall cultic stands and the chalices, the two types mentioned above. Because of the typological similarity between them, it was included among the chalices. This vessel has a very high base reminiscent of a cultic stand. The chalice stands to a height of 57 cm, with no fenestrations fashioned in the tall pedestal, unlike those seen in cultic stands or incense burners (see below). The bowl has a triangular rim, like the type CH II chalices, but it is shallower and measures 20 cm in diameter, like the type CH I chalices. The rim, curving sharply inward and pinched outward, can be considered a development of the type CH IIc rims, whereby the rim is now more pinched and extends beyond the edge of the bowl, with the ridge being not as delicate as the one seen in type CH IIb.

No similarly sized chalices were found in other sites. In Tell Abu Hawam, the upper part of a chalice (a bowl and rim fragment) was found in a locus close to the surface containing mixed materials. The author mentions the possibility such chalices might have originated in the northern coast of Israel and southern Lebanon and that it has a post-LB II date (Yoselevich 2004, 43, type CH 2, n. 5, pl. 2.7). Finding a similar, albeit smaller chalice in an LB II repository near Tel Qashish suggests that the chalice from Tell Abu Hawam should also be dated to no later than LB II. Similar rims from Pella, dating from the Late Bronze, have been published, as well as a similar type from the Iron Age I strata (Grutz 2007, 35–36, fig. 8.1.1.8).

GOBLETS (GO)

The assemblage contains forty-one goblets, making up 18 percent of the pottery assemblage. All the goblets have tall trumpet bases and cups which are as high as their bases or slightly higher. They have been divided into eight subtypes based on differences in carination and (or) the slanting of the vessels' wall. Most goblets are undecorated. Decorations characterize types GO IV and V and have also been noted on two type III goblets,[9] two type VI goblets, one type VII goblet, and on the human-faced goblet. Thus, nine of the goblets in the assemblage are decorated, making up 22 percent of all the vessels of this type.

Type GO I: Goblet with a vertical, slightly concave wall (fig. 25.18.1)

Only one vessel belonging to this type was found in the assemblage. The vessel has a simple, slightly tapered rim. Its aperture is 14 cm in diameter, similar to that of its bottom part, above the connection to the base. On the upper part of the base is a prominent ridge not present on other goblets in the assemblage. No parallels of this type were found.

Type GO II: Goblet with a rounded wall (fig. 25.18.2)

This type is also represented by only one specimen. It has a simple, rounded rim and a vertical wall that curves on its lower third, where it connects to the base.

Parallels: A goblet with decoration remains on its rim and wall was found at Deir 'Alla and dates to the end of LB I (Franken 1992, fig. 3-7.10).

Type GO III: Goblet with a partly inverted wall (fig. 25.18.3–4)

Only two goblets could be ascribed to this type. Eleven additional goblets with straight or slightly inverted walls were not restored, and their fragments were only counted. It was not possible to deduce from these if the bottom third of the wall, in the medial base connection, was originally curved or carinated. Goblets with an inverted or a straight wall make up 37 percent of all goblets in the assemblage. Like type GO II, the wall curves where it connects to the base. The partially preserved goblet illustrated in figure 25.18.4 shows a wavy horizontal red-painted decoration along the central part of its wall, and almost vertically arranged red-painted stripes on its base.

Parallels: Megiddo Stratum VII (Loud 1948, pl. 72.10); Deir 'Alla, end of the LB II and beginning of the Iron Age I (Franken 1992, figs. 4-14.14, 4-15.17–18, 4-20.6).

Type GO IV: Decorated goblets with an inverted wall (fig. 25.18.5–6)

Two goblets belong to this type. They have inverted walls with a mild carination at their lower third. Above this carination, the wall is decorated with two bichrome panels separated by an applied ridge affixed to the middle of the wall. The decoration on the goblet in figure 25.18.5 is made of triangles, with black triangles delineated by a red horizontal line in the bottom panel, and inverted, red triangles delineated by a black line in the upper one. The upper panel on the goblet in figure 25.18.6 is adorned with a wavy, red decoration, while the bottom panel is divided into metopes adorned with a black geometric pattern of Xs set within a black frame and separated by a vertical black line.

---

9. One goblet, missing the rim, was therefore not restored.

Type GO V: A decorated goblet with a tall, cylindrical neck (fig. 25.19.1)

This singular vessel has a cylindrical neck with a simple, slightly everted rim. An accentuated carination is seen in the lower part of the vessel's wall. The wall, including the area of the carination, was decorated with a monochrome lattice of diagonally crossing red stripes.

Parallels: A similarly shaped goblet was found at Tel Mevorakh, Stratum XI (LB I), with a bichrome decoration of horizontal strips divided into metopes (Stern 1984, fig. 7.2). A similarly shaped goblet from Tel Lachish has a larger diameter and is ascribed to the Fosse Temple I (Tufnell, Inge, and Harding 1940, pl. XLVII.220). Another goblet was found at Tel Ḥazor, Area C, Stratum Ib (Yadin et al. 1958, pl. XC.5–6).

Type GO VI: Carinated goblets with an S-shaped profile (figs. 25.19.2–6; 25.20.1–6; 25.21.1–3)

These are the most common goblets in the assemblage and include twenty-three complete vessels, making up 56 percent of the goblet assemblage.[10] They have inverted walls, with simple rims bending outward and a rounded carination on the lower part of the wall. The carination can be mild, as illustrated in fig. 25.19.2–4, or accentuated and protruding to the extent of forming a ridge, as illustrated in fig. 25.20.1–6.

Parallels: Ḥazor Stratum 1b and Area H–Stratum 1b (Yadin et al. 1958, pls. LXXXV.10, CXXVIII.4; 1961, pls. CCLXXIII.19, CCLXXX.6); Deir ʿAlla, from the end of the LB II to the Early Iron Age I (Franken 1992, figs. 3-7.9, 4-14.12, 4-15.20); Tell Kazel Stratum 6 (Badre and Gubel 1999–2000, figs. 16.a, c; 17.b); Tel Lachish–the Fosse Temple II (Tufnell, Inge, and Harding 1940, pl. XLVII.227).

Type GO VII: Goblets with an inverted and grooved wall (fig. 25.21.4–5)

Two goblets in the assemblage are ascribed to this type. The goblet in figure 25.21.4, made of reddish clay, is adorned with a red wavy decoration on the upper part of the wall and its rim. The goblet in figure 25.21.5 is the only one in the assemblage made of buff-colored clay. The well-levigated and light-colored clay is reminiscent of the eggshell-type bowls and goblets, but the goblet from Tel Qashish has a thicker wall. Parallels to type GO VII goblets were found at Deir ʿAlla, where they appear from the end of the LB II onward (Franken 1992, fig. 4-14.12).

Type GO VIII: Human-faced goblet (fig. 25.22)

The human-faced goblet is a unique artifact among the repository vessels, differing from all the other goblets in the presence of a modeled face on its front and its overall morphology.[11] It is 30 cm high, taller than any of the other goblets in the assemblage (15–20 cm high). Also, the upper part of the vessel's curved wall is inverted, unlike the mild carination or straight wall seen in the upper part of the other goblets. In addition, the vessel's preservation context differentiates it from the rest of the goblets, and, in fact, from all the other vessels in the assemblage, since while most goblets were discovered intact or complete and sometimes only two parts needed to be adjoined, the human-faced goblet was found broken (perhaps intentionally) into five pieces.

The modeled face was retrieved in excavation unit Basket 2200 (elevation 26.56 m ASL; figs. 25.23–24) while the rest of the cup was restored from five separate baskets (2070, 2100, 2153, 2190, 2200). The uppermost basket was at an elevation of 27.25 m ASL and the lowermost basket at 26.38 m ASL (table 25.1). Thus, the vessel was restored from fragments that were recovered from the upper part of the cave, as well as from the floor of the cave. Since the goblet is complete, we may assume that the vessel was brought there intact for the interment ceremony, when it was perhaps intentionally broken into several pieces. The head was first discarded and placed on the floor of the cave, while the other four pieces of the goblet were buried at subsequent levels.

---

10. Nine goblets counted by their preserved rims were not restored.

11. For a detailed discussion of this vessel see Ziffer et al. 2018.

KRATERS (K)

Six kraters were found, making up 3 percent of the ceramic assemblage, which can be divided into two main types:

1. Type K I, with a rounded body.
2. Type K II, carinated.

Type K Ia: Open rounded krater

These kraters (fig. 25.25.1–2), with a curved wall, an outwardly folded rim, and a broad disk base, have two loop handles that extend from the rim to midway up the wall. The kraters are wide, with orifices ranging between 34 cm (fig. 25.25.2) and 40 cm (fig. 25.25.1) in diameter. Similar kraters were found at Tell Abu Hawam (Stratum V; Artzy 2007, fig. 9), where, although the petrographic analysis has still not been completed, they are ascribed to the Late Bronze Cypriote plain white wheel-made ware (Artzy 2007, 364).

Type K Ib: Incurved rounded or carinated krater with a thickened rounded rim

This type (fig. 25.26.1–2), with an incurved wall and a thickened, rounded and everted rim, has a body varying in form from rounded to carinated without a neck. Two similar types were reported in the Megiddo publications: in the first type, the rim is more vertical and thickened and is characteristic of Strata VIII–VIa; in the other, the thickened rim is more inverted but less accentuated and is characteristic of Strata VIIa–VI (Ilan, Hallote, and Cline 2000, 211).

Parallels of the second: Deir el-Balaḥ, thirteenth century to the early twelfth century BCE (Killbrew 2010, fig. 4.1.4);[12] Beth Shean Stratum VII (James and McGovern 1993, fig. 43.4); Megiddo Stratum VIII(?) and VIIa (Ilan, Hallote, and Cline 2000, fig. 9.11.1, 7; Loud 1948, pl. 69.11); Tel Qasile Strata XI and X (Mazar 1985, figs. 27.10, 44.29, 45.21). In Amihai Mazar's (1985, 47) opinion, the multitude of par-

allels from northern sites, among them Megiddo and Taʻanach, is indicative of the vessel's northern origin.

Type K II: Carinated krater with a simple vertical rim

A complete krater and a diagnostic body fragment of another krater belong to this type (fig. 25.26.3–4). Kraters of this type have a delicate ridge at the base of the neck, a carination in the middle of the wall, two loop handles, and a low ring base. These kraters were found in two assemblages at Tel Qashish proper, the first ascribed to Stratum VIIb and the second to Stratum VI (Ben-Tor and Bonfil 2003, fig. 108.8). It seems that these vessels were used from the LB I until the beginning of the LB II (Bonfil 2003, 281, type K 1). Other parallels come from Hazor Area D–LB II, Area C–Stratum 1b, Area H–Stratum 1a, Area A–stratum 8 (1b) (Yadin et al. 1958, pl. XCIX.5; 1960, pl. CXIX.4; 1961: pl. CCLXXX.10; BenTor et al. 1997, fig. II.18.27); Tell Kazel, from the courtyard, level 6 (Badre and Gubel 1999–2000, fig. 17a); Tell Dan, from Tomb 387, dated to the LB IIA (Biran, Ben-Dov, and Arensburg 2002, fig. 2.54.14).

COOKING POTS (CP)

There are five cooking pots in the assemblage, making up 2 percent of all the recovered vessels. These are open and carinated shapes, with a round base and without handles. They have been divided into two main types, CPI and CPIIa–b, based on differences in the shape of the rim (gutter, flared, or short triangular), and the extent of the wall's inclination. Despite the low number of cooking pots in the assemblage, it should be noted that most of them (60 percent) have a short triangular rim (type CPIIb), while only one pot has a flared rim (type CPIIa), and another one has a gutter rim (type CPI).

Type CPI: Cooking pot with gutter rim

Only one cooking pot (fig. 25.27.1) of this type was found in the assemblage, with a guttered rim and an upright rim concave on the inside.

Parallels: This type appears in Tel Qashish Strata VIIb–IXa. The gutter rim is characteristic of Strata IXa–VIII, where the rims are more accentuated compared to those of Stratum VIIb (Bonfil 2003, 285, type CP I, fig. 119.1–2). In Yoqneʻam, this type

---
12. There it occurs with a pair of handles; however, in the Late Bronze Age this type is more common without handles (Killebrew 2010, 80).

appears in small numbers in Strata XXIII–XIX, making it impossible to draw any definite chronological conclusions (Ben-Ami and Livneh 2005, 279, type CP CIIc; Ben-Ami 2005, fig. IV.10.3). At Dan, Tomb 387, these are dated to the LB IIA (Biran, Ben-Dov, and Arensburg 2002, fig. 2.55.17).

Type CP IIa: Cooking pot with flaring triangular rim

One cooking pot of this type, with a flaring triangular rim with an extending down edge, was found in the assemblage (fig. 25.27.2). This type, common throughout Canaan (for additional parallels, see Killebrew 1999b, form CA 18a, 85), is characteristic of the LB II, occurring in many rim shapes and carination variants. These are the most predominant vessel type at Tel Miqne, where a good parallel dates from the LB II (Killebrew 1999b, 84–85, fig. 1.1).

Type CP IIb: Cooking pots with short triangular rim

In vessels of this type, the edges of the triangular rims slightly detach from the vessels (fig. 25.27.3–6), a feature that characterizes cooking pots dating from the end of the LB II (Ben-Ami and Livneh 2005, 279, type CP CIIa2). At Tel Qashish proper, this type is known from Strata VI–V/IV, but it is already present in Strata VIII and VIIb assemblages (Bonfil 2003, 286, type CP IIIe; Ben-Tor and Bonfil 2003, figs. 112.18, 128.1, 130.15). In Yoqneʻam, these cooking pots first appear in Stratum XXb; their numbers increase in Strata XXa–XIXb, becoming the most dominant type in Stratum XIXa (Ben-Ami and Livneh 2005, 279; Ben-Ami 2005, figs. III.8.18, III.14.28, III.16.20, III.19.15–16, III.23.14, III.24.14).

Additional parallels: Tell Kazel Stratum 6 (LB II, Badre and Gubel 1999–2000, fig. 17g); Ḥazor Area F–Stratum 1, Area E–LB I, Area H–Stratum 2 (Yadin et al. 1958, pl. CXXXIX.18; 1960, pl. CXLII.1; 1961, pl. CCLXV.5); Tel Yinʻam Building 2, Stratum XIIA (mid-thirteenth century BCE, Liebowitz 2003, fig. 31.7).

STORAGE JARS (SJ)

The assemblage includes a single storage jar, making up 0.4 percent of all the ceramic vessels. The jar, type SJ I, was found standing near the eastern side of the cave.

Type SJ I: Small Jar

This is a small, ovoid jar, with a tall, cylindrical neck, a thickened and rounded rim, rounded shoulders, a stump base, and two handles attached to the middle of the wall (fig. 25.28.1). No traces of decoration were found on the jar or its handles. Nevertheless, because of its diminutive size (just 35 cm high), it can be ascribed to the group of small decorated jars (Amiran 1963, 174).

Parallels: Small decorated jars were found at Tel Qashish proper, in Strata VIIb–VI (Ben-Tor and Bonfil 2003, 253, fig. 112.20). Another, similar jar, with a slightly everted rim, was found in Stratum VI. A small jar with a concave rim was found in one of the tombs in Tell Abu Hawam (fourteenth century BCE, Anati 1959, fig. 7.5). Small jars are also known from the Fosse Temples I and II at Lachish (Tufnell, Inge, and Harding 1940, pl. LVII.390–391).

JUGS (J)

Ten jugs, making up 4.2 percent of all the vessels, are present in the ceramic repertoire: Eight of these have with a trefoil rim, one has a triangular rim and the last one shows a rounded rim.[13]

Type J Ia: Jug with a trefoil rim and a rounded base

Four jugs (fig. 25.29.1–4) belong to this predominant jug type: the jug in Fig. 25.29.2 has a rounded body; the two in Fig. 25.29.3–4 have an elongated body; the jug in Fig. 25.29.1 has an elongated body with a mild carination in its middle, below the shoulder of the vessel. Jugs with a pinched rim, wide neck, and a rounded base, already known in the Middle Bronze Age II, continue into the Late Bronze Age.

Parallels: Tel Mevorakh Stratum XI (LB I, Stern 1984, fig. 8.5); Yoqneʻam Stratum XIXb (Ben-Ami 2005, fig. III.15.12); Beth Shean Stratum N-4 (LB IIB, Panitz-Cohen 2009, pl. 2.6); Tel Kazel Stratum 5 (1300 BCE–end of LB II, Badre and Gubel 1999–2000, fig. 38.g); Tel Ḥazor Area C–Stratum 1b, Area D (LB II), Area F–Stratum 1b (Yadin et al. 1958, pls. XC.10, CVIII.5–6; 1960, pls. CXXXII.7, 10).

---

13. Three jugs were not restored or drawn.

Type J Ib: Jug with a trefoil rim and a ring base

A single, complete jug is ascribed to this type (fig. 25.30.1). It is identical to type J Ia, except for the ring base.

Parallels: Tell Kazel Strata 3 and 4 (Iron Age I), with a stripe-painted decoration (Badre and Gubel 1999–2000, figs. 43.f, 46.d); Megiddo Stratum VIII (Loud 1948, pl. 59.1); Tel Yin'am Stratum XII (Liebowitz 2003, fig. 12.2).

Type J II: Jug with a round rim and a ring base

Only one jug in the assemblage belongs to this type (fig. 25.30.2). It has a spherical body, a cylindrical neck with an everted triangular rim, and a ring base. A handle, incised on the outside, prefiring, extends from rim to shoulder. The incised decoration includes three parallel grooves that run from the upper part of the handle to its joining to the shoulder. The spherical shape of the jug and the incised decoration on its handle are characteristic of bronze jugs, which are round and with handles adorned with an incised lotus pattern, a motif known from New Kingdom Egypt. A bronze jug was published from Tomb 118 at Deir el-Balaḥ, and other bronze jugs from Tomb 33 were mentioned, all dating from the Ninteenth to Twentieth Dynasties (Dothan 1979, 66–68, ills.148–149, 152)

Parallels: Tell Qashish Stratum VIIa (LBI; Ben-Tor and Bonfil 2003, fig. 105.5).

Type J III: Jug with a shoulder handle

This jug type (fig. 25.30.3), with a shoulder handle and a ring base, resembles Middle Bronze II and Late Bronze I jugs. Ruth Amiran (1963, 178) suggested this type of jugs disappears in the LB III when the jug with a loop handle extending from rim to shoulder becomes predominant.

JUGLETS (JT)

The pottery assemblage includes ten locally produced juglets, making up 4.2 percent of all the repository vessels. These are all dipper juglets with a low neck and a pinched, everted rim. They have been divided into three subtypes according to the shapes of their bases: rounded, pointed, or stump.

Type JT Ia: Dipper juglets with a rounded base

Three juglets of this type were retrieved from the repository (fig. 25.31.1–3). The handle on the juglet in figure 25.31.1 is missing. The juglet in figure 25.31.2 has a pronounced shoulder, and the highest part of its handle is leveled with the rim. In juglet figure 25.31.3, however, the handle raises slightly above the rim.

Parallels: Ḥazor Area F–Stratum 1b, Area C–Stratum 1b, Area D–Stratum 1, Area E (LB II), Area H–Strata 1a–1b (Yadin et al. 1958, pls. XCVI.17, CXXXIV.2; 1960, pls. CXX.9; CXXXI.4, 15; 1961, pl. CCLXXXI.9).

Type JT Ib: Dipper juglets with a pointed base

Two juglets found in the repository have a pointed base (fig. 25.31.4–5). These elongated juglets, with a simple pinched rim, have either a handle leveled with the rim or slightly above it. Parallels: Many parallels of these juglets have been found, for example, in a tomb at Tell Abu Hawam (fourteenth century BCE, Anati 1959, fig. 7.8); in Tel Aphek Strata X13–X12 (Gadot 2009, fig. 8.8.1); in Ḥazor Area C–Stratum 1b, and Area H–Stratum 1a (Yadin et al. 1958, pls. CVIII.10, CXXXIV.3; 1960, pl. CXX.4, 6; 1961, pl. CCLXXXI.5); and at Deir el-Balaḥ, dated from the thirteenth century to the beginning of the twelfth century (Killebrew 2010, fig. 4.4.2, 8), and in Tomb 118, where the juglets are dated to the end of the Late Bronze Age and the Early Iron Age I (Dothan 1979: 124, tomb 118).

Type JT Ic: Dipper juglets with a stump base

Four of the juglets have a thickened stump base (fig. 25.31.6–9), which is sometimes button-like (fig. 25.31.9). The juglet in figure 25.31.7 has a more prominent shoulder. The juglet in figure 25.31.9, with a simple and everted rim, has a more cylindrical and accentuated neck.

Parallels: At Deir el-Balaḥ, where similar dipper juglets were found in coffins dating from the thirteenth century BCE (Dothan 1979, II.23, 26); Tel Aphek Stratum X11 (Gadot 2009, fig. 8.8.2); Ḥazor Area C–Stratum 1b (Yadin et al. 1960, pl. CXXXI.16–17; 1961, pl. CCLXXV.5).

PILGRIM FLASKS (FL)

The assemblage includes two flasks: One, missing its neck, rim and one of its handles, was found in the cave (Locus 225, Basket 2135), while the other was found intact in the secondary cache (L226, Basket 2080). The flasks were divided into two types, distinguishable by the location of the handle's joint: in type FL I, the handles emerge from the upper part of the shoulder; in type FL II, they emerge from the neck, below the rim and wind around the neck of the vessel.[14]

Type FL I: Pilgrim flask

A round flask with a lentoid cross-section (fig. 25.32.1). Two handles are drawn from the upper part of the shoulder to the body of the vessel, which is adorned with a decoration of brown concentric circles. This type is known from the early fourteenth century BCE and continues into the thirteenth century (Killebrew 2010, 99).

Parallels: Deir el-Balaḥ type A1 (see Killebrew 2010, 99–100 for other parallels); Tel Lachish–a similar flask, ascribed to the Fosse Temple III (thirteenth century BCE; Tufnell, Inge, and Harding 1940, pl. LIVB.349); Aphek Stratum X13-X12, dated to the LB IIB (Gadot 2009, fig. 8.9.10); Hazor Area F, Stratum 1b (Yadin et al. 1960, pl. CXXX.13).

Type FL II: Pilgrim flask

A round flask with a lentoid cross-section and a low neck (fig. 25.32.2). The two handles, extending from the shoulder to under the rim, were attached to it by spreading the clay to form petals around the neck. The simple, everted rim rests on top of the handles. This vessel is also decorated with red concentric circles.

Parallels: Two flasks from the last layer of the Late Bronze Age destruction in Yoqneʿam Stratum XIXa (Ben-Ami 2005, figs. III.24.27, IV.21.3). These flasks are a known element in the ceramic repertoire, beginning in the fourteenth century and continuing in the thirteenth century (Killebrew 1998, 127, form CA 28a). They are the most prevalent type in Deir el-Balaḥ, with or without decoration, and flasks of a similar type were found in the cemetery excavated by Trude Dothan and were dated to the end of the thirteenth century BCE (Killebrew 2010, 110, type B: 2). Parallels were also found in the LB II Mycenaean tomb at Tel Dan (Biran, Ben-Dov, and Arensburg 2002, fig. 2.61.67), and in Tel Yinʿam Stratum XIIA, dated to the mid-thirteenth century BCE (Liebowitz 2003, fig. 47.7).

CUP AND SAUCER (CS)

Two composite vessels are included in the assemblage, that is, cup and saucer, making up 1 percent of all the vessels found in the repository cave. There are minor differences between the two vessels, perhaps because they are unique and not mass-produced, unlike, for example, bowls and jars. The vessel in figure 25.33.1 (Basket 2128), with a slightly cut rim, has a hemispherical saucer base, rounded or slightly carinated on its upper part (fig. 25.33.1). In the second vessel (Basket 2121; fig. 25.33.2), the inner cup, with a simple and everted rim, is higher than the saucer. Composite vessels of this kind are already known, in small quantities, from the Middle Bronze Age, but become more common in LB II–Iron Age I contexts, whence most of the examples were found (Uziel and Gadot 2010, 43). Most were found in cultic assemblages: in Lachish, for example, twenty out of twenty-nine such-like vessels originated in cultic assemblages, while three others derived from a single *favissa*; in Ḥaẓor, many of these vessels have a clear cultic association (Uziel and Gadot 2010, 49).

Parallels: Beth Shean Stratum VIII (James and McGovern 1993, fig. 18.16); Megiddo Strata VIIa–VIII (Loud 1948, pl. 67.7, 70.15); Tel Yinʿam Stratum XIIA, dated to the mid-thirteenth century BCE (Liebowitz 2003, fig. 42.6). These vessels also continue into the Iron Age I, for example in Tel Qasile, where a similar vessel (with a pinched mouth) from Stratum X was published, found in the entrance to the inner sanctuary (Shrine 300) together with a low, cylindrical stand (Mazar 1985, 79, fig. 45.2).

---

14. This classification is based on Killebrew's division of Deir el-Balaḥ flasks.

LAMPS (LP)

Seventeen lamps are included in the assemblage, making up 7 percent of all vessels.[15] The lamps were divided into two subtypes, based on differences in the shape of their rims: simple or flaring. This typology pertains only to the completely preserved lamps.

Type LP Ia: Lamps with a plain rim

These lamps, with a rounded base and a sharply pinched mouth, have a rim that continues their body outline (figs. 25.34.1–6; 25.35.1). They are known from the beginning of the Late Bronze Age.

Parallels: Aphek Strata X12–X11 (see Gadot 2009, 234, table 8.44 for additional parallels).

Type LP Ib: Lamp with a splayed rim

These lamps are identical to the previous type, except for their simple splayed rims (fig. 25.35.2–3). The presence of lamps, both with splayed and plain rims, is an indicator of the last phase of the Late Bronze Age (Beck and Kochavi 1985, 33).

Parallels can be found at Hazor Area F, Tomb 8144-8145 (Yadin et al. 1960, pl. CXXXV.2), and Aphek-Antipatris Stratum X11 (Gadot 2009, fig. 8.13.4).

STANDS (ST)

Seven stands (figs. 25.36–39, 40.1), that is, tall pedestals above which a bowl or another vessel could be placed, were uncovered in the repository, making up 3 percent of the ceramic assemblage. The stands have been divided into four types:

1. Type ST I, a tall, painted, fenestrated stand with a small, schematic human figure sculpted in one of its fenestrations.
2. Type ST II, a tall, hollow fenestrated stand.
3. Type ST III, with jar-like, carinated or rounded shoulders and a cylindrical body.
4. Type ST IV, a small, nonfenestrated hollow cylindrical stand.

---

15. Eight lamps were not restored or drawn.

Type ST I: Tall, cylindrical, painted, fenestrated stand

This hollow stand (fig. 25.36), preserved to a height of 65 cm, is incomplete, missing the rims of both the upper and lower orifices. Two loop handles are attached to its upper part, and square fenestrations are cut along the vessel's length—four fenestrations on the back and five on the front. A framed schematic human figure is seen in the facade of the uppermost, fifth fenestration on the front side of the vessel.[16] Traces of red paint, including vertical, curving lines running the length of the stand, are still visible.

Parallels: A tall cylindrical stand with two loop handles on its upper part from a Stratum-V temple at Beth Shean (Rowe 1940, pl. XIV.2).

Type ST II: Plain cylindrical stand

Three stands of this type were retrieved from the assemblage (figs. 25.37.1–2, 25.38). They are similar to the type ST I stands, but with round rather than square fenestrations and without the framed sculpted human figure. No traces of painted decoration were found and probably did not survive. These stands, also hollow and cylindrical, have a pair of loop handles attached on opposite sides of the vessel. The conical, everted shape of the stand's upper part is identical to that of its base, albeit that the diameter of the upper orifice is significantly smaller than that of the lower one.

Despite the similarity in shape among the three stands belonging to this type, they are not identical. The vessel in figure 25.37.1, 80 cm high, has four round fenestrations on both the front and back sides, and the pair of opposite handles are connected to the vessel at the height of the third fenestration. The second stand (fig. 25.37.2), also 80 cm high, has three fenestrations on each side, and loop handles attached to the stand in its middle, by the second fenestration. The third stand (e), only 60 cm high, has three round fenestrations on one side and two on the opposite side, with loop handles attached near the upper, third fenestration.

---

16. The figure disintegrated while undergoing restoration and therefore the documentation includes field photographs taken while removing the stand at the time of excavation, as well as a photograph taken by E. Kamaisky prior to the pottery restoration in the laboratory.

Parallels: The bottom part of a similar stand was found in Beth Shean, in the Stratum-V temple assemblage (Rowe 1940, pl. XVII.8).

Type ST III: Jar-like stands

Two stands belong to this type. These stands (fig. 25.39.1–2), cylindrical and hollow, have a prominent shoulder and a short rim, similar to jars. A pair of opposite loop handles are attached either beneath the shoulder (fig. 25.39.1) or on the upper part of the wall (fig. 25.39.2). The bases are wider than the shoulders. Two oval-like fenestrations, facing each other, were opened on both sides of the vessels.

Parallels: The Bet-She'an Stratum-V temple assemblage (Rowe 1940, pls. XV.2–4; LIXA.1–2; LXA.1–2; LXIA.1–2, 4; LXIIA.4).

Type ST IV: A small stand

This diminutive 16-cm high stand is cylindrical and has a tall stem (fig. 25.40.1). Its trumpet-like bottom part is wider than its upper aperture. This vessel differs from the other stands in the assemblage by its diminutive size and the absence of fenestrations and handles, probably inherent to its small size. Vertical scraping marks, evident on the body of the vessel, might have been intentionally made to imitate metallic stands.

Parallels: No comparable stands were found. A somewhat reminiscent vessel from Tell Abu Hawam was published as a chalice (Anati 1959, 97–98, fig. 8.17–18), that is, the upper part of the stand was interpreted as a bowl. However, given the similarity between these two vessels, perhaps the chalice from Tell Abu Hawam was also used as a stand.

Stands: Discussion

The assemblage comprises seven hollow, cylindrical stands. Scholars ascribe the tall cylindrical stands to the group of tower-like stands (Katz 2006, 91). This group is divided into three types:

1. Tall stands, with or without an upper bowl.
2. Tall, square stands with an upper tray.
3. Low, square stands, with or without an upper tray (Katz 2006, 91, 117).[17]

The upper part and the base of the type ST 1 stand did not survive; however, based on a comparison with type ST II stands, it can be assumed that its upper part was everted.

Tel Qashish vessels belonging to types ST III and IV have a narrow orifice atop which a bowl (more than 10 cm in diameter) or another vessel could be placed. Unlike these stands, Tel Qashish ST II vessels have a large aperture of at least 20 cm in diameter, greater than the diameter of most Tel Qashish bowls—except for the type BL IV bowl, which could have been placed on top of these cylindrical stands.

Type ST I stand is atypical of the assemblage. A schematically represented human figure was initially present in the upper fenestration of the stand. A parallel can be found among the Beth Shean Stratum V cultic vessels (Rowe 1940, pls. XVII.1, LVII A.1–2). Pirhiya Beck (1994), and subsequently Irit Ziffer (2011, 391–92), showed that the front in these stands simulates the appearance of the temple and the image of the goddess in it, or some symbol belonging to her cult. In a stand from Megiddo Stratum VIIB, discussed by them in this respect, a tree, flanked by animals, depicts events taking place in the inner sanctuary, while the treetops and the water streams represent passing into the temple (Ziffer 2011, 391–92; Beck 1994, 441). Thus, perhaps, in the Tel Qashish stand, the upper fenestration simulates the inner sanctuary of the temple and the image of the goddess in it, while the passage into the temple is represented by streams of water indicated by red-painted wavy lines.

INCENSE BURNER (IB)

One vessel in the assemblage was defined as an incense burner (fig. 25.40.2). Like the chalices, the incense burner has a tall pedestal and an open bowl above it; however, unlike them, the incense burner has two facing rounded fenestrations, cut on both sides, and two loop handles that extend from below the base of the bowl to the sides of the vessel, typical

---

17. For this *contradictio in terminis*, i.e., tower-like stands with low stands, cf. Kletter 2010a.

of stands. Signs of burnishing were discerned on the vessel's exterior, perhaps in imitation of a metallic vessel.

Parallels: The bottom part of a cylindrical vessel from Tel Yoqne'am Stratum XXI (Ben-Ami and Livneh 2005, fig. IV.21.9).

Imported Wares: Mycenaean Pottery

Seven Mycenaean closed vessels, dated to the Late Helladic (LH IIIB1–LH IIIA2), were found in the assemblage: four stirrup jars, two flasks, and one piriform jar, making up 3 percent of the assemblage. Five vessels were found grouped—three in the southern corner of the cave, and the other two on the southeastern side of the cave. The vessels were found complete but for the stirrup jar Basket 2115, which was discovered in fragments.

PIRIFORM JARS

Type FS 48: Small piriform jar

This 13-cm high vessel (fig. 25.41.1), piriform at the bottom and with a rounded shoulder in its upper part, has a low slanting-outward neck and a torus base. The three small vertical strap handles are flanked by decorative painted bands. The vessel is decorated with geometric designs, and, below the handles, the horizontal thin-strips decoration delimits the decorative strip running between the handles. Its diminutive size is characteristic of piriform jars attributed to the LHIIIB1 (Mountjoy 1986, 97).

Parallels: The body of a similar jar was found in a temple in Amman, dating from the LB II (Hankey 1974, fig. 2.8).

FLASKS

The assemblage included two imported flasks. These were divided into two types based on the decorative design appearing on the body of the vessels: One has a (monochrome?) painted concentric-lines decoration, while the other shows horizontal decorative lines surrounding the wall of the vessel.

Type FS 189(?): Flask with a vertical design

This 13-cm high spherical flask (fig. 25.41.2), made of two joined vessel parts, has a narrow neck and an everted rim with a ridge at its base, and a ring base. The handles are vertical and flattened and extend from the center of the neck to the shoulder. This type is always decorated with concentric circles separated by a petal or a curly motif on the side panels, but no such decoration was noted on the flask from the Tel Qashish repository cave. Flasks of this type are known from a temple in Amman, Jordan, and date from the end of the LHIIIA2 (Hankey 1974, fig. 8.96).

Type FS 190–e

This spherical flask (fig. 25.41.3), with a long narrow neck, a triangular rim, and a concave base, has two vertical handles that extend from the center of the neck to the sloping shoulder. The body is decorated with alternating narrow and wide bands. This design reaches the base of the usually undecorated handles.

Parallels: The assemblage from the temple at Deir 'Alla (LHIIIA: 2, B: 1; Franken 1992, fig. 4-20.15); Ḥazor Stratum 1b (LHIIIA2, B1; Yadin et al. 1960, pl. CXXXVII.7–8).

STIRRUP JARS

Four stirrup jars (fig. 25.42) were retrieved from the repository cave: one was found intact (fig. 25.42.1), one was found in several fragments retrieved from three separated baskets (2115, 2090, 2133; fig. 25.42.2), and two were found complete except for the rim (fig. 25.42.4) and the handle (fig. 25.42.3–4).

Type FS 166: Conical–piriform stirrup jar

This vessel has a conical, piriform body, a rounded shoulder, and a narrow torus base (fig. 25.42.1). The shoulder is adorned with a multiple stem (FM 19) decoration. This type dates from the early and late LHIIIA2.

Parallels: A similar vessel was found at Tel Yin'am in a building dating from the LB II period (Hankey 2003, fig. 33.3, photo 5.1).

Type FS 178 and 180: Squat stirrup jar

A stirrup jar (fig. 25.42.2) with a squat-globular shape, a rounded shoulder, a low ring base, a long and narrow false neck with a convex disk on the upper part, and a tall mouth with a rounded rim. The handles are painted in a single color in all known types, except on the upper part, where the triangles are present. The disk capping the false neck is decorated with concentric circles.

Parallels: A similar vessel, dating from the transition phase between LHIIIA2 and LHIIIB1, was found in a Late Bronze II destruction layer at Tel Yin'am (Hankey 2003, 155, fig. 38.1). Another vessel, dating from the LHIIIB1 was published, from Tomb 613 at Deir el-Balaḥ (Dothan and Nahmias-Lotan 2010, fig. 7.1.3).

Type FS 171: Globular stirrup jar

This globular jar (fig. 25.42.3), missing the handles, has a rounded rim and a prominent concave base. The decoration includes painted lines on the mouth's rim and on and at the base of the false mouth. The decoration on the body includes a series of thin lines delineated by broad bands. A decorative band is also painted on the base of the vessel. Globular stirrup jars were common throughout a long period; however, the absence of decoration on the shoulder of the vessel dates the jar to the LHIIIB1 and not the LHIIIA2 (Mountjoy 1986, 79).

Parallels: Ugarit (Hirschfeld 2000, cat. nos. 138–140); Deir el-Balaḥ Locus 1392 (upper; Dothan and Nahmias-Lotan 2010, fig. 7.1.2).

Type FS 178(?): Squat stirrup jar

This vessel (fig. 25.42.4) is less squat than the previous one. Its circumference is at least equal to its height and possibly greater. The vessel has a shallow ring base and is decorated similarly to the preceding globular FS 171 vessel. This type continues into the LH IIIB (Mountjoy 1986, 203).

Imported Wares: Cypriot Imports

Eighteen Cypriot pottery vessels (fig. 25.43), making up 8 percent of all vessels, were found in the repository cave. These comprise two base ring II bowls (= 0.1 percent), four white slip II bowls (= 1.7 percent), one base ring II flask (= 0.4 percent), and eleven white shaved juglets (= 5 percent). They are discussed in detail by Celia Bergoffen (ch. 27, this volume). A few items were submitted for INAA analysis (Yellin, Boulanger, and Glascock, ch. 28, this volume).

Faience

A Faience bowl

The only nonceramic vessel in the assemblage is a hemispherical faience lotus bowl (fig. 25.44). This bowl is decorated on the outside with alternating white and yellow floral corolla with pointed petals in relief. This object reflects Egyptian influence and is ascribed to the group of vessels referred to as the international western Asiatic vases (Peltenburg 1972, 133–136).[18]

Parallels: Beth Shean Stratum VI-lower (first half of the twelfth century BCE, Rowe 1940, pl. XXI.31); the inner sanctuary of the temple at Tell Kazel in Syria, Stratum 6, dating from the LB II (see Badre and Gubel 1999–2000, figs. 10.e, 12.I; see also p. 139 for additional parallels).

Conclusions

Dating

The ceramic assemblage presented above derives from two caches. The main cache was found in the repository cave, whose roof had caved at a later time, a conclusion reached during the excavation, when the vessels were found in a cluster, piled one on top of the other and alongside each other without any notable stratification (fig. 25.45). The second, secondary cache was found in a bedrock pocket outside the cave.

Many pottery types found in these repositories are not chrono-typologically sensitive, making it often impossible to distinguish between earlier and

---

18. The water lily, or Nymphaea, is known in Egyptian literature as "lotus," appearing in Egyptian architecture and art (Pommerening, Marinova, and Hendrickx 2010). Over the years, the floral motif was adopted by the population of the Levant and the Eastern Mediterranean, as evidenced by this object.

later. Vessels dating from the LB IIA and possibly even earlier are alongside vessels dating from the end of the LB IIB; for example, the open bowls with a straight or curved wall and the carinated bowls with a cyma-shaped profile appear together with open carinated bowls of the LB IIB tradition, which do not characterize the last phase of the Late Bronze Age.

Pirhiya Beck and Moshe Kochavi (1985, 33; Gadot 2009, 201) discussed the chronological aspect of the carinated LB bowls and noted that, although these appear in the governor's house in Aphek in Stratum X14, not a single carinated bowl was found in Stratum X12, meaning that the layer should be dated to the early thirteenth century BCE. They noticed a similar phenomenon in the last phase of the Fosse Temple at Lachish, in Ashdod Stratum XIV, and Tell Beit Mirsim Stratum C, all dated to the thirteenth century (Beck and Kochvi 1985, 33).

Based on this typological conclusion, Beck and Kochavi (1985, 33) contended that the end of Aphek's Stratum XIII is parallel to Stratum 1a at Ḥazor—where carinated bowls were dated by Yigael Yadin to the second quarter of the thirteenth century—and that this date should reflect the beginning of the period. They (1985, 38) concluded that Ḥazor Stratum 1a and Aphek Stratum XIII are among the first settlements destroyed in the early thirteenth century, while Megiddo, Beth Shean, and Lachish continued to exist under Egyptian hegemony until the mid-twelfth century and even later.

In addition, some vessel groups in the Qashish ensemble include types which can be dated to the beginning of the Late Bronze Age, such as the cooking pot with a gutter rim (type CP I).

Since the ensemble found in the cave most likely represents a one-time deposition, the latest-datable vessels determine the sealing date of the repository, while earlier vessels in the assemblage represent heirlooms brought in/collected by the worshipers after they were no longer used. Thus, the assemblage should be dated to the LB IIB (late thirteenth century BCE). Among the vessels that can be attributed to this period are the Mycenaean IIA and IIB vessels, the chalices with a triangular rim, cooking pots, and Cypriot pottery (white slip II Late Cypriot and BR II bowls; Bergoffen, ch. 27, this volume). The presence of these vessels indicates that the assemblage is contemporary with Tel Yoqneʿam Strata XIXa–XIXb;

Tel Qashish Stratum IV–V; Megiddo Stratum VIIb; Beth Shean Stratum VII; Tell Abu Hawam Stratum V; Lachish, Fosse Temple III; Tel Yinʿam Stratum XIIa, and others.

Context

The assemblage comprises about 236 vessels. Some were found intact, while most of them, complete, broke when the ceiling of the cave caved in or from the sheer weight of other vessels deposited on them.[19] The vessels were deposited in an orderly fashion: Bowls were stacked in groups one inside the other, the Mycenaean vessels were placed in one corner of the cave, Cypriot juglets in another corner, and so forth, and most of them were not deliberately broken at the time of deposition. The care taken when depositing the vessels, combined with the cultic nature of some of them, led the authors, as one possible interpretation, to associate the concealment with a repository of a local temple or shrine (van den Brink, Segal, and ʿAd 2012).

The fact that complete vessels were buried is evident from the data in table 25.1. Only 56 vessels, making up about 24 percent of the assemblage, were restored from various excavation baskets. Most of the vessels were restored from the baskets collected the same day, and others from baskets collected the previous day or later. Only a few vessels originated in baskets from different elevations, such as, for example, Goblets 2101, 2130, 2234/5, and the human-faced goblet 2200, which include body sherds from the bottom of the cave and were restored with fragments from Basket 2070, collected at the very start of the excavation. The molded human face was found on the soil covering the bedrock floor of the cave, and it was restored to its original state as a tall cup with sherds from baskets from the upper levels of the cave.

Since the majority of vessels were found complete, it might be assumed that some vessels, including the goblets, might have been intentionally broken to be used in the interment ceremony. The human-faced goblet was broken into at least five pieces: the face was discarded first, followed by pieces of the vessel

---

19. Some vessels could not be restored due to budgetary limitations.

placed or discarded as high up as the upper deposition levels within the cave.

The secondary cache (Locus 226) is also of interest in this respect: two of the vessels found in it (Bowl 2088 and Jug 2206) were restored with fragments deriving from baskets originating in the main cache (Loci 219 and 225). Bowl L226/B2088 was restored from sherds coming, inter alia, from baskets within the repository cave differing by one meter in elevation. There was also an approximately 2-m difference in height between the loci baskets within the cave containing fragments of jug L226/B2206 (table 25.1). The placing of the vessels and (or) how they were broken suggests that some goblets were deliberately smashed and discarded or placed in the cave alongside complete vessels that were deposited intact. Also, a few vessels were buried concomitantly in the main and secondary caches, with at least two being broken and their pieces buried in both caches.

Among the vessels characteristic of temple assemblages can be mentioned the stands, the goblets—including the human-faced goblet (Ziffer et al. 2018)—the cup and saucer, and the chalices which are also known from burials, domestic assemblages, and boat hulls (Grutz 2007; Yoselevich 2004). The rest of the vessels, including the bowls, lamps, cooking pots, juglets, jugs, flasks, and other, are household vessels, and nothing specific in them may point to the nature of the assemblage. Their quantitative division (figs. 25.46) also shows a high percentage of tableware, such as bowls (40 percent), versus only a few storage vessels such as jars (only one jar was found in the assemblage). This division is similar to those in other cultic assemblages. In the three Fosse Temple phases at Lachish, bowls constitute the most prevalent vessel type (Tufnell, Inge, and Harding 1940, 79): In the Fosse Temple I, bowls make up 45 percent of all the vessels; in the Phase II temple, bowls make up 43 percent of the total; and in the Phase III temple they make up as much as 48 percent of all the vessels (Tufnell, Inge, and Harding 1940, 79). In the cultic assemblage from Deir 'Alla, bowls are also the most quotidian vessel found in every room (Franken 1992, 164).

Petrographic analysis of the cultic vessels (Cohen-Weinberger, ch. 26, this volume) show the examined vessels—such as the human-faced goblet, the stands, the goblets, the chalices, and the cup and saucer—were made of indigenous clay in a local workshop that produced cultic vessels alongside domestic pottery. Using the same clay to produce cultic and noncult-related vessels was also found in other cult assemblages, such as in Ḥorbat Qitmit, 'En Ḥaẓeva, and Tel Yavneh (Kletter 2010b, 197).

The excavation results indicate that the disposal of temple objects in the repository cave was a one-time event and that the cave was explicitly adapted to conceal the vessels inside it. Interment of cultic artifacts in the Late Bronze Age is a rare phenomenon and occurred in only a few sites. At Lachish, small pits containing cultic objects were found in the immediate vicinity of the fosse temple in all its phases; although the excavators characterized them as refuse pits, their proximity to the temple and the nature of their contents, which included cultic objects, lead to the conclusion that these are caches of cult items from the nearby temple (Kletter 2010b, 202). Contemporary with the Fosse Temple III, a Stratum VII building with pits existed on the acropolis, where a temple was constructed in Stratum VI (Ussishkin 2004, 198). In this stratum, several pits were dug in the eastern part of the temple's courtyard. Two caches of vessels near the temple's southeastern corner (L3027, L3078) were identified as *favissae* (Ussishkin 2004, 217, 257). A pit (L2156) containing numerous ritual artifacts and a basalt libation table, were also revealed in the open area outside the Orthostat Temple in Area H at Ḥaẓor (Yadin et al. 1989, 247).

Another LB I and LB II cache can be associated with the deposits in Area D (L407) at Shiloh. The excavators of the site believe the finds indicate that a temple was situated on the tell and that the cultic objects found there were used during the Late Bronze Age in an open sanctuary compound, being buried in a *favissa* after they were no longer used (Bunimovitz and Finkelstein 1993, 128). This *favissa* was dug up and removed as a result of the construction works carried out at that place in the Iron Age (Lederman and Finkelstein 1993, 43–47).

A repository (*favissa*) exposed in the center of the southern temple at Ḥaẓor is attributed to the Middle Bronze Age and the transition to the Late Bronze Age (Weinblatt-Krauz 2013). The repository pit was 0.6–1.0 m in diameter and more than 4 m deep. Cultic vessels, some of them in a complete state, were found in the pit, together with animal bones mostly intentionally broken (90 percent; Weinblatt-Krauz 2013, 79).

Some cultic items from the Philistine temple in Tel Qasile were found in a pit or *favissa* (L125), probably after temple 200 was abandoned (Mazar 1980, 24–25). Among the artifacts in this pit was an anthropomorphic vessel broken into small fragments, a zoomorphic rhyton, bowls, goblets, juglets, lamps, and bones (Mazar 1980, 25).

A large cache, comprising thousands of vessels from the Iron Age, was discovered at Tel Yavneh (Kletter, Ziffer, and Zwickel 2010). The vessels discovered in the pit are cultic artifacts brought from a nearby temple. The vast majority of the vessels were found broken. Some had been deliberately destroyed before being discarded in the pit, while others had been shattered when they were thrown away (Panitz-Cohen 2010, 128; Kletter 2010b, 194). Traces of soot were discerned on the bowls and chalices.

The assemblage from 'En Ḥazeva is ascribed to a later Iron Age phase. In this case, a *favissa* comprising cultic items, some of these anthropomorphic vessels, bowls, goblets, and other, was excavated near a temple (Ben-Arieh 2011). Since all the vessels were restored, it can be concluded that they were brought intact to their place of interment (107, 111).

Based on the *favissae* assemblages mentioned above, six characteristics distinguish the Tel Qashish cache:[20]

1. Place of interment. In all instances, the *favissae* are related to a nearby temple and are located in the temple courtyard or close by. The cache from Tel Qashish, as already noted, was discovered at some distance from the mound, with no contemporary architectural remains nearby.
2. All caches (*favissae*) are actually pits dug in the ground, often just small. At Tel Qashish, a small natural cave had been adapted for serving as a cache and was utilized, and steps going down to it were cut in the bedrock, possibly indicating repeated use of the cave.
3. In the Tel Qashish repository cave, the time of use is not prolonged and, in fact, entails a one-time deposition. In most caches, in contrast, the vessels had been used in the temple for long periods and were buried in the pit for any of three reasons: after they broke, because of changes/evolution in form and design of the vessels, or after implementing religious reforms.
4. The condition of the vessels. The artifacts from all caches were found broken, often having been intentionally destroyed before deposition. At Tel Qashish, apart from the human-faced goblet and two other goblets, all the vessels were found complete, and some were even intact. Moreover, the vessels had not been thrown into the cavity but carefully arranged inside it.
5. No signs of usage or wear are evident on the vessels from Tel Qashish. No soot was noticed on the chalices or most lamps. In fact, except for two or three lamps showing signs of burning, none of the other vessels evidenced signs of usage, wear, or thermal shock (unlike the repository in Yavneh, see Namdar, Neumann, and Weiner 2010). The soot on the lamps might indicate they were last used at the time of the actual interment, perhaps conducted after sunset.[21]
6. No animal bones were discovered inside the vessels, near them, or in the overlying fill. This absence is remarkable since animal bones in all the caches mentioned above are an integral part of the concealed ritual assemblage.

Summing up, the Tel Qashish cache is a collection of both quotidian vessels and cultic artifacts dating from the LB II. The differences between the burial of cultic objects in this cache and other caches (*favissae*) led to the conclusion that the Tel Qashish cache cannot be considered a *favissa*, that is, the concealing of cultic objects buried after they were no longer used in a temple (Kletter 2010b, 204–5). At Tel Qashish, the reason for burying ritual artifacts might thus be related rather to a specific event occurring in the region (e.g., conquest, religious coercion) during which the vessels were hidden.

---

20. Differences observed among the *favissae* reviewed above stem from the nature of the ritual and chronological and/or regional distinctions; however, these cannot be discussed here.

21. It should be mentioned that the chemical analyses performed on the Qashish vessels (particularly the chalices) produced only negative results (Namdar, ch. 29, this volume).

References

Aharoni, Yohanan
1987 *Eretz Israel in Biblical Times: A Geographical History.* Jerusalem: Yad Ben-Zvi. [Hebrew]

Amiran, Ruth
1963 *The Ancient Pottery of Eretz Yisrael.* Jerusalem: Bialik; Israel Exploration Society. [Hebrew]

Anati, Emmanuel
1959 "Excavations at the Cemetery of Tell Abu Hawam (1952)." *'Atiqot* 2: 89–102.

Artzy, Michal
2007 "Tell Abu Hawam: News from the Late Bronze Age." In *The Synchronisation of Civilisations in the Eastern Mediterranean in the Second Millennium B.C. III: Proceedings of the SCIEM 2000—2nd EuroConference, Vienna 28th of May–1st of June 2003,* edited by Manfred Bietak and Ernst Czerny, 357–66. Contributions to the Chronology of the Eastern Mediterranean 4. Vienna: Österreichischen Akademie der Wissenschaften.

Badre, Leila, and Eric Gubel
1999–2000 "Tell Kazel Syria: Excavations of the AUB Museum, 1993–1998, Third Preliminary Report." *Berytus* 44: 123–203.

Balensi, Jacqueline
1980 "Les Fouilles de R. W. Hamilton a Tell Abu-Hawam, Niveaux IV et V." Strasbourg: Universite des sciences humaines.

Beck, Pirhiya
1994 "The Ta'anach Cult Stands: Iconographic Traditions in the Iron I Cult Vessels." In *From Nomadism to Monarchy. Archaeological and Historical Aspects of Early Israel,* edited by Nadav Na'aman and Israel Finkelstein, 417–46. Jerusalem. [Hebrew]

Beck, Pirhiya, and Moshe Kochavi
1985 "A Dated Assemblage of the Late 13th Century B.C.E. from the Egyptian Residency at Aphek." *TA* 12: 29–42.

Ben-Ami, Doron
2005 "The Pottery of the Late Bronze Age." In *Yoqne'am III: The Middle and Late Bronze Ages; Final Report of the Archaeological Excavations (1977–1988),* edited by Amnon Ben-Tor, Doron Ben-Ami, and Ariella Livneh, 165–240. Qedem Reports 7. Jerusalem: Hebrew University of Jerusalem.

Ben-Ami, Doron, and Ariella Livneh
2005 "The Typological Analysis of the Pottery of the Middle and Late Bronze Ages." In *Yoqne'am III: The Middle and Late Bronze Ages; Final Report of the Archaeological Excavations (1977–1988),* edited by Amnon Ben-Tor, Doron Ben-Ami, and Ariella Livneh, 247–348. Qedem Reports 7. Jerusalem: Hebrew University of Jerusalem.

Ben-Arieh, Sara
2011 "Temple Furniture from a Favissa at 'En Ḥaẓeva." *'Atiqot* 68: 107–75.

Ben-Tor, Amnon, and Ruhama Bonfil
2003 "The Stratigraphy and Pottery Assemblages of the Middle and Late Bronze Ages in Area A." In *Tel Qashish: A Village in the Jezreel Valley; Final Report of the Archaeological Excavations (1978–1987),* edited by Amnon Ben-Tor, Ruhama Bonfil, and Sharon Zuckerman, 185–276. Qedem Reports 5. Jerusalem: Hebrew University of Jerusalem.

Ben-Tor, Amnon, Ruhama Bonfil, Yosef Garfinkel, Raphael Greenberg, Aren M. Maeir, and Amihai Mazar
1997 *Hazor V: An Account of the Fifth Season of Excavation, 1968.* Jerusalem: Israel Exploration Society; Hebrew University of Jerusalem.

Ben-Tor, Amnon, Ruhama Bonfil, and Sharon Zuckerman
2003a *Tel Qashish: A Village in the Jezreel Valley; Final Report of the Archaeological Excavations (1978–1987).* Qedem Reports 5. Jerusalem: Hebrew University of Jerusalem.

2003b "Introduction." In *Tel Qashish: A Village in the Jezreel Valley; Final Report of the Archaeological Excavations (1978–1987),* edited by Amnon Ben-Tor, Ruhama Bonfil, and Sharon Zuckerman, 1–6. Qedem Reports 5. Jerusalem: Hebrew University of Jerusalem.

Biran, Avraham, Rachel Ben-Dov, and Baruch Arensburg
2002 *Dan II: A Chronicle of the Excavations and the Late Bronze Age "Mycenaean" Tomb.* Jerusalem: Nelson Glueck School of Biblical Archaeology.

Bonfil, Ruhama
2003 "Pottery Typology of the Middle Bronze Age II and the Late Bronze Age." In *Tel Qashish: A Village in the Jezreel Valley; Final Report of the Archaeological Excavations (1978–1987),* edited by Amnon Ben-Tor, Ruhama Bonfil, and Sharon Zuckerman, 277–318. Qedem Reports 5. Jerusalem: Hebrew University of Jerusalem.

Brink, Edwin C. M. van den
2014 "Tel Qashish (Rakevet Ha-'Emeq)." *HA-ESI* 126. http://www.hadashot-esi.org.il/report_detail_eng.aspx?id=14714&mag_id=121.

Brink, Edwin C. M. van den, and Uzi 'Ad
2011 "Tel Qashish: Preliminary Report." *HA-ESI* 123. http://www.hadashot-esi.org.il/report_detail_eng.aspx?id=1894&mag_id=118.

Brink, Edwin C. M. van den, Orit Segal, and Uzi 'Ad
2012 "A Late Bronze Age II Repository of Cultic Paraphernalia from the Environs of Tel Qashish in the Jezreel Valley." In *Temple Building and Temple Cult: Architecture and Cultic Paraphernalia of Temples in the Levant (2–1. Mill B.C.E.)*, edited by Jens Kamlah, 421–34. ADPV 41. Wiesbaden: Harrassowitz.

Bunimovitz, Shlomo, and Israel Finkelstein
1993 "Pottery." In *Shiloh: The Archaeology of a Biblical Site*, edited by Israel Finkelstein, Shlomo Bunimovitz, and Zvi Lederman, 81–196. SMNIA 10. Tel Aviv: Tel Aviv University.

Dothan, Trude
1979 *Excavations at the Cemetery of Deir El-Balah*. Qedem 10. Jerusalem: Hebrew University of Jerusalem.

Dothan, Trude, and Tamar Nahmias-Lotan
2010 "Mycenaean and Minoan Pottery." In *Deir El-Balah: Excavations in 1977–1982 in the Cemetery and Settlement; Volume II: The Finds*, edited by Trude Dothan, and Baruch Brandl, 117–135. Qedem 50. Jerusalem: Hebrew University of Jerusalem.

Franken, Hendricus J.
1992 *Excavations at Tell Deir 'Alla: The Late Bronze Age Sanctuary*. Louvain: Peeters.

Gadot, Yuval
2009 "Late Bronze and Iron Age Pottery." In *Aphek-Antipatris II: The Remains on the Acropolis; The Moshe Kochavi and Pirhiya Beck Excavations*, edited by Yuval Gadot, and Esther Yadin, 182–341. SMNIA 27. Tel Aviv: Tel Aviv University.

Garstang, John B. E.
1922 "Report: Tell el Kussis." *BBSAJ* 2: 16–17.

Giveon, R.
1954 "'Emeq Yizreel." *Teva Va-Aretz* 10: 515–18. [Hebrew]

Grutz, Robert
2007 *Late Bronze and Iron Age Chalices in Canaan and Ancient Israel*. BARIS 1671. Oxford: Archaeopress.

Guy, Philip L. O., and Robert M. Engberg
1938 *Megiddo Tombs*. OIP 33. Chicago: University of Chicago Press.

Hankey, Vronwy
1974 "A Late Bronze Age Temple at Amman: I. The Aegean Pottery." *Levant* 6: 131–59.
2003 "The Mycenaean Pottery from Tel Yin'am." In *Tel Yin'am I: The Late Bronze Age; Excavations at Tel Yin'am 1976–1989*, edited by Harold A. Liebowitz, 153–58. Studies in Archaeology 42. Austin: Texas Archeological Research Laboratory, the University of Texas at Austin.

Hirschfeld, Nicolle
2000 "Introduction to the Catalogue." In *Céramiques Mycéniennes d'Ogarit*, edited by Marguerite Yon, Vassos Karageorghis, and Nicolle Hirschfeld, 75–161, 211–51. Ras Shamra-Ogarit 13. Paris: ERC-ADPF; Nicosia: Fondation A. G. Leventis.

Ilan, David, Rachel S. Hallote, and Eric H. Cline
2000 "The Middle and Late Bronze Age Pottery from Area F." In *Megiddo III: The 1992–1996 Seasons*, edited by Israel Finkelstein, David Ussishkin, and Baruch Halpern, 186–222. 2 vols. SMNIA 18. Tel Aviv: Tel Aviv University.

James, Frances W., and Patrick E. McGovern
1993 *The Late Bronze Egyptian Garrison at Beth Shan: A Study of Levels VII and VIII*. University Museum Monographs 85. Philadelphia: University Museum, University of Pennsylvania.

Katz, Hava
2006 "Architectural Terracotta Models from Eretz Israel from the Fifth to the Middle of the First Millennium B.C.E." PhD diss., Haifa University. [Hebrew]

Killebrew, Ann E.
1998 "Ceramic Typology and Technology of the Late Bronze II and Iron I Assemblages from Tel Miqne-Ekron: The Transition from Canaanite to Early Philistine Culture." In *Mediterranean Peoples in Transition: Thirteenth to Early Tenth Centuries BCE*, edited by Seymour Gitin, Amihai Mazar, and Eliezer Stern, 379–405. Jerusalem: Israel Exploration Society.
1999a "Ceramic Craft and Technology during the Late Bronze and Early Iron Ages: The Relationship between Pottery Technology, Style, and Cultural Diversity." 2 vols. PhD diss., The Hebrew University of Jerusalem.
1999b "Late Bronze and Iron I Cooking Pots in Canaan: A Typological, Technological, and Functional Study." In *Archaeology, History and Culture in Palestine and the Near East: Essays in Memory of Albert E. Glock*, edited by Tomis Kapitan, 83–126. ASOR Books 3. Atlanta: Scholars Press.
2005 *Biblical Peoples and Ethnicity: An Archaeological Study of Egyptians, Canaanites, Philistines, and Early Israel, 1300–1100 B.C.E.* ABS 9. Atlanta: Society of Biblical Literature.
2010 "Canaanite Pottery." *Deir El-Balah: Excavations in 1977–1982 in the Cemetery and Settlement; Volume II; The Finds*, edited by Trude Dothan, and Baruch Brandl, 75–109. Qedem 50. Jerusalem: Hebrew University of Jerusalem.

Kletter, Raz
2010a "The Typology of the Cult Stands." In *Yavneh I: The Excavation of the "Temple Hill" Repository Pit and the Cult Stands*, edited by Raz Kletter, Irit

Ziffer, and Wolfgang Zwickel, 25–45. OBO 30. Fribourg: Academic Press; Göttingen: Vandenhoeck & Ruprecht.

2010b "Conclusions: Repository Pit–Favissa–Genizah." In *Yavneh I: The Excavation of the "Temple Hill" Repository Pit and the Cult Stands*, edited by Raz Kletter, Irit Ziffer, and Wolfgang Zwickel, 192–210. OBO 30. Fribourg: Academic Press; Göttingen: Vandenhoeck & Ruprecht.

Kletter, Raz, Irit Ziffer, and Wolfgang Zwickel
2010 *Yavneh I, The Excavation of the "Temple Hill" Repository Pit and the Cult Stands*. OBO 30. Fribourg: Academic Press; Göttingen: Vandenhoeck & Ruprecht.

Lederman, Zvi, and Israel Finkelstein
1993 "Area D: Middle Bronze Age Stone and Earth Works, Late Bronze Age Dumped Debris and Iron Age I Silos." In *Shiloh: The Archaeology of a Biblical Site*, edited by Israel Finkelstein, Shlomo Bunimovitz, and Zvi Lederman, 35–48. SMNIA 10. Tel Aviv: Tel Aviv University.

Liebowitz, Harold A.
2003 *The Late Bronze Age: Excavations at Tel Yin'am 1976–1989*. Studies in Archaeology 42. Austin: Texas Archeological Research Laboratory, the University of Texas at Austin.

Loud, Gordon
1948 *Megiddo II: Seasons of 1935–1939*. OIP 62. Chicago: University of Chicago Press.

Mazar, Amihai
1980 *Excavations at Tell Qasile I: The Philistine Sanctuary; Architecture and Cult Objects*. Qedem 12. Jerusalem: Hebrew University of Jerusalem.
1985 *Excavations at Tell Qasile II: Various Finds, The Pottery, Conclusions, Appendices*. Qedem 20. Jerusalem: Hebrew University of Jerusalem.

Mountjoy, Penelope A.
1986 *Mycenaean Decorated Pottery: A Guide to Identification*. Studies in Mediterranean Archaeology 73. Göteborg: Astroms.

Namdar, Dvory, Ronny Neumann, and Steve Weiner
2010 "Residue Analysis of Chalices from The Repository Pit." In *Yavneh I, The Excavation of the "Temple Hill" Repository Pit and the Cult Stands*, edited by Raz Kletter, Irit Ziffer, and Wolfgang Zwickel, 167–73. OBO 30. Fribourg: Academic Press; Göttingen: Vandenhoeck & Ruprecht.

Panitz-Cohen, Nava
2009 "The Local Canaanite Pottery." In *Excavations at Tel Beth-Shean 1989–1996, Volume III: The 13th-11th Century BCE Strata in Areas N and S*, edited by Nava Panitz-Cohen, and Amihai Mazar, 195–284. Jerusalem: Israel Exploration Society.
2010 "The Pottery Assemblage." In *Yavneh I. The Excavation of the 'Temple Hill' Repository Pit and the Cult Stands*, edited by Raz Kletter, Irit Ziffer, and Wolfgang Zwickel, 110–147. OBO 30. Fribourg: Academic Press; Göttingen: Vandenhoeck & Ruprecht.

Panitz-Cohen, Nava, and Aren M. Maeir
2004 "The Pottery Assemblage." In *Bronze and Iron Age Tombs at Tel Gezer, Israel: Finds from Raymond-Charles Weill's Excavations in 1914 and 1921*, edited by Aren M. Maeir, 9–41. BARIS 1206. Oxford: B.A.R.

Peltenburg, Edgar J.
1972 "On the Classification of Faïence Vases from Late Bronze Age Cyprus." In Πρακτικα του Πρωτος Διεθνους Κυπρολογικου Συνεδριου, edited by Vassos Karageorghis and A. Christodoulou, 129–36. Nicosia: Hetaireia Kupriakon spoudon.

Pommerening, Tanja, Elena Marinova, and Stan Hendrickx
2010 "The Early Dynastic Origin of the Water-Lily Motif." *Chronique d'Egypte* 85.169–170: 14–40.

Raban, Avner
1982 *Archaeology Survey of Israel: Nahalal Map (28), 16–23*. Jerusalem: Archeological Survey of Israel.

Rowe, Alan
1940 *The Four Canaanite Temples of Beth-Shan, Part I: The Temples and Cult Objects*. Publications of the Palestine Section of the Museum of the University of Pennsylvania 2. Philadelphia: University of Pennsylvania Press.

Stern, Ephraim
1984 *Excavations at Tel Mevorakh (1973–1976), Part II: The Bronze Age*. Qedem 18. Jerusalem: Hebrew University of Jerusalem.

Tufnell Olga, Charles H. Inge, and G. Lankester Harding
1940 *Lachish II (Tell ed-Duweir): The Fosse Temple*. London: Oxford University Press.

Ussishkin, David
2004 "Area P: The Level VI Temple." In *The Renewed Archaeological Excavations at Lachish (1973–1994), Volume I, Part II: The Bronze Age Stratigraphy and Architecture*, edited by David Ussishkin, 215–81. 4 vols. SMNIA 22. Tel Aviv: Tel Aviv University.

Uziel, Joe, and Yuval Gadot
2010 "The 'Cup and Saucer' Vessel: Function, Chronology, Distribution and Symbolism." *IEJ* 60: 41–57.

Weinblatt-Krauz, Dalit
2013 "The Favissa of the Southern Temple in Area A." *NEA* 76.2: 76–81.

Yadin, Yigael, Yohanan Aharoni, Ruth Amiran, Trude Dothan, Immanuel Dunayevsky, and Jean Perrot
1958 *Hazor I: An Account of the First Season of Excavations, 1955.* Jerusalem: Magnes; Hebrew University of Jerusalem.
1960 *Hazor II: An Account of the Second Season of Excavations, 1956.* Jerusalem: Magnes; Hebrew University of Jerusalem.

Yadin, Yigael, Yohanan Aharoni, Ruth Amiran, Trude Dothan, Moshe Dothan, Immanuel Dunayevsky, and Jean Perrot
1961 *Hazor III–IV: An Account of the Third and Fourth Seasons, 1957–1958 (Plates).* Jerusalem: Magnes; Hebrew University of Jerusalem.

Yadin, Yigael, Yohanan Aharoni, Ruth Amiran, Amnon Ben-Tor, Trude Dothan, Moshe Dothan, Immanuel Dunayevsky, Shulamit Geva, and Ephraim Stern
1989 *Hazor III–IV: An Account of the Third and Fourth Seasons of Excavation, 1957–1958 (Text).* Jerusalem: Israel Exploration Society; Hebrew University of Jerusalem.

Yoselevich, Noga
2004 "The Utilization of Chalices as Incense Burners on Boats and in Coastal Sites." MA thesis, University of Haifa. [Hebrew]

Ziffer, Irit
2011 "Diminished Sanctuaries for Grassroots Piety: The Case of the Cult Stands from the Repository Pit at Yavneh." *ErIsr* 30: 380–96. [Hebrew]

Ziffer, Irit, Edwin C. M. van den Brink, Orit Segal, and Uzi 'Ad
2018 "A Unique Human-Head Cup from the Environs of Tel Qashish in the Jezreel Valley, Israel." In *The Adventure of the Illustrious Scholar: Papers Presented to Oscar White Muscarella,* edited by Elizabeth Simpson, 406–20. CHANE 94. Leiden: Brill. DOI: 10.1163/9789004361713_023.

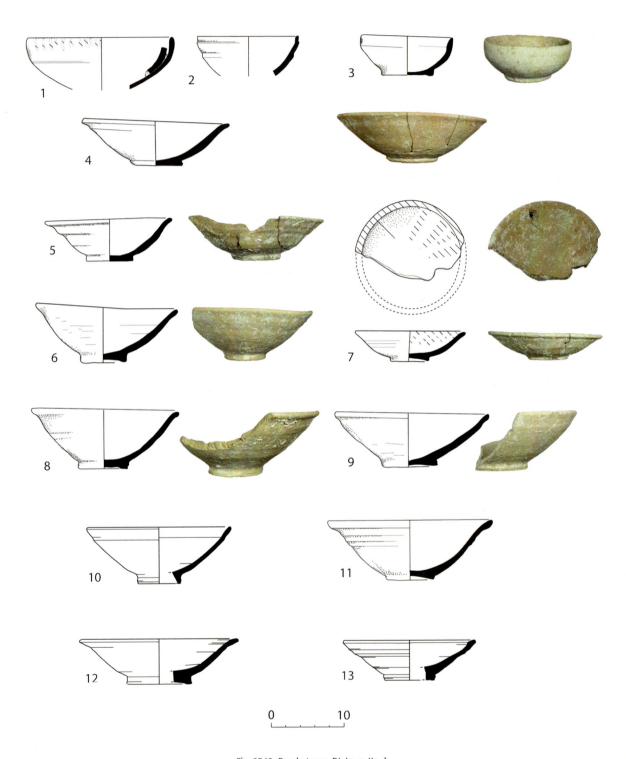

Fig. 25.10. Bowls types BL Ia–c, IIa–b.

No.	Locus No.	Reg. No.	IAA No.	Type	Level	Description	Parallels
1	225	2246		BL Ia	26.32–26.20	Clay: brown-pink yellow; a red paint decoration on the rim.	Megiddo II (Loud 1948, pl. 65.9); Beth Shean III (Panitz-Cohen 2009, pl.19.15); Beth Shean (Killebrew 1999a, fig. III.III.1.6).
2	225	2246/10		BL Ib	26.32–26.20	Clay: buff; core: light gray; grits.	Tel Qashish (Ben-Tor and Bonfil 2003, fig.104.2); Tel Yin'am (Liebowitz 2003, fig. 35.1).
3	219	2096	12-568	BL Ic	27.37–27.29	Clay: brown-greenish; core: gray; grits.	Tel Qashish (Bonfil 2003, fig.113.20, type BVI.c); Tel Miqne-Ekron (Killebrew 1999a, Fig. III.III.2.9).
4	225	2149	12-583	BL IIa	26.69	Clay: brown; core: gray; grits.	Dan II (Biran, Ben-Dov, and Arensburg 2002, fig. 2.29.16).
5	225	2239		BL IIa	26.31–26.22	Clay: brown-gray; core: light gray; grits.	Yoqne'am III (Ben-Ami 2005, fig. III.18.27).
6	225	2225		BL IIa	26.47–26.29	Clay: buff; grits.	Yoqne'am III (Ben-Ami 2005, fig. III.4.5); Tel Qashish (Ben-Tor and Bonfil 2003, figs. 107.10, 108.2); Aphek-Antipatris II (Gadot 2009, fig. 8.2.4); Hazor I (Yadin et al. 1958, pls. XCV.12, CV.5–6).
7	225	2235	12-637	BL IIa	26.50–26.44	Clay: brown-gray; core: gray; grits; a red paint decoration inside the bowl and the rim.	
8	225	2216		BL IIa	26.40–26.36	Clay: pink; core: light gray; grits.	Yoqne'am III (Ben-Ami 2005, figs. III.8.8, III.24.7); Tel Qashish (Ben-Tor and Bonfil 2003, fig.108.2); Hazor I (Yadin et al. 1958, Pl. CXXXIII.5).
9	225	2209		BL IIa	26.54–26.45	Clay: light brown-pink; core: gray; grits.	Hazor I (Yadin et al. 1958, pl. XCV.12).
10	225	2182		BL IIa			
11	225	2213/3		BL IIa	26.71–26.36		
12	225	2220/5		BL IIa	26.55–26.28		Tell Abu Hawam (Anati 1959, fig. 8.10).
13	225	??		BL IIb			Tel Miqne-Ekron (Killebrew 1999a, figs. III.III.1.2, III.II.4.9); Tel Yin'am (Liebowitz 2003, fig. 1.6).

338 Salvage Excavations at Tel Qashish (Tell Qasis) and Tell el-Wa'er (2010–2013)

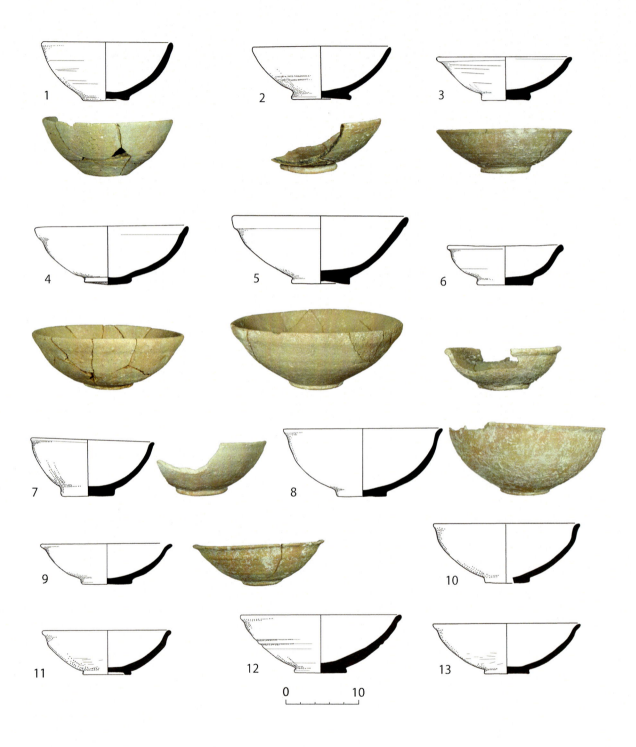

Fig. 25.11. Bowls types BL IIIa–b from Locus 225.

No.	Reg. No.	IAA No.	Type	Level	Description	Parallels
1	2114		BL IIIa	27.01–26.92	Clay: brown-gray; core: gray; grits.	Tel Gezer (Panitz-Cohen and Maeir 2004, pl. 2.5); Yoqne'am III (Ben-Ami 2005, fig. III.4.9); Aphek-Antipatris II (Gadot 2009, figs. 8.2.1, 8.3.1); Hazor I (Yadin et al. 1958, pl. LXXXV.6; 1960, Pl. CXVII.7); Beth Shean (Killebrew 1999a, figs. III.II.57.3, 61.7; III.III.1.6).
2	2170		BL IIIa	26.60–26.55	Clay: brown and brown-yellow; core: dark gray; grits.	Hazor I (Yadin et al. 1958, pls. LXXXV.6, CXXV.10); Aphek-Antipatris II (Gadot 2009, fig. 8.3.1); Tel Qashish (Ben-Tor and Bonfil 2003, fig.112.2).
3	2229	12-585	BL IIIb	26.47–26.40	Clay: light brown; grits.	Tel Qashish (Ben-Tor and Bonfil 2003, fig.107.10); Hazor I (Yadin et al. 1958, pl. LXXXVII.3); Hazor II (Yadin et al. 1960, pl. CXXVIII.16).
4	2138		BL IIIb	26.89–26.77	Clay: brown/pink-brown; core: gray; gray and white grits.	Tell Abu-Hawam (Balensi 1980, pl. 5.12).
5	2256/3	12-633	BL IIIb	26.32–26.00	Clay: brown-red; core: pink.	Hazor I (Yadin et al. 1958, pls. LXXXV.7, LXXXVII.2, LXXXIX.1, CV.24).
6	2063/1		BL IIIb			
7	2110		BL IIIb	26.91	Clay: light brown; core: gray; grits.	Yoqne'am III (Ben-Ami 2005, fig. III.16.11, 13); Hazor I (Yadin et al. 1958, pl. CV.26).
8	2194		BL IIIb	26.64–26.54	Clay: brown; core: gray; grits.	Yoqne'am III (Ben-Ami 2005, fig. III.18.27); Hazor II (Yadin et al. 1960, pl. CXVII.38); Tell Abu-Hawam (Balensi 1980, pl. 5.4).
9	2131/1	12-638	BL IIIb	26.86–26.79	Clay: brown–brown green; core: dark gray; grits.	Yoqne'am III (Ben-Ami 2005, figs. III.8.8; III.14.16, 18); Tell Abu Hawam (Anati 1959, fig. 8.8).
10	2123/5		BL IIIb	26.86–26.79	Clay: brown-green outside and orange inside; core: gray; grits.	
11	2133/3+ 2169		BL IIIb	26.64	Clay: brown; core: gray; grits.	Tell Abu-Hawam (Balensin 1980, pl. 5.6).
12	2231		BL IIIb	26.43–26.36	Clay: gray-green; core: gray-green; grits.	Tel Mevorakh (Stern 1984, fig. 1.10).
13	2133/4		BL IIIb	26.89–26.51	Clay: brown-pink; core: dark gray.	

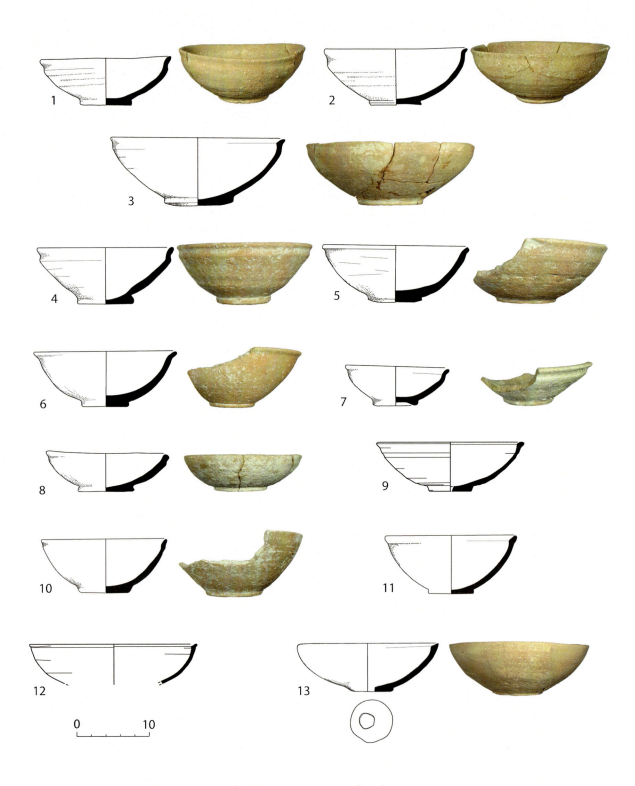

Fig. 25.12. Bowls types BL IIIb (cont.), IIIc.

No.	Locus No.	Reg. No.	IAA No.	Type	Level	Description	Parallels
1	219	2097	12-566	BL IIIb	27.33–27.27	Clay: brown; core: gray; grits.	Tel Qashish (Ben-Tor and Bonfil 2003, figs. 100.5, 130.7); Megiddo III (Ilan, Hallote, and Cline 2000, Fig. 9.14.3).
2	219	2085	13-14	BL IIIb	27.57–27.45	Clay: brown; core: gray; grits.	Yoqneʻam III (Ben-Ami 2005, fig. III.14.14); Tel Gezer (Panitz-Cohen and Maeir 2004, pl. 2.11); Tel Qashish (Ben-Tor and Bonfil 2003, figs.108.5, 130.7).
3	219	2088		BL IIIb	27.49–27.37	Clay: brown-pink; core: gray-green: grits.	Yoqneʻam III (Ben-Ami 2005, figs. III.14.15, III.16.12); Tel Qashish (Ben-Tor and Bonfil 2003, figs.108.5, 130.7); Aphek-Antipatris II (Gadot 2009, fig. 8.43.20); Hazor II (Yadin et al. 1960, pl. CXVII.38).
4	225	2143	12-586	BL IIIb	26.80–26.73	Clay: brown; core: gray; grits.	Tel Gezer (Panitz-Cohen and Maeir 2004, pl. 2.11); Tel Qashish (Ben-Tor and Bonfil 2003, fig.130.7).
5	225	2127		BL IIIb	26.86–26.79	Clay: brown; core: pink-greenish; grits.	Yoqneʻam III (Ben-Ami 2005, fig. III.16.13); Hazor II (Yadin et al. 1960, pl. CXXVIII.19).
6	219	2129		BL IIIb	27.03–27.01	Clay: brown; core: gray.	Yoqneʻam III (Ben-Ami 2005, fig. III.16.12); Aphek-Antipatris II (Gadot 2009, fig. 8.43.20); Lachish II (Tufnell, Inge, and Harding 1940, pl. XLIB.109).
7	225	2234/5		BL IIIb	26.50–26.19		
8	225	2131/2		BL IIIb	26.86–26.79	Clay: light brown; core: brown-gray.	
9	225	2220/6		BL IIIb	26.55–26.28		
10	225	2159	13-2	BL IIIc	26.71–26.63	Clay: brown; core: gray.	Megiddo III (Ilan, Hallote, and Cline 2000, fig. 9.10.18).
11	225	2164		BL IIIc	26.63–26.60	Clay: brown–brown-yellow; core: dark gray; grits.	
12	225	???		BL IIIc			
13	225	2153/1		BL IIIc	26.84–26.47	Clay: brown; core: gray-green; grits; a hole at the base.	Yoqneʻam III (Ben-Ami 2005, fig. III.24.6); Hazor I (Yadin et al. 1958, pl. CV.29); Hazor II (Yadin et al. 1960, pl. CXVII.28); Tell Abu Hawam (Anati 1959, fig. 8.5); Tel Yinʻam (Liebowitz 2003, fig. 30.1, 4).

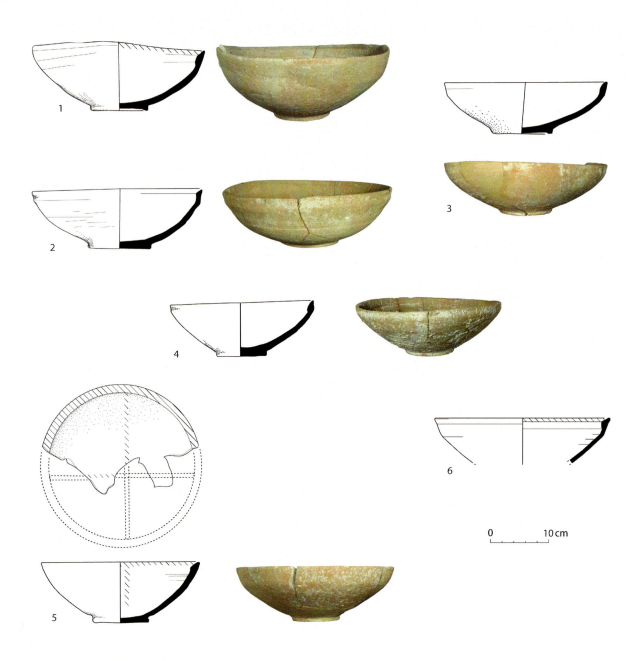

Fig. 25.13. Bowls type BL IV.

No.	Locus No.	Reg. No.	Type	Level	Description	Parallels
1	225	2145	BL IV	26.87–26.73	Clay: brown-yellow; paint decoration on the rim and a cross decoration inside; grits.	Tel Gezer (Panitz-Cohen and Maeir 2004, pl. 1.18); Yoqne'am III (Ben-Ami 2005, figs. III.4.16, III.16.7); Aphek-Antipatris II (Gadot 2009, fig. 8.2.8); Tel Qashish (Ben-Tor and Bonfil 2003, fig. 130.9); Megiddo II (Loud 1948, pl. 65.13); Tel Miqne-Ekron (Killebrew 1999a, fig. III.II.4.11).
2	219	2124/1	BL IV	27.09–26.86		Tel Gezer (Panitz-Cohen and Maeir 2004, pl. 1.20); Hazor II (Yadin et al. 1960, pls. CXVI.5, CXVII.37, CXXVIII.24); Giloh (Killebrew 1999a, fig. III.III.2.1).
3	225	2158	BL IV	26.7	Clay: light brown; core: dark gray; grits.	Hazor II (Yadin et al. 1960, pls. CXVI.5; CXXVIII.23, 24); Tel Gezer (Panitz-Cohen and Maeir 2004, pl. 1.18); Yoqne'am III (Ben-Ami 2005, fig. III.4.16), Dan II (Biran, Ben-Dov, and Arensburg 2002, fig. 2.54.11); Tel Qashish (Ben-Tor and Bonfil 2003, fig. 100.7).
4	225	2191	BL IV	26.50	Clay: brown; core: gray; a burnish evidence inside.	Megiddo III (Ilan, Hallote, and Cline 2000, fig. 9.10.18).
5	225	2133/2	BL IV	26.89–26.51	Clay: brown; core: gray; a brown strip decoration on the rim and a cross inside; grits.	Yoqne'am III (Ben-Ami 2005, figs. III.16.7, III.18.15); Hazor II (Yadin et al. 1960, pls. CXVI.5, CXXVIII.23); Dan II (Biran, Ben-Dov, and Arensburg 2002, fig. 2.54.2); Tel Miqne-Ekron (Killebrew 1999a, fig. III.III.1.2).
6	219	2117	BL IV	27.13–26.86		

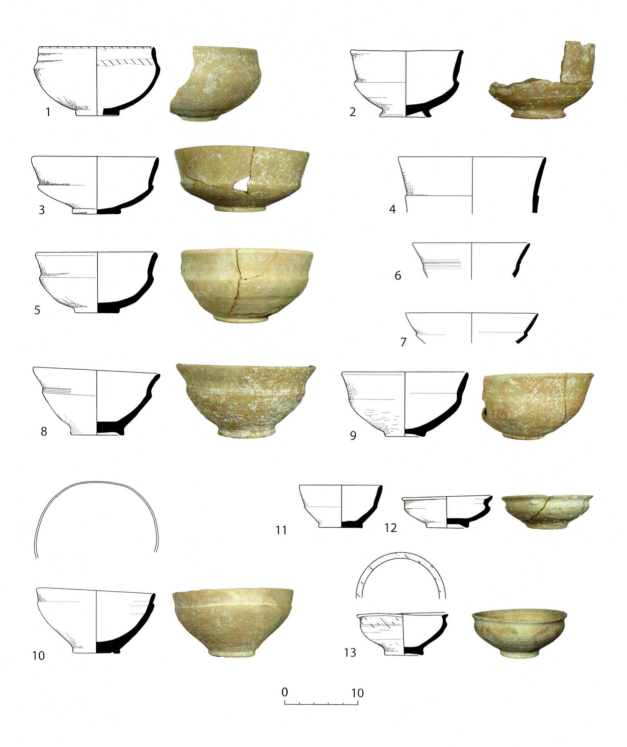

Fig. 25.14. Bowls types BL V, VIa–b, VII.

No.	Locus No.	Reg. No.	IAA No.	Type	Level	Description	Parallels
1	225	2230		BL V	26.45–26.38		Megiddo III (Ilan, Hallote, and Cline 2000, fig.9.10.14); Dan II (Biran, Ben-Dov, and Arensburg 2002, fig. 2.30.7 [goblet]).
2	225	2241		BLVIa	26.31–26.23	Clay: brown; core: brown-gray.	Aphek-Antipatris II (Gadot 2009, fig. 8.4.2).
3	219	2117/2	12-584	BLVIa	27.13–26.86	Clay: pink; core: gray.	Hazor I (Yadin et al. 1958, pls. XCVI.4, 5, 7; CXXXVI.7); Hazor II (Yadin et al. 1960, pl. CXVIII.8); Hazor V (Ben-Tor et al. 1997, fig. II.15.3).
4	225	2246/10		BLVIa	26.32–26.20	Clay: buff; core: light gray; grits.	
5	219	2087	12-639	BLVIb	27.47–27.45	Clay: brown-pink; core: light gray; white grits.	Tel Qashish (Ben-Tor and Bonfil 2003, fig.104.5); Hazor I (Yadin et al. 1958, pls. XC.3, XCV.13); Hazor II (Yadin et al. 1960, pl. CXVIII.6); Dan II (Biran, Ben-Dov, and Arensburg 2002, fig. 2.54.5); Tel Yinʿam (Liebowitz 2003, fig. 8.1).
6	225	2145/10		BLVIb	26.87–26.78	Clay: light brown; core: gray-yellow; gray grits.	Dan II (Biran, Ben-Dov, and Arensburg 2002, fig. 2.29.17).
7	219	2117		BLVIb	27.13–26.86	Clay: brown-pink; core: gray.	Tel Yinʿam (Liebowitz 2003, fig. 42.1).
8	225	2252	12-588	BLVIb	26.32–26.17	Clay: brown; core: gray; grits.	Tel Qashish (Bonfil 2003, fig.130.1); Hazor I (Yadin et al. 1958, pl. CVI.6).
9	225	2213/1		BLVIb	26.71–26.36	Clay: brown; core: light gray; grits.	Tell Kazel (Badre and Gubel 1999–2000, fig. 22r); Tel Qashish (Ben-Tor and Bonfil 2003, figs. 104.5, 112.6); Hazor I (Yadin et al. 1958, pl. CV.9); Hazor II (Yadin et al. 1960, pl. CXVIII.11); Megiddo II (Loud 1948, pl. 65.15); Beth Shean III (Panitz-Cohen 2009, pl.15.2, 23); Tel Yinʿam (Liebowitz 2003, fig. 20.1).
10	225	2243	12-587	BLVIb	26.33–26.21	Clay: brown and brown-yellow; core: brown-green; grits.	
11	225	2220/4		BLVIb	26.55–26.28	Clay: brown; core: gray; red paint traces on the outside.	Tel Miqne-Ekron (Killebrew 1999a, fig. III.III.1.13).
12	225	2234/3		BLVII	26.50–26.19	Clay: brown; core: gray; a red painted decoration on the rim and a red cross decoration inside the bowl.	
13	225	2263	12-569	BLVII	26.26–26.10	Clay: brown-green; grits; a brown wavy paint decoration from the rim to carination.	Tel Yinʿam (Liebowitz 2003, fig. 21.6).

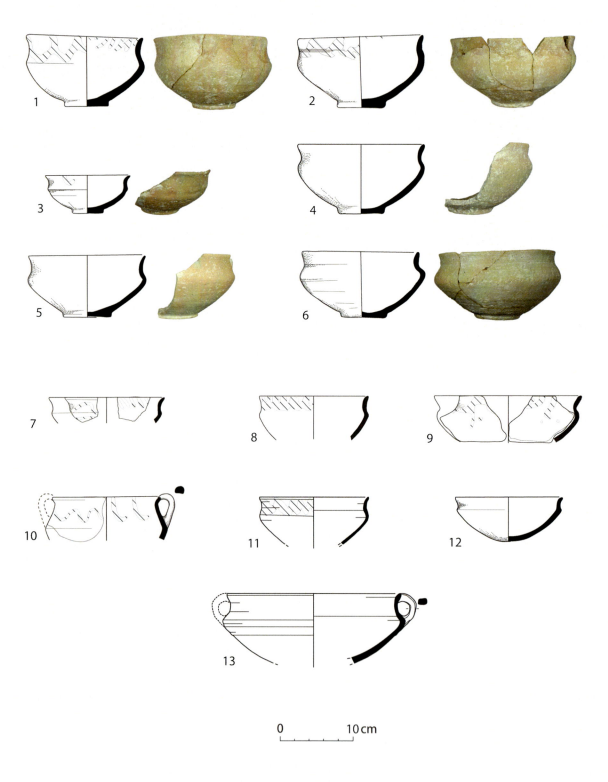

Fig. 25.15. Bowls type BL VIII (Locus 225).

No.	Reg. No.	IAA No.	Type	Level	Description	Parallels
1	2218		BL VIII	26.51–26.46	Clay: light brown; core: gray; a red paint decoration on the rim; grits.	Hazor I (Yadin et al. 1958, pl. LXXXVII.7); Hazor III–IV (Yadin et al. 1961, pl. CCLXXII.27); Yoqne'am III (Ben-Ami 2005, fig. III.18.34).
2	2227/1		BL VIII	26.47–26.36	Clay: brown/pink-brown; core: greenish-gray; a red paint decoration outside the rim.	Yoqne'am III (Ben-Ami 2005, fig. III.8.2), Hazor I (Yadin et al. 1958, pls. LXXXV.14); Megiddo III (Ilan, Hallote, and Cline 2000, fig. 9.14.4).
3	2149/1		BL VIII	26.69	Clay: brown; core: dark gray; grits.	Yoqne'am III (Ben-Ami 2005, fig. III.24.10).
4	2174		BL VIII	26.46–26.43	Clay: brown gray; core: gray.	Yoqne'am III (Ben-Ami 2005, fig. III.18.34); Hazor I (Yadin et al. 1958, pl. XC.2).
5	2193		BL VIII	26.55–26.51	Clay: light brown; core: gray; grits.	Yoqne'am III (Ben-Ami 2005, fig. III.18.35); Hazor I (Yadin et al. 1958, pl. LXXXV.16).
6	2180	12-567	BL VIII	26.58–26.54	Clay: brown-greenish; core: brown; grits.	Tel Qashish (Ben-Tor and Bonfil 2003, fig. 130.10); Yoqne'am III (Ben-Ami 2005, fig. III.18.35).
7	2234	12-636	BL VIII	26.50–26.19	Clay: pink; a red paint decoration.	
8	2234/20		BL VIII	26.50–26.19	Clay: brown-yellow inside and orange outside; core: gray.	
9	2234/10		BL VIII	26.50–26.19	Clay: pink; core: gray-green; a red decoration inside and out.	Tel Yin'am (Liebowitz 2003, fig. 11.4).
10	2077		BL VIII		Clay: pink; core: brown; gray grits; red paint decoration.	
12	2239/1		BL VIII	26.31–26.22	Clay: brown yellow; core: brown-gray; grits.	Yoqne'am III (Ben-Ami 2005, fig. III.18.27).
11	2123		BL VIII	26.86–26.79		
13			BL VIII			

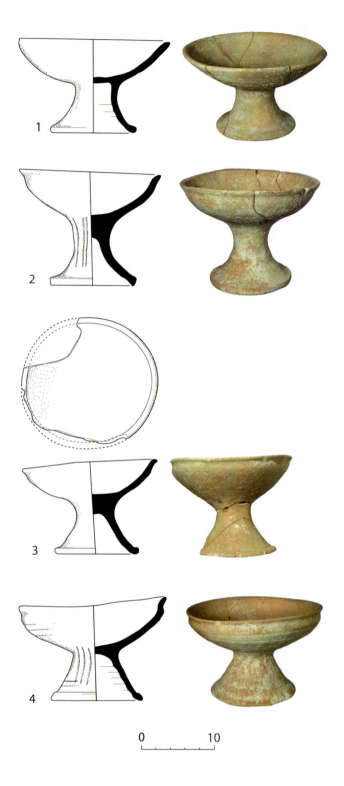

Fig. 25.16. Chalices types CH Ia–b.

No.	Locus No.	Reg. No.	IAA No.	Type	Level	Description	Parallels
1	225	2175	12-576	CH Ia	26.67–26.60	Clay: brown; core: brown, gray at the base; grits.	Hazor II (Yadin et al. 1960, pl. CXXIX.19); Tell Deir 'Alla (Franken 1992, fig. 5-3.10); Tell Abu-Hawam (Balensi 1980, pl. 8.5).
2	225	2264		CH Ib	27.08–26.93		Tell Abu-Hawam (Balensi 1980, pl. 8.7).
3	226	2082		CH Ib	28.53		Megiddo II (Loud 1948, pl. 74.17).
4	225	2205	12-575	CH Ib	26.66–26.45	Clay: brown; core: gray; grits.	Yoqne'am III (Ben-Ami 2005, fig. III.18.39); Tel Nami (Yoselevich 2004, pl. 1.10).

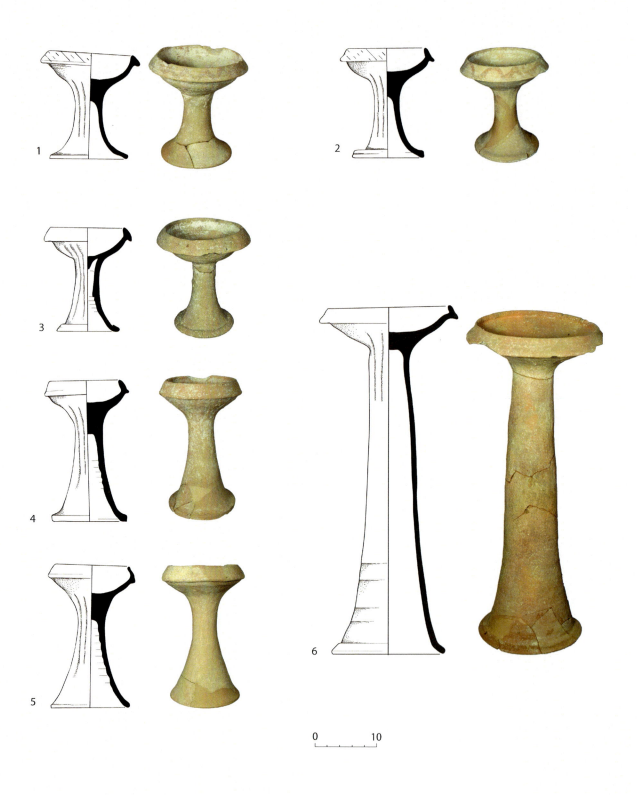

Fig. 25.17. Chalices types CH IIa–c, III.

No.	Locus No.	Reg. No.	IAA No.	Type	Level	Description	Parallels
1	219	2093	12-574	CH IIa	27.17–26.98	Clay: pink; core: light brown; grits; a red paint decoration on the rim.	Tel Mevorakh (Stern 1984, fig. 1.23); Tell Abu Hawam (Yoselevich 2004, pl. 2.4).
2	225	2232	12-550	CH IIb	26.44–26.37		Tel Nami (Yoselevich 2004, pl. 2.1); Megiddo II (Loud 1948, pl. l.72.12; Grutz 2007, fig. 7.3.1.2).
3	225	2258	12-551	CH IIb	26.26–26.19	Clay: brown-green; core: gray; grits.	Yoqne'am III (Ben-Ami 2005, fig. III.14.20); Megiddo Tombs (Guy and Engberg 1938, pl. 60.30; Grutz 2007, fig. 4.5.5); Tel Nami (Yoselevich 2004, pl. 1.6); Tell Deir 'Alla (Franken 1992, fig. 5-13.8).
4	219	2103	12-547	CH IIc	27.05–26.92	Clay: brown; core: gray; grits.	Tel Nami (Yoselevich 2004, pl. 1.4); Tel Yin'am (Liebowitz 2003, fig. 27.2).
5	225	2113	12-548	CH IIc	27.08–26.93	Clay: brown-pink; core: gray.	
6	225	2112	12-624	CH III	27.01–26.78	Clay: brown; core: dark gray.	Pella (Grutz 2007, fig. 8.1.1.8); Tell Abu Hawam (Yoselevich 2004, pl. 2.7).

Fig. 25.18. Goblets types GO I–IV.

No.	Locus No.	Reg. No.	IAA No.	Type	Level	Description	Parallels
1	219	2109		GO I	27.27–27.15	Clay: pink; core: light brown; grits.	
2	225	2171	12-594	GO II	26.58–26.57	Clay: gray and brown-green; core: gray and brown grits and medium–large-sized white grits.	Tell Deir 'Alla (Franken 1992, fig. 3-7.10).
3	225	2070/1	12-597	GO III		Clay: light brown; core: gray; grits.	Megiddo II (Loud 1948, pl. 72.10); Tell Deir 'Alla (Franken 1992, figs. 4-15.17, 4-20.6).
4	225	2214		GO III	26.44–26.38	Clay: brown; core: dark gray; a red-paint decoration inside and on the rim.	Megiddo II (Loud 1948, pl. 72.10); Tell Deir 'Alla (Franken 1992, figs. 4-14.14; 4-15.17, 18).
5	219	2100	12-552	GO IV	27.25–26.92	Clay: pink; core: gray; a red and black paint decoration.	
6	219	2130	12-598	GO IV	27.09–26.98	Clay: pink; core: light gray; grits; a brown-paint decoration outside and a red-paint (zigzag) decoration on the rim.	

Fig. 25.19. Goblets types GO V–VI.

No.	Locus No.	Reg. No.	IAA No.	Type	Level	Description	Parallels
1	225	2161	12-615	GO V	26.65–26.52	Clay: light orange; core: light gray; a red paint decoration.	Lachish II (Tufnell, Inge, and Harding 1940, pl. XLVII.220); Tel Mevorakh (Stern 1984, fig. 7.2); Hazor I (Yadin et al. 1958, pl. XC.5–6).
2	219	2106	12-614	GO VI	27.09–26.98	Clay: light brown–brown yellow; core: brown-green; and white and brown grits.	Tell Kazel (Badre and Gubel 1999–2000, figs. 16.a, 17.b).
3	225	2162	12-612	GO VI	26.72–26.47	Clay: brown-pink; grits.	
4	225	2242	13-13	GO VI	26.35–26.23	Clay: light brown–yellow; core: gray-yellow; grits.	Tell Deir 'Alla (Franken 1992, fig. 4-15.20).
5	225	2224	13-4	GO VI	26.38–26.31	Clay: brown-yellow; core: yellow-gray; grits.	Hazor I (Yadin et al. 1958, pl. LXXXV.10); Hazor III–IV (Yadin et al. 1961, pl. CCLXXIII.19).
6	225	2251	12-572	GO VI	26.28–26.19	Clay: light brown-pink; grits.	

356 Salvage Excavations at Tel Qashish (Tell Qasis) and Tell el-Wa'er (2010–2013)

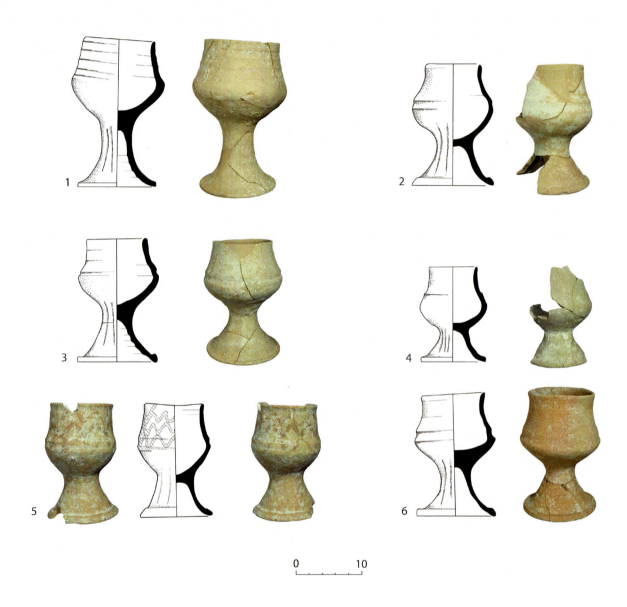

Fig. 25.20. Goblets type GO VI (cont.).

No.	Locus No.	Reg. No.	IAA No.	Type	Level	Description	Parallels
1	225	2234/1	12-571	GO VI	26.50–26.19	Clay: pink; core: green; grits.	Hazor I (Yadin et al. 1958, pl. CXXVIII.4); Tell Deir 'Alla (Franken 1992, fig. 4-15.20).
2	219	2105		GO VI	27.28–27.19	Clay: brown-orange; core: gray; grits.	Tell Kazel (Badre and Gubel 1999–2000, fig.16.c); Hazor III–IV (Yadin et al. 1961, pl. CCLXXX.6).
3	219	2101	12-613	GO VI	27.17–26.13	Clay: brown-yellow; core: light brown; grits; a paint decoration outside.	
4	225	2234/7		GO VI	26.50–26.19	Clay: brown-pink; core: light gray; brown grits.	Tell Kazel (Badre and Gubel 1999–2000, fig.16.c); Hazor III–IV (Yadin et al. 1961, pl. CCLXXX.6).
5	225	2185	12-616	GO VI	26.57–26.42	Clay: light orange–pink; core: light gray; a red and brown paint geometric decoration.	Lachish II (Tufnell, Inge, and Harding 1940, pl. XLVII.227); Tell Deir 'Alla (Franken 1992, fig. 4-15.20).
6	225	2140	12-602	GO VI	26.77–26.64	Clay: brown; core: light brown; grits.	

358 Salvage Excavations at Tel Qashish (Tell Qasis) and Tell el-Wa'er (2010–2013)

Fig. 25.21. Goblets types GO VI (cont.), VII.

No.	Locus No.	Reg. No.	IAA No.	Type	Level	Description	Parallels
1	225	2196	12-596	GO VI	26.52–26.40	Clay: brown-pink; core: brown yellow; grits; red paint.	
2	219	2092	12-600	GO VI	27.29–27.13	Clay: brown; grits.	Tell Deir 'Alla (Franken 1992, fig. 3-7.9).
3	225	2139	12-595	GO VI	26.72–26.54	Clay: brown; black; grits.	
4	219	2119	13-3	GO VII	27.16–27.06	Clay: brown; core: gray and black; grits; a red paint decoration on the rim (zigzag) and base (lines).	Tell Deir 'Alla (Franken 1992, fig. 4-14.12).
5	219	2104	12-599	GO VII	27.13–27	Very well-levigated; clay: buff; core: buff.	

360 Salvage Excavations at Tel Qashish (Tell Qasis) and Tell el-Wa'er (2010–2013)

Fig. 25.22. Human-head goblet, restored (Locus 225).

No.	Reg. No.	IAA No.	Type	Level	Description	Parallels
1	2200	12-573	GO VIII	26.56		

Fig. 25.23. Human-head goblet fragment prior to restoration.

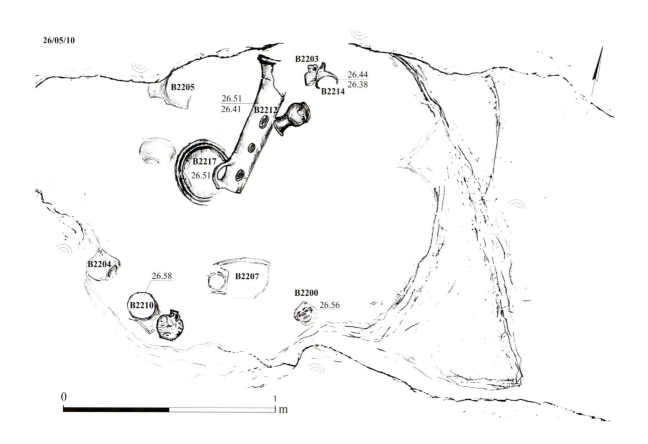

Fig. 25.24. Drawing of the vessels at the bottom of the repository cave.

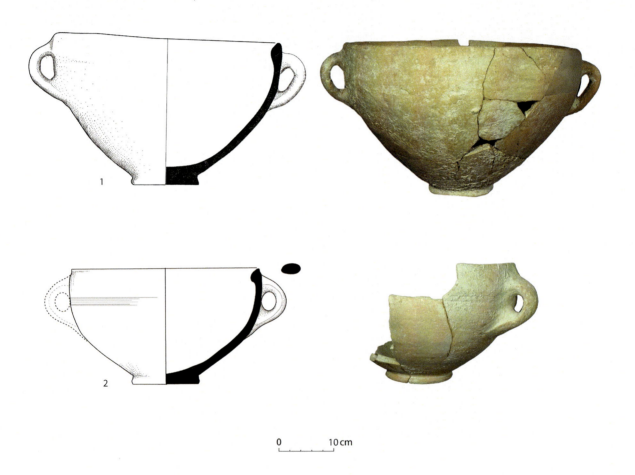

Fig. 25.25. Kraters type K Ia (Locus 225).

No.	Reg. No.	IAA-No	Type	Level	Description	Parallels
1	2210	12-631	K Ia	26.58–26.45	Clay: green-buff; core: light gray.	Tell Abu Hawam (Artzy 2007, fig. 9).
2	2166		K Ia	26.73–26.64	Clay: pink; core: light gray.	Tell Abu Hawam (Artzy 2007, fig. 9).

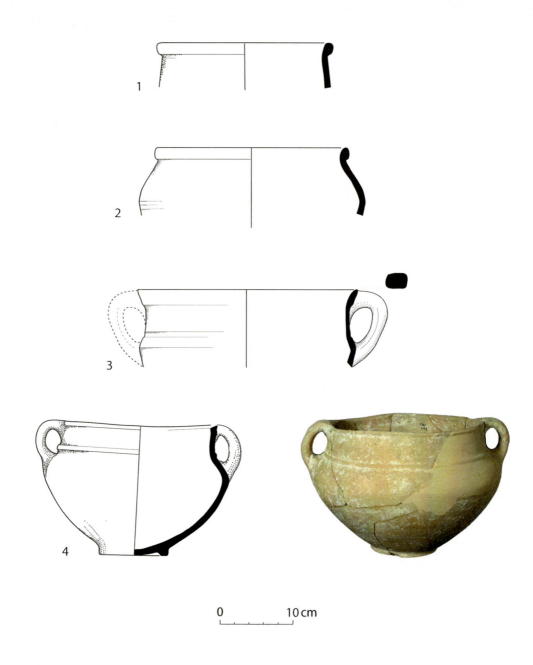

Fig. 25.26. Kraters types K Ib, II.

No.	Reg. No.	IAA No.	Type	Level	Description	Parallels
1	2026		K Ib		Clay: orange, core: gray-green; gray and brown grits.	
2	2153/1		K Ib	26.84–26.47	Clay; brown-pink; core: gray.	Deir El-Balah (Killebrew 2010, fig. 4.1.4); Megiddo III (Ilan, Hallote, and Cline 2000, fig. 9.11.1, 7); Megiddo II (Loud 1948, pl. 69.11); Tell Qasile (Mazar 1985, figs. 27.10, 44.29, 45.21); Beth Shean (James and McGovern 1993, fig. 43.4).
3	2256		K II	26.32–26.00	Clay: pink-yellow; core: gray.	
4	2167	12-632	K II	26.57–26.53		Hazor V (Ben-Tor et al. 1997, fig. II.18.27); Hazor I (Yadin et al. 1958, pl. XCIX.5); Hazor II (Yadin et al. 1960, pls. CXIX.4); Hazor III–IV (Yadin et al. 1961, pl. CCLXXX.10); Tel Qashish (Ben-Tor and Bonfil 2003, fig. 108.8); Tell Kazel (Badre and Gubel 1999–2000, fig. 17a); Dan II (Biran, Ben-Dov, and Arensburg 2002, fig. 2.54.14).

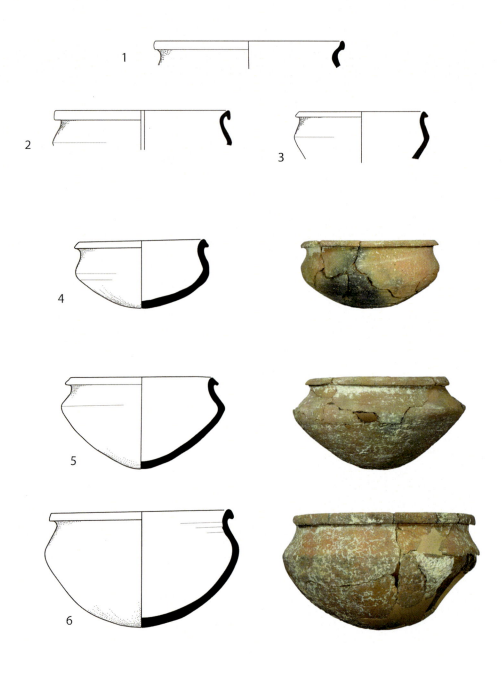

Fig. 25.27. Cooking pots.

No.	Locus No.	Reg. No.	IAA No.	Type	Level	Description	Parallels
1	225	2073		CP I		Clay: brown-orange; core: gray.	Dan II (Biran, Ben-Dov, and Arensburg 2002, fig. 2.55.17); Yoqne'am III (Ben-Ami 2005, fig. IV.10.3); Tel Qashish (Bonfil 2003, fig. 119.1–2).
2	225	2179		CP IIa	26.72–26.57	Clay: brown-orange; core: brown yellow; grits; soot traces.	Miqne-Ekron (Killebrew 1999b, fig. 1.1).
3	225	2056		CP IIb		Clay: dark brown; core: gray; grits.	
4	219	2098	12-589	CP IIb	27.31–27.14	Clay: brown; core: brown.	Yoqne'am III (Ben-Ami 2005, figs. III.8.18, III.14.28); Tel Qashish (Ben-Tor and Bonfil 2003, fig. 112.18).
5	225	2217	12-565	CP IIb	26.55–26.39	Clay: brown; core: dark gray–black; grits.	Yoqne'am III (Ben-Ami 2005, figs. III.16.20; III.19.15, 16; III.23.14; III.24.14); Tel Qashish (Ben-Tor and Bonfil 2003, fig. 128.1); Hazor II (Yadin et al. 1960, pl. CXLII.1); Tell Kazel (Barde and Gubel 1999–2000, fig. 17g); Tel Yin'am (Liebowitz 2003, fig. 31.7).
6	225	2234/4		CP IIb	26.50–26.19	Clay: brown; core: brown gray.	Tell Kazel (Badre and Gubel 1999–2000, fig. 17g); Tel Qashish (Ben-Tor and Bonfil 2003, fig.130.15); Yoqne'am III (Ben-Ami 2005, fig. III.14.28), Hazor I (Yadin et al. 1958, pls. CXXXIX.18); Hazor III–IV (Yadin et al. 1961, pl. CCLXV.5).

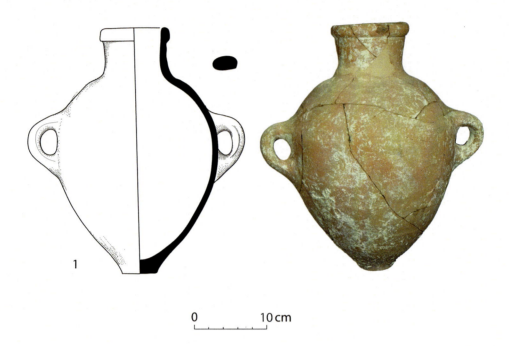

Fig. 25.28. Storage jar type SJ I (Locus 225).

No.	Reg. No.	IAA No.	Type	Level	Description	Parallels
1	2262	12-564	SJ I	26.18–26.07	Clay: brown; core: brown and black at the base.	Tel Qashish (Ben-Tor and Bonfil 2003, fig.112.20); Tell Abu Hawam (Anati 1959, fig. 7.5); Lachish II (Tufnell, Inge, and Harding 1940, pl. LVII.390, 391).

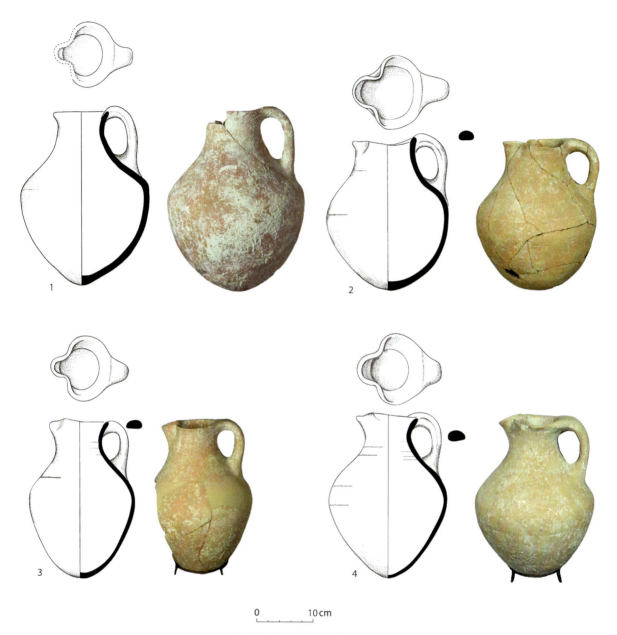

Fig. 25.29. Jugs type J Ia (Locus 225).

No.	Reg. No.	IAA No.	Type	Level	Description	Parallels
1	2116		J Ia	26.98–26.73	Clay: light brown-orange; core: light gray.	Hazor II (Yadin et al. 1960, pl. CXXXII.7); Beth Shean III (Panitz-Cohen 2009, pl. 2.6).
2	2099	12-562	J Ia	26.90–26.69	Clay: brown; core: dark gray; grits.	Yoqneʿam III (Ben-Ami 2005, fig. III.15.12); Tell Kazel (Badre and Gubel 1999–2000, fig. 38.g).
3	2206		J Ia	26.59–26.49	Clay: brown; core: brown-gray.	Hazor I (Yadin et al. 1958, pls. XC.10, CVIII.5); Tel Mevorakh (Stern 1984, fig. 8.5).
4	2155	12-563	J Ia	26.84–26.63	Clay: pink; grits.	Hazor I (Yadin et al. 1958, pl. CVIII.6); Hazor II (Yadin et al. 1960, pl. CXXXII.10).

370 Salvage Excavations at Tel Qashish (Tell Qasis) and Tell el-Wa'er (2010–2013)

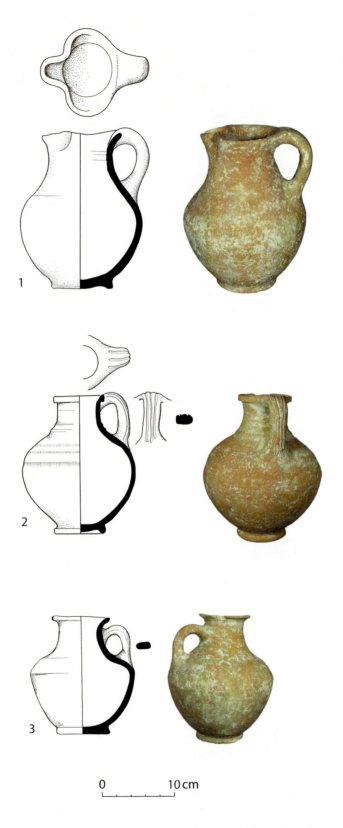

Fig. 25.30. Jugs types J Ib, II–III (Locus 225).

No.	Reg. No.	IAA-No	Type	Level	Description	Parallels
1	2187	12-553	J Ib	26.62–26.59	Clay: brown; grits.	Tell Kazel (Badre and Gubel 1999–2000, figs. 43.f, 46.d); Megiddo II (Loud 1948, pl. 59.1); Tel Yin'am (Liebowitz 2003, fig. 12.2).
2	2157	12-618	J II	26.71–26.52	Clay: brown orange; core: gray.	Tel Qashish (Ben-Tor and Bonfil 2003, fig.105.5).
3	2165	12-619	J III	26.56–26.43	Clay: brown–yellow; core: gray.	

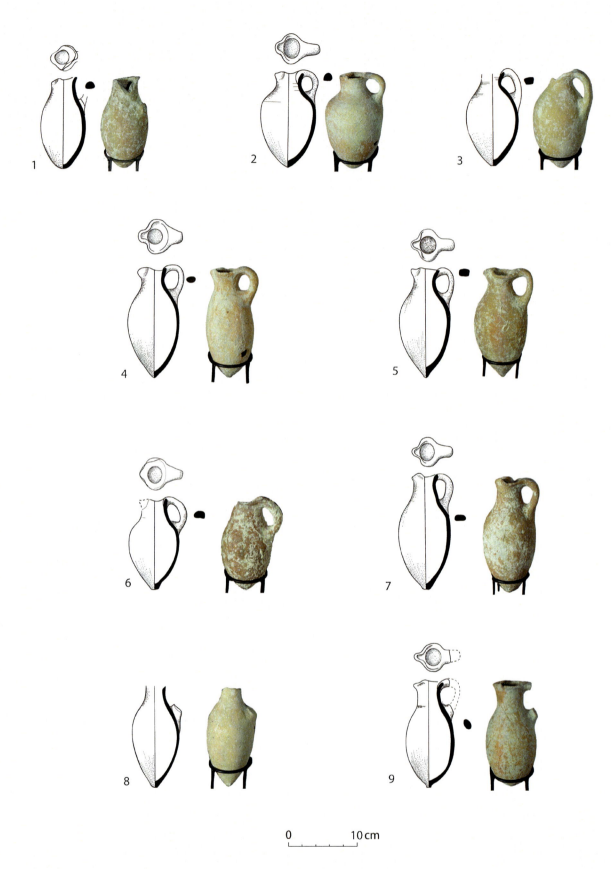

Fig. 25.31. Juglets.

No.	Locus No.	Reg. No.	IAA No.	Type	Level	Description	Parallels
1	225	2238		JT Ia	26.34–26.27	Clay: brown; core: gray.	Hazor II (Yadin et al. 1960, pl. CXXXI.15).
2	225	2186	12-581	JT Ia	26.65–26.59	Clay: light brown–light brown pink.	Hazor I (Yadin et al. 1958, pls. XCVI.17, CXXXIV.2); Hazor II (Yadin et al. 1960, pl. CXX.9); Hazor III–IV (Yadin et al. 1961, pl. CCLXXXI.9).
3	225	2247		JT Ia	26.27–26.20	Clay: light brown; core: light brown.	Hazor II (Yadin et al. 1960, pl. CXXXI.4).
4	219	2091	12-579	JT Ib	27.27–27.20	Clay: brown-pink; core: brown; white grits.	Hazor I (Yadin et al. 1958, pls. CVIII.10, CXXXIV.3); Hazor II (Yadin et al. 1960, pl. CXX.6); Hazor III–IV (Yadin et al. 1961, pl. CCLXXXI.5); Deir El-Balah (Dothan 1979, p. 55, fig. 125 [Tomb 118]); Killebrew 2010, fig. 4.4.8).
5	225	2173	12-620	JT Ib	26.59–26.54	Clay: brown-orange.	Hazor II (Yadin et al. 1960, pl.CXX.4); Aphek-Antipatris II (Gadot 2009, fig. 8.8.1); Tell Abu Hawam (Anati 1959, fig. 7.8); Deir El-Balah (Killebrew 2010, fig. 4.4.2).
6	225	2257		JT Ic	26.25–26.18	Clay: brown; core: gray.	Hazor II (Yadin et al. 1960, pl. CXXXI.16).
7	225	2178	12-582	JT Ic	26.55–26.43	Clay: brown.	Hazor III–IV (Yadin et al. 1961, pl. CCLXXV.5).
8	225	2211		JT Ic	26.43–26.37	Clay: brown-pink; core: green-brown.	Aphek-Antipatris II (Gadot 2009, fig. 8.8.2); Hazor II (Yadin et al 1960, pl. CXXXI.17); Deir El-Balah (Dothan 1979, ills. 23, 26).
9	219	2095		JT Ic	27.32–27.24	Clay: brown-orange; core: green.	Hazor III–IV (Yadin et al. 1961, pl. CCLXXV.5).

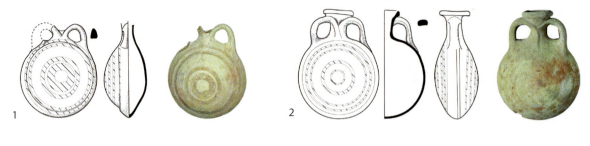

Fig. 25.32. Flasks.

No.	Locus No.	Reg. No.	IAA No.	Type	Level	Description	Parallels
1	225	2135	12-555	FL I	26.68–26.61	Clay: red; light slip with brown concentric circles.	Aphek-Antipatris II (Gadot 2009, fig. 8.9.10); Hazor II (Yadin et al. 1960, pl. CXXX.13); Lachish II (Tufnell, Inge, and Harding 1940, pl. LIV B.349).
2	226	2080	12-640	FL II	28.50–28.43	Clay: green; fragments of red concentric circles.	Yoqneʿam III (Ben-Ami 2005, figs. III.24.27, IV.21.3); Hazor II (Yadin et al. 1960, pl. CXXX.12); Dan II (Biran, Ben-Dov, and Arensburg 2002, fig. 2.61.67); Tel Yinʿam (Liebowitz 2003, fig. 47.7).

Fig. 25.33. Cup and saucer (Locus 219).

No.	Reg. No.	IAA No.	Type	Level	Description	Parallels
1	2128	12-592	CS I	27.09–26.96	Clay: light brown–pink; core: brown; grits.	Beth Shean (James and McGovern 1993, fig. 18.16); Tel Yinʿam (Liebowitz 2003, fig. 42.6).
2	2121	12-593	CS I	27.13–27.01	Clay: brown-yellow; core: gray; gray grits.	Tell Qasile (Mazar 1985, fig. 45.2); Megiddo II (Loud 1948, pl. 67.7, 70.15).

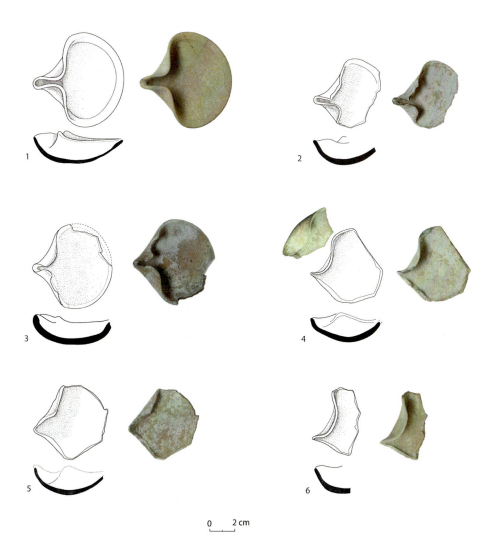

Fig. 25.34. Lamps type LP Ia (Locus 225).

No.	Reg. No.	IAA No.	Type	Level	Description	Parallels
1	2184	12-634	LP Ia	26.59–26.54	Clay: pink; grits.	Aphek-Antipatris II (Gadot 2009, fig. 8.13.4); Tell Kazel (Badre and Gubel 1999–2000, fig. 23.b); Dan II (Biran, Ben-Dov, and Arensburg 2002, fig. 2.61.75).
2	2237	13-5	LP Ia	26.38–26.26		Hazor II (Yadin et al. 1960, pl. CCLXXV.14).
3	2223	13-6	LP Ia	26.55–26.42		Tell Kazel (Badre and Gubel 1999–2000, fig. 23.f); Hazor II (Yadin et al. 1960, pl. CCXCIII.12).
4	2261		LP Ia	26.28–26.19	Clay: light brown–yellow; grits.	
5	2228		LP Ia	26.47–26.44	Clay: brown; core: brown.	Hazor I (Yadin et al. 1958, pl. CX.1).
6	2183		LP Ia	26.59–26.55	Clay: brown-yellow; core: light gray; grits.	

Fig. 25.35. Lamps type LP Ia (cont.), Ib (Locus 225).

No.	Reg. No.	IAA No.	Type	Level	Description	Parallels
1	2141		LP Ia	26.75–26.66	Clay: brown; core: gray-black.	Hazor I (Yadin et al. 1958, pls. XC.11, CXXV.23, CXLV.10); Hazor II (Yadin et al. 1960, pl. CCXL.8).
2	2254	12-635	LP Ib	26.19	Clay: brown; core: brown-gray.	Hazor II (Yadin et al. 1960, pl. CXXXV.2); Aphek-Antipatris II (Gadot 2009, fig. 8.13.4).
3	2204		LP Ib	26.71–26.64	Clay: brown; core: gray; gray and brown grits.	

25. A Late Bronze Age II Cultic Repository near Tel Qashish in the Jezreel Valley, Israel

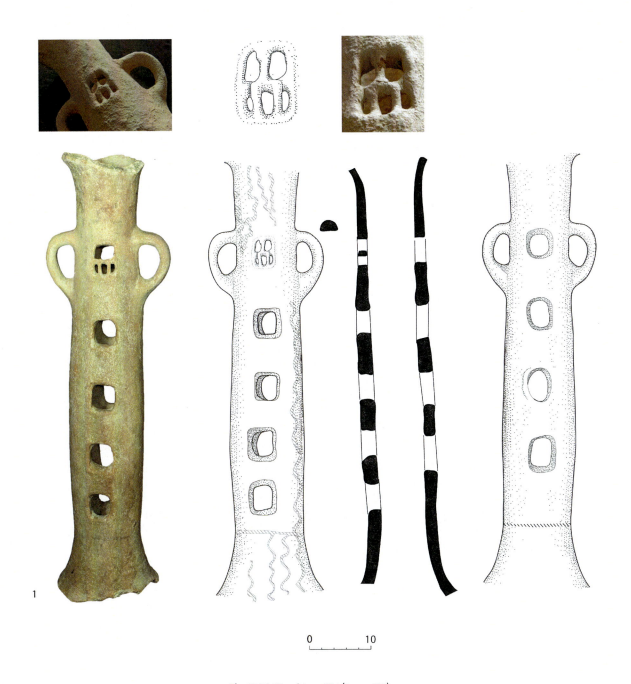

Fig. 25.36. Stand type ST I (Locus 225).

No.	Reg. No.	IAA No.	Type	Level	Description	Parallels
1	2111	12-627	ST I	27.18–26.91	Clay: brown–brown gray; core: gray; red decoration.	Beth Shean (Rowe 1940, pl. XIV.2).

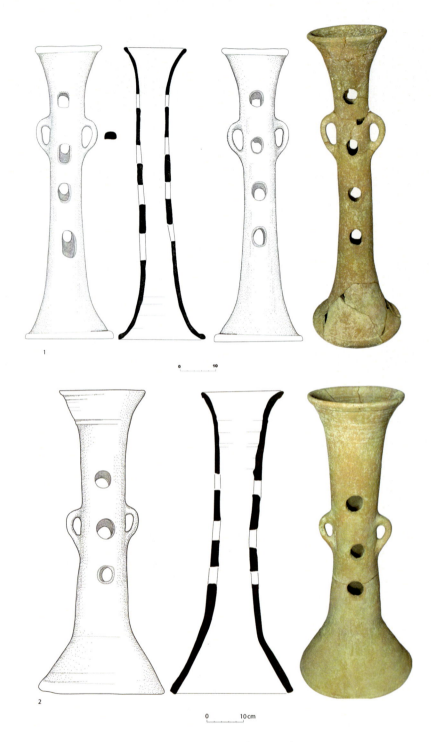

Fig. 25.37. Stands type ST II (Locus 225).

No.	Reg. No.	IAA No.	Type	Level	Description
1	2212	12-630	ST II	26.52–26.41	Clay: brown-gray; core: gray.
2	2107	12-629	ST II	27.01–26.78	Clay: brown-buff; core: gray; grits.

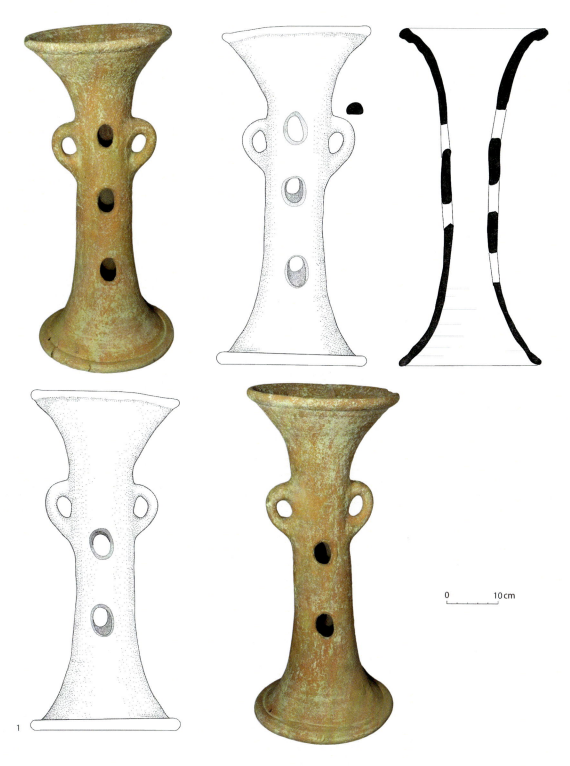

Fig. 25.38. Stand type St II (cont.) (Locus 225).

No.	Reg. No.	IAA No.	Type	Level	Description	Parallels
1	2094	12-628	ST II	27.00–26.69	Clay: brown-orange; core: gray; grits.	Beth Shean (Rowe 1940, pl. XVII.8).

Fig. 25.39 (this page and adjacent). Stands type ST III (Locus 225).

25. A Late Bronze Age II Cultic Repository near Tel Qashish in the Jezreel Valley, Israel 381

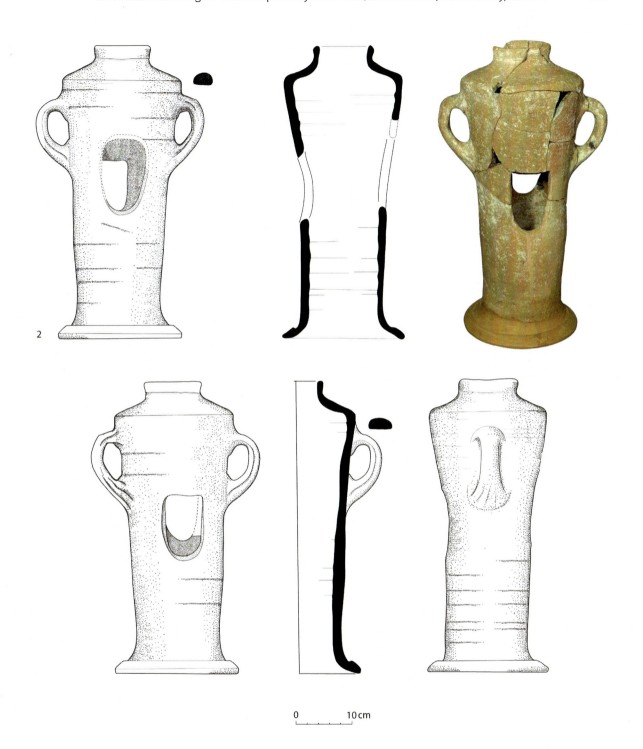

No.	Reg. No.	IAA No.	Type	Level	Description	Parallels
1	2260	12-625	ST III	26.32–26.22	Clay: brown; core: black.	Beth Shean (Rowe 1940, pls. XV.2, 4; LXA.1, 2; LXIA.4; LXIIA.4).
2	2245	12-626	ST III	26.36–26.19	Clay: pink; core: dark gray; grits.	Beth Shean (Rowe 1940, pls. XV.3; LIXA.1, 2; LXIA.1, 2).

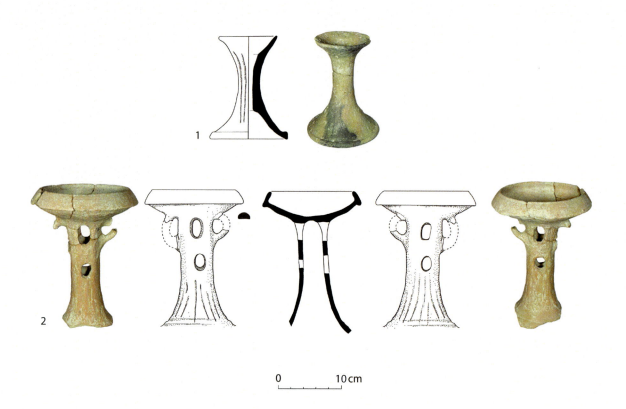

Fig. 25.40. Stand type ST IV and incense burner (Locus 225).

No.	Reg. No.	IAA No.	Type	Level	Description	Parallels
1	2226	12-577	ST IV	26.38–26.28	Clay: pink/white- buff; core: gray.	Tell Abu Hawam (Anati 1959, fig. 8.17, 18).
2	2189	12-549	IB	26.62–26.54	Clay: brown-pink; core: gray; grits.	Yoqneʻam III (Ben-Ami and Livneh 2005, fig. IV.21.9).

25. A Late Bronze Age II Cultic Repository near Tel Qashish in the Jezreel Valley, Israel

Fig. 25.41. Mycenaean pottery: Piriform jar and flasks (Locus 225).

No.	Vessel	Reg. No.	IAA No.	Type	Level	Parallels
1	Piriform jar	2142	12-560	FS 48 Myc IIIB1	26.78–26.65	Amman (Hankey 1974, fig. 2.8).
2	Flask	2199	12-557	FS 189 Myc IIIA2 late	26.55–26.46	Amman (Hankey 1974, fig. 8.96).
3	Flask	2192	12-559	FS 192, LH IIIb?	26.61–26.39	Tell Deir 'Alla (Franken 1992, fig. 4-20.15); Hazor II (Yadin et al. 1960, pl. CXXXVII.7, 8).

Fig. 25.42. Mycenaean pottery: Stirrup jars (Locus 225).

No.	Vessel	Reg. No.	IAA No.	Type	Level	Parallels
1	Stirrup jar	2134	12-556	FS 166, FM 19, motif multiple stem curved.	26.89–26.75	Tel Yin'am (Hankey 2003, fig. 33.3, photo 5.1).
2	Stirrup jar	2115	12-561	FS 178, 180 Squat stirrup jar, FM 18 motif—flower on shoulders, FM 48.	26.97–26.74	Tel Yin'am (Hankey 2003, fig. 38.1); Deir El-Balah (Dothan and Nahmias-Lotan 2010, fig. 7.1.3).
3	Stirrup jar	2147	13-7	FS 171	26.67–26.51	Deir El-Balah (Dothan and Nahmias-Lotan 2010, fig. 7.1.2); Ras Shamra-Ugarit (Hirschfeld 2000, cat. No. 138–140).
4	Stirrup jar	2146	12-558	FS 178?	26.68–26.59	

386 Salvage Excavations at Tel Qashish (Tell Qasis) and Tell el-Wa'er (2010–2013)

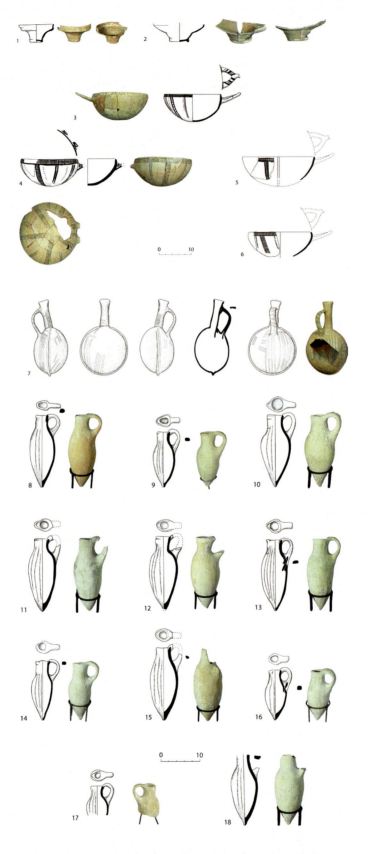

Fig. 25.43. Cypriot pottery.

No.	Vessel	Reg. No.	IAA No.	Level	Parallels
1	Base-Ring II Y-shaped bowl	2117/1	12-570	27.13–26.86	Bergoffen, ch. 27, this volume.
2	Base-Ring II Y-shaped bowl	2246/1		26.32–26.20	Bergoffen, ch. 27, this volume.
3	White-Slip II bowl	2118	12-590	27.12–27.07	Bergoffen, ch. 27, this volume.
4	White-Slip II bowl	2144	12-591	26.65	Bergoffen, ch. 27, this volume.
5	White-Slip II bowl	2100	219	27.25–26.92	Bergoffen, ch. 27, this volume.
6	White-Slip II bowl				Bergoffen, ch. 27, this volume.
7	White-Shaved juglet	2120	12-580	27–26.90	Bergoffen, ch. 27, this volume.
8	White-Shaved juglet	2248	12-622	26.28–26.24	Bergoffen, ch. 27, this volume.
9	White-Shaved juglet	2150	12-621	26.68–26.61	Bergoffen, ch. 27, this volume.
10	White-Shaved juglet	2137	13-8	26.87–26.80	Bergoffen, ch. 27, this volume.
11	White-Shaved juglet	2136		26.89–26.79	Bergoffen, ch. 27, this volume.
12	White-Shaved juglet with pierced handle	2249	13-9	26.26–26.18	Bergoffen, ch. 27, this volume.
13	White-Shaved juglet	2232	12-578	26.44–26.37	Bergoffen, ch. 27, this volume.
14	White-Shaved juglet	2151	226	28.48–28.41	Bergoffen, ch. 27, this volume.
15	White-Shaved juglet with pierced handle	2236	13-10	26.39–26.26	Bergoffen, ch. 27, this volume.
16	White-Shaved juglet	2203		26.55–26.51	Bergoffen, ch. 27, this volume.
17	White-Shaved juglet	2168		26.59–26.51	Bergoffen, ch. 27, this volume.
18	Base-Ring II flask	2179	12-554	26.72–26.57	Bergoffen, ch. 27, this volume.

388 Salvage Excavations at Tel Qashish (Tell Qasis) and Tell el-Wa'er (2010–2013)

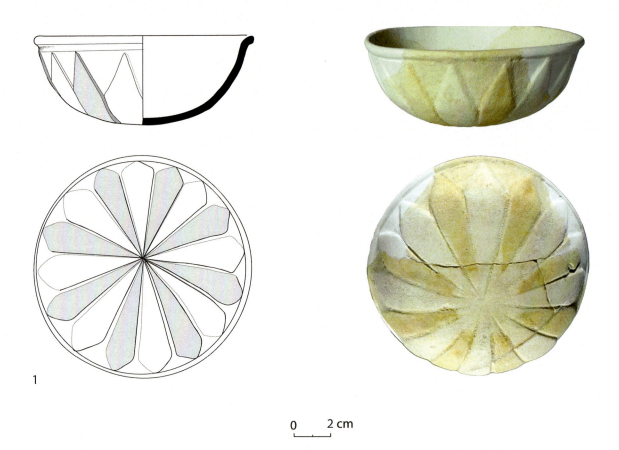

Fig. 25.44. Small faience bowl (Locus 225).

No.	Reg. No.	IAA No.	Level	Parallels
1	2202	12-623	26.39	Tell Kazel (Badre and Gubel 1999–2000, figs. 10.e, 12.I); Beth Shean (Rowe 1940, pl. XXI.31).

25. A Late Bronze Age II Cultic Repository near Tel Qashish in the Jezreel Valley, Israel 389

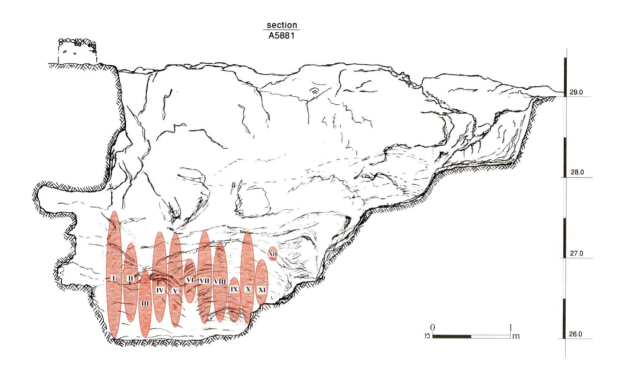

Fig. 25.45. Section of the repository cave showing the height range of the types found in the cache.

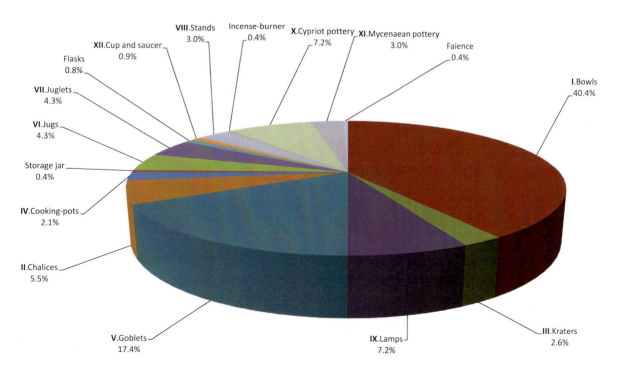

Fig. 25.46. Pie chart showing the numerical distribution of pottery types in the cave's repository.

Table 25.1. List of restored pottery vessels.

No.	Vessel	Type	Locus	Reg. No.	Res.	H. Level	L. Level
1	Goblet	III	219	2070/1			
			219		2070		
			219		2090	27.57	27.13
2	Bowl	IIIb	219	2088		27.49	27.37
			226		2080	28.50	28.43
3	Goblet		219	2090/1		27.57	27.13
			219		2067		
			219		2070		
			219		2090	27.57	27.13
4	Goblet	IV	219	2100		27.25	26.92
			219		2079		
			219		2117	27.13	26.86
			219		2124	27.09	26.86
			225		2133	26.89	26.51
			225		2213	26.71	26.36
5	Goblet	VI	219	2101		27.17	26.13
			219		2070		
			225		2133	26.89	26.51
			225		2153	26.84	26.47
6	Chalice	IIc	219	2103		27.05	26.92
			219		2067		
			225		2182	26.64	26.38
7	Goblet	VII	219	2104		27.13	27.00
			225		2145	26.87	26.73
			225		2163	26.72	26.43
8	Goblet	VI	219	2105		27.28	27.19
			219		2070		
			219		2090	27.57	27.13
9	Goblet	VI	219	2106		27.09	26.98
			226		2080	28.50	28.43
10	Stand	II	225	2107		27.01	26.78
			219		2100	27.25	26.92
			225		2188		26.53
11	Goblet	I	219	2109		27.27	27.15
			219		2124	27.09	26.86

No.	Vessel	Type	Locus	Reg. No.	Res.	H. Level	L. Level
12	Chalice	III	225	2112		27.01	26.78
			219		2100	27.25	26.92
13	Chalice	IIc	225	2113		27.08	26.93
			219		2090	27.57	27.13
14	Bowl	IIIa	225	2114		27.01	26.92
			225		2133	26.89	26.51
15	Mycenaean stirrup jar	FS182	225	2115		26.97	26.74
			219		2090	27.57	27.13
			225		2133	26.89	26.51
16	Bowl	VIa	219	2117/2		27.13	26.86
			225		2123	26.86	26.79
17	Milk bowl		219	2118		27.12	27.07
			219		2098	27.31	27.14
18	Goblet	VII	219	2119		27.16	27.06
			219		2100	27.25	26.92
			219		2117	27.13	26.86
			219		2124	27.09	26.86
19	Cup and saucer		219	2128		27.09	26.96
			219/225		2077		
20	Goblet	IV	219	2130		27.09	26.98
			219		2090	27.57	27.13
			219		2100	27.25	26.92
			219		2124	27.09	26.86
			225		2133	26.89	26.51
			225		2153	26.84	26.47
			225		2182	26.64	26.38
21	Goblet	VI	225	2140		26.77	26.64
			225		2182	26.64	26.38
22	Cypriot milk bowl		225	2144		26.65	26.65
			225		2133	26.89	26.51
			225		2163	26.72	26.43
			225		2182	26.64	26.38
			225		2213	26.71	26.36
23	Bowl	IV	225	2145		26.87	26.73
			225		2153	26.84	26.47

No.	Vessel	Type	Locus	Reg. No.	Res.	H. Level	L. Level
24	Mycenaean globular stirrup jar	FS171	225	2147		26.67	26.51
			219		2100	27.25	26.92
			225		2153	26.84	26.47
25	Bowl	IIa	225	2149		26.69	
			225		2133	26.89	26.51
26	Bowl	IIIc	225	2153/1		26.84	26.47
			225		2099	26.90	26.69
27	Bowl	IV	225	2158		26.71	26.63
			219		2117	27.13	26.86
			219		2124	27.09	26.86
			225		2133	26.89	26.51
28	Krater	Ia	225	2166		26.73	26.64
			219		2122	27.09	26.98
			225		2182	26.64	26.38
29	Goblet	II	225	2171		26.58	26.57
			225		2123	26.86	26.79
30	Bowl	VIII	225	2174		26.46	26.43
			225		2213	26.71	26.36
31	Chalice	Ia	225	2175		26.67	26.6
			225		2153	26.84	26.47
32	Incense burner		225	2189		26.62	26.54
			225		2094	27.00	26.69
33	Bowl	IV	225	2191		26.50	
			225		2153	26.84	26.47
			225		2163	26.72	26.43
			225		2213	26.71	26.36
34	Goblet	VI	225	2196		26.52	26.40
			219		2093	27.17	26.98
			225		2131	26.86	26.79
			225		2153	26.84	26.47
35	Human-head cup	VIII	225	2200		26.56	26.56
			219		2070		
			219		2100	27.25	26.92
			225		2153	26.84	26.47
			225		2190		26.38
36	Faience		225	2202		26.39	26.39
			225		2208	26.43	26.37

No.	Vessel	Type	Locus	Reg. No.	Res.	H. Level	L. Level
			225		2221	26.36	26.33
37	Chalice	Ib	225	2205		26.66	26.45
			225		2133	26.89	26.51
38	Jug	Ia	225	2206		26.59	26.49
			226		2081	28.52	28.48
			225		2153	26.84	26.47
			225		2169	26.64	26.64
			225		2182	26.64	26.38
39	Krater	Ia	225	2210		26.58	26.45
			225		2133	26.89	26.51
			225		2182	26.64	26.38
			225		2213	26.71	26.36
			225		2227	26.47	26.36
			225		2234	26.50	26.19
40	Stand	II	225	2212		26.52	26.41
41	Bowl	VIb	225	2213/1		26.71	26.36
			225		2195	26.58	26.43
42	Goblet	III	225	2214		26.44	26.38
			225		2153	26.84	26.47
43	Cooking pot	IIb	225	2217		26.55	26.39
			225		2127	26.86	26.79
44	Bowl	VIII	225	2218		26.51	26.46
			225		2133	26.89	26.51
45	Goblet	VI	225	2224		26.38	26.31
			225		2133	26.89	26.51
			225		2213	26.71	26.36
			225		2234	26.50	26.19
			225		2227/2	26.47	26.36
46	Goblet	VI	225	2234/1		26.50	26.19
			225		2153	26.84	26.47
			225		2182	26.64	26.38
			225		2213	26.71	26.36
47	Bowl	VII	225	2234/3		26.50	26.19
			225		2207	26.54	26.46
48	Bowl	IIIb	225	2234/5		26.50	26.19
			219		2070		

No.	Vessel	Type	Locus	Reg. No.	Res.	H. Level	L. Level
			225		2227	26.47	26.36
49	Goblet	VI	225	2242		26.35	26.23
			225		2234	26.50	26.19
			225		2240	26.34	26.24
50	Bowl	VIb	225	2243		26.33	26.21
			225		2234	26.50	26.19
51	Goblet		225	2244		26.36	26.21
			225		2256	26.32	26.00
52	Base ring		225	2246/1		26.32	26.20
			225		2213	26.71	26.36
			225		2246	26.32	26.20
53	Goblet	VI	225	2251		26.28	26.19
			225		2234	26.50	26.19
			225		2256	26.32	26.00
54	Chalice	IIb	225	2258		26.26	26.19
			225		2240	26.34	26.24
55	Stand	III	225	2260		26.32	26.22
			225		2212	26.52	26.41
			225		2234	26.50	26.19
			225		2256	26.32	26.00
56	Storage jar	I	225	2262		26.18	26.07
			225		2156	26.69	26.61

Chapter 26

Petrographic Study of Late Bronze Age II Vessels from the Cultic Repository near Tel Qashish

Anat Cohen-Weinberger (*Petrographic Laboratory, Israel Antiquities Authority*)

This study presents petrographic results of the pottery assemblage discovered in a Late Bronze Age repository pit (*favissa*) near Tel Qashish.[1] These objects, bearing cultic characteristics, were apparently used in a not-yet-found nearby cultic place (see Segal, 'Ad and van den Brink, ch. 25, this volume). Studying pottery from a cultic context is of special interest, and a few questions emerged in the process: Did the worshipers bring the vessels with them from their hometowns, or did they acquire them at the cultic place? Where were the workshops located? Next to the cultic place, near Tel Qashish? Were the vessels made especially for cultic purposes, or had these been formerly used as daily life objects? Does a variety of used raw materials suggest that the vessels were made by several workshops? Does highly homogeneous raw material in the cultic assemblage suggest that a single workshop manufactured the vessels, especially, for the cultic place? It is noteworthy that, in an area where limited potential clay sources for pottery are exposed, all workshops had to use the same soil or clay/marl formation, making it hard to distinguish, petrographically, between various workshops. On the other hand, in an area with a variety of potential clay sources, different fabrics can be used and be related to a single workshop (e.g., for different vessel types) or to different workshops.

The provenance of the raw materials used for making the vessels of the cultic place may help to delineate the geographical borders it served or, alternatively, reflect the trade relations and interregional connections of the population it served. The aforementioned scenarios indicate that petrographic study results of cultic assemblages may raise as many questions as they answer, as shown by previous provenience studies of pottery found in cultic repositories and sanctuaries from various periods. One of the examples of such studies in Israel is the Chalcolithic sanctuary in Ein Gedi (Goren 1995). Although there seems to be a general agreement that Ein Gedi served as a regional sanctuary for pilgrimage from close-by and far-away regions (Goren 1995; Ussishkin 2014), the petrographic analysis shows uniformity in the raw material used for the cultic ceramic vessels (Goren 1995, 296). This uniformity was explained as representing a situation where locally made vessels were acquired purposefully as offerings for the shrine by pilgrims that came from remote locations (Goren 1995, 296, but see Goren's [2014] recent view on the function of the site).

A petrographic study of miniature vessels from the Middle Bronze Age II temple at Nahariya suggested that several local fabrics were used (Namdar, Cohen-Weinberger, and Zuckerman 2018). The low quality of Nahariya's vessels indicates that they were made especially as one-time use offerings and not for repeated daily use. Homogeneity of the fabric

---

1. This chapter was submitted in 2013; minor updates were made in 2020.

was also attested within the ceramic objects from the Iron Age repository pit at Yavneh (Ben-Shlomo and Gorzalczany 2010, 150). A study of pottery from the Iron Age Edomite temple in ʿEn Ḥaẓeva suggested high homogeneity in raw materials as well (Cohen-Weinberger 2011, 188). Another pottery study, from a Persian sanctuary at Miẓpe Yammim, indicated that the objects originated in different geographic regions, including remote (Phoenicia) and local (Galilee Mountains) sites (Berlin and Frankel 2012, 25; Shapiro and Berlin 2012, 69). These are only some examples of previous studies dealing with the provenance of cultic assemblages found in different contexts, and they represent varied situations concerning the purchase mechanism of offering objects. These aspects will be examined in the current study by identifying the provenance of the cultic assemblage from the Late Bronze repository near Tel Qashish.

Method

The current study includes sixteen samples taken from the pottery found in the repository, following a naked-eye examination of the whole assemblage leading to the selection of a representative sample for petrographic analysis. The samples include bowls, krater, cooking pot, jugs, jars, a human-head cup, goblets, and stands, all of which underwent petrographic analysis. Imported vessels from Cyprus and Greece, also present in the assemblage, were not included in the current study.

The geological setting of the excavated site is important for the present analysis. The petrographic method is based on the assumption that ancient potters used local clay units and tempers, which must, thus, reflect the geology of the production site (e.g., Arnold 2006). Hence, the fabric of the vessels is compared to the local geological setting of the site. The unknown cultic place that the vessels in the repository belonged to had probably been used by the Late Bronze inhabitants of Tel Qashish and (or) Tel Yoqneʿam, or by other adjacent sites. For this reason, it is necessary to compare the petrographic results to the local raw materials used for pottery in these sites.

Comparative data for the local raw materials used for pottery by the Late Bronze Age inhabitants at Tel Qashish and other adjacent sites are absent. The most relevant available data are the fabrics of the Early Bronze Age pottery from Tel Qashish (Goren 1991; Porat 2003; Cohen-Weinberger, ch. 17, this volume), and perhaps also the Amarna tablets from Yoqneʿam and the fabric of the Iron Age Pottery from Yoqneʿam (Buzaglo 2004; Goren, Finkelstein, and Naʾaman 2004).

Geological Setting

The site is located about 140 m north of Tel Qashish, on the northern bank of the Kishon River that is covered by alluvial sediments derived from the surrounding sedimentary and volcanic rocks. North and northeast of the site, sedimentary rocks, mainly chalk and limestone of the Eocene Adulam, Timrat, and Maresha formations are exposed. These formations are also exposed at Tel Qashish (Sneh, Bartov, and Rosensaft 1998; Sneh, pers. comm. 2012). In a recent archaeological excavation at Qashish, a few meters west of the current site, an Early Bronze site was found lying on basalt bedrock (van den Brink et al., chs. 11 and 13, this volume; Yannai, ch. 12, this volume). The Jezreel Valley southeast of the site is characterized by alluvium and a few Miocene basalt exposures. West of the site, the northeastern flank of Mount Carmel exposes mainly chalk of the Cenomanian Isfye and Arqan formations, dolomite and limestone of the Turonian Bina Formation (Sneh, Bartov, and Rosensaft 1998; Segev, and Sass 2009). Chalk of the Mount Scopus Group is exposed on a hill sloping eastward from Mount Carmel and facing Tel Qashish, on the western side of Road 70. The Mount Carmel sedimentary rocks are accompanied, in several localities, by volcanic intercalations of basalt and tuff (Picard 1956; Sass 1968, 115–16; Bein and Sass 1980). The dominant volcanic rocks are pyroclastic of basic composition and demonstrate undersea explosion (Sass 1980). About 2 km southwest of the site and in Naḥal Raqefet, a Late Cretaceous basaltic flow as well as tuff and spilitic basalts crop out (Segev and Sass 2009). Upper Cretaceous to Paleocene marl and chalk of the Ghareb and Taqiye formations are exposed about 3 km from the site, on the southern slope of Naḥal Yoqneʿam (Segev and Sass 2009). The primary soils in the vicinity of the studied site are brown and light rendzina that develop on the chalk units northeast and east of the site; alluvial brown grumusols in the Kishon River and

26. Petrographic Study of Late Bronze Age II Vessels from the Cultic Repository near Tel Qashish

Table 26.1. Inventory of analyzed vessels.

Sample no.	Locus	Basket	Type	Petrographic group	Fig. no.	Fig. no. in ch. 25, this volume
1	225	2094	Stand with windows	A	26.1	25.38.1
2	219	2100	Goblet decorated with red and black	B	26.3	25.18.5
3	219	2104	Goblet	C	26.4–5	25.21.5
4	219	2106	Small goblet	A		25.19.2
5	225	2127	Bowl	A		25.12.5
6	225	2193	Bowl (carinated)	A	26.2	25.15.5
7	225	2200	Human-face goblet	A		25.22.1
8	225	2206	Jug	A		25.29.3
9	225	2210	Krater	B		25.25.1
10	225	2212	Stand with windows	B		25.37.1
11	225	2217	Cooking pot	D	26.6–7	25.27.5
12		2217/2	Bowl (carinated)	B		25.14.3
13	225	2231	Bowl	E	26.8	25.11.12
14	225	2234/3	Bowl	B		25.14.12
15	225	2245	Stand	B		25.39.2
16	225	2262	Small jar	A		25.28.1

the Jezreel Valley; and terra rossa and rendzina soils on Mount Carmel (Ravikovitch 1969; Dan and Raz 1970; Dan et al. 1975).

Results

The analyzed vessels were divided into five petrographic groups. Members of a petrographic group share similar petrographic properties in clay and tempers. These groups were determined only by the qualities of the raw materials, regardless of the vessel's typology, its chronological affinity, and the geographic location of the site. Thus, this classification into groups serves as an independent method for classifying ceramic assemblages. The proposed origin relies on the mineralogical and lithological properties of the clay and tempers and their suggested geological contexts.

Group A (n=7): This group is characterized by foraminiferous clay with a few silt-sized quartz grains (fig. 26.1). The foraminifera assemblage within the matrix is of Eocene age and includes the planktonic genera *Acarinina, Morzovella, Subbotina, Bulimina,* and *Globorotalites*.[2] Terra rossa soil nodules were added to the calcareous matrix. The nonplastic components (f:c ratio$_{\{0.062mm\}}$≈90/85:10/15) include mainly poorly sorted rounded chalk fragments, a few basalt fragments (fig. 26.2), angular fine quartz grains, micritic and sparitic limestone and tufa fragments, rarely chert fragments, and mollusk shell fragments.[3] The foraminifera in the chalk fragments are of the same genera as those in the matrix. A few discrete fine-sand-sized basalt-derived minerals such as plagioclase, iddingsite, and chlorite appear in the paste. The basalt fragments are usually fine (≈300μm) and are identified as alkali-olivine basalts with alterations to iddingsite and chlorite. The pla-

---

2. Foraminifera determinations were made by Lydia Grossowicz from the Geological Survey of Israel.
3. The f:c ratio expresses the relative proportions of the fine (f) and coarse (c) components of a fabric. In this case, the boundary between these two components is 0.062mm, which is the boundary between silt to sand size (Kemp 1985, 22).

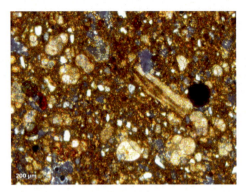

Fig. 26.1. Stand. Petrographic Group A. Foraminiferous clay. ×50, xpl.

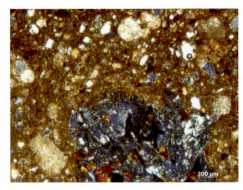

Fig. 26.2. Bowl. Petrographic Group A. Basalt fragment embedded in foraminiferous clay. ×50, xpl.

Fig. 26.3. Goblet. Petrographic Group B. Calcareous clay with silt-sized quartz grains. Basalt fragment and ferruginous nodule with silt-sized quartz grains. ×50, xpl.

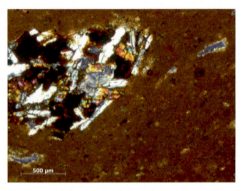

Fig. 26.4. Goblet. Petrographic Group C. Basalt fragment embedded in calcareous clay with fine rounded red opaque iron minerals. ×50, xpl.

gioclase feldspars in some basalt fragments are identified as labradorite, a common plagioclase mineral in the basalts of northern Israel. This raw material was identified as rendzina soil occurring widely on chalky rocks in the Mediterranean climate of Israel (Wieder and Adan-Bayewitz 2002, 397–406). The age of the foraminifera suggests rendzina soil that developed on Eocene chalky rocks. This soil appears locally at the site and along the lower Galilee as well as in Ramot Menashe. The nonplastic components characterized the drainage basin of the Jezreel Valley and the Kishon River and were most probably collected there. The results suggest manufacturing in the very close vicinity of the site, for example, in Tel Qashish, Tel Yoqne'am, or another close site. Two bowls, a small goblet, a human-head cup, a jug, a small jar, and a single stand belong to this group (table 26.1.1, 4–8, 16).

Group B (n=6): This group is characterized by calcareous, optically active clay with about 2–10 percent silt-sized quartz grains (fig. 26.3). A few discrete foraminifera appear in the clay but cannot be clearly identified. Poorly sorted (fine-sand-sized up to 2mm) ferruginous nodules containing silt-sized quartz grains appear in a single bowl and a goblet (table 26.1.2, 14). The nonplastic components (f:c ratio $_{\{0.062mm\}}$ ≈95/90:5/10) consist of mainly rounded to subangular basalt fragments (fig. 26.3) and basalt derived minerals, mainly iddingsite and chlorite. A few chalk and calcrete fragments of up to 2mm appear in the clay. Calcrete is the dominant nonplastic component in a single bowl table 26.1.14). Rarely, mollusk fragments, calcite, sparitic calcite, and chert fragments, and rounded quartz grains (probably quartz geodes) also appeared. Elongated voids, which evidence vanished straw, are attested in the stands (table 26.1.10, 15) and a bowl (table 26.1.14). The raw material of this group was identified as soil. The soil was not identified, but the nonplastic components can be related to the site's close vicinity. Two bowls, one krater, two stands, and a single goblet belong to this group (table 26.1.2, 9–10, 12, 14–15).

26. Petrographic Study of Late Bronze Age II Vessels from the Cultic Repository near Tel Qashish

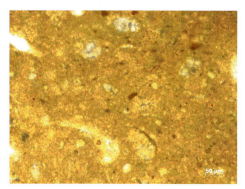

Fig. 26.5. Goblet. Petrographic Group C. Calcareous clay with foraminifera and mollusk fragments. ×100, ppl.

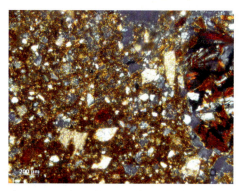

Fig. 26.6. Cooking pot. Petrographic Group D. Basalt fragment embedded in ferruginous silty clay. ×50, xpl.

Fig. 26.7. Cooking pot. Petrographic Group D. crushed calcite fragment embedded in ferruginous silty clay. ×50, xpl.

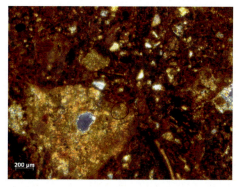

Fig. 26.8. Bowl. Petrographic Group E. Travertine fragment embedded in calcareous clay. ×50, xpl.

Group C (n=1): This group is characterized by light calcareous clay with fine rounded red opaque iron minerals (fig. 26.4). The clay is also characterized by foraminifera and fine mollusk fragments. The foraminifera are very badly preserved, and the genera *Acarinina*, *Textularia*, and *Subbotina* are attested. Other microfossils such as radiolaria and mollusk fragments are also present. The foraminifera assemblage suggests a Paleogene source. The nonplastic components (f:c ratio $_{\{0.062mm\}} \approx 98:2$) consist of a few fine mollusk fragments and, rarely, basalt fragments (figs. 26.4–5). This raw material was identified as marl. The marl of the widely exposed Taqiye Formation is a likely source, although the closest exposures to the site are on the southern slope of Naḥal Yoqneʿam, about 3 km southwest of the site. The presence of nonplastic basalt components posed limitations on the source possibilities and support identifying the exposures to Yoqneʿam's vicinity. A single goblet belongs to this group (table 26.1.3).

Group D (n=1): This group is characterized by ferruginous silty clay (fig. 26.6). The silty fraction consists mainly of quartz grains, but a considerable amount of plagioclase grains is also recognizable. The nonplastic components (f:c ratio $_{\{0.062mm\}} \approx 85:15$) consist of poorly sorted crushed calcite fragments, as well as basalt fragments with alterations to iddingsite and chlorite (figs. 26.6–7). Rarely, fine rounded chalk fragments are also present. The calcite fragments were deliberately added to the paste. The petrographic analysis result points to brown basaltic grumusol as possible raw material. Thus, local production in the area of the Jezreel Valley or the lower Galilee is suggested. A single cooking pot (table 26.1.11) belongs to this group.

Group E (n=1): This group is characterized by calcareous silty (2 percent) clay. The nonplastic components (f:c ratio $_{\{0.062mm\}} \approx 90:10$) consist mainly of tufa fragments and mollusk shell fragments with some basalt fragments (fig. 26.8). Quaternary tufa dominates the lithology of Beth Shean Valley (Schulman 1962; Horowitz 1979, Kronfeld et al. 1988; Shaliv, Mimran, and Hatzor 1991; Hatzor 2000). Previous petrographic studies of pottery from Tell Beth Shean and Tel Reḥov indicated that the clayey units of the tufa-rich Reḥov Formation were widely used for pottery making. The unique combination of tufa and basalt rocks in the Beth Shean Valley is reflected in the thin sections of the vessels made in this valley (e.g., Cohen-Weinberger 1997, 1998, 2009; Cohen-Weinberger and Goren 2011; Mazar, Ziv-Asudri, and Cohen-Weinberger 2000). A single bowl (table 26.1.13) belongs to this group.

In summary, all the analyzed vessels were divided into five petrographic groups (groups A–E). Most of the analyzed vessels (thirteen out of sixteen) belong to group A or group B. This result represents the whole repository assemblage, noted already in the initial naked-eye examination. The vessels of group A were made of rendzina soil and were most likely produced in Tel Qashish or its close vicinity. The raw material of group B vessels was most likely derived from the nearby Kishon River or the Jezreel Valley. Groups C–E are each represented by a single sampled vessel. The raw material of group C was identified as marl of the Taqiye Formation that was probably quarried in the vicinity of Tel Yoqneʻam, but other sites, such as Megiddo, cannot be ruled out as a possible source. The raw material of group D was identified as brown basaltic grumusols that was most likely collected from the Jezreel Valley. The raw material of group E was identified as a unit of the Reḥov Formation exposed in the Beth Shean Valley.

Discussion

The petrographic analyses of the Late Bronze Age vessels from the Tel Qashish repository indicate that the vessels were manufactured from a variety of clay sources. The vessels related to petrographic groups A–D were most likely manufactured in the repository's close vicinity. Their raw material fits, in general, the geology of the Jezreel Valley. A single bowl was made of a raw material (group E) commonly used in Beth Shean during the LB IIB–Iron I (Cohen-Weinberger 2009). This bowl reflects interregional relations between sites located tens of kilometers apart and can be interpreted as an offering brought by a worshiper from the Beth Shean Valley or, alternatively, as a vessel acquired by inhabitants of a close-by site that subsequently offered it in their cultic place.[4]

The initial naked-eye examination of the whole assemblage indicated that groups A–B are seemingly the most common. The petrography shows no correlation between the vessel types and the petrographic groups, and a single type can relate to different groups (table 26.1). Since distinguishing between groups A and B based on naked-eye examination is difficult, a quantitative correlation between a specific type and a petrographic group is not feasible for the whole assemblage. Each of the main petrographic groups (A and B) contains various vessel types. Group A comprises types with an apparent cultic affinity, such as goblets and stands, and vessel types that are common in dwelling assemblages, such as bowls, jugs, and jars. The affinity of the latter to cultic purposes is not yet clear.

Generally, potters used a conservative approach to raw materials due to the economic risks involved in experimenting with new clays. Thus, the use of different raw materials may distinguish potters or workshops from each other and, accordingly, the acquisition of vessels by the worshipers at several local workshops may be considered (Costin 2000, 387–88). Nevertheless, the picture is more complex due to the various factors described below. The pottery assemblage in the cache could present a time span during which a single workshop switched from one raw material to another (Costin 2000, 387). Vessels that required specific technological affinities, such as cooking pots, were made from different raw materials, perhaps in the same workshop, together with other forms. This scenario can explain the raw material observed in the cooking pot sample (group D). However, the cooking pots are negligible in the assemblage. Multiclay sources are also present in domestic assemblages, as reflected by many petrographic studies of pottery. Therefore, the vessels related to groups A–E could have originated in a single adjacent inhabited site, where they may have been previously used.

---

4. The mixed population (Egyptian and Canaanites) of Beth Shean during the Egyptian domination (Mazar 2009) makes interrelations even more interesting. The origin of this bowl in another site within the Beth Shean Valley inhabited by a Canaanite population should also be considered.

However, the multiclay sources and the imported vessels from Greece and Cyprus, together with the occurrence of vessel types such as jars and cooking pots that do not bear cultic affinities, support the interpretation that the vessels were not acquired from a single workshop that locally manufactured the offering vessels specifically for cultic purposes.

Notwithstanding, the pottery assemblage found in the cache, with a high percentage of bowls versus storage jars and cooking pots, is not common in dwelling contexts, and the presence of types such as stands, goblets, and chalices indicates that at least part of the vessels were explicitly made for cultic purposes.

Further information and petrographic data of the daily use vessels from Late Bronze strata at Tel Qashish and other adjacent sites such as Tel Yoqneʻam will contribute to our understanding of this cache.

References

Arnold, Dean E.
2006 "The Threshold Model for Ceramic Resources: A Refinement." In *Ceramic Studies: Papers on the Social and Cultural Significance of Ceramics in Europe and Eurasia from Prehistoric to Historic Times*, edited by Gheorghiu Dragos, 3–9. BARIS 1553. Oxford: Archaeopress.

Bein, Amos, and Eytan Sass
1980 "Geology." In *Atlas of Haifa and Mount Carmel*, edited by Arnon Sofer and Barukh Kipnis, 14–17. Haifa: Applied Scientific Research Co.; University of Haifa.

Ben-Shlomo, David, and Amir Gorzalczany
2010 "Petrographic Analysis." In *Yavneh I: The Excavation of the "Temple Hill" Repository Pit and Cult Stands*, edited by Raz Kletter, Irit Ziffer, and Wolfgang Zwickel, 148–66. OBO 30. Fribourg: Academic Press; Göttingen: Vandenhoeck & Ruprecht.

Berlin, Andrea M., and Rafael Frankel
2012 "The Sanctuary at Mizpe Yammim: Phoenician Cult and Territory in the Upper Galilee during the Persian Period." *BASOR* 366: 25–78.

Buzaglo, Eyal
2004 "Petrographic Investigation of Iron Age Pottery Assemblages from Megiddo and the North." MA thesis, Tel Aviv University.

Cohen-Weinberger, Anat
1997 "The Typology and Petrography of the Egyptian Pottery from Tel Beth Shean in the Light of the Renewed Excavations." MA thesis, Hebrew University of Jerusalem. [Hebrew]
1998 "Petrographic Analysis of the Egyptian Forms from Stratum VI at Tel Beth-Shean." In *Mediterranean Peoples in Transition: Thirteenth to Early Tenth Centuries BCE; In Honor of Professor Trude Dothan*, edited by Seymour Gitin, Amihai Mazar, and Ephraim Stern, 406–12. Jerusalem: Israel Exploration Society.
2009 "Petrographic Studies." In *Excavations at Tel Beth Shean 1989–1996, Volume III: The 13th–11th Century BCE Strata in Areas N and S*, edited by Nava Panitz-Cohen and Amihai Mazar, 519–29. Jerusalem: Israel Exploration Society; Institute of Archaeology, Hebrew University of Jerusalem.
2011 "Provenance of the Clay Artifacts from the Favissa at ʻEn Hazeva." *ʻAtiqot* 68: 185–89.

Cohen-Weinberger, Anat, and Yuval Goren
2011 "The Clay Sources of the Theater Pottery Workshop: A Petrographic Study." In *Bet Sheʼan II, Bayŝan: The Theater Pottery Workshop; The Bet Shean Archaeological Project 1989–1999*, edited by Rachel Bar-Nathan and Walid Atrash, 215–28. IAA Reports 48. Jerusalem: Israel Antiquities Authority.

Costin, Cathy Lynne
2000 "The Use of Ethnoarchaeology for the Archaeological Study of Ceramic Production." *Journal of Archaeological Method and Theory* 7: 377–403.

Dan, Joel, and Zvi Raz
1970 *Soil Association Map of Israel, 1:250,000*. Beit Dagan: Volcani Institute.

Dan, Joel, Zvi Raz, Dan H. Yaalon, and Hanna Koyumdjisky
1975 *The Soil Association Map of Israel, 1:500,000*. Beit Dagan: Volcani Institute.

Goren, Yuval
1991 "The Beginnings of Pottery Production in Israel: Technology and Typology of Proto-Historic Ceramic Assemblages in Eretz-Israel (6th–4th Millennia B.C.E.)." PhD diss., Hebrew University of Jerusalem.
1995 "Shrines and Ceramics in Chalcolithic Israel: The View through the Petrographic Microscope." *Archaeometry* 37: 287–305.
2014 "Gods, Caves, and Scholars: Chalcolithic Cult and Metallurgy in the Judean Desert." *NEA* 77.4: 260–66.

Goren, Yuval, Israel Finkelstein, and Nadav Naʾaman
2004 *Inscribed in Clay: Provenance Study of the Amarna Letters and Other Ancient Near Eastern Texts*. SMNIA 23. Tel Aviv: Emery and Claire Yass Publications in Archaeology.

Hatzor, Yosef H.
2000 *Geological Map of Israel 1:50,000, Sheet 6-I, II, Bet-Sheʾan*. Jerusalem: Geological Survey of Israel.

Horowitz, Aharon
1979 *The Quaternary of Israel*. New York: Academic Press.

Kemp, Rob A.
1985 *Soil Micromorphology and the Quaternary*. Quaternary Research Association Technical Guide 2. London: Quaternary Research Association.

Kronfeld, Joel, Johann Carl Vogel, Eliahu Rosenthal, and Mina Weinstein-Evron
1988 "Age and Paleoclimatic Implications of the Bet Shean Travertines." *Quaternary Research* 30: 298–303.

Mazar, Amihai
2009 "Introduction and Overview." In *Excavations at Tel Beth-Shean 1989–1996, Vol III: The 13th–11th Century BCE Strata in Areas N and S*, edited by Nava Panitz-Cohen, and Amihai Mazar, 1–32. Jerusalem: Israel Exploration Society.

Mazar, Amihai, Adi Ziv-Asudri, and Anat Cohen-Weinberger
2000 "The Early Bronze II–III at Tel Beth Shean: Preliminary Observations." In *Ceramic and Changes in the Early Bronze Age of the Southern Levant*, edited by Graham Philip and Douglas Baird, 255–78. Levantine Archaeology 2. Sheffield: Sheffield Academic.

Namdar, Dvory, Anat Cohen-Weinberger, and Sharon Zuckerman
2018 "Towards a New Understanding of MB IIB Cult Practices: Residue and Petrographic Analyses of Seven-Cupped Bowls from the Shrine of Nahariya." In *Tell it in Gath: Studies in the History and Archaeology of Israel in Honor of Aren M. Maeir on the Occasion of His 60th Birthday*, edited by Itzhaq Shai, Jeffrey R. Chadwick, Louise Hitchcock, Amit Dagan, Chris McKinny, and Joe Uziel, 723–46. ÄAT 90. Münster: Zaphon.

Picard, Leo
1956 *Geological Map of Israel, Series C, Zikhron Yaʿakov, 1:100,000*. Jerusalem: Geological Survey of Israel.

Porat, Naomi
2003 "Petrography of the Early Bronze Age II–III Pottery." In *Tel Qashish: A Village in the Jezreel Valley; Final Report of the Archaeological Excavations (1978–1987)*, edited by Amnon Ben-Tor, Ruhama Bonfil, and Sharon Zuckerman, 161–64. Qedem Reports 5. Jerusalem: Hebrew University of Jerusalem.

Ravikovitch, Shlomo
1969 *Israel: Soil Map. 1:250,000*. Reḥovot: Faculty of Agriculture, Hebrew University of Jerusalem.

Sass, Eytan
1968 "Geology of the Umm El Fahm Area, Northern Israel." *Israel Journal of Earth Sciences* 17: 115–30.
1980 "Late Cretaceous Volcanism in Mount Carmel, Israel." *Israel Journal of Earth-Sciences* 29: 8–24.

Schulman, Nachman
1962 "The Geology of the Central Jordan Valley." PhD diss., Hebrew University of Jerusalem.

Segev, Amit, and Eytan Sass
2009 *Geological Map of Israel 1:50,000. Sheet 3-III, Atlit*. Jerusalem: Geological Survey of Israel.

Shaliv, Gabriel, Yaʿakov Mimran, and Yosef Hatzor
1991 "The Sedimentary and Structural History of the Bet Sheʾan Area and Its Regional Implications." *Israel Journal of Earth Science* 40: 161–79.

Shapiro, Anastasia, and Andrea M. Berlin
2012 "Petrographic Appendix." In "The Sanctuary at Mizpe Yammim: Phoenician Cult and Territory in the Upper Galilee during the Persian Period," by Andrea M. Berlin and Rafael Frankel. *BASOR* 366: 69–74.

Sneh, Amihai, Yosef Bartov, and Marcelo Rosensaft
1998 *Geological Map of Israel 1:200,000, Sheet 1*. Jerusalem: Geological Survey of Israel.

Ussishkin, David
2014 "The Chalcolithic Temple in Ein Gedi, Fifty Years after Its Discovery." *NEA* 77.1: 15–26.

Wieder, Moshe, and David Adan-Bayewitz
2002 "Soil Parent Materials and the Pottery of Roman Galilee: A Comparative Study." *Geoarchaeology: An International Journal* 17: 393–415.

Chapter 27

The Cypriot Pottery from the Late Bronze Age II Cultic Repository near Tel Qashish

Celia J. Bergoffen (*Fashion Institute of Technology, NY*)

Eighteen Cypriot pottery imports were found in the Late Bronze Age II repository near Tel Qashish: two base ring II bowls (fig. 25.44.1–2), four white slip II bowls (fig. 25.44.3–6), one base ring II flask (fig. 25.44.7), and eleven white shaved juglets (fig. 25.44.8–18).

Base Ring II Bowls

The repository yielded two large fragments of base ring II Y-shaped bowls with wishbone handles, Paul Åström's type IF. One is of the small variety (ca. 11.0 cm in diameter), Åström's type IFh (Åström and Popham 1972, 178), and is completely desurfaced (fig. 25.44.1). The second one (fig. 25.44.2), of standard size, Åström's type IF (Åström and Popham 1972, 175), also with an almost entirely worn outer surface, was probably originally covered with a dark gray slip, as are virtually all the bowls of this type.

The small base ring II bowl type, measuring between 8 and 10 cm in diameter, is rarely found in Canaan. Examples are known from Tell el-'Ajjul tombs dated to the fourteenth and thirteenth centuries; from Tell er-Ridan, dated to the thirteenth century; and from a pit in Deir el-Balaḥ Stratum IV dated to the end of the Late Bronze Age.[1] Unlike the normal-sized bowl, ubiquitous in settlements, almost all known examples of the small base ring II bowl in Cyprus and Canaan were found in funerary or cultic contexts. The use of small or miniature base ring II bowls as grave gifts in Canaan echoes their votive function in Cyprus, for instance, in the Athienou sanctuary, and at Enkomi, in the shrine of the Horned God (Dothan and Ben-Tor 1983, 41, fig. 18.3–5). This variety (type IFh) may have a later chronological distribution than type IF but is also found in fourteenth-century contexts.

White Slip II Bowls

The four white slip II bowls are represented by two almost complete vessels and two rim sherds, all decorated in ladder lattice pattern style (fig. 25.44.3–6). The cursory style of painting, lack of dots along the rims, and very pale brown slips on the bowls (fig. 25.44.3–4) are characteristic of the white slip II late type (Popham 1972, 456, fig. 57), predominantly found in thirteenth-century settlement contexts, as in Tell Aphek (Stratum X12), Tel Gerisa, and Deir el Balaḥ VI, and in later LB II levels at Tell Jemmeh.[2] In

---

1. Tell el-'Ajjul tombs 1119, 1514, 1515, 1816 and 1863, and the thirteenth-century Tomb 3 at Tell er-Ridan, Bergoffen 1989, catalog numbers 652, 653, 654, and 1649; Petrie 1931, pl. XLVIII, type E2; 1932, pl. XXVIII, type E2; and 1934, pl. LXVIII, type 19E2; Brandl 2010, 104–5. Merrillees 2010, fig. 8.1.25, and pl. 40.17. The LH IIIA2 stirrup jars from Tell el-'Ajjul tombs 1119 and 1816 most likely date these burials to the fourteenth century.

2. Gadot 2009, 239–40; the unlabeled ladder-lattice-pattern-style sherds illustrated in Merrillees 2010, photo 8.4 may have come from the crater's fill (Deir el-Balaḥ Stratum

general, Cypriot bowls are far more prevalent in settlement than funerary contexts. However, there are also instances of white slip II late bowls in tombs, as in Tell er-Ridan (tombs 3 and 6) and Tell el-Ajjul (tomb 1815; Bergoffen 1989, catalog nos. 1664, 1667–1668, 1204).

Base Ring II Flask

The large base ring II painted flask, about 23 cm in height (fig. 25.44.7), has a marked circumference ridge. Large flasks, ranging from approximately 22 cm to 26 cm in height, are much less frequently found in the Levantine or Egyptian import repertoire than the small flasks comparable in size to the base ring juglet. As customary in closed base ring vessels, the neck was made separately and inserted into the body. The handles on large flasks and jugs are often crooked, perhaps because their length made them more liable to sag or warp during the firing process (fig. 25.44.7). The chronological range of the large base ring II flask in Canaan is the fourteenth and thirteenth centuries BCE.

White Shaved Juglets

Eleven white shaved juglets (fig. 25.44.8–18) were retrieved from the repository, ten of them complete, and one fragmentary. Only two have the piercing handles characteristic of Cypriot juglets (fig 30.44.13, 16), although, as Yuval Goren (1992, 24*, 175) demonstrated, the handles of white shaved juglets made in Cyprus sometimes do not pierce the vessel wall. Canaanite versions of these juglets are identical in form and color to the Cypriot imports but may be distinguished by their coarser fabrics and heavier weights, and by their handles that never pierce the vessel's wall.

The white shaved juglets in this assemblage range from about 12.5 to 19 cm in height (from base to rim), clustering around 18 cm, conforming to the standard sizes for this vessel type. The predominance of white shaved juglets over base ring juglets in this assemblage is noteworthy. During the fifteenth to fourteenth centuries, base ring juglets are the dominant small containers in both funerary and cultic contexts, while white shaved juglets play a relatively minor role. The latter become prevalent only later in the Bronze Age (fourteenth to thirteenth centuries BCE).[3]

Conclusions

This small collection is typical of thirteenth-century BCE assemblages, which are typologically and quantitatively more restricted than those of the fifteenth to fourteenth centuries BCE and often include late white slip II normal and late style bowls, white shaved juglets, and base ring II bowls.

VI), which yielded approximately a hundred white slip II and white slip II late sherds (Bonnie Gould, pers. comm.; Merrillees 2010, pl. 31.9–20; Bergoffen 2014, 664, 666–67, fig. 11.8c, d, j, k, n).

3. E.g., in the Nineteenth Dynasty fortress of site A-289 in North Sinai, and at Level X in Tel Sera' (Bergoffen 1989, catalog nos. 8–9, 12, 16–44, 1602–1603, 1607, and, possibly residual, 1609–1611, ascribed to level IX). Tell Aphek Stratum XII (thirteenth century) also comprises vessels with applied rather than pierced handles (Gadot 2009, 240–41).

References

Åström, Paul, and Mervyn R. Popham
1972 *The Late Cypriote Bronze Age Architecture and Pottery*. Swedish Cyprus Expedition 4.1C. Lund: Swedish Cyprus Expedition.

Bergoffen, Celia. J.
1989 "A Comparative Study of the Regional Distribution of Cypriot Pottery in Canaan and Egypt in the Late Bronze Age." PhD diss., New York University.
2014 "Bronze and Iron Age Cypriote and Aegean Imports." In *The Smithsonian Institution Excavation at Tell Jemmeh, Israel, 1970–1990*, edited by David Ben-Shlomo and Gus W. Van Beek, 657–720. Smithsonian Contributions to Anthropology 50. Smithsonian Institution Scholarly Press.

Brandl, Baruch
2010 "The Stratigraphy of the Settlement." In *Deir el-Balaḥ: Excavations in 1977–1982 in the Cemetery and Settlement Volume I; Stratigraphy and Architecture*, edited by Trude Dothan and Baruch Brandl, 63–208. Qedem 49. Jerusalem: Hebrew University of Jerusalem.

Dothan, Trude, and Amnon Ben-Tor
1983 *Excavations at Athienou, Cyprus 1971–1972*. Qedem 16. Jerusalem: Hebrew University of Jerusalem.

Gadot, Yuval
2009 "Late Bronze and Iron Age Pottery." In *Aphek-Antipatris II: The Remains on the Acropolis; The Moshe Kochavi and Pirhiya Beck Excavations*, edited by Yuval Gadot and Esther Yadin, 182–341. SMNIA 27. Tel Aviv: Tel Aviv University.

Goren, Yuval
1992 "Petrographic Analyses of White Shaved Juglets from Tomb 26 at Palmaḥim." *'Atiqot* 22: 15*–26*. [Hebrew, English Summary 174–75]

Merrillees, Robert S.
2010 "Cypriot Pottery." In *Deir el-Balaḥ: Excavations in 1977–1982 in the Cemetery and Settlement Volume II; The Finds*, edited by Trude Dothan and Baruch Brandl, 137–43. Qedem 50. Jerusalem: Hebrew University of Jerusalem.

Petrie, W. M. Flinders
1931 *Ancient Gaza I*. London: British School of Archaeology in Egypt.
1932 *Ancient Gaza II*. London: British School of Archaeology in Egypt.
1934 *Ancient Gaza IV*. London: British School of Archaeology in Egypt.

Popham, Mervyn R.
1972 "White Slip Ware." In *The Late Cypriot Bronze Age Architecture and Pottery*, edited by Paul Åström and Mervyn R. Popham, 431–71. Swedish Cyprus Expedition 4.1.C. Lund: Swedish Cyprus Expedition.

Chapter 28

Provenience of Late Bronze Age II Pottery from the Cultic Repository near Tel Qashish

Joseph Yellin (*Institute of Archaeology, Hebrew University of Jerusalem*)
Matthew T. Boulanger (*Department of Anthropology, Southern Methodist University*)
Michael D. Glascock (*University of Missouri Archaeometry Laboratory, University of Missouri Research Reactor*)

Eighteen LBA II pottery vessels from a recent salvage excavation on the edge of Tel Qashish (van den Brink, Segal, and 'Ad 2012; Segal, 'Ad, and van den Brink ch. 25, this volume) were subjected to neutron activation analysis (NAA). Sixteen analyzed vessels were found in a cultic cave repository (Area B), while two vessels, found on the tell, were included for comparison purposes. The eighteen pots were analyzed with two objectives in mind:

1. To determine the origin of pots, which, on stylistic grounds, appeared to be imports from Cyprus and the Mycenaean world.
2. To determine which pots were locally made—the provenience of the pottery will most certainly cast some light on the nature of the cult.

The pottery from the cave was analyzed at the University of Missouri Research Reactor (MURR), while the pottery from the tell was analyzed at The Hebrew University of Jerusalem (HUJ). Previous analytical results from Tel Qashish showed the characteristics of pottery local to the region; these results allowed to determine which of the eighteen pots from Area B are local and which are imports.

The excavation, carried out on the edge of Tel Qashish in what is believed to be a cultic repository of the Late Bronze Age II (LBA II), yielded many complete vessels, with some of them, based on stylistic considerations, appearing to be imports.[1] Eighteen vessels were subjected to instrumental neutron activation analysis (INAA; Yellin, Boulanger, and Glascock 2015). Table 28.1 lists the vessels analyzed and summarizes the results of the study. Sixteen of these vessels come from Locus 225, the cultic repository, while two vessels, from the tell itself, Locus 219, were also tested to determine if, stylistically, local vessels from both assemblages were the same.[2]

The vessels were sampled at the Israel Antiquities Authority facility in Har Ḥotzvim, Jerusalem, where the finds were already under study, restoration, and photography. Great care was taken in sampling the pottery to leave a minimum of marks on it by using diamond tools to clean the surface where a sample was to be taken, followed by a clean diamond drill to powder pottery from the cleaned surface with minimal damage.[3] The powder was collected on aluminum foil and subsequently transferred to a plastic vial. The tools used to sample the pottery are presented in figure 28.1, and figures 28.2–3 show a

---

1. For full details on Area B and the cultic repository, see Segal, 'Ad and van den Brink, ch. 25, this volume.
2. For a full description of the vessels and similar types, see Bergoffen, ch. 27, this volume.
3. The diamond drills were driven by a Wolf Mini Grinder MD128 (Dremmel-like) motor at the end of a flexible shaft. This arrangement enables a high-precision control of the drilling.

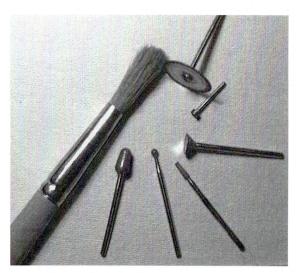

Fig. 28.1. Diamond drills used to sample pottery.

Fig. 28.2. Vessel B.2156 after sampling.

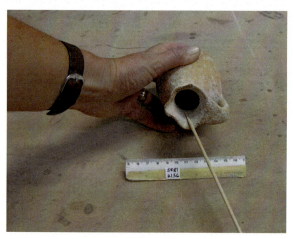

Fig. 28.3. Vessel B.2156 before sampling.

vessel before and after sampling. After cleaning the surface, the vessel was sampled to a depth of approximately 1 mm. The mark left on it by the sampling is clearly visible, but it will be less noticeable once it is restored by cleaning the whole surface. Neutron activation analyses were carried out at MURR.[4]

Pottery sherds from the 1980s excavation at Tel Qashish itself (Ben-Tor, Bonfil, and Zuckerman 2003), many dating from the Early Bronze Age, were analyzed by neutron activation at the Archaeology Institute of the Hebrew University of Jerusalem. The present report deals only with the pottery from the recent excavation adjacent to Tel Qashish, but the previous analytical work provides a strong clue about the composition of local pottery.[5]

Methodology

The methods used to analyze the pottery at MURR and the HUJ have been described in past publications (Glascock, Speakman, and Neff 2007; Yellin 2007; Yellin and Maeir 2007), with the procedures used at the HUJ being similar to those used in Berkeley (Perlman and Asaro 1969). Thus, we shall not go into those details in this report.[6]

Results

A summary of the samples' provenience is given in table 28.1 (all tables can be found at the end of the chapter). Analytical results for the eighteen pots analyzed at MURR are given in tables 28.2–3. Also shown in table 28.2 is the composition of pottery from the Argolid (Zuckerman et al. 2010). For reasons stated below, we are basing our conclusions, as much as possible, on the rare earth elements (REE).

Local Pottery
(QASH01–QASH03, QASH05, QASH08, QASH10, QASH13–QASH18)

The pottery from Early-Bronze-Age Tel Qashish, previously analyzed in Jerusalem (unpublished), exhibits very high values of barium, as do most of

---

4. For details, see Glascock, Speakman, and Neff 2007, and references therein.
5. Tens of potsherds were subjected to INAA at the Hebrew University. The results were not published.
6. For some details on how provenience is determined once the compositions are obtained, see Yellin and Killebrew 2010.

the eighteen pottery vessels from the LBA II cultic repository from the edge of the tell.[7] Barium concentrations vary from approximately 1000 ppm to 1 percent. Specimens exhibiting similar characteristics and dating from different periods and the same location are good evidence that the pottery was made of local clay sources. Moreover, the region is known to be rich in the mineral barite (barium sulfate), which explains the high barium concentrations found in the pottery. Similar high values of barium have been observed in other nearby sites, including 'En Ḥaggit (Yellin et al. in press), Tel Yoqne'am, and Tel Qiri (barium values were not published, but see Sharon, Yellin, and Perlman 1987).

One of the many potsherds from the tell (as opposed to the cultic repository on the edge of the tell), exhibiting high barium values, was taken to serve as a representative of the pottery composition local to the region of Tel Qashish. The composition of the specific sherd, QASIS66, is shown in table 28.2. Table 28.3 shows the barium concentrations and calcium concentrations for this sherd and all the QASH samples. The two samples from the tell, QASH01 and QASH18 (Locus 219), also present very high barium values.

A preliminary comparison of this Tel Qashish sample with samples from other sites measured in the past by the INAA at the Laurence Berkeley National Laboratory was performed using a Euclidean-distance search against the LBNL ceramic database (Asaro and Adan-Bayewitz 2007; Boulanger 2012).[8] Results are generalized from ten LBNL specimens, with the lowest mean Euclidean distances calculated against each Qashish specimen. Specimens QASH01–QASH03, QASH05, and QASH12–QASH18 are most closely related to archaeological specimens from Megiddo, Akko, and Ḥazor. Megiddo, located about 12 km southeast of Tel Qashish, showed the closest relationship, suggesting a regionally localized production. The results for QASH08 and QASH10 were inconclusive and require further examination. However, QASH08 shows some similarity with the pottery from the coastal area of Ashdod.

Mycenaean-Style Pottery
(QASH 6, 9, 11)

Mycenaean-style pottery has been found in many sites in Israel, and the chemical composition of true Mycenaean pottery is well known.[9] For a signature of true Mycenaean pottery, a reference group of 297 samples, MYBE ref., from Zuckerman et al. 2010, was taken. The MYBE reference is from the University of Bonn (see also Mommsen et al. 1988).

Three pottery vessels, QASH06, QASH09, and QASH11, were classified as Mycenaean based on stylistic considerations. The REE patterns of QASH06 and QASH09 are similar, differing from that of QASH11, suggesting a similar geologic origin for QASH06 and QASH09 and a different one for QASH11. Also, the REE patterns of QASH06 and QASH09 are similar to the pattern of the reference-composition MYBE, as shown in figure 28.4, where the REE compositions of the vessels and the reference MYBE are plotted.

The data (table 28.2) were first adjusted to eliminate dilution due to different calcium concentrations and were subsequently normalized to the C I chondrite composition (Anders and Ebihara 1982; Wasson 1985; Wasson and Kallemeyn 1988), as also shown in table 28.2.[10] The REE elements have similar chemical properties, and thus, their relative distribution in the earth is not sensitive to clay-forming geochemical processes.[11] Nevertheless, the relative distribution is affected by geophysical processes that cause fractionation due to differences in the physical properties of the REE. Thus, over geologic time,

---

7. The classification of the pottery as either local or imported under the column heading "Description" in table 28.1 is based on a preliminary visual observation provided by the excavators before any rigorous stylistic analysis was undertaken. For convenience, we use this initial visual classification in the headings of this and the next two sections where we test the visual hypothesis.

8. These past measurements are archived at MURR.

9. For reports on INAA analyses of Mycenaean pottery in Israel, see, e.g., Yellin 1984; Yellin and Maeir 1992; Ben-Shlomo, Maeir, and Mommsen 2007; Liebowitz and Yellin 2009; Zukerman et al. 2010. For reports on INAA analysis of Mycenaean pottery from other sites, see, e.g., Asaro and Perlman 1973; Mommsen et al. 1988, 1996; Yellin 1998; Mommsen, Beier, and Hein 2002; Yellin 2007.

10. The C I chondrite composition is the composition of the solar nebula from which the solar system formed.

11. Rare earths are trivalent, but europium can also be bivalent and cerium quadrivalent. This different behavior of europium and cerium can lead to anomalies in the concentration of these elements.

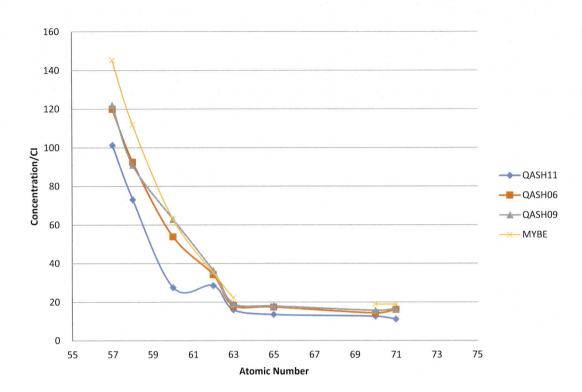

Fig. 28.4. REE pattern for three Tel Qashish pottery vessels classified on stylistic grounds as Mycenaean.

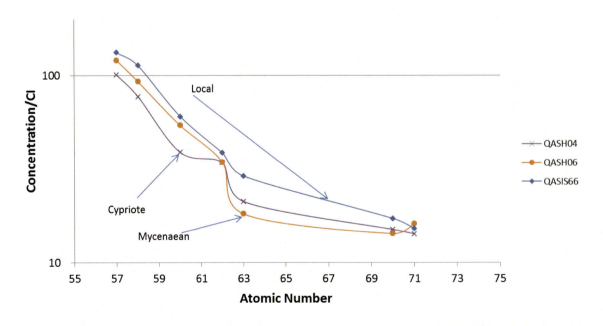

Fig. 28.5. REE pattern for three local and imported pots from Area B.

significant changes occurred in the REE distribution in clays, and this can be used to identify different geologic regions. The REE pattern exhibited by QASH06 and QASH09 is similar to the REE pattern of Mycenaean pottery, MYBE, the latter originating in the region of Mycenae.

A study of the LBNL data archive, similar to the study described above, yielded that QASH06 and QASH09 are most closely related (in the sense described above) to compositions of the Mycenaean pottery in the LBNL data archive, while QASH11 is most closely related to Cypriot pottery.

Cypriot-Style Pottery
(QASH 4, 7, 12)

Figure 28.5 shows the REE distribution in QASIS 66 along with the REE distribution of the Cypriot-style vessel QASH04 and the Mycenaean-style vessel QASH06. The REE plots show that these three objects have different geological histories and, thus, origins. In table 28.2 is given the composition of group ETS 1, traced to Cyprus (Gunneweg, Perlman, and Yellin 1984), but two elements are not reported (Nd, Tb). Based on the REE, QASH04 is a good match for this group. Sample QASH07 has a very high (about 1 percent) concentration of barium. Such high barium concentrations have not been reported for Cypriot pottery and are characteristic of the local Qashish vessels. While a Cypriot origin cannot be ruled out, this is highly unlikely, unless the high barium value is the result of contamination from the environment where the vessel was embedded. Sample QASH12 also has a high barium concentration, but here, too, there is no Cypriot reference material with such levels of barium concentrations.

To get a more precise definition of the origin of the imported vessels, it is necessary to use data from several sources, for example, LBNL, MURR, HUJ, and Bonn. Although data from these laboratories are comparable, no extensive interlaboratory studies have been carried out by all the laboratories, and studies carried out in the past may need refinement.[12]

In this study, laboratory comparability was avoided, and, where possible, local and imported wares were separated based on REE patterns. It was also decided to avoid direct element-by-element comparisons because of the high barium concentrations and their highly varying levels. Only the geographic region that the imported wares came from was sought, not a particular potter's workshop or even a particular settlement.

Further evidence bearing on local pottery can be obtained from the microscopic examination of thin sections of pottery. Studies combining INAA with petrographic thin-section analysis have been carried out in the past on pottery from Israel (e.g., Goldberg et al. 1986; Porat et al. 1991; Maeir, Yellin, and Goren 1992; Ben-Shlomo, Maeir, and Mommsen 2007; Waksman et al. 2008). Unfortunately, only three vessels tested by INAA (QASH01, QASH08, QASH05) were also examined by thin section. The results for these three vessels are consistent with the INAA results reported by Anat Cohen-Weinberger.[13]

The LBNL INAA data archive was searched for compositions similar to the Cypriot style pots QASH04, QASH07, and QASH12, resulting in a Neolithic sherd from Cyprus being the best match for QASH04. No Cypriot matches were found for QASH07 or QASH12.

Conclusions

The high concentrations of barium observed in QASH01–QASH03, QASH05, QASH08, QASH10, and QASH13–QASH18, coupled with the fact that the geological region of Qashish is rich in the mineral barite, leaves little doubt that these pots are local. Also, high values of barium observed in Early Bronze Age pottery from Tel Qashish (unpublished) supports this conclusion. Furthermore, high barium concentrations have also been observed at other nearby sites, for example, Ḥaggit, Megiddo, Qiri, and Yoqneʿam. Evidence from the LBNL INAA data archive suggests that these vessels are indeed local

---

12. INAA pottery measurements conducted at the HUJ were compared with INAA carried out, on the same pottery, at MURR. Also, the same pottery was measured by ICP-AE and ICP-MS at the Israel Geologic Survey. A good agreement was obtained for most elements. The results were not published but confirmed good comparability between MURR and HUJ INAA. The study was performed on pottery from Cyprus and Israel.
13. For the petrographic thin-section analysis of local wares from the cultic repository, see Cohen-Weinberger, ch. 26, this volume.

to the region of Qashish–Megiddo–Yoqneʻam, with the possible exception of QASH08 and QASH10 which may originate elsewhere. The best matches for QASH08 come from the coastal region of Ashdod.

Of the three Mycenaean-style pots, QASH06, QASH09, and QASH11, QASH06 and QASH09 exhibit an REE pattern similar to Mycenaean pottery from the region of Mycenae, while QASH11 has a different pattern which also differs from the local pottery, thus needing further study. Evidence from the LBNL INAA data archive strongly suggests that QASH06 and QASH09 are from the region of Mycenae while QASH11 may be Cypriot.

Only one of the Cypriot pots, QASH04, has a Cypriot composition. Of the other two Cypriot-style pots, QASH07 has a concentration of barium not observed in Cypriot compositions and suggests a local origin. The Cypriot-style pot QASH12 needs further study. Evidence from the LBNL INAA data archive on the Cypriot-style pottery is inconclusive. Nevertheless, a local provenience is suggested for QASH07 and QASH12, while for QASH04, a Cypriot origin is likely. It should be stressed that this is one of the very first times that the MURR archive of the LBNL INAA data was used in conjunction with new data for delimiting the pottery's possible origin points rather than finding exact matches.

All the pots were sampled shortly after their discovery and before they underwent any cleaning/conservation treatment, and the areas sampled were cleaned with an abrasive tool (diamond) before sampling. Although unlikely, the cleansing of the pottery's sample surface may not have been done deep enough, thus accounting for some of the variations in barium concentration.

References

Anders, Edward, and Mitsuru Ebihara
1982 "Solar-System Abundances of the Elements." *Geochimica et Cosmochimica Acta* 46: 2363–80.

Asaro, Frank, and David Adan-Bayewit
2007 "The History of the Lawrence Berkeley National Laboratory Instrumental Neutron Activation Analysis Program for Archaeological and Geological Materials." *Archaeometry* 49: 201–14.

Asaro, Frank, and Isadore Perlman
1973 "Provenience Studies of Mycenaean Pottery Employing Neutron Activation Analysis." In *Acts of the International Archaeological Symposium "The Mycenaeans in the Eastern Mediterranean," 27th March–2nd April 1972, Nicosia*, 213–24. Nicosia: Department of Antiquities.

Ben-Shlomo, David, Aren M. Maeir, and Hans Mommsen
2007 "Neutron Activation and Petrographic Analysis of Selected Late Bronze and Iron Age Pottery from Tell es-Safi/Gath, Israel." *JArS* 35: 956–64.

Ben-Tor, Amnon, Ruhama Bonfil, and Sharon Zuckerman
2003 *Tel Qashish: A Village in the Jezreel Valley; Final Report of the Archaeological Excavations (1978–1987)*. Qedem Reports 5. Jerusalem: Hebrew University of Jerusalem.

Boulanger, Matthew T.
2012 "Salvage Archaeometry: Lessons Learned from the Lawrence Berkeley Laboratory Archaeometric Archives." *SAA Archaeological Record* 13: 14–19.

Brink, Edwin C. M. van den, Orit Segal, and Uzi ʻAd
2012 "A Late Bronze Age II Repository of Cultic Paraphernalia from the Environs of Tel Qashish in the Jezreel Valley, Israel." In *Temple Building and Temple Cult: Architecture and Cultic Paraphernalia of Temples in the Levant (2.–1. Mill. BCE)*, edited by Jens Kamlah, 421–434, pls. 55–62. ADPV 41. Wiesbaden: Harrassowitz.

Glascock, Michael D., Robert J. Speakman, and Hector Neff
2007 "Archaeometry at the University of Missouri Research Reactor and the Provenance of Obsidian Artifacts in North America." *Archaeometry* 49: 343–57.

Goldberg, Paul, Bonnie Gould, Ann E. Killebrew, and Joseph Yellin
1986 "Comparison of Neutron Activation and Thin-Section Analyses on Late Bronze Age Ceramics from Deir el-Balaḥ." In *Proceedings of the 24th International Archaeometry Symposium*, edited by Jacqueline S. Olin and M. James Blackman, 341–51. Washington, DC: Smithsonian Institution Press.

Gunneweg Jan, Isadore Perlman, and Joseph Yellin
1984 *The Provenience, Typology and Chronology of Eastern Terra Sigillata*. Qedem 17. Jerusalem: Hebrew University of Jerusalem.

Liebowitz Harold, and Joseph Yellin
2009 "Instrumental Neutron Activation Analysis of Two Vessels from Tel Yinʻam." *Leiden Journal of Pottery Studies* 25: 103–18.

Maeir, Aren M., Joseph Yellin, and Yuval Goren
1992 "A Re-evaluation of the Red and Black Bowl from Parker's Excavations in Jerusalem." *OJA* 11: 39–53.

Mommsen, Hans, Thomas Beier, and Anno Hein
2002 "A Complete Chemical Grouping of the Berkeley Neutron Activation Analysis Data on Mycenaean Pottery." *JArS* 29: 613–37.

Mommsen, Hans, Thomas Beier, Anno Hein, C. Podzuweit, E. B. Pusch, and A. Eggebrecht
1996 "Neutron Activation Analysis of Mycenaean Sherds from the Town of Ramesses II near Qantir and Greek–Egyptian Trade Relations." In *Archaeometry 94: The Proceedings of the 29th International Symposium on Archaeometry, Ankara, 9–14 May 1994*, edited by Ş. Demirci, A. M. Özer, and G. D. Summers, 169–78. Ankara: Tübitak.

Mommsen, Hans, E. Lewandowski, J. Weber, and C. Podzuweit
1988 "Neutron Activation Analysis of Mycenaean Pottery from the Argolid: The Search for Reference Groups." In *Proceedings of the 26th International Symposium on Archaeometry Held at University of Toronto, Toronto, Canada, May 16th to May 20th, 1988*, edited by Ronald M. Farquhar, R. G. V. Hancock, and L. A. Pavlish, 165–71. Toronto: University of Toronto.

Perlman, Isadore, and Frank Asaro
1969 "Pottery Analysis by Neutron Activation." *Archaeometry* 11: 21–52.

Porat, Naomi, Joseph Yellin, Lisa Heller-Kallai, and Ludwik Halitz
1991 "Correlation Between Petrography, NAA, and ICP Analyses: Application to Early Bronze Egyptian Pottery from Canaan." *Geoarchaeology* 6: 133–49.

Sharon, Ilan, Joseph Yellin, and Isadore Perlman
1987 "Marked Cooking Pots from Tel Qiri." In *Tell Qiri: A Village in the Jezreel Valley; Report of the Archaeological Excavations, 1975–1977*, edited by Amnon Ben-Tor, and Yuval Portugali, 224–35. Qedem 24. Jerusalem: Hebrew University of Jerusalem.

Waksman, S. Yona, Edna J. Stern, Irina Segal, Naomi Porat, and Joseph Yellin
2008 "Elemental and Petrographic Analyses of Local and Imported Ceramics from Crusader Acre." *'Atiqot* 59: 127–90.

Wasson, John T.
1985 *Meteorites: Their Record of Early Solar-System History*. New York: Freeman.

Wasson, John T., and Greg W. Kallemeyn
1988 "Composition of Chondrites." *Philosophical Transactions of the Royal Society* A325: 535–44.

Yellin, Joseph
1984 "Provenience of Selected LB and MB Pottery from Tel Mevorakh by Instrumental Neutron Activation Analysis." In *Excavations at Tel Mevorakh (1973–1976), Part Two: The Bronze Age*, edited by Ephraim Stern, 87–100. Qedem 18. Jerusalem: Hebrew University of Jerusalem.
1998 "The Small Mycenaean Vessels from Athienou, Cyprus." *Chemistry and Chemical Engineering* 33: 21–24. [Hebrew, with English abstract]
2007 "Instrumental Neutron Activation Based Provenance Studies at The Hebrew University of Jerusalem, with a Case Study on Mycenaean Pottery from Cyprus." *Archaeometry* 49: 271–88.

Yellin, Joseph, Matthew T. Boulanger, and Michael D. Glascock
2015 "A Chemical Signature for Ancient Pottery from Tel Qashish." Abstract of a paper presented at the Eighteenth Annual Meeting of the Israel Analytical Chemistry Society, January 14–16, Tel Aviv. https://bioforumconf.com/analytica-abs/outofhtml/isranalytica_2015/achemicalsign_Joseph_Yellin.html.

Yellin, Joseph, Matthew T. Boulanger, Michael D. Glascock, and Samuel R. Wolff
In press "Instrumental Neutron Activation Analysis on Collared-Rim Pithoi." In *'En Ḥaggit: A Middle Bronze II and Iron Age I Rural Site in Northern Ramot Menashe, Israel*, edited by Samuel R. Wolff.

Yellin, Joseph, and Ann E. Killebrew
2010 "The Origin of Egyptian-Style Ceramics from Deir El-Balaḥ: Conclusions from Neutron Activation Analysis." In *Deir El-Balaḥ: Excavations in 1977–1982 in the Cemetery and Settlement, II; The Finds*, edited by Trude Dothan, and Baruch Brandl, 57–74. Qedem 50. Jerusalem: Hebrew University of Jerusalem.

Yellin, Joseph, and Aren M. Maeir
1992 "Origin of the Pictorial Krater from the 'Mycenaean' Tomb at Tel Dan." *Archaeometry* 34: 31–36.
2007 "Four Decades of Instrumental Neutron Activation Analysis and Its Contribution to the Archaeology of the Ancient Land of Israel." *Israel Journal of Earth Science* 56: 123–32.

Zuckerman, Sharon, David Ben-Shlomo, Penelope Mountjoy, and Hans Mommsen
2010 "A Provenance Study of Mycenaean Pottery from Northern Israel." *JArS* 37: 409–16.

Table 28.1. Pottery from Area B analyzed by INAA.

Sample ID	Basket	Locus	Figure	Origin	Description[a]
QASH01	2106	219	15.2	Local	goblet
QASH02	2157	225	25.2	Local	jug
QASH03	2113	225	13.5	Local	chalice
QASH04	2150	225	38.9	Cypriote	Cyp juglet
QASH05	2217	225	22.5	Local	Cooking pot
QASH06	2115	225	37.2	Mycenaean	Myc stirrup jar
QASH07	2179	225	38.18	Uncertain[b]	Cyp flask
QASH08	2206	225	24.3	Local[c]	Jug
QASH09	2147	225	37.3	Mycenaean	Myc
QASH10	2135	225	27.1	Local[d]	Flask
QASH11	2192	225	36.3	Cypriote[e]	Myc flask
QASH12	2236	225	38.15	Uncertain[f]	Cyp juglet
QASH13	2161	225	15.1	Local	Goblet
QASH14	2156	225	–	Local	Dipper juglet
QASH15	2198	225	–	Local	Stand/Goblet
QASH16	2254	225	30.2	Local	Lamp
QASH17	2258	225	13.3	Local	Chalice
QASH18	2129	219	8.6	Local	Bowl

a These are based on a preliminary visual observation given the authors before a rigorous stylistic analysis was carried out.
b Needs further study.
c Possibly from the coastal area of Ashdod. Needs further study.
d No useful information was found in the LBNL archive.
e Needs further study.
f Needs further study

Table 28.2. Rare earth composition of pottery from Area B and references.

Element[a] >> Atomic No. >>	La 57	Ce 58	Nd 60	Sm 62	Eu 63	Tb 65	Yb 70	Lu 71
QASH01	23.52	50.91	23.47	4.77	1.085	0.61	2.30	0.355
QASH02	27.83	62.14	31.59	5.68	1.246	0.65	2.89	0.383
QASH03	23.80	50.42	20.16	4.99	1.177	0.68	2.30	0.331
QASH04	19.26	38.49	14.38	4.13	0.962	0.77	1.94	0.289
QASH05	21.67	67.51	18.82	4.69	1.083	0.64	2.31	0.329
QASH06	25.55	51.46	22.21	4.61	0.918	0.57	2.05	0.364
QASH07	28.18	66.72	35.93	5.65	1.245	0.75	2.76	0.396
QASH08	26.07	61.65	25.67	5.42	1.134	0.62	2.89	0.411
QASH09	24.49	47.70	24.47	4.60	0.915	0.55	2.11	0.351
QASH10	27.16	51.20	27.95	5.00	1.012	0.61	2.20	0.346
QASH11	18.54	34.92	9.76	3.30	0.692	0.38	1.55	0.215
QASH12	12.75	19.61	12.86	2.52	0.556	0.32	1.33	0.227
QASH13	23.38	56.04	27.97	4.91	1.116	0.64	2.28	0.345
QASH14	21.47	49.45	19.21	4.36	1.006	0.55	2.14	0.293
QASH15	18.26	36.91	21.02	3.96	1.042	0.52	1.73	0.287
QASH16	17.68	39.97	21.03	3.62	0.817	0.43	1.74	0.277
QASH17	22.89	53.77	28.34	4.67	1.053	0.55	2.23	0.302
QASH18	21.11	56.50	20.08	4.41	0.981	0.57	1.92	0.279
QASIS66	27.70	61.70	24.43	5.09	1.44	na	2.43	0.33
MYBE ref[b]	31.1	62.5	26.1	4.76	1.13	0.67	2.73	0.42
ETS-1[c]	20.70	41.80	-	3.85	1.03	-	2.16	0.32
CI Chondrite[d]	0.236	0.616	0.457	0.149	0.056	0.036	0.159	0.025

a Values are in parts per million (microgram/gram).
b Zuckerman et al. 2010.
c Gunneweg, Perlman, and Yellin 1984.
d Anders and Ebihara 1982.

Table 28.3. Concentration of barium and calcium in percent.

Sample ID	Basket	Locus	Ba%	Ca%
QASH01	2106	219	0.50	20.74
QASH02	2157	225	0.68	15.39
QASH03	2113	225	0.24	18.76
QASH04	2150	225	0.08	18.68
QASH05	2217	225	0.29	10.72
QASH06	2115	225	0.19	9.75
QASH07	2179	225	1.08	8.87
QASH08	2206	225	0.50	4.45
QASH09	2147	225	0.09	14.90
QASH10	2135	225	0.25	16.58
QASH11	2192	225	0.17	22.41
QASH12	2236	225	0.14	30.63
QASH13	2161	225	0.65	14.01
QASH14	2156	225	0.49	21.62
QASH15	2198	225	0.14	20.45
QASH16	2254	225	0.75	20.59
QASH17	2258	225	0.85	14.14
QASH18	2129	219	0.24	17.42

Chapter 29

Residue Analysis of Chalices from the LBA IIA Cultic Cache from Tel Qashish

Dvory Namdar

(*Department of Plant Sciences, Agricultural Research Organization, Volcani Center, Bet Dagan, Israel*)

From March to May 2010, a salvage excavation was conducted by the Israel Antiquities Authority along the north and west margins of Tel Qashish in the Jezreel Valley (fig. 29.1) prior to laying a gas pipeline. The area was excavated down to the natural bedrock consisting of Eocene chalks. The bedrock surface was covered with a layer of colluvial sediments (thickness ca. 0.25–0.50 m).

In a narrow bedrock cavity (depth ca. 3 m), whose original entry was from the southwest, a cache of Late Bronze Age IIA ritual ceramic vessels was uncovered (figs. 29.2–3).[1] The excavators assume that the finds are possibly vessels from a temple, deposited in the cache through some kind of ritual. Evidence of Early Bronze Age I occupation was found on top of this cavity's roof, which had collapsed in antiquity, creating a bedrock depression filled and sealed, over time, by colluvial sediments.

The LB II cache assemblage of cultic ceramic artifacts comprises over two hundred complete specimens, including pottery vessels locally produced and imported from the Eastern Mediterranean, that is, Mycenae and Cyprus. The local vessels included a human-faced goblet, four tall cylindrical stands (braziers) with round or rectangular fenestrations, scores of chalices and small, plain stands, incense burners and oil lamps, disk-based bowls, goblets, plain jugs, small dipper juglets, and a few cooking pots.

The excavators hoped that a careful study of the wealth of finds from this cache would provide a deeper understanding of the actual cult practices in an assumed provincial LB II temple or shrine that should have existed in the site's vicinity, a type of shrine not found in previous excavations conducted at the site (Ben-Tor et al. 2003). Therefore, samples from numerous vessels found in the cache were taken for residue, petrographic, and INAA analyses, to assess their original contents and provenience.

Only local items were sampled for residue analysis. Samples were taken on-site during the excavation season. Contact with bare hands was limited to a minimum, and the samples were not washed or handled in any way. Sediments associated with the ceramic items and further allocated sediments were sampled to serve as controls (table 29.1).

Materials

Five chalices, found in different areas of the cave, were chosen as the first extracted batch for assessing the general preservation state of the samples in the cave. The chalices from Qashish were analyzed together with eight samples from two other, completely unrelated sites in Israel, to monitor any fortuitous contamination due to lab work.

---

1. Dating was based on the locally produced and imported ceramic vessels.

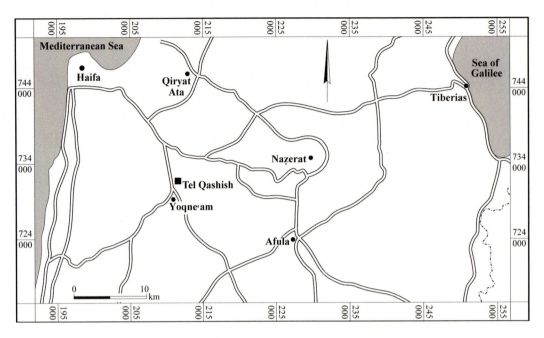

Fig. 29.1. Schematic map of northern Israel on which the location of the site is marked.

Fig. 29.2. The items found in the cave.

Fig. 29.3. Sampling during excavation. Handling the sampled items with bare hands was restricted to minimum.

Methods

The extraction and analysis procedures of the lipids followed Dvory Namdar et al. 2013. All the glassware was soaked overnight in fuming nitric acid, washed carefully with distilled water, and then washed with acetone followed by dichloromethane, and dried in a fume hood. Sherd fragments were broken off the ceramic vessels with pliers, further fragmented and ground manually to a powder with the help of an agate pestle and mortar. Samples (1 g each) were ex-

29. Residue Analysis of Chalices from the LBA IIA Cultic Cache from Tel Qashish

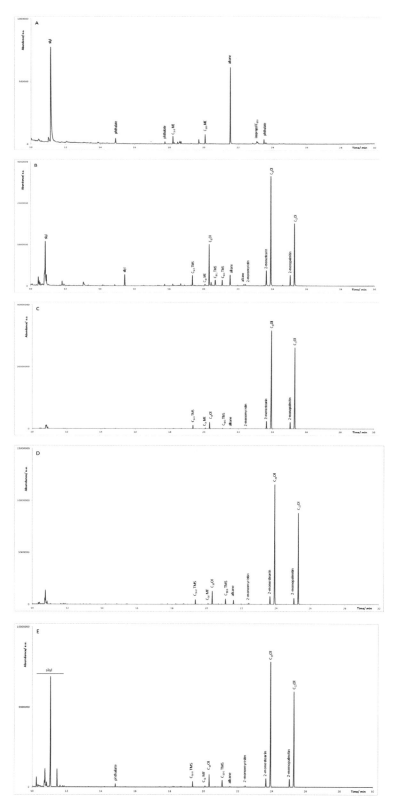

Fig. 29.4A–E. Chromatograms of the analyzed samples: A. Chalice 2329; B. Chalice 2331; C. Chalice 2332; D. Chalice 2335; E. Chalice 2336. Cx:y, Cx:yME, Cx:yTMS—a fatty acid with x carbons chain and y degree of unsaturation, and its methyl ester and trimethylsilyl forms; Cxol—alcohol with x carbons chain.

tracted twice with 10 ml of dichloromethane:methanol (2:1, v/v) followed by sonication for 10 minutes. The tubes were centrifuged for 5 minutes at 3500 rpm to separate the ceramic powder from the solvents. The supernatant was removed to a clean glass vial. The accumulated solvents were evaporated under a gentle stream of nitrogen. Prior to analysis, 50 μl of N, O-bis (trimethylsilyl) trifluoroacetamide containing 1 percent trimethylchlorosilane was added to the dry extracts, followed by heating at 65° C for 20 minutes. One μL of each sample was injected into the gas chromatograph (GC) with the mass selective detector (MSD) in a splitless mode.

Results

The results of the extraction of the five Tel Qashish sampled chalices are presented in the chromatograms incorporated in figure 29.4A–E. The results of the total lipid extracts are summarized in table 29.2.

Discussion and Conclusions

All the chalice extracts from Qashish presented a similar assemblage of compounds. The pit where the chalices were found yielded no internal stratigraphy or layers. All the analyzed chalices were found lying in a moist chalky bedrock environment. The assemblage points to no known organic source other than organic-soil contamination (Tisdall, and Oades 1982; Haynes, and Naidu 1998). The high similarity between the five extracts strengthens the conclusion that these molecular assemblages are likely to be driven from the burial environment. The humid chalk permeability inhibited proper surface water drainage, exposing the chalices to constant humidity. These conditions are likely to have washed away the original organic materials introduced into the chalices in antiquity. The current assemblage reflects the organic composition of the accumulated material in the cave, absorbed, over time, into the ceramic walls of the vessels. The high concentrations of monoacylglycerols seem to fit this proposed scenario. After reaching this conclusion, the residue analysis of the ceramic items found in the cave was halted.

References

Ben-Tor, Amnon, Ruhama Bonfil, and Sharon Zuckerman
2003 *Tel Qashish: A Village in the Jezreel Valley; Final Report of the Archaeological Excavations (1978–1987)*. Qedem Reports 5. Jerusalem: Hebrew University of Jerusalem.

Haynes, Richard J., and Ravi Naidu
1998 "Influence of Lime, Fertilizer and Manure Applications on Soil Organic Matter Content and Soil Physical Conditions: A Review." *Nutrient Cycling in Agroecosystems* 51: 123–37.

Namdar, Dvory, Ayelet Gilboa, Ronny Neumann, Israel Finkelstein, and Steve Weiner
2013 "Cinnamaldehyde in Early Iron Age Phoenician Flasks Raises the Possibility of Levantine Trade with South East Asia." *Mediterranean Archaeology and Archaeometry* 13.2: 1–19.

Tisdall, Judith M., and J. Malcolm Oades
1982 "Organic Matter and Water-Stable Aggregates in Soils." *Journal of Soil Science* 33: 141–63.

Table 29.1. List of on-site samples, during the excavation.

Lab. No.	Locus	Basket	Type	Description
2318	225	2253	Jug	
2321	225	2255	Bowl/jar	
2323	225	2252	Bowl	
2325	225	2251	Goblet	
2327	225	2250	Lamp	
2328	225	2203	juglet	
2329	225	2177	Chalice	
2330	225	2148	Chalice/goblet?	
2331	225	2113	Chalice	
2332	225	2263	Chalice	
2334	225	2190	Chalice	
2335	225	2130	Chalice	
2336	225	2259	Chalice	
2337	225	2259	Chalice	
2338	225	2224	Chalice	
2339	225	2196	Chalice	
2340	225	2242	Goblet	
2341	225	2119	Chalice/goblet?	
2342	225	2214	Chalice/goblet?	
2343	225	2244	Chalice	
2344	225	2090	Bowl	
2346	225	2090	Bowl	
2348	225	2121	Cup and saucer 1	Lower part
2349	225	2121	Cup and saucer 1	Upper part
2350	225	2128	Cup and saucer 2	Upper part
2351	225	2128	Cup and saucer 2	Lower part
2352	225	2101	Goblet	
2353	225	2143	Bowl	
2354	225	2181	Bowl	
2355	225	2114	Bowl	
2356	225	2149	Bowl	
2357	225	2262	Jar	
2319	225	2253	Soil from jug 2318	
2320	225	2255	Soil from bowl 2321	
2322	225	2252	Soil from bowl 2323	
2324	225	2251	Soil from goblet 2324	

Lab. No.	Locus	Basket	Type	Description
2326	225	2250	Soil from lamp 2327	
2333	225	2263	Soil from chalice 2332	
2345	225	2090	Soil from bowl 2344	
2347	225	2090	Soil from bowl 2346	
2300	225		Sediment	Between vessel concentrations
2301	225		Sediment	Sediment left of 2300
2302	225		Sediment	Sediment left of 2301
2303	225		Sediment	Sediment above 2300 and 2301
2304	225		Sediment	Sediment, burnt(?), in the northern area of the cluster
2305	225		Sediment	Sediment from a concentration of chalice fragments
2306	225		Sediment	Sediment under a special, already removed chalice
2307	225		Sediment	Sediment under a fenestrated stand
2308	225		Sediment	Yellow patch on the cave's wall
2309	225		Sediment	Brown sediment (bioturbation fill) on the cave's wall
2310	225		Sediment	Sediments under/near vessel with flaring rim
2311	225		Sediment	Limestone from the cave's wall
2312	225		Sediment	Cave wall above the initial level of vessels
2313	225		Sediment	Sediment from a vacant area between vessel concentrations
2314	225		Sediment	Sediment from a dark patch on the cave's wall
2315	225		Sediment	Sediment from an area empty of vessels
2316	225		Sediment	Brown sediment outside the pit—control EBI area
2317	225		Sediment	

Table 29.2. List of the compounds identified in the lipid extracts of five chalices from Qashish. Cx:y, Cx:yME, Cx:yTMS—a fatty acid with x carbons chain and y degree of unsaturation, and its methyl ester and trimethylsilyl forms; Cxol—alcohol with x carbons chain; MAGx—monoacylglycerides with x-carbons chain attached to the glyceride-backbone.

Lab. No.	Figure No.	Total lipid extract
2329	29.4	Phthalate, silyl, C16:0ME, C18:0ME, isopropylC18, alkane
2331	29.5	Silyl, C16:0TMS, C18:0ME, C18Ol, C18:1, C18:0TMS, alkane, MAG14, MAG16, MAG18, C20Ol, C22Ol
2332	29.6	C16:0TMS, C18:0ME, C18Ol, C18:0TMS, alkane, MAG14, MAG16, MAG18, C20Ol, C22Ol
2335	29.7	C16:0TMS, C18Ol, C18:0TMS, alkane, MAG14, MAG16, MAG18, C20Ol, C22Ol
2336	29.8	Phthalate, silyl, C16:0TMS, C18Ol, C18:0TMS, alkane, MAG14, MAG16, MAG18, C20Ol, C22Ol

Index

Abu Ghosh, 229–30
Abu Hawam, Tel, 313, 315, 318–19, 321–23, 326, 329, 337, 339, 341, 349, 351, 363, 368, 373, 382
Abu Shusha, Tell, xvii
Abu-Salah, D. 79
Acheulian, 29, 291
Adulam Formation, 13, 29, 241, 246, 396
Affūla, 303
Afula, 276, 299
Ajjul, Tell el-, 403–4
Akko, 409
alcohol, 419, 422
Aphek, Tel, 290–91, 315–16, 323–25, 329, 334, 403–4
Aphek-Antipatris, 315, 325, 337, 339, 341, 343, 345, 373–76
apse, 59–62
Asawir, 'Ein ('En Esur), 97, 131, 161, 163–66, 241, 244–45, 248, 262, 299
Ashdod, 314, 329, 409, 412, 414
Ashkelon, 229, 283, 290–92
Atlit-Yam, 290
auroch (*Bos primigenius*), 271, 273
Azor, 70

bacterium rhizobium, 290
barium, 408–9, 411–12, 416
barley (*Hordeum vulgare*), 287–90
beer, 290
Beit Mirsim, Tell, 329
Beth Shean, 97, 161–64, 292, 299, 313–15, 317, 321–22, 325–26, 328–29, 334, 337, 339, 345, 365, 369, 374, 377, 379, 381, 388, 399–400
Beth-Yerah, Tel, 162, 299–300, 301
boar (*Sus scrofa*), 271, 274
burial (of cattle), 276–77

caprines, 89–90, 269–77
cattle, 89–90, 269–77, 300
cattle burials, 276–77
cereals, 285–93, 300
chlorite, 219, 397–99
chondrite, 409, 415
cloaca, 222, 288, 311, 422

Dabbesheth, 6, 307
deer, 269–77, 300

Deir 'Alla, 313, 318–20, 327–28, 330, 349, 349, 351, 353, 355, 357, 359, 383
Deir el-Balah, 321, 323–24, 328, 365, 373, 385, 403, 412–13
diversity, 281
donkey, 89–90, 269–77

Ein Gedi, 395
'En Shadud, 97, 110, 161–65, 275, 298–300
'En Zippori, 249, 298
emmer wheat (*Triticum dicoccum*), 117–18, 287–90
Enkomi, 403

faba bean (*Vicia faba*), 288, 290
faience bowl, 312, 328, 388–89, 392
fruit, 289–93, 296

gazelle (*Gazella gazella*), 89, 270–71, 275, 279, 300
Gesher Benot Yaaqov, 291
Gezer, 314–16, 339, 341, 343
Ghassulian, 86, 229
grape (*Vitis vinifera*), 289, 291, 293
grumusols, 18, 13, 15–16, 18–19, 20, 28, 107, 110, 113–14, 219, 121, 396, 399–400

Har (Ha)Haruvim, 244
Hazor, 315, 317, 321, 324–25, 337, 339, 341, 343, 345, 347, 349, 355, 357, 365, 367, 369, 373–76, 383
Helkath, 6, 307

Jericho, 25, 164, 290
Jezreel Valley Regional Project (JVRP), xvii, 3, 5–7, 10

Khirbet el-Batrawy, 229
Khirbet Kerak Ware, 220, 222
Kinneret, 227
Kishon River, 3–4, 6–7, 9, 13–17, 25–26, 38, 41, 55–56, 91, 95, 107, 113, 219, 269, 271, 274, 282, 285, 297, 301, 396, 398, 400

Lachish, 313–15, 320, 322, 324, 329–30, 341, 355, 357, 368, 374
lentil (*Lens culinaris*), 120, 123, 130, 288–93, 300
Leviah, 220
lotus, 323, 328

Mansura, Wadi, 26–27, 35, 37–38, 40–41
marl, 21, 217, 219, 395–96, 399–400

Megadim, Tel, 299
Megiddo, Tel, 4, 6, 9, 97, 223, 225, 247, 276, 282–83, 298–300, 302, 313–19, 321, 323–24, 326, 329, 337, 341, 343, 345, 347, 349, 351, 353, 365, 371, 374, 400, 409, 411–12
Megiddo East, Tel, xvii
Mevorakh, Tel, 313, 315, 318, 320, 322, 369
Midrakh ʿOz, 221
Mimes, 324, 369
Miocene bedrock, 13, 17, 115, 217, 298, 396
Miqne/Ekron, 229, 314–17, 322, 337, 343, 345, 367
Mousterian, 7, 55
Museum, Kibbutz Ramat HaShofet, 241, 244
Mycenaean, 312, 324, 327–34, 329, 383–84, 389, 391–32, 407, 409, 417

Nahariya, 395
Nami, Tel, 290, 318, 349, 351
Nazareth, 3–4, 29, 95, 239, 241
Neandertals, 9 25–27, 38, 41
Neutron Activation Analysis (INAA), 407–8
Nymphaea, 328

oak (*Quercus calliprinos*), 13
Ohalo II, 291–92
optically stimulated luminescence (OSL), 15–16, 19–20, 27

Pella, 319, 351
Philistine, 331
pig (*Sus scrofa*), 89, 270–71, 274–75

Qiri, Tel, 409, 411
Qiryat Ata, 97, 120, 161, 163–65, 227, 229, 274–75, 298–300, 302–3
Qiryat Haroshet, 6
Qitmit, 330

radiocarbon dating, 25, 118, 120, 287, 289, 300–301
Ras Shamra/Ugarit, 385
ritual, 9, 102, 104, 247, 330–31, 417
ryegrass (*Lolium* cf. *temulentum*), 287

seals/sealing, 223, 225, 298, 300
Senonian, 13, 27, 217, 219
shell, 128, 219, 397, 399
Shiloh, 291, 330
Shimron, Tel, xvii
Shiqmim, 292
silo, 62, 118–20, 130, 1652, 240, 288, 292, 297, 300
spindle whorl, 228, 232–33

tabular scrapers, 87, 240, 245–47, 251, 300
Tel Erani C horizon, 70
threshing 288, 290–91
Thutmose III, 6, 307
tournette, 112, 227, 229, 232–33, 237, 300
travertine, 399, 402

Ugarit, 328
ungulates, 271

vertisols, 13, 28, 220

weeds, 287–289, 291–293, 295–296
wool, 275, 300

Yaqush, 302
Yavneh, 311, 330–31, 396
Yiftahʾel, 9, 69–70, 79, 91, 165, 275, 290
Yoqneʿam, 4, 6–7, 9, 13, 27, 55, 95, 99, 219, 302, 313–18, 321–22, 324, 327, 329, 337, 339, 341, 343, 347, 349, 351, 367, 369, 374, 382, 396, 398–401, 409, 411–12

zoomorphic rhyton, 331
Zuckerman, Sharon, v